WARRIOR-PIONEERS

Extracts from the Boone Papers

Volumes 4C-13C
of the
Draper Manuscripts

Anne Crabb

HERITAGE BOOKS
2019

HERITAGE BOOKS
AN IMPRINT OF HERITAGE BOOKS, INC.

Books, CDs, and more—Worldwide

For our listing of thousands of titles see our website
at
www.HeritageBooks.com

Published 2019 by
HERITAGE BOOKS, INC.
Publishing Division
5810 Ruatan Street
Berwyn Heights, Md. 20740

Copyright © 2019 Anne Crabb

All rights reserved. No part of this book may be reproduced or transmitted in any form or by any means, electronic or mechanical, including photocopying, recording or by any information storage and retrieval system without written permission from the author, except for the inclusion of brief quotations in a review.

International Standard Book Number
Paperbound: 978-0-7884-5845-3

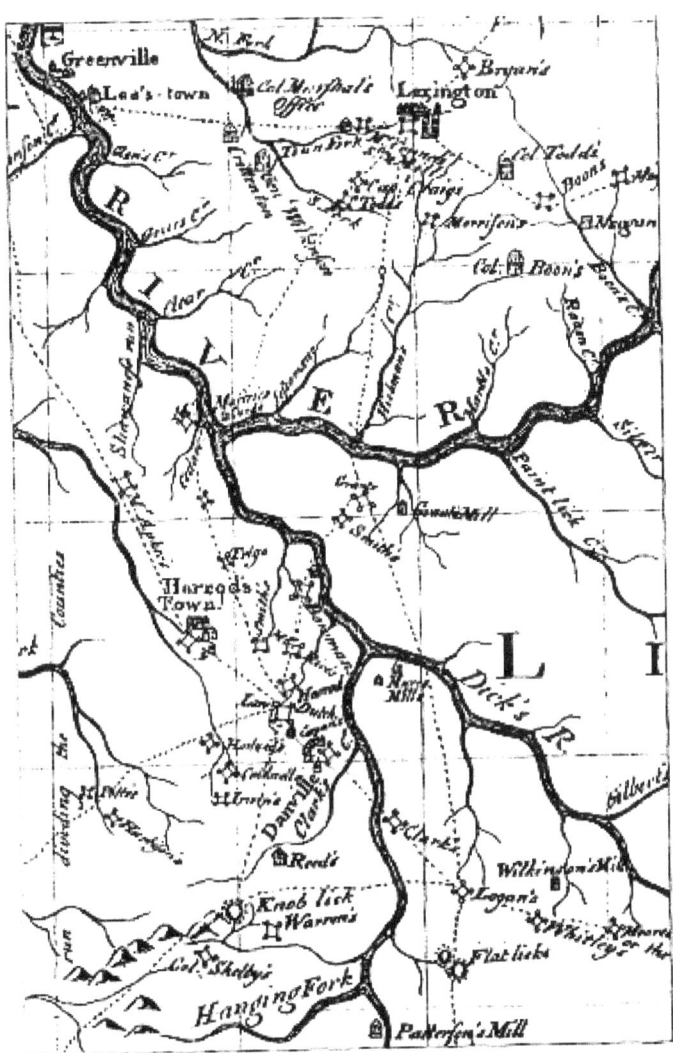

Center portion of John Filson's map of Kentucky, 1784,
showing Kentucky forts and stations

CONTENTS

Introduction xv
Note to Reader xvii

Note: All letters are addressed to Lyman Copeland Draper unless otherwise noted. Eyewitness or contemporary accounts are designated *.

Volume 4
R. M. Snoddy letter, Armstrong, Mo., 1890 1
*Capt. Wm. Russell letter from Preston Mss., 1775 1
Hanging Maw/Scolacutta, 1796, from *New York Magazine* 2
*Petition re: Hanging Maw, 1797 2
Mr. Ed. Sutton re: Daniel Boone tree / soapstone, 1876,
  from *Chicago Times* 4
History of the First Settlements of Scott County, Va. 5
Judge M. B. Wood, 1883, "Some Unrecorded Events" 5
D. M. Wood letter, Estillville, Scott County, Va., 1883 11
Notes on LCD map of Kentucky rivers, forts, and towns to the Ohio
  River 12
Notes on LCD map: Kentucky to Ohio River 12
Elijah Bryan letter, St. Charles County, Mo., 18__ 13
LCD questions for Elijah Bryan, 1884 13
LCD notes on Elijah Bryan interview 14
Elijah Bryan letter, 1884 17
Elijah Bryan letter, 1884 18
Elijah Bryan interview, 1884 18
Daniel Boone and Sons Crossing the Missouri River in 1802 18
LCD references for a map of notable places in pioneer Kentucky 20
LCD to Miss Emily Bryan, Nevada, Mo., July 12, 1888 20
LCD to Miss Emily Bryan, 1888 22
LCD questions to Miss Emily Bryan 23
Abner Bryan's Recollections, 1890 23
Abner Bryan interview near Guadaloupe, Ca., 1890 25

Abner Bryan interview near Guadaloupe, Ca., 1890 28
Abner Bryan interview, 1890 28
Abner Bryan letter 31
LCD questions to James Bryan, 1890 34
*James S. Stonestreet letter, Clark County Ky., 1853 34
*James S. Stonestreet letter, 1853 35
Daniel Boone's account book 36
LCD re: Shane's error 36
*Daniel Boone to William Preston, 1776 37
*Arthur Campbell to William Fleming, Washington County, Va., 1778 37
*William Hancock's Deposition, 1778 38
*Daniel Boone to Col. Shelby, 1778 38
LCD Memo on sending militia to Kentucky in 1778 39
LCD notes on Daniel Boone in Kentucky 1770, 1776, 1779 39
Daniel Boone's deposition, 1795, re: recapturing the girls 39
"Ms. Letter[s] of Daniel Pennington to the author," c. 1854 41
*Michael Stoner deposition, 1816 41
Samuel McAfee Duncan letter, Nicholasville, Ky., 1885 41
Samuel McAfee Duncan letter, 1885, with margin notes 42
Samuel McAfee Duncan letter, 1887, with map of Boone's Cave 43
Notes on J. D. Spratt map of Kentucky place names 43

Volume 5

Long Hunters of Kentucky., Louisville, Ky. Public Library, 1874 43
Robert Wickliff letter, Lexington, Ky., 1848 44
Robert Wickliff letter, Lexington, Ky., 1848 44
Robert Wickliff letter, Lexington, Ky., 1848 45
Life of John Todd 46
Robert Wickliff letter, Lexington, Ky., 1849 58
James Spilman letter, Paint Lick, Ky., 1849 65

Volume 6

Samuel Alley letter, Metamora, In., 1884 65
Notes on J. D. Imboden map, 1884: Black's Fort Area 66
Notes on a map by J. H. Duff, 1888: Powell's and Clinch Valleys 67

LCD notes on Daniel Boone in 1774 68
LCD notes on John M. Stoner's letter, Nov. 1853 68
Thomas Hanson's Journal [excerpt from McAfee's Scrap Book] 68
*Daniel Boone deposition re: recalling surveyors in 1774 68
W. D. Hixson letter, Maysville, Ky., 1885 69
*Daniel Boone deposition, 1794 69
*Michael Stoner deposition, 1816 69
W. D. Hixson letter, Maysville, Ky., 1885 70

Volume 7
Plan of works at Indian Old Fields, Clark County, Ky. 70
Memo for Indian Old Fields 72
Indian Old Fields in May 1775 72
*William Frazier, 1825 re: Indian Old Fields 72
Notes on lands ceded by the Cherokees 73
LCD note: Daniel Boone left Boonesborough in 1775 73
*Edward Mills to Mark Alexander, 1776 73
*Col. William Fleming to Col. Preston re: Daniel Boone in 1776 75
LCD notes on Col. Daniel Boone in 1776 75
Will B. Rodman letter, Washington, D. C., 1890 76
*Benjamin Sharp letter, Warren County, Mo., 1845 78
*Benjamin Sharp letter, 1845 81
LCD notes on Benjamin Sharp's letter 85
Benjamin Sharp letter, 1845 85
LCD notes on Benjamin Sharp's death... 86
John T. Teass letter, Otter Hill, Bedford County, Va., 1883 87
N. S. Halbert letter, Crawfordsville, Miss., 1882 88
Notes on Baylus Cade map 89
*Ralph Clayton letter, Walnut Plains, Mo., 1877, re: visit with Daniel
   Boone in 1818 89
Newspaper account of Clayton's visit with Daniel Boone 90
Notes on Thomas Teas. 90
Mrs. Elizabeth L. Wood letter, 1883, with map of Teas Valley 92
Letter from Thomas Callaway[?] 92
Notes on Thomas Callaway letter 92

v

George W. Stoner letter, Bath County, Ky., 1868 92
Richard Henderson's Treaty in March 1775 93
*William Cocke's Statement 93
LCD notes on the capture and rescue of the Boone and Callaway girls in 1776 95
*Daniel Boone deposition, 1817 96
*Flanders Callaway deposition 97
*James Ray deposition, 1818, on Edward Boone 97
*John Stephenson deposition, 1818, on Edward Boone 98
*John McIntyre deposition, 1818, on Edward Boone 98
*Peter Scholl deposition, 1818, on Edward Boone 98
*Daniel Boone deposition re: re-capture of girls 100
LCD notes on the pursuit after Edward Boone was killed in 1780 100
LCD: speculation and names of those reporting on the location of Boone and Callaway girls' recapture 101
LCD: Where girls recaptured in 1776 101
V. B. Young re: the rescue party for the girls 102
V. B. Young: notes on map showing girls' rescue location 102
B. F. Maxey letter, Fleming County, Ky., 1885 102
B. F. Maxey letter 102
James Wade letter, Virginia, Ill., 1883 102

Volume 8

Beal Ijames letter, Calahan, Davie County, N.C., 1884 105
LCD notes on Boone land granted in 1753 in Rowan County, N.C. .. 106

Volume 9

S. A. Yates letter, Gap Creek, Ashe County, N.C., 1883 106
S. A. Yates letter, Gap Creek, Ashe County, N.C., 1884 108
LCD questions to S. A. Yates 110
S. A. Yates note 110
Thomas Bouchelle with Mrs. Jemima Brown's Statement, 1884 110
Mrs. Brown's statement, 1884: Incidents of the Big Siege 114
A.S. Yates letter, 1884 114
Notes on map by T. C. Land, Wilkes County, N.C., 1885 117

T. C. Land, Mt. Zion, Wilkes County, N.C., 1885 117
T. C. Land letter, 1885 118
T. C. Land letter, 1886 118
T. C. Land letter, 1886 118
Jonathan Horton letter with map of Yadkin area, Horton, N.C., 1884 .. 119
Thomas S. Bouchelle re: The Hossey Raid 119
T. S. Callaway letter, South Fork, N.C., 1884 121
Notes on T. S. Callaway letter 122
LCD questions for Mrs. Prudence Callaway, 1883 122
Jim[?] Dene Callaway letter, Maple Spring, N.C., 1883 122
John H. Thompson letter, Wilkes County, N.C., 1887 123
LCD questions for Mrs. Prudence Callaway 124
John H. Thompson letter, Reedy Branch, N.C., 1887 124
Jesse Yates letter, Stony Hill, N.C., 1884 124

Volume 10
Elijah Dougherty letter with notes on map of Yadkin River area, 1884
.... 126
Elijah Dougherty, 1884, "Scenery of the Mountains" 126
Notes on map of D. B. Dougherty, Boone County, N.C., 1884 127
W. H. Weaver letter, 1884 127
Notes on map of Elijah Dougherty: Boone's Ford, c. 1772 128

Volume 11
*William Cradlebaugh deposition, 1832 128
*William Cradlebaugh Pension Statement, 1832 128
*Thomas Hall Pension Statement, 1832 129
*John Stephens Affidavit, 1832 130
*Jesse Hodges Pension Statement, 1832 131
*Joseph Jackson statement, 1832 132
*Oswald Townsend Pension Statement, 1832, with Joseph Kennedy
   and Richard Gentry statements 132
LCD references for Ansel Goodman 133
*Joseph Kennedy statement for Oswald Townsend, with statements
   of Oliver Steel and Richard French 133
*Ansel Goodman Pension Statement, 1832, with R. T. Letcher

statement ... 136
*Richard Wade Pension Statement, 1832 ... 138
*Anselm [sic] Goodman statement for Richard Wade, 1833 ... 139
*George Richardson Pension Statement, 1832, with Noah Lunsford and E. J. Bullock statements ... 140
*Arabia Brown Pension Statement, 1832 ... 142
*Ancel Goodman statement for Arabia Brown ... 142
*Josiah Phelps: Pension Application ... 143
*Josiah Phelps Pension Statement, 1832 with Thomas Jerman, Jr., Humphrey Jones[?], and James Paseleye statements ... 144
LCD notes on Josiah Phelps ... 145
Col. Wm. Russell's Services ... 145
Brandywine Battle, 1777 ... 146
LCD sources for the Paint Creek Expedition of August 1778 ... 146
LCD on Daniel Boone in 1778, notes on court-martial ... 146
*Joseph Jackson Interview, 1844 ... 146
*Daniel Boone Deposition 1777, Mason County, Ky. ... 160
*Jesse Hodges' statement on Paint Creek Expedition ... 161
LCD note. Bartlett Searcy ... 162
*Petition of Sarah Brown to the Journal of the House of Delegates, 1778 ... 162
John N. James to Mann Butler, 1835 ... 162
Boone at the Three Forks of Johnson in 1778 ... 164
Notes on map by W. D. Hixson, c. 1884: trail from Limestone to Lower Blue Licks ... 164
Fragment: Notes on old fort ... 165
Douglas Brynner[?] letter, Ottawa, Canada, 1884 ... 165
LCD: Paint Creek Expedition, 1778 ... 165
*Henry Hamilton letter to Guy Carleton, 1778 ... 165
H. D. Hixson Memos, 1886 ... 167
*Stephen Cooper interview, Yolo County, Ca., 1889 ... 167
Mrs. Z. H. Maupin interview, Kansas City, Mo ... 171
LCD notes in Daniel Boone in 1779 ... 172
LCD Memo: Mrs. Joseph B. Boyd, Notes on Henry Hamilton and Boone, Ambrose White and Moses McIlvaine ... 173
W. D. Frazee letter, Indianapolis, In., 1872 ... 174

R. T. Durrett to LCD, 1884 176
R. T. Durrett to LCD, 1884 177

Volume 12
*Henry Hall interview, Bourbon County, Ky., 1844 178
Memorial of Maj. John L. Martin to Congress, 1836 183
    Affidavits:
        *William Cradlebaugh 184
        *Jesse Hodges 184
        *Maj. Joseph Kennedy 185
        *Maj. Bland W. Ballard 185
        *Simon Kenton 186
        *Col. Daniel Trabue 186
        *Benjamin Briggs 187
        *Abraham Estes 187
        *Jesse Hodges 187
Maj. John L. Martin letters, Lincoln County, Ky., 1852 189
Maj. John L. Martin letter, 1851 190
*Payroll of Capt. John Martin, April 21-May 27, 1781 192
*Col. James Davidson interview, Frankfort, Ky., 1844 193
*Ann Casey Montgomery interview, Columbia, Ky., 1844 194
*Thomas Stotts interview, Adair County, Ky., 1844 195
*Robert Fletcher interview, Adair County, KY., 1844 196
*William Dudley interview, 1844 196
*General James Ray, notes by Mann Butler, and letters from Gen.
    Ray's son, Dr. John Ray, Madisonville, Ky., 1843, 1845 198
*Mrs. Ann Harrod Declaration, 1842, Boyle County, Ky 208
    Depositions:
        *Benjamin Briggs 209
        *Mrs. Elizabeth Thomas, 1842 209
*Mrs. Ann Harrod's Declaration of Dec. 1842, from Notes by Gen.
    R. B. McAfee 210
*Col. William Christian to Col. William Preston, 1781 211
*John Tayloe Griffin Fauntlroy letter, Buchanan County, Mo., 1845 .. 211
*Mrs. Ann Harrod from the *Western Christian Advocate* 221
*Mrs. Elizabeth Pogue Thomas interviews, Harrodsburg, Ky., 1844 .. 221
*Herman Bowmar letter, Versailles, Ky., Jan. 9, 1843 230
LCD notes on Herman Bowmar letter of March 1845 235
*Col. Joseph McDowell interview near Danville, Ky., Fall 1844 236
*Mary Logan Smith letter, Bardstown, Ky., 1844 237
*Mary Logan Smith letter, Bardstown, Ky., 1845 239

*John L. Ballinger letter, Frankfort, Ky., 1845.................................244
*Hon. John McKinley interview, Louisville, Ky., 1846......................247
Mrs. G. R. C. Floyd interview, Louisville, Ky., 1846 247
Benjamin Logan Obituary, 1802..248
*Elijah Farris interview, Washington County, Ky., 1844....................249
Hunting expedition, Indians in Rockcastle County, Ky. [fragment].....253
*Elijah Farris interview, Lincoln County, Ky., 1844 253
*Armistead Miller interview, Lincoln Co., Ky., 1844.........................255
Isaac Shelby Obituary..259
Isaac Shelby's Monument, Obituary 260
*Sol Clark Interview, Pontotoc, Miss., 1842 260
* Interviews with William Whitley [Jr.], George Nokes and Morgan
    Vardeman, Lincoln County, Ky., 1844...261
*Morgan Vardeman interview, Lincoln County, Ky., 1844 278
*Morgan Vardeman interview 280
*Gen. Christopher Rife interview, Casey County, Ky., 1844..............280
*Samuel Davis letter, Harrodsburg, Ky., 1854 285
Mrs. M. T. Daviess letter, Harrodsburg, Ky., 1854 285
Samuel Frazee interview, Bracken County, Ky., Nov. 1845 286
Jeff Patterson[?] interview[?], son of Col. Robert Patterson 287
*Col. Patterson's Deposition, 1815 287
Indian attack on Farris family [fragment] 287
*Statements on Bowman's Campaign by Richard Rue and
    Samuel Davis, Harrodsburg, Ky., 1854..288

Volume 13

V. B. Young letter, Owingsville, Ky., 1883 288
LCD notes on whisky bottle incident..289
H. C. Anderson letter, Haywood Co., Tenn., 1884.............................289
LCD notes on Daniel Boone and Tarleton in 1781.............................290
Thomas Walker letter, 1781 and accounts of Tarleton in Virginia...... 290
*Col. William Preston to Col. John Floyd, 1781 292
LCD notes on Daniel Boone in 1781 293
*Col. William Christian to Col. William Preston, 1781 293
*Hon. Marshall McCue Manuscript on Tarleton invasion, 1781.........294
LCD list and chart of those killed and wounded and those who
    escaped at the Battle of Blue Licks on August 19, 1782 297
LCD notes on Col. Daniel Boone in 1782 297
W. D. Hixson, Maysville, Ky., 1886 diagram of Estill's Defeat
battleground 297
John F. Estill, Lewisburg, W. Va., 1891 298

Conley's Heirs v. Chiles, Kentucky Court of Appeals, 1831 300
Depositions regarding Estill's Defeat:
    *Joseph Proctor, 1816 300
    *James Berry 301
    *John Lane 301
    *Stephen Hendricks, 1818 301
    *Enoch Smith 302
    *David Lynch 302
    *Frederick Couchman 302
    *Samuel South, 1818. 302
    *John Harper 303
LCD references for W. D. Hixson's map 303
Conley's Heirs v. Chiles: Chief Justice Robertson's Opinion 303
D. W. Hazelrigg letter, 1842 304
D. W. Hazelrigg essay on James and Samuel Estill 304
William Estill letter, Winchester, Tenn.,1845 309
Dr. William Estill letter, Winchester, Tenn., 1845 311
Wallace Estill letter, Madison Co., Ky., 1846 311
Wallace Estill letter, 1846 317
Letter of "FF," 1826, to Mr. Hunt of *Hunt's Western Review* 318
*"Grandmother Tomlinson's Story" [siege at Bryan's Station]........... 320
*Joseph Ficklin letter, Lexington, Ky., 1845 325
The History of Black Hoof, A Chief of the Shawnee Nation............... 328
*Joseph Ficklin letter, Lexington, Ky., 1846 331
*Joseph Ficklin letter, 1846 332
*Joseph Ficklin interview, Fall 1846, with diagram of
    Bryan's Station. 332
Diagram of Bryan's Station as in 1781 343
LCD to Joseph Ficklin, 1847 343
*Joseph Ficklin letter 344
*Joseph Ficklin comments on Maj. Robert Todd 345
T.[?] Russell letter, Lexington, Ky., 1859 345
*LCD Notes on Joseph Ficklin's Papers 345
*Mrs. Elizabeth Arnold letter, Versailles, Ky.,1845 345
*Blue Licks Campaign – British Account 347
*Elizabeth (Betsy) Payne letter, Scott County, Ky., 1846 348
*Elizabeth (Betsy) Payne letter, 1846 349
*Elias Kincheloe letter, Chaplain, Ky., 1847 353
Obituary for William Polk 353
*Elias Kincheloe letter, Chaplain, Ky., 1847 354
*Elias Kincheloe letter, Chaplain, Ky., 1847 355

*Elias Kincheloe letter, Chaplain, Ky., 1848 355
*Elias Kincheloe letter, Chaplain, Ky., 1848 356
Notes on newspaper account: attack at Kincheloe's Station 357
LCD notes on Kincheloe's Station attack 357
Newspaper account, 1851 re: Kincheloe's Station attack 358
Frank Waters letter, February 1862 359
*Frank Waters letter, 1862 359
*The Early Pioneers of Kentucky: Philemon Waters' Captivity 359
LCD questions for Frank Waters, 1862 365
Frank Waters letter, Cave City, Ky., 1872 367
"Incidents of Early Settlement in Kentucky," *Cist's Advertiser*, 1851. 368
*Appointment of Philemon Waters to Captain of Militia: Copy of
    original document signed by Benjamin Harrison and Philemon
    Waters, 1784 369
LCD questions to Maj. Thomas H. Waters, 1862 370
Thomas C. Waters letter, Lexington, Ky., 1862 370
Thomas C. Waters letter, Lexington, Ky., 1863 373
Fanny Young letter, Millville, Mo., 1863 374
LCD questions to relatives of Philemon Waters 375
Letter from son of Philemon Waters, 1862 375
Frank Waters letter, 1862 375
Notes on Hand-drawn map Blue Licks Battleground 376
W. H. Sterling letter, 1886 376
Notes on John Vawter letter, Morgantown, Ind. 377
John Vawter letter writing for *Phoebe Vancleve Harris, 1854 377
Philip S. Bush letter, Covington, Ky., 1867 379
LCD notes on Capt. John Craig and Jeremiah Craig 380
William McMurtry letter, Oakland, Ca., 1890 380
LCD notes on William McMurtry letter 381
William McMurtry letter, 1890 381
Capt. Lewis Rose by Gen. R. B. McAfee, 1849 382
Capt. McMurtry, Rose, and Jesse Yocum 383
William McMurtry letter, 1890 386
*Extract of letter of Joseph McMurtry, 1791, in Kentucky Gazette 386
Notes of Gen. R. B. McAfee on Capt. Lewis Rose, John McMurtry,
    and James Ledgerwood 386
William McMurtry letter, Los Gatos, Ca., 1890 Notes on McMurtry
family origins.. 387
John McMurtry - notes from his grandson, William McMurtry, Los
    Gatos, Ca., Jan. 31, 1890. 387

Appendix: Volumes 4-13 Findings Without Transcriptions or Notes
.... 391
Acknowledgements and Glossary 401
Index 403

INTRODUCTION

"An eye for nature and a soul for God."
This well applies to Daniel Boone.
-LCD

O, we ought never to have left Carolina...
Since we have come here we have had
a great many hardships to undergo.
I never could do much with a gun...
-Ann Harrod

    Lyman Copeland Draper's collection focused on what he called the "Trans-Allegheny West" during the Revolutionary War years. This area included the western Carolinas and Virginia, the entire Ohio River Valley, and parts of the Mississippi River Valley. Draper's collection is described as the "largest single first-hand account of the settlement of the region."
    Letters and interviews in his collection date from the 1840s to 1891. Emphasis is on the western frontier (Kentucky) during the Revolutionary War. Kentucky had been an Indian hunting ground when white people, led by Daniel Boone and others, settled there in 1775. The small population of the earliest Kentucky forts - Boonesborough, Harrodsburg, and Logan's - defended this frontier against the Indians and British, and provided manpower for expeditions of George Rogers Clark against those enemies from the north.
    The collection of 491 volumes is divided into sections, some of which have been calendared and indexed. The C Series, known as the Boone Papers, has not been calendared and there is no guide to this collection apart from Josephine Harper's *Guide to the Draper Manuscripts*, which gives a description of each volume in the collection. The collection is held by the Wisconsin Historical Society where Lyman Copeland Draper was employed as librarian, historian, and recording secretary during the last half of the nineteenth century.
    Reuben Gold Thwaites, in *How George Rogers Clark Won the Northwest*, quotes Draper as saying, in 1857, that he had amassed "10,000 foolscap pages of notes of the recollections of the warrior-pioneers, either

written by themselves, or taken down." And he still had more than thirty years to go in his travels. During fifty years; Draper visited more than once in Kentucky, Missouri, Indiana, Virginia, Tennessee, Ohio, and further west. Among the Indian tribes he visited were the Mohawks, who gave him an Indian name meaning "The Inquirer." In 1890, the year before his death, he was interviewing in California.

To prepare for his trips, Draper wrote to postmasters in small towns asking for names of the oldest residents. After introductory letters to those persons, Draper followed up with a list of questions, or he arrived for a visit, notebooks in hand. His correspondents wrote in the spelling of the day or in some that they invented, with or without punctuation, or they dictated letters to their ministers or their grandchildren to send to Draper. They sent "likenesses" of their ancestors, and complained afterward in letters to Draper because he never returned them.

The C Series of the collection, from which this work is drawn, contains thirty-three volumes of source materials for Draper's intended biography of Daniel Boone, now published in Lyman Draper's and Ted Blue's *Life of Boone*. The C Series is arranged in rough chronological order. At intervals in each volume, Draper gave a list of events in Daniel Boone's life for a particular year, and in some cases, a list of published sources for those events. Volumes 1, 2, and 3 of the C Series are chiefly Boone genealogical data pertaining to England and Pennsylvania and are omitted here.

In this work letters, interviews, military correspondence and other documents are selected from Volumes 4 through 13 of the Boone Papers. Extracts from these ten volumes include more than 80 first-hand accounts. Draper's correspondents related their stories of Indian captives, raids on isolated cabins, and prolonged sieges on the Kentucky forts. The mythology surrounding Boone is somewhat balanced by Draper's correspondents, many of whom knew Boone personally.

Daniel Boone, born in 1734 in Pennsylvania, came to Kentucky in April 1775, opening the Wilderness Road with his woodcutters to settle what had been an Indian hunting ground. He brought his family to Kentucky in September of that year, the first family to settle in Kentucky. The Boones lived in Kentucky for more than twenty years before moving to Missouri. Boone died there in 1820, leaving relatives and neighbors who would welcome Draper to their firesides.

NOTE TO THE READER

This work is not a word-for-word transcription. Only selected letters and interviews are extracted/transcribed. The Table of Contents includes those items for which there are extracts/transcriptions. An Appendix provides a list of other items discovered in the reading of the microfilm.

Draper's system of numbering pages is retained throughout the body of this work, including the index. To explain: the first number is the volume number, the letter following it is the series (C in this work), and the next number is the page number. For instance, an interview appearing in volume 7 on page 5 would be numbered 7C5.

To account for interviews with more than one page, Draper additionally assigned numbers 1,2,3, etc. So if the interview contained 3 pages it would appear as 7C5-5(1,2,3). Cardinal numbers are omitted within letters/interviews. After the first page, numbering appears within a letter or interview as **(1)**, **(2)**, etc. Therefore the last page of 7C5-5(1,2,3) would be designated **(3)**.

The original notebooks are filled with the varying handwriting, spelling, punctuation, and factual errors of Draper's many correspondents. Some entire pages or portions of pages are illegible due to old ink which has faded, or which has bled through from the reverse side. As well, there are torn pages and tight bindings which obscure words. "Best guess" transcribing is all that is possible in many instances.

To maintain continuity in the narrative, some words or phrases, and sometimes entire paragraphs or pages have been omitted. For a complete transcription, the reader should consult the microfilm.

Draper's notebooks differed in size. Josephine Harper in her *Guide* to the collection describes the small notebooks used for some of the interviews as "pocket memoranda books bound together." In these notebooks, four pages are microfilmed to a page with four page numbers in one corner. Sequence is difficult to determine in many cases. Draper's memos and notes appear within brackets followed by Draper's initials, "LCD" as in his original notebooks. His underlining has been omitted.

Remarks of the transcriber are italicized; explanatory words/spelling have been added in brackets without initials. Illegible or obliterated words are indicated by _____. Punctuation is added sparingly; original spelling and capitalization is usually retained.

Some page numbers are uncertain due to blurred ink or mis-numbering. No doubt a few volume and page numbers have been recorded in error here. While some interviews and letters are transcribed in their entirety, some are omitted or only briefly mentioned. Terminology which would be considered improper today is used throughout by Draper and his correspondents: "whites," and "Indians," "savages," etc., appears frequently here. Hand-drawn maps were sent to Draper; place names are listed for those when legible.

Draper inserted small three-digit numbers throughout the manuscripts. No one seems to know what these signify and they have been omitted, but most were retained by the transcriber in case someone figures that out.

One might wonder about the retelling in the 1880s of an event which took place 100 years earlier. Then one might consider the rich oral history passed down when there were few books, when paper was scarce. Also to be considered is that those who lived in Missouri during the early 1800s could have heard Daniel Boone himself telling of his adventures in Kentucky. As one pioneer said, "The story was told and told again and again, until the children knew it by heart."

Each time the microfilm was re-visited, more and more information was found. The purpose of this work was not to make a complete transcription, however, but to make available some of these most valuable accounts of a vital era in our history, to make more widely available Lyman Draper's tribute to Daniel Boone and the pioneers. These same pioneers, hearing of his adventures, became adventurers and defenders of the frontier as well, as far west as California.

Volume 4C contains 160(1) numbered pages

4C2, 4C6(1) R. M. Snoddy letter, Armstrong, Mo., Aug. 8, 1890.
This letter appears to have been written in pencil and traced over in ink. The writer's grandfather was John Snoddy, of Snoddy's Fort in Virginia. He was an early Kentucky pioneer. Some pages are omitted.

     John Snoddy died in Madison Co Kentucky some seventy-five or eighty years ago. My father was about twenty one years old at the time of his father's death, and moved to Missouri directly after his death. Uncle John Snoddy moved some eight or ten years later. He was of the same name as my grand father
     I know nothing of any old papers. I know He was one of the first settlers in Kentucky. He was from Virginia.
R. M. Snoddy

4C8 "Capt. Russell writes," June 12, 1775. LCD handwriting citing Preston Mss Papers, vol. iv.

     Shawnee chief Cornstalk had just visited with Capt. Russell to discuss keeping Indian tribes peaceful at the beginning of the Revolutionary War. Capt. Russell credited the Cherokees with the attack on Daniel Boone's men in March 1775, at a site known afterward as Twitty's Fort.in today's Madison County, Kentucky. William Twitty and a Negro man were killed.

Capt. Russell writes:

     The Cornstalk left me last Thursday & in the space of four days' conversation, I discovered that it is the intention of the Pick tribe of Indians to be troublesome to our new settlements whenever they can & he further assured me that the Mingoes behave in a very unbecoming manner, frequently upbraiding the Shawanoes in cowardly making the peace and calling them the Big Knife people so that the Cornstalk cannot well account for their intentions. If this be true and a rupture between England and America really commenced, we shall certainly receive trouble at the hands of those people in a short time as they got news of other battles [near Boston] in the Shawnee towns eight or ten days before the Cornstalk came here, though I am confident the Shawnees will always be our friends. The Cornstalk brought me two of the horses taken by that party of Cherokees who murdered the people in Kentucke in March. The Shawnees took the rascal who had them, but he made his escape from them; it is supposed he returned to the Cherokee Nation. It appears to have been the Picts [Piqua] who fired on Boone's camp when the two men were killed out of his party.

1776 – Indians in Kentucky. Hildreth's Pioneer History, 99. Collins' Kentucky,, ii, p. 50.

Here a note states that "due to a mistake in numbering there are no pages 10 – 19" in the microfilm.

4C21 LCD handwriting: Scolacutta or Hanging Maw.
Died in Tennessee. A great and beloved chief of the Cherokees, aged about sixty-five years - a man distinguished for his love of peace, and exertions for its preservation between his nation and the United States. In his death humanity has lost an able supporter.
N. Y. Magazine, May 1796

4C22-22(1,2) Report of the Committee of Claims on the Petition of the Widow of the Late Scolacuttaw, or Hanging Maw, One of the Chiefs of the Cherokee Nations of Indians, 17th January 1797.
Referred to the committee of the whole House, to Whom is committed the report of the Committee Of Claims on the petition of James Ore. Published by Order of the House of Representatives

(1) REPORT

The Committee of Claims, to whom was referred the petition of the widow of the late Scolacuttaw, or Hanging Maw, one of the Chiefs of the Cherokee Indians. That the complaints against the conduct of one John Beard, and a number of armed men, who, she states, in the year 1793, contrary to law and the good faith of government, attacked the dwelling house of the petitioner and her husband; killed and wounded a number of well-disposed Indians; burnt and destroyed and carried away their property, and wounded the petitioner. She now prays that some provision may be made for her.

After examining the statement made by the petitioner, and the facts upon which she rests her present application, the committee have found some difficulty in deciding what measures would be most available for the House to adopt.

Previous to the attack on the Hanging Maw, the frontier settlers of Tennessee and the Indians in that quarter had been guilty of mutual acts of aggression and hostility. A party of the Indians had killed some settlers;

their trail was discovered, conducting across the Tennessee [River]. This circumstance induced a belief in their pursuers, that the Hanging Maw had been concerned in that business; and occasioned his being wounded, and the misfortunes complained of by his widow. The general opinion, however, represents the Hanging Maw as having been uniformly friendly to the settlers, as vigilant to apprize them of the approach of banditti, and constant in his exertions, on all occasions, to compose differences between them and his nation, and withall as possessing considerable influence over the Indians. The same disposition is also attributed to his widow, the present petitioner; who, instead of exercising her people to acts of retaliation, has abated nothing in her friendship to the white people.

(2) *Two or three words are missing on some lines.*

All these circumstances seem to countenance ___ ___ required for her, a pension from the government, or some ― other relief from the Legislature. Such a provision ___ might also be considered as extending its influence beyond the particular object; or, as an inciting cause to other Indians to pursue a familiar line of conduct, under circumstances alike cruel and distressing, should they happen.

But, on the other hand, it is to be considered there are citizens on the frontiers who have suffered injuries as cruel, and deprivations as severe, by the Indians; and who have been thereby left in situations of distress that would equally call for assistance from the Legislature. Questions arise whether both descriptions of suffering ought to be provided for - Whether the abilities of government would be competent to meet all possible claims of this nature. And whether help can be extended by law, to the one, and consistently refused to the other.

It may be said, that those who settle upon the frontiers, voluntarily assume all the risques and dangers attached to the position; and, therefore, can have no just claim upon government for consequences resulting from their choice; whilst, on the contrary, policy requires that the minds of the Indians, who may be roused to hostility by acts of the settlers, should be quieted by small pecuniary interpositions.

Under these views of the subject, the committee have hesitated what report to make - but, upon the whole, as the authority vested in the Executive Department is competent to meet this claim; and should the petitioner, from her sufferings and her attachment to the United States, appear to the Executive to be entitled to any annual relief, as it may be afforded out of the appropriations for contingent expenses in the Indians Department, without an interference of the Legislature; and, as this mode will probably involve the fewest difficulties, the committee think she should apply to that department; and that the prayer of her petition ought not to be granted...

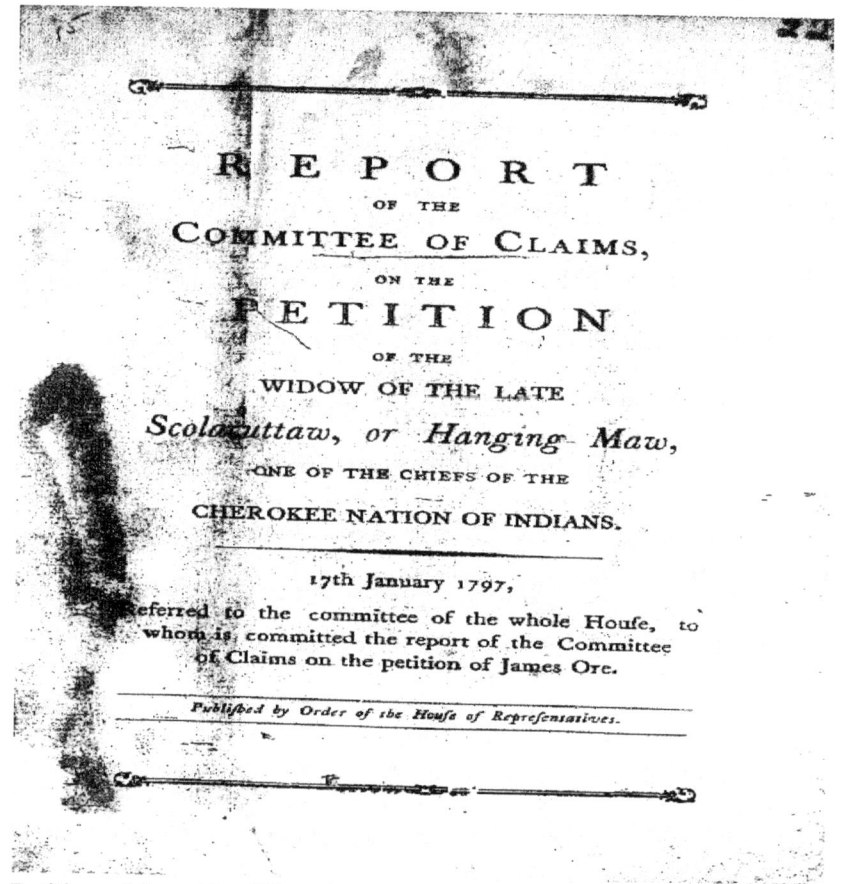

Petition of the wife of Hanging Maw to the Virginia Legislature, 1797

4C23 The Herald of Springfield, Ky., says: "Mr. Ed. Sutton, living near Willisburg, in this county, says that while chopping into a tree which was hollow, he observed on the inside a piece of Mineral, which, after being taken out, proved to be a soapstone, with the name of Daniel Boone written upon it, together with the date, 1776. We understand that this fact is vouched for, and that the strange relic was shown at the celebration on the Fourth of July." Chicago Times, July 11th, 1876.

1776 – Boone on Lawrence & Bracken: <u>Collins' Ky</u>. ii, 563

4C24 Newspaper clipping from <u>The Progressive Age</u>, Estillville, Scott County, Va., Thursday, September 27, 1883.

"History of the First Settlements in Scott County" by Peter Honneycutt. Number One.

> *This is the account of the men in Porter's fort in Virginia coming to Kentucky after being summoned to the aid of Fort Boonesborough during the siege of 1778. There are many errors. Mentioned: Col. John Snoddy, Patrick Porter, William Cowan, John Cowan - all emigrants from Ireland and all brothers-in-law, having married sisters before coming to the New World. They built Snoddy's Fort and brought their families out near Castlewoods in the Spring of 1777. Patrick Porter moved to Clinch River in now Scott County and built a mill on Fall Creek, the first mill west of Clinch Mountain. His oldest son was Samuel Porter. Stuffy Cooper shot the mooner at the siege of Boonesborogh with a steel-barreled gun called a yager, pronounced yawger. Samuel Porter, Cooper and John Arter mentioned.*

4C26, 26(1-16) Judge M. B. Wood letter, Estilleville, Va., April 9, 1883

My Dear Sir,
    I have found my notes and also had another personal interview with my old friend who is yet alive. I send you enclosed the result of both. I hope it will help to fill up some of the gaps in Boone traditions and be of some service to you. I may find among my papers some more notes that will be worth mentioning to you, but I think that the enclosed "account" contains about all that can be gotten in this section.
    About ten years ago there was held in Kentucky a kind of Boon centennial.
    May God preserve you to finish the work which will surely be for you a work of love, and then may you yet live to enjoy the praise it will surely call forth.

                                        Truly &c
                                        M. B. Wood

4C26(2-16) Mr. Lyman C. Draper

The following account of Daniel Boone is from Thomas W. Carter, the youngest of eleven children of Dale Carter who married Catherine Porter about the year 1786. Catherine Porter was the daughter of Patrick Porter and was born in Surry County, North Carolina in 1763. When she was six years of age, her father with Col. William Snoddy, William Cowan and John Cowan emigrated from North Carolina and settled in Castle Woods which is now in Russell County, Virginia.

Snoddy, Porter and the two Cowans came from Ireland and all married sisters. They built a fort which was called Snoddy's fort. Patrick Porter's wife preserved with great care the traditions of her family and on her death bed bequeathed some valuable relics to her daughter Catherine Carter, who inherited her mother's curiosity and fondness for the traditions of her family. With equal care she preserved and transmitted them to two of her sons who have preserved with great fidelity her recollections of early times of the country.

One of these sons was Thomas W. who is a man now 72 years of age. He has a very retentive and accurate memory and from his earliest years has collected and preserved much interesting information relative to the settlement of this section. **(3)** He is simple and has none of the marvelous about him. His means of information were ample, his curiosity active & his recital of that information carries with it the weight of truth.

He is and always has been accounted honest and respectable and influential. He was elected Sheriff of the County before the war.

The other son above referred to as an antiquarian, died some years ago in Russell County very wealthy. He was a lawyer of considerable local notoriety. During his life he held various important offices.

(4) Some Unrecorded Events in the Life of Daniel Boone

Col. [John] Snoddy, Patrick Porter, William Cowan and John Cowan were born in Ireland. They married four sisters and emigrated to America about the middle of the last century. They settled in North Carolina in Surry County. Then they became acquainted with Daniel Boone who lived in that section. In 1769, they determined to leave that country and seek a home on the then western frontier. Being well acquainted with Daniel Boone, they tried to induce him to emigrate with them but he declined to do so. They however collected their up effects and with their families came to Castle Woods in what is now Russell County on the western border of Virginia. Here they built a fort and erected some log cabins and began a settlement. This was the first fort and first settlement made west of Clinch Mountain. The fort was known as Snoddy's fort.

In the same year that they left North Carolina, Boone started on his first trip into Kentucky. This little settlement at Snoddy's fort was not disturbed for two years and the Cowans had begun to erect another fort at a short distance. **(5)** While the men were at work on it one day, John Cowan and his wife Ann started to carry some rations from Snoddy's Fort to the men at work on Cowans fort. They left their two little children, boys, one about two years of age, the other eight months. They had proceeded but a short distance and were passing through a rye field when the Indians fired on them. John was killed and his wife taken prisoner. The Indians were about fifty in number and led by the notorious Simon Girty. [LCD: error] At the same time they made a break for the fort in which but one man had been left. His name was John Arter. He heard the Indians fire on Cowan and boldly rushed out and fired and killed the foremost Indian making toward the fort. The Indians supposing there must be others, fell back. This enabled the whites to collect up and enter Snoddy's fort which they lost not a moment in doing.

About midnight the Indians made an attack on the fort which was repulsed. Ann Cowan, who was a prisoner, says they lost four killed in their night attack. Two Indians then left and carried Ann Cowan away with them. They held her as a prisoner for seven years and six months until General Wayne's **(6)** campaign when she was released and conveyed to Philadelphia. Patrick Porter went there for her and brought her back to her home.

The first attack on Snoddy's Fort was made in the month of May. The following spring, about first of March, Daniel Boone started from North Carolina with his first colony for Kentucky. He crossed Clinch river at the old Neil ford and went up the Devils Race Path and crossed Powell Mountain near the head of Wallen Creek. On this trip there were with Boone eighteen men besides women and children. They were down Wallen creek to the Gap where it breaks through Wallin ridge. Just as Boone's party were entering the gap they were attacked by twenty-seven Indians. At the first fire of the Indians Boone's oldest son was killed, and there they buried him. Some fired and killed an Indian and before the Indians could carry him away, Boone had reloaded his gun and wounded another. The Indians then fell back. Boone had intended to go through the gap and camp in the level country beyond but it was late in the evening and he selected his camping ground in the gap. There was a dry hollow which led up into a gorge of the ridge and in the wet season the water running down the hollow had **(7)** dirt from under the roots of a beach tree forming a fair shield from the wind. Here Boone put the women and children and posted sentinels all around his camp. A few of his followers followed the Indians some distance in their retreat down the creek, but night coming on they returned to their camp.

About midnight they discovered that the Indians were stealthily approaching their camp and of course they were soon ready for them. They waited till the Indians got in range when they suddenly fired on them. The Indians were not expecting this and hastily fell back. The next morning Boone and the men with him followed their trail down the Creek. They saw traces of blood and supposed some of the Indians had been killed or wounded in their night attack. They advanced cautiously until they came to the mouth of the creek where it empties into Powell river. On a bluff or spur on the opposite side of the river they saw the Indians hovering over the fire. Boone's party shot at them but it is probable without result. The Indians however scampered away. They then returned to their camp and held a counsel at which it was determined to fall back to Snoddy's fort for it was believed that the Indians had collected a large force. **(8)** Accordingly they went back and followed the Clinch river to Snoddy's , which place they reached in safety After being there a few days, the entire party returned to North Carolina except Boone and his family. Boone procured a house for his family and provisions, and on 5th May with Samuel, a son of Patrick Porter aged about Seventeen, started to Kentucky on his second trip.

They moved cautiously. Explored the Big Sandy river to the mouth. They went down the Ohio some distance and the country opening up in exploring South. They came to Licking river where they discovered an Indian trail which they followed till they came to the Blue Lick crossing. The Indians had been there and had left a vessel in which they had made salt. Boone and his companion got some salt which they carried with them. Believing the Indians would return at night, they concealed themselves and lay all night watching for them. Next morning they followed the trail down Licking river to its mouth, but the Indians had crossed ahead of them. They saw several of their bark canoes tied to the opposite bank of the Ohio.

They continued their explorations but found no Indian villages. Boone picked out a place **(9)** at the Kentucky river to erect a fort. Here they prepared venison and provisions for their homeward journey. They marked their road from the side of Boone's fort through to Snoddy's fort. They took pains to select the best route and plainly mark it. Their families had long since given them up for lost for it was late in October when they returned to Snoddy's fort.

Boone rested here a few days and leaving his family in their present quarters, returned to North Carolina and in the following March he returned to Snoddy's fort with a colony of emigrants numbering 108 souls. They had prepared baskets made of fine hickory or splits of proper size and fastening two of them together with ropes they put a child in each basket and put on a horse across a pack saddle. They had poultry with them which they carried in the same way. They also had with them hogs and cattle. In morning they made a terrible racket for the horses, cattle and hogs had bells on.

In the company of emigrants was Daniel Boone's brother Squire and his family. They rested some days at Snoddy's fort and Daniel Boone led the whole party into Kentucky and settled at Boonesborough.

After a while Daniel Boone was captured by the Indians and Squire Boone collected his and his brother's, Daniel Boone's, families, left Kentucky and [went] **(10)** back to Snoddy's Fort. They all believed that Daniel Boone was dead. Squire Boone remained with his own and Daniel's family at Snoddy's Fort about two years at the end of which time Daniel Boone made his appearance. In a day or two after Daniel's arrival at the fort, Squire Boone left with his family and returned to North Carolina for the two brothers had a serious [disagreement].

_____.*

*LCD note says there is no information about this. *See 4C27(1)*

The following describes the journey of a man from Fort Boonesborough who was sent as "Express" to Porter's Fort in western Virginia to ask for help during the siege of September 1778.

He reached Snoddy's Fort in the evening. Every available man [went] to the aid of Boone. The next morning 27 men volunteered to go under the command of **(11)** young Samuel Porter who knew its Country. Seven or eight women were put to moulding bullets, others were put to cooking rations at which duties they willingly served all night. Next morning Samuel Porter with his 27 brave followers took up the march into this dark and bloody ground and marched on foot almost day and night and reached Boonesborough in five days at about 10 o'clock.

Porter formed his men like the letter V. [They] converged on the fort to the joy of the besieged. They rested a few hours and then went out to survey the enemy. They could see the Indians on the opposite bank of the Kentucky River.

They discovered an Indian in a tree watching the movements of the besieged. One of Porter's men named Cooper had a long range yager gun. [They] asked him if he could not bring the Indian down from the tree. Cooper said he would try. There was a stump in the front yard & they brought out a chair and placed at the stump in which Cooper seated himself and placed his gun upon the stump. The Indian in the tree watched the maneuvers and believing himself to be perfectly safe on account of the great distance, he came down from the tree, turned **(12)** the insulting part of his body to the besieged and defiantly patted it. Cooper took deliberate aim and at the crack of his gun the Indian jumped into the air and fell over the cliff and his lifeless body lodged in a crab apple tree.

In a few days Col. Smith arrived with 100 cattle and supplies and 100 men. After waiting a day or two they made reconnaissance as far as the Ohio River, but finding no Indians they returned to Boonesborough and Col. Smith and Porter's men returned to Virginia. Porter and two of his men remained with Boone. Cooper and John Arter were the 2 who remained with Porter. They were in the fight at Blue Licks. John Arter was one of the slain but Porter and Cooper were unhurt and remained with Boone till the next summer when they joined Col. Bowman.

Bowman with a small force crossed the Ohio River near the boundary line between Ohio and Indiana. *End of page illegible, concerns Porter being injured in the knee* **(13)** completely disabling him.

At this time a Negro woman who had been captured by the Indians made her way to Bowman and told him to fall back for Black Fish was coming with 500 warriors. Bowman credited her information sufficiently to act on it. He [had] to retreat.

Cooper carried his friend Porter about a half a mile with his gun when luckily an Indian pony bridled and saddled came up with the little army. They put Porter on it, when sure enough Black Fish came in sight. Bowman posted his men in a low sunken piece of ground. Porter could only hope for safety on sticking to the pony. The Indians advancing with terrible yells, the pony became unmanageable and broke and ran through their line. Porter said he passed within ten feet of Black Fish. He said Black Fish was the most powerful man he ever saw. He looked like he would weigh about 230 pounds and he distinctly saw the foam in each side of his mouth. Three fleet warriors immediately started after Porter. He urged his pony on for some distance without gaining on his pursuers when coming to a little ravine he turned up it. At this the Indians who were well acquainted **(14)** with the country set up a fierce yell of delight. Porter looked ahead and saw the cause of their exultation, for a large log lay across the ravine and there was no way to go around it. The moment was critical. The pony ran at the log and made an effort to leap over it but fell back. The Indians came on at a short distance giving yells. In this supreme moment the pony frightened by the yelling made another effort and cleared the log and Porter felt safe. In a moment he was on the top of the ridge and the Indians gave up the chase. He turned his horse and fired at them and then rode rapidly along the ridge for some distance. It was about one hour by noon. He could plainly hear the roar of Bowman's guns.

Just before dark he came to a beautiful open place of some two or three acres. He dismounted as best he could to fix his handkerchief on his knee and let his pony graze. He unbridled [the horse] and crawled about to allow the pony to graze in fresh grass. When darkness came he crawled to the root of a tree, put his pony's bridle over his arm and soon fell asleep. Late in the night he awoke to find the pony gone.

(15) Porter saw the pony grazing some little distance off, but it came back to sniff his hand and Porter was able to catch it and crawl back on it. He headed in the direction he thought Bowman would be, was hailed by 3 of Bowman's sentinels, one of them his friend Cooper, who said: "My God, Porter, are you yet alive?" They crossed the Ohio River at the French trading post where Louisville now stands. Here he remained til his wounds were well and near Christmas he went back to Boonesborough. The following June he left for his home at Snoddy's Fort. He was 27 days on the road.

Upon his return, he joined Col. Lewis in his campaign against the five tribes. At the close of the campaign he returned to his home and was attacked by consumption. After lingering two or three years, he died.

Cooper, who had remained at Boonesborough, came back to Snoddy's Fort and said when he left Boone was preparing to go west, **(16)** that the country where he lived had become too thickly settled.

Snoddy moved to Kentucky and settled in Madison County. The Cowans went to West Tennessee. Samuel Porter left no issue because he was never married.

4C27(1-6) D. M. Wood letter, Estillville, Scott County, Va., April 23, 1883 *Some pages omitted.*

In my Boone notes sent you on 8th instant I intended to tell you in a private note of Daniel and Squire Boone's disagreement. It was thus - when Daniel returned to Snoddy's fort from his captivity, he found his wife with a baby about 6 or 8 months old which was acknowledged by the natural offspring of Squire.

(1) Fort Black-e-more and all old persons in speaking of the old pioneer, call him Black-e-more.

Your first enquiry was about the mention I made in my letter of 29 March of Joseph Blackmore & David Cox leaving Boone in 1769. I send you copy of notes taken several years ago which will give you all I have been able to find at present...

Snoddy and Porter and Cowan came to Castlewood's in 1769. In summer or fall, erected some cabins, returned to North Carolina for their families.

I don't think I stated this in copies sent you, but it was so related to me by Carter. When they returned with their families, parties named by Mr. Dickenson came out with them - he fixed the date of Bush's Fort and Castle's settlement 1770 or 1771, 1 or 2 years after Snoddy came. Bush [fort] was a different form from Snoddy's, Dickenson says, no information from Castle's after the first settlement.

M. D. Wood

4C30 *Rough map by LCD. Place names north-to-south clockwise: Cincinnati, Licking River, Ohio River, Maysville, Lower Blue Licks, Big Sandy River,* **A.** *West Fork, Whitesburg, [easternmost]; Hinksons's Fork of Licking, Boone Creek; [southernmost]: Winchester, Clark County;* **B.** *Lulbegrud Creek, Red River, Boonsboro, Kentucky River, Jessamine County, Lexington, Dick's River, Harrodsburg, Kentucky River, Stanford - near which was Logan's Fort.*

4C31 References for Draper's map. *Many are not legible.*
A. Young's Salt works - 10 miles west of Prestonsburg - where Boone wintered about 1769.
B. Lulbegrud Old Indian Town - where Finlay traded with Indians &c prior to 1769.
C. Boone's Cave - with "D. B. 1770" cut on a tree immediately above - & where Boone camped in 1770
D. Boone's ramblings in 1770 &c
E. E. Two caves - known as Boone's - where his initials & 1773 were carved, now defaced.
F. Boone's first Fort at Boonesboro - not the one given in Hall's Sketches, Collins &c
G. Harrodsburg Fort - locality
H. where the girls were captured
I. Boonesboro <u>new</u> fort east side of the Lick Branch, at Boonesboro
J. Locality of Logan's Fort - a mile north of Stanford
K. Blue Licks - where Boone surrendered the Salt boilers - south side of river
Crossed out: L. Plat of Indian camp - & also treaty & treachery at big siege of Boonesboro
crossed out: M. Piqua on Ohio - now Benton 6 miles from Springfield -

which Clark attack'd in 1780

N. Locality of Edward Boone's death by Indians, & Daniel Boone's escape.

O. Locality of Bryan's Station, 6 miles from Lexington, attacked by Indians in 1782.

P. Blue Lick battle ground - nearly a mile north of the Licks & crossing of river

crossed out: Q. In Ohio - where Boone and Indian t---- in 1782

S - Locality of Boone's Station - 12 miles from Lexington - about 8 miles from Boonesboro.

About the mouth of Dick's river are some lofty cliffs, where Boone, according to a vague tradition, jumped down, I presume, to escape Indians; I have only given it as uncertain tradition: A Sketch of the lofty scenery there would make a fine sketch. [Plans for illustrating biography of Daniel Boone. LCD]

4C33 Elijah Bryan letter, May --, 18--, St. Charles [County, Mo.]

Elijah Bryan was born in 1779 in Kentucky and died in 1896 in Missouri at age 96. This letter, ink badly faded, seems to consist of answers to Draper's questions. Draper's notes in the margin list the topics.

An interview with Elijah Bryan in Missouri is recorded in Draper's S Series. That series of interviews is designated "Trip Vol. 2, 1868." The Elijah Bryan interview is found in 23S242. Draper must have begun a correspondence with Elijah Bryan after visiting him.

Pages 4C33 and 4C33(1) are mostly illegible. Elijah Bryan's answers to Draper's questions are given here where possible. Two pages are numbered 4C33(2). Sequence is followed here rather than page numbers.

4C33 Draper's questions for Elijah Bryan, Dec. 19, 1884.

1. What year Boone & sons cross Missouri [River] when frozen?
2. The year carved on the cottonwood [tree]?
3. Was it 1808 or 1802, your father, Jonathan Bryan died?
4. Where Merrimack Springs located?
5. When Flanders Callaway & wife die?
6. Page 9, your son's book on <u>Missouri Pioneer Families,</u> mentions about Boone shooting down a large buffalo bull in front – was it not a cow?
7. Was this incident in Kentucky in 1769 or 1770?
8. How Boone & Stuart were captured, & how escape?

9. Boone's Indian name & meaning? Did he save ammunition when a prisoner to aid in his escape?
10. Long shot at big siege of Boonesboro & killing a negro?
11. Throwing tobacco in Indian's eyes?
12. Yadkin – meaning
13. Any Kentucky explorations between 1771 & 1773? LCD

4C33(2) LCD heading on Elijah Bryan's answers: Boone in Kentucky, 1769-1770

So where Boone met & shot a buffalo heifer was about 30 miles southwest of the Blue Licks – which must have been perhaps between Lexington & Paris.

One account says 35 miles from Lexington to Blue Licks.
[Question 6] Boone in Kentucky, 1769-70.

The Statement in my sones book was not right. In Kentucky there was no prairies but cane breaks. I recollect well Boone said he shot down a nice 2 year old heifer, thought to have a good breakfast out of her, but the buffalo came so thick and fast he had to back to a tree and stand there for two hours without his breakfast. The buffalo on both sides of him often so near he had to punch them with his gun. He happened to be about middle of the drove. The first of the drove was the cows and calves, then 1-2-3 years old mostly, then came the bulls in the rear and all the time so thick he had to punch them with his gun.

After they had gawn [gone] he said they made a big wide road, and that led him to the Blue Lick; he followed them, he thought, 30 miles.* This was on his first trip to kentuckey.

*So where Boone met & shot a buffalo heifer was about 30 miles s.w. of the Blue Lick – which must have been perhaps between Lexington & Paris. LCD.

[Question 8]. I have no recollection of the Stewart affair.

(3) 9th. Boone's Indian Name

I know the Indeans gave a name but have forgotten it; I think I feel well enough, I think I wrote that you can make out to read it. it is now the 24th of June.

Boone's Captivity – 1778

When Boone was captured as you say with the salt boilers, he was out hunting for meet for the salt boilers to live on. the Indians had discovered him first and surrounded him so as to capture him and did so. It was the Shawnees; he understood their language and bargained with them to have the men all surrender if they would not kill any of them. Boone had all to surrender. The Indians was 3 to one. I have no recollection of any bargain about his escape.

As to his saving ammunition when he made his escape, he was sent with 2 squas [squaws] about 8 miles to a sugar camp to bring home what was there and a gun and some powder with led [lead] was with the gun. He said he fixed every thing so the two squaws could ___ it. The gun he was to cary. He told the he was going home to see his white squaw. They layed hold of him and begged him go back with them. He said they cried heartily. He said they sat on their ponies as far as he could see them. He really felt sorry. **(4)** He saw the warriors were then busy hunting to prepare for the siege of Boons Borough. He knowed they was to start in 2 or 3 days. He has to pass through the country where they were hunting. He said he kept a sharp look-out and got home safe in 3 days and nights, and found the fort quite unprepared for the siege. He said he fully believed the Indians would have taken the fort if he had not got home quick enough. In 3 days [it was several weeks], here they came and pretended they wanted to make peace. And the next day there was 6 Indians and 6 whites to meet at a stump 80 yards from the fort gate. Boone said he knew it was to be the beginning of the battle, for the men all to be ready and when ever the Indians attempted to drag off the whites, to fire on the bunch.

The next day in due time 2 Indians instead of 6 came and soon concluded the treaty and Indians proposed a dance. So they locked arms, 2 Indians to each white man, and at once made the attempt to drag off the whites, and according to orders, the men at the fort fired and killed 3 Indians. That broke up the dance. They were all ready 150 yards off, and fired as the men ran to the fort. One ball struck Squire Boone in the heel. All got in to the fort safely but Boone wounded in the heel; he was a brother of old Daniel's.

4C33(2) *Duplicate page number. Top of page illegible, mentions Merrimac Spring.*

You ask me when Flanders Callaway or where he died; Can not tell; they was buried about one mile north of where Boone and wife was, on T. Lammes farm, their son in law. I have lived 8 years in sight of their graves. There are head and foot stones, but not lettered. In those dayes there was no such thing as regular graves stones. My father made the stones at Boones and his wifes graves, of a kind of chalk stone with a

Knife. Think they was about 8 inches square. When Boone and wifes bones were removed to Kentucky, the graves was not filled up and the stones fell in, and the one at her grave broke in two. Was 30 years after Boone's removal, I concluded to have the graves filled up, and the stone set up, and on making inquiry, I found the stones had been taken to Fayette College.

LCD martin notes. Boone & the buffalo drove in Kentucky in 1770.
No recollections of Boone & Stuart's captivity. About Samuel Adams & James McAfee's buffalo adventure: see Collins' Kentucky, ii, 607. Savage buffalo fights: Bradbury's Travels, p. 182; ____'s French & Indians of Illinois River, 2nd edition, 184-186. Danger of buffalo gangs ____ ____, Roosevelt I, 151, 157.

(5) You ask me about Boon's long shot. This was the 14th Day of the seage. *The siege lasted 9 days.* There had been firing day and night without an intermission of one hour. This was about 2 o'clock p.m. Boone said there come several shots across the river into the fort. He watching close where shots came from and bang went the gun. He saw the smoke away up a big forked hickory tree. [Boone then fired] "old tick-licker". *Boone's name for his gun, according to Elijah Bryan...*
  Squire Boon that was shot in the heel had made a wooden canon. they had loaded it with one pound of powder, fired their wooden cannon at the Indians. Boon said it made them jump about.
  (6) Boone never drank whiskey or used tobacco; he was a decent man if he was a backwoods man.
  This is the 3rd of August. This finishes the last letter.

  Your letter of July 27th.
  Jesse Boone, a cousin or nephew [of] ole Daniel, I can only say this was some relation, left in Powell's Valley.
  Daniel Boone's wife gave up Boone *for dead during his captivity.* She with her children went back to Powel's valley. After [the siege] of Boonesborough, Boone went after her and found her with some of the family.
  You ask me about the Yadkin – I only know it was the name of the river, my grandfather and some other friends had a fishery. My father thought they was the biggest fish in the world. My father was born July the 15th, 1759 and died [in] 1846.
  I was born may the 5th 1799.
  My father, James Bryan, helped fight that Battle at King's

Mountain.

LCD margin notes for this and the following letter: The tobacco story a hoax; Boone never used whisky nor tobacco; Shad catching on the Yadkin; Jonathan Bryan's birth & death; Elijah Bryan's birth-date; James Bryan at King's Mountain; Loutre Island & Creek, Col. Hale Talbott, Indian Phillips & Charette, Boone's Camp, Ancient Stone Houses.

Elijah Bryan letter. 4C33(5)

4C34–34(1,2) Elijah Bryan letter, Wentzville, St. Charles County, Mo., Oct 23, 1884 *The letter is only partly legible. LCD questions run up and down the margins. Omitted here: mention of William T. Lamme, who was the son-in-law of Flanders Callaway, and a discussion of Charette village and creek. Indian Phillips is described here as a French man, but another writer names him as Phil Nail from North Carolina. See DM 8C11(2).*

L C Draper: I supose you will be surprised to get a letter from me; I received a letter from _____ Bryan with your letter the 11th of Oct.

In the fall of 1808 a man by the name of Hale Talbott* settled the Loutre Island. Talbott had 4 or 5 sons, some daughters – in time of the war of 1812 there was a company of rangers from the Misssippi.

Draper's comment on Hale Talbott not found

(1) Indian Phillips I recollect well. He was tall spare made man & I think he was a French man – had an Osage squaw for a wife and lived in Charette village that was a French and Indian village …

Flanders Callaway was the father of Capt. James Calloway. Philips once made an arrangement with my brother in law to go hunting, asked "have you plenty of bullets" – my sister told him "no," and he said he might go to the (2) the lead mine and get some. In about an hour, came back with a shot pouch full of lead ore, his arm full – went to a flat rock and laid on his ore directly. may be living yet for what I know

I will give you a little history of Warren County. About 3 miles north east of Marthasville and one mile north of the Dutch College is a stone house about 10 or 12 feet long and about 8 feet wide about 5 feet [LCD: high?]…

LCD margin note: See Mr. Bryan's letter, May 13, 1885, first page – showing this was Dec. 25, 1802.

4C35 Elijah Bryan letter, Nov. 27, 1884

You will see by the different dates that I have written this letter by piecemeals. I received this morning a letter from Mr. S. Bryan, St. Louis, Mo., urging me to answer your request. I have had a very severe spell of neuralgie, which delayed my writing from time to time.

I remember another one of the Charette village settlers. John Manial was one I could not think of, had an Osage woman for a wife with four or five children. My best respects to you.

Elijah Bryan

4C36-36(3) Elijah Bryan letter, Dec. 16, 1884
LCD heading: Green's Bottom, Mo., & Col. Boone & Sons crossing the Missouri, Dec. 25, 1802. *Letter written by Elijah Bryan's daughter.*

Mr. Lyman C. Draper

Father requests me to say he has neglected answering your letter of Dec. 1. Green's Bottom is on the north side of the river. "Pioneers of

Missouri" not at hand, will have to depend on memory. Your letter has made me reflect more about the Boones than I ever had before.

Nathan Boone was in the prime of man-hood, had just married a beautiful girl...

When they came to the river, weather severely cold, no chance of crossing, ice running thick. Old Daniel Boone was up the river, cut his initials on a tree in a large cottonwood grove, **(1)** now the station on the road called South Point is located there. Not likely that they had been on a hunting expedition, but do not know. The father and son made their camp ready for the night. In the morning the river was frozen over. The proposition made was for each to get two long dry poles, take them one in each hand and try to cross the river. Nathan being a keen, active young man, likely said I'll go foremost, then Daniel M. Boone followed, then the old Colonel. Nathan and Daniel M. got over but the old man [Daniel] broke in. D. M. attempted to go and help him. Nathan went safely across, made up a fire. The old man, by the aid of his poles got out **(2)** of the water. They warmed and dried him, then set out for their home on Femme Osage, about 12 miles.

About 1801 or 1802 the Spanish Governor sent Boone to pilate [pilot] my Father to the great Merrimac Springs, and iron ore bank. After returning, the Governor offered my Father a grant of ten thousand acres and the loan of ten thousand pounds for ten years to build iron-works at the Merrimac Springs. It was then a wilderness of 80 or 100 miles from any settlement, in the direction the Boones would come after crossing on the ice. The Spanish government sent the Boones various trips and ways. They had no difficulty in crossing the river when they went to show Father.

I can't give the pages you asked **(3)** for as my book is not at home.

Boone in Kentucky 1770

Boone encountered the great drove of buffaloes in what is near the great Bluegrass land of Kentucky. I have frequently heard him say he stood with his back to a tree and they passed on each side, at least two hours, so thick he had no possible chance of excape; the buffalo were all marching; the cows and calfes in front, yearlings and two years old next, they followed the residenters – patriarchs of the flock – brought up the rear. One was crippled, but the drove went on without loss of time. As to Boone hunting alone, I have no recollection, or information about it. Father says he has done the best he could to give the desired information. He is suffering very much with neuralgia in head & breast. Nathan Boone was a wonderful man, had he had the opportunity, his history would be

almost equal to that of his Father. God bless your ___.
    Elijah Bryan written by his Daughter S.[?] C.[?] Bryan

4C37 LCD References for a map[?]
- A. Young's Salt works – 10 miles west of Prestonsburg – where Boone visited...
- B. Lulbegrud Old Indian Town – where Finley traded with Indians &c prior to 1769
- C. Boone's Cave – with "D.B. 1770" cut on the tree immediately above – where Boone camped in ___.
- D. Boone's ___ connected with his ramblings in 1770 &c.
- E. E. Two Caves – known as Boone's – where his initials & 1773 were carved ___ ___
- F. Boone's first Fort at Boonesboro – <u>not</u> the one given in Hall's Sketches ___
- G. Harrodsburg Fort – locality
- H. Where the girls were captured – *where they were rescued
- I. Boonesborough <u>new</u> fort – east side of the Lick Branch, at Boonesborough
- J. Locality of Logan's Fort – a mile north of Stanford
- K. Blue Licks – where Boone surrendered the Salt boilers – south side of ___ ___
- L. [crossed out: Plat of Indians camp]
- M. [crossed out] Piqua in Ohio, now Boston, 6 miles from Springfield where Clark ___ ___
- N. Locality of Edward Boone's death by Indians, & Daniel Boone's escape.
- O. Locality of Bryan's Station, 6 miles east of Lexington, attacked by Indians in 1782.
- P. Blue Lick battle ground – nearly a mile north of the Licks & crossing ___
- Q. [crossed out] In Ohio where Boone ___
- R. [crossed out] Boone burned an Indian town in 1782
- S. Locality of Boone's Station – 12 miles from Lexington, about 8 miles from Boonesborough

4C40 LCD to Miss Emily Bryan, July 12, 1888. *Mary Emily Bryan, born in 1834, was the daughter of Elijah Bryan. The letter and LCD questions are filmed out of order.*

Miss Emily Bryan –
    Respected Lady

You will be able to see by the enclosed that, like other mortals, I have my afflictions – but try to bear them as best I can – I feel more than ever, that my duty is, to work while the day lasts, & do what I can to complete my labors.

Your brother at St. Louis, has informed me, what I was glad to learn, that your remarkable father is still spared, & his brother also…

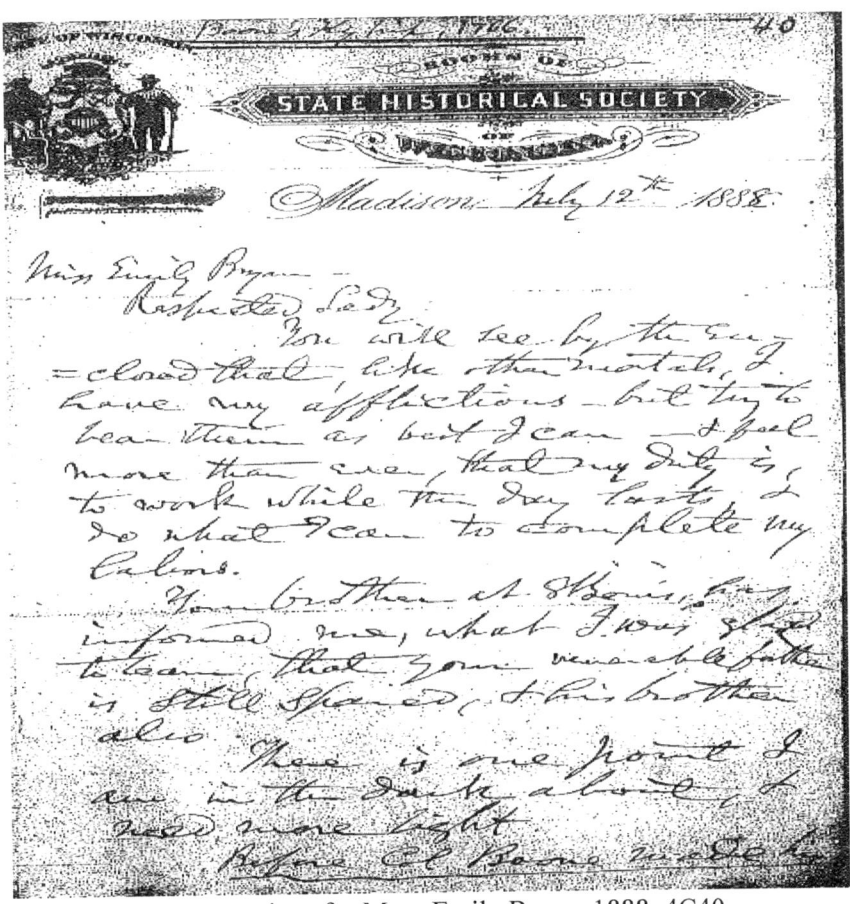

LCD Questions for Mary Emily Bryan, 1888. 4C40

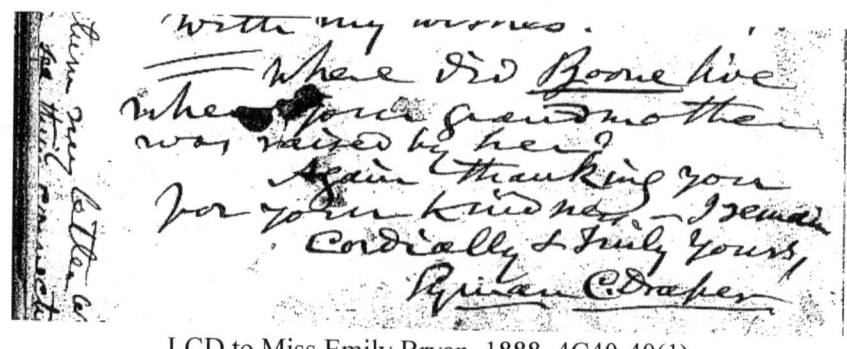

LCD to Miss Emily Bryan, 1888. 4C40-40(1)

4C41(1-3) Mary Emily Bryan letter, Nevada, Mo., Aug. 15, 1888

(1) I have talked with both father and uncle & both believe the circumstances of which you inquired with regard to Daniel Boone is correct and authentic. Father is in his 90th year... his memory of things past is remarkable. He is feeble but not childish and foolish. Uncle James is stout & hearty & at 82 walks all about the neighborhood, plowed & tended corn this summer. He seems almost like a man in the prime of life.

Miss Emily Bryan note Sept. 10, 1889
– about Alexander McKinney, that he died on Charette Ceek, Warner County, about 45 years ago, hence about 1844. Son Marion McKinney, Fayette, Howard County, Mo.

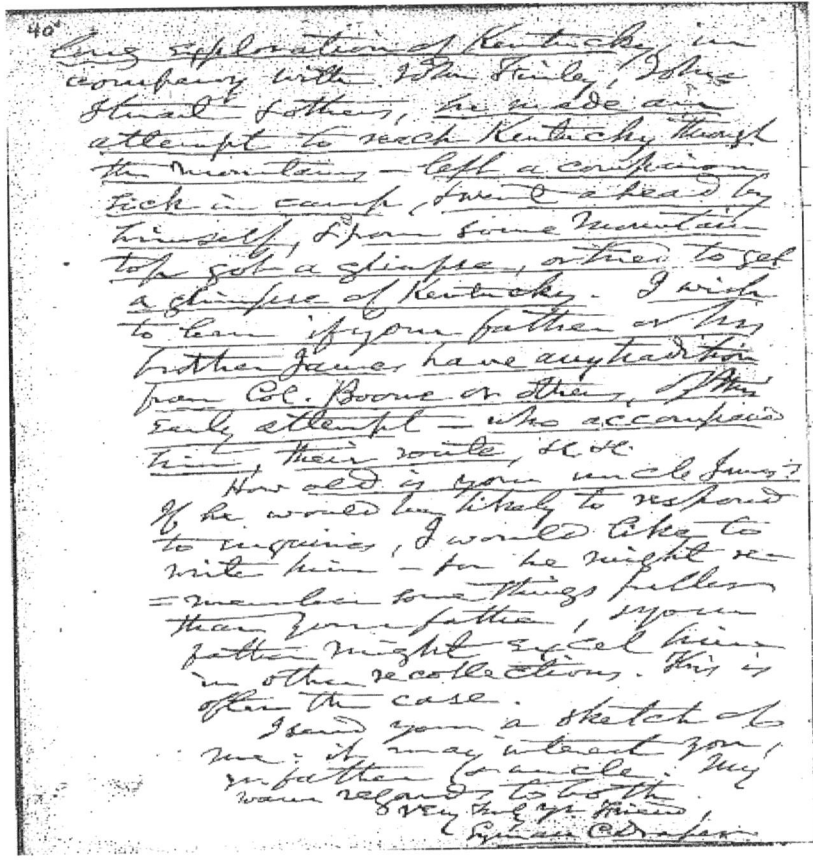

4C42 LCD questions (for Mary Emily Bryan?), Aug. 30, 1888.

What year father and uncle remember hearing Boone say about his first attempt to reach Kentucky and failed? Was Boone alone when he encountered the big ___ buffalo in Kentucky? *Other topics: Mrs. Hays at the big siege, Boone's other trips to Kentucky, James Bryan's relationship to Joseph Bryan and when they lived in Kentucky, etc.*

4C43-43(1) Abner Bryan letter, Oso Flaso, San Lus Obispo P.O., California. Nov. 6, 1889. LCD margin note: Abner Bryan's Recollections of Col. Daniel Boone &c.

Abner Bryan lived in St. Charles County, Missouri among the Boone and Bryan families until 1845, when he and a large family group left for California. During their six months journey, Abner's wife Mary died. He married a second time and lived in California into the 1890's.

Dear Sir, I send you a book which will give you more information perhaps than I can give you. You can read it & if you do not come soon here, send it to Guadaloupe. Would be glad to see you.

There is one hunting trip Col. Boone, Jesse* & Nathan took which is not in the Book. They went across the Missoury River to the Merimack river late in the fall. The winter set in very cold. They started for home. When they got to the river it had blocked up with ice. Each one got a long pole, started across. about the middle of the river the Old Man fell through the ice, lodged on his pole and came out. Had a cold bath.

We live three miles north of Guadaloupe. If you ever come down, any person in San Luis or _____dy can tell you where Osa Flasa is.

Exchuse [sic] the scribbling. I am old man Born March 17th 1809 one mile and half of where Col. Boone died; helped cary him in his coffin. The book will tell you where died all about it.

Henrey Boggs used to live in S____, a grandson of Col. Boone. An older brother lives in Nappa Valley. Henrey can tell you where he lives.

Yours &c
Abner Bryan

*Really Daniel. M. Boone – Jesse did not remove to Missouri till shortly before Col. Dl. Boone's death. LCD

Abner Bryan Letter, 1889. 4C43

4C44-61 Interview from Abner Bryan near Guadaloupe, Cala, Feb. 12–13-14, 1890. *In notes from Draper's interviews with Abner Bryan, pages are not numbered in the usual way.*

    Abner Bryan was born in St. Charles County, Missouri on March 19, 1802, the son of Jonathan Bryan whose father got his thigh broken & died of it about 1806 or 7. Jonathan Bryan died at age 87 in 1848.
No particular recollection of traditions of the Boones & Bryans in the Yadkin country - only at Shoals of Yadkin, catching plenty of shad.
    1773 - Thinks none of the Bryans were of Boons party when his son James, with other youths in rear, driving cattle, were killed. *This refers*

to the Powell's Valley Indian attack when the Boones with other families turned back from their first attempt to settle in Kentucky.

Panther Adventure

While yet young in North Caralina, Daniel Boone & other young fellows were out hunting & came on a panther. Heard its screeching & coming nigher & nigher - the others fled, but Boone stood his ground, shot & kild the animal, as it was in the act of springing at him, which secured him much eclat in all his region.

Captivity Near Blue Licks in 1778

February 1778 - While Daniel Boone was out hunting for meatt for the salt boilers, was chased & caught. While returning with Indians towards Blue Licks, Boone considered the matter, concluded he had better get the men to give up & save their lives. They were out numbered, & Indians agreed to treat them well. Boonesboro was too weak to resist - as the men were mostly away, & pickets in decay [around the fort] - so Boone told informant. So the men gave up. Boone was blamed by a few - but when tried, acquitted.

This refers to Boone's being court-martialed for offering to surrender the salt boilers, which Boone thought would prevent the Indians from attacking the fort and capturing the women and children.

1778 - Expedition Indian towns. *This has been called the Paint Creek Expedition; it took place in August 1778, just before the Siege of Booneborough.* Indians stole horses - Boone & party followed - saw by this it was a small party - came to a point of prairie, & saw the Indians camp fire at a distance, & concluded to wait till in night or next morning & creep & fire on them; but **45** when night came, the men backed down & declined to go; when Boone said he would go & kill one anyhow. An Indian dog began to bark - an old Indian at the fire raised up & encouraged on the dog. In the fire light, Boone could see a silver half moon ornament on the Indian's breast, aim'd at it, shot him through & fell dead. The other Indians- from 6 to a dozen – fled. So Boone related to informant.

Boone Kills 2 Indians

About 1770 - Boone was by himself - discovered 2 Indians fishing, sitting on a log. Boone was walking along on the bank, & heard a noise & peeped over & saw them. He said heard a gun crack that sounded very much like Tick-Licker [Boone's name for his gun], & they both fell off into the water; & he bore off to the mountains to the east & circled around to his camp. He did not say outright that he killed the Indians - but evidently took aim so as to kill them both by same shot.

4C46 Big Siege of Boonesboro, September 1778

While [Boone was] a prisoner, Indians had assigned him a lengthy pan handle to carry; & when about to run the gauntlet, squaws & boys with switches - Boone threatened to knock them over with his long Iron pan handle, & they desisted & so he escaped without receiving a blow. He was adopted *into the Shawnee family of Black Fish*. They tried to get Boone to hoe corn… the Queen Mother, by hoeing [to show Boone how], he would cut & slash & cut up the corn. He was obstinate. They undertook to whip him into it. He would push over one squaw on to the ground, but kept out of the way of his Indian mother - so they had to let him alone. Boone never was much in raising corn… **47** Black Fish saw the process at a distance and seemed to enjoy it - came up & patting Boone on the shoulders said good warrior, & rescued him from the squaw corn hoers. Boone would fix & repair their gun stocks & help them hunt & they began to have confidence in him, so he ventured away further till finally he escaped. Reaching Kentucky river, found a canoe with a hole in it, he repaired it with bunches of leaves for a plug & got over. It was knowing of this intended Expedition *against Boonesborough* that led him to escape.

1778 – Treaty *during Siege of Boonesborough*

Only remember Squire Boone was one of the treaty makers, with Daniel Boone. Duquesne [DeQuindre?] & Black Fish demanded a surrender, which Boone declined; & then to hold a council between the fort & Where Indians were camped - did so. Indians proposed to shake hands - 2 Indians to a white man. This the 2nd day of the treaty, to confirm the treaty. Boone told the men to fire on the Indians if they showed treachery. While fleeing Squire Boone was wounded. Split logs set up endwise as pickets in which leaden balls were shot. **48** Indians undertook to undermine the fort from the river, when one of the men in the fort would pitch over stones upon them.Some wished their fellows [to] stop lest the Indians would get mad.

Squire Boone made a wooden cannon banded with the iron, which when the Indians were marched away, the cannon was fired at them. The Indians would [say] "Dam you - fire your wooden cannon again."

During the Siege, a Negro with the Indians peered his head in the fork of an oak tree on opposite bank of river, to set shots at the defences of the fort. Boone, watching for the opportunity, shot the Negro through the forehead, 180 yards. Boone's gun carried an ounce ball.

Understood the Negro belonged to some one in the fort and ran away; and early in siege would dare his old master to come out & dine with him.

The leaden balls from the picketing was a happy supply, when lead was scarce.

1779 - Removal to Kentucky

Mrs. Boone had returned to North Carolina. After the siege, Boone returned there & all with the Bryants went to Kentucky in fall of 1779. James Bryan & sons Jonathan, David, & others of the family - a large party of emigrants - don't remember about the swivels [cannon] - no attack on emigrants.

49 After the Bryans had got well settled at the Station, they learned that the location had been entered by a Virginian & sent word by a young man returning to Virginia, that they would give a certain amount for the place - the young man stopping at one Rogers in Virginia, indiscreetly described the valuable Bryan Station location, & freely told of his mission; & while the young man tarried to visit with his kin folks, Rogers got ahead of him & bought the place - & going to Kentucky, drove off the Bryans from their hard earned improvements.

1776 - Girls captivity.

When Boone & party the 2d day came in sight of Indians, Boone seeing an Indian behind a log with his leg stretched over the log - & Boone shot & broke the Indian's leg. "That's father" said Jemima, & Indians ran off.

4C50-54 LCD interview with Abner Bryan near Guadalupe California, Feb 12-13, 1890, [Bryan] born in 1802 in St. Charles County, Mo., son of Jonathan Bryan

Blue Lick - Boone commanded one party. Boone warned them if they crossed, they would get into a trap & get defeated. Boone commanded the left wing. Indians encompassed them. Either Todd or Trigg fought till only 4 men were remaining & Boone trying to get below down the river, from the crossing, saw an Indian in the act of tomahawking his son (whom Boone had tried to carry off when he had to abandon him) when Boone shot the Indian & escaped.

1786 - Logan's campaign. Tom Kennedy's saddle got loosened, &

he had to stop to repair the strap, & dashed up among some squaws & slashed his sword, scattering them. Returning to Kentucky would hollow - "who hacked the squaws" - another would respond - "Tom Kennedy" & a third would yell "That's so" - so Kennedy felt nettled, & reported to Logan - but the matter dropped.

Moluntha was taken & asked if he was at Blue Licks. he said yes & making a motion of scalping around the crown of his head, & holding up his fingers gave the idea how many he had scalped there - when a squaw axe cleft his skull.

51 Mrs. Susan Hays, Boone's daughter, was pretty good looking woman, medium sized - rather slim. Jemima Callaway - medium sized - fine woman

Boone Returns from Missouri to Kentucky

Is quite certain Col. Daniel Boone did return to Kentucky after he settled in Missouri. He sold his land, & took the proceeds & went to Kentucky & paid up his old debts. Returned with four bits in his pocket & said he had now paid his old debts, could now die happy. No one could say he was dishonest.

Boone said when in Kentucky he identified a piece of land where a corner was located in a swamp & said he stood within three feet of where he buried a corner stone, marked with the owner's name or initials mark on it - dug & found it. Boone so related to informant. Don't know in what part of Kentucky & perhaps this account when he went back to pay his debts.

Once, before the War of 1812, probably about 1808, Col. Boone & sons D. M. & Nathan were out hunting & a very cold spell came on. They started to return home - this on south side of Missouri well up M-------ck river & came to the Missouri, found the river frozen. Fearing it was not sufficiently strong, each provided himself with a pole to use upon the ice in case they should break through, to hold on to & aid in getting out. Col. Boone about half way over broke through & with his pole on the ice, scrambled out with his gun, traps, & blanket, & furs, D. M. [Daniel Boone's son] proposed to aid him; but the **52** old Colonel kept him off for safety, else he too might break through. Nathan went to northern shore & built a fire by which for his father to warm & dry his clothes. Don't know about their hunting success, but the cold spell drove them home.

Sink Hole battle. - Thinks Nathan Boone was there [a mistake I think: LCD] & when afterwards asked why they did not fire the wagon battery & run it into the hollow, said he did not think of it.

Rock River Rapids - D. M. Boone was along on boat when

attacked; kept loading & firing as he supposed; but afterwards discovered much to his astonishment that he had not fired his gun - & had several loads rammed upon each other.

Tobacco Story

Boone had a small patch of tobacco, & only a rail pen. Indians came, & Boone hailed them as old friends, snatched up an arm full of the dried tobacco, & jumped with it upon the Indians & filled their eyes with the blinding particles & escaped. Heard others, not Boone, speak of the affair.

Boone's Spanish grant was sold.

53 Robert Ramsey & family were attacked while Mr. & Mrs. Ramsey were milking cows in the door yard & dashed towards the house. Killed Mrs. Ramsey & Ramsey got into the house & pushed the bed stead against the door, & kept the Indians out. But tomahawked 3 children & Col. Boone, no doctors, did what he could in caring for their wounds. R. Ramsay was a one legged man, was wounded in the affair, but recovered. All the children died within 4 days. This was near Marthasville [Missouri]. In the house, Ramsey had a tin horn, which he blew, & Indians recognizing it was an alarm, fled away. This was just after sun rise. It is a mistake in saying Abner Bryan was at Ramsey's that morning; he & Jesse Caton heard the firing & wondered why it was.

About 1812 - Grand River, Boone, H— Logan & John Davis went on hunting expedition to Grand River… Osage River Expedition - took Derry… Boone was taken sick, & thought he would die - directed how to take his tomahawk & cut out a grave, designating the place.

54 Can tell nothing of John Coalter, Jenkins Williams, nor Indian Phillips, nor when Stephen Hancock died.

1815 - Capt. James Callaway's death. He was a large vigorous man. Indians committed depredations, & Callaway raised his company. Indians left some of the stolen horses tied, & went back on the trail, expecting to be pursued. Callaway's party seeing their horses & Lt. Jonathan Riggs warned Callaway that they would be ambushed. Callaway called him a coward. Went on, waylaid, & Callaway while on his horse was shot, as was the horse, & Callaway plunged into the swollen stream. Riggs became a Colonel & a man of prominence.

No knowledge of Loutre Island previously known as Duchane's Island. Mr. Bryan tells of evidently Kenton supposed killing a man who recovered & of his riding on the colt when a prisoner.

4C55-61 Abner Bryan interview.

No traditions of Gen. George Rogers Clark.
Elijah Bryan [living in Nevada, Missouri] born May 5, 1799
James Bryan in Nevada, Missouri, born July 29, 1800[?].

Hunt 1808 or thereabouts – On return, Col. Boone thought one direction would lead to the Missouri river – less observant than when younger - while Nathan insisted that his father was wrong. He led the way, & reached the river as he had prognosticated. Nathan Boone (so said Jonathan Bryan, informant's father), could shave the hair from a deer's pelt in five minutes - in one third the time of ordinary hunter. While dogs were tusseling with a black bear, Nathan could run up and Stab him fatally without endangering himself. He was a wonderful man and a woodsman & hunter.

Daniel M. Boone [son of Daniel Boone] was no hunter - very excitable - rather short heavy built man. Not so well acquainted with Indian fighting as his father or younger brother Nathan. He had a light voice, much like a woman.

Daniel Boone was about five feet eight inches, broad shoulders, and strong limbed. Instead of being a "rough pioneer," he in his old age exhibited a mild, pleasant and interesting appearance, communicative, especially to the young, in relating his early experiences.

Remember Col. Boone had a number of books which he had read, and evinced an acquaintance with them. Was no farmer.

56 Mr. Abner Bryan thinks his idea of Col. Daniel Boone revisiting Kentucky comes in part from his own boy recollection of it at the time, & partly from hearing his father, Jonathan Bryan, & Col. Boone speak of the matter; & thinks it was about 1809 or 1810 & alone on horseback. That returning from Kentucky, Boone felt happy to think he had paid up Kentucky debts contracted in part by his land litigations there - that no man could say Boone was a dishonest man - now was ready to die.

The statement in Pioneer Families of Missouri p. 47 would indicate that the Shobe sale was in 1815, too late for Daniel Boone going to Kentucky.

Col. Boone's sickness - Was taken sick at Flanders and Jemima Callaway's. Dr. Jones attended him (no recollection about over-eating sweet potatoes) & recovered; but before recovering his strength, concluded to return to Nathan Boone's, about 13 miles distant. Dr. Jones warned him if he did, he would be likely to have a relapse & die. Boone said he thought not as he could take it easy pace on "old R—," his family horse. But the relapse came, about a week later.

Boone never lost a tooth. Boone had made a black walnut coffin which was used for someone dying there - don't **57** know who he was; then Boone had another coffin made from a cherry tree lumber.which he polished & often slept in. This was the one found decayed when the remains were disinterred in 1845. The burrial was a very large one - people attending from many miles around. Could have been no Legislative delegation attending the funeral - perhaps at Jesse Boone's funeral. Boone's death occurred about the time of the admission of Missouri to the Union.

Rev. James Craig preached the sermon: what Boone had done for his country in exploration and settlement of the west, & defence of the country. Only an ordinary preacher, yet did pretty well.

Mrs. Grant (sister of Daniel Boone) had the dropsy, nine gallons of water were taken from her at different times.

Mrs. Coshow (Bryan's Missouri Families, pages 133 & 138) can tell nothing more than that he was early killed by the Indians - when, where & how, can't tell - nor any thing about his being with Daniel Boone. Mrs. Coshow married Jonathan.

58 Death of Capt. Wm. Hays - Dec. 13, 1804 - given in <u>Pioneer Families of Missouri</u>, p. 90. Daniel Boone thought him a quarrelsome man. Hays supposedly whipped his wife Susannah Boone Hays badly, reports were that Daniel Boone whipped William Hays badly. Mrs. Bryan doubts it.

James Davis was a shoemaker, was summoned on the grand jury. Started to hunt his horse to ride to court, & passing by Capt. Hays, the latter saw him & asked him in. Davis declined as he said he was in a hurry to find his horse to ride to court as he was on the Grand jury. Hays said if he wouldn't come in, he would make him, & went in & got his rifle & followed. Coming near Davis, the latter dodged behind a tree, & Hays dodged up to same tree on opposite side, still cursing Davis, & bantered him to shoot, when Davis, in self-defence, did so & killed Hays. The only witness was a son of Hays, a youth, Daniel.

Col. Daniel Boone, knowing Hays was of a quarrelsome disposition, went alone on Davis bond of $3000, to appear at court. He was tried & acquitted.

While in Kentucky, Hays badly cut a man with whom he was scuffling in playfulness, & got mad & came near killing him.

Femme Osage - origin of name - see <u>Pioneer Families of Missouri,</u> p. 66

59 The payment of his Kentucky debts could hardly have been by sale of his land confirmation in Dec. 1813 (p. 43 <u>Pioneer Families</u>) – for he was too old to have gone to Kentucky after that date.

    Green River Hunting Expedition – p. 14; Mr. Bryan, after further thought, says while he is not certain, rather thinks that Boone discovered a lone Indian going from the direction of one of his traps with a beaver. When out of sight, Boone went to the trap, & found a beaver had been caught & was missing. Thus as Indians had discovered his traps, & kept them, evidently with a view to appropriate further catchings, & so Boone removed his trips to another stream. Compare this with Nathan Boone's statement.

    I think Col. Nathan Boone's notes show that when Col. Daniel Boone's claim was confirmed – Dec. 1813 – some Kentuckian to whom Boone had sold Kentucky land, of which a better title turned up, & seeing Boone's claim confirmed, came on & claimed for his pay – hence Boone sold his land…

    Jackson or Fish of Shawanoes was taken prisoner when a boy* in Kentucky at an early day – his brother James Jackson came to persuade him to return home; but he would not leave the Indians, said the whites would not respect him. He was only an Indian. James identified him by particular marks, which the Fish recognized.

*See Joseph Jaackson interview in 11C

    60 Mrs. Susanna Hays – Boone's daughter – Hays whipped her badly & it was reported that Col. Boone went & whipped Hays as badly. Mr. Bryan has doubts about it. Mr. Bryan has no recollection of seeing her – she died in her 40th year, says <u>Pioneer Families of Mo.</u>, p. 6

    1770 – Daniel Boone said he & Stewart were out hunting & [Indians] surrounded them, & made them prisoners, did not keep them long before they got away.

    Don't know who the man was who came out with Squire Boone, perhaps Jesse Boone on one occasion, & on another.

    1804 – John Davis & Lewis Jones went from Loutre region, joined Lewis & Clark & went along to the eastern foot of Rocky Mountains – did not enlist – went as volunteers; came across a party of Indians who robbed them of their guns, ammunition & other things; gave them an old gun, a poor blanket, a little powder & lead, & let them go. Killed a deer & skinned it – meat for food. And Green took the green deer skin, cut holes in it, to run through for his arms, with the hair next to the body. Finally got into the settlement & had to cut off the skin. Davis had the old blanket for his protection. He married Susan Bryan, the daughter of Henry Bryan. Davis was a large, stout man. Davis died long after the war about 1852 or later, had a son, Clark Davis, a saddler, may yet be living. His father, John Davis, lived on Bear Creek, Montgomery County.

61 Allen's Biographical Dictionary says:
In 1800, Boone discovered the Boone's Lick Country. In 1800, also, Daniel Boone visited the headwaters of the Grand Osage & spent the winter upon the head waters of the Arkansas.

At the age of 80, in company with a white man & Negro, laid under strict obligations to carry him back to his family dead or alive, he made a hunting trip to the head waters of the Great Osage, & was successful in trapping beaver & other game. This is wrong as to date - Allen's Biography…would have made the time of the hunt with the Negro & a white man in 1814, when it was several years before.

[Newspaper clipping at bottom of page]
Vernon's Early Settlers. A Reunion of the Pioneers and Their Friends Held at Vernon. Special to the Republic – 1890, Nevada, Mo. July 31. The old settlers and pioneers of Vernon County held their annual reunion at Sulphur Springs, two miles north of this city, today. Addresses by local orators and a basket dinner were the features of the day. There were perhaps 1000 people on the grounds, only a few of whom were old pioneers. Among the latter was James Bevan, aged 84, born in St. Charles County, Missouri, who came to Vernon in 18—. He has a brother living in Nevada.

4C62 LCD questions To James Bryan, Sept. 24, 1890
1- Whether Daniel Boone ever visited Kentucky after he settled in Missouri, also when & circumstances
2 - His hunting trips in southwest Missouri
3 - Particularly the trip with Henry Logan & John Davis to Grand River, date not exactly determined - when it took place – where - & incidents.
Whether Boone & others went as far as Yellow Stone River.
Is John Davis's son Clark Davis. Pioneer Families of Missouri, p. 253) is yet living & where. LCD

4C66-66(1) James S. Stonestreet letter, Clark County, Ky., August 24, 1853. Was in Harmar's Campaign &c.

Dear Sir.
 I received your letter a few days ago. I have learned since I wrote to you that the Samuel Boone I know was not the brother of Daniel Boone, but the son of Samuel Boone, Daniel's brother, who I am informed died in

Fayette County in the year 1808 or 1809.

  I have seen Mrs. Vaughn. She says her father Col. Holder died on the 30th of March 1799. She fixed the date by the birth of her oldest son. She also says that the party who rescued the three girls captured by the Indians near Boonsboro were headed by Col. John Floyd and not by Dan. Boone.

  I have seen a gentleman who was acquainted with Jesse Cofer. He could give no information of his early adventures but says he removed with his family to the state of Missouri, he thinks about thirty years ago. I have no further information concerning Peter Scholl, and know nothing of Philip Goe.

  I have seen an intelligent neighbor of Capt. William Bush. His information is that Capt. W. Bush was born in Orange County, Virginia, that he came to this country with Daniel Boone the second time Boone came out. He was in the fort at Boonsboro when it was besieged by the Indians, was on captain Harmer's campaign, and was ingaged in many small encounters with the Indians. He **(1)** secured a large tract of land across the river from Boonsboro and four or five of his brothers afterwards came out & settled around him. It is still called the Bush Settlement. He died in this county about forty years ago, and left a large family of children, now all dead but two. One son, Willis Bush, lives in Gallatin County [Tennessee]. The Bush connection in this county is counted by hundreds, perhaps a thousand or more. Col. Pleasant Bush who married his cousin, a daughter of Capt. Wm Bush, is now State Senator from this district, and Col. James Bush another nephew is our county Judge.

                Yours &c
                Jas Stonestreet

4C67-67(1) James Stonestreet letter, Clark County Ky., Sept. 13, 1853

Dear Sir

  I received your letter of the 2d ult. by the last mail. I answered your second letter some weeks ago. I suppose you had not received it when you wrote. In answer to your last letter, I never was at the mouth of Red river, the greater part of which overflows in very high floods. Below the mouth there is no bottom. Opposite the mouth on the south side of the Kentucky River there is a large bottom of several hundred acres which does not overflow except a small strip.

  I am well acquainted with the mouth of Hickman creek I lived near there some six years. There is very little bottom on either side of the river. There is a singular hill with steep sides below the mouth of creek.

More than three hundred feet high in the form of a sugar loaf and a valley some fifty yards wide between it and the main hill. It looks as if the river might have run there in former times. I append on the next page a diagram of the locality.

A young man by the name of Goe came unexpectedly to my house last week. He says his grandfather's name was Philip Goe, that his father moved some years ago from this county and now lives about eight miles **(1)** up the Kentucky river above Irvine, the county seat of Estill county, that he is kin to the Boones but knows nothing of the history of his grandfather. I mentioned in my last letter that I had seen Mrs. Vaughn who informed me when Col Holder died. She also said that Fanny Calloway one of the three girls captured by the Indians. She afterwards married Col. Holder and was her step mother.

Respectfuly Yours &c
James Stonestreet

P. S. I know nothing about the mouth of Little Hickman. The Bottoms on the Kentucky River are seldom more than fifty yards wide and change from one side of the river to the other, rarely any bottom but on one side and every high flood, the most of them overflow.

J.S.

A plat in the middle of this last page above the postscript shows rivers and turnpikes going out from a center-point. Clockwise place names: Turnpike to Lexington, Hickman Creek, small creek, Turnpike to Danville, Kentucky River.

4C75 Daniel Boone's account book
No date is legible and only a few names are legible: Wm Moore, Edmon Smith, Daniel Boone, James Black, Fredrick G_____ly.

4C75(1) *LCD speculation on Shane's error re: the year of Daniel Boone's trip 1774-1775 to Charleston, South Carolina. Boone could have visited Charleston only after his return to North Carolina in the fall of 1778 & prior to his removal from the Yadkin to Kentucky in fall of 1779.*

In that interim he might have done so – might have driven cattle there, or something of that kind. On the whole, I think this trip was a part of the Florida exploration in 1766 – when John Field was one of the party. Some of the party gambled, "a watch played away at dice." Col. John Field was killed in 1774 at Point Pleasant battle is another reason for placing trip prior to that date. LCD

4C77 Daniel Boone to William Preston *in Boone's handwriting*
                                         Boones Borrogh Sep the 7 1776
Dear. Colonel
        As Col. Floyd is going in, it is not worth my while wrighting any thing But my best Respects to you and your family. When Major Campbell was out he told me there was a Little money left - and desired you might take your pay out of it for the powder and Lad [lead?] he sent me which I told him I was willing   he sent me word to sell it at ___ shillings a pound and the lead at ten pence and in the S____s had one pound of it and 2 pound of lead. I have sent you Majr. Campbells Latter that you may se it. I am Sir your humble Sarvant
                                                       Daniel Boone

4C77(1) LCD note: See Col. Campbell Sept. 7, 1776

4C78 *This letter is partly illegible.*

Arthur Campbell to William Fleming
Washington [County, Virginia]
July 31, 1778

Sir:
By the enclosed Copy of a Letter and deposition will be made known the probable distress of the Garrison at Boonesborough. We have a report that no Militia will be Ordered to join General McIntosh on the Western Expedition. If that expedition should be dropt this year again it will be unfortunate for the Western frontier as by the accounts of the prisoners the Commandant at Detroit has effectually set against us the most vindictive Indian Tribe Yet. No doubt he profits much in a private way by the plunder of our frontier. I propose sending Major Smith [William Bailey Smith] of This County with some Militia to the relief of Kentucky. will you please to communicate the matter to the Lieutenant of Montgomery [County, Virginia] who I understand is now in your County and could one Company be sent from That county. I think I can raise two out of this and I hope to have Them ready to March from the neighborhood of Mockison Gap by the 15th day of August. Should not there be a call for Militia to go on the Expedition. I hope the relief of Kentucky may prove an essential service. I have sent on the Kentucky packet to Williamsburg by Express as assind [assigned] and expect an Answer will be back by the 15th of next month.

Open the Kentucky packet, and write if proper to the Governor. Attention is too much enjoyed with the affairs Eastwardly, or else They don't feel for the miseries that happen on the Western frontier.

                              I am Sir Your very Humble Servant
                              Arthur Campbell

4C79 *William Hancock, captured in February 1778 with Daniel Boone's saltmakers, had just returned to Fort Boonesborough on July 17 after escaping from captivity.*

William Hancock's deposition. Boonesborough, 17th July 1778, Kentucky SS

    The deposition of William Hancock, being first sworn on the Holy Evangelists, is as follows: This deponent saith, that the 5th of this instant he was in company with twelve Frenchmen in Big Chillacotha Town, at which time there was a Grand Council held with the principal Indians from different nations. There were considerable presents made them by the French from Detroit, two of whom were a Captain and an Ensign, and that they informed him they were coming at least two hundred men strong against this garrison. This deponent saith, that the Indians informed they should come four hundred strong, and offer the English flag to the inhabitants, and if the terms were rejected, they intended to batter down our fort with their swivels, as they are to have four sent them from Detroit, which will be conveyed up the Mawmee river, and down the Great Miami to the Ohio, and thence up the Kentucky to Boonesborough. This deponent further saith, that the French and Indians intend to be around our fort, and live on our stock, till they starve us out. Further this deponent saith not.
                                        Sworn before me.
                                        Richd. Callaway

Page before 80
        Boone – Callaway
        Col. Arthur Campbell.
        Maj. Daniel Smith – to Ky.
        A party goes within 5 miles of Chillicothe.

4C80 Daniel Boone to Col. Arthur Campbell or Evan Shelby
                        Boonesborough, 18th July 1778.
Dear Colonel:
    I have inclosed the Deposition of Capt. Daniel Boone with that of Mr. Hancock, who arrived here yesterday and informed us of both French

and Indians coming against us to the number of near four hundred, which I expect here in twelve days from this. If men can be sent out to us in five or Six weeks, it would be of infinite service, as we shall lay up provisions for a siege. We are all in fine spirits, and have good crops growing, and intend to fight hard in order to secure them. I shall refer you to the bearer for particulars of this country.

I am yours &c
Daniel Boone

To Cols. Arthur Campbell,
or Evan Shelby
a copy

N.B. The original is in the hand write of Mr. William Bailey Smith and he first signed his own name which is the cause I understand of a blunder in the language.

R. C. [Richard Callaway?]

4C81 LCD Memo – The Journal of the Governor & Council of Virginia of August 12th, 1778 shows: "A letter from Col. Arthur Campbell and sundry papers from Kentucky giving information of the French & Indians at Detroit having a design to make an attack upon the forts in Kentucky. " The Governor was advised to give Col. Campbell directions to send not under 100, not over 150, militia, officered in the usual manner, for the relief of Kentucky.

4C82 Boone in Kentucky – 1770 – 1776 – 1779.
Depositions from Clark County, Ky. Records
_____ Broadhurst, Winchester, Ky., Oct. 23, 1883

Dear Sir; I have received several letters from you in regard to copying some old depositions of Daniel Boone which are filed in the Clerk's office of the Clark County Court. I have never copied these depositions before, because I thought they were uninteresting and not worth what they would cost you to have them copied…

4C83-87 Daniel Boone's camp returning from Recapturing the Girls – 1776. Boone's Deposition for Watson. *Not in LCD handwriting. Deposition was given on Oct. 22, 1795.*

The Deposition of Daniel Boone in order to prove and establish the entry of William Watson containing 955 acres… Deponent deposeth and saith that on the 16th day of July 1776, on my return from retaking my Daughter from the Indians, we, deponent & company, lay all night on Flat Creek at the mouth of a small Branch a small distance from a Cabin on the east side of said Creek, & in the year 1780. On the 15 day of May, I Entered 955 acres of land for William Watson beginning six miles nearly south west of the upper salt spring at Daniel Boone's old camp at the forks of a branch on [the] War Road, running up the Branch on both sides... and in the year 1785, I Surveyed the said land and the cabin was then standing **84** and that we now stand near the spot where Deponent and company lay that night viz the 16th of July 1776.

Question: Col. Boon, were you employed to make said entry?
Answer: To be sure, I was.
Question 2. Were there any writings passed between you & any person touching the said business?
Answer: I do not recollect that there were.
Question 3. Were you to receive anything for making these entries?
Answer: Yes, I was paid for it.
Question [number?]. Did you know this to be Flat Creek when you made the entry?
Answer: I think I did certainly know because of Hammond's & Henderson's entries.
Question 4. Were you employed to show as well as to survey said Land?
Answer: I was not employed nor received anything but the Surveyors fees.
Question 5. Were you acquainted with the upper salt spring on Lickin at that time?
Answer: I was.
Question 6: What course do you at this time suppose the said upper salt springs to be?
85 Answer: I now suppose it to be nearly north.
Question 7. What distance do you suppose to be from here from this old camp to the upper salt springs?
Answer: I suppose 8 or 9 miles – but at that time I did not think so much.
Question 8. Did you make or cause to be made any special mark at the old camp or place of beginning?
Answer: I did not.

The Deponant then according to request proceeded to find the place where a cabin stood ...but when we came there appeared nothing but some vestages of an old camp where some cutting had been (viz) one old stump, which Deponent supposed might have been cut for a cabin.

We then proceeded to ascertain the distance from said old encampment to the beginning of said survey...

86 Agreeable to an order of the Court of Clark County in July 1795, this day Daniel Boon came before us, Elisha Collins and Joseph Scholl, Commissioners appointed agreeable by the Court... that he was then on the place alluded to in the Entries made by Boon for Leonard Hall, assignee[?] of Benjamin Barton, that this was the spring, the fork of the creek and Buffalo Trace.

Question: What sum of money did Boon receive of Leonard Hall to locate the Hall entries?
Answer: Deponant doth not remember what sum but was satisfied and at the time the Entries was made for said Hall.
87 Question: Whether he, Boon, is not to receive a certain sum of money from Hall for showing the said Land marks mentioned?
Answer by Deponant: That he has not received one Shilling nor was never offered any sum by Hall but that he, Boon, intended to charge Hall for his trouble and further saith not.

Daniel Boon
Joseph Scholl
Elisha Collins

4C99 "From Ms. Letter[s] of Daniel Pennington to the author", c. 1854. *John Stuart was married to Hannah Boone, sister of Daniel. They had three young daughters at the time he was killed by Indians in Kentucky. Hannah and her second husband, Richard Pennington, had four children: Joshua, Daniel, Stuart, and Abigail Pennington. The children were named in a letter of Thomas L. Pennington, grandson of Hannah Boone Pennington, to LCD in 1853 (DM 23C40-40(1).*

4C130 Deposition of Michael Stoner, living Wayne County, Ky. in 1816, "deposes and says that in 1772 Francis Ward, William Miller and myself was at the Blue Licks in Madison County in the spring of the year and the said Ward told me that Daniel Boone had showed them licks to him, that one was called Blue Lick, and the other Joe's Lick. In the year 1774, in the summer, said Boone and myself came out and crossed Station Camp Creek. He then told me the Red and Blue Licks was on the head of the Creek."

4C133-133(1) Samuel McAfee Duncan letter, Nicholasville, Ky., July 21,

1885

Dear Sir your letter of 15th was handed to me this morning. I never received yours of May 1st. In answer to your query concerning Marble Creek Cave, I can inform you that the Cave is small, and would probably safely hide three or four persons. It is about thirty five or forty miles from the ruins of Boonesboro, and is about a mile or perhaps two miles from the mouth of Marble Creek, so nine miles northeast of Nicholasville and fourteen southeast of Lexington.

The initials of Daniel Boone are not there at present. Whether Boone was in the cave, or whether he cut his initials at the time he was at Boonesboro is a question I cannot answer.

(1) I believe he was much in that portion of our county as there was a good road as early as 1790 from Boonesboro to Richmond in Madison County, and from Richmond to Lexington. The Road is now called the Tates Creek Pike, Richmond is 19 miles from Nicholasville. Boone had many relatives in Madison County in Pioneer times.

Very truly
Your Friend
Saml McAfee Duncan

4C150-150(1) Samuel M. Duncan letter, Nicholasville, Ky., Sept. 2, 1885

I have not been able to visit the cave at the mouth of Hickman but will do so as soon as I have more time to Spare. I have it from good authority that the dates of 1780-2-3-4 are not to be Seen in the cave at the mouth of Hickman. I have believed for years that a Mr. D. Burchell cut his own initials, and cut the dates there to induce Harvey Lindsy to believe that Daniel Boone had cut them. It was done in order to make Lindsy believe it was Boone, in order to establish a Post office to be called Boone's Knob.

I sent you an account of the story about an Indian leaping over the great cliff **(1)** at Brooklyn. This was published in the <u>Casket of 1828.</u>* I have seen many men who remembered the story as it is told by the old ferry man. You may have a copy, if it will do you any good. If not return it to me as it relates to historical fact entirely forgotten by the present generation.

Truly
Saml. M. Duncan

LCD notes: *Not in Casket of 1828 – it must have been in 1831, or 1833 or later. The Indian's Leap – 100 feet down into the Kentucky river – apparently about 1782, just before the Siege of Bryan's Station, "late in the spring" – it may have been 1780. The story is too marvelous – too many Indians slain to be true. If it had been true, or anything like it, Boone would have mentioned it in his narrative & other early writers would have done so.

Boone forgot not to mention the Crab Orchard incidence, where only one Indian was killed.

4C157 *This seems to be the end of Draper's questions to Samuel M. Duncan.*
Indicate on the rude plat below, the localities of Camp Nelson, the cave of "DB 1773" - & Boone's Knob. Place names on map: Boons Knob, Camp Nelson, Cave 1773, Big Hickman, Little Hickman, Kentucky River, Jessamine ____, Burns Knob, Montgomery County.

Note of Samuel M. Duncan
Oct. 1887
I am always glad to hear from you. I am active in manhood yet but my memory and eye sight is failing me. I am poor in this worlds goods, but I envy no man for his wealth. I own a small home and have never been married. My sister lives with me.

4C159 *J. D. Spratt map with some legible place names: Licking River, Clark County, Montgomery County, Peyton Lick, Hinkston Creek, Battleground Estill vs. Indians, Mt. Sterling, Stephens Station, Slate Creek, Mill Creek, Salt Lick Creek, Marshall, Olympia Station, Morrison's, East Fork, Bald Eagle Branch, upper Blue Lick, Cassity Creek, Flat Creek, Owingsville.*

Volume 5C contains 100(3) numbered pages

5C1-1(1) Long Hunters of Kentucky

Public Library Paper, Louisville, Ky. Jan. 17, 1874.
… the section of a beech tree cut upon Beargrass, upon which is inscribed the name of Daniel Boone ninety-nine years ago. An additional proof where the Long Hunters camped (which no history has before shown) is the names of Knox's party plainly to be seen upon the beech

trees in the same vicinity.

    <u>A Century Tree</u> – Col. Wm B. Allen… has sent to the cabinet of the Public Library the block of a beech tree, which from its size and rings of annual growth make it one hundred years old. In the heart of this tree are several ten-penny nails, horizontally and firmly fixed in the solid wood of a healthy growth, not a speck of rottenness being about it. Strange how incidents can become witnesses in after ages, as does this in proof of the record of the history that Col. James Knox and his long hunters (two years in the dark and lonely wilderness) camped near this tree in 1770, one hundred and four years ago. The nails must have been driven in to this tree when a sapling and time imbedded them in its heart. A man who was cutting wood at Col. Allen's place, near Greensburg, told him he had found nails in the heart of a large tree…

5C47-48 Robert Wickliff letter, Lexington, Ky., Dec. 25, 1843

My Dear Sir,

    I have received by mail your letter, & a letter from Mr. Vander____ requesting a sketch from me (&/or you) of the lives of Col. William ____ and of Col. John Todd. I have had a sketch of each of the gentlemen, & would now lend them… [but] fear you will not think them worth the Postage & shall keep them until you write me how I am to send them to you…

                                                         Robert Wickliff

5C49-49(1,2) Robert Wickliff letter, Lexington, Ky., October 23, 1848

Dr Sir

    I have just reached home & opened your very Interesting Letter of the 16th of October on My Table. And will when I can steal as much time to answer most of your inquery. I never knew you had called on me untill I received Your Letter. I once prepared (I think for you) a Sketch of The Life of General John Harlan, grand father to the young man of the same name that fell at Buena Vista (but not seeing nor hearing from you) I tore it up. I write Badly, am old & over charged with ____ & you will please to excuse me if I do not **(1)** Send you my ____ very shortly. For I am sure I cannot work on it for some time to come. I am out of practice but I am alone in the world, Blacks exceeding two hundred… What I send you shall possess verity but will be rough [in] **(2)** my crude style…such however as I can send you I will & that as soon as I can.

                                                           Yours Respy
                                                           Robert Wickliff

5C50-50(1,2) Robert Wickliff letter, Lexington, Ky., Nov 18, 1848

Dr Sir
    Sent you a rough sketch of John Todd history and a rough pen mark of the buffaloe road ___ battleground ... if you think it worth the postage, Give you the life of General John Harlan (of the Revolution)... The sketch given ... by a son of John Harlan who was too young to know anything of his father's history when he was killed, but has taken family statements, a part of which is in ___. [Regarding false statements that] John was raised a hunter & was always in the woods with his Gun – So far from this being correct, his father was a man in comfortable circumstances – had a country store when the revolution broke out, & John kept it for him...
    I can give you a short sketch of Col. James Knox after whom our Knox County was called... James Knox was in Kentucky in the fall of the year 1768, & named Dicks River after the Isham[?] Dick who pioneered him to it. Boone never saw the country until 1769.
    ...The John Howard & Sallie of whom you inquire I know nothing. Of the John Howard, brother-in-law to Col. Preston, I do, & presume he was no relation to the former Howard. **(1)** Judge Twyman lived about ten years since in the county of Scott where he resided for many years. Samuel Johnson lived in Lexington at the time ___ the Blue Licks & settled and married in that part of Fayette which is now Jessamine County where he lived many years & died about thirty years past. Henry Wilson – the only survivor that was at the Battle of the Blue Licks - nearly one hundred years old... in the county of Montgomery in this state when I saw him last, in his proper mind
    (2) ...He said he was informed by the Indians ... in the Battle, that but for Harlan's advance that few of the whites would have escaped...communicated to him by several Indians & at different Times...[at] Indeans treaty...who were in the battle & survived. Should you desire a Sketch of John Harlan... Wishing you success in your undertaking I am Dear Sir your obedient Servant
                                                           Robert Wickliff

5C51-51(18) The Life of Colo. John Todd

This account is undated and is not in Draper's handwriting. The unnamed writer mentions that pioneer Henry Wilson is nearly one hundred years old at the time this account was written. Henry Wilson, who was at Harrods Station and later lived in Bourbon County, Ky., died in 1848.

The writer seems to have eyewitness facts of the Battle of Blue Licks and to have been in the battle and at the burying of the dead.

A discussion of strategy between Col. Todd and Daniel Boone just before the beginning of the battle at Blue Licks is given, with Daniel Boone telling the other officers how he knew the Indians were planning an ambush.

John Todd married Jane Hawkins in Virginia about 1780; they traveled to Kentucky on horseback during that bitter winter. Their daughter and only child, Mary Owen Todd, was born in Kentucky a few months later. (John Todd's mother's maiden name was Owen.) Mary Owen Todd married first James Russell, and second, Robert Wickliff. She died in 1844 in Kentucky. It was Robert Wickliff who sent this account to Lyman Draper.

Col. John Todd was a native of the state of Pennsylvania, son of David Todd, a farmer of that State. The family of Todd were originally from Ireland, but the Mother of John Todd was from Wales or descended from Welch parents. Col. Todd at an early age left his parental residence to reside with this paternal uncle, John Todd, a distinguished Divine, who had established at his residence in the state of Virginia an academy at which his Nephew John received the rudiments of a good education, both Literary & scientific, & aided in his studies by his Uncle who had an extensive library.

He left his hospitable mansion with advantages superior to most youths of his time, for added to a thorough acquaintance with the classics, he had acquired a pretty considerable knowledge of mathematics & had read & studied History & Geography with great success so that he was well prepared to commence the study of Law.

At a period before the revolution broke out, he was admitted to the practice of Law & selected as the scene of his future usefulness the village of Fincastle, then the seat of Justice for Fincastle since named by the revolutionary Legislature of Virginia, Botetourt County. It was here that the youthful Todd became acquainted & a favourite with Colonels Preston, Christian, Flemming & other distinguished men of western Virginia. His habits, like his acquirements, were ___ solid, so that he was soon possessed of a good practice & before the revolution broke out had acquired some Capital. His character gave him unlimited credit, but when ____ of **(1)** Henderson's purchase of the Cherokee Indians & the adventures of Boone reached the settlements of Virginia, Col. Todd yielded up his practice & embarked his fortunes with those of Henderson's company. We find from scraps of manuscripts still existing preserved that he was an active member of Henderson's Legislative Council & a locator of considerable bodies of land under Henderson.

However he did not long remain with Col. Henderson before he learned from Doctor Walker's extension of the line between Virginia & North Carolina that Henderson's purchase lay wholly within the State of Virginia (that refused to ratify Henderson's purchase from the Indians).

Col. Todd immediately determined to submit to the will of his adopted State & withdrew himself altogether from Col. Henderson's party, & yet the kindest feelings & sympathys are said to have always existed between Henderson &Todd, & Todd & all the distinguished followers of Henderson, although Henderson's settlement was broken up & his purchase from the Cherokee Indians of what is now the State of Kentucky abandoned. The State of Virginia in considerations of the sum advanced by the Company to the Indians granted to them 150,000 acres of land on the Ohio river, around what is now the town of Henderson [Kentucky]. Col. Todd appears not to have been a beneficiary in the Grant but to have remained in the country aiding & assisting the settlers under the State of Virginia in the bloody war that was raging between the United States & England & her savage allies.

It appears from the deposition of May or others that Col. Todd accompanied Gen. George Rogers Clarke on his expedition against Kaskaskie & Vincennes in which a handful of volunteers with no other weapons than Rifle & tomahawk reduced **(2)** two British garrisons, that of Kaskaskia & Vincennes defended by Col. Hamilton & his British regulars. After the capture of these forts from England, the State of Virginia ____ed all the territory lying west of the Ohio to the Pacific Ocean into a county with She called the county of Illinois.

Col. Clark was created a general with the supreme command of all the forces belonging to the state west of the Alleghany Mountains. Col. John Todd was created Colonel commandant of the county of Illinois & further invested with all the civil & executive powers within said county exercised by the Governor of Virginia in the rest of the State of Virginia. He was further invested with power in conjunction with the Governor of Virginia to raise a regiment either by Drafts or by voluntary enlistment for the defence of the county of Illinois, to be styled the Illinois regiment, & to commission the officers &c. This act was passed at the session of

1778... & was to continue in force one year. Col. Todd immediately set to work, & organized the regiment & repaired to Kaskaskee which he made the seat of his government. Here he formed a compleat municipal government by appointing & commissioning all necessary officers, & by the wisdom & energy of his government, the Creoles of the country were contented & happy under their change of master, & continued to display the greatest Loyalty to the State of Virginia...

The State of Virginia passed an act by which they created two regiments for the defence of the west & two Regiments for the defence of the east of the States. It is believed that Col. Todd was appointed to the command of one of those regiments & Col. C____ to the other, but as the records & papers of the times when such appointments should have been made **(3)** were destroyed by the British during the revolutionary war when they took possession of Richmond, the Capitol of Virginia, no commission has ever been found that he was appointed to the command of either of them. The presumption is that he had his commission with him when he was killed at the battle of the Blue Licks, but Col. Whaly & Major Netherland both swear that he did belong to the regular army.

Whaly, being a Lieutenant, swears further that he served with him upon a court marshal [sic] of regular officers at Louisville. Added to the testimony of these witnesses, papers left with his widow & some now existing in the Archives of Virginia, prove the fact that he was a Colonel in the regular army on the Virginia State line establishment.

In May 1780, Col. Todd was elected a delegate to the house of representatives of Virginia, which office he accepted & returned to the settled or eastern part of Virginia for the first time after he left it, which must have been about the year 1775...

As Colonel commandant & Governor of the County of Illinois, & as Colonel commandant of his regiment on State ____ establishment, he had still a dearer object to his heart to visit. He had while a school boy & student contracted an engagement of marriage with Jane Hawkins, eldest daughter of John Hawkins, Esqr., of Hanover County in the State of Virginia. The youth of the parties when this tender engagement was made rendered a postponement proper until he had established himself in the practice of his profession. But before the ____ for the consummation of their vows had arrived, the revolution broke out & Col. Todd had other scenes & jeopardies to pass through than those which him & his fair one had contemplated. However, the parties, true to their pledges, determined that nothing but death should **(4)** repeal their vows or finally separate them. In 1780[?] they were allowed to meet & marry while war & blood-shed still convulsed the state from the Capital to its western limits. During the session 1780[?], much business was done & Col. Todd seems to have taken the leave upon all important measures affecting western interests. The county of Kentucky was divided into three counties, To wit – the counties of Fayette, Lincoln & Jefferson. Col. Todd was appointed Colonel commandant of the county of Fayette.

The amount of private business done by Col. Todd as well as publick duties performed by him the few months he remained in Virginia would seem almost incredible, yet such was his industry & activity that he was not only an active & leading member in the house, but was incessantly employed every moment he could spare…

When the Legislature adjourned, he had to avail himself of the depth of one of the severest winters ever felt in America (the winter of 1780) to repass the dreary wilderness which lay between the Capitol & the scenes of his future destined home. Yet duty impelled his return & his wife preferred to [endure?] hardships & encounter dangers however great to again being separated. Her Father died wealthy & she had been surrounded by comforts & friends, but she braved the winter, the savages & with her husband set out from her widowed Mother's comfortable mansion (in the county of Hanover) on horseback without a guard to protect them.

They passed the settlements of Virginia, crossing her mountains covered with snow until they penetrated the wilderness that lay **(5)** between the Alleghany mountains and the settlements of Kentucky (who that has ever passed the road since the Indian murders have ceased) over the mountains & rivers of that wilderness that will not wonder at the firmness of Mrs. Todd & even that of her husband in daring to attempt a passage through it in such a winter. Many of the streams they had to cross were large rivers that were too deep to be forded, such as the Kanawa[?], The Holston, the Clinch, the Powel, the Cumberland & Rocastle rivers, besides others of lessor note too numerous to mention. These were not forded & there were no ferries. The country had no inhabitants but Indians & the Traveller no vehicle to cross over them on but such feeble rafts as he could construct out of logs & chunks of wood he could tie together with grape vine or hickory withes. Yet on the rafts constructed by Col. Todd & servant he would first pass over wife & then swim by the side of the raft his horses, one at a time.

The passage of a stream always consumed a day & sometimes two days, but they finally reached the first settlement about the 15th of February 1781 & was hospitably received & entertained by his friend & companion in arms, Lieut. Benjamin Logan.

There Col. Todd & his lady rested a day & proceeded to the fort that stood at the centre of where the city of Lexington now stands. Although Col. Todd & his wife were met by kind friends & some relations in Lexington, such had been the severity & length of the winter that the Buffaloe & other game had become poor & most of it had since left the usual hunting grounds ... The people were reduced to such a degree of distress that they had scarcely a piece of poor Buffaloe ___ to divide with them. Bread there was none in the fort. Old inhabitants used to speak of this winter as a time of the most intense suffering. They knew that spring would come & **(6)** their hunters would supply them with meat & this hope gave them consolation so that they passed their season of suffering without complaint, although they knew that they could have no bread until they grew another crop of corn.

The year 1781 was a year of their great peril & bloodshed. The British Government, determined to break up the settlements in Kentucky, had by rewards for scalps in blankets, guns, & tomahawks, armed the whole of the savages of the North & South against the feeble forts of Kentucky.

Yet in this year, 1781, through scenes of bloodshed & daring, Col. Todd was engaged incessantly in his pubic duties in Kentucky & Illinois. He visited the seat of Government of Illinois in the latter part of 1781 for the last time & returned to Lexington during the following spring, where he remained endeavouring to settle his family & to cultivate a piece of corn land, until the Indians between three & four hundred strong invaded the country. [They were] led by Mulunthy [Moluntha], a Shawnee chief, & Simon Girty, a white man who becoming disabused with the whites had left Pittsburg about the beginning of the revolution & joined the Indians & became famous for his achievements & cruelty upon the whites. This army of Indians was well supplied with arms & ammunition after having swept one or two forts, laid siege to Bryants Station about five miles from Lexington, where Col. Todd was then residing.

Upon intelligence reaching Lexington of the precarious condition of Bryant's station & that the Indians had burnt Craigs station in the same neighbourhood, Col. Todd & others at Lexington immediately prepared to give succor to the besieged before they were victimized by the savages. They despatched couriers to all the forts in the country that could from their distance aid the besieged, summoning every **(7)** man that could be spared from those forts to rendezvous at Lexington as soon as possible. Col. Logan's fort was the most distance. By the night of the second or third day of the siege, there reached Lexington about one hundred twenty brave men, some of them the first men in the country... it is believed there never were assembled in the same number of volunteer soldiers more talented &

worthy. They had waited until the volunteers from Harrods station, a distance of ten[?] miles had arrived & all they could hear from Col. Logan that he was actively engaged in collecting volunteers together to push forward to the relief of Bryant's fort. It was concluded, however, not to wait longer for Logan as the fort was in danger of falling into the hands of the savages every moment.

Col. Todd set off from Lexington with all the men he could raise, ignorant of the actual force of the enemy, was soon at Bryant's Station with the heartfelt gratification to see the fort still standing. The Indians had retreated as he approached. After halting at Bryant's...to receive an additional force, & also hoping to hear from Col. Logan, having but a supply for few days of provisions, he concluded to wait no longer, but to pursue the Indians & bring them to battle – if not to drive them from the country, concluding if they were not pressured & offered battle that they would follow other & weaker forts & then disperse into small parties to ambush & murder, as well as to steal & destroy the stock of the villagers.

The Indians took up their line of march upon the buffaloe road that led from the neighbourhood of Bryant's station to the Blue Licks. Todd, with his whole force consisting of about 180 mounted guns, & footmen pursued them, but could **(8)** not overtake them as he desired to do & bring them to action before they crossed the Licking river. However, on approaching the summit of the river hill which overlooked the bottoms on the North side from whence the large salt spring flows into the river, the advanced guard discovered three Indians run out of the glen or open space around the Lick. This was immediately reported to the commander, who sent for Daniel Boone to advise with him.

On Boon's approaching Todd, Boon was heard to say "Colonel, they intend to fight us," to which Todd replied, "how do you know?" Boon answered, "they have been for some time concealing their numbers by treading in each others tracks," & pointing the Colonel to the trail, "don't you see they are doing so? This is invariable with them when they wish to seduce a pursuing enemy into an ambush." Todd enquired of Boone what kind of land there was on the other side of the river. He answered very favourable to an ambush, & that he suspected they were waylaying the road near where the river makes narrows.

On this, Col. Todd had Maj. Trigg, Captains Harlan, Lindsy & other officers brought to him & Boone repeated what he had informed Todd, & his belief that the Indians were lying in ambush at the point of the road called the narrow. Col. Todd then enquired of Boon the kind of land further on the Buffaloe road than the narrow, & the practicability of retrograding a short distance & crossing the river & falling into the rear of the Indians undiscovered. Boone stated that it might possibly be done, by going down or up the river about a mile or two & then turn, striking into the road about three miles ahead of where they were.

While this council was going on McGary, a Subordinate **(9)** in the command from Harrods' Station, Clapped spurs into his horse & plunged into the river (then about midsides of a horse deep), crying out to all that was not damned cowards to follow him. He rode across & about a third or fourth of the command followed him. Todd & the other officers appeared to pay no attention to McGary, but finally concluded that the chance to avoid a discovery of the Indians was a bad one, & that the best course to pursue was a direct pursuit. The order to march was given, Col. Todd taking the position he had kept from Lexington at the head of the column, preceded by an advance guard of twenty-five men under Capt. Harlan. On the open space or field in the North bottom of Licking [River] a halt was called.

Two experienced hunters & Indian fighters well acquainted with the road & the ground near it, were selected & directed to take the main Buffaloe road leading out of the Licks, & to pursue until it forked into three forks, to examine carefully on each side of the road if they saw any Indians to immediately return & report. These man being started, for the further marching of the Column it was directed to be drawn up & then to be divided in three lines. The right line or column was to be moved under the command of Major Trigg, & the left line under the command of Capt. Boon, & Capt. Harlan was directed to take position with his twenty-five picked men as an advance guard.

Todd, taking the command & leading the center line, in this position they remained until the two spies returned & reported that they had gone as far as the three forks of the road. Carefully going & coming, they examined on both sides of the road for Indians in ambush, but that they saw none & did not believe there was any between the river & the forks.

On this intelligence being secured, the whole were set in motion in pursuit. The lines marching **(10)** the distance of about eighty yards apart, & the advanced guard about 80 or 100 yards ahead of all. In this manner they moved in perfect order, with their arms first examined & prepared for action, untill they reached near the narrows, when some half dozen guns were fired into the front of Trigg's column, killing the Major & several others. In a few minutes the engagement became general, & Trigg's column having lost its commanding officer, gave way in great confusion.

This exposed Todd's command in flank to the Indians fire, which a part of his men received with much gallantry & spirit, returning the Indians fire with coolness & effect, but Capt. Boone returning the enemies fire from the left line, his main force was soon directed to the centre, where Harlan & Todd were engaged. The gallant Harlan stood fighting until every man of his twenty-five but three were cut down, when he fell covered with wounds. Never did man fight more bravely than Harlan did, & his men were alike brave. They proved by their deaths, & like him, ____ with their blood.

 Col. Todd & those nearest to him retreated last, but were mostly slain, forgot all that retreated & escaped but one man, Capt. Samuel Johnson, could give an account of Todd's condition & death. He saw him just as his horse's head was turned in the retreat with the blood gushing out of his body before & behind, a ball having, as he supposed, passed through the centre of his body. Todd was almost alone behind of the retreating party, apparently senseless. Thus fell John Todd, a purer & braver man never lived.

 In the battle also fell many men of talent & rank in the country who were engaged in the appropriation of lands, such as William Stewart, William McCracken & others.

 But of all the gallant spirits Kentucky had to mourn, none save Todd himself was so much lamented **(11)** as Captains Harlan & Lindsay. They were citisen soldiers trained by Clark, were among the first immigrants to the country & shared & braved every danger & fought in almost every battle with the Indians, were with Clark & distinguished themselves in his wonderfull winter campaign through the swamps & snow of Illinois. When he reached Kaskaskie & took it after crossing stream & flats covered with water, a distance of more than one hundred miles, surrounded & took St. Vincent & Colonel Hamilton & his command of British regulars.

 Gen. Clark always spoke of Harlan & Lindsay as two of the best subalterns he ever commanded. In one conversation about the battle he informed the writer of this, that in the treaties & intercourse he held with the Indians, they said but for the stand that Harlan with his advanced guard made, that but few of the whole command would have ever reached their homes. Of the one hundred & eighty that went into battle, not more than one hundred escaped.

 The Indians took but few prisoners. It is said only three prisoners taken ever returned to the country. All the rest were murdered, amidst the general gloom & common danger which this disastrous battle threw over Kentucky. Some of the fugitives who fled & left their fellow soldiers to bleed & die, were guilty no doubt of raising rumours unfavourable to the conduct of Col. Todd & his officers, to offer some apology for their escapes as so many were overtaken & murdered. Unfortunately, ____ scribblers have narrated those tales as true until the History of the State is in danger of being tinctured with their falsehoods, though none pretended that Todd did not act bravely **(12)** until he fell, none imputed cowardice to any of his Captains, his gallant Major, who poured out their blood for their country.

Lindsey & all near him fell. Trigg & all near him fell. Todd & all near him fell, & so did all those near & that fought with the chivalrous Harlan. But there were those that threw down their arms & ingloriously fled, & such are generally the manufacturers of falsehoods & slanders upon those they desert or leave to do the fighting & die.

One of those tales was that Todd & his officers, fearing that Logan & his officers would come up & Logan take the command, whip the Indians & take the glory of the victory, hastily brought on the action & was overpowered by the numbers of the enemy. Another was that they were pressed into the ambush by McGary, without order, were taken by surprise while in disorder & thus lost the battle. Facts should have warned the Historians of the falsity of these reports.

First, Col. Todd & his officers could not have apprehended that Col. Logan being present would be entitled to the command, because as before stated, Col. Todd was commissioned Colonel commandant & Governor of the county of Illinois in the beginning of the year 1778 when Gen. Logan held a commission as Captain in the county of Kentucky, as did Col. Todd. Again Col. Todd was, about 1779, commissioned a Colonel (as is believed, in one of the western regiments on State establishment in 1780) in the division of the county of Kentucky. Todd was appointed Colonel commandant of the county of Fayette, so that it is now unlikely[?] that Gen. Logan or Todd either thought of who should command when both should go into action. Todd certainly ranked Logan & every other officer in the country except Gen. Clark, but other circumstances endorsed such gro---lling Jealousy. Improbably, Logan & Todd **(13)** were companions in all the common dangers that surrounded them & afflicted their country, were bosom friends. Their families were connected by the marriage of Col. Todd's younger brother to Logan's niece & that brother went into battle with him. But the fact that the battle was fought on the 19 of August 1782 near the Blue Licks, & Col. Logan did not reach Bryant's station until the morning of the 21st, a distance of at least thirty miles from the battlefield proves that Todd could on no occasion have desired aid from Logan. From the battle to the Ohio river at the mouth of ____nna Creek, was about twenty–seven miles & a good road, by which but for the battle the Indians would have crossed the river before Logan reached Bryants station, so that a distance of sixty miles would have to be traversed before Logan could have reached the ___ & then not found an Indian.

Judge Twyman was the first man ___ ___ in the battle that saw Logan at Bryant's station, which he reached about ten o'clock on the 20th. Another man had a few minutes before brought the news who had stopt at his own house to see his family, but the sad news was, through his intelligence of the defeat, given to Logan. Twyman being a young man & a stranger in the station, was ushered into the presence of Logan to detail what he had witnessed. Logan received him with great emotion & shed tears as he related the disaster which had befallen… Logan returned as did his command, from there went from Bryant's Station to their homes.

But on the 28th, Simon Kenton took with him a sufficient number of men to bury the dead & on the 29th [?] reached the battle ground when he performed as far & as well as he could. He found Col. Todd's body & recognized it near the spot where Capt. Johnson saw him last. He was stripped & scalped. Assisted by Henry Wilson, buried him at the root & under the shade of a white oak tree, out of which Henry Wilson cut a block & formed the head of a cane.

That a few years before the death of Mrs Wickliffe, the only child of Colonel Todd, Henry Wilson conveyed **(14)** a testimony of the high regard he had ever held & cherished for her father.

Wilson still survives in his perfect health & sense, at the advanced age of nearly one hundred years, and has been for many years the only survivor of those who shared in that disastrous battle. Nor can the want of caution be charged upon any of those men who fought & on that day died for their country, that ever knew personally or by report, Boone, Lindsay, & Harlan & many others that commanded & directed the movement of the force into the ambuscade. None believe that more could have been done by others than was done to avoid disaster.

Spies had searched out the ground & reported no Indians were in ambush, the three lines were nevertheless divided, so that in the advance forward the whole narrow should be occupied by the forming of the advance column. In case of an attack & the surprise of one column might not derange the other two, the first shot brought ___ the command of the right line & that line gave way leaving the balance of the army so weakened that they had to fight more than two Indians to each white man. Indians whose nations had contended with the whites every inch of ground from the shores of the Attlantick to the North western bank of the Ohio, Indians the most warlike known in history, headed by two of the most experienced chiefs that ever led them into action.

The facts relative to Col. Todd, his death & the battle of the Blue Licks are devised from his surviving relatives. The letter of Gen. Clark to the Governor of Virginia & conversations with Gen. Clark, the letters of Capt. Daniel Boone giving an account of the Battle & the positions he occupied in it, from Judge Twyman & Capt. Sam C. Johnson who was in the battle, from Simon Kenton & Henry Wilson, who assisted in burying of the dead. Twyman's account is graphic & supported by every incident of the battle, the fabulous tale is that, Todd, Trigg, Boon, Harlan, Lindsey, & McBride & all the other gallant spirits that fell **(15)** who had fought to conquer in many a hard-contested field...

A miserable braggart such as McGary... McGary was only an ensign & according to Twyman, stood so low, that his counsel was not asked, & that, piqued at neglect shown him, he ventured the attempt to break up or distrust the consultation going on. That he was a savage monster is proven by the fact that when Gen. Logan captured the chief Molunthy in the year 1786, he with his wife & children were peaceable as all thought when he was placed under guard. McGary rushed through the guard & hewed down the captive Indian warrier with an ax. This character in after life was infamous... that the most distinguished gentlemen & Indian warriors that the country then or ever had, would yield up command & follow such a being into action, much less into an ambuscade, but it is not the whole sketch of the battle. A batch of contradictions... makes the officers throw up their command & follow the lead of a braggart & ruffian & Col. Todd & Major Trigg fall into the rear & follow the disordered mass without an advance guard, & without even sending spies to search for the enemy, the author might well be deceived by his informants... his first statement however is that Todd & Trigg were in the rear, McGary leading Boone, Harlan, & McBride in the ___, the front is attacked & Trigg & Todd in the rear killed & Harlan & the forces of McGary killed in the ___, but the front man, McGary, is unharmed. An apprehension that the Indians would attempt to get in the rear of the whites alarmed the rear & they retreated & yet Todd & Trigg in the rear already killed & Harlan & McBride are killed also, when the retreat commenced. Strange it is indeed that the two officers in the rear should have been killed before the rear was even fired upon. The high standing & amiable character of the author of the sketches forbids all who know him from even a suspicion that he did not sketch the account of the battle **(16)** from what he believed to be unquestionably true, yet the greatest men that ever adorned Kentucky & the result of the action prove ___ unintentional errors.

Gen. Clark's statement is positive that Capt. Harlan with his advance of twenty-five men were all killed but three, before the centre &

Boone's lines retreated. Capt. Johnson lived in Lexington, was a single man, of great prowess & acknowledged worth & led his company immediately after the commander into the battle, was among the last that left his position & as he did so, observed his Colonel, friend & neighbor sitting apparently senseless & dying upon his horse, the blood gush out behind & before a wound through his body. The Indians having passed over the dead bodies of Harlan & his command within a few paces of ___ & Todd.

He, Todd, was found & buried near the place where he was last seen by Johnson. Twyman's statement that he had been but a short time in the country, was a young Virginian, that had come to the country to take up lands, that he joined the volunteers & marched with them but did not select any particular company to march with, that he stood near Col. Todd when he sent for Boon, overhearing their conversation until the council of officers was called, & then retired only out of their way, that he was present & saw McGary plunge in the river & heard him call upon all but damned cowards to follow him, that not more than a third or a fourth of the men followed him, that he, Twyman, passed the river after the order to cross was given. That he saw the spies start & return & the men turned into three lines & Capt. Harlan take the guard. In this position they ascended the River hill, Todd leading the centre **(17)** column on the Buffaloe track, that he being attached to no command ascended the hill out of line near to the command. That he was about ten steps from the commander when the first guns were fired by the Indians & being between the lines of Todd & Trigg, he turned his eyes towards where the firing was & saw several horses running loose without riders but with Bridles & Saddles on. Among them he recognized Major Trigg's horse, some that he well knew. He showed the place where he was & Todd & Trigg fell when the first guns were fired & assisted the writer & servant to gather up the bones that lay heaped upon the earth & to deposit them under a cover of stones where they remained years ago. He also affirms the fact that Logan was at Bryant's Station at 10 o'clock on the 20th, the day after the battle. Boone himself says that he commanded the left column or line & the writer of the sketch says that he escaped by crossing low down the River & was attacked immediately upon the top of the curve, his way was aided by the river hill & precipices. Whereas if he had of been at the head of the centre as the writer s___s, places him, his escape would have been impossible.

The writer is in possession of other facts, tending to prove the error of the sketches of the battle of the Blue Licks… But he feels the memory of the brave men over whose memory a shade has been cast, to add one more evidence or testimony in their behalf.

In the month of April, the writer's Father descended the Ohio with his family to Kentucky. On the day that he left for Kentucky his brother-in-Law (the late Gen. John Hardin), presented him a young man in apparent destitution by the name of Neal, who was taken prisoner at the battle of the Blue Licks, was then on his return to his friends in Kentucky, the young man was given his passage & on his way **(18)** ___ narrated the particular events of the action to Capt. Lewis Thomas, also a passenger. After he had done so, Thomas replied such were the facts. The men & not the officers were to blame for the defeat. The young man answered that the defeat was owing to a part of the men breaking & running & a large body of them not running into action. But, said he, never did men & officers fight better than these did, that fought at all, & the best proof of it is that they were nearly all killed or taken prisoners.

Young as I was then the impression made upon my mind was what it is now, That is that the battle was lost by a failure of the rear to go into action & the retreat of Trigg's men after he fell.

5C54(1-7) Robert Wickliff letter, Lexington, Ky., Jan. 28, 1849
Wickliff discussed the aftermath of the Battle of Blue Licks, naming those he thought had buried the dead on the battleground.

Dear Sir

I have delayed writing in answer to your letter of the 2nd of December longer than intended, hoping to be able to give you some information on the new subjects which you present for my consideration. In this I have failed & must beg you to understand that I cannot garnish what I write with imaginary incidents. My object has been & is only to detail what either I know or have heard & believe & where I fail to be ___ in my narratives, that I do so because I do not think myself at liberty to use the Poets license.

As for instance, you say I disagree with [Henry] Wilson &c, who say Logan buried the dead & I say Kenton buried the dead &c. I was informed by Kenton himself that he went out with the party that buried the dead. Henry Wilson told me he assisted in burying the dead, but said nothing as to who headed the burying party. Until I saw your statement that you had it from Wilson & others that Logan headed the party that buried the dead, I never heard a surmise that Logan had any hand in burying the dead. Their statements may be true on my own knowledge &, on the distinct information of others, I know nothing to the contrary. Yet I believe it is wholly a mistake. I have not the least idea that Logan went a mile beyond Bryant's Station, & conversed with Judge Twyman & Capt Johnson, who were in the battle, & both Wilson & Kenton who assisted in burying the dead. I have often & over again conversed with others relative to Logan's movement & have never been informed that he approached the battle ground nearer than Bryant's Station & did not reach Bryant's Station until the day after the battle. Though for all I know, he might have gone with the burying party. But scarce as he must have been of provisions & threatened as was his own weak station with daily assaults from the enemy, it is not likely that he detained his force & marched with it forty miles to bury the dead. I think Kenton told me the dead was buried some four or five days after the battle & that the slain were all putrified & black so that few could be recognized. I have no doubt myself that Col. Logan commenced his return the same day he reached Bryant's Station, & in less than two days him & his command were with their families that needed their protection. Yet Sir, take this as an opinion.

I know nothing of the tale that Col. John **(1)** Todd & Levy [Levi] Todd attempted to relieve Bryant's Station & that they were defeated & believe it is a mistake or a poet's creation. It is possible that the tale grew out of the fact that Sharp, McConnell & Levi Todd were sent by Col. Todd to try to get into the station to advise them to hold out until he could come to their relief. These three men in attempting to approach the Station fell into an ambush of the Indians, were fired on & McConnell killed. Sharp & Todd escaped. This statement I had from Sharp's son & was no doubt correct.

Nor do I know anything of the story of Gen. Clark's & John Todd's having come down the Ohio together & hiding powder, that Todd went back for it & was defeated. I believe that tale not true for the following reasons: Todd's residence was in Virginia – Bottetourt, & Clark's in some place below the Blue Ridge. Besides, I have strong evidence both from papers & facts that John Todd was never in Virginia from 1778 until 1780, when he went as a delegate from the country of Kentucky, & returned back to Kentucky through the wilderness in the winter 1781. As I have already written you, in 1781 he might have headed a party to bring to Lexington ammunition deposited at Limestone for all I know, but I believe it is not so. John Todd was then governor of the Illinois country & Illinois constantly employed him. It is not likely that he was engaged in the petty business of packing into the Station powder & lead.

John Howard, my father-in-law, is not the imagined John Howard. I have no information relative to the Sallie & John Howard you enquire after. John Howard, the Father of Gen. Benjamin Howard & brother-in-law of Col. William Preston, was an excentric old man when I knew him. He was a gentleman of fine education & good fortune, youngest son of Col. ___ Howard who was a planter on James River, & often a member of the Colonial House of Burgesses in Virginia & was descended from the English Howards.

There was nothing in the life of John Howard, his son, worth a page in history. He was an early adventurer into Kentucky & resided at one time nearly six months by himself on the Kentucky River near the mouth of upper Howard's Creek, there being two creeks called after him, both emptying into the Kentucky River. This I think was in the year 1777 or 1778. He was at the Battle of Guilford and taken Prisoner after being cruelly mangled & cut down, his right eye was cut out & his **(2)** nose cut into. He was always a devoted Christian of the Presbyterian Church & a Radical Republican, although his Father was an Episcopalian & a descendant of the ancient British aristocracy. He lived to the age of 104 years. His remains repose on the military survey acquired under the Proclamation of 1763.

Major Wales, [and] family, have always been among the poor & obscure & I do not know the name of any of his surviving heirs. I knew his son Jacob, but I believe he has been dead many years.

Of Douglas, the surveyor of whom you make enquiry, I know nothing except what I learn from his surveys. He was a Scotchman & must have died or left the United States before the revolutionary war.

Of the person Neal that was taken at the Battle of the Blue Licks, I know nothing more than what my last letter contains. I do not say that he fell in with my Father on his way down the river as you seem to infer from your letter. But I intended to say that at the instance of Col. Hardin, my Father gave him his passage home or down the river. What became of him I know not, nor do I recollect his Christian name. My Father, Charles Wickliffe, left G____ or the mouth of Georges Creek in the month of April 1784, & landed at where Louisville now stands on the Ohio on the 1st day of May 1782. I was then ten years old & my residence has been in Kentucky ever since.

As I promised, I will now state what I know of Col. James Knox. Col. Knox was by birth an Irishman as I have always understood, but was in early life a great hunter & devotedly attached to the woods & hunter's life. Of his life & its incidents, I can say but little, for although I was well acquainted with him & often conversed with him, I do not recollect of his ever speaking of his adventures in the western wilds but twice. The first was in company with my brother-in-law, Gen. Benjamin Howard, and the second was at the last interview I ever had with him. His narratives were in each substantially the same & were as followith: That before 1768, he had become acquainted with the wilds & hunting grounds east of the Cumberland range of mountains lying on the Clinch & Powell rivers. That in the beginning of the year 1768, he became acquainted with Powell's Valley & in that valley fell in company with a Cherokee Indian that spoke English and called himself Dick with whom he concluded to hunt for some time. While hunting with Dick **(3)** the Indian informed him that he had repeatedly crossed the Cumberland mountains & travelled through a beautifull country, abounding in Game, to the Ohio. He also described to him the Cumberland Gap & the Cumberland River & a river still further on which emptied itself into another river & that into the big river (Ohio). Col. Knox with great difficulty prevailed upon the Indian to go with him & show the river & country he described. They passed the Cumberland mountains at the Gap & pursued a Northwestwardly direction, crossing the Cumberland river & other streams until they reached Dicks River, a principle branch of the Kentucky [River]. Here they made a halt. Dick insisted upon returning & rejoining the hunting party of Cherokees to which he belonged. He described to Knox the course of the river into the Kentucky, & the Kentucky into the Ohio. After spending a night & part of two days, he left Knox not far from where the town of Danville now stands & Knox never heard of him again. This was late in October 1768. Knox being alone hunted & examined the fertile lands around him a few days & then returned nearly on the same rout which the Indian led him. But after reaching a point not far from Raccoon Spring [in the forks of Laurel River - see map of Ky. in 3rd edition of Imlay. See also Mr. Wickliffe's letter of Nov. 18, 1848. LCD] - built him a camp & remained at it until after Christmas of that year. On Christmas Eve, he provided himselfe with thirty six Buffalo marrow bones for his Christmas festival.

After Christmas, Col. Knox returned to Virginia & was one of the company of long hunters, as they were called from being absent from the settled parts of Virginia twelve months in a single hunt. Their principle camp was called by them their station Camp & was upon what was called in early times Station Camp Creek, but now called Robinson's Creek. [LCD note mentions Laurel River, Greene County, Ky.]

This company reached Kentucky in 1770. Daniel Boone it is

admitted never saw Kentucky until 1769, about one year after Knox visited it & returned to Virginia or Carolina. There are afloat various storys of adventures such as that of Sallie, John Howard, ____, & Findley, but I have ever doubted the verity of those tales about those adventurers. Poetry & Falshood has made Boone the pioneer & discoverer of Kentucky, when Boone had as little claim to the credit of being such as Americus had of being the discoverer of America, yet immortalized in story & song while the real discoverers & first pioneers are forgotten.

Knox was a man of Fortune, Talents, & Veracity & not a doubt existed **(4)** that he was in Kentucky in 1768 & that he named Dick's River after Dick the Indian, which name it bears to this day. Now is there a doubt that the company of Long Hunters consisting of Knox & Henry Skaggs & others were the cause of the emigration of the McAfees & Boone, piloting Henderson & Company. Most of these hunters, Knox being one, returned to the Western part of Virginia & of North Carolina after exploreing the interior & fertile parts of Kentucky & spread abroad the reports of its surpassing fertility & vast herds of wild game.

Here it is worthy of notice that the first emigrants that set out for Kentucky was from Botetourt County, the residence of Knox & most of the long hunters. According to all history, James & Robert McAfee set out for Kentucky in 1773 & they & their companions made in that year the first permanent Settlement in the country near where the town of Harrosburgh now stands. Although these men left their cabins & improvements, they did so with intention to return to them with their families, which they did & are now buried upon their lands and a part of the fruits of their interprise still in possession of their Descendants.

True, in 1774 [1775], Boone, who had been absent from the country for several years, piloted Henderson & his associates to the Banks of the Kentucky river. But Knox & the long hunters caused not only the settlement of the McAfees in 1773 & that land of speculators ___ visited Kentucky in 1774; I have no doubt that James Knox was the first white man that ever visited the rich & fertile lands in Kentucky - that constitutes the region in which Danville, Lexington &c, are situated. It is possible that Findly & company may have before Knox ever saw Kentucky, crossed the Cumberland range of mountains & been in the mountainous section of what is now called Kentucky. I am certain they never saw the interior of the country.

The best evidence of the exploration of the interior of any part of Kentucky is the narrative of William Jordan[?] (who I well knew, delivered to William Stone, who detailed it to me). William Jordan's account of himselfe was that he was at Fort Duquesne (Pitsburgh) when the French evacuated ___. That he went with the part of Frenchmen to Kaskaska & remained in that country until the year 1753 when he & a friend, whose name I think was McCall, agreed to leave & make their way to the western part of Virginia on foot. They started, depending on their guns for supplies, & struck the Ohio river below the mouth of Green river, & then struck their course eastwardly, passing through what is now called the Green river country **(5)** & crossing the Kentucky river where it appeared to break through the mountains & pursued their course through the mountain range until they reached the Cowpasture settlements. This, I think, is on one of the tributaries of the Jackson or James river. There they halted & Jourdan settled & married a sister of John Jackson, the Brother-in-law of the McAfees. Of what became of McCall, Stone could not relate. Jordan described the game in the low lands through which he passed south of the Green river as remarkable, gently abundant, so much so, that he did not believe that they had ever been hunted by white men or Indians.

John Jackson was an early adventurer to the Country but whether he came with the McAfees the writer does not know. He first settled in what is now the county of Marion in the year 1783, & his Brother-in-law Jordan soon followed him & settled upon Cartwright's ___ where he died & where the bones of himselfe & wife repose. Jordan was, at the time he gave Stone the account of his adventures in 1763, nearly eighty years of age & as far as the writer ever heard, a fair character, both as an honest man & a man of veracity.

Two incidents have come to my knowledge to confirm Jordan's narrative. The one is that Major Long, acting as Deputy Marshall of Kentucky, was sent by me (about thirty years ago) to serve process from the Federal Court on some people living on the Kentucky river above the town of Irvine. On his return informed me that while he was performing that duty, he was shown a beech tree standing on the bank of the Kentucky river a few miles above the court house or county Town, near which McCall 1763 was plainly & anciently marked. This tree stood on the Kentucky river about the point Jordan said he crossed it.

The second incident is that in Collins Life of Edmund Rodgers it is stated on the authority of the Hon. Joseph R. Underwood that he, Rodgers, found a Beech tree standing on the East Bank of the east Fork of Little Barren River marked as followith: James McCall, Mecklenburg[?] County North Carolina June 8th 1770.

The writer knew Henry Skaggs well. He was always respected to have been one of the pioneer hunters upon the waters of Green river & known to have come to **(6)** Kentucky with Knox in 1770. I never saw those trees but Long & Edmond Rodgers were truthfull men & of the truth of their statements no earthly doubt can exist. While I admit my connecting the marking of the two trees rests upon conjecture, still I have always been satisfied that Jordan's narrative was unquestionably true & that his companion McCall marked the Beech [tree] on the Kentucky [river].

Skaggs lived on the waters of Green river and died at an advanced age. No tradition has ever referred to a human Being being in Kentucky in 1770 except the Long hunters. I infer that McCall & Skaggs visited Green river in 1770 & while there, McCall cut his name & residence upon the Beech tree found by Edmund Rodgers… The writer is unadvised when Col. Knox settled in Kentucky, but it must have been at a very early period as he was residing with Gen. Logan's family in his fort during time of the Indian wars and was an extensive locator of lands under the laws of Virginia in various parts of Kentucky. He was very highly esteemed as a man of talents & worth, & an accomplished gentleman. He was often a member of the Legislature from the county of Lincoln when General Logan claimed before the Senate, the office of Governor upon the ground that the Electors had first given him a plurality of votes over Garrard, but refused to declare him elected & had then struck off the name of Col. Todd by which Garrard had a majority over him.

Knox was Logan's neighbor, friend & senator, but he was one of a majority that thought the Senate had no jurisdiction over the subject, but was bound to accept the man whom the Electors returned as elected. A coolness is said to have existed between Logan & Knox until the day of Logan's death. Knox, however, late in his life married the widow of Gen. Logan… distributed most of his fortune among the Children of Gen. Logan.

(7) *Paragraphs on the naming of Knox County, Kentucky are omitted here.*

As to the story of Major Trigg's sword being found in Licking River, I am confident there is no truth in it. The same sword was said to be Todd's & I was written to, to know if I wished it. I investigated the story & am satisfied that it was a sword belonging to neither Todd nor Trigg. Both from the place where it was found, and from the fact that it is so inferior an affair, that neither Todd or Trigg would have owned, much less wore it in the action [at Battle of Blue Licks.]

I gave you the statement about the spies sent forward by Col. Todd before the Battle of the Blue Licks as I had it from Judge Fryman Johnson & others. I have no doubt Mr. Wilson is mistaken. Is it likely the spies would have passed & repassed through the ambuscade, seeing the Indians, certainly not. Still less is it likely that Todd's command being told of the ambuscade & where it was, would have fell into it.

Mr. Wilson was but a private & talks of the camp may have misled him, or his memory become feeble as to so minute a fact; that he is mistaken there can be no doubt.

I am, as you will perceive from my former Draft, but a poor Draftsman & as I have no notes of the battle ground; the points where Trigg fell, Todd fell as well as where I placed the bones under a cover of rocks can be but conjectural. I will, however, give you the scratching of the pen of which you may make a draft.

Yours respectfully –
Robert Wickliffe

Postscript is in different handwriting.
P.S. this is a copy by a young clerk & must be very inaccurate as you'll perceive. I send it only as notes to yourself – when you send me ____
____ I think I can send you something worth the postage.
R.W.

[See also R. Wickliffe's first letter - Nov. 1, 1845. Briggs – McCormick's & Kenton's Notes. LCD]

5C84 James Spilman letter, Paint Lick [Madison County], Ky., May 17, 1849. *Topic in this letter and another from Paint Lick concerns a Capt. Miller.*

Volume 6C contains 105(2) pages

6C70-70(1-2) Samuel Alley letter, Metamora, Ind., April 28, 1884 *Letterhead: The Alley Telephone Company, Inventors and Manufacturers of the Alley Telephone. Lines built and Warranted at a Distance of 2 1-2 Miles.*

Yours of 22d inst received. Will give you what I recall hearing about Daniel Boone. Boone was not disposed to molest the Indians if he was not molested. The Indians would try by divers [diverse ways] to capture Boone by pretending to be friendly, but he was equal to them in every emergency.

Boone's family remained in the fort while he Boone was out on expeditions. **(1)** At that time it was considered Boone understood Indian warfare better than any man living.

My father's sister (Fannie Napper) and five children were killed and scalped by Indians near Ft. Blackamores. I was born in a few yards of the fort in 1801 and have just returned from a visit to my old birthplace; the ground where the fort stood is being cultivated. A very large apple tree stands near the fort that my father set out. It is called to this day the John Alley apple tree.

Yours
Samuel Alley

(2) Once when Boone was gone some 2 or 3 years his wife had a child and she was wonderfully mortified over the matter, but on Boone's arrival he acted as if nothing unusual had happened and played and tossed the little fellow up as though it was his own. The little mishap never caused any family trouble as long as they lived at Ft. Blakemore [Blackmore].

6C80 J. D. Imboden. I submit below a ____ sketch showing the relative position of these gaps.

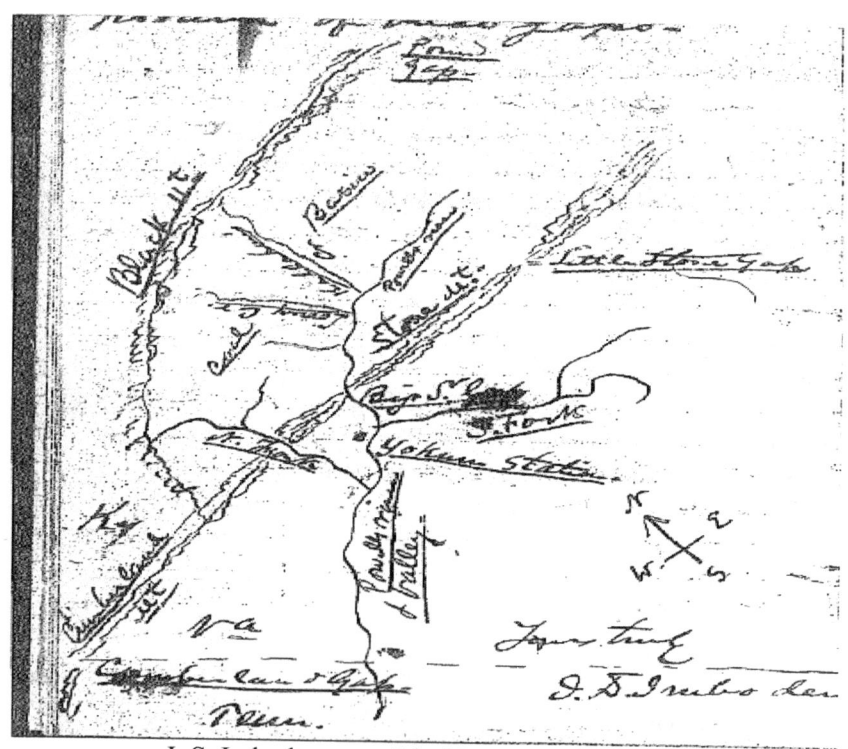

I. S. Imboden map. Black's Fort area. 6C80

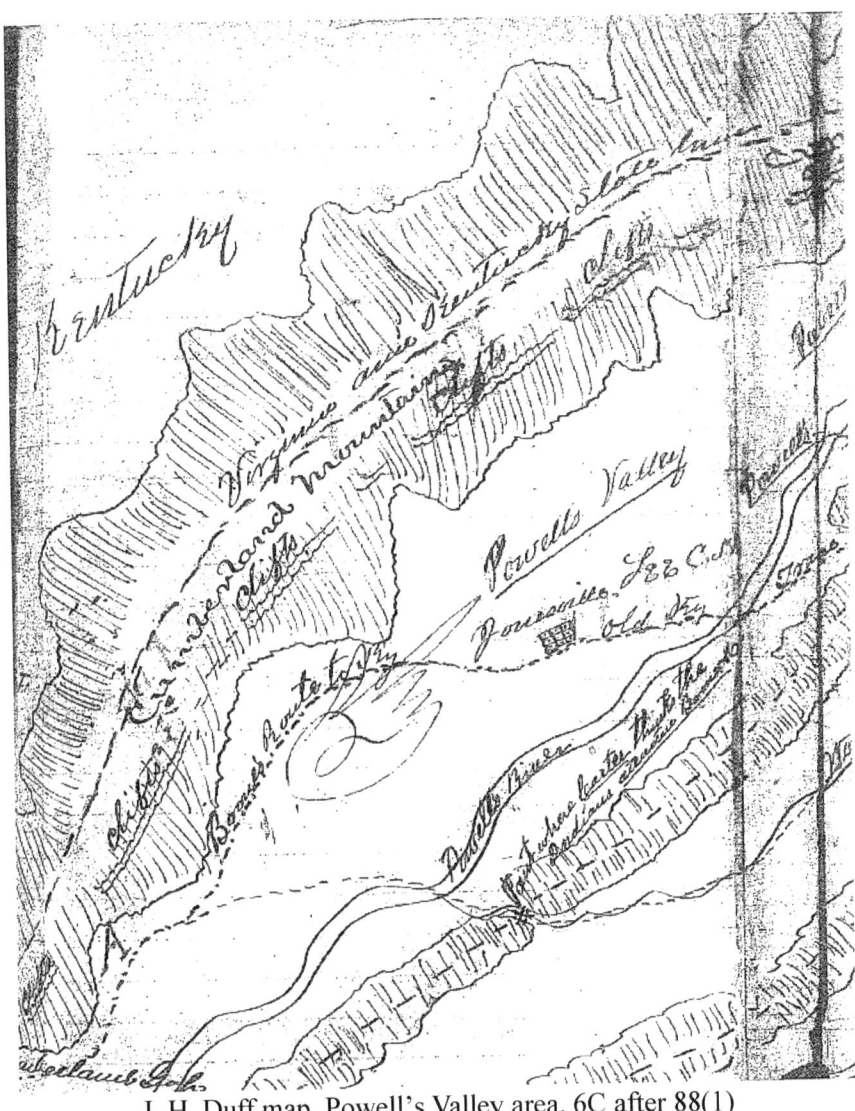

J. H. Duff map. Powell's Valley area. 6C after 88(1)

6C89-90 J. H. Duff Map of Powell's & Clinch Valleys, 1888.
Four-page map. Place names which are legible: Powell's Valley, Clinch Valley, Holston River, Tennessee line, Estillville, Moccasin Creek, Copper Creek, Station where Boone was stationed, stock land, Fort Blackmore, Carter's Fort, Fincastle Road, Stony Creek, Wallens Creek, Boone's Route, Powell's Valley where Indians attacked and killed Daniel Boone's

son. *Another page of this map: Cumberland Mountains, Jonesville, Powell's River, Powell's Mountain, North Fork of Cinch River, Scott's Ford, Stickleyville*

6C93-99 LCD Sources/Notes for Col. Daniel Boone in 1774
Moore's Fort or Fort Byrd on south side of Clinch, Blackmore's Fort on north side of Clinch, John Blackmore Sr. and Jr .went to Nashville in 1779, Martin's Old Station called "The Block House," Cowan killed, James Mooney killed at Point Pleasant, Cowan's Fort or Fort Preston.

6C94 LCD notes: John M. Stoner's letter, Nov. 1853, shows that Boone & Michael Stoner had a "small party" with them when they went to recall the surveyors. This corroborates Thomas W. Carter's statement that Samuel Porter was one of the party - & Capt. John Gass, that his father, David Gass, was also along.
    Joseph Curd, Donelson's Line, Capt. John Ashby was with Hancock Taylor in going in a canoe from Kentucky to North Carolina, 1758, William Crabtree, etc.
    Sources listed include Shane Collections, Bath Co p. 51; 1758; William Crabtree, Bedford County, Va. service – sources given.

6C96 Thomas Hanson's Journal; American Archives I, 707, 708, 787; Gen. McAfee's Sketch in Scrap Book.

Lower part of page: Aug. 28th, 1774, Capt. Russell writes: "An express from Boone Overtook me this day & informs me of Boone's return, to go on the Expedition." A[rthur] Campbell, Aug. 28th writes: "... relieve Floyd's anxiety, I wrote presingly to Boone to raise men to join Floyd. I have been informed that Boone tracked a small party of Indians from Cumberland Gap, to near the settlements."
    Arthur Campbell writes Sept. 29th: "Mr. Boone is very diligent at Castlewoods, & keeps up good order." Maj. Campbell writes March 1: Boone's information about attack on Blackamores, Cherokees; Boone to meet Capts. Russell & Shelby by 15th Nov. at mouth of Dick's river.
Col. Campbell Oct 9th – Boone & Smith pursue Indians
Oct 13th Capt. Daniel Smith – Boone to be Captain

6C102 Heading: Boone recalls the surveyors in Kentucky in 1774

Daniel Boone in a deposition concerning his visit in 1774, says:
    "I was at General Lewis' house a few days before I started. He

directed me to cross the Cumberland mountains at Sounding Gap (now called Pound-gap), an old war road that would convey me to the waters of Big or Little Sandy. Governor Dunmore however changed the route and ordered me after I crossed the mountains to take the Kentucky and meander to its mouth. "

The above received from W. D. Hixson of Maysville, Ky., Oct. 18, 1884. LCD.

6C103 W. D. Hixson note about depositions, Maysville Ky., Nov. 12, 1885

Also copy of all Boone's Depositions relative to visits in 1774.
In going over Fayette Records I found nothing else of interest.
Yours
W. D. Hixson

Deposition of Daniel Boone taken in Kanawha County Virginia, April 22, 1794 to be [read] in the suit of Boffman's Heirs vs. Hickman's

This day came Daniel Boone before us Justices and made oath that to the best of his knowledge that about the last or first of June 1774, one James Blackman [asked] me to locate, enter and direct the survey of 4000 acres as soon as time would permit and lodged with me Col. Preston's certificate for the entry – and on the 26 day of June same year, I was employed by Governor Dunmore to go out to that country to give the surveyors notice of the breaking out of the Indian war and I took with me one Michael Stoner and on the Creek that goes by the name of Hickman Creek, about three or four miles below Colonel Levi Todd's, I cut the first letters of said Hickman's name on a water oak with a large stone grown in the fork in the presence of said Stoner I returned home and wrote Col. Preston the Entry for him.

6C104 Michael Stoner's Deposition, 1816, [living in] Wayne Co., Ky.

"In the year 1774 & in the summer Boone & myself came out, and crossed Station Camp Creek. He then told me that the Red and Blue Licks were on the head of that Creek."

Above sent me [LCD: by W.D. Hixson] appended to, & part of, a deposition relative to a trip to Kentucky by Stoner & Thomas Ward & others in Spring of 1772 - & placed among papers of trip 1773 &c.

Mr. Hixson (now with me – June 1-2 1890) says this date 1774 is an error; that when he referred to & explained the original, he found it 1772. LCD

6C105 Heading: Boone's age – Col. Andrew Lewis – Boone's Trip to Kentucky in 1774. Information sent by W. D. Hixson, 1885.

Have returned from Greenup – send you date &c of Boone's deposition relative to his visit to Kentucky in 1774. Maysville, Ky., Dec. 5, 1885. W. D. Hixson [LCD handwriting]

The Deposition of Daniel Boone and others taken at the home of Flanders Callaway in the County of St. Charles, Missouri territory, on the 6th day of October 1817, agreeable to two dedimusses. Two Justices of the Peace for that county, to be read in evidence in certain suits in Chancery now depending in the Greenup County, Court in the State of Kentucky wherein D. Trimble and J. Young are Complainants and A. Buford and others, Defendants.

The Deponent being about 84 years of age* and being duly sworn and interrogated, deposes & says:
Question by Complainants: Were you well acquainted with the Ohio River from what is now called Big Sandy to what is now called Little Sandy Creek as early as May 1784 or previous to that time? If you will please state what was the reputed distance between the two Creeks?
Answer: I was not personally acquainted but by good information. In the year 1774, I was requested by Governor Dunmore to go to Kentucky and bring in the Surveyors. I was at General Lewis's own house, a few days before I started, and he undertook to give directions how to travel and where to find the surveyors.

* LCD: Hence born: 1817
     <u>84</u>
    1733

Volume 7C contains 120 numbered pages.

7C1 Plan of Works at Indian Old Fields, Clark County, Ky.
Place-names: Howards Creek, Lulbegrud Creek.

Key:
1. White oak (marked C. C.)
2. White oak blacked and marker found
3. Old intrenchment 13 [18?] poles diameter
4. Old intrenchment 21 [27?] poles circumference

5. A Lick.
6, 7. Part of old town.
8. Beasly's cabin - tree marked W. B. [William Beasley]
9. A Lick.
10. Falls of Branch
11. Gate Posts.
12 to 12. North extension of town
13. Block house
14. Spring
15. Pigeon Roost
16. [6 small circles arranged in 3 parallel rows] Old buildings.

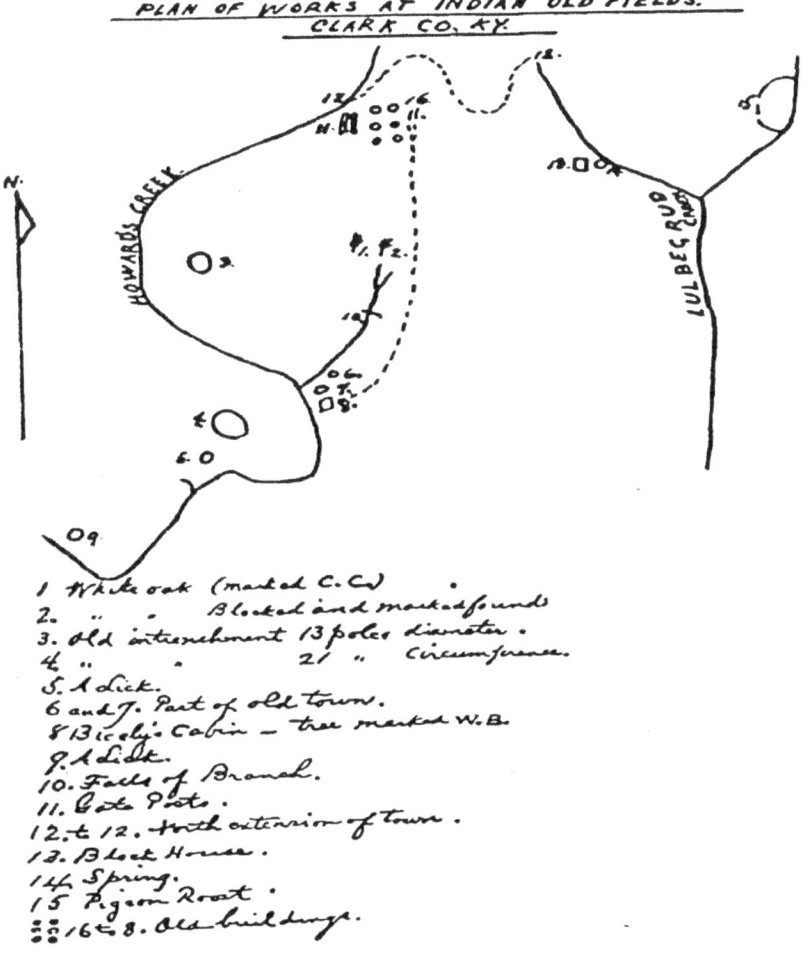

Plan of Works at Indian Old Fields, Clark County, Ky. 7C1.

Memo. For Indian Old Fields

I am inclined to think this is the spot where Findlay traded with the Indians, and that it is the location of the Indian town given on Evans's Map Es-kip-pi-ki-thi-ki. Or it have been the Blue Lick town where Maginty and his companion were captured in 1753, or the one spoken of by Croghan in vol 1, Va. State Papers. LCD

7C3 *Not in Draper's handwriting.*

In May 1775, Col. Marquis Calmes, Sr, and Marquis Calmes, Jr., Cuthbert Combs, Enos Combs, Benjamin Combs, Joseph Combs, and John Combs came down the Ohio. A portion of the Company, under Cuthbert Combs, landed at Cabin Creek, and came along the war road and buffalo trace to Boonesborough. Here Calmes constructed a canoe and descended the Kentucky River to meet the others of the party who had descended the Ohio. On reaching Boonesboro, the party was joined by William Calk, Enoch Smith, Benjamin Berry, and Robert Whitledge and all together (eleven persons) proceeded to the "Indian Old Fields," in what is now Clarke County, where liking the situation, but perceiving that there was not enough land for all, Berry, the two Calmes, and Cuthbert and Benjamin Combs gave the others fifty shillings each not to make any improvements between Lulbegrud and Howard's Creeks. The party encamped on a branch of Lulbegrud, erected a cabin, planted corn, and afterwards, employed Major and William Beasley to take care of the corn and make additional improvements. At this time there were distinct traces of recent settlement there. Corn rows, ruins of houses, cleared grounds, with stumps surrounded by sprouts, and two gate posts with iron bands on them. The ruins of cabins consisting of dirt thrown up, were in two rows of fifty or sixty yards long, twenty or thirty feet wide between them. Evidences of recent habitation and fortifications, showing that it had been also the resort of the mound builders." A station was afterwards built on the spot where Beasley's cabin stood.

7C4 William Frazier in 1825, testifies that he settled in "Indian Old Fields" in 1793. "In 1794 he saw the appearance of an old town where the dirt had been thrown up for their buildings in two rows or lines of buildings fifty or sixty yards long, with a street about twenty or thirty feet between, which place the deponent showed to the surveyor this day. There was, also, in 1794, an old post standing there with a strip of iron on it."

7C6 *Map of lands ceded by Cherokees showing Ohio River, Kanawha, Connaway. Place-names include Scioto River, intersecting Ohio River, Conhaway River, Louisa River, New Province. Tryon Mt., Reedy River, Donelson line.*

The land between the new Province and Louisa river was ceded by the Cherokees but, without a special order from the King, was not to be granted to or occupied by any of his white subjects. The Louisa river and Holston to the Holston river were the boundaries agreed upon by Atta Kula Kulla, Mr. Cameron.

N. B. This is commonly called Donelson line.

7C11 [LCD notes]
    June 14, 1775 Daniel Boone left Boonesborough to get his family at Blackmore's Fort in Powell's Valley, his men accompanying him for salt.
    July 18, 1775 Boone not returned yet - Mrs. Boone not delivered a few days since. Mrs. Boone had a son about July who died in infancy (said Nathan Boone to me: LCD).
    Sept. 8, 1775 Boone & McGary parties arrived Harrodsburg and Boone's group was at Boonesborough about Sept. 6-7.
    Wm. Bush one of Boone's party on his return trip to Kentucky (Collins II, p. 131).
    Late 1775 Col. Callaway's family came to Kentucky (from Clinch) and may have reached Clinch in time to return with Boone.
    February 1776 Boone took a winter hunt in Morgan County, Kentucky, name carved on a tree.

7C14 Edward Mills to Mr. Mark Alexander, Feb. 14, 1776
N*ot LCD handwriting.*

    For Mr. Mark Alexander
    p. Jno Mills Marcht. in Baltimore Town

    On separate page written as a title:
    Colonial letter
    Watauga to Kentucky
    Containing[?] of Daniel Boone.

Unnumbered page before 7C15; ink covers top of page.

Dr Sir

In the year '72 I Receiv'd a Small Present by my Son from you and if it is to grate an Imposition on Good Neature [Nature] I should still be your Petitioner for some Cloathing. You may be Shure that it is Necessity that obliges me to Make such a request as the Indean wars almost Broke me up. And if it is not by the immedit ____ of God is Likely to Brake out again this Spring and no other hopes to the contrary but our making Peace with England. They have begun already and has taken three Sculps [scalps] and two Prisoners into Detroit where they are Incouraged by the Commanding officers of that Post by the reward of fifty Dollars a head but where they have Done that mischief * is Near Seven hundred miles from us at a New Settlement Call'd Cantuck and which is the Gardin of America. I was to view it last summer and found it to be one continued Meadow cover'd with Blue Grass and Clover and when I left there which was the last of May the grass was never as high as my shoulders. I was Piloted to it by a Gentleman that has frequented that Country near ten years. that the Part of it where we ware is the most Convenient of aney in that Country not exceeding five miles from the Ohio and a fine streame running thro' the Land as big as the m__ falls and is yet undiscovered but by a few Peopple and if it Please God to Grant us Peace I do intend to settle there this spring and if you have a mind to be an adventurer, send your Commands with my son by whome you will receive this and you may Depend that I will Improve Land for you upon as Reasonable terms as you could Define and will be greatly to your advantage if your inclination could let you to come out and for what other information you want Johnny can inform you. So concludes with my best wishes and am

                                          Sir. Your Most Humble
                                          And obedient Servant
                                          Edward Mills

14th Feby. 1776
*Saml. Sanders was one of the
Prisoners – taken near Boonesboro,
Dec. 23 – Hall's Romance of the West [LCD]
And McQuinney's one of the scalps.
        American Archives iv, 559-60.

Samuel Sanders and William McWhinney, young teen-agers, were hunting across the Kentucky River from Fort Boonesborough in 1775 when Indians captured Sanders and killed McWhinney. Arthur Campbell who was hunting with them, escaped.

Edward Mills letter, 1776. 7C14

7C15 LCD notes on Daniel Boone in 1776

Letter of Col. William Fleming to Col. William Preston
    Col. Wm. Fleming writes Col. Preston from Bottetourt County: This forenoon Boone delivered here 700 lbs powder – 100 of which is ordered for the Point, 400 is allotted for your County to the use of the committee. In consequence of an order from the Committee of Safety, I have ordered four men as an escort to the waggon. Should you think them too slender a guard, you can reinforce them, or discharge them altogether, & order a guard of your militia. I had no letter from Williamsburg.

Edmund Pendleton wrote June 20th, 1776, to Col. Preston for Committee of Safety.
    "Ordered that the Committee of Fincastle County deliver to Col. Russell or order so much of the powder lately sent to that county as may be necessary, for the use of the said six companies."

This would seem to show that Boone went to Williamsburg on some pubic business in April or May 1776, & on his return had this powder placed in his charge. Perhaps it was the need of powder in Kentucky that prompted Boone's Mission – rifles he succeeded – as 700 pounds were allotted for Fincastle County as Preston then resided in Fincastle as the address of his letters of this period show…

7C17 LCD notes on Col. Daniel Boone – 1776.
Fleming's Ms. Papers – Capt. Matthew Arbuckle, Fort Randolph, Aug. 18,

1776

After mentioning the capture of the Boone & Callaway girls, says: Doubts about Indians preserving peace, "as they have now the Cornstalk away at Fort Detroit treating with the English, and are constantly backwards and forwards on that course."

... Walker, and his fellow commissioners, Pittsburgh, Aug. 31, 1776, "Yesterday we received alarming intelligence from the Lower Shawnese Town. A general Confederacy of the ___ tribes seems to have been formed in order to strike our frontier settlements – the ___ & Ottawas to attack Pittsburg; the Shawanoes & Delawares & Mingoes, & other nations to fall on the settlements on this side of the Ohio. They notified the Governor & Council of Virginia and County Lieutenants of neighboring counties."

James Cooper killed on Licking - & Hinkston's Station breaks up &c. Floyd in Notebook "2", 87, 90-91
Forting at Harrodsburg & Royal Spring – Note-Book "2" p. 90.

Fleming Ms. Papers – Capt. Mathew Arbuckle, Randolph, Aug 15, 1776, to Col. William Fleming, Fort Randolph. [copy]

I was informed some time ago, the Shawnees & Cherokees had taken 3 women prisoners from Cantuckie, and got one scalp. Therefore dispatched three of my men to demand the prisoners, if in possession of the Shawnees, to be immediately delivered up. Two of the women were daughters to Col. Callaway, at Cantuckie, and the other a daughter of Col. Boone's at Cantuckie likewise. This day the men are returned, with one of the Shawnee chiefs, and a brother of Cornstalk's, who inform me that after having taken the prisoners from Cantuck, the whites followed & retook the prisoners, killing two of their men. Upon this I informed them the fate of the Cherokees, & that our people would without dispute cut them all off, which seemed to have a great effect upon them. I look upon it not to be lasting.

7C20-20(1) Will B. Rodman letter, Washington, N.C., Oct. 22, 1890

Dear Sir

Yours of 11 Sept. was handed to me on yesterday. John Gray Blount died in December 1832 or 1833. All of his children are now dead. I was about 16 years of age when he died, and had lived with him as one of his family until his death. It was always known in the family, that he had been with Boone in Kentucky and Tennessee, and had acted as Clerk to Boone when he (Boone) married the first couple ever married in Kentucky or Tennessee – which of the two states it was, I do not remember with certainty. I do not remember ever hearing my grandfather personally speak of his connection with Boone.

There was preserved in the family, an old hunting shirt said to have been won by my grandfather while in Kentucky, which was destroyed during the late civil war, with all the old papers of my grandfather, which were of much historical interest. As I never fully examined these, I am unable to say whether they contained any memorials of that **(1)** part of his life. He and his brothers, William and Wiley, obtained grants for large bodies of land in Tennessee.

I do not know what man named Bryan you refer to as having visited Boone.* The only family so named that I know of now is represented by the Hon. W. P. Bynum, lately one of the Judges of the Supreme Court of this State and now residing in Charlotte, N.C.

LCD note: *Error – if I mentioned Bynum, as it seems I did, I intended John George Blount. LCD

There is no evidence that any justices were appointed for the Kentucky portion of Fincastle County; & this wedding of Flanders Callaway & Jemima Boone took place before Kentucky County was organized. If appears certain, then, that as courts were provided for the Transylvania government, Boone was made a justice under that organization, & thus was empowered to perform the marriage ceremony.

Samuel Henderson's daughters' letters may tell about the wedding. LCD

Following are the legible portions of a series of letters from Benjamin Sharp to LCD in which Benjamin Sharp covered a wide range of topics. In his pension statement (DM 1OO 64-68), Benjamin Sharp described extensive service in North Carolina and Virginia during the Revolutionary War. He was to have marched to Kentucky just after the attack on Martin's and Ruddell's Stations in 1780, but the expedition did not proceed.

Benjamin Sharp said he was born in Lancaster, "now Dauphine" County, Pennsylvania in 1762. He resided in Lee County, Virginia after the Revolution before moving to Missouri where he became acquainted with Daniel Boone. The handwriting of Benjamin Sharp is very dense.

7C21–21(1, 2) Benjamin Sharp letter, Warren Co Mo., May[?] 25th, 1845

This is a partial transcript with numbered answers to Draper's questions, which are missing. Topics pertain to incidents occurring mostly in western Virginia during the mid-1770s. Question 9 concerns the attack at Ruddle's Station in Kentucky.

In the Cherikee war I was but a little over fourteen, and am now in the eighty fourth year of my age.

I will then take your inquiries as they stand in your letter.

First of the Cherikee War of 1776. I have no doubt but Capt. John Campbell commanded a Company at the battle of the Island Flatts. After I was married and settled, he purchased land near me and became my neighbor, and for several years we lived in the strictest habits of friendship and intimacy but I cannot recollect of ever hearing him say anything about Eatons Station or the Island battle.

Capt. Cock's flight from the battle was notorious at the time to everyone. I omitted it from an unwillingness to wound the feelings of his descendants. My brother, Thomas Sharp, was his lieutenant and when the battle ended, Capt. Cock was missing and supposed to be killed, and strict search was made for him, and when he could not be found, some ____ were thrown out that he had been away, which was warmly resented by my brother. However on their return to the fort, they met Capt. Cock returning with these[?] men. He appeared greatly agitated; he said he was separated from the men, and chased off by the Indians, and then ran to the fort to bring on a reinforcement. I am certain at that time that I never heard of his killing one of the pursuing Indians. It was said that he served credit in Gen. Jackson's Creek War, and ____ his character by killing an Indian in one of Jackson's battles, which is the only Indian I ever heard of his killing.

I believe it was Capt. Buchanan who was left to guard the fort at Eaton's, but I cannot be certain.

2nd Information by Nancy ____s's son and

3rd by Col. Logan's daughter. It is probable that Wm. Casey and Robert Harrod might have killed, or mortally wounded, one or more of the Indians in their **(1)** defense of Nancy. That any Indian was killed I never heard till I saw your letter, although I was present and witness of the whole affair. John Logan I have no doubt [was?] with Mr. Cummings waggon, as he lived in the fort but I question his being there as an officer, having in particular the command. When parties went out, they were seldom under the direction of an officer. If Mr. Lyon was an officer, I never knew him as such.

The man's name that was killed at Casey's field was Daniel Mungle, and the man that was shot, tomahawked and sculped and yet survived, was Arthur Blackeburn. The man that was killed at the waggon was Andrew Cara____, and the wounded man was James Piper - the fore finger of his right hand was shot off.

The number of men composing either of these parties I can say nothing about.

4th Was the Indian Camp above Montgomeris on the north, or middle fork of Holston? The Camp was on the north branch of the middle fork of Holston river within some six or eight miles out of Abingdon. Who commanded the party or the numbers of the whites or Indians, the length of time has passed my recollection.

Capt. Andrew Colville was commander of the fort but not with the party. Some supposed that the number of the Indians was twenty four, from twenty four notches cut on the handle of a war club that was taken, but that was mere conjecture, as the notches might have been cut for a different purpose.

5th [and 6th?] Who were the two men killed at the neighbouring fort? The neighbouring fort was Briants fort about six miles from Blacks. The name of one of the men was James Young; the other was his servant from Black's fort. The name of the one that escaped was John Bennum. The name of the one that was killed was Douglas,* his given name I think was John.

7th The company [that] were to escort provisions &c at Black's was under command of Capt. Andrew Colvill.

8th Of the officers who went from Fincastle County on Christians Campaign, I can only mention with certainty Col. William Russell. I cannot say that William Campbell, Daniel Smith, or John Logan was on the expedition...

9th I never understood that any were killed at Riddles Station. The British planted their artillery against the fort and summoned them to surrender. The men at once saw that they could not defend the fort against the British cannon. They therefore stipulated for protection against the Indians, and surrendered to the British officer. The number taken I never knew. My brothers-in-law who were taken, with their wives and families. were Capt. John Dunkin, and Francis Berry.

10th. Mr. Henry Hamblin lived on Clinch not far from a place called Castlewoods, when Mrs. Hamblin so bravely defended her house against eleven assailing Indians. He had moved to big mockison Creek, north of Clinch mountain and the next year his family was again attacked, Mrs. Hamblin was killed with others of the family and one of his little boys carried prisoner to Detroit. Some years after Mr. Hamblin lived for several years within a mile of me.

*See Mrs. Sarah Shelby's notes.

Thus my dear Sir, I have rubbed up every nerve and fiber of my memory, if possible to brighten it, so as to shed light on the subjects of inquiry, but in many instances I found the rust so corrosive that it will not wipe off; but if anything I have said will benefit to you, I tender it cheerfully. It is a pitty that these things had not been inquired for **(2)** at an earlier day, before so many of the actors in them had quit the stage. The only ones who can now be resorted to for information are here and there an old superannuated man whose faculties are all impaired, and many of whom were boys when the events happened, and in the giddy rounds of youth, suffered their impressions to pass off like the darkening Shadows of an evening Sun.

    I am at present in corrispondence on these subjects with my relation, Samuel H. Laughlin of Tennessee, who is collecting historical materials I expect for your use, and for the use of a Colonel Ramsey who is about to write a history of Tenesee; but if any thing further occurs to your mind, in which you think I can serve you, your application will be cheerfully Minded to.

                        With very much respect, I am &c.
                        Benj. Sharp

P. S. I am in possession, by common report, of an affair of Lieut. Samuel Newels; but like all my other communications, I cannot give the date. Lieut. Newel was stationed with a few men in Powells Valley to guard the rockey station, the only settlement then in the Valley. One day by some means, they became suspicious that Indians were lurking about. In the evening some travelers from Kentucky arrived at the fort, and a fear was suggested that the Indians might that night steal their Horses, to prevent which they carried rails from a fence, and made a high pen against the wall of the fort in which the[y] put the Horses. But the Indians in the night opened the pen, and carried off the Horses, and in the morning Newel with his party went in persuit; he followed their trail over Wallins ridge, and over powels mountain, and in the mean time it begun to drizzel rain. Newel was marching at the head of his men down the mountain, approaching a creek called blackwater, on which there was much cane, when he discovered an Indian sitting on a log by the side of the cane with his head sheltered from the rain by his blanket. Newel made no alarm, but raised his gun and fired, he shot the Indian through the body, and the ball entered the head of another who sat behind him on the ground. The other Indians fled into the cane. Thus without any other gun being fired were two Indians killed, and the travelers Horses recovered.

B. S.

N. B. You must do the best you can with interlining and a p____ing hand; within a five month, I have become so subject to something like mental absence, that I cannot write without leaving out words.

7C22-22(1) Benjamin Sharp letter, Warren County, Mo., March 14, 1845

Mr Draper
Dear Sir   A few days ago a paper called the Western Christian Advocate fell into my hands in which I find an article headed "A Sketch of the Life of the Rev. J. Proctor an early settler," which calls to my mind one of the most fierce and sanguinary actions, to the members engaged, that occurred during the whole of the Revolutionary struggle; and least [lest] you should not have obtained a correct version of it, I send it to you in the words of the Advocate.

"Rev. Joseph Proctor was born in Roan County, N.C. and removed from there to the long Islands of Holston in 1777 where he enlisted as a regular soldier in the revolutionary army for four years. In 1778 he was ordered to Kentucky, and stationed at Boonsborough and Estills Station. He was in Boonsborough during the nine days siege in 1778, and by his gallantry contributed much to the protection of the inmates and the defeat of the besiegers. From this period untill the month of March 1782 he was constantly and bravely engaged in guarding the settlers, and protecting the imigrants against the constant incursions of the Indians.

On the 19th of March, 1782, rafts without any one on them were seen floating down the Kentucky river past Boonsborough. Inteligence of this fact was immediately dispatched to Capt. James Estill at his Station fifteen miles distant from Boonsborough. Capt. James Estill lost not a moment in collecting a force to go in search of the Indians. From his own and the nearest Stations he raised twenty five men. Joseph Proctor was of the number. While Capt. Esitll and his men were on this inspection, the Indians suddenly appeared around his Station at the dawn of day on the 20th of March. [They] killed and scalped Miss Gass, took Monk, a slave of Capt. Estill, captive. The Indians hastily [retreated?] in consequence of an exaggerated account which Munk gave them of the strength of the station, and the number of fighting men in it.

No sooner had the Indians commenced their retreat, than the women in the fort (the men being all absent except one on the sick list) dispatched two boys, the late Gen. Samuel South, and Peter Hackett, to take the trail of Capt. Estill and his men and overtake them [to] give information of what had transpired at the fort. The boys succeeded in overtaking Capt. Estill early on the morning of the 21st between the mouth of drowning creek and red river. After a short search Capt. Estill's party struck the trail of the retreating Indians. It was resolved at once to make persuit, and on the ever memorable 22nd day of March 1782, in the now county of Montgomery, in the vicinity of Mt. Sterling, Capt. Estill's party came up with the Indians. They proved to be Wyandotts, and twenty five in number, exactly that of Capt. Estill's. The ground was highly favourable to the Indian, made for warfare, but Capt. Estill and his men, without a moment's hesitation, commenced an attack upon them, and the latter as fearlessly engaged in the bloody contest. It is however, painfull to record that at the very onset of the action, Lieut. Miller of Capt. Esitlls party, with six men then under his command, ingloriously fled from the field. Hence Estills party numbered eighteen, and the Wyandotts twenty five. Between these parties at the distance of fifty yards, the battle raged for the span of two hours. Deeds of daring were common. On either side, wounds and death were inflicted, neither party advancing or retreating. Every man to his man, and every man to his tree. Capt. Estill was now covered with blood from a wound received early in the action, nine of his brave companions lay dead upon the field, and four others were so disabled by their wounds as to be unable to continue the fight. Capt. Estill's fighting men were now reduced to four, one of whom was Joseph Proctor, the subject of this notice.

Capt. Estill, the brave leader of this Spartan band, was now brought into personal conflict with a powerfull active Wyandott warrior. The conflict for a time was fierce and desporate and anxiously watched by Proctor **(1)** with his finger on the trigger of his unerring rifle. Such however was the struggle, that Proctor could not shoot without endangering the safety of his Captain. Estill had had his right arm broken the preceding summer in an engagement with the Indians, and in the conflict with the Wyandott warrior, that arm gave way, and in an instant the savage foe buried his knife in Capt. Estills breast; but in the same moment Proctor sent a ball from his rifle to the Wyandotts heart. Thus ended the memorable battle, which lacks nothing but the circumstance of numbers to make it one of the most memorable in ancient or modern times. The loss of the Indians was even greater than that of the whites. There is a tradition derived from the Wyandott towns that but one of the warriors engaged in that battle ever returned to his nation. During this bloody engagement the coolness and bravery of Proctor was most conspicuous, but his conduct after the battle elicited the warmest commendation. He brought off the field of battle, and most of the way to the station, a distance of forty miles, on his back, his badly wounded friend, the late Col. Irvine, so long and so favourably known in Madison [County, Kentucky].

In the engagement at the Pickaway towns on the grait Miami, Proctor killed an Indian chief. He was brave and fearless, and an ardent friend to the institutions of his country; he made three campaigns into Ohio, and fought side by side with Col. Daniel Boon, Col. Callaway and Col. Logan."

What follows respects Mr. Proctor's conversion and ordination into the Methodist Ministry, in which I suppose you would not be much interested. I have only to clar— your indulgence, for my hand shakes so unmercifully that I expect you will have trouble in making out my scrawl.

I am most respectfully &c.
Benj. Sharp

Memo by LCD: The newspaper in the spring of 1845 had this item: "The Rev. Joseph Proctor, for 36 years a preacher of the gospel in Kentucky, died in December last, and was buried with military honors! He had been a noted Indian fighter in early times."

The Pension Census gives his residence in Estill County, Ky., & gives his age 86 in 1840; & hence must have been in his 91st year at the time of his death. LCD

Benjamin Sharp's answers to LCD questions, April 10th, 1845

1st My impression is, that the man who escaped from the camp where ____ ____ were killed at the ford of Wallins Creek in 1773 was Isaac Crabtree; the name of the 5th man killed I do not remember. At that time I was but 11 years of age. It was said that one man was missing who never was found or heard of. I afterwards lived nearly twenty years within 1 ½ miles of the defeated camp, and my people found the bones of a man between two high hedges of rocks on a ceder hill, about half a quarter mile above the camp, which we suposed was his remains.

2nd. The attack on the Cummins party was in the woods; the Indians were concealed in ambush, and the party knew nothing of them til they were fired upon.

3d   Gen. Ben. Logan came to Black's fort in 1776, perhaps in August, or first September; his appearance created great excitement, for it flashed upon the minds of every one, that some fatal disaster had happened in Kentucky. Of course, the people all crowded round him. He made no secret of his business; he enquired for Nathan Reid (afterwards Capt. Reid of the U. States army, who had come from Kentucky just before) said Reid had wounded his honor in the tenderest part, and he had followed him determined to kill him. Reid was not at Black's; and it was said that Logan overtook him at Kincannons fort. How the thing was settled I do not know; but I do know that neither Reid nor Logan was killed or wounded. How Gen. Logan traversed the wilderness either coming or going I cannot tell, but my impression is, that he came to and returned from Blacks fort on Horse back and alone. This information you have forced from me with much reluctance, and I shall be truly sorry, if in stating these facts, I should wound the feelings.

(1)   4th   I have some vague recollection of aid being sent to Kentucky perhaps in '78 but what aid was sent, or by whom, I cannot say. I lived immediately on the frontier, and I presume the aid was sent from a more interior part of the country.

5th   It is my impression that it was Col. John Montgomery who conveyed the British Governor [Henry Hamilton] and prisoner captured by G. R. Clark at Post Vincent, through the Holston settlement. He also conducted the Cherokee deputation to the seat of government in '77. He was a young man of much promise; he raised a regiment on state establishment to defend Clark's conquest of post Vincent, but of his future services, or what became of him, I can give no information.

6th   Cleveland's position was the south side of Kings mountain, and from some cause he did not arive at it till near the close of the action, but at a time when the battle was raging with its gratest fury. His regiment came up with intrepid bravery, and the Colonel dismounted from his wounded Horse within 8 or 10 steps of the spot I occupied. The Tories were executed after night by the light of a large fire made of lightwood, commonly called pine knotts. Capt. Snody ____ these as a Tory, was not the man you speak of. I knew the Capt. Snody you speak of and know him to be a staunch Whig.

7th   The ages and date of the deaths of Capt. Dunkan and my brother Thomas, I have no [way] of ascertaining. Perhaps Col. Laughlin, Duncan's grandson, can satisfy you as to him.

8th   Faithfully to delineate the characters of men who have left behind them a number of respectable descendants is a point of much delicacy. The general character of the Campbells, Shelby and Russell was, that they were true friends to their country, brave officers, respectable neighbours, and useful citizens, but for entering into the peculiar traits of each ones character I must beg to be excused.

9th   Gen. George Rutledge was one of my early friends. We were together in the battle of Kings Mountain. He was certainly the man who shot the British commander through the head, for when his gun fired he exclaimed to those around him that he had shot him in the eye. He became very popular in his county, served on the convention that framed the Constitution of Tenesee, and was frequently a member of one or the other branches of the legislature, but towards the end of his life, I am told he became rather intemperate. The Colonels Scott, Anderson, and Pemberton were respectable men.

7C23(3) LCD notes on Benjamin Sharp's letter of April 14, 1845

Fight on Middle Fork of Holsten & Island Flat battle – 1776
Campaign 1780-1781
Capt. James Thompson
Casey's Field & Cummings Fights
Col. John Montgomery
King's Mountain – Campbell & Cleveland,
    Tories, killed & hung
The Round Meadows
Col. Jos. Martin's scout in 1779
Sketch of the Sharp family
Col. A. Bledsoe
Boone's Defeat in 1773
Ben. & John Logan, 1776
Capt. Jas. Montgomery & Jos Black
John Campbell's character
Col. Sam Newell

7C24-24(1,2) LCD notes on Benjamin Sharp's letter from Warren County, Mo., June 14, 1845

  Wallin's Creek Defeat 1773, Isaac Crabtree escaped; previous letters name those killed. 1776 - Ben Logan at Black's Fort; John Montgomery and Laughlin.
  (2) Boone's defeat – 1773
Fight at Casey's 1776
Gen. Ben. Logan

Col. John Montgomery
King's Mountain & Ben. Cleveland
George Rutledge
Anderson – Pemberton
Col. Henry C. Clark

7C25-25(1) Benjamin Sharp letter, Warren County, Mo., August 25, 1845

Mr. Draper -
Dear Sir. Since the receipt of yours of the 6th inst., I have written to a Grand Son, and two grand daughter[s] of the late Col. Henry Clark for such information as they can give of the life and services of their Grand father. I have also instituted an enquiry among the Descendants of Col. Daniel Boon in this State, touching the incidents of his life after his removal to Missouri.

I settled in St. Charles County in the fall of 1816, and from that time till his death, I was acquainted with Col. Boon. He was a fine looking old man, of firm and manly stature. His mind possessed considerable native strength, without much of that polish seldom attained in woods and uninhabited wilderness. Much legendary stuff has been reported and published about this man; such as him and his wife making long trips by themselves up the Missouri, and returning with each a canoe loaded with furs and wild geese feathers; His capturing a wild savage man and bringing him down, who was only cloathed with long hair like a Bear, &c. Col. Boon died in his bed, in this County of St. Charles, and was intered on the farm of David Briant, now Warren County, and but a month or so ago the remains of him and his wife were disinterred, at the request of a committee from Kentucky, and carried to that state, with a view I supose of paying due respect to his memory. Kentucky certainly owed this man a considerable debt of gratitude, and ought to have acknowledged it in his life time by some more substantial benefit. When I obtain what information I can on these subjects, I will write you again.

I was intimate in the family of Rev. Charles Cummings. **(1)** I well remember Sally Bledsoe from her Girlhood, and long before she was the wife of D. Shelby.

Flanders Calaway, the Son in law of Col. Boon, and his wife has been dead for several years, but in prosecuting the enquiry which I am instituting in the Boon connection here, proper care will be taken to peruse his printed narrative, and if I can obtain it, it shall be forwarded to you. One of the legends about Col. Boone which have found its way into a work which ought to be of some importance, called the Book of the Unites

States, and which I ought to have mentioned in its proper place, is that Col. Boon was found dead in the woods, on his knees, with his Gun presented over the trunk of a tree, Just in the act of shooting at some game. What a pitty that writers of historical sketches, should delight so much in the marvelous to render these productions incredible.

Yours in Sincerity &c
Benj. Sharp

Memo. – Maj. Sharp, Col. S. H. Laughlin wrote me, died Jan. 1st, 1846 – but I failed to get the Boone notes prepared for me, after repeatedly writing for them, & once calling on his grandson of same name, at Danville, Mo.

LCD notes in the margin and a follow-up letter mention Benjamin Sharp's death. Sharp's grandson of the same name wrote the letter at page 7C26 (not included here). The letter is dated 1853 and written from "Danville" - no state given.

7C35(1-5) John T. Teass letter, Otter Hill, Bedford County, Va., Oct. 22, 1883 *In this letter, it is told that Thomas Teas' life was saved by an Indian to whom he had given salt some years earlier. See 7C56.*

Mr. L. C. Draper,
Dear Sir

I received a letter from my sister Mrs. Ed Wood, Warrenton, Mo. inclosing a letter from you making inquiries about my Grandfather, Thomas Teass. What information I can give you I will do it chearfully. Thomas Teass was born in Lancaster County, Penn. about 1744, died in New London, Campbell County, Virginia, May 3rd, 1821.

Was captured by the Indians about 1774 - do not know by what tribe. He and a party whose names **(1)** I do not know were on a hunting expedition, and also of discovering lands on Ka [Kanawha?] and Coal rivers. The party seperated some where on Ka. river, with the understanding to meet at the Falls. One party went on horse-back across the mountain, and my Grandfather with the other party went up the river in a canoe, & were attacked at or near the Falls by Indians. The party on horse-back made their escape, came home, and said the party in the canoe were all killed, judging from the firing. I guess my Grandfather was the only one taken alive.

I have heard it said he fought to the very last and when captured they said he was too brave a man to be killed and they would take him prisoner; so it was he was captured and taken to Fort Pitt, now **(2)** Pittsburg and when the council met was sentenced to be burned to death at the stake. The faggots were all prepared, and an old Indian Chief interceded for him, and said he would adopt him as his son. The chief asked him [Teas] if he knew him. He said he did not. Then the chief asked him if he remembered giving an Indian a half pint of salt at the mouth of Coal [river], which he remembered, and was told it saved him his life. He was with him two years & was then brought by him into Greenbrier County and was told to go home. The first night after being released, he slept in a hollow log and the Indians came and camped near the log and set on the log. I have herd they made their fire on one side of the log.

(3) He went back again on the same business, and was captured; and to punish him a sick Indian was strapped on his back and carried a long distance, and was released by promising them he would never come back on their lands again; but not satisfied he went back the next fall and the Indians got after him and chased him on a ridge until he came to a precipice. He thought if he made the leap it would be instant death and if he did not, the Indians would capture him and rather than be tortured by them, he chose death and made the leap. The Indians looked over the precipice and said scary - which is called Scary to this day. But fortunately for him, he (4) received no injuries from the leap.

Teass' valley was his hunting ground and was discovered by him. He was a Tanner by trade, and also a skin-dresser; sunk a vat at Mouth of Coal to dress deer skins. I have herd on one occasion that a deer came up to him and licked salt from his hand. He said it was an evil omen, and packed up immediately and came home, and never went back any more.

There are many more incidents connected with his adventures which I deem unnecessary to mention. What I have written you I got from my father and aunts. I heard a gentleman say he saw a history in Fayette County, West Va. which mentioned him and told (5) of his adventures with the Indians. If you know any thing about the book you will confer a great favor by telling me how I can get it. For any information I can give, I will do it very cheerfully

     Yours Most Respectfully
     John T. Teass
   Address Potter Hill, Bedford County, Va.

7C37 N. S. Halbert letter, Crawfordsville, Lowndes County, Mississippi, 1882

This letter cites a newspaper article dated 1877 and written by a clergyman. It concerns an incident during the French and Indian War in which Daniel Boone killed an Indian who had his knife drawn. See Ralph

Clayton letter below.

7C41-42 *Map of Teays Valley drawn by Baylus Cade in 1889: legible place names include Great Kanawa River, Putnam County Line, Trace Fork, Charlie's Creek, Killgore's Creek, Big Hurricane Creek, Teay's Valley*

7C43-43(5) Ralph Clayton letter, Walnut Plains, Mo., May 30, 1877 "Reminiscences of Daniel Boone" *from Ralph Clayton's visit with Boone in 1818. LCD handwriting*

I have recently seen in the public as well as in history, pieces [on] Col. Daniel Boone, and have, on good authority, pronounced them fabrications.

In the fall of 1818, three gentlemen and myself from Rockingham and Augusta counties, Virginia started to explore the west and Missouri in particular. If Col. Boone was yet living, intended to go and see him. Col. Miller, one of my companions, replied "Yes – that [is my] intention, for Col. Boone is my mother's cousin; therefore I think it my duty."

We had the pleasure to land in what was then the town, now city, of St. Louis [in] November, and were informed that Col. Boone was living on or near the road to the Boone's Lick country, the region of our destination. We were informed that the Colonel was at Captain Callaway's, his son-in-law's.

(1) We arrived there on the thirtieth, and spent that night, and part of the next day with Col. Boone, whom I found as interesting a gentleman as I ever conversed with. Col. Miller asked "Uncle Daniel, how are you?" He said, "I was eighty four years old* on the twenty-second of October. If I had not over-heated myself running after my horse, a short time ago when he got loose from me, and I took a cold, I now would have been out in the woods ahunting."

I asked him if he had ever seen the book called the "Mountain Muse," written by Daniel Bryan. He said he had, and regretted that he could not sue him for slander, and added that such productions ought to be left until the person was put in the ground. He took occasion to remark that there was a small pamphlet+ that he had written some thirty years before, every word of which was correct to the best of his knowledge. The Colonel observed that Bryan, in his book, had made him a host - that he had killed a host of Indians. "But," said he, "I never killed but three that I claimed, but many was the fair fire I have had at them. The first I ever [was]

+Doubtless Filson's narrative
* Draper's calculation of Daniel Boone's age: 1818
                                                1734
                                                  84

(2) in Pennsylvania, when Stevenson was ____ council with a tribe of Indians, and I was there as wagon-master, and went across the bridge on business. On my way back, I was overtaken by a big Indian, half drunk. He drew his knife on me, flourishing it over his head, boasting that he had killed many a Long Knife, and would kill some more on his way home, and charge the murders on the tribe who were then engaged in the treaty."

Col. Boone said he was unarmed, and was very cautious in approaching the dangerous Indian, and kept at a distance from him for a while. As the fellow reached the bridge, he stopped, repeating his savage threats. Col. Boone said, in relating the incident, "I thought at the time that the blood-thirsty Red Skin had killed his last victim - that it was high time an end should be put to his bloody career." Looking around and seeing no person, Boone watched his opportunity; and quickening his own pace as the Indian started, overtaking him about the middle of the bridge, as he was about to turn round when Boone gave him a sudden push, that precipitated him over one side.

(4) Boone and Callaway girls captured. *Newspaper article included in this letter is omitted here.*

(5) Col. Boone – Reported Death

This statement appeared in the papers in Virginia in 1819, a year before the Colonel died. I have asked different members of his connections if they knew the date of Col. Boone's death, but none of them could tell. He died on the 24th of September 1820, and the old <u>St. Louis Republican</u> was in mourning for him.

I could relate different anecdotes of Col. Boone from good authority, but as this is too long, let it suffice.

R. C.

Memo – Transcribed from the preceding original statement, sent me Feb. 22d, 1883, by Ralph Clayton, his birth-day, nintey-five years of age. LCD

7C44 *Printed version of eyewitness account of visit with Daniel Boone in 1818 in Missouri. Boone was age 84 on 22 Oct. 1818. Boone and Callaway girls captured.*

7C56(1-5) Thomas Teas* was from Campbell County, Va.

Thomas Teas discovered Teas's Valley in about 1782, located thousands of acres of land including the greater portion of Teas's Valley. Surveyed in 1783 and obtained patents in 1795. He was captured by the Indians on Coal River and was returned in three years. LCD

(1) His son Stephen Teass settled at Coals Mouth on the Kanawha River but he returned to Campbell County where he lived to a good old age. He died in 1829. He married a Miss Lee of French descent.

Scarry Creek where the first Battle of the Great Rebellion was fought in West Virginia was named by Thomas Teass from having a dreadfull scare by the Indians. Tacket Creek near mouth of Coal takes its name from Hannah Tackett, one of the pioneer women who was captured at the same time.

(2) Thomas Teass while surveying in the Kanawha Valley with a small squad of men saw a number of Indians on a hill not far away. They felt uneasy but as only one Indian advanced they met him kindly.

After a great many words and signs he made them understand he wanted salt. Thos. Teass had about a half Gallon of salt which he handed to the Indian telling him to help himself. The Indian took about half of the salt and after thanking them over and over again he went away. He little thought this little act of kindness would be the means of saving his life; but so it proved a year or two after.

(3) When Thos. Teass was captured by the Indians, he had in his possession 1 rifle gun, 1 pocket knife, 2 pieces of gold which were given back to him when he was [saved] from the steak [stake], by the old indian. He kept them 3 years and finally gave them to a young Indian chief to conduct him to the white settlement with some others, among whom were Mrs. Erskine,** (4) Thomas Teass, Col. Crawford, Hannah Tackett, and others [who] were captured. The children were killed, the women retained for cooks. The men sentenced to be burnt at the stake. Col. Crawford and others were burned; and when Teass' turn came, he was also bound to the stake, and the pine knots filled around him. He had witnessed the burning of others, and we can imagine what his feelings were when he heard the command to light the pine knots. But the Great God who orders all things, decreed it otherwise.

An old Indian (5) who had been sitting and watching him sadly arose and stepped quietly to Teass, and unbound him, saying "You must burn me before you burn white man. White man Indian's friend. White man give me salt."

They unloosed him and thus the life of Thos. Teass was saved by the gift of salt. The old Indian took him and put him to cooking when they went out on a long hunting excursion. For his first meal, he boiled a pot of venison, put in a little salt (he had with him) and a large hand full of Indian meal which thickened the broth into soup. The Indians were pleased and as he sat a little ways off, he heard them say "pretty good cook."

* *Thomas Teas was mentioned in the captivity narratives of* ***Margaret Pawley Erskine. She told that they returned together from Indian captivity to western Virginia about 1784.* See "What Shall I Do Now?" The Story of the Indian Captivity of Margaret Paulee, Jones Hoy and Jack Callaway 1779 - ca. 1789. Anne Crabb, *Filson History Quarterly*, Oct. 1996

7C58 Map of Teas Valley and LCD memo: Wrote to Mrs. Elizabeth L. Wood, Warrenton, Mo., who replied Aug. 28, 1883. "I am sorry that I cannot answer your inquiries correctly. Thomas Teass, my grandfather, died in New London, Campbell County, Va., when I was very young..."

LCD note: Thomas Teass was an inhabitant of Greenbriar County, Va., Sept. 1781. <u>Calendar Va. State Papers,</u> ii, 469.

7C65 Letter from Thomas Callaway[?], the "oldest Callaway now living." *The writer learned from his grandfather, also named Thomas Callaway, who died in 1818, that Thomas Callaway had emigrated from England. The writer is a son of John Callaway, who was a Marshall in East Tennessee in 1824. This is a 4-page letter and is legible. The letter is not signed, seems to stop mid-stream, perhaps due to a page missing in the microfilm.*

7C67 *Signature gives abbreviation for first name, perhaps Thos. Callaway. Capture of the Boone and Callaway girls in 1776 is discussed and Dr. James Callaway, Joseph Callaway, Elijah Callaway, Samuel Callaway are mentioned.*

7C72-72(1) George W. Stoner letter, Bath County, Ky., Nov. 1868. He was born in 1787.

It is said the Indians [when the Boone and Callaway girls were captured in 1776] were taken on a small branch of Flat Creek about 15 miles above the mouth of Flat Creek. Indians were a little north of the branch, south-western part of Bath County, on George Hamilton's farm – some 38 miles from this spot to Boonesboro & probably nearer 50 miles the way they trailed the Indians.

Mr. Caleb Ratliff, an aged settler, says the girls' rescue was made opposite the mouth of Bald Eagle Creek, Branch of Flat Creek. **(1)** But Richard Robinson, nearly 80, & raised in the country - & on the whole, better authority than Mr. Ratliff, & now residing in Bethel, Bath County – says the rescue took place at the mouth of Miner's Branch*, a western tributary of Flat Creek... *more speculation follows... the asterisk refers to a small map designating Eagle Creek, and to Draper's note below.*

*I must have noted Mr. Robinson's statement above from Mr. Stoner, or someone else – as it is erroneous. For I wrote to Mr. Robinson & he replied Feb. 5, 1869, saying he understood they camped near Minor's Branch – the Indians & their captives – don't know where the girls were retaken.

7C75 Heading: Henderson's Treaty, March 1775
Seizin - Possession of an estate or freehold giving possession of a tract of land, as in the Henderson &c. purchase of 1775, John Fa___ was deputed by the Cherokees to make the transfer.

To Col. Wm. Crawford's will, made May 16, 1782, was appended a curious memorandum, in imitation of the old English feudal feoffment – that on the day of the date thereof, full and peaceable possession of said land being taken and had by said Crawford, the same was by him, then and ___ in due form, by <u>turf and twig</u>, delivered to Harrison (to whom the land was conveyed). <u>Veech's Monongahela of Old</u>, 121.

7C76-76(1-2) Partial statement of Col. William Cocke. LCD heading: Copy of Col. Wm. Cocke's Statement – taken from the original.

Dunmore, March 1774. *A similar statement is found also in Draper Mss 32C84, titled "Fragment of Col. Wm. Cocke's, copied from a dilapidated paper found among Cocke's papers." The two statements are not identical, but nearly so. The three paragraphs from Cocke's Papers are followed by Draper's comments.*

Cocke's Mission to Boone. April 1775.

That he, Daniel Boone, had prevailed on fifteen men to assist him in erecting some small huts for defence, & that he would make a stand if possible & that he should confide in our giving him assistance. Feeling as I did for their distress, I proposed that any one [who] would venture with me that I would go on to join Boone to spirit up the brave men with him, and assure them of the general determination to join him with about forty who were then with Col. Henderson. But no person would be prevailed on to go with me to encounter so dangerous an undertaking. I then consented to go alone, and did actually perform that dangerous enterprise.

About the month of June [LCD: 1775], I returned to Holston, and on my way back fell in with Samuel Newell, James Davis, William Griffith, Peter Shoemaker and one Campbell in Powell's Valley. The Indians attacked the camp, shot Shoemaker with several shot[s] through the back of the neck, who fell, and to all appearance seemed past recovery, but suddenly recovering, shot an Indian with his own gun, and, seizing Campbell's gun that lay near him shot a second Indian, which so confused the Indian and (at that moment) were at a small distance running up toward the camp, the Indians fled; and we **(1)** sustained no other loss than that of Shoemaker's losing an ounce or two of blood, and the inconvenience of a few days unpleasant feelings with the wounds.

In March 1774, I returned to Amelia County, Virginia. Lord Dunmore, with whom I was personally acquainted, having spent some time with him, sent me a Captain's Commission, and a letter requesting that I would see him at the Palace. I attended him at his request, & after the most polite & friendly treatment he spoke as if with the deepest concern at what he called the rebellion, & assured me that he always looked upon me as a loyal subject, & that there was nothing that he could do to serve me that he would not gladly do - complimented me on the great expectations he had of my becoming serviceable to the King & country, should a disturbance (or what he termed a rebellion) take place between the two countries. I did not hesitate a moment to inform him that I would not deceive him; and that I would assist in defending the rights and liberties of my country to the last extremity. He endeavored to prove to me that my resolution was rash & hasty, and said he hoped I would consider better when I took into view the just claim of our Sovereign & the power of the crown, & the weakness, and above all, the divisions that were in the country. My determination was fixed. I returned to what was then called Fincastle, the Wolf hills, near Abingdon – called my company together **(2)** & endeavored to impress on their minds the value of our Liberties, the benefit of self-government, and the necessity of being firm and united: declared myself to be what I believe the God of nature had made me & will continue to be, a friend to Liberty and Equal Rights, to free representative government founded on the principles of our happy Constitution.

This is a fragment of evidently a more lengthy narrative of early border events written by the late Colonel or Judge William Cocke, once U.S. Senator from Tennessee. He was, as this paper shows, & "Hall's Sketches" corroborate, one of the first party that pioneered the way in the settlement of Kentucky in the Spring of 1775 - & the year previous, '74, had a singular interview with Gov. Dunmore of Virginia. – and the evidence, that the Governor had designs against the good people of America previous to his Indian campaign in the fall of that year, when, it is believed, he conciliated the good wishes of the western tribes in behalf of the King, & against the Colonies. Baltimore, Md., June 4th. 1845. LCD

PS – The original from which the above is copied, I found among Col. Cocke's papers in possession of his daughter Mrs. Jack, of Grainger County, Tenn. – Aug. 1844. LCD

Addenda – See Col. Henderson's Manuscript letter, July 20th, 1775, about the little fight in Powell's Valley, 23rd June: see, also, Nathl. Hart's letter in the "Commonwealth."

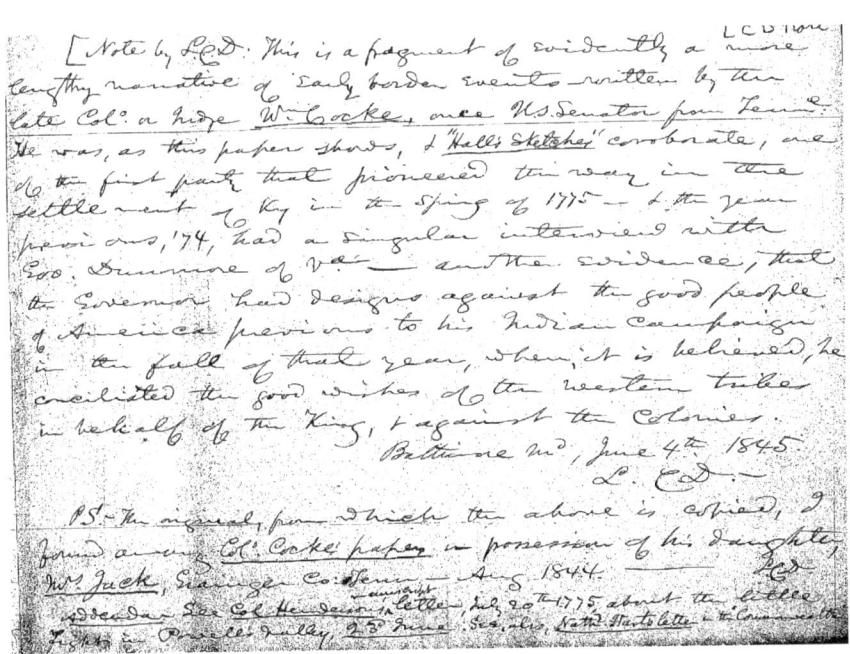

LCD Notes on Col. William Cocke's Papers. 7C76(2)

7C77-77(1-3) *LCD notes on capture and rescue of the Boone and Callaway girls in 1776.*

(1) The Cherokees had sent a tomahawk belt with two scalps to the Shawanese, informing them that they had struck the white people, and it was his opinion that the Shawanese would join, provided the other nations did. - <u>American Archives</u>, Fifth Series, ii, 514-515.

The above shows that the Cherokees of the party who captured the Boone & Callaway girls were ambassadors from their people, who had commenced war upon the whites, inviting the Shawanese to join them, probably meeting the Shawanoe party in Kentucky, informed them of the digging up of the tomahawk in the Cherokee country, & persuaded them to unite with them in striking the whites on the Kentucky [River]. It seems [that] they came across a couple of solitary whites in the wilderness, killed them, & then captured the girls.

Memo – This report of Wilson's originally appeared in Hildreath's <u>Pioneer History of Ohio</u>, pp. 98-100, in 1848 - & ____'s Archives, into which it is copied, was not printed till 1851.

(2) Arbuckle's Account – Capt. Matthew Arbuckle writes Col. William Fleming, from Ft. Randolph, Aug. 15, 1776: "was informed some time ago, the Shawnees & Cherokees had taken three women prisoners from Cantuckee, and got one scalp. I therefore dispatched three of my men to demand the three prisoners (if in possession of the Shawnees) to be immediately delivered up. Two of the women were daughters of Col. Callaway, and the other a daughter of Col. Boone, at Cantuckee likewise. And this day the men are returned again with one of the Shawnee chiefs, & brother of Cornstalk's, who informs me that after having taken the prisoners from Cantuckee, the whites followed and retook the prisoners, and killed two of their men. Upon this, I informed them of the fate of the Cherokees, and that our people would, without dispute, cut them all off, which seemed to have a great effect upon them, and they promised to hold a lasting peace; but this I dispute, as they now have the Cornstalk away at Fort Detroit treating with the English, & are constantly backwards and forwards on that course – so that the peace (3)   with them I look upon not to be lasting. I am ever on my guard for fear of a surprise. The traders got quantities of goods from the English at Detroit & have for some time, as the traders informed my men while at the towns. They had received sundry quantities of goods from thence for the use of the Indians."

7C80-81 Deposition of Daniel Boone taken this 22nd day of September 1817 at the house of John B. Callaway in St. Charles County, Missouri Territory. LCD note: These depositions furnished me by W. D. Hixson, of

Maysville, Ky., Oct., 1884. LCD

Daniel Boone, aged 85 years and first duly sworn… That the war-road leading from the mouth of Cabin Creek to the Upper Blue Licks along which [I] pursued the Indians at the time they killed my brother Edward Boone in the year 1780 in the month of October same year, is and was the main upper War-road leading from the mouth of Cabin Creek to the Upper Blue Licks; and that we returned home from the pursuit, the road leading from the mouth of Cabin Creek past the Stone Lick, and this Upper War-road about that time to my knowledge was more traveled than the other considerably; and what they now call the two lower roads was by me and many others called one and the same road because they forked about 3 or 4 miles from the Upper Blue Licks and came together below the Stone Lick [on] **(1)** Cabin Creek where the Widow Rowland lived when I made a chain of Surveys for Lawrence Slaughter, Boone and others [to] a number of buffalo paths until we come within a mile of the mouth of Cabin Creek and then proceeded on to the Ohio river at the mouth of Cabin Creek [to] Stockton Spring where Stockton afterwards built a station and then we turned down to the Lower Blue Licks.

Question: When did you become first acquainted with the road spoken of?
Answer: In June or July 1776 at which time we followed the Indians almost to the North fork of Licking. [LCD: July 1776, pursued Indians who captured the girls] But never heard neither of the roads called upper or lower war roads until the trip in October 1780.
81 Question: Did the whole of our company, in October 1780, pursue the Indians to Cabin Creek – If they did not, state who did and where did they stop.
Answer: Jacob Stucker, Charles Gatliff and some others, probably 9 or 10, the balance stopped at the Junction of the Stone Lick road. My son Israel went with us to see the river.

Flanders Callaway, aged 63, at the same time and place deposes that he came to Kentucky in 1775, and continued 7 or 8 years & then returned to Virginia and back again the same fall – that he became acquainted with the Upper Blue Licks in 1775 and hunted from that time about 6 or 7 years about the Upper Blue Licks and between the Licks and Boonsboro. In the year 1775, I met at Upper Blue Licks a party of Indians, "five men, __ squaws, and seven children."

Draper's notes in the margin: Girls captured, July 1776.

Edward Boone killed, Oct. 1780. Flanders Callaway hunts & meets Indians at the Upper Blue Licks in 1775. *Draper calculated Daniel Boone's birth year again as 1733 by his being age 84 in 1817.*

7C82 LCD heading: Edward Boone killed, Oct. 1780. *Deposition is in the same handwriting as the above depositions.*

Deposition of James Ray at the dwelling of John Haggin, Mercer County, [Ky.] Oct 24th, 1817

That he was one of the Company that pursued the Indians in the month of October 1780. Captain Charles Gatliff commanded at the time Edward Boone was killed. We pursued the Indians to the Upper Blue Licks and then along a plain road till we came to another road in the neighborhood of Limestone. Colonel Daniel Boone said that road we came to was the Lower Blue Lick road, and that it led to the Lower Blue Licks. Here a council of war was held at the forks of the road. The Counsel composed of Boone, Gatliff and myself as I was second in command. We concluded to go to the Lower Blue Licks.

7C83 Extract from Deposition of John Stephenson taken May 5th, 1818 in Christian County, Ky.. LCD heading: Edward Boone killed, Oct. 1780.

That sometime in the fall of the year 1780, I went in company with Daniel Boone, Charles Gatliff and others and buried Edward Boone on Grassy Lick, who was killed by the Indians. From there took the trails of the Indians and followed them along a path until we struck a creek which the company said was Cabin Creek and went on down the creek. I think the main body went down to the mouth of Cabin Creek and when they came back to us they said the Indians had crossed the Ohio river and were gone.

Extract from Deposition of John McIntyre

That he went in company with Colonel Daniel Boone, Charles Gatliff, James Estill, James Ray, Wm. McConnell and a number of others, perhaps 60 or 70, for the purpose of burying Edward Boone & to pursue the Indians that killed him &c.

7C84-87 The deposition of Peter Scholl, taken at the house of L. P. Dorsy, Mason County, Ky., April 17, 1818. LCD notes: Edwd. Boone killed Oct. 1780. 1776 Boone & Callaway girls, where re-taken.

[I] was one of the company that pursued the Indians that killed Edward Boone, my wife's father, in October 1780; and after burying said Boone, we followed the trace of the Indians to the Upper Blue Licks until we came to what is now called Fleming Creek, where they had roasted their meat. Thence a branch that led down between two knobs, and just before we got to the Knobs, the Indians parted, and a part of them went over the left hand knob and come to the road on the other side at a pealed tree, thence along the road until we came to the North Fork, as Colonel Daniel Boone called it at that time, where there were a number of camps, pealed and chopped trees, and a large long clay lick in the bank of said North Fork, on the north east side.

85 I set my pocket compass to know the course in case we should be defeated, through some marshy ground leaving the knob on our right-hand, we came over on the waters of Cabin Creek and then asked Colonel Daniel Boone where he thought the Indians would cross the Ohio river. He said he thought they would cross at the Mouth of Cabin Creek, if we did not overtake them. After going down Cabin Creek [to] a large bend, the war road went across the white oak point, and on the point there were many trees pealed, and the picture of a turtle and I think of a deer.

After going some distance, Captain Charles Gatliff spoke to Colonel Boone and requested him to send some spies forward to see if they had crossed the Ohio river; the object was if they had crossed, the company need not go all the way. Some of them went about one mile and a half, and I think the same place shown to me yesterday [by] Elias Hood and on their return they said the Indians had crossed the Ohio river at the mouth of Cabin Creek on the lower side of said creek.

We then went back some **86** short distance, then held a council. Some wanted to go back the same way and others wanted to go the trace by the Lower Blue Licks. Mutually agreed to return by the Lower Blue Licks, came to a stone lick where the men stopped and cracked hickory nuts and rested about one hour, and then went down the creek. After going two or three miles from the North Fork where the land was rich, Colonel Boone spoke to me to stop behind and there was Israel Boone and Israel Grant behind. Colonel Boone proposed to turn to the left hand and hunt. We did so and killed a buffalo, and went on to overtake the company which was to camp at the Lower Blue Licks that night. When we came to the Lower Blue Licks we saw nothing of the Company and we crossed Licking and went over to a big flat creek and there we came up with them and the company parted. Gatliff and his company went to Bryant's Station.

87 Colonel Boone, myself and others went to Boone's Station, where we fell in company with Bartlett Searcy and related to him the route we had pursued the Indians. Searcy said we had went the Upper War road to the mouth of Cabin Creek which he stated to be a great crossing place for the Indians, that he [Searcy] was well acquainted with the road and he believed it to be the same [route taken] at the time they took two of Colonel Callaway's daughters and one of Colonel Boon's, who were retaken two or three miles south of the Upper Blue Licks.

Scholl in answer to question states that John McIntyre was one of Strode's men but they did not go on to Cabin Creek.

Scholl gives his age as 63 and states that he came to Kentucky in the fall of '79 by the wilderness road. That he was to hunt for four families and they were to raise 4 acres of corn for him.

The above copy of Peter Scholl's deposition was sent me, in Oct. 1884, by W. D. Hixson, of Maysville, Ky. LCD

7C91 LCD - Capture of Boone & Callaway's Daughters, 1776. Boone's deposition concerning the re-capture of his daughter.

On the 16th of July 1776 on my return from retaking my daughter from the Indians, we lay all night on Flat Creek at the Mouth of a small branch, a short distance from a cabin on the east side of said creek where I afterwards entered 955 acres for William Watson South of the Upper Licks 8 or more miles.

"William Watson enters 955 acres upon a treasury warrant, beginning six miles south-west of the Upper Blue Lick Spring, at Daniel Boone's old camp at the forks of a branch on the war-road, running up the branch on both sides..."

[See confirmation on middle of next page. Entered May 15, 1780. LCD]
[Above copies rec'd from W. D Hixson. LCD]

7C92 Pursuit of the Indians who killed Edward Boone, in Oct 1780

Here Draper quoted from the above depositions as to the location of the rescue of the Boone and Callaway girls in July 1776. He gave references from Collins History, ii: 526, 655; from Bradford's Notes on Kentucky, p. 24; Collins, ii, 526.

LCD: the pursuing party went 5 miles first day, 30 miles the second, & 5 miles the third. John Floyd's letter does not agree about the short distance the first day; but says 30 miles the second day, and ten miles on the third – the latter pursuing a buffalo road (Butler, 23). Thus, calling the first day 5 miles, it was 45 miles from Boonesboro to where the girls were retaken.

The maps show 40 miles, straight line measurement, from Boonesboro to the Upper Blue Licks.

7C93 *LCD speculation on the location of the rescue of the Boone and Callaway girls and a list of those telling of the event: George Bryan, Josiah Collins, Septimus Scholl, Mrs. Cunningham and Robin Moore. These appear to be brief statements about locations extracted from interviews by LCD in which he lists all the sources for the statement, such as Shane, Collins, etc. Much is illegible.*

7C95 LCD - Where Girls Recaptured & 1st night's camp on return.

There seem to have been two war roads of the Indians – one, I judge, by the Lower Blue Licks – the other east of Lulbegrud Creek to Upper Blue Licks & Cabin Creek as shown by Filson's map. (This latter must have forked north or near Lulbegrud, in early times leading to the Shawanoe Town at the mouth of Sciota.)

When the girls were captured, the Indians took through the cane country – with no path – evidently intending to strike the war road at Upper Blue Licks, & must have reached Cassidy's Creek, on its upper part, apparently some 5 or 6 miles from the Upper Blue Licks, for there is no part of that stream nearer, apparently.

The girls were retaken (I think) about ten o'clock in the forenoon; they were all, no doubt, weary from travel & anxiety, & hence did not hurry very much on their return march that day – perhaps had to kill meat for their sustenance. Not caring to return by the route through the cane they came, & Boone knowing of the old war road, steered for it, taking a somewhat south or southeasterly course, & passing perhaps two or three miles south of the Lower Blue Licks, & then reaching the Old War Road, following it in a southerly direction, & where it crossed Main Flat Creek – or perhaps its western upper Fork, Bald Eagle, there encamped for the night – Boone's Camp. They would seem to have been about twelve miles from the place of rescue on Cassidy's Creek.

The fact of Boone & rescuing party camping there – in now Bath County – has no doubt given rise to the tradition that the rescue took place there – Collins' Kentucky, Bath County, ii p 50 – on Bald Eagle, 3 miles east of Sharpsburg.

Bath County map sent me by V. B. Young shows the locality of the spring on the Hamilton place north of Bald Eagle, & up Flat Creek.

This Boone's Camp on Flat Creek or Bald Eagle, where they camped Tuesday night, July 14th, was some thirty-five miles from Boonsboro – which they reached the next day, Wednesday.

7C97 V. B. Young named the men in the rescue party for the captured girls: D. Boone, John Floyd, John Holder, Flanders Callaway, Samuel Henderson, and others. Betsy Callaway & Sam Henderson married on Aug. 7, 1776 by Squire Boone in Boonesborough.

7C99-99(1) V. B. Young. *Map where girls were rescued. Along the side of this map is written: Turnpike road from Mt. Sterling to Owingsville. Place-names: Main Flat Creek, Fork of Flat Creek, Spring, Hamilton's House, Hills Brough, Dirt road leading to J. W. Fassetts house. Hughes grave.*

(1) Explanation of map

7C100(2) B. F. Maxey letter, 1885. *Boone and Callaway girls captured. He was born in Montgomery County, Ky., now in Fleming County, Ky., since 1863. Jacob Cassity mentioned.*

7C108 B. F. Maxey's notes on a map.

 The map that is before me is laid off into precincts, 18 in[ches] by 14, & the paper I have is too small; but it will give you an idea of the locality at any rate.
 I said to you, I think, that the old trace left Flat Creek at Bald Eagle, but upon examining the map, & on reflection, I see it left Flat Creek above Miner Branch, a half mile below David Hughes, and passed out at the head of Bald Eagle to Bethel Ridge, & the head of Little Flat Creek & Cassidy.
 Moorefield is in Nicholas County, on the road from Sharpsburg to Carlisle.
 I believe I have said to you all I can that is strictly true.

7C115(1-5) James Wade letter, Virginia, Ill., Oct 29, 1883
LCD: Boone & Callaway Girls Captured – 1776. Red River Scout – Morgan's Station.

Dear Sir
 I yesterday received your Book and also your letter putting me in mind that I had not answered yours of August 27. About the time I received your letter I lost a near & dear Relative which has made me forget

your letter… I will now try to answer your questions…

1st My Grandfathers name was Dawson Wade.

2nd What year he came to Kentucky I cant say. Whether Grandfather ever lived on Greenbrier in west Virginia I cant say or what I said before about Greenbrier I don't recollect, but he lived in Burbon County on Stoner creek… Stoner is a memorable landmark of Kentucky to this day. It passed through Bath County, about 2 miles from **(1)** where I was born.

3th [sic] My information is that Father was at Boonsborough when the Girls were taken: have herd Father tell all the particulars but do not now recollect any more that Father said. They were able to follow them as the Girls had Shoes & occasionally they would Screw their heels in the Ground so as to make it plain, but the Indians discovered it & removed their Shoes & placed mockisons on them. After that one of the Girls who wore a red Shawl would every now & then drop a piece of the fringe. This is about all I can now recollect.

4th I do not recollect anything about Boone's being Shot at in Bath County.

5th It was not during a tour of scouting that Father rode upon the Indian camp. It was on a small stream called Little Slate about 2 miles from its mouth; it empties into Big Slate.

6th The Scouting party who went out on Red River was on that trip commanded by Capt. James Lane (a man I have often seen). I will give you father's words as nigh as I can. He said they had traveled all day and were very tired; they went down a steep hill some 100 yards & came to a bench or level place some 20 yards wide – then a clift some 50 feet down to River. **(2)** There they camped, making a fire by a big log. Not having seen any sign of Indians all day, they felt pretty safe & being tired, the men soon began to lay down. The captain said someone must stand guard.

  After the Captain lay down they began to make excuses to each other – one was tired, another had a sore foot, & so on, until no watch stood, but all went to sleep. Just before daylight they were attacked.
The fire had burned under the log & was a better fire on the opposite side. Just before the attack, 2 of the men had gotten up and went over the log & sat down on the ground & was talking when the attack was made.

  At the first fire, one of the men fell over, so the other one said when he came in to the Station. Father said when he woke, every man was gone. He satched [snatched] his gun & started up the Hill; when he had gone about 20 steps, he heard to his right someone groaning. He made for him, as maybe could do him service. Just before reaching him he [saw] the tomahawk strike him. He then turned, reached the top of the hill, but could **(3)** rase but one man who said his comrade was shot by his side the first fire, & father said one was killed on the hillside, so they made their way in best they could.

Captain Lane ran into a thick bunch of Laurel and before he knew, came near falling over the clift. He was close to camp where he could see all the Indians maneuvers. After daylight the Indians got breakfast by the fire, put up a mark & shot at it for an hour or two before leaving. When gone, Capt. Lane came out & found one man killed – the man that was shot at the fire was the same man that was tomahawked on the hillside. He was shot in the groin.

7th He was in the Blue lick defeat. I do not know what company he was in.

8th I do not know who was his Captain on Wayne's Campaign. When he went across the River, he saw the Road was full of moccasin tracks (perfectly flattened). I don't recollect whether the tracks were going up or down.

9th Father died the 8th day of June 1844. He was no pensioner. He said he had done no more for his country than he owed it ___ and would take no pay. He was often solicited to apply, but always refused.

(4) 10th You say Morgan Station was taken in 1793. I cant say anything about dates – for these things I heard related when a boy & was much interested in them; but not in dates. For some time before the Station was attacked, times had been quiet & the Station was out of Stockading – down in places &c. Father had just come in to the Station & turned his Horse into the Stable. There was but one other man in at the time, all the rest were out – some one & some another, when the cry was "Indians coming." He went out, they being on high ground above the station, & saw them coming in single file. I think he said 30 or 33. Just then a man coming in from the field, angling across the line of the Indians, was in 50 or 75 yards of the Indians before he saw them. He stopped a second, the foremost Indian beckoned to him to come to him; the man sprang away when the foremost Indian dropped on his knee & fired; the whole line fired – all missed. Father hollowed "fly to the Block House." When they all got in they found **(5)** their were only 2 guns that was available. So it was every man for himself. The man that had been shot at had a wife & small children. He picked up the largest & the smallest & made their escape. The other man's wife clung to him for some 20 steps; he broke her hold & escaped; she was taken prisoner. Father said he went to the stable to get his horse; but the horse was so frightened he could not get hold of him. He threw the stable door open & the horse went clear Father ran down & jumped the pickets on the south side of the Station. He said it seamed to him he was right in the midst of them; they commenced firing & kept it up as long as they had any chance. When firing ceased, he cast his eye back over his shoulder & found 2 Indians were after him; he said he was satisfied then for he did not believe their was an indian that could catch him. They ran him about 2 miles and returned.

On their return they passed by an old lady who had made her escape on the first announcement of Indians, and had went as far as she could & cralled under a rock that projected out of the hill-side. She said the 2 Indians that had followed Father, on their return, came so close to her that she could have reached out and taken them by the foot. She said they were panting like they were very tired. There was only one man killed & 26 prisoners **(6)** taken – Women & children. There gathered a force of 30 men by the next morning at the Station & started in pursuit; after following some distance they began to press the Indians and they began to kill their prisoners who could [not?] keep up. One little girl who they had scalped & tomahawked & left for dead, the men in pursuit found, & she recovered.

I believe I have given you all the information I can. When I heard Father talk and tell those things, I was but a boy; some things were indelibly impressed upon my mind while dates I paid no attention to. In the same county in which Father lived (Bath), lived some of Father's old comrades in those times; they used to come & see father most every year as long as they were able. I believe they were all dead before Father died. I here give you some of their names:
Luke Hood
Wm. Suddith
John Trumbo
John Iles
John Warner
Jas. Lane

I tender you my thanks for your Book & would like to have one of your Books

J. A Wade

Volume 8C contains 200(1) numbered pages.

8C11(1-3) Beal Ijames letter, Calahan, Davie County, N.C, July 17, 1884. LCD heading: Huntsville – Dutchman's Creek – Phil Nail – John Boone on Hunting Creek

Dear Sir I rec'd your letter of June 5th & also the book you sent for which am very much obliged… I have been trying to get up some information…

I will send you a history of Col. Daniel Boone & his ancestors &c, written many years ago... I will say however that Squire Boone, father of Daniel Boone, settled on the Yadkin...

(1) ... at a place known today as Boone's Ford. Colonel Daniel Boone, when he left his father, crossed over on the west side of the river & moved up the river about 30 miles & settled in the bend of the river, near where Huntsville, a little village in Yadkin County, now is. Dutchman's & Sugar Creeks are west of the Yadkin river. Dutchman's is a low swampy stream. *Mentioned: Conrad's line, Holden, Cooley*

(2) ... And the Nail you enquired of was Phillip Nail, a young man at the time & accompanied Col. Daniel Boone in his first trip over the mountains. He came back & was generally known at "Indian Phil." He sickened & died & was buried at a place where Bethel Church was years afterward built.

(3) *Discussion of John Boone's daughter who married Samuel Little, whose children all emigrated west.* John Boone married a widow Wells & moved to the western part of Tennessee, Gibson County, where he died. He has several children in Tennessee.

8C92 *Plats of the Boone Lands granted in 1753, in Rowan County, now Davie County, N.C.* LCD notes: George, Squire & John Boone's Lands. "Boone's Bottom" on east side of the Yadkin. Plats: George Boone's Survey of 640 acres; John Boone's Survey of 640 acres; Jonathan Boone's Survey of 640 acres

Volume 9C contains 244 numbered pages

9C2 Map by W. E. White, Taylorsville N.C., Oct 26, 1887. *Wilkes County N.C., Yadkin river, Walker & Alexander, Catawba County, Iredell County, Catawba River, Brushy Mountain, Alexander C____, Boone's Home.*

9C58(1-3) S. A. Yates letter, Ashe County, Gap Creek, North Carolina, Oct. 5th, 1883. LCD heading: Boone on Yadkin, North Carolina; Boone Mustering - living at mouth of Lewis' Fork; His Captivity & escape - siege of Boonesboro, 1778.

Accounts of two of Boone's escapes were probably blended here. The account begins with the earlier escape with the dog chasing him; the last statements pertain to his return to Fort Boonesborough in June 1778. This account continues with the 1778 siege at that Fort in September of that year.

Mr. Lyman Draper Dear Sir: as reply to your wanting information concerning the Early life of Col. Daniel Boone when he explored North Carolina is a difficult matter for me to ascertaine; but to the best of what I am able to tell you he was in this county about the date of 1765. I have heard my father say many times that my Grandfather, John Yates, said that he had seen Daniel Boone & mustered with him in Old Wilkes County; & he also said that Boone lived at the mouth of Lewis' fork Creek where it emptys in the Yadkin River - lived there one summer & hunted & fished.

My Grandfather, John Yates, was in the Revolutionary war - was a private Soldier under Colonel Ben. Cleveland. My Grandfather was in the Battle of King's Mountain.

I will relate to you what I have heard my mother say about Col. Daniel Boone. She said that she was Born in Boone's Forte in Kentucky in the year 1784. My mother & Boone **(1)** were neare relations, am not prepared at the present time to relate our kindred; but I will write to you a gain and tell you all about it.

I am going to tell you some tails that I have heard my mother relate about Boone & the Indians. I heard her say that Boone was out hunting one day & three Indians attacked him with their guns - commenced firing at him & he Returned the fire at the Indians. They fought for a long time & they took shelter behind trees & so did Boone & they fought untill Boone's ammunition gave out. The fight was so tight that they shot Boone's tomahawk belt from around his Body; then Boone took his Gune Breach foremost & walked up to the Indians & surrendered him self to the Indians. The indians had Boone then for a considerable time, and they watched Boone very close for fear of his Runing a way from them. Boone Studyed many plans how to Get away. The Indians tied Boone every night fast & tight, & one Indian lay on Each Side of Boone.

One night while at Supper Boone, full of tricks, had taken his knife and tied **(2)** it up in his moccasin. When supper was over Indians commenced hunting for Boone's knife - hunted up and down for it & threw Boone's moccasins over & gave it up as lost. The Indians & Boone all lay with the moccasins under their heads for pillows: time came for going to bed, when two stout Robust Indians ___ Boone and lay down on Each Side of Boone. Boone lay wide awake untill all the Indians went fast to sleepe; then Boone took his moccasins from under his head, took out the Knife & cut himself loose from the Indians & Raised up Easly & put on his moccasons, & went to their Guns, & took the best gun in their Camp & tomahalk & sliped off in the Darkness of night.

Boone had not got far till he heard the Indians Raise & Call for

"Daniel" — in the darkness of night & raised up clinching ____ another, saying "is dis you, Daniel Boone" & "dis you Daniel Boone," "no Daniel Boone here, now."

Boone was running in this time & the Indians hunting for him; they set ther track dog after Boone & it commenced yelping & following on Boone's track, & soon overtook him; but Boone drew his tomahalk and kild the Indean track Dog, & Run on with Speed **(3)** all night & all the next day untill he came to Kentucky River where his own fort was. When on the other side of the River, Boone hollowed Loudly, when one of his own daughters says "there is father's Voice." He was immediately — over the River & welcomed in. Next morning by day light the indeans were at the other side of the river & Called for "Daniel Boone" to come out, they wanted to have a talk with him.

[This escape would appear to have been in 1769: LCD]

So Boone went down to the River to Chat with the Indians. Before leaving the fort Boone told the people in the fort that if the Indians went to lay hold of him, to fire on the Indians. Sure enough three made a lunge for Boone, & Boone fled for refuge to the fort. The Indians then commenced a Battle which lasted three days [nine days] which proved successful for Boone & his people who w— the fort after the fight was over; there was three or four hundred pounds of balls picked up that struck the side of the fort & fell.

I will write to you again When I have time to see some of my relatives who are older than I am. very Respectfuly

S. A. Yates

9C60-60(1) Mrs. Sarah Yates letter, Gap Creek, N.C., March 25th, 1884. *Words cut off in the margins are supplied as well as can be guessed.*

Mr. Lyman C. Draper - Dear Sir: I Received your letter of Enquiry; in due time I am going to give you the best information that I am able to give - 1st as to my gran father, John Yates, & Boone, I have heard my father Say that Boone & Grandfather Yates used to muster together at the old muster ground about 5 miles west of where old Wilkesboro now stands. What the name of the muster ground was at that time I am not able to describe: in this day and time it bears the name of Hay six muster ground. As to the militia officers I am not able to give their names.

2. As to my mother's maiden name, it was Willcox - Sarah. Her father's name was Samuel Willcox. His wife's maiden name was Ann Gordon.

Boone was my mother's uncle. Mother was born January the 28th, 1785 in Daniel Boone's Fort in Kentucky, died June the 17, 1858. Aged 73 years - 4 months, and 20 days.

3rd As to Boone killing any of the Indians after his return, I have heard my mother say that after the battle was over, that Boone & his men discovered — River Runing Red muddy & Boone said to his men — Indians have been here in the night and took ___ from the fort to the river and are going to undermine our forte and dig under the Fort & kill – all - then Boone & some of his best men ___ out and cut a large white oak and made them – wooden cannon, and sunk them a pit just about the depth that they expected the Indians would come from the River. Boone loaded his Cannon ___ with powder & other materials; and sure enough Boone and his men heard the Indians digging and jabbering, and Shortly the Earth began to break in - then Boone and his men touched match **(1)** to the wooden cannon and such screams & yells was hardly ever heard - the great ___ of the wooden cannon Brakin the earth in on the Indians and killing or wounding them without number.

4th As to Lewis and his bear fight I have heard my father talk some about Lewis being a-bear hunting & shooting a Bear and wounding it; & before Lewis could reload his gun, the bear caught him and dredfully wounded him. Lewis belonged in some of the Eastern County, below Wilkes 50 or 60 miles. As to his (Boone's) hunting Company I am not able to give thur names

5th as to — Boone & my Grandfather Yates hunting together I never heard my father say anything about thur hunting Exploits.

6th as to the locality of the Big Lump I am very well acquainted with that mountain. It is a very Large round-up mountain, very high, high as the Blue Ridge. Boone had a camp 3 miles north of the top of the Big Lump in a large flat Gap of the Blue Ridge and it is called Daniel's Gap to this day.

  As to telling you about Boone's name being cut on trees it would have been Grown out Long Days before now. I have heard Recently of Boone's name being cut in a Rock a considerable distance from where I live. My health has been very poor all the Winter and Spring - so I am not able to go round but very little; but if – live and get able to ride Round, I will go to — & see whether that is true or not about Boone's name being cut in that Rock.

  I am 60 years of Age the — Day of April next. Very Respectfuly your — friend, from

                S. A. Yates

9C61 LCD questions to S. A. Yates

9C62(1) S. A. Yates. *She wrote that Daniel Boone shot an Indian and of Indians gobbling like turkeys. Yates supposes that her grandfather Wilcox was in the fort during the Siege.*

From what my mother always told me. I and Daniel Boone are 2nd cousins. Grandfather and Daniel Boone's father all left Pennsylvania together."

9C63(1) S. A. Yates [LCD: This happened about 1780.]

I am going to relate to you a circumstance that happened to my grandfather's brother Isaiah[?] Wilcox while they were in Boone's Fort. They heard a turkey gobbling, as they supposed. Issia Wilcox says to the other boys in the Forte – "I will go and kill that turkey," and away went Wilcox and never [heard of] any more. It was an Indian gobbling instead of a turkey & he killed Wilcox. Wilcox wore a cap that had a large ivory button. In two or three days this same Indian came to the bank of the river about 3 hundred yards from the Fort & climbed up a sycamore tree and patted his [behind] at the people in the Fort, had Wilcox's cap with the ivory button on his head. He made it a regular business for several days & the boys got to shooting at the Indian and this made him very saucy. There was an Irish man in the Fort who said "Just let me try him one pop," then loading his gun he shot the Indian who fell into the river.

I am not very well; must close, ever your best friend. If I can be of any service, I am willing to give you any information that I can. God bless you!

9C68(1-11) Thomas Bouchelle letter, Idlewild, N.C., July 28, 1884
Mrs. Jemima Brown's account was dictated to Thomas Bouchelle; she was a Boone relative through the Wilcoxon line.

Dear L Draper:
Dear Sir: Mrs. Jemima Brown received a communication from you to which she desires me to reply and furnishes me various crude & incomplete narratives, as she remembers them. Mrs. Brown's age is 75 and she is the mother of 22 children all by her first husband, William Phillips.

Mrs. Brown is the daughter of Hugh Yates and his wife Sally who was Sally Wilcoxon, daughter of Samuel Wilcoxon, who was brother to Daniel Boone's mother, and accompanied Boone to Kentucky, where his daughter Sally was born in Boone's fort, on the Kentucky River.

Now, Mrs. Brown came from Maryland in the first place – her maiden name was Annie **(1)** Jordan. Her daughter, Sally Wilcoxon married Hugh Yates, was the mother of a number of Children. She died In Wilkes County, N.C. just before the late civil war commenced, or 23 years ago, say twenty three years. She was "going on 75 years" when she died – 23 or more years since her birth in Boons fort in Kentucky. If she had nearly completed her 75 year it would make the time fully 98 years.

Hugh Yates died July 15th 1870, aged 93. Mrs. Brown says his age was supposed to be greater than ninety three – as "Grandpa had his age put back on account of the war." This is as near as Mrs. Brown can fix the date of Boones settlement in Kentucky – she does not know how long they had been in the fort before the birth of her mother.

(2) Daniel Boone lived about the forks of the Creek (Lewis fork of Yadkin) near Holeman or Holeman's Ford, Wilkes County now. He married the daughter of a 'Tory' down the country somewhere, a very nice woman &c.

Boone did not stay long settled at our place - not longer than it would take him to consume the timber for firewood, so far around his house, that he could no longer brush his cabin with the laps or top branches of the falling trees. This was Daniel's own boast. Daniel's Gap of the Blue Ridge was named for Daniel Boone. Had a hunting camp there. His name was cut on a tree near a fine spring there. Road from Wilkesboro to Jefferson now passes thro' this gap.

Mrs. Brown's recollection is not as good as we could wish. Says she used to hear her uncles, the Wilcoxsons **(3)** tell their stories until she would get scared & leave the house to avoid hearing more.

She says that Boone was several times captured by the Indians – once in 1778 he was taken far north of the Ohio River and was left by the Indians with the women & children of their camp. As a good guard and hunter &c – He soon announced his intention to return to Kentucky. The women tried to dissuade him. "It was too far. He would starve &c." said they. But finding that he was determined - "Well if you will go, child, you must take something to eat." So they baked Ashe cakes for him to take along with him. He took an old gray pack horse & a gun. Rode down the horse before reaching the Ohio River. Hid the saddle in a hollow tree, crossed the Ohio River on a Buckeye chunk, putting his gun on the log before him.

(4) Captured on another occasion – provisions exhausted – Indians unsuccessful in hunting – Boone & Indians all about to starve. Boone asked to be allowed to hunt, was refused at first. Afterwards when starvation was imminent, they told him to go hunt. Boone succeeded in killing a buffalo & brot in some of the meat. Indians rejoiced noisily & catching Boone, tossed him up in the air & caught him as he came down & otherwise so roughly handled him that Boone was being overcome with their kindness, and begged them to let him go as such treatment would soon kill him in his then weak and half starved condition.

They kept Boone tied at night, between two Indians. Boone made no attempt to escape for some days, but at the feast of Buffalo meat, Boone succeeded in concealing a knife (5) in his moccasin, with which he cut the thongs that bound him and stole away from his Sleeping guard. But while yet in hearing his guards awoke and aroused the entire party and they ran around calling "Is that you Boone?" Boone noted their movements & finally made good his escape.

Daniel Boone and Neddie Boone his brother were at one time pursued by Indians: were hungry & tired - when coming to some Black-walnut trees, 'Neddie' sat down to crack and eat some of the nuts. But Daniel seeing a bear cross a hollow, started in pursuit and stopping to drink some water, heard the firing of guns & heard Indians exultingly exclaiming that they "had killed Daniel Boone." Boone profited by the mistake of the Indians & escaped.

(6) They (the emigrants from North Carolina) forted on Kentucky River. They had two forts. The upper Fort was taken by the Indians soon after Daniel went to the lower Fort. Indians attacked lower Fort: tried to dig under it. Boone & comrades hollowed out a white oak log, charged it with powder & missiles, and at a favorable moment discharged it in the mine killing most of the party.

Indians endeavored to entrap Boone by inviting him over the river for a friendly talk [at the treaty talk at the siege of Boonesborough]. Boone agreeing, if they would leave their guns at a certain place and two only go to a designated point that he would meet them unarmed. They did so and with 'we have you now Boone' the two powerful savages produced cords or thongs with which to (7) bind Boone. But the cautious Daniel had placed six trusty friends well around at a convenient place with instructions to act in case of treachery. These men killed the Indians and Boone again escaped the clutches of his savage foes.

The Girls Captured

After having been long penned up in the Fort, the settlers seemed to have respite from the presence of their foes. Some of the young women, desired to go out and stroll along the river bank. For a time Boone resisted their entreaties, but at length gave permission to his daughter Jemima & her friend Miss Fanny Callaway to go out for not longer than two hours. If they staid longer, he would look after them. The two hours having passed & the young ladies not having returned, Boone set out in search with one companion, John Callaway*, who asked leave to accompany him. He was brother to Fanny Callaway, & a suitor for the hand of Jemima Boone - but not favorably regarded by Daniel Boone.

[*Flanders Callaway, a cousin, Fanny's, I think. LCD]

(8) They soon discovered the mark of an Indian canoe on the margin of the stream; and prints of moccasined feet – and signs of a struggle – succeeding in getting on the trail of the party. They followed for some days watching their chance at a favorable location, choosing their time, they attacked the Indians from two quarters, firing and making all the noise they could & calling our "Run! Gals, run!" The gals did run. Boon & Callaway immediately retired. Indians did not follow. The weather was cold and Boone and Callaway took off their undergarments for the girls to wear as the Indians had deprived them of portions of their clothing.

After this Boone withdrew his former refusal to C[allaway]'s and Jemima's marriage.

The following is the substance of Mrs. Brown's statement. She desires me to convey her thanks to Mr. Draper for the book he sent her; and intimates that another similar favor would be much appreciated.

I can add but little more to this – I believe in a former letter I mentioned that when I was a child, or perhaps a boy of 8 years, my father pointed out to me apple trees that had been there & old man had told him they marked the site of Boone's cabin. The location was a few hundred yards above the junction of Lewis Fork with Yadkin river, and of course "in the Fork." If my memory (10) serves me, the tree stood on ground slightly elevated from the river "bottom" but not on the plateau of the river hill. Lewis fork joins the river from the north side 7 miles west of Wilkesboro.

Mrs. Sarah Brown of Wilkesboro, who was a relict of Colonel Nat. Gordon & is now the widow of Col. Hamilton Brown & another of Ham.

A. Brown of Columbia, Tenn – tells me in reference to Boone that she knows nothing about him other than what she had learned from history generally. She states that Boone's name was on a tree on the bank of _eddies River above the Gordon mill site, and at the foot of a bluff that is north of the olde Gordon homestead – and that many **(11)** years since a musket was found in one of the grottoes of this bluff. It was nearly eaten up with rust and the stock much decayed, and gave no clue to its owner, and nothing subsequently learned about it.

It is due you that I explain my neglect to write you sooner.

I had no information of my own to communicate – and sickness & death & sorrow in my own household turned my thoughts to other subjects.

Mrs. Brown at my request gave me her statement only a few days since. Hoping the communication may be of use to you in fixing the date of Boone's settlement in Kentucky and perhaps in corroborating other statements you may have. I have the honor to be

Very respectfully yours
Thos. S. Bouchelle

9C75 LCD heading: Incidents of the Big Siege – 1778. *Much of this account is illegible; only a fragment is given here.*

Mrs. Brown gives some incidents...

Israel Wilcoxson wore a star on his hat and was killed by an Indian – under what circumstances not stated. The hat and star were captured by the Indian who climbed a tree over the river and placing the hat on his ramrod waved in triumph in view of the besieged, supposing himself to be out of range of the rifles in the fort. But someone in the fort double-loaded his gun and with careful aim fired and the Indian fell into the water.

9C77(2) *Aley Yates says (about the mooner at the siege of Boonesborough) "he showed his prankes."*

9C79(1-4) A. S. Yates [Aley Yates] letter, Stoney Hill P. O. Wilkes County, N.C.

Aug. 2, 1884

Mr. L. C. Draper - Sir I will relate to you a few more incidents of Daniel Boone.

1st. The Indians had Boone a prisoner in the state of Kentucky & their object was to put him to Death by Scalding him with the water thickened with meal likened unto sizing. In this preparation all the Indians stood round the Pot (which was boiling) with their Ladles in hand expecting to keep him in the middle & all to dip with ladles & pore on him till Death effected. (Boone now was striped [stripped] except napkin to hide his nakedness.) Boone, now knowing that Death was at hand, resolved what to do & being quick thoughted, he Jumped at a little Indian which was nigh & Threw him in the boiling pot prepared for him self & while the Indians was giting him out, Boone leaped off & got away & reaching the forte telling his friends his narrow escape...

2nd. The Indians had Boone a prisner in the state of Kentucky near the Kentucky River, about 2 days travel from the Fort. They had had him some time, began [to allow] him to Carry an old shackling gun: now leaving their little Town where they lived, going out on a hunting expedition and took Boone with them, going on & killing every thing whos hide was valuable & makeing Boone skin and stretch the Hides. Camping out, covered their Tents with bark to keep there hides dry (being near a Creek).

They now made preparations to take their fur to Market - made them some bark canoes & loaded them with their furs aiming to start the next day. (The Indians mode of sleeping was to lay in a ring with all their feet in towards a little fire in the middle - setting their guns up & putting their butcher knife in their mockesan, wrapping **(1)** strings round them & put them under there head leaving a watchman siting up to watch for enemy. That night Boone complained of being sick, got lief to sleep on one side & not in the middle. After keeping them up late as he could, for the purpose of making them sleep sound, he watched who had the best mockesans & butcher knife & finally supposeing them to be asleep he slipped up, taking the best gun, butcher knife, pair of mockesons, a tin tumbler.

He went to the spring, now waiting a while to see if he was missed & if so to tell them he went to get water & had these things to gard himself. Now not being apprehended he goes & gets their canoes (which they had laded with their furs), takeing them some distance up the Creek & hideing them close to the bank under the groath which closely over hung the Creek. Leaveing then he goes on to the Foart - after some little time which Boone thought there was no danger - he took a croud [crowd] & went back & got the furs & took it to market. Now he reaped the benefit of his labor which he said was his whole study while the Indians had him skinning for them.

3rd. [LCD: Oct. 1780] Once Boone left The Fort on a rambling expedition, was traveling along & as he was allways watching for the Indians he saw a croud some little distance off, who happened to see him about the same time. Now they were full bent to catch Boone & he running with all his mite, now they having a little yellow dog, set it after Boone — the dog soon overtook Boone snapping & biting at his legs but as soon as Boone reached the top of a ridge, he choped the dog & killed him with his tomahock & went on & made his escape.

4th. Once Boone being out had a sorry gun & about out of ammunition, met with a nice young Indian man who had a fine gun & plenty ammunition. Boone bantered him for a match which made the Indian laugh who was keen for the shooting. Boone getting him to set down his gun to take a leaf against a beech tree, & while he **(2)** was tacking up the leaf had his back to Boone. Boone shot him dead - took his gun & ammunition & went on. When he told the incident to his friends, they told him he aught not to have killed the poor man. But Boone told them the Indians were so bad to kill & scalp the whites, that it was no matter for him.

5th Boone once was a prisoner of the Indians. They had had him a good while, untill there was a good deel of confidence obtained by the Indians. The Indians now was going to move now. They put all the old women & children on horses & placed Boone on a very poor horse. **(3)** Now all the young stout men & squaws went before, a-foot, leaving Boon to come on with the old folks & to take care of them. After traveling some distance Boone commenced Saying the [to] the old squaws as follows "Granny, I have been gone from home a long time & I must go Home to see my wife & Children; they will all perish." She say "O no, child, you must stay with us" - he says "no, I must go & you just let me have some bread or I will starve." She says "Well, child, if you will go, you shall have some bread," telling him to get it. Boone opened the sack taking 2 or 3 Pones - left them & went to the Fort.

May God bless you in all your undertakings

Aley Yates

(4) P.S. The Big Lump is a high peak of the Blue Ridge & no Gap nor name of any gap a bout it.

I have made Inquiry, cannot learn whether there is any place by the name of stairs of Standing Stairs.

These Boone traditions I learned from my Husband's Mother who was a Daughter of Sam Wilcox, who lived in the Forest with Boone. I guess it all to be true.

Please let me know if you get this, & whether it is any information or not.

Aley Yates

9C84 T. C. Land, Mt. Zion, Wilkes County, N.C., 1885
Map showing Cook's Gap, Sander's Gap, Deep Gap, Boone, New River, Watauga River, Valle___, Phillip's Gap, Mt. Zion, ___ Holman's Ford, The Dotted line is Boone's route, Boone's Residence, Beaver Creek, Holman's ford, Boone's Route, Yadkin River, Elk Creek, South Fork, Bald Knob, North Fork, Ridge, Stony Fork.

9C87-87(1) T. C. Land letter, Mt. Zion, Wilkes County, N.C., Sept. 28, 1885.

L. C. Draper, Esqr.

    Mr. Proffit, [one] of the oldest inhabitants of Lewis's fork, informed me that it was old Thomas Holman who first settled at lower Holman's and that it was his son Thomas Holman who settled at upper Holman's ford. Mr. Proffit informed me that the way he recollected so distinctly was that old Thomas Holman had an excellent gun of which he was very proud and at his death he bequeathed his son Thomas with the request that if there should be a son in the Holman family by the name of Thomas the gun should be given to him. William Holman, son of Thomas Holman of upper Holman's ford, located on Lewis Fork, Proffit's settlement and he named one of his sons Thomas. In due time, the gun was given to him. Mr. Proffit informed that he had seen the gun many times.

(1) *Margins on right side of second page are cut off, obliterating whole words. Heading on the 2nd page: Lewis Green's Adventure, Dan'l & Jesse Boone, 1770. Second paragraph on this page follows*

    Mr. Profitt also informed me that the following circumstance was what gave rise to the name Lewis's fork. Three men had them a camp near the mouth of the creek which they occupied while hunting. The name of one of the men was Lewis Green. I did not learn the names of the other two. On one of their hunting excursions they had killed and dried a great deal of meat and they had killed a great many wild turkeys and had deposited the feathers in a hole in their camp. About this time, a bear attacked them and tore up Lewis Green so badly that his partners fled and left him for dead. But he finally revived sufficiently to enable him to crawl to the scaffold from which the meat was hung and in some way or other managed to excavate the dirt from the fork upon which the scaffold was erected so as to lower the meat so he could reach it and thus managed to keep from starving to death. He made him a bed in the turkey feathers and remained in the camp all winter, his wounds healing up in the meantime, and the turkey feathers adhering to his wounds. The flesh had grown over some of them so that they stuck fast to his body. The next Spring his partners went back to the old camp to get their comrade's bones to bury them. When they got on the hill near the camp, one of them fired off his gun and Lewis Green – still living at the old camp – answered them and was able to return home with them. The creek was then named Lewis's fork in honor of Lewis Green.

    Mr. Proffit also informed me that Jesse Boone, a cousin of Daniel Boone, once accompanied Daniel to his camp on the waters of the Kentucky River on a hunting excursion and during their stay, Jesse killed two deer, while Daniel killed eighty.

    By conversing with the oldest inhabitants of this locality, I find that Boone traveled a great many different routes, but they were principally to and from his hunting camps. The one which I mapped out to you some time ago is believed to be the one traveled when he moved his family to Kentucky. If I can obtain any more traditional history which I think will be of any [use] to you, I will take pleasure in doing so.

I am Very truly yours, &c
T. C. Land

9C88-88(2) T. C. Land letter, Mt. Zion, Wilkes County, N.C., Oct 21, 1886. *The first two paragraphs give a description of a map. Third paragraph follows.*

9C88(1) Mr. Proffit was personally acquainted with Jesse Boone, and learned the particulars relative to his and Daniel's hunt in Kentucky from him (Jesse). Their camp in Kentucky was near the Blue Lick where they procured their salt. Mr. Proffit took a trip to Cheslowa Creek, McMinn County, Tenn., where he met Jesse Boone and learned the particulars before mentioned. Jesse was a farmer at that time. Jesse was a well appearanced man, of medium size and of excellent character. He was residing in the locality above ___ ___ [when last] heard from.

9C 91-91(1) T. C. Land letter, Mt. Zion, Wilkes County, N.C., May 4, 1886

Lyman C. Draper, Esqr.
    Dear Sir:
    After some delay I take pleasure in responding to yours of the 28 March. I have recently visited Mr. William Proffit, but could obtain but

little additional history from him in addition to what he had already given. Mr. Proffit informed me that he frequently met and conversed with Jesse Boone in McMinn County, Tenn. in the year 1833 and he supposed from Jesse's appearance that he was then about 50 years of age. Jesse's oldest daughter was named Sallie and married a Mr. Edmundson. Mr. Proffit did not recollect Edmundson's given name. He informed me that Jesse was a man of medium size, well proportioned and he suposed he would weigh about 160 lbs. and was quite a kind hearted, affable and genial gentleman. Mr. Proffit **(1)** had often conversed with Jesse relative to his and Daniel's celebrated hunting excursion on the head waters of Kentucky River, but could not recollect the exact locality of their camp. Mr. Proffit says it was 72 deer that Daniel killed while Jesse killed but two. He says he knows that 72 was the number, for since he (Mr. Proffit) returned to N. C. he has often conversed with friends relative to Daniel & Jesse Boone's hunting excursion and all agreed that they were satisfied that Jesse was highly elated over killing the two deer as Daniel was over killing Seventy two! I am satisfied that the above statement is correct and the mistake making Daniel's number 82 instead of 72 was in me, and not in Mr. Proffit. Mr. Proffit had never heard of Jesse Boone ever taking any part in the Revolutionary war.

I don't know whether I will be able to obtain anymore traditional history or not, but if I should obtain any, I will take pleasure in transmitting it to you.

Wishing you abundant success, I remain Truly Yours &c.
T. C. Land

9C102 Map from Jonathan Horton of Horton, N.C., 1884
Clear map "of the Yadkin area of North Carolina. Place-names: Elk Creek, West Camp Creek, Blue Ridge, Three Forks, Cooks Gap, Yadkin Spring, Blowing Rock, Buffalo Creek, Winding Stairs, Deep Gap, Stoney Fork, Gap Creek, New River, Big Lump, Lewis Fork, Patton's Old Field, Beaver Creek, Boone's house, Bend [of New River], Yadkin River, some topographical detail, Blue Ridge Mountains.

9C129(1,2) Thomas S. Bouchelle - The Hossey Raid – Indian captivity story

The last Indian Raid that I learn of is known as the Hossey Raid. Old man Hossey was settled on Rock Creek (a small tributary of the Yadkin that flows in on the North side of the stream, between Mulberry and Roaring Rivers. His farm was on the Yadkin river at mouth of the creek and his plow horse subsisted principally on the pea vines that was so abundant in that day, and ranged along the borders of the Cane-brakes. This cane was quite common at the fishing ___ in my boy hood, but now it is rarely the case that a specimen is left to grow long enough to attain a sufficient size for this purpose.

  Hossey sent his daughter to drive up the old plow horse preparing to commencing the day's plowing, whose bell was heard at a little distance. The bell was heard to rattle as tho' the animal was moving, quietly. A little further off, presently the young woman was heard to scream, and the bell ceased to rattle. Hossey discovered that his daughter had been decoyed & captured by Indians who were rapidly bearing her off on "Old Gray." The settlers were notified and collected a force to follow and attempt a rescue. The Indians proceeded to Hollman's Ford where they were reinforced by the accession of another considerable party of Indians. They retired along the divide between Lewis Fork & Stone's Fort and were brought to bay by their pursuers near **(1)** Lewis Fork church, where the rolling hills cease, and the divide rises abruptly to a single ridge of considerable height, the narrow ledges of whose profile is distinctly marked upon the sky. In the fight that ensued two Indians were killed and one white man was wounded. The Indians retired along this narrow ridge, the whites following, but no opportunity for a favorable attack occurred until after crossing the head waters of Stony Fork and crossing the Blue Ridge at, or west of, the Deep Gap. The Indians awaited their pursuers & were overtaken at a knob a few miles west of the Deep Gap. In the battle here fought, one white man was killed and the Indians again retired and were pursued or at least followed to the Watauga River some 4 miles further, when the pursuit was abandoned. It does not appear that the captive was rescued or that any considerable advantage was obtained over the Indians. It seems that the Indians chose their own ground to fight on, and their own time for retiring with their booty. These, I suppose, were Cherokees.

  And right here I would like to put a **(2)** question. Can you cite me to the authority for the following statement? The Tuscaroras occupied a considerable portion of North Western North Carolina, and as the whites were increasing their settlements in the eastern part of the country - they, the Tuscaroras, being a warlike race, tried to excite the Indians of the East to hostilities to the whites, and for the purpose pulled up stakes and moved in a body to the ___ but here they failed in their efforts to excite their neighbors to a general war. They then moved on north and joined the Confederacy known as the "six nations." By this general migration they left this portion of the country and the magnificent Valley of the Yadkin unoccupied by the red man and open to the settlement of the whites. The Cherokees fearing the return of the warlike tribe abstained from occupying the territory of their former neighbors. Information on this head would be thankfully received.

I cannot give you the meaning of the word Yadkin. This river further south in this state and in South Carolina bears the name of Great Pedee. Capt. M___ Moore of Lenoir, Caldwell County, N. C. may be able to give you the information. He has been interesting himself in obtaining the meaning of Indian names of North Carolina Rivers. And from the Editor of the "Lenoir Topic" you might get some information concerning the Boone family as they are men in that county (Caldwell) who — to be descended from the Boone family.

Mrs. Brown is in very feeble health now.

Yours Truly,
Thos. S. Bouchelle

9C130-130(1,2) T. S. Callaway letter, South Fork, N.C., June the 25th 1884

Dear Sir:

I have a few minutes to give attention to your letter of enquiry. I will commence at no. 4 of your letter of March 15th (the fourth question). I know nothing of grandfather [LCD: Benj. Cutbirth] accompanying Boone on his removal to Kentucky. I know very little of Boone's difficulty with the Indians on his way to Kentucky, only I heard my Father say they had a fight on the way and Boone's son was kiled.

I cannot tell you any thing about the route that Boone traveled from North Carolina to Kentucky. Some Say he cross the Blue Ridge at the Boaring Gap and crost the new River about the State line and by the way of the Blue spring on the Holston and at Abingdon. But my opinion is that he crossed the Blue Ridge at Reddies River Gap and past immediantly [sic] by where **(1)** I now live, and near Jefferson, the county seat of Ashe, and up the North Fork of New River, and through Tenn. and so on to Powell's Valley.

I am satisfied beyond a dout that George Boone, Daniel's Brother, who followed him to Kentucky some time afterwards, past this way; that he camped at a certain place on a leading ridge, within a mile and a half of my house, from the fact that I heard my Father say so. That he turned off of the ridge on to the head of a branch to camp and that branch has always gone by the name of Boones Branch until this day. That in Serching for water he found a peculiar rock, and set it up against a tree near his camp. That rock stands now at the head of Grand Father Callaways grave - it is about the sise of an ordanary fence rail, and stands at least six feet above the ground and must be two or three feet in the ground: it is a mixture of sand and flint.

(2) The Big Lump is a Peak on the Blue Ridge between the head of Reddie's River and Lowrence Fork, and about four miles from where I live.

I think I have answerd all of your enquiries as fare [sic] as I am able to do. I regret veary much that I know so little about all these matters that you are looking after. I might have known it all if I had enquired more Perticularly of my Father and Mother in their lifetime, tho the things were not thought about in those days.

I Reman veary Respectfully yours
T. S. Calloway

9C133 T. S. Calloway letter. *"Grandfather" Benjamin Cutbirth, Sr. on a hunting trip, explored to the Mississippi River about 1765 or 1770. Lewis Green, wounded by a bear, gave Lewis's Fork its name.*

9C135 "Early Boone Traditions - Route over the Mountains" [Questions] To Mrs. Prudence Callaway, Maple Springs, Wilkes County, N.C., Aug. 15, 1883

Topics addressed: Boone's return with the young panther after his long Kentucky hunt; how long did Susan Dula live in Boone's family and was it during Boone's long absence in Kentucky, when did she die; an insult by a runaway negro to Boone's daughter; anything learned from your Grandfather Howard about Boone, etc.

9C137,137(1), 138 Jim[?] Denes Callaway letter, Maple Spring, N. C., Dec. 5th, 1883

Mr. Draper Sir:

I think Susan Dula died about the age of 90 years. I know nothing of the Negro. Daniel Boone married my aunt Howard's sister Rachel [LCD: Rebecca] Briant. I can tell nothing of Samuel Callaway. **(1)** Susan Dula was an Ellison, married John Brown; he died & she married John Dula. She died at widow Horton's close to the mouth of Beaver Creek about 25 years ago.

My grand mouther [sic] let me ___ Daniel Boon to the door on his return from Kentucky after an abbsense of 7 years & requested her and grand father to go home with him and see him and wif[e] remarried.

(138) Allen Hicks has the history of Daniel Boone. Jonathan has the history of North Carolina.

I refer you to them.

Jim[?] Denes Callaway

Postmarked "Lewis Fork, N.C., Dec. 8th, 1883. LCD

9C139-139(1) John H. Thompson letter, Wilkes County, N.C., January 12, 1884

L. C. Draper – dear sir: after my Best respects you wanted to no how old Benjamin Howard was when he died. He died in June 1829 aged 84 years and Prudence Howard died September 1823 aged 77. Cornelius Howard and Joshua Howard were brother-in-laws to Daniel Boone. Joshua Howard married Etta Bryan; Cornelius married Polly; Boone married Rachel [really Rebecca. LCD].

As nigh as we can get at it, Susan Dula's age is she was born in 1768. She lived to be near 80, nigh as we can git at it.

We have no account of Susan Dula ever living in Boone family. She was born in sight of where Boone last lived on the Yadkin River.

Cornelius Howard and Benjamin Howard were brothers – Joshua Howard was a nephew.

I have been trying to gather something for you. The first account we have of Boone he was born in Surry County – he then moved 8 miles above Wilksboro on the north side of the river near the mouth of Lewis Fork.

In traveling with an aged gentleman many years ago, he showed me the trace of the ford that **(1)** Boone made, and said that in years past that it went by the name of Boone's Ford. This present ford across the river is called Holman's Ford – about 150 yards above the old ford.

The next we hear of Boone, he lived four miles above Holman's Ford on the north side of the Yadkin near the mouth of Beaver Creek. This is the place he lived that was spoken of on the other page when Benjamin Howard and his wife went home with him from his seven years trip west.

The next we hear of Boone, there is a place on the west side of the Blue Ridge on the head waters of New River called Boone's Camp. The old sign of his camp is seen yet.

The next we hear of him is at a place called Boone's Path in Lee County, Va., also a place called Boone's Fork, Letcher county – the post office is Rosedale; also a place called Boone Ville is in Kentucky, the county I don't recollect.

This is about all we no about Daniel Boone with the exception of a small book or a pamphlet that I have heard of lately; it gives a short sketch of the travels and escapes with the Indians – if you want the Book please write to me, and give me some time, and I will try to hunt it up. My address is Reedy Branch.

So no mor at present
John H. Thompson

9C140 Questions for John H. Thompson – July 27, 1884. Inquiries for Mrs. Prudence Callaway.

Questions concern William Colley and Joseph Holden, the particulars of Col. Boone and his wife meeting when he returned from his long Kentucky Hunt – "tell me all about it." "A son of Col. Boone told me about some robbers. Can you and Mrs. Callaway tell me about this matter?"

9C142 John H. Thompson letter, Reedy Branch, N.C., May 25, 1887.

Mr. Draper – After my best respects in compliance - there must have been much joy when Boone and his wife met. Joshua Howard lived in Wilkes but died in Burke County, his age 55 years. Cornelius Howard lived in Rowan County, his age 75 or 80 years. From Benjamin Howard to where Daniel Boone lived [is] 4 miles. About the robbers we don't know anything.

Green and the bar fight I don't know anything about.
Hugh McGary I don't know anything about.
The pamphlet I spoke about I can't find.
I have found an old history and a sketch of Boone's trip on it. If you want it, I will send it. Yours   J. H. Thompson

9C204-204(3) Jesse Yates letter, Stony Hill, N.C., Jan 11, A. D., 1884

Boone Killing Bears in Mulberry Trees

...what is now known as Boone's camp rock – this rock has been described heretofore. Elk Creek took its name on account of the vast number of elk that hearded their in gangs. The land bordering on this creek, the most part is very hilly, generly putting in to the creek vary steep covered with Blue rock[?] & rough. The Bottoms along this creek are vary narrow, but productive of corn, wheat, rye, oats & potatoes, &c.

Boone also had a camp on the Catawba River, now Burk County (in this State) west of Wilkes [County]. The Cherokee Indians then inhabiting the Country a little west of this river.

My grandfather accompanied Boone to this Camp & they then went on a hunt some 20 or 30 miles west near the Cherokee nation. They killed, I think he said, 2 deer & 1 Elk, hanging them up in Som trees to remain until they went to camp & returned after their game &c. And while engaged in hanging up their deer & Elk, I think Yates said some 7 or 8 Indians come on them & took their game. Tyed my grandfather's and Boon's hands with a rope of Some kind **(2)** ... The Nation of these Indians included the Junction of these states: western part of N.C., S. C., Ga., Tenn., Ala. The Indians when they arrived the next day at their town built a fire & made some stuff they called conahama, which was mush of some beat indian corn and was preparing to burn them to death – Yates & Boone being then & their tied. While in this arrangement, a fire occurred, their town being on fire. The wigwams smoked & flamed. The Indians being greatly excited all ran to extinguish the fire, leaving Yates & Boon their tied. Yates said he burnt the rope from his hands, Boone doing the same. They seized their guns & left. They did not think the Indians followed them.

Boone had some other camps on and near Watauga River & on New River &c.

Now my grandfather, John Yates, & Daniel Boone killed much game in company when quite young. That must have been between the dates of 1760 & 1770, Say 1762-3-4-5-6 &c.

The Bottom land bordering on the Yadkin River & its many tributaries was beautifully covered with cane, mulberry trees, black walnut, cherry and other groath &c. The mulberry trees produced **(3)** fruit we call mulberries... and when the fruit was ripe which is about April & May, the Bear would clime those trees to eat those Berries. Yates & Boone often came on them while the Bear was up there eating berries & had much sport in shooting & killing the bear.

I understand Aley Yates, widow, heard her grand father John Yates, say much about Daniel Boone which I hope she will communicate to you.

I give the name of Col. Jonathan Horton, who married a kindsman [sic] of Daniel Boone, heretofore I think his wife can tell you much about Boone. Mr. Col. Jonathan Horton, Boon Court house, Watauga County, North Carolina.

If I can assist & give you any information please write to me & I will try to do so.

Your friend
Jesse Yates

Volume 10C contains 93 numbered pages.

10C24 Notes on scenery with a map of the Yadkin River area by Elijah Dougherty, 1884: "You ask for a map. I have done it very hastily, so I can send it by mail, this morning. I have been housed up from first of Feby till now by bad weather till I am geting old and frail, cant attend to business much. You ask if I got the Book on Agriculture from you, I received the Book all right for which I return thanks. it is a Book that interests me very much. I have delayed writing a good while trying to get up reliable facts for you. I perceive you want to get a history of facts and not fiction, a history that reliable and authentic.

Elijah Dougherty.

10C41 Elijah Dougherty - "Scenery of the Mountains & Boone's Hunting Life"

You said something of the scenery of these places, or some of them. The Scenery in many places along the described route is very Grand and magnificent, particularly on the Stone mountain at the place where the star route crosses, looking toward the west you can see mountains that seems almost lost in the mist distance.

"Distance lends inchantment to the view"
"And robes the mountains in their azure hue"

The Town of Boone shows by the Barometor to be the highest town in the State of North Carolina. This mountain country has many things to attract the attention of the lovers of nature scenery: its boundless forrest, its beautiful clear, and cool springs, which break out at the foot of the mountains, and upon their sides, and even on their high summits are often found beautiful springs gushing out and running down their sides like threads of silver meandering through the forrest till they mingle their limpid waters with the larger streams and with them roll on till they reach the great father waters…and with that mighty river to the gulph of Mexico.

It seems that Boone spent a good part of the prime of his life amid these hills, and streams, and mountains of this section of country, at a time when it was nearly in its primeval state, at a time when all the wild animals that roamed through the country were abundant. There is no doubt but what he enjoyed it well. Boone was a child of Nature, and enjoyed a wilderness life. His name is enrolled in the list of the great men of our

Country.

10C56 *Map - D. B. Dougherty 22 June 1884. Boone County, N.C.*
Map covers 2 pages. Place-names: Boone North Carolina, Three Forks of New River, Road to Wilkesboro, Yadkin River, Rich Mountain, Blowing Rock, Tennessee State Line, Carter County, TN, horse shoe, Roans Creek, Stone Mountain, Johnson County, TN., Forge Creek, Ashe County, Meat Camp Creek, Deep Gap, Cook's Gap, Boone's Camp on Boone's Branch of Elk, mouth of Beaver Creek, Wilkes County, Blue Ridge, Phillips Gap, North Fork of ___ River, E Forks N. Fork, Elk Creek, Jesse ___ ___ for Boone, Cove Creek, Baker's Gate where the road now crosses Stone Mt into Tenn, old Vandergriff Gap, Meadow Creek,. The dots indicate Boone's trails. The dotted lines made with ink indicate the old trails as near as I can give. NB This map places Boone too far south, ought to be nearly west from Wilkesboro.

10C69-69(1) W. H. Weaver, June 8, 1884
 Refers to LCD letter of May 15 and continues on the Stairs and location of same, Roan Creek, Laurel, Holston River, where Abingdon now stands.

 (1) "Daniel Boon killed a Bar on this tree 1775" – this was cut out of a tree on Reed Creek west of Abingdon & if marked by him must have been done when he removed his family to Kentucky, as he made his first trip through this Country at an earlier date, in 1760 & 1765.

 It might be possible [to get] the information - by Enquiry of old people - & mapping Important places.

 I refer you to Col. Thos. L. Triston of Charlottesville & Hon. T C. Clingman of Asheville, N.C. as men best-versed in the traditional history southwest Virginia and Mountains of North Carolina of any I could refer you to.

Very Respectfully yours
W. H. Weaver

10C77 Map. I.D. Imboden 3 pages. "I am almost ashamed to send so rough a tracing."
Clear Map of western Virginia, Tennessee, North Carolina showing Wilkes County., Blue Ridge, Yadkin County, old Boone homestead, Watauga River, Sullivan County, Washington County, Iron Mountain, Taylorsville, Walker Mountain, Clinch Mountain, Moccasin Gap, Cassellswoods (Castlewoods), Big Stone Gap, Abingdon, "State Line,
" "Bar" Tree, Big Island, Kingsport, Wise County, Russell County, Stone

Mountain, etc..

10C79 Map: J. D. Imboden, 30 Sept. 1884. *Heading for this map: Boone at Roan's Creek - Boone's Ford c. 1772, White top branch of Laurel, Va. and Tenn. State Line, Johnson County, Taylorsville, Doe Mountain, Little Doe Creek, Stone Mountain, Shady Valley, Beaverdam Creek, Holston Mt., South Prong, Watauga River, Boone's Ford, Carter County, Tenn., Iron Mtn., Boone Farm owned by B___, Cobbs Creek, Boone homeplace.*

Volume 11C contains 113(3) numbered pages.

11C6-6(1) Deposition of William Cradlebaugh, age 88 on 3rd August 1832 when deposition taken. He came to Boonesborough in 1776* & continued to hunt provisions for the Fort, & to act as a spy and serve in different campaigns for 6 or 7 years. Lived in Madison County, Kentucky since 1776 and has no documentary evidence to prove his services, but can prove them by Col. Samuel Estill, Maj. J. Kennedy, and Yelverton Peyton.

William Cradlebaugh (his mark)

*In depositions given in Circuit Court cases in Madison and Fayette Counties, Ky.., William Cradlebaugh said he was living at Fort Boonesborough in 1775.

Jesse Hodges, resident of Madison County, Kentucky knew him [William Cradlebaugh] since 1777. Cradlebaugh was a private in Capt. Daniel Boone's Company at Fort at Boonesborough [and in the Companies of] Capt. John Holder and Capt. Callaway. [Cradlebaugh was] absent at times between 1777 - 1779 on Indian expeditions. Cradlebaugh served with Col. Bowman, Col. Thos. Kennedy, and Daniel Boone.

Jesse Hodges
(his mark)

11C10 Pension Application of William Cradlebaugh, State of Kentucky, Madison County. April 29, 1833 – attested.

This day personally appeared before me Henry B. Hawkins, a justice of the peace in & for the County of Madison aforesaid, William Cradlebaugh, a resident of said county and an applicant for a pension under the act of Congress passed June 7th, 1832 & whose original declaration was made before me on the 30th August 1832, who being first duly sworn according to law states upon oath that in 1776 he came from North

Carolina to Kentucky. That in same year he volunteered as a private in Capt. Daniel Boone's Company at the Fort or Garrison of Boonesborough. He cannot now state whether he enlisted or volunteered for any specified length of time but he knows well that he continued as a soldier in the Company of Capt. Daniel Boone & of Capt. John Holder & Capt. Callaway, who commanded the fort at Boonesborough. Subsequently to Capt. Boone or after he was promoted to do regular Garrison duty at Boonesborough for more than three years from the time he volunteered or enlisted except when absent on expeditions against the Indians. In such cases as many usually went as could be spared from the fort so that a sufficient guard was left. He states that according to his best recollection he served upon Campaigns against the Indians under Col. Bowman, Gen. Clark, Col. Thos. Kennedy and Daniel Boone not less than Six Months. He cannot from his loss of memory and great age recollect the different years when he served on these Campaigns but knows it was during the Revolutionary War.

He states during his services at Boonesborough his whole business was to do Garrison duty, to spy for Indians and to hunt for provisions for those in the fort. He knows that he served as a soldier at the fort at Boonesborough during the Revolutionary War & in campaigns against the Indians during the same period a good deal more than two years for such service. He trusts he will receive a pension; he claims that his age & poverty render it doubly desirable.

William Cradlebaugh

11C11-11(1-2) Thomas Hall pension statement, resident of Montgomery County, Ky., Jan. 7, 1833

...That he enlisted in the Army of the United States at Boonsborough, Lincoln County in the state of Virginia, now Kentucky, in the year 1779 for the term of during the War with Capt. John Holder, and served in the regiment of the Virginia line under the following named officers: That he resided in the county of Lincoln when he entered service, under the command of Capt. John Holder.

Col. Boon and Logan and Gen. Clark in the year 1779, about the last of March of that year, was stationed some time at Boonsborough and was then marched to the lower Blue Lick against the Indians [LCD: August 1782], under Col. Logan but the enemy fled and we were marched across the **(1)** country to Salt River, where the Indians had burnt Kincheloe Fort and were murdering the frontier inhabitants but we soon dispersed them. After our arrival we were then marched to Strode Station to guard that fort. After being stationed at that point for some months, we were marched to

Boonsborough and from there to the Upper Blue Licks under command of Maj. [William] Hoy where we had a pretty severe engagement with the Indians.

From there we were marched back to Boonsborough where we were stationed principally until the termination of the war, engaged, however, during the whole period in occasionally and frequent scouting along the frontier settlement. In fact our whole service partook a good deal of the nature of a frontier guard.

After the termination of the revolutionary war, I was regularly discharged at Boonsborough and received a discharge given to the best of my recollection by Gen. Clark which is now lost. [He] states that he was born in the year 1759 in the County of Prince William and State of Virginia and is at present a resident of Kentucky in the County of Montgomery. He states that he is infirm and in very needy circumstances, and although he cannot now recollect the precise date at which he was stationed at the different points or the number of the regiment to which he was attached, he is certain that he rendered the services as stated in his declaration and in the evening of his life appeals to the **(2)** government of that country whose independence he contributed to establish for such compensation as the justice of his claim may entitle him to receive.

Thomas (X his mark) Hall

LCD notes:
Thos. Hall - 1782 – with Col. Logan at the Blue Licks, & then went across the country where the Indians had taken Kincheloe's Station, dispersed them. Also in Maj. Hoy's fight at the Upper Blue Licks.

11C14 The affidavit of John Stephens taken at Frankfort [Ky.] on the 30th day Nov. 1832 to be used on the behalf of John Mitchell, an applicant to be placed on the Pension Roll. Deposeth that in the year 1782 he was a volunteer soldier in Capt. Robert Johnson's Company, who composed a portion of Boon's Regiment, that said regiment of Boone was attached to Gen. George Rogers Clark's Brigade, that John Mitchell was in said company with the affiant and we went to the mouth of Licking River where Cincinnati now stands and there Daniel Boon's Regiment joined said Clark and went to New Chillicothe on the Big Miami in Ohio.

Clark took the town and destroyed everything the Indians had and took some prisoners that was with this affiant during the whole tour of duty, that he was well acquainted with said Mitchell and is yet acquainted with him, that the tour of duty was performed in five or six months including the time of going and returning. This affiant has understood that said Mitchell was in other tours of duty. That after his return home this affiant left the station called Bryants & went to Gilbert's Creek where he lived.

John Stephens

11C16 Pension Application of Jesse Hodge[s], State of Kentucky, Madison County

On the 4th day of September 1832, personally in open Court, before Richard Turner, sole and presiding Judge of the Court for the circuit of Madison aforesaid. Jesse Hodge[s] a resident of Madison County Kentucky, aged 72 years in November next, doth on his oath make the following declaration in order to obtain the benefit of the Act of Congress passed June 7, 1832. That he Entered the Service of the United States under the following named officers and Served as herein Stated.

That he enlisted in July 1777 in Bedford County, Virginia for Eighteen months under Captain Charles G. Watkins, in what he understands was the State Troops of Virginia. He enlisted to come to Kentucky to defend the Western Country. John Milam was Lieutenant and David Crews, Ensign. We were immediately marched to Boonesboro in the now County of Madison, where he continued to do duty as a Soldier guarding the Fort, Spying for Indians and hunting for meat for the people in the Fort. He was there during the great Siege of 1778 of 11 days by 300 - 400 Indians. That he continued at Boonesborough after the 10 months' time was out, did duty as a Soldier and a Spy to the end of the War. In May 1779, he went on a campaign against the Indians. John Holder, Captain, Col. Bowman commanded. In 1780, served on a campaign across the Ohio against the Indians - went to the Pickaway Towns, was in the Battle, burnt the cornfields - General George Rogers Clark, Commander.

He also Served as a volunteer on a Campaign in 1782 under Gen. Clark against the Indians across the Ohio - that in all his Services he was a volunteer. That from the time he Enlisted in ___ till 1783, he was actively Engaged as a Soldier or Indian Spy.

That he was born in Goochland County, Virginia, was residing in that County when he Enlisted in Bedford County, Virginia, that he had resided in the bounds of the now County of Madison since 1777. He had no documentary evidence in his possession to prove Service, can prove them by Major Oswald Townsend & Joseph Jackson. He hereby relinquishes every claim whatever to a pension or annuity except the present and declares that his name is not on the Pension roll of the agency of any State. Sworn & Subscribed the day and year aforesaid.

Jesse Hodge

11C17 Joseph Jackson for Jesse Hodges

I, Joseph Jackson, a resident of Bourbon County, Kentucky, do certify that I have been well acquainted with Jesse Hodges, who had subscribed and Sworn to the foregoing declaration, since July 1777, that at that time I enlisted with said Hodges in Bedford County, Virginia for 18 months, under Capt. Charles G. Watkins in the Virginia State Troops. That we immediately marched to Boonsboro in November or December 1777. I left Boonsboro under Capt. Daniel Boone for the lower blue Licks, was taken prisoner by the British and Indians, and remained a prisoner several years. I have known said Hodges ever since, and his character has always been that of a good Soldier and an honest man. I believe him to be 72 years of age and that his Declaration is Strictly true.

Joseph Jackson (X his mark)

11C21-22-23 Pension Statement of Oswald Townsend

On this 12 day of August 1832 personally appeared in Open Court before Jas. Degarnett [Dejarnett], Richard Broaddus & H. B. Hawkins, Justices of the County Court for the County of Madison aforesaid, now sitting. Oswald Townsend, a resident of the County of Madison aforesaid, aged 74 years, who being first duly sworn according to law, doth on his oath make the following declaration in order to obtain the benefit of the Act of Congress passed June 7th, 1832. That he entered the service of the United States under the following named Officers & served as herein stated. That in the Fall 1775 he came from Mecklenburg County in Virginia to Kentucky & went into the Fort or Station at Boonesboro, that during the remainder of that year & the years 1776 & 1777 he continued at Boonsboro acting as a spy for the defence of the Fort against the Indians & as a hunter to procure provisions for those in the Fort. That during said years he was in three or four Skirmishes with the Indians. That during the year 1777, the Indians made several attacks upon the Fort at Boonsboro, where he was engaged in its defence as an Indian Spy. That in 1779 he was employed under Henderson from North Carolina, who with Dr. Walker & others from Virginia, undertook to run the line between North Carolina & Virginia, as a hunter & Indian Spy. That late in the year '79, he came again to Boonsboro & continued there as a Hunter & a Spy till the Spring following. That in the Spring 1780 he started out with Henderson, who was running **(22)** said division line between North Carolina and Virginia ____ on the part of North Carolina & continued with him as a hunter & Spy for some time. That in the Fall of 1780 he returned to the Fort at Boonsboro where he continued as a hunter for the Fort and Indian Spy till 1782. That he was in the Blue Lick defeat & went on three campaigns across the Ohio against the Indians. That he has no documentary evidence to prove his services, but can prove them by Maj. Kennedy. He has lived in Madison County for 50 years. He hereby relinquishes any claim whatever to a pension or annuity excepting the present & declares that his name is not [on] the pension roll of any agency in any State.

Oswald Townsend

We, Joseph Kennedy & Richard Gentry, residents of Madison County, do hereby certify that we are well acquainted with Maj. Oswald Townsend who has subscribed & sworn to the foregoing declaration, that we believe him to be 74 years of age, that he is represented & believed in the neighborhood where he resides to have been a soldier of the Revolution, Indian fighter & Spy. Said Kennedy states that he has known him since 1776 & knows he performed services as in his declaration set forth. We both concur that his statement is true. Sworn & Subscribed the day & year aforesaid.

Jo. Kennedy
Richard Gentry

And the said Court do hereby declare **(23)** their opinion after the investigation of the matter. The Court further certifies that Jos. Kennedy and Richard Gentry, who have signed the preceding Certificates, are residents of Madison County aforesaid, are credible persons of good character & that their statement is entitled to full credit.

Richd. Broaddus
James Dejarnett
Henry B. Hawkins

11C23(1) LCD references for Ansel Goodman

11C24, 25-25(1), 26 Statement of Joseph Kennedy for Oswald Townsend, State of Kentucky, Madison County.

Joseph Kennedy, a resident of the County aforesaid, being first sworn before me Thomas Branston [Bronston], Justice of the peace in &

for the County aforesaid, states that he came to Kentucky in the year 1776, on the 1st day of April. In that year or early in 1777 he became acquainted with Maj. Oswald Townsend of the County aforesaid & whose original declaration for a pension this affiant attached his certificate. He knew said Townsend at the Fort at Boonesboro in the County aforesaid in the year 1777 & from that time to this. That said Townsend in the year 1777 acted as a soldier in said Fort & as an Indian Spy, that this affiant was a fellow Soldier & an indian Spy with said Townsend. That said Townsend was a good soldier & an active Spy. We were both in Old Capt. Daniel Boone's Company. Continued a soldier & an Indian Spy & out on Campaigns across the Ohio against the Indians most of the time till the close of the Revolutionary War.

This affiant was frequently with said Townsend as a soldier & spy after 1777 during the Revolutionary war. This affiant knows of his own personal knowledge that said Townsend served as a soldier & Indian spy during the revolutionary war a good deal more than two years, that he was in actual service much longer than that period. This affiant could detail, if necessary, a good many skirmishes & battles with the Indians, in which he & said Townsend were together, but presumes the detail would be unnecessary. This **(25)** affiant & said Townsend have lived in the now County of Madison most of the time since 1776. Affiant is 73 years of age. Said Townsend has always sustained a good character. Affiant further states that his health at this [time] will not permit him to attend at the seat of justice to give his testimony.

Jo. Kennedy

Subscribed & sworn before me a justice of the peace in & for County of Madison aforesaid this 1st day of March 1833 - and I certify that Maj. Joseph Kennedy is a credible person on oath, a man of high standing & excellent character and that in consequence of bodily infirmity he is unable to attend any of the Courts. Given under my hand the date aforesaid.

T. S. Bronston

State of Kentucky, Madison County & Circuit Sct. On this 7th day of March 1833 personally appeared in Open Court before the Hon. Richard French, presiding Judge of the Circuit Court for the County & Circuit aforesaid now sitting, Oswald Townsend, doth on his oath make the following declaration supplementary to his declaration made before the County Court on the 13th day of August 1832. The said Townsend further states that when he first entered the fort at Boonesborough in the fall 1775, he was enrolled and served in **25(1)** Daniel Boone's Company who was then Captain. There was then few or no Colonels or Majors in Kentucky. During the remainder of the war 1775 & the years 1776 & 1777, he acted as a guard for the Fort at Boonesboro & Indian Spy in said Boone's Company.

In the years 1781 & 1782, he also served as a guard for said Fort, Hunter & Indian Spy except when out on campaign against the Indians across the Ohio & elsewhere, that his best recollection is that in 1781 [1780 over-written] & 1782 he was in Capt. John Holder's Company & that Daniel Boone was Colonel, also Colonel Bowman. He states that he served as a private volunteer in Defence of the Fort at Boonsboro in Madison County aforesaid & as an Indian Spy during the Revolutionary War more than four years & for such service he claims a pension. That he was at the fatal Battle of the Blue Licks in 1782 & many other engagements with the Indians.

That he can prove his services by his neighbor Maj. Joseph Kennedy & knows of no other person whose testimony he can procure to establish them. Richard Gentry is also his neighbor & has & can testify concerning his services. Oliver C. Steele, a clergyman, can testify concerning him &c.

He states that he was born in in Granville [County], North Carolina in the year 1758. That he has no record of his age, that he came to Kentucky in 1775 & has resided in this County of Madison aforesaid ever since. That in 1781 & 1782 he knew Col. John Todd who was killed at the Battle of the Blue Licks or Blue Lick defeat – he also knew **26** Gen. George Rogers Clark & Col. Ben Logan, Col. McGary & others. He states that he has no written discharges & does not recollect that he ever received any.

Oswald Townsend

I, Oliver C. Steele, clergyman residing in the County of Madison aforesaid, hereby certify that I am well acquainted with Maj. Oswald Townsend, that he is represented & believed in the neighbourhood where he resides to have been a soldier of the Revolution & an Indian spy & that I concur in that opinion. I further certify that said Townsend is a man of good character & standing.

O. C. Steele

The Court further certifies that Maj. Joseph Kennedy, whose affidavit has been taken to be used in this case & is now before the Court, is a resident of the County of Madison is a person of good character & in consequence of disease and infirmity is unable to attend Court.

Richard French

11C28 Statement of R. T. Letcher

I certify that Ansel Goodman, the applicant, is reported to me to be a preacher of the Gospel and a man unreproachable character. I further certify I have had a personal acquaintance with the witness Arabia Brown upwards of twenty years and that he is man of truth and respectability.

R. T. Letcher

11C28-32 Ansel Goodman, Pension Application State of Kentucky, ____ County

On this twenty ninth day of October 1832 personally appeared in open court it being a court of Record setting in and for the county af[oresaid] Ansel Goodman resident of said county, aged about eighty years, makes the following declaration in order to obtain the benefit of the act of Congress passed 7th June 1832.

That in the state of Virginia in the County of Bedford in the year, as well as he can now remember, 1777, he enlisted in the service of the United States under Capt. Charles Watkins and was ordered to Kentucky with the balance of the Company for the purpose of assisting the inhabitants in their battles against the British and Indians. That the Company was composed of fifty odd men, that they were promised forty shillings per month and the period of their Enlistment was for six months. That very soon after their enlistment they were marched to Kentucky by their Captain at Boonesborough on the Kentucky [River] in the now state of Kentucky which was a Fort, sometimes called a Station, at which place we found Col. Daniel Boon and some men and families under his command. We were placed under the command also of Col. Boone and acted in the capacity of defenders of the Fort against the enemy, and also as Indian Spies.

Some considerable time after being so employed upon constant duty and very short allowance, himself and as well as he can now recollect about thirty others under the command of Col. Boone were ordered out on an expedition to make salt for the use of those in the Fort. They marched to a place about 70 or 80 miles from the Fort then and now known and called the Blue Licks.

After being there about three weeks engaged making salt, Col. Boone was absent from the Company hunting and trapping when a party of the Shawnees of about one hundred Indians commanded by their Chief, Black Fish, fired Several guns at him as he, Boone, told this applicant, and run him some distance and he, Boone, discovering he would be taken, stopped and gave up. The Indians then marched with Col. Boone to where the balance of us were and we were ordered by Col. Boone to stack our guns and surrender. We did so.

We were all taken first to the Indian towns over the Ohio River on the Little Miami. Some of the company were taken to the British. This applicant and a few others were retained by the Indians. And from the day he was taken up to the time he run off, a period of Eight months, he suffered missery and wretchedness, hunger, cruelty, and oppression of almost every sort. The night after he was taken his arms were tied behind him, a rope or buffalo tug tied fast around his middle and then made fast to an Indian on each side of him, and the one around his arm was made to go around his neck, and tied fast to a tree, and in that position he had to sleep upon the Snow.

A little while before he reached the Indian Town he was compelled to strip himself, and was entirely naked, his arms again made fast and a load of Bare [bear] meat packed upon him. It was a heavy load. Indeed he was packed heavily from the time he was taken until he arrived at the Town. Just as he got there he was met by many Indians from the town and run the Ganttlet with the load of meat and was very severely beaten and Abused in the race. Before they got in sight of the Town he was made to sing as loud as he could hollow [holler]. The object of that afterwards learnt was to give notice of their approach. After running the Ganttlet he and the other prisoners were ordered to dance like the whites. A Negro who was prisoner with them [the Indians] acted as interpreter.

Col. Boone was taken a while to the British and they gave him a little horse and a saddle and he returned with the Indians and was taken off with a party [of] mostly Squaws to make salt. There he made out to run off and got back to Boonesborough safely.

This applicant, having said as he before mentioned, eight months he in company with two others, George Hendrick and Aaron Terman, run away, having learnt from some of the Indians before they started that there was some white men at the falls of the Ohio. They made their course that way. Before they arrived there, being ___ pressed with hunger, they were getting some red haws when a party of Indians came upon them and after a chase retook George Hendrick, but his other companion and himself arrived at the Falls [of Ohio]. He remained there upwards of two months having engaged as a soldier and performed duty under Capt. Wm. Harrod. He has no discharge, no written evidence of the services whatever from the time of his enlistment until he got back to Virginia, one year and nine months. He can prove by a living witness, Arabia Brown, of the County

Garrard the fact of his enlistment and his service. He hereby relinquishes every claim Whatever to a pension or anuity except the present.

Ansel Goodman
(his mark)

Memo - Ansel Goodman Enlisted in Capt. William Harrod's Company at Falls of the Ohio September 23, 1778, discharged October 27th following. Aaron Foreman enlisted in the same company on the same date and was discharged January 2, 1779. See Harrod's Payroll in Bowman Papers. LCD

11C33 Richard Wade Pension Statement in Cumberland County, Ky.

Age 81. Born Goochland County, Virginia on 26 October 1752. In March 1777, served at Williamsburg under Col. Johnson. In July 1777, went to Bedford County and enlisted with Capt. Charles Watkins to guard the frontier, went to Boonesborough, arriving 12 October 1777. From this place I, with 28 or 29 others, were ordered to go to the Blue Lick with Daniel Boone to make Salt for the garrison, where we remained until the 8th day of February 1778, where we were taken prisoner by the Indians commanded by old Black Fish, taken to the Indian towns on the Miami River.

Some of the Prisoners were taken to Detroit, soon after, but John Brown and myself remained until after they were done planting corn. We were then taken to Detroit and given or Sold to the British, where we remained [until] the next Summer, when Seven of us Escaped and Started home. A few miles above where the little River, St. Joseph and St. Mary's meets, we were then taken by the Maumee Indians, and carried back to Detroit. We were then put in irons aboard a Ship and sent down to Montreall, where we were kept in prison until the month of July 1781, six of us to wit: John Brown, John Morton and myself, from Virginia, & James Flack. George Finley & William Marshall of Pennsylvania were taken out of the prison to work on a mill race, from where we escaped and after nine days travel being through the wilderness, we came to the head waters of the Connecticut River, to a Station commanded by Capt. Lovell. He sent a guard with us the next day 18 miles to Gen. Bayley who give us a pass to the Governor, John Hancock, at Boston. On our arrival there the Governor gave us a pass with orders to draw provisions homewards.

We proceeded as far as Carlisle in Pennsylvania, where Brown and Morton went on to Virginia, the Pennsylvanians to their home, I to Fort Pitt to get a passage down the River. I arrived at the Falls of the Ohio about three weeks before Christmas in 1781, and there give my pass to

Gen. George Rogers Clark, and returned to Boonesborough. In my absence, Capt. Watkins had returned to Virginia, and I understood was in the battle of Guilford. I never received a discharge nor any pay as a soldier.

I do not know whether I was ever exchanged as a prisoner or not. After my return I was called on to march against the Indians and being as I thought unable to ___ over the duties, I did not go. I was called up to be tried before a Court Martial held at Harrodsburg, where Gen. Clark was present. He asked if I was not the man who had just returned from Canaday, and was assured that I was, he said that they had no right to prevail on me to Serve until I was exchanged.

I served afterwards on Scouting parties at various times under Capt. Thompson, and Capt. Charles Kavanaugh. At the time of the battle of the Blue Licks, I had been left to guard the Fort. I went and assisted in burying the dead among whom were Cols. Todd and Trigg and another Col. whose name I have forgot.

I never held any Commission. I have no record of my birth except in my bible in my handwriting which I took from my Grandfathers Bible and my age was recorded by the Parson at Dover Church (Mr. Douglas) who also christened me & married me, and christened two of my children.

I have never applied for any pension. I have no documentary Evidence of any service and know of no person living by whom I can prove my service Except George Richardson now living in this County & Ansel Goodman living in the County of Russell Same State. I hereby relinquish every claim whatever to a pension or annuity except the present.

I have lived in Madison County Kentucky until about December 1801 and from that time in Wayne County, Kentucky, until lately, and now live alternately with my Grandson in Wayne County & my Son in law in Cumberland County.

Sworn and Subscribed the day and year aforesaid

Richard Wade, Senr.

11C38-39 Anslem Goodman for Richard Wade in Russell County, Kentucky on July 16, 1833

This day Anslem Goodman came personally before me a Justice of the Peace in and for the County of Russell and state aforesaid, and made oath that he knew Richard Wade of Cumberland County in the Company of Capt. Charles Watkins which was raised in Bedford County, Virginia and marched to Boonesborough in Kentucky about the year 1777. I did not see him Enlist but he was considered a Soldier in the company to the best of my recollection.

He was taken prisoner with one Daniel Boone and about 24 others by Black Fish & party at the Blue Lick on Licking River. We were taken to the Indian Towns on the North Side of the Ohio; I believe that Wade and Some others were taken to the British and I understand they went to Montreal and Quebec and returned away by the Eastern States.

I escaped from the Indians about the year after I was taken and returned to the falls of ohio and after Staying there about a month I returned to Virginia. I have since Seen Wade at his house once or twice in Wayne County or Cumberland county near the line, but I am so forgetful I will not be certain. I saw Capt. Watkins in Virginia after I returned. I do not recollect that I got a discharge. I think Wade was a little older than me, I think. I am now in my 81st year.

Anselm Goodman (X his mark)

11C41-41(1), 42, 43 George Richardson Pension Statement

On this ___ [blank] of December 1832 personally appeared in open Court now sitting, George Richardson, a resident of ___ County, aged 75 years, who being first duly sworn according to law on his oath doth make the following statement or declaration in order to obtain the benefit of an Act of Congress passed June 7th, 1832. That he entered the service of the United States under the following named officers and served as hereinafter stated.

In 1774, I went a tour driving beef cattle for the use of the army in the Shawnee expedition under Capt. Taylor. This tour lasted not less than two months.

In 1777, I enlisted a volunteer under Capt. Watkins for 6 months in defence of Kentucky, was stationed at Boonsboro and was discharged 1778 by Capt. Watkins after serving eleven months.

In 1778, I went a tour in McIntosh's campaign as a driver of pack horses loaded with flour from Fincastle, Bottetourte County, Virginia on toward Pittsburg, commanded by Capt. McReynolds and was discharged by him after 41 Days service.

In 1779, I went a militia tour for 3 months under Capt. Adams and was discharged by him at the lead mines on New River in Virginia. I was out 3 months.

The first of 1780, I went a tour driving a United States Waggon for the use of a company of new recruits to Petersburg commanded by Capt. Cummins. From thence I went to Richmond and **41(1)** gave up the wagon & team to the wagon master as I was directed. I was gone this time two months.

In 1780, I went a militia tour under Capt. Selfridge in the South States. I was with the army under Gen. Gates before his defeat at Camden. I was gone this tour 3 months.

In 1780, I went for 8 months under Capt. Tate and Capt. Webber. I was discharged by Capt. Webber in 1781. I was in that tour through North and South Carolina, wintered at Cheraw Springs on Big Pedee. I was gone 8 months.

In 1781, I was employed by Capt. Irvine in providing beef for the armoury Kept at New London Bedford County, Virginia where I served 6 months for which I was allowed 2 tours, for which I got a receipt But lost it among all my papers by the destruction of my house by fire.

In 1782, I was engaged by the Agent of the United States in gathering the scattered property belonging to the U. S. in Bedford & Campbell Counties, Virginia such as cattle & horses. I was engaged in this business not less than 2 moths.

I was in no engagement during my revolutionary services. I resided in Bedford County, Virginia when I entered the services. I was drafted when I served under Capt. Selfridge and served as a draft 3 months. I served as a substitute for Henry Ward 8 months. All the rest – a willing volunteer.

I was born in Bedford County Virginia [in] 1758. I have no record of [my] age and never had. I have lived since the war in Bedford & Camell [Campbell] Counties, Virginia until 34 years ago when I moved to Tennessee where I lived 4 years and then moved to Cumberland County, Kentucky where I now live. I was known to Gen. Green, Col. Washington, **(42)** Gen. Lee & Col. White.

I received several discharges from the service But they were lost amidst the universal destruction of my property by fire. There are many persons in my neighborhood who are ready and willing to testify as regards my veracity and services in the Revolutionary army, among whom I will name John Emerson, Milton King, Dr. Joel Owsley &c. I hereby relinquish every claim to any pension or annuity except the present. I served in all 3 years and 2 months and for this I claim a pension.

       Sworn to and subscribed
       George Richardson

We, Noah Lunsford, a Clergyman residing in the County of Cumberland State of Kentucky, and Edwd J. Bullock, residing in the same state & hereby certify that we are well acquainted with George Richardson, that we believe him to be 75 years of age, that he is reputed and believed in the neighbourhood where he resided to have been a soldier of the revolution and that we concur in that opinion.

Noah Lunsford
E. J. Bullock

And the said Court do hereby declare their opinion after the investigation of the matter **(43)** that the above named applicant was a revolutionary soldier.

Wm Spearmen J. P. C.C.[Justice of the Peace of Cumberland County, Ky.]
G. Shugarb J.P. C.C.
Charles Palmore C. C.

11C44 Arabia Brown Pension Statement

      Arabia Brown of Bedford County, Virginia under Capt. Watkins. Arabia Brown was an Indian spy for Daniel Boone. Was under Boone's command when they were making salt at Blue Licks. That shortly after he was taken prisoner, he got away from the Indians and returned to the Fort and was engaged in the most active and dangerous service for eight months instead of six. That his duty was acting with his company to go forth from the Fort looking out for Indians and Indian signs in order to give the alarm to the Fort in case of danger.

      That he was allowed one single pint of corn per day for 3 months of his service, and that he had to grind himself on a hand mill. That the balance of the time he had nothing furnished him but meat and that there was nothing else to give them.

      The reason why he served 8 months [instead of 6] was that he could not get back to Virginia until Squire Boone, a brother of Daniel Boone, was despatched with this affiant and others to Virginia to get more men. That he remained in Virginia some ten years after his return and then removed to Kentucky upwards of forty years ago and has been living in the now County of Garrard long before it was a county.

Arabia Brown (his mark)

Memo. Brown's statement – this certificate appended to Ansel Goodman's pension statement seems conclusive that Arabia Brown was not one of Boone's salt boilers & fellow prisoners with the Indians. LCD

11C46 Ancel Goodman for Arabia Brown

      L. Landrum, a justice of the peace of Garrard County, Kentucky, took the deposition of Ansel Goodman. aged 80 and resident of Garrard County. Goodman states that he is well acquainted with Arabia Brown who has applied for a pension. They enlisted at the same time (1777) in the same county (Bedford County, Va.) under the same Capt. Charles Watkins & were sent to Boonesborough, Kentucky. Brown was taken prisoner at the Blue Licks by Indians.

11C48 Pension Application of Josiah Phelps (S 31451)
State of Kentucky Madison County *Subsequent three pages are not numbered.*

On this 4th day of December 1832, personally appeared in open Court before the Worshipfull the Court of Madison now Setting, Josiah Phelps, a resident of Madison county state of Kentucky, aged 77 years, who being first duly Sworn according to law, doth on his oath make the following declaration, in order to obtain the benefit of the Act of Congress passed June 7, 1832.

That he entered the service of the United States under the following named officers, and served as herein Stated. That in the fall of the year 1777, while on his way from the State of Virginia to Kentucky, (then Virginia) on the north fork of the River Holston, he entered the Service of the United States and had his name enrolled under Capt. Richard May, and marched to Boonsborough on the Kentucky River, and remained there as a guard until the last of June 1778. Some of the Men called it Enlisting under Capt. May. Deponent does not know whether it was So or not. He received no bounty but said Capt. May seemed to lack men to make up his Company. He agreed to have his name enrolled, it might properly speaking be called volunteering, as the defendant thinks,

In July 1778, he again entered the Service as a Substitute for Robert Bowman under Captain John Montgomery at the falls of the Ohio, now Louisville, and marched under Col. George Rogers Clark to the Town called Kaskaskie, then held by the British, and then returned back to Boonsborough. He was engaged in this Expedition three months. There was a Capt. Helm and Capt. Bowman under Col. Clark.

That in the Spring of the year 1779, he went on an Expedition under Col. Bowman against the Shawnee Indians, and had two Engagements with them, one in Chillicothe, and the other in the woods near the Town. He was Engaged in this tour upwards of 3 weeks.

In the Summer (he thinks June) 1780, he was Sent by Capt. James Patton from the falls of the Ohio River to a Fort on the Mississippi River a few miles below the mouth of the Ohio River with an Express to

Col. George Rogers Clark, to return with his troops to the falls of the Ohio, as he understood, for the purpose of marching against the Shawnee Indians. He was one month Engaged in this service.

In the latter part of the Summer 1780, he volunteered again under Capt. William Oldham, and was again under Col. Clark, and marched against the Towns of the Pickaway Indians. There was a pretty Severe battle between us and the Indians, fifteen or twenty killed on each Side. We destroyed their Towns, and all their Corn &c. He was engaged upwards of one month in this service.

In the year 1781 or 1782, he again volunteered under Capt. James Sturges, in his Home company, and was again under Col. G. W. Clark. We marched against the Shawnee Indians, had a little skirmishing with them and took some prisoners. He was engaged in that Service upwards of one month. This ends his Services.

He was engaged in the service of his country, where all his Services are put together, thirteen months and one half. He never received a discharge for any part of his services, and has no documentary Evidence, and knows of no person whose testimony he can procure who can testify to his services.

He was born in Buckingham County, Virginia on the 11th of Feb'y, 1755. He has a record of his age at his present residence in his Family Bible, which he took from that of his Father. He was on his way to the western Conty [Country] when he entered the service, and resided in what is now the State of Kentucky during the balance of his service except when out on Expeditions against the Indians &c.

He has resided in the County of Madison State of Kentucky ever since the War and now resides in the same County where he had resided upwards of 40 years. He always volunteered his Services, except in the instance before Stated. He has already Stated all the names of the officers he can recollect, and the circumstances of his services.

He never received a discharge. He is known in his present neighbourhood to the Reverend Thomas Jerman, Jr., and James Pasley and Col. Humphrey James, who is 52 years old. He hereby relinquishes every claim whatever to a pension or annuity except the present.

Josiah Phelps Seal

11C50 Josiah Phelps Pension Statement, 1832 with Thomas Jerman, Jr., Humphrey Jones[?], James Paseleye statements

Thomas Jerman Jr., a Clergyman residing in the County of Madison, Humphrey James [Jones?], & James Pasley, residing in the same, that we are well acquainted with Josiah Phelps, who had Subscribed and Sworn to the above declaration; that we believe him to be 77 years of age; that he is reputed and believed in the neighborhood where he resides to have been a Soldier in the Revolution, and that we concur in that opinion. Thomas Jerman, Jr. States that he is 52 years of age, and James Paseley states that he is 66 years of age.

                                        Thomas Jerman Jr
                                        Humphrey Jones [James?]
                                          Jas. Paseleye

11C51 LCD notes on Josiah Phelps
1777 – arrived at Boonesboro under Capt. May
1778 – at capture of Kaskaskia
1779 – on Bowman's Expedition
1780 – June - goes Express to Gen. Clark at Ft. Jefferson
1780 – on Clark's Campaign
1782 – on Clark's Campaign

11C52 Col. Wm. Russell's Services
1776 June 20th - Edmund Pendleton to Preston – says Col. Wm. Russell is to command rangers on frontier of Fincastle by appointment after Virginia Convention.
Aug. 27 – On Holston preparing for Christian's Expedition
1777 Feb. 28 – writes from Col. Wm. Campbell's saying he had the day before received orders to join Gen. Washington & intends starting about 20th. Col. Russell in Green's Division in Germantown. Sparks v. 462
1778 March 1 – at Camp Valley Forge: says Gen. M____ being gone home, the command of the Brigade devolves on me till his return. Expecting to be ordered to Ft. Pitt with his regiment on the Detroit expedition.
Oct 7 – near West Point – in a better country foraging than when at White Plains
Oct. 23 – ditto
1779 July 9 – Camp Smith's Cove: says the 5th & 11th Regiments are incorporated, which he commands, & then annexed to the 2nd Regt, as is done on all marches, he commands the whole…
July 25 – The Virginia Division commanded by __ Stirling, Wooford, Muhlenberg's brigade march for ____ tavern, 20 miles back towards Jersey, where expected to be posted a considerable time, then on the ____ of the American Army.

11C53 1777 – Sept 1 Brandywine Battle
Col. C. C. Pickering's Note of Sept 24, 1777, p. 50 of Papers in Battle of Brandywine published by ___ Hist. Society, it is mentioned that Gen. ___ desired to halt Spotswood & Stevens regiments – indicating that they formed his brigade – hence Col. Wm. Russell's regiment was most likely in Muhlenburg's brigade.

11C57 LCD sources for the Paint Creek Expedition of August 1778: Boone's Narrative; Filson, p. 67; Bradford's Notes, p. 32; Almon, vol. vii, 340; McClung's Sketches; "Marshall mentions it only in a general way;" Western Magazine. ii 213; Hunt's Review, iii, 262; Trabue's Memoir; Ben. Briggs Notes; Capt. John Gass Notes & Letters; Jos. Jackson's notes; Kenton's Ms. Statement; Collins Kentucky ii, 664; Wm. Hancock's deposition in R.H. Collins transcript; Jesse Hodges depo[sition] Nov 20, 1817 in R. H. Collins

11C61 LCD notes on Daniel Boon in 1778: Court martial, Boone's profane letter.

After a full investigation Boone was not only honorably acquitted of every charge, but soon after advanced to the rank of Major, and received the grateful plaudits of his countrymen. [LCD sources are listed here for Boone's good conduct.]

After Boone's return from captivity to Boonesboro - Ms. depo[sition] or Ms. letter perhaps will show date of his return - he wrote a letter to his wife denying the story of his Toryism - using profane language, which Mrs. Boone cut out of the letter: See Shane's copy of Daniel Bryan's statement. The good Mrs. Boone, acting like the angel of mercy, who is represented, on a similar occasion as dropping a tear on the unguarded words, was blotting them out forever.

After the big Siege & trial, Boone returned to North Carolina. I judge from what J. C. Barkley states (next page), that Boone hunted back of the settlements of Rowan frontier, perhaps with John Cathey - & that fall & winter made quite a collection of pelts & furs – the easiest articles to transport on pack-horses to the Charleston market – about 250 miles from the upper part of Roan [Rowan] County to Charleston.

11C62-62(1-37), 63 Interview with Joseph Jackson, Bourbon County, Ky., April 1844.

Joseph Jackson was one of Daniel Boone's saltmakers captured by

Indians in February 1778; he stayed with them for about twenty years before returning to Kentucky, where he drew a pension. Joseph Jackson was an eyewitness to many of the campaigns and battles between the Indian tribes and the settlers in Kentucky and Ohio. After returning to Kentucky, he married and had a family. Patrick Scott, in his interview with Shane, said that Jackson hung himself not long after this interview. Jackson's gravestone gives his death date as May 10, 1844.

Boone & his party captured 7th Feb. 1778, at the Blue Licks

From Joseph Jackson, a survivor of the party, born & bred in Bedford County, Virginia, Dec. 15, 1755, and now residing near Jacksonville, Bourbon County, Kentucky.

Joseph Jackson came to Kentucky in the summer in 1777 in Capt. Chas. G. Watkins' Company of about 50 men for the protection of the Country from Bedford County, Virginia.

Early in January 1778, Daniel Boone & twenty eight others went from Boonesboro, where Watkins' company was stationed, to make salt at the Lower Blue Licks. They were to stay a month, & then be relieved by Capt. Watkins and a party from the fort of about the same number. Of Boone's party, Mr. Jackson recollects the names of George Hendricks, William Hancock [Stephen Hancock's name crossed out], Benjamin Kelly, Nathaniel Bullock, John Holley, James & Micajah Callaway, Daniel Asbury, William Tracy, Ansel Goodman, Jesse Copher, William & Samuel Brooks, Jack Dunn - these with Boone & Jackson (my informant - LCD) were among the **(1)** captives - & ten others not recollected.

Jesse Hodges, before the capture, had made two trips from Boonesboro to the Licks, & each time packed in a horse load of salt, & he was not among [those] captured. Boone about the 1st of Feb. went to visit his beaver traps on Hinkson, which done, he had packed a large horse load of buffalo meat & commenced his return for the Blue Licks...

Four Indians were despatched from their camp on Hinkson **(2)** to the Blue Licks to see if anyone was there. When they reached there it was snowing so fast that they did not discover the men, & while on their way to rejoin the party, they met Boone with his horse loaded with buffalo meat - this was the 7th Feb. 1778. It was still snowing so fast that they got within thirty steps of him before he saw them. He at once jumped from his horse, & ran about six miles before the Indians overtook him. Three of the four pursued. One stripped Boone's horse & mounted him, following in his rear, & the other two aimed to out flank him. When the two flankers were within a few steps of him, they made an ineffectual shot at him & were about to shoot a second time, when Boone, weary & exhausted, surrendered. Boone now recognized in the mounted Indian one who had robbed him twice or thrice before.

All three **(3)** now came up & shook hands with Boone, & he gave himself up. The Indians said they were going to take Boonesboro. Boone began to devise the best mode of procedure in such an emergency.

(He well knew that Boonesboro was not in a condition to withstand an attack from so large a party & at that season of the year when an enemy was little expected. There was a fair prospect of the place being taken by surprise. At all events, it was not properly stockaded for defense. As things appeared to Boone…the Indians would go & take Boonesboro. His mind, then, turned on the point, how he could effectually turn the Indians from their purpose. -LCD)

When he was conveyed to the Indian camp & had an interview with the chiefs, he at once set himself about dissuading them from going to Boonesboro. He said that none were there but women and children **(4)** and old people, & that the weather was too cold and inhospitable [to] remove them to the Shawanese towns, that all the young men were at the Licks making salt. He would surrender them all if they would agree to let Boonesboro alone till spring, when the weather would be mild & they could be removed with comfort & safety. To this proposition they acceded. Boone well knew he had yet a difficult service to perform - to prevail on his men to surrender themselves.

On the next morning, 8th February, all went for the Licks, & as they neared the place, Boone was sent ahead some little distance (perhaps was threatened if he did not). When the men first saw him, they thought Watkins was at hand with his relief party; but a moment after, seeing the Indians, they seized their arms & were ready for battle - when Boone came near enough **(5)** to call "Don't fire! If you do, all will be massacred." The Lieutenant ordered the men (26, himself included) to form a ring & lay down their arms in the center & the Indians came up, & formed a circular line within & without the whites, & then ordered the prisoners to sit down. The men, on account of high water in the river which had submerged the Salt springs, had not been able for several days to make salt, & were camped on the point on the South bank of the river, & directly opposite the ford. Flanders Callaway & another person were out spying at the time, & escaped being taken.

The Indians now held a council. It was proposed to kill all the prisoners except Boone, & make him pilot them to Boonesboro & get the people there & carry them to the Indian towns. One Indian would speak and sit down, & then another; & thus about two hours were consumed in deliberation. Neither the Frenchmen **(6)** nor the Girtys made speeches - or if they did they were not recognized as whites; indeed, the Girtys were painted & dressed as the Indians were. It was not known among the prisoners that the Girtys were of the party until a day or two's march on their way to the Indian towns. Simon Girty voted for mercy - favored Boone & his party, & advised kind treatment. When the Indians spoke, the Negro Pompey sat beside Boone & interpreted all that was said, but in a voice so low that the others did not hear. Finally Boone was permitted to make the closing speech & said in substance:

"Brothers! What I have promised you, I can much better fulfil in the spring than now. Then the weather will be warm, & the women & children can travel from Boonesboro to the Indian towns, & all live with you as one people. You have got all the young men. To kill them, as has been suggested, would displease the Great Spirit, & you could not then expect **(7)** future success in hunting nor war. If you spare them they will make you fine warriors, and excellent hunters to kill game for your squaws and children. These young men have done you no harm; they unresistingly surrendered upon my assurance that such a step was the only safe one. I consented to their capitulation on the express condition that they should be made prisoner[s] of war & treated well. Spare them, and the Great Spirit will smile upon you."

During the delivery of Boone's unvarnished speech, the last one which the whites understood, & by which they learned the subject under deliberation was one of life or death to them. Under such circumstances, it is not strange that they should catch with eager solicitude every word that dropped from Boone's lips, & felt a deep suspense until the vote was taken. **(8)** The result was announced, 61 for sparing the prisoners, to 59 for death - but <u>two</u> majority. (I cannot think Boone voted, as Jackson says, for if he did there could not have been <u>two</u> majority in a vote of 121. LCD)

In five minutes after, all the salt, some 300 bushels, was wasted & scattered about, picked up their knap-sacks, & at once commenced their return march for the Indian towns. They struck for Limestone on the Ohio, passing Johnson's Fork at its mouth where was a canoe which they had made on their march out, to cross over.

On the morning of the 9th February, an Indian who had been carrying along one of the salt kettles now told James Callaway to carry it; he said he would not. The Indian still insisting, & Callaway still obstinate, the Indian finally drew **(9)** his tomahawk & raised it when Callaway bent forward his head to receive the blow, at the same time taking off his hat & patting the top of his head with his hand, saying, "Here, strike! I would as lief lie here as go along. I won't take your kettle!" The Indian with a dry smile, turned away, put up his tomahawk, & carried his kettle himself.

At the Ohio River, where Maysville now is* [see notes in appendix. LCD], there was a large boat made of four buffalo hides, in which they crossed coming out. It was fitted up with a rude framework & would carry about twenty persons. This boat was kept there for several years for crossing the river.

When they reached Little Chillicothe (contra-distinguished from Old Chillicothe on the Sciota) on the Little Miami, the Indians had a great war dance. The next day, Ansel Goodman came in with two Indians who had him in charge & returned to a place where the Indians had left some articles on their way out. On reaching the town, Goodman had **(10)** to run the gauntlet, but being expert on foot, he passed the ordeal, so fatal to many, without injury.

*McDonald's Kenton & Nathan Boone and the course leading to the Shawnee towns leads me to think this incorrect & that it must have been near the Little Miami. LCD

The Indians proceeded to adopt several; while these were sold to the British at Detroit, at a bounty of one hundred dollars each - scalps commanded only fifty dollars - & these were generally paid in goods. Among the number adopted were Boone, Micajah Callaway, the two Hancocks [only William Hancock was captured], Dunn, Hendrick, Kelly, Holley, Goodman, & Jackson (my informant - LCD). Tracy, Asbury, Coker [Cofer/ Copher], the two Brooks, Bullock, & James Callaway were carried to Detroit & there sold. Kenton was captured that fall, & when at Detroit, he escaped together with Coker [Copher] & Bullock. Samuel Brooks attempted to run away, was retaken, put in confinement & died. James Callaway was carried down the Lakes, put on board a British vessel, which was captured by our allies, the French, & it was several years before he returned to Kentucky.

Jackson remained with the Indians until the year 1799.

(Becoming, as I could not but **(11)** infer, in every sense an Indian, & as I doubt not, fought against Harmar, St. Clair & Wayne, & perhaps Bowman. When he left the Indians, he returned to Kentucky & married & raised a family, in Bourbon County, now enjoys a pension for his revolutionary Service. April '44 - LCD)

It should have been stated in the proper place, that on the very night after the Indians had left the Blue Licks with their prisoners, Capt. Watkins reached there with his relief party, & kindled up a fire to camp for the night, thinking that as the kettles were gone [that] Boone & the men had returned to Boonesboro, & they had missed each other. But after a little, discovering an Indian <u>bow,</u> Watkins & his men now understood what had happened & thought it prudent to leave, & soon conveyed the melancholy tidings to Boonesboro.

Boone had agreed to go with the Indians to Boonesboro. It was now Summer, & preparations began to be made for the expedition to Kentucky. Boone went with **(12)** the party to the Salt springs on Sciota, on the opposite shore of the river from Old Chillicothe. On their return home to Little Chillicothe, they concluded to kill some bears for meat for the squaws when the warriors were absent on the expedition. Some of the squaws were along with the party. The horse that Boone rode had a couple of kettles fastened on behind, which had been used for salt boiling. Hearing some turkies gobble at a little distance, the Indians ran off to kill them, when Boone cut the tugs which made the kettles fast, & said to the squaws that he wanted to go & see his squaw & children, & dashed off. The guards raised a cry & the Indians soon started in pursuit. Boone rode at full speed until his horse was broken down, & left him with the perspiration streaming from his body. Then he dashed ahead on foot, would frequently break his course by **(13)** running across fallen trees across his path; & thus while his pursuers would be puzzled to find his trail again, he would gain upon them, & finally so far outstripped them that they gave up the chase.

After crossing the Ohio, Boone stocked his rifle barrel & lock on a wide stick with a crack at the breech, & killed a deer. This lock & barrel he had agreed to stock for an Indian at the town on Paint Creek, which he shortly did after his 19 men went to attack. Also got of the Indians 3 or 4 balls, some powder to try the gun so as to be sure of getting it right. & had these up in his shirt flap.

Addenda. Dunn was the first to escape, then William Hancock who got lost, weak & hungered, set himself down in despair, when observed a couple of chumps [axe marks on a tree] near each other in a position which reminded him of a sudden that the spot was where he had formerly camped when out hunting. Now knowing his whereabouts, he bent his course for Boonesboro without difficulty. Kelly escaped when Girty was attacking Wheeling [not the attack of '77 – I have since learned it was in that of Sept. 1782. LCD]

(14) John Holley, who had been in Braddock's defeat (& one of the salt boilers with Boone at the Blue Licks) escaped in '82, when Gen. Clark went against Piqua - which see.

When the Indians had gone against Boonesboro in 1778, Ansel Goodman, George Hendricks, and another young man (who had got lost from Kenton on some horse serape, & went to the Indians of his own accord, recruited from almost starvation) attempted to run away to Kentucky, & met the Indian army returning. The young man was killed, Hendricks was taken by the Wyandotts, & Goodman escaped. After a while, the Wyandotts carried him to Detroit & sold him, & finally, it is believed, he got back to Kentucky.

Boone's Expedition to the Rocky Fork of Paint Lick [1778]

This town, against which Boone carried on his little expedition, was a small one on the head of the Rock Fork of Paint Creek & it was one [where] Boone got his rifle barrel to stock. When within a few miles of the town, they discovered two Indians on **(15)** horseback mounted on one horse – shot one, the other escaped. Boone & his party heard guns firing in almost every direction from Indians collecting for the Kentucky Expedition & hence they had to be wary & cautious. Not to betray themselves to the foe, Boone's party had refrained from killing game until they were well nigh starved. At length seeing a gang of buffaloes, they killed one & ate a hearty meal.

Just as they were making off from their camp, they discovered by the sign where two Indian spies had been posted behind a tree watching their camp, attracted, doubtless, by the firing in killing the buffalo. The grass & weeds were tall & troublesome, & it was so difficult to get through that the men would take turns in taking the lead to break the trail. Jesse Hodges was one of this party. [Boone returned, with a <u>certainty</u> that the enemy would soon appear before Boonesborough. LCD]

(16) Attack on Boonesboro [1778]

The negro Pompey was killed, think he was shot by John Martin. After this, the men in the fort would call out, "where is Pompey?" The Indians would reply "he's asleep."*

A couple of Indians were seen behind a log on the hill side on the north bank of the river opposite to the fort. [John] Martin, with his old yeager & ounce balls, levelled away when one of them poked up his head, & shot him through. The —— jumped up & ran off. It was a very long shot. Martin raised his back sight to take good aim for a long shot.

<u>Cotta-wa-na-go,</u> or <u>Black Fish,</u> was the leader of the Indians,

aided by Black Beard, Black Hoof & others - some 5 or 6 hundred. Don't recollect whether Girty was there. This party was chiefly Shawanoes. DeShane, the interpreter for ____ Wyandotts & Ottawas, was along. On the return of the Indians to their towns, they retook Hendricks & Goodman escaped.

* [LCD note at end of this page is illegible, seems to be an explanation of the Indian word for sleep.]

11C62 (17) Bowman's Campaign.

This was against Little Chillicothe, the Indians called it, or New Chillicothe of the whites. About a month before Bowman's attack, the French trader Laramie, with Black Stump & the Yellow Hawk, two chiefs & with them about 400 warriors, went & settled up Sugar Creek, a little distance above Cape Girardeau, to settle on Spanish Grants. [LCD note: "Shawnee V." or White river Map]

When Bowman appeared, an Indian who had gone out to hunt was killed on his return, & this gave the alarm. About 75 warriors now ran off at the first alarm. The squaws & children, over 200, mostly ran to the council-house. There were not over 25 warriors left, with some boys with guns included, not over 40 in all.

Black Fish & a party went to see what shooting it was that caused the alarm, when Black Fish received a severe wound in his right knee. The ball ranged along up his thigh out at his thigh joint, shattering the bone (he must **(18)** have been in a creeping, recumbent, or squatting position). He called upon the Indians not to leave him for he said they would all die together. The cry went over one to another to "run to the council-house & fight as long as they lived."

Black Fish was taken to his own cabin, some 30 yards west of the council-house, with 3 or 4 warriors with him. Several other cabins were occupied by the Indians, so that not over 6 or 8 guns were in the Council house. This could, at first, have been easily taken, but after all the squaws & children were in, the doors were made fast with --enches. This building was about 60 feet square, one story of round hickory logs - gable ends open and low, could easily have been scaled. Before getting to the council-house, one squaw had her thigh broken just at the door. She recovered - lay outside all the time.

(19) In the council-house was the old conjurer, Astakoma, well nigh a hundred years old. He kept constantly calling out & encouraging the men. It must have been him that Maj. Bedinger heard & thought was Black Fish.

Bowman got to the town in the early part of the night, posted themselves on three sides of the town, when an Indian hunter was killed, after which a large number of the whites shot off their guns to <u>alarm</u> the Indians. The moon rose about midnight. Then several board houses, save 10 or 12, on the south side of the town, were fired & burned.

One Armstrong had got a stroud petticoat, half covered with silver broaches, & foolishly put it on, & stood some 200 yards from the council-house toward the Miami, & looking towards the council-house, his arms akimbo. An Indian crept out after day, **(20)** got under the bank of the bench or ridge, & got sufficiently near, without being discovered by Armstrong, shot him through the heart.

The Indians shot two persons posted behind a large forked cherry tree, 150 yards to the south of the council house.

Mr. Jackson thinks the firing was considerably intensified around the town & from behind the white oak log, to the south east of the council house not over 30 yards off. When the men abandoned the log, the sun was about 2 hours up. They went first to an empty cabin where they each seized a plank[?] & put them over their heads with an angle behind protecting their bodies & thus escaped over the fork of Massie's Creek nearby, & dropped them as they entered the corn field. One of the men was found lying behind the log[?] flat upon his face. The Indians turned him over **(21)** to see where he had been shot when he opened his eyes, & it turned out that he had fallen asleep from excessive fatigue. He got up, & a very aged warrior begged that he might kill him, as it would be the last opportunity he would have. He hacked him down without the least resistance, not even uttering a word.

Joseph Jackson (my informant: LCD) was at this time a prisoner, & at the first alarm, seized an Indian's rifle in a cabin & made for the woods, but was retaken by some Indians. The gun was taken from him, & he conveyed to the council house & tied to one of the posts that support the roof. And there remained during the whole attack.

The squaw & children kept up a great noise, don't recollect about any particular speech, but plenty of hollowing & whooping. Both the conjurer & Black Fish encouraged the Indians during the attack. Even after **(22)** the whites had gone, Black Fish exhorted the warriors to be watchful lest the whites return.

A very old Negro warrior who had long lived with the Indians, told the whites that Girty was not far off with 400 warriors. He was probably then at Detroit.

After Black Fish was wounded, Black Hoof and Black ____ took the lead as chiefs. Bowman's men got some two or three hundred horses.

They had fled to avoid ___ __ & hence were there and mostly taken. About 10 o'clock on the day Bowman left ___ the afternoon a fight ensued. The Indians lost a warrior killed & scalped. The whites halted & watched several hours – men so exhausted, that they would frequently fall asleep on their post. When the Indian was killed, the whites made a rally & dashed out – whether on foot or mounted don't recollect - & rescued the dead Indian from his ____, carrying him off & took his scalp. Jesse Hodges told Jackson this. Some spies followed Bowman to see that he crossed the Ohio.

(23?) *Page number and part of page is illegible.*

(24) Kenton, Clark, & Montgomery – 1778 – by Jos. Jackson
The man named Clark here is not George Rogers Clark.

Had the Indians discovered Bowman's approach [at a] day's notice, they must have vigorously defeated, for the warriors from the Michalacheck, Piqua on Mad River, & Wakatomika would have numbered about 400.

Kenton, Clark & Montgomery found some mares & colts at the Flag Lick, 7 or 8 miles from Little Chillicothe, at an Indian sugar camp where John Redan, a noted Indian warrior, kept a large herd of horses. Kenton & his party got several, but the Ohio was so rough that the horses would not swim over. Start & then return, & his companions concluded to wait til it got calm. While thus waiting, the three sons of Kedan, viz – Kaskaskia, Wesketo, & Wa-we-ou-eem went to salt the horses & found them gone. They pursued on, killed Montgomery, took Kenton. Clark secreted himself under the root of a tree on the bank, the dirt partly washed from under it. One **(25)** of the Indians stood upon the roots of the tree, but did not discover the fugitive and he escaped. Montgomery, rising the river bank in the bushes, met an Indian. Both exchanged shots. Montgomery was shot through the head, & the Indian's powder horn was torn to pieces.

Kenton ran a quarter of a mile before he was taken, conveyed to Little Chillicothe, & being a horse thief, was tied on a wild colt, never before haltered. Kenton's feet [were] fastened under the colt's belly, a 3 or 4 year old, but the colt would not be driven away from the town. After several ineffectual efforts to get him started, gave it up, & took Kenton off. [It] seemed a Providential escape, for he himself expected to have been torn all to pieces. Jackson was an eye-witness. Then Kenton was made to run the gauntlet there, & also at every place from there on to Detroit.

(26) Campbell's Boats Taken, 1779

In the month of October 1779, a party of Shawanoes captured two boats, called Campbell's boats, loaded with Spanish goods, destined for Fort Pitt. Among the articles on board were a large number of barrels of flour. There were four boats [in?] company - seeing Indians, all on board went on shore at the mouth of Pond Creek, now Mill Creek, but finding the Indians too strong, they retreated to their boats. Two of the boats got off; while the other two being unable to get off, were taken. A good many whites were killed & Campbell himself was taken prisoner. Girty was with this Indian party, & he favored Campbell by taking him around Chillicothe so as to avoid his running the gauntlet. The flour was in tight barrels. The boats were scuttled & sunk in the mouth of Mill Creek – flour sunk with the boats, the Indians not liking it as well as their pounded corn. Two years after, when the corn was destroyed, they used to go & raised the sunken flour; it was wet an inch or two in from the staves, & was good as well. Jackson ate of it. Girty so told it.

(27) Capt. Thompson's Intended Expedition.

About 1778, Capt. Thompson of the British at Fort Erie, planned an expedition against Falls of Ohio (hence I should think it was as late as the summer of '79 – for in '78 there could hardly be said to have been a sufficient settlement to warrant an expedition of any moment – LCD). Had his Negroes, & a large body of Indians. At Piqua (of Mad River, doubtless – LCD) the river being very low, an old Indian conjurer predicted that before a week should pass it would rain so heavily that the river would overflow its banks; & in case his prediction proved true the conjurer was to have a horse. It did rain as he said it would, producing a great freshet. He went to claim his reward, & Thompson refused it. The old man said, "the man who buys water, & won't pay, shall meet with no success. Your expedition shall prove a failure, & you yourself will get drowned."

On this expedition Girty got intoxicated, & in a quarrel with Thompson, the latter gave him a severe **(28)** blow over the head, the mark of which he ever after carried. From some cause the expedition miscarried, & never reached its destination. On Thompson's return he took the schooner *Nancy* for Fort Erie, got drunk, fell overboard & was drowned. Jackson heard the old Indian's prediction. "I did not think," said Jackson, "that he could make rain, but he was pretty weather wise."

[Memo. This, I suspect, was an Expedition in fall 1781, against the Beargrass Settlements: See vol. 4, trip 1863, p. 198 & 199 & references. LCD]

Col. Richard Callaway was raised in Bedford County, Virginia, was a colonel of the county where Jackson knew him. It was a Shawanoes party who killed him near Fort Boonesborough. Jackson saw his scalp, & knew it by the long black & grey mixed hair.

Clark's Campaign of 1780

The white man that the Indians took at Piqua of Mad River (who was probably the same who deserted from the whites) was condemned by the Indians to be shot, & five were detailed to shoot him at Wakatomika. This was after Clark had destroyed Piqua, & the Indians had ___ not over 20 warriors. This loss was what incited **(29)** the Indians to seek vengeance on the White man & he was shot. The Shawnees lost more (not over 20 in all) warriors here at Piqua in '80, than in St. Clair's defeat.

Jo. Rogers (Jackson thinks his name was Jo.) was taken prisoner prior to '78. He got shot through the belly & suffered greatly before he died. It was said he was going to join the whites when he was shot. *This was David Rogers, who was thought to be an Indian when he was shot by the white men he was attempting to join.*

The house in which the Indians threw themselves was a body of a house without a roof, & perhaps rudely fortified. Jackson recollects the substance of Henry Wilson's narrative of this campaign, & thinks it about right. After the fight at Piqua the Indians commenced gathering at Wakatomika, but Clark returned home. It was this campaign that caused the final abandonment of Little Chillicothe & the settlement of Piqua of Big Miami. Mr. Jackson is confident the Indian loss did not exceed twenty.

(30) Blue Lick Defeat 1782

But a very few of the Shawanoes were on this campaign, but two from Chillicothe of Mad River. The expedition was composed chiefly of Chippeways, & was at Detroit without the knowledge of the Shawanoes. It was said to number 600. Simon Girty was then at Detroit, but kept coming & going backwards & forwards from Detroit to the Indian towns. He drew captain's pay. James Girty was not probably on the Blue Lick campaign – he then resided at Chillicothe on Mad river.

Clark's Campaign of 1782

It was on this campaign that an Indian was shot while on horseback as told by Col. Jef. Patterson, at Piqua on Big Miami. This town was settled by the Little Chillicothe people in 1780 when they abandoned their town on the Little Miami, just prior to Gen. Clark's appearance there that year. It was Moluntha's queen that was taken prisoner, & a Mrs. Long, a white woman, was with **(31)** her & taken at the same time. A young squaw ran down the bank & was shot in the river, a white man having nearly overtaken her in the water, as another on the bank shot her.

On the east side of the river, John Holley, who had been in Braddock's defeat (& was captured with Boone in Feb. '78. LCD), was rescued by the whites some little distance above Piqua. On the opposite side Holley had tied his horse & was rummaging in a cabin, some Indians in company, when whites came in sight, the Indians with him dashed off, & he <u>pretending</u> to be bothered in untying his horse, thus delayed until the whites came up. Don't recollect about George Girty being there, as Henry Wilson relates – only recollect that there was a night fight. George Girty then lived at Wapakonetta, but may have been at Piqua.

There were four Cherokee conjurers at Piqua who foretold that the whites would invade their country **(32)** in less than two weeks. Joseph Jackson (my informant: LCD) was immediately sent to recall the hunters in Big Swamp, south of Little Chillicothe & towards the Rocky Fork of Paint Creek, but did not find them. Clark arrived with his army while Jackson was absent & in less than half the time predicted by the conjurers, Jackson does not know how (if at all) they got wind of it. A Frenchman kept the store at Laramie's – the successor of Laramie (who had gone to Missouri, vide p. 50). This store was taken in the night by a detachment of Clark's army, & a Negro was captured there.

Logan's Expedition – 1786

At Mackachake, Moluntha, the successor of Munsska as king of the Shawanoes had a little ___ of his own near Meckachake, had in his hand accommodation given him by the whites, & was disposed to peace, when McGary tomahawked him. He was quite aged, & was <u>not</u> at Blue Licks, & misunderstood McGary's allusion. *McGary had asked Moluntha about the Battle of Blue Licks just before he killed Moluntha.*

Moluntha had been at a treaty (probably Clark's at the mouth of Big **(33)** Miami in '85) & there got his paper, & a cocked hat, which had he wore on this occasion, & his white official robe. McGary killed Moluntha (Jackson thinks – but is probably mistaken. LCD) & aimed to kill Moluntha's wife & actually cut off three of her fingers.

The day after, two Indians, one a wounded one, got into a tree lap, & killed five or six whites before they in turn were killed.

Simon Girty

Girty used to say that he was a spy at Pittsburg & was to have had two dollars a day, & they would not pay him. Got vexed & joined the Indians. He ___ with the Mingoes; could speak that tongue best, but Shawanoe, Delaware & others well. He would live sometimes in one town, & sometimes another - kept changing.

Girty said he had interceded for [Col. William] Crawford to be spared – even got on his knees, & begged this favor, as Crawford was an old friend. The reply of the Indians was that as Crawford was the commander of the whites, he must suffer; that they **(34)** must have revenge for Williamson's cruel tragedy at the Moravian towns on the Muskingum. If Crawford had been but a private soldier, Girty's request would have been granted. As it was, they could not spare him, unless Girty would take his place at the stake. After Crawford was burned (no women were suffered to be present at the burning of captives, lest their children should be marked or disfigured), his bones were gathered up, & tied up & fastened on a pole near where he suffered.

Takataneka, a Shawanoe town, furnished some warriors who fought Crawford's army, & perhaps there were a few other Shawanoes, but they were chiefly Wyandott, perhaps some Ojibewas, whom Girty most generally commanded. It was near Wapetomika (as Jackson thinks) where Crawford was burned. It was shortly after Crawford's death that Girty narrated these particulars to Jackson (my informant – LCD).

(35) (Neglected to ask whether Girty opposed Harmar? LCD) He took part against St. Clair. The Indians numbered 900. Jackson counted them, 600 of whom were Chippeways. They discovered St. Clair in the evening, fell back & attacked him next morning. Jackson does not think Girty was in Wayne's fight. About that time he [Girty] got drunk, & jumped from an upper story window of a house in Detroit, & got much bruised & injured, & was unable to go to war.

Girty was cruel, yet often showed evidence of human feelings. He greatly favored Boone & his party when captured in '78 & used his influence against killing them. [He] was kind to Campbell (Colonel John Campbell, of Louisville: LCD) in '79, saved Kenton from the stake, interceded for Crawford &c.

[See notes of Maj. Ballard in small Notebook, Nov. 1844 where Girty aided in ___ Mrs. Polk, captured at Kincheloe's . LCD]

James & George Girty were less prominent among the Indians. Jackson thinks Simon Girty was never [prominent?] - only a British emissary. George Girty died in a drunken frolic, a little after Wayne's victory. LCD note: This must be an error as to Simon - as he had not then joined the Indians.

(36) Influence of Cols. McKee & Elliott, Loughey's & Harmar's defeats at the Mouth of Sloan Creek

Colonels McKee & Elliott kept the Indians at war with the Americans in order to retain possessions at Detroit, and not surrender Detroit to the United States.

At Loughey's defeat, a prisoner of the name of George Ash was made to decoy the whites on shore.

Harmar's Defeat

The Indians thought Maj. Fontaine <u>mad</u> to rush single-handed among the Indians & thus sacrifice himself. After the last fight, a large Indian _____ of several hundred Chippewas & Wyandotts arrived & they invoked the Great Spirit to give them some sign if it were wrong to attack the whites. That night there was an eclipse of the moon. They agreed to attack Harmar next morning if all was propitious, but <u>sign</u> was too visible & conclusive to be mistaken. They obeyed the supposed **(37)** wishes of the Great Spirit - & thus, probably, Harmar's escaped a signal defeat.

At the fight between the mouth of St. Josephs & St ____, an Indian had his thigh broken – laid hid in the woods days, then crawled out – when, to his surprise, he saw the whites marching towards him. He cut his ____ with his knife. [This must have been Hurstborne's fight, it seems to me – LCD.]

Hamtramack & Whitley never made their appearance. The Indians were intent watching Harmar, learned a week before his arrival that he was coming, from spies. Had Hamtramack & Whitley approached as designed, the Indians would doubtless have been taken by surprise.

Black Hoof's wife was a daughter of Nelly Dougherty, taken in Braddock's war.

63 Joseph Jackson says he was never, while with the Indians, from 1778 to 1799, in a skirmish or battle; that the Indians never <u>force</u> their prisoners, nor even their own people, to go to war.

The two Ruddells, taken at Ruddell's Station in 1780, were Stephen & Abram – sons of Capt. Ruddell.

April 1844.

L. C. Draper

11C64 The Deposition of Daniel Boone taken agreeable to an order of the

County Court of Mason [Ky.] according to an Act of the Assembly entitled an act to ascertain the boundaries to lands and for other purposes.

This deponent being proven, deposes and Saith "That on the 17th of June 1778 being on his way from the Indians (in captivity: LCD), came to this place, being a large open place of ground at a buffalo road and the forks of three branches of the waters of Johnston's fork," which said land the said deponent entered for James Peake [in] January 1780. Being further questioned as to whether he was at the spot prior to the time you entered the land for James Peak, answered "I was, for I was here on the 19th[?] day June 1778, roasted some meat and got drink near the mouth of the three branches." Sworn to the 3rd day of July 1797.

11C65-66 Paint Creek Expedition – 1778 Extracts from Deposition of Jesse Hodges taken at the dwelling of Overton Harris, Madison County, Ky. on March 4th, 1815

Jesse Hodges, Nov. 20, 1817. In 1778 he in company with 18 men started from Boonesboro to take an Indian town on Paint Creek. Passed the Lower Blue Licks, and crossed the Ohio near the mouth of Cabin Creek which said creek appeared to have considerable notoriety at that time and is the same creek that is called by that name at this time.

Simon Kenton, who was then called Simon Butler, was our best pilot and well acquainted with this point of the country. We left the way that the road passed to Limestone between Johnston's Fork and Mayslick, and I remember seeing marks on the road in some places, but don't remember [how] we traveled so I could have returned the same way immediately afterwards. And saith that the buffalo roads were so numerous, and the marked ways so common....

Question: Who was in company with you?
Answer: John Kennedy, John Logan, John Callaway, Edmund Fear, Daniel Boone, Alexander Montgomery, John Stapleton.
Question: When you, Simon Kenton, Boone, and others went the Expedition against the Paint Creek Indian towns, in August '78 – how far did you strike Cabin Creek above the mouth of said creek?
Answer: I can't say, but I think about 3 or 4 miles.
Question: When you returned home, after crossing the Ohio River the same trip, did you not travel most of the way from there to Licking River through the woods, and was not the grass and pea vines so thick that it was with great difficulty and labor for you to travel, and did you not have to change your leader frequently?

Answer: Yes, and we crossed the Ohio below Limestone, and Licking below the Lower Blue Lick. We were hard pressed by the Indians who were pursuing us.

[LCD note listing sources for Paint Creek Expedition: See Collins' Kentucky ii, 59; 664 and depositions – Simon Kenton, Aug 23, 1821; Jesse Hodges - given above -] Nov. 20, 1817; March 4, 1818; Stephen Hancock, May 23, 1808.]

11C71 LCD note. Bartlett Searcy, one of Boone's captive salt makers evidently accompanied, by force or finesse, Gov. Henry Hamilton from Detroit to Vincennes in November or December ,1778 and then perhaps ran away and reached Kentucky.

John Todd told George Rogers Clark that Bartlett Searcy was captured, was with Hamilton in Detroit, and Vincennes, Nov-Dec 1778, then ran away to Kentucky

11C75 Journal of the House of Delegates, 1777 - 1780

Tuesday, December 1, 1778

Resolved, that it is the opinion of the committee, That the petition of Sarah Brown, an ancient widow, who had four sons in Captain Boone's company of militia, two of whom were taken prisoner by the enemy at the Salt Springs, and are in captivity, and the others continue in the service of this state, by which means the petitioner is left in distress for want of the common necessaries of life, praying relief, is reasonable; and that the petitioners ought to be allowed the sum of 30 lbs. for her present relief.

Journal of the House of Delegates
Friday, December 28, 1781

...Resolved that it is the opinion of this committee, that such parts of the petition of the said John Brown, Richard Wade and John Morton, as pray that they may severally be allowed the full pay of a soldier, from the time they were taken prisoners by a party of the Indians at the Salt Springs, in the county of Kentucky, which happened on the 8th day of February, 1778 whilst in the service of the State, until the __th of September 1781, the time that they effected their escape, is reasonable; and that the auditors of public accounts ought to settle the pay due to them in specie.

11C76-76(2) John N. James letter, Urbanna, Ohio, Nov. 12, 1835 to Mann Butler in Louisville, Ky.

Notes taken of Simon Kenton

My Dear Sir
    Yours is received, and when a little less pressed for time than I am just now, I will give you some definite account of my purposes and plans in the History of Ohio. My object now is to volunteer something to yourself, as you tell me that your new edition is going through the press. In your first edition pp. 97-98, you describe the siege of Boonesborough in the same spirit with Mr. McClung and adopt his criticism on the contest of folly between Boon and Duquesne. The censure is plausible as the facts are told but they are not correctly given.

    In one of my visits to Simon Kenton, I had McClung's book with me and read him the passages reflecting on Boone. With an emphatic nod of the head he replied, "they may say what they please of Daniel Boone, he acted with wisdom in that matter." He was in a poor state for defense, and he wanted to gain time, as he expected succor.

    The project of the treaty served to ___ the object. A good deal of form was used in the treaty. A table was taken out and covered, a clark [clerk] was seated at it and writings were drawn and signed. A chief then addressing Boone "said it was usual with them, in making friends, to shake hands; but when they made a long and lasting peace, they caught each other by the shoulders and brought their hearts together." Advancing with extended arms, he offered to embrace Boone, who did not show interest. At the same time as if by accident, some Indians stood near each white man, and this was the signal for the forcible capture which they evidently meditated. Before going out, Boone had given orders to the men in the fort to fire into the whole crowd outside if anything happened. They did so and many were killed. "He told me it was his pointed orders to the men he had stationed in the two basteens [bastions] to shoot without one moments delay and with good aim at the enemy."

    When the Indians and the French commander were undermining from the river, Boone had a box fixed with ropes so as to draw up to the pickets, so that they could see the work. He commenced digging in the block house and dug out the whole floor to the depth of four feet, he could have thus killed any number of men that could enter from a mine. Drewyer [Drouillard] and the Indians also told me their plan was broken in on by wet weather, and they quit on that account.

    I copy from the notes I made at the time **(2)** and as I wrote while he talked; you may rely on my accuracy. I preserved as nearly as possible the very language used, for I then meditated a sketch of his own times in his own <u>cabin talk.</u>

Kenton was not present at the siege, but was at Boonesboro very soon afterwards and had the detail from Boone himself. The vigorous truth of his statement is confirmed by the character of Boone as exhibited in all his other conduct. The imputation on the prudence of your Kentucky Hero is wiped away; and my Ohio Chief is also vindicated from the bold artifice of proposing that two Indians should shake hands with one white man. His skilful dissimulation & poetic language wholly escaped the pedantic writer of Boone's Narrative.

I hope this is not too late for you to make that correction, which I am sure you will feel inclined to.

Yours Respectfully,
John N. James

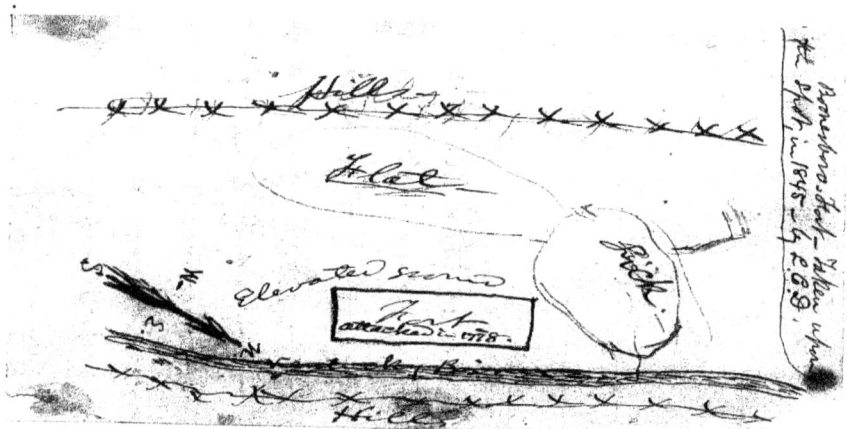

LCD drawing of Fort Boonesborough Taken Upon the Spot in 1845.
11C78

11C89 Boone at the Three Forks of Johnson – 1778.
See Collins' Hisory of. Kentucky ii, p. 555; copies Boone's depositions 1795 & 1794, as furnished me by R. L. Collins.

W. D. Hixson, of Maysville, Ky., a good local antiquary, pointed out to me on the Atlas of May's Lick township this locality & the spring below Frank Pogue's as the place where Boone camped in 1778, when escaping from the Indians, as referred to in Collins' Kentucky., as cited above. Hixson so told me when he visited me July 15 &c, 1884. LCD.

11C93 Description of a map of the Limestone - Lower Blue Licks area :

This trail left the main trail from the mouth of Limestone to the Lower blue Lick at or near Mayslick crossing Johnson to the lower blue lick - both on Licking [River]. Two houses labeled "Morrow," other place names: Buffalo Wallow, Bear Wallow, old trail [dots] which follow a road, Big Spring, Elizaville Turnpike Road [northeastern quadrant], Mays Lick and Flat fork Turnpike. Traces of old fort with small mound in center [marked out as a square 175 yards by 175 yards and near main Flat Fork]. Other places and names on the map: residence of Frank Pogue, Kenton's cabin, John William's Preemption Entry of 1798; old plum orchard; traces of old fort; Big Spring; 3 mounds are designated.

11C94 *Fragment. Not LCD handwriting.*
You will see that the old fort (or earthworks which it __, was square, and was laid out to the cardinal points – whether intentional or accidental I don't pretend to say. Also on every point overlooking valley road was a small mound with one Skeleton – except one, and that contained two, what I took to be male & female.

11C95 Letter of Douglas Brynner[?], Ottawa, Canada, May 24, 1884.
LCD heading: Boone's Captivity – Feb. 1778.
Letterhead: Department of Agriculture, Ottawa, Canada

Dear Sir,
      You will find herewith a copy of the letter you wanted, which I have done at odd minutes, it not being worthwhile to get anyone to copy it. There is an extract from a letter of Rocheblave's in French, of which I have made a very rough translation, but which gives the full sense of the extract.
                                      Yours truly
                                        Douglas Brynner[?]

LCD margin notes:
Boone & Party captured – taken to Detroit &c.
John Morton
Edwd Hazle

"Placarts" – Circulars of American prisoners – a sort of British decoy.
See Hildreth's <u>Pioneer History,</u> 126-128.
McKee, Elliott, & Girty join the British
Lt. Gov. Abbott & Piankeshaws.
Rocheblave – bad disposition of Indians.

11C96(1-3) Gov. Henry Hamilton to Guy Carleton, British Governor of Canada, March 29 to April 25, 1778.

All parties going to war are exhorted to act with humanity as the means of seeing a sincere peace when His Majesty shall be pleased to order the hatchet to be buried.

<u>March 11th</u> One hundred and twenty fine warriors, Mingoes, Shawnese, & Delawares with a number of wives & children came to this place. They have accepted War Belts.

<u>March 29th</u> Addressed the Lake Indians and all the Western Nations for the Six Nations, by which they declare their resolution to support Government and revenge themselves, desiring all the nations of the Confederacy to act as one man - thanking them at the same time for the zeal and spirit with which they acted last year.

<u>April the 1st</u> Forty Shawanese arrived barring [bearing] four prisoners, whom they delivered to me soon after.

(2)   <u>April the 5th</u> Mr. Charles Baubin who acts at the Miamis came in from a scout, not having been able to prevail on the Miamis to act with spirit. He with a young man named Lorimier engaged four score Shawanese from Tchelacase on Pecomi to go towards the Fort on Kentucky River, east of the Ohio into which it discharges directly opposite the great ____ or Rocky River. The Fort is about 130 miles from the mouth. The number of men in it about 80. Here they had the good fortune to make prisoner Captain Daniel Boone, with 26 others, whom they brought off with their arms without killing or losing a man. The savages could not be prevailed on to attempt the Fort, which by means of the prisoners might have been easily done with success.*

*That is, by threatening to kill or burn the prisoners, if they should refuse to give up the fort. LCD

(3)   These Shawanese delivered four of their prisoners to me, but took Boone with them expecting by his means to effect something. [The Indians evidently retained Boone to take with them & use him in their expedition against Boonesboro – but he gave them the slip. LCD]

By Boone's account, the people on the frontiers have been so incessantly harrassed by parties of Indians they have not been able to sow grain; and at Kentucke will not have a morsel of bread by the middle of June. Cloathing is not to be had, nor do they expect relief from the Congress. Their dilemma will probably induce them to trust to the savages, who have shewn so much humanity to the prisoners & come to this place before winter.

Daniel Boone says Boonesborough is an easy mark.

The Placarts for this place having found sway among the inhabitants & one in particular, several Prisoners who were saved by the Indians, * was seen in the hands of Mr. Morgan at Fort Pitt, who refused to let it be public.

April the 20th – Edward Hazel who has undertaken to carry a letter from me to the Moravian Minister at Kershayking. He brought me a letter & newspaper from Mr. [Alexander] McKee who was Indian agent for the Crown and has been a long time in the hands of the Rebels at Fort Pitt, at length has found the means to make his escape with three other men, two of the name of Girty (mentioned in Lord Dunmore's list), Interpreter, and Matthew Elliott, the young man who was last summer sent down from this place a prisoner. This last person I am informed has been at New York.

*See Hildreth's Pioneer History, p. 126-28.

11C97 H. D. Hixson Memos – Sept. 1886

1778 – Boone captured – That Boone & Wm. Bickley (as stated by W. Bickley, Jr.) used to hunt in the Millersburg region, & it was somewhere there that Boone was captured in Feb. '78.

That some depositions (perhaps William Brooke – one of the captives) in Bourbon County, Kentucky records, states where Indians made a canoe & crossed Licking, some miles below the Lower Blue Licks, at perhaps mouth of Indian Creek, south side of river, & the stump was shown where they cut down trees to make a canoe for crossing when en route to Millersburg region. Boone was captured on <u>south</u> side of river, & the salt boilers were on the <u>south</u> side too.

That the Salt Spring on the south side was the one used, as flat – overflowed in high water, & on till about 1784.

11C98-104 Interview with Stephen Cooper, 1889.
Heading: Big Siege of Boonesborough, 1778.

Stephen Cooper, son of Sarshall Cooper, near Winters, Yolo County, California. Oct. 16th, 1889.

Born in Madison County, Ky., March 10th, 1797 & was removed to Missouri in 1807 when 10 years old, settling in the Boone's Lick settlement. ,Grandson of Frank Cooper, who migrated from some part of Virginia* to Boonesboro, perhaps before the big siege of 1778, with several children, and certainly before Blue Lick defeat, in which his son Ben participated. Col. Ben - the oldest. Sarshel among them (another son of Sarschel Cooper).

Frank Cooper married Ruth Hancock, daughter of Stephen Hancock, who was 13 years old when she went to Boonesboro. She was there in the Big Siege. It was a six [nine] days attack.

Boone when a prisoner promised to give up the fort to the Indians - promised everything. Three days before the fight or attack, the Indians - 600 in number - came up. Pompey, a Negro on horseback, rode up, & announced that Captain Blackfish wanted to see Captain Boone. Boone went out alone, when Blackfish demanded the surrender of the fort according to promise. Boone said he could not comply, as while [he was] a prisoner, another man had been appointed to fill his place.

Then a council was held. Names of whites who participated not recollected. It was agreed that the Indians were to return to their country, & the whites were to abandon the Kentucky country as the Indians' land. They were to shake hands in the Indian mode: two Indians to one white man, and at the elbow. As this elbow-shaking was in progress, an Indian nearby fired a signal gun, when all the Indians seized their white counsellors, each two Indians making an effort to clinch fast his fellow associate. But all the whites snatched or wriggled themselves loose and escaped. As Daniel Boone was escaping an Indian threw a tomahawk at him, which struck between the shoulders, & knocked him down, but he quickly recovered himself & made good his escape.

Then commenced the Six days' Siege. The Indians shot arrows on the cabin roofs, & set them on fire. The whites with squirt guns endeavored to extinguish the fire - this was the third day after the commencement of the attack. Then fortunately it commenced raining, which continued three days, & so saturated the ground that the subterranean attempt to undermine the fort from the river bank below, caved in. The whites had countermined, & the mining approached within a few feet of each other. A fort Negro had dug a hole, when they, the whites, removed the garden fence away to frustrate their evening's design of setting the fort on fire, & got a shot at them, & retiring & re-loading crept up for a second fire. The Indians, having watched the locality from which the flash of the first fire had issued in the dark, watched & shot the Negro dead. *This man was named London; he was one of two persons killed in the fort during the sige..*

Don't remember about Pompey's death. No recollection of blame of Boone for his promises of surrender when a prisoner.

Just before leaving, the Indians killed cattle and destroyed the corn, so as to compel the retirement of the whites from the country within the time they had agreed to evacuate at the council preceding the attack.

Just after the retirement of the Indians the next day, Kenton came to Boonesboro alone, and stated that the other stations had learned (by the discoveries of their Scouts) of the attack, and were anxious to know the result.

*Col. Ben. Cooper's pension statement will probably show his birth-date. LCD

Frank Cooper married Ruth Hancock, daughter of Stephen Hancock. Stephen Hancock was about 5 feet 10 inches high, moderate size, died about 1816.

Col. Daniel Boone – no recollections of hearing of any part of his career before settling in Kentucky, save in a general way that he was a year or two in Kentucky exploring. Thinks he used to hunt in the Salt Lick country, & perhaps discovered the Salt Springs there. No recollection of Boone's Missouri hunts. No knowledge of the tobacco story.

Nothing of Indian Phillips - & nothing in particular of Point Sable.

Thinks Boone returned from Missouri to Kentucky about 1801. That Mrs, Boone had a child (**101**) in his absence & and she said to him on his return: "you had better have staid at home & got it yourself." [This, of course, refers to a much earlier period – about 1771. LCD]

Daniel Boone's brother George was at heart a Tory, but shared in the defence of Boonesborough during the big Siege.

Attack on Wood's family [1783]

Mr. Wood built a new cabin, & stayed away over night perhaps hunting & next morning he was the first to open the door of the cabin & was shot down by the Indians outside and one of the latter dashed in before the door could be closed & barred. After he had forced himself in, the door was barred lest others should come in also. A Negro had a tussel with the Indians when a twelve year old daughter of Woods seized a broad-axe, & hacked the Indian till she finally beheaded him. Mr. Woods' wife was Betty Cooper, a sister of Sarshall Cooper; she afterwards married a Mr. Peak. Don't know the 12 year [old] girl's first name, nor what became of her.

Forts in Boone's Lick Country [Missouri] – Kinkead's Fort [and] Fort Hempstead

The forts were 8 or 10 miles apart. No Hempsteads there

then (hence the Fort must have been named out of compliment to Captain Hempstead. LCD].

(102) Dodge's Expedition 1814

No knowledge of Dodge's prior services. Capt. Sarshal Cooper, in whose company was the narrator, Stephen Cooper, who with his brother Joseph, reconnoitered the Indian fort, found it. The Indians had discovered the approach of the whites, & took to the bushes. All were searched for & taken without any shedding of blood.

Dodge came on to Cooper's fort. There Capt. Sarshal Cooper joined him, with his company of 116 men. Crossed the Missouri River at Arrow Rock, three miles above Cooper's Fort; & after crossing the river, organized for the march, & kept on till dark. Joseph & Stephen Cooper then went to reconnoiter – discovered the fort abandoned, got back & reported, when Dodged marched in the night. About an hour before daylight reached the fort with orders to rush on the fort if an enemy were there, & if they fired, to know what they fired at.

Capt. Hempstead came up with a boat, no recollection of a company with him; found the Indians had been taken. The bucks were marched down afoot & then others of the Indian prisoners were sent down by Hempstead.

Col. Ben. Cooper was cutting off Indian packs with his pipe tomahawk, to relieve **(103)** the stolen horses, when Dodge's adjutant (name not recollected) said: "Old man, you are too hasty." Cooper slapped the adjutant's jaws with the side of his tomahawk. When the latter designed to report the matter to Dodge, Joseph C. Brown, one of Dodge's staff, interposed, saying "Better not do so; the old man has more friends than any man in the army."

Old Butler, a Guinea Negro, remained at Boone's Lick settlement. When the rest ran off; he fed & took care of the abandoned horses, and raised about 100 hogs. He rode one of the horses to Ft. Hempstead, when he was ordered to strip & be whipped. He appealed to his accusers whether he was to be whipped for saving their horses and raising their hogs. The response was "Let him go," so Old Butler was not humiliated for his noble & trusty conduct.

Julien [Dubuque? LCD?] went up the Missouri with a cargo of goods to trade with the Indians – powder, lead, and whisky, not a large amount. He was ordered to desist, but persisted, saying he had a permit to trade. But Col. Ben Cooper, not relishing the idea of having possible hostelry supplied, leveled his rifle, & compelled Julien **(104)** and his party to surrender themselves & goods. The latter were never called for, & were supposed to have been furnished by the British Government as Indian supplies for their allies.

Capt. Sarshal Cooper was killed about 15th May 1815, in his own house. The Indians had picked a hole in the chimney, & shot through it at Cooper's Fort, where Col. Ben Cooper, Sarshal Cooper only had cabins. Stephen Cooper, son of Capt. Sarshal Cooper, fired on the Indians from a loop-hole. Sarshal Cooper commanded at Cooper's Fort. Don't know Sarshal Cooper's age - not old enough to have taken part (as his brother Ben did) in the Indian Wars of Kentucky. He married Stephen Hancock's daughter, Ruth, already mentioned.

11C105-106 Notes from Mrs. Z. H. Maupin, about 56 years old. Her first husband was Henry G. McKinney. Address in care of Mr. Taylor at Bolene & Ewing, Kansas City, MO. She had a Manuscript book of John McKinney on early Kentucky events.

J. Wiseman Bryan, son of Abner Bryan…grandson of Jonathan Bryan of Missouri, Santa Clara. Can tell where his father resides (Guadaloupe, Santa Barbara County). Younger brother of Elijah & James Bryan of Nevada, Missouri.

Says she heard from her aged ____ that 200 families – persons – came with Daniel Boone from Carolina to Kentucky & most of them settled at Bryan's Station. [This must have been in 1779. LCD].

When Jonathan Bryan moved to Missouri, some came in keel-boats by water. Thinks Daniel Boone & Jonathan Bryan visited Missouri before moving there – on a hunting & exploring trip, through St. Charles, Warren & Montgomery Counties as afterwards constituted, & resolved to locate at (**106**) Femme Osage. Spent a winter in the woods, & their horses wintered on the wild cane and other wild food. They wrapped up in skins, & lay on brush piles of nights.

11C107-108 LCD: Col. Daniel Boone – 1779.

Some trip to Charleston [South Carolina?] …. John Cathey went to Charleston with Boone, packing in skins and furs, & returning with salt, powder, lead, & necessaries. This [was] preparatory to Boone's going to Kentucky. Also that Boone went to Virginia to attend to land matters, most likely to secure lands perhaps in place of those located under the Transylvania Company.

From Notes taken of John Tanner, Aug. 1844, of Grainger County, Tenn. – born in 1759, Sept. 16th

"In July 1779, Mr. Tanner says he went with Daniel Boone, his family, and a few other adventurers to Kentucky, passing through Moccason Gap, down Wallen's Creek, to Cumberland Gap, thence by the old trace to Boonesboro. Both Boone and his wife said on that trip that the very day she reached her friends on Yadkin, Boone reached Boonesboro from his captivity, in July 1778. Boone now [1779] settled his new Station. Tanner went on to Bryan's Station &c."

"Samuel Boone (nephew of Col. Daniel Boone) says Daniel Boone raised a company in Rowan County, N.C., which he joined. Marched from Rowan County on Sept. 15th, 1779, reaching Boonesboro in October. Pension Statement, ii, p. 2. "

See ScrapBook iii, p. 4, for names of emigrants of Boone's party." *[16E 4, or volume 16 of Draper's E series, is written in the margin, but does not contain the names of the emigrants]*

Samuel Boone's Father, also named Samuel, moved to Kentucky in 1779 in company with Daniel Boone, from Daniel Bryan's 2nd Statement, Sept. 1842, p. 1.

(108) LCD notes Daniel Boone -1779

Boone as one of the Trustees for Boonesborough – refused to serve.
   Hening's Statutes x:134, xii :603.
Gov. Hamilton "speaks of Boone's kindness." "Gov. Hamilton saw Boone in his captivity." Roosevelt, ii: 86 note

Cannon in Kentucky

[George Rogers] Clark had cannon at Fort Jefferson in May 1780. First cannon in Kentucky were those brought by Col. [Henry] Bird in June 1780, but those brought by Boone in fall of 1779 to Cumberland River take precedence. Samuel Gibson, who went from Tennessee to Kentucky in about 1794, says: "Boone hid two swivels he was trying to get to Boonesboro, in a hollow tree, at the Cumberland River." Shane's Collection, ii, Montgomery County, p. 4

"Probably the cannon were left at mouth of cannon creek, a western branch of Yellow Creek, some four miles above the mouth of the latter. See Map of Geological Survey of Eastern Kentucky, 1886."

The lower part of this page is LCD's list of sources for Bowman's Expedition.

11C109 Heading: Col. Boone & his cannon
See following page for LCD explanation of addressee.

27 Dec. 1817

   In the year '79 my Father left at the old ford of Cumberland in the wilderness two small pieces of cannon. He has heard by some since that they were brought years ago to Frankfort for the protection of the ____. Will you be so good as to make some inquiry. It may so be calculated they were the property of the State of Virginia and might have had them brought in to that place. That place is in Rockcastle or Knox [County, Kentucky]. Seen them in 1791 on my way to the Eastward. They are on our own private property, a present from Col. Carter of South Carolina to my Father, and owing to the death of some horses we were ____ to leave them in the wilderness. Any person living near the old ford can give you information about them as they remained there many years. If they be at Frankfort, it is nothing but right that I should be paid for them. [if] you obtain information you will please drop me a line on the subject.

J. B. Boyd

11C110 Memo. The preceding copy was furnished by Mrs. Joseph B. Boyd after her husband's death at Maysville, Kentucky, who made a large autograph collection among them the papers of Judge John Coburn – a friend of the Boones. Hence the preceding letter was doubtless addressed to Judge Coburn. Mr. Boyd in his lifetime sent me a copy of the same letter, among the transcripts he transmitted to be bound in a volume. LCD

[Henry Hamilton, Governor of Detroit, meets Boone – it was in May 1780. Roosevelt i:139; ii: 86. Notation is made of Gov. Hamilton meeting Boone – if in 1779 in Kentucky, it is a mistake as Boone was then in North Carolina. LCD]

[Daniel Boone was not in captivity in 1780. LCD]

[Ambrose] White & [Moses] McIlvaine captured at Boonesborough: Shane's Collections ii, Montgomery County, 5-6; G. M. Bedinger's Notes; Trip 1860, vi: 30; Shane ii, Bath County, 65; Montgomery County, p.4; Trabue's Narrative; Shane iii: 138; 140-41, 157. LCD

For the capture of Ambrose White and Moses McIlvaine, see DM12CC 125.

Oct. 1779 – Condition of Boonesboro or Boone's Station: Trip 1860, vi:20-36.

11C111(1-6) W. D. Frazee letter, Indianapolis, Ind., Oct. 23, 1872
LCD: Joseph Doniphan kills two Indians with one shot.

Your letter of inquiry sent to my uncle, Gen. A. W. Doniphan, has been sent to me by him.

Now on the shady side of fifty, have to some extent lost my interest in such subjects. When I was but a youth, I wrote a biographical sketch of my Grand Father Frazee. My Grand Father Doniphan [came] to Kentucky. Grand Father Frazee was living in Mason County, Kentucky about summer of 1774, while my Grand Father Doniphen did not arrive until 1778. He taught school at Boonesborough in 1779. He had seventeen scholars; he returned to Virginia about the spring of 1781, was married to the sister of Captain Bob Smith in 1783. Served as Justice of the Peace in his native county of Stafford during the years of 1786 & 1787. General Washington brought a number of suits before him that are recorded in the old Docket that is now in my possession. Rents, Negroes, & Tobacco in the old book. He moved with his family to Mason County [Kentucky] in the spring of 1792 and settled 4 miles ___ Germantown on the road to Washington, Kentucky. **(1)** He died at his dwelling, though the Washington Paper said "Old Squire Joseph Doniphan is dead, he was found dead at a Deer lick – when found his gun was cocked, and was pointing to the lick. He had on eye closed, and his finger was on the trigger, and had a deer come in even after his death, by a spasmodick move of his finger the gun might have been discharged, and the deer killed, and this highly gifted pioneer and bosom friend of Daniel Boone might have carried out in death what he followed so long in life."

My mother who is now 78 years old was born & raised in Mason County, Kentucky. I have this day been talking to her – she says Grand Father Doniphan came to Boonesborough about 1778 with ___ Hancock, James Kea & John South from Virginia. My mother says a wealthy Spaniard of note

[LCD: ___ Cyclopedia of Biography says 1813 – 11,200.]

(2) landed on the Potomac shore, and called upon her Grand Father, [said]

that our family was of Spanish origin, that the name was Phan and the Dou was a title of honor prefixed to it. That he gave him a small golden wedge that was handed down in the family for many years.

During my Grand Father's first stay in Kentucky he had many narrow escapes and hair breadth adventures among the Indians. I have heard [sic] of a family tradition that may have occurred with my Grand Father in 1779. While out hunting, making the circuit of a hill, he discovered that 2 Indians were on his track. Running to the creek he crossed on a log, hid behind a tree on the opposite bank until the Indians came upon the log to cross. Getting them in range, shot them both off at once.

Once when camped in a canebrake, with **(3)** Kea, who was partly deaf. Hearing the Indians were near, like other partially deaf men, talked very loud even when He whispered. In a loud but as he thought in a very low tone whispered back, "I wish I was at home, with my wife & children." Grand Father with his hand on his mouth & the other around his throat, he choked him still.

Grand Father taught school only about six months. His school was small, seventeen scholars. Taught more as an accommodation, received but little compensation besides his board. A friendship then formed between him & Boon that is to this late day cherished by their descendants.

[In] 1843 in company with Major Nathan Boon – descended from Greensupsburg to Cincinnati – he spent quite a time in making inquiries about our family. I dislike to record many things that I might get wrong as I have to depend solely on my **(4)** memory, except a few trivial papers and my Grand Father's old Docket.

My Grand Father owned a large farm and more than forty Negroes. My Mother was raised to labor. I now have at my house cotton cloth with silk stripe that she raised the cotton, graded it, spun it & wore it, in 1806 or 1807. She says she was 12 or 13 years old.

I think that Gen. A. W. Doniphan [was] the best orator, & the most successful criminal Lawyer in Missouri. His services have frequently demanded one thousand dollars, & once or twice he has obtained as high as ten thousand in a single case.

They are the only two surviving children of Joseph Doniphan. My Mother still writes a fine hand & reads fine print without the aid of glasses & could always do so.

(5) My oldest uncle, George Doniphan, of Augusta Kentucky, had heard of my Grand Father talk of his school at Boonesborough in 1779 being the first ever taught in the state.

An old joke was played off on [my uncle] in 1810 at Greenupsburg, Kentucky. Harriett Boon, the daughter of Jesse Boon, Daniel's fourth son, was a beautiful girl of 17 and full of fun. Her Father was about to move to Missouri, paying a visit to Uncle Hockidays who married my Aunt Margarett Doniphan. That night (purely for mischief) she told Uncle Tom that she loved him & never could love anybody else so much. He replied that he never expected to marry her or any one else. Harriett putting on a very serious ___ told him that she would take poison and kill herself that night. **(6)** He would ask himself can it be possible that she was in earnest. After dressing, he came down & informed Uncle Hockiday, who got out of bed, took the lantern & walked over to Jesse Boon's, waked him up. After imparting the information, the lantern in hand, they marched downstairs, where they found Harriett reposing calmly in the arms of sleep. "Halloo Harriet, what have you been telling Tom Doniphan?" It would have amused a Stoic to have heard her clear ringing, rolicksum laugh, as she replied. "I had entirely forgotten it." But not wishing to take the job of writing the early history, I'll bring this letter to a close & assure I may write you a letter about Samuel Frazee, My Grand Father on my Father's side.

Yours Truly
W. D. Frazee

11C112-112(1) Heading: Boone's Pre-Emption & Settlement Right, 1779. Henderson Grant to Boone in 1779.
R. T. Durrett letter, Louisville, Ky.

Feby 26. 1884

Hon. Lyman C. Draper –
  Yours of the 16th was duly received. My Dear Draper
  Glad to learn from it that you had duly considered the question of Boone's residence. I did not want the old hunter turned out in the woods and settled on a farm as indefinite as the whole realm of Kentucky by you, as had been done by his other biographers. In Henderson's Transylvania domain, he selected a thousand acres at a place called "Stockfield. "But he lost it. George Meriwether laid a survey right square over it, and got it. His settlement and preemption right, however, was on Cartright's Creek about 5 miles from its mouth. It looks like the old fellow may have had a cabin on 400 acres at this point. It was regularly surveyed for him in 1783, and he claimed it as his settlement right under the act of 1779. Cartright's Creek is a branch of the Beech Fork of Salt river. I will look further into the matter when I have time.

(1) I am sorry that the Clark petition is to end with no connection with the petition for the town of Louisville. In George Croghan's Journal of 1765 (<u>Butler's Kentucky</u>, appendix, edition of 1836 page 462) he states that he was at the mouth of the Scioto when a flood rose 9 feet above a 40 foot bank and drove the inhabitants from the town there. I know he [Croghan] was here with Gist in 1750 but I fear that is not the date because Gist in his Journal reports of the thunderstorm on the Kentucky Shore, while Croghan says the flood drove them to that shore thus indicating a previous date. I should like the date of this flood if it can be fixed any nearer than 1750.

Truly
R. T. Durrett

11C113 (1-3) R. T. Durrett, Louisville, Ky., March 1, 1884

    Yours of the 28th Feb., My Dear Draper, has reached me being the long sought petition of our early people for a town at the Falls. You can't well estimate the amount of obligation you have placed me under by sending a copy of this document. I have been for years trying to get hold of it. Possibly since you took the copy, the original has disappeared from the Archives of Virginia, for the search has there been made for me without success. I have the plat of the town to which the petition refers. It was found among the papers of William Johnston, an early Clerk of our Courts and Board of Trustees.

    (1) Neither Evans nor P___ gives any clue to the date of the flood that swept away the Shawnee town at the mouth of the Ohio. I had examined these and other contemporary authorities before I wrote you. Don't bother yourself about hunting down the question unless you had accidentally fallen upon it in previous research. I thought of writing an article on the <u>Floods of the Ohio</u>, and as this was the earliest within my search, I was anxious to fix its date.

    What I wrote about the early home of Boone is conjectural but worthy of your regard. I have since looked into the matter a little and find I could not have been far from right in what I stated. I will give the facts more explicitly, and leave you to judge for yourself.

    (2) In 1776, Daniel Boone seems to have selected for himself a thousand acres of land, and surveyed it, and named it Stockfield. This was under the Transylvania auspices, and of course, like all other lands under that title, was lost. In 1780, George Meriwether laid a land warrant on the Stockfield tract, and covered the thousand acres of Boone. Whether he bought Boone's right to it, or merely took it up as wild land, does not

appear.

The case of _____ against Meriwether, reported in the 4th vol of Bibb's Kentucky Reports, page 138, shows such facts with regard to the Stockfield tract. In after years, the tract of land between Estill's Station and Silver Creek took the name of Stockfield because of the abundance of cane with which it supplied the cattle for grazing. Could it have been possible for the old pioneer when he located this 1000 acres under Henderson & named it Stockfield to have had in his head the purpose of a home of that name, but Meriwether seems to have gotten the land, and that was the end of any such notion if he had it.

(3) In 1780, March 9th, Boone entered 500 acres on Elkhorn. July 17th, 400 acres on Licking, Oct 4, 500 acres on Boone Creek; but none of these entries seem to have been surveyed.

On the 10th of January 1785, Thos. Whitledge, a deputy for George May, surveyed for Boone his settlement right of 400 acres about five miles from the mouth on Cartright Creek. Cartright Creek being a branch of the Beech Fork of Salt River. Again, on the 11th of January 1788, Boone's preemption was surveyed adjoining his settlement. These surveys being made for Boone, at intervals so far apart, and for his Settlement and preemption lands, (evidently under the law of 1779, 400 acres for a Settlement and 1000 acres preemption) make a pretty strong presumption that Boone had a house on this 400 acres and lived on it. These are the facts, and you can draw your own conclusions. It is not likely that other facts can be added.

Truly
R, T. Durrett

Volume 12C contains 82 numbered pages.

12C1-1(12) *Pages skip from 1(1) to 1(3).*

From Henry Hall, a Survivor, in Bourbon County, Kentucky. Born near Philadelphia 24th May 1760. Notes taken in April 1844, Bourbon County, Kentucky. LCD: Bowman's Campaign 1779.

Draper interviewed Henry Hall and Joseph Jackson (see 11C62) in the same month and year in Bourbon County, Kentucky. Draper compared some of Henry Hall's statements to Jackson's in this interview.

Bowman's Campaign - 1779

Mr. Hall was in William Harrod's Company of about 60 men from the Falls of Ohio. Edward Bulger, who was subsequently killed at the Blue

Licks, was Ensign of Harrod's company. Mr. Hall doesn't think James Harrod nor John Haggin were out - recollects but four companies, commanded by William Harrod, Benjamin Logan, Levi Todd and John Holder. Bowman's men numbered altogether about 230 men. Rendezvoused at the mouth of Licking. William Harrod's company reached there first, & turned in to killing buffalo **(1)** bear & deer for provisions. Killed some game at Big Bone Lick, & there got some of the bones of the mammoths.

Harrod brought 3 keel-boats & 3 canoes & in these all the troops crossed at the mouth of Licking, save 32 who were left to take care of the boats. No cabin was built. They lived in the boats, & kept plying up & down until the troops returned, thus kept moving about, thinking it less dangerous than to remain stationary. Left the mouth of Licking on Friday morning, May 25th, & reached the vicinity of the town [Little Chillicothe] on Sunday eve, May 27$^{th.}$ Halted in the prairie a few hundred yards east or perhaps south east of the town, the dogs barking, while the captains went to reconnoitre.

[LCD: while copying these memos, I have referenced to Gen. Daniel Smith's Journal of '79 & '80. I find that the last Friday in May '79, was the 28th, & that the Monday following was the 31^{st,} I would naturally think that Mr. Hall mistook the date (28th May) of starting from the Mouth of Licking for the date of the attack.]

Mr. Hall thinks it was after midnight when they reached there. Don't recollect about the moon, but it was quite foggy. The captains were gone near an hour. A disposition of the men was now made: William Harrod's company were to attack the east on upper end of the town, while the other captains went further around.

One of Capt. William Harrod's men named Hatton, seeing an Indian coming into town, shot him & he fell, & Hatton ran up to take his scalp, when one of the others, mistaking him for an Indian, fired & very slightly wounded Hutton [sic] in the side. At this alarm some five or six Indians came running out of the cabins & shot at the men & were shot at in turn (& probably Black Fish was here wounded, as Mr. Jackson says). Then the Indians retired, & the fog again settling, it was thought **(3)** best to remain as they were, & while thus lying upon their arms, two Indian drums were beat in the town at a loud rate. Some of the Indians <u>did</u> throw themselves (as Jackson says) into some cabins near the council-house, & from them fired, &c. Laid still for an hour or so, when daylight came, commenced fighting & continued some time. In a cabin Mr. Hall saw an

Indian repeatedly remove a shingle from the roof & shoot out. Hall & some others were posted behind a deserted cabin; a left handed gunner was needed to get a good shot at the opening in the roof. Hall, who could shoot as well left or right handed, watched, & when the Indian's gun was seen to take its place in the aperture, Hall took aim a little above & fired. This hole was closed, & no more firing from that quarter. William Hickman, of Harrod's company, ran from behind the cabin where Hall was, & took post **(4)** behind the white oak log, & exposing himself too much, was shot through the forehead. The sun was then an hour high.

The Indians hollowed out, proposing that they would fight the whites out in the woods & Bowman seemed to accept, & ordered the men to fall back into the woods & form. The men were in confusion & did not obey. Shortly after however, they fired some 10 or 12 cabins at the east end of the town. These were set on fire chiefly with the aid of small bags of powder, which were found scattered more or less in almost every cabin - furnished doubtless by the British. This was about 9 or 10 o'clock in the morning. Then gathered up the horses around the town - got some five or six hundred. Got strouds, clothes, leggings, shirts (one of which Hall had, having on it 100[?] broaches) & a variety of English goods.

While retreating out of **(5)** town, Jerry South was shot between the shoulders, the ball passing through his body & lodging under the skin of his breast. He was packed on a horse, with some one behind to hold him on. He died the 2nd day after.

Commenced the return march about eleven o'clock, & went some distance - 2 or 3 miles - towards Detroit. [Going towards Detroit must be an error - went perhaps southeast to Xenia, then tacked to southwest. LCD] Then Bowman ordered the spies to ___, & steer for the mouth of the Little Miami. Bowman was advised to ambush the trail, as the Indians were seen following at a distance. When the whites would leave a small prairie, the Indians would be seen entering it on the other side.

Got some 6 or 8 miles & just crossed a creek when they found themselves surrounded by the Indians. The ground was a pretty good piece. The Indians had, in this particular, no advantage: timber thick **(6)** on the north east side, & pretty much barren on the other sides, with scattering trees & shrubbery. It was now about one o'clock. The men had thus far marched in three lines, with the horses within the lines. A hollow square or circle was now formed, & a scattering fire commenced which soon became quite brisk.

During the fight John Moredock was shot in the head. Thomas Guthrie was shot in the mouth, though not dangerously. Someone was shot in thigh & was lying down in the hollow square. Seeing the firing slack on one side of the line, & some Indians attempting to cut him off, mounted a horse & dashed off, hotly pursued by three Indians. He managed to escape them, though several times they came in view.

At night he lay down, fastening the bridle to his wrist & fell asleep - and woke, found the horse gone, & felt that he must perish in his lonely & almost **(7)** helpless situation. But overpowered with fatigue & weariness, he soon again fell asleep. Awoke by the singing of birds at day break, & was rejoiced to find his horse close by him! Crept up & got on; & that day fell in upon Bowman's trail & overtook the troops.

After fighting some time, Hall got a fair shot not over ten steps off at an Indian loading his gun. The Indian jumped up several feet & fell, when Hall had to escape from several Indians around him.

Edward Bulger proposed, as the only way of extricating themselves, to mount several of the horses, dash out, rouse up the Indians from their coverts, fire & return. Accordingly, Bulger, Hall & three others thus made a sally & returned. Every one of the five horses were shot; some fell dead as they re-entered the hollow square or circle. It made no great difference, as the horses were Indian plunder.

This new mode of carrying on operations placed **(8)** the Indians, instead of the whites, as heretofore, on their defensive. Other horses were mounted. The number of men increased a little, & again dashed out, Between that & dark made some six or seven sallies, the last one near after dark, when the flashes of the guns on the sides were distinctly visible. The Indians now drew off. Bowman renewed his march - went two or three hours, passed through a piece of swampy ground, & down a branch or creek. When emerging from the low ground, a halt of two hours was ordered for the men to rest, & then resumed the march.

The men were in great confusion & anger - some blaming Bowman for bad management, & for not taking a more vigilant part himself. While thus bandying complaints a great many of their horses strayed off. Men were nearly starved.

It should be remarked, that on Sunday evening **(9)** while lying on the prairie for the officers to reconnoitre, it was quite cold, & the men took their blankets & threw them around them. In these were their small supply of provisions, & when they were ordered to take their respective positions in surrounding the town, they left their blankets there. When they left next day, they were too much confused to re-possess their blankets, & thus lost their provisions. Had Bowman been attacked during this return march, after the afternoon fight, it must have resulted disastrously.

Mr. Hall thinks Bowman's loss was seven or eight killed, & three or four wounded. At the mouth of the Little Miami they found the boats, which had been directed to be there. Crossed the Ohio, got but 163 horses over, were slower in getting back to the Ohio than in going out.

(10) Had the sale [of plunder] on the south bank of the Ohio, a little above the mouth of the Little Miami. The property sold a mounted, when apportioned off, to about 110 pounds to each man. Little, however, was ever collected or distributed - & thus as it proved in the sequel, each got what he bid off.

Capt William Harrod, with 61 others, went up the Ohio to Red Stone in the two keel boats &c & took along several bones & tusks got at the Big Bone Lick.

Logan's Campaign, 1786.

Mr. Henry Hall was out on this campaign. Were some 8 or 9 hundred men. Cols. James Garrard, Benjamin Harrison, Thomas Kennedy, & Hugh McGary were the principal officers under Logan.

When Logan reached Mickacheck, some 18 or 20 Indians remained, & the men rode after & killed them most all. Capt. Irvine & others were pursuing an Indian with a broken thigh, & did not rush upon **(11)** him as quick as they ought. He snapped several times at Irvine, who thought the gun was empty. Finally the Indian shot him in the breast, while on horseback. Irvine died that night. Rhody Stafford was on the look for the same Indian (hid in the tall grass - vide Gen. Lee's Statement. LCD) & leaning forward in the search when he received a shot under the collar bone. Then one of the men ran up & shot the Indian in the head. Stafford died at Maysville on the return of the troops. William Rout was wounded.

Moluntha's Town was about a mile from Meckacheck, at the head of the prairie. There was Moluntha & his queen & several others, some 15 or 20 prisoners, one or two of whom were white girls. One of these was badly cut by one of the Colonels mistaking her for an Indian. After the prisoners had been taken an hour, McGary went up to Moluntha, who had about **(12)** his person a good many silver trinkets & jewelry, & asked "Do you remember the Blue Lick defeat?" "Yah, I do," replied Moluntha, upon which McGary cussed him & snatched a squaw hatchet from the queen & with two blows killed Moluntha. Don't recollect about McGary cutting the queen's fingers off. McGary was much blamed. It had been strictly ordered that no prisoners, after having surrendered, should be injured. No recollection about McGary's justifying himself for the act.

The next paragraph is partly obliterated by ink from other side or has been deliberately marked through.

Next day went & took McKee's Town, 6 or 7 miles off. It was

deserted. Burned these & some half a dozen of the towns on the Big Miami. At McKee's ___ ___ house ___ log, had windows & ___. The fighting ___ ___ ___ the killing of Moluntha at his own town. At McKees Town, killed hogs & beef cattle. All the towns were burned.

12C2 *The top of this page is numbered 12C1(12), and the lower half is numbered 12C2 for the beginning of John Martin's Notes.*

12C2–2(24) Memorial of Major John L. Martin to Congress – 1836. Nov. 14th, 1844, Paris, Ky.

To the Honorable Congress of the U.S. –
Your memorialist, John L. Martin, begs leave to represent that his father, John Martin, a native of Orange County, New York, came to Kentucky early in the spring of 1775, simultaneously with Boone, Harrod, & the first adventurers to the western wilds.

(2) In 1812 or 1813 my ancestor presented a Petition to the Legislature of Kentucky in order to receive a remuneration for his services.

(3) The committee who sat upon the subject suggested my father was wrong in appealing to Kentucky. It was the duty of Virginia to pay all demands of that kind. I withdrew the Petition, where it remained until 1832.

(4) I find in possession of his children, a petition to the Legislature to pay a certificate given to my father on the first of May 1777, by Col. John Bowman for four horses appraised to 101 pounds, leaving his services for an adjustment in another manner. Having at the time an application held under advisement by Gov. John Floyd [of Virginia] for the ___ of military lands. In one of the Pay roll testimonies ___ ___.

(5) Shortly after the rejection of the horse claim by Virginia, I employed a gentleman to procure the interests of my ancestor's descendants. A few weeks afterwards the law of 1831 was passed, my assistant procured the copy of Martin's Payroll to show that he was attached to the Illinois northwestern regiment under Colonel & General George R. Clark. The claim was rejected by the secretary of the Treasury, Mr. Du___. In a few days afterward, the Department was destroyed by fire, all the testimony ___ ___ were burnt.

(6) The testimony of Gen. Robert Pogue, Gen. Squire Grant, Gen. James Ray, & William Cradlebaugh, all of whom were personally actors in that memorable contest & known to the representation of Kentucky, stated they knew Capt. John Martin intimately, & that he was in the State Line of Virginia, & independent of all important campaigns &

other expeditions of military duty, was stationed at Grant's, Bryant's, Logan's, Harrod's, McAfee's, Boone's, & the Falls of Ohio Stations, from the commencement of hostilities to the termination in 1783.

William Cradlebaugh recounted a circumstance, [as] Col. Clark who arrived in the country at about the same **(7)** time to attach Martin to his regiment, or at least to command his services continually. That early in the spring of 1778, the Indians came to Boonesborough & stole a portion of the inhabitants' horses, & returned for their towns north of the Ohio. The consequence was Capt. John Martin with a few volunteers pursued & came upon them before day light, upon the buffalo road where the town of Washington [Ky.] now stands. Discovered the encampment under the obscurity of the night. They placed themselves under the cover of the cane, under a general agreement that no man should fire until the Indians commenced their march in the morning. Contrary to the understanding & expectation, one of the savages [woke? LCD] about daylight & walked past the sentinel smoking a pipe, without weapons of offense or defence. Joseph Drake, the last in the line, fearful of discovery, raised his rife & in a moment a ball passed **(8)** through the head of the Indian, he leaping up some height, falling in the buffalo road where he [was] walking, upon his face.

In a few minutes afterwards the Shawnoe warriors ran up until they saw the body of their kicking warrior in the agonies of death, which brought their foreman in front of Martin, the trigger of his gun being previously set he brought to bear upon the enemy, at about five paces apart the Indian & himself firing simultaneously, both shots taking effect – Martin picking up his adversary's gun before the smoke had left the tuch-hole; this circumstance being called afterwards by the inhabitants Martin's Shawnee duel.

[Martin was shot in the left shoulder. Martin ran upon the Indian who, wounded, as blood indicated, & dropping his gun, ran off with the others, got the Indian plunder in budgets. Martin had about 18 men? LCD.]

On the 1st of May 1779, Capt. Martin placed or **(9)** rather were pressed into the service, four horses appraised at 101 [pounds] by Col John Bowman, which horses were stolen by the Indians & never reclaimed.

Capt. John Martin died 28th April 1821, aged 85, in Lincoln County, Kentucky.

Jesse Hodges deposes that in the spring of 1778, four horses placed in the service by Capt. John Martin were stole by the Indians & never reclaimed.

The [Land] Commissioners were sitting at Falls of Ohio on 20 Nov. 1779, for adjusting disputed titles to the Kentucky lands. [Those] present [were] Stephen Trigg, Edmund Lyne & James Barbour.

"When Martin this day claimed a settlement & pre-emption to a tract of land lying on the South fork of Licking Creek, on the south side thereof, about five miles from Riddle's Station, with the letters JM on a tree at a small spring, by improving the same & raising a crop of corn in the year 1775 & residing in the country since. **(10)** Martin's right to a settlement of four hundred acres including the said improvement & the pre-emption of one thousand acres adjoining, & that a certificate issue accordingly."

[Depositions]

The affidavit of Major Joseph Kennedy, of Madison County, Kentucky, aged 75, saith he came to Kentucky on the first of April 1776 [1775], and in January or February 1777, the Indians commenced hostilities at Boonesborough by killing one man & wounding another, which induced us to take refuge at the station. Joseph Kennedy went to said Station for the first time, & then & there became acquainted with Capt. John Martin. We were enrolled under the command of Capt. Daniel Boone in January or February 1777, & engaged in the defence of the infant settlements & stations there in the country against the hostile savages with which we were infested from the different Indian tribes.

(11) Signed & sworn to on the 22nd of January 1835, before George Alcorn, Justice of the Peace for ____ County, Kentucky.

The affidavit of Major Bland W. Ballard of Shelby County, Ky., aged 76 years, taken on 31 August 1835 before James Barnett, Justice of the Peace, of Shelby County, saith that in the year 1779, he became acquainted with Captain John Martin at Boonesboro & was attached at that time to Capt. John Martin's company & immediately under his command as a captain until I was placed at other Forts or stations, that he knew Martin from first acquaintance until the termination of the Revolutionary War.

(12) In the winter of 1779 or early '80, Capt. John Martin with others erected a Station at or near his first settlement in the country, on the waters of Licking, known by the name of Martin's Station. In the summer of 1780, Col. Bird & a portion of Indian allies captured said station & another called Ruddle's. And in 1780, Col. George Rogers Clark & I, said Kennedy, was on said expedition, & Capt. John Martin was on the same. I saw Martin at the Blue Licks in August 1782, helping to bury the dead. In said year George R. Clark commanded an army against the Shawny Indians & Capt. John Martin on same campaign in command of his company.

After my first acquaintance with Capt. John Martin, he was

located at other Forts or Stations from those I was placed in. Capt. J. Martin, so far as I know or believe, continued an active & usefull officer until the end of the Revolutionary War, distinguished for his enterprise & gallantry.

(13) The affidavit of Gen. Simon Kenton, formerly one of the inhabitants of Kentucky, and now of the state of Ohio, Logan County, aged 79 years saith he came to Kentucky in 1775. When I arrived in Kentucky, I became acquainted with Capt. John Martin, the founder of a station of his name. Capt. **(14)** John Martin together with myself and a few others were continually, after the declaration of war 1776, in the protection & defence of the country until the termination of the Revolutionary War with Great Britain, under the immediate command of Colonel or General George R. Clark, & formed a portion of Clark's North Western regiment.

I say with the utmost confidence that no man or officer of his grade rendered more important or signal services in the west during the Revolutionary contest against the Western Indians than Capt. John Martin did.

Sworn to before James Crews & John R Parkerson on 9th April 1834, Logan County, Ohio.

The affidavit of Col. Daniel Trabue of Adair County, Ky., taken in open court, now 75 years old, saith he came to Kentucky in February or March 1778, & at that time was attached & belonged to Col. George R. Clark's north western **(15)** regiment. Upon my arrival in the western country became acquainted with Capt. John Martin who was engaged in the service as a captain under Col. George Rogers Clark & formed a part of his northwestern regiment. Capt. John Martin continued an active & useful officer during the years 1778, 1779, & 1780, he being stationed at Logan's, Boonesborough, Harrod's & a part of said years at the Falls of Ohio station.

That in the fall of 1778, information was brought to Logan's Station by William Patten that Boonesboro was taken & all the inhabitants massacred, which report at that time was believed, the consequence was that great dismay and alarm prevailed. Capt. Benjamin Logan & the inhabitants of the Fort prevailed on Capt. John Martin to go to Holston for men to maintain the Fort & country. Martin performed the same unaccompanied by soldiers or any individuals. [He] returned immediately bringing 100 or 200 soldiers & their officers with them, which was **(16)** of great indispensable importance at that period of difficulty & distress in the country, amongst whom was Capt. Adams & company.

I know these facts most certainly, for I now have the original Journal or Book before me where I recorded these circumstances just related. The expedition of Martin was executed at a hazard and difficulty that no man in the station was willing to encounter but himself. It was at the greatest possible peril that he performed the enterprise.

The Southern Indians that were at the siege of Boonesboro were at the time on their return immediately upon a considerable portion of Martin's rout to Holston. I was, during Capt. Martin's trip to Holston, stationed at Logan's Station by Col. George R. Clark & in a short time a portion of the soldiers on Holston returned. I issued provisions to them for that purpose & Capt. John Martin continued in his duties [as] **(17)** officer in the western country til the final termination of the Revolutionary War.

Benjamin Briggs of Lincoln County, Ky., 70 years old, states that he became acquainted with the late John Martin at Logan's Station in 1778, & continued to be well acquainted with him up to the time of his death. He saw him very frequently at Logan's Station, Harrodsburg, at Boonesboro, & knew him from that period until his death, he having died in Lincoln County within a few miles of the residence of this affiant. He was famous with the early settlers for **(18)** his speed in running, & his skill as a marksman, & his bravery as an officer. No call was ever made upon him that he was not prompt & ready to oblige. No man of his day rendered more valuable or signal services to the country than Capt. Martin did. [He] was at the taking of Kasksaias & Vincennes under Colonel or Geneneral George R. Clark in the year 1778 or 1779, but in what character he aided this deponent does not know as he was not himself present, but many of his neighbors & acquaintances were upon that campaign. He states further that in the year 1782, Capt. Martin commanded a company in the expedition led by Gen. George R. Clark against the Pickaway Towns. This affiant was himself upon that expedition, though attached to a different company.

(19) Given under my hand at Stanford [Ky.], 27th May 1833 – sworn to before John E. Weight, Justice of the Peace for Lincoln County, Ky., 16 Jan. 1834. Signed – Benj. Briggs.

Affidavit of Abraham Estess of Lincoln County, Ky., aged 75 years, states that he came to Kentucky in 1780 and continued to live in the neighboring stations in the capacity of guard, became acquainted with Captain John Martin in 1781.

(20) I say with utmost confidence that Capt. John Martin did as much, if not more than any other officer in bringing about that happy event of Liberty, Independence, & an exemption from the tomahawk & scalping knife. Sworn to 3 Oct. 1833.

The affidavit of Jesse Hodges of Madison County, Ky., near

Boonesboro where he has lived since 1777, aged 75 years. Saith he came to Boonesboro in 1777, then an infant settlement of Kentucky, in company with a corps of men for the purpose of defending the settlement against the assaults of tribes of Indians. **(21)** That in spring of 1778 the Indians came to Boonesboro & stole horses & Captain Martin & a few others pursued the Indians and overtook them at or near where the town of Washington [Ky.] now stands. Martin & one of the savages exchanged shots simultaneously at a few paces apart, both taking effect, Martin picking up the rifle of his enemy before the smoke left. Martin I know was badly wounded – I dressed [his wound: LCD] many times before his recovery.

A short time after in the spring of 1778, I believe from my best recollection, there was taken from the public service four horses **(22)** by the Indians which were placed in the service by Capt. John Martin, one of which name being "Bull" which together with others brought the buffalo meat & provisions to the station that we lived in. John Martin continued an active officer, distinguished for his gallantry, enterprise & bravery. Sworn to by J. Hodges, 25 January 1835, before Elkanah Bush, Justice of the Peace.

Martin [was] in Western Pennsylvania where he had a sister married & settled, & there heard about Kentucky, a fine country as represented by the accounts of the Long hunters & that any one was entitled **(23)** to a settlement right who would make a crop of corn. He joined Capt. John Hinkston, John Haggin, Samuel McMillen, Lilas Fain, Michael Stoner, Oswald Townsend, & others, came down the Ohio. This was in 1774 & were arrested by the war of the Shawnees, tarried at some point until Feb. 1775 when they reached Kentucky. Came up Licking [River] & commenced a settlement subsequently known at Hinkston's station, a mile below the mouth of Townsend. In a few days thereafter Martin left alone & went up Licking [River] & up Stoner on South Licking & made a settlement where his Station was subsequently located & there raised corn that year.

Sometime after corn was gathered, one day alone he discovered a large party of Indians, fled to Hinkston's, gave notice that Indians were in the country. Hinkston & the men with Martin pursued the Indians but soon abandoned the pursuit (likely these Indians would have been the same who attacked McClellan's &c – LCD).

He was at Boonesboro **(24)** in March 1780, when Col. Callaway was killed, and aided to bring in Callaway's dead body, & Pemberton Rollins, who was mortally wounded. He was out in pursuit of the Indians who captured Montgomery's Station & the Montgomery family in the Spring of 1781, & that Ben. Logan was some distance behind. Martin was engaged with his company that year, 1781, in making pirogues where Frankfort now is, for the use of Gen. Clark's intended expedition against Detroit.

He was six feet high, heavily formed, fair skin, blue eyes, & blue [sic] hair: He was (as some of notes will show – LCD) a Captain on Logan's Expedition of 1786. In 1760 he was one of the thousand men furnished by the Province of New York for the Northern frontier – was a grenadier – fought three days & all were much blackened with smoke & powder [at Ticonderoga? LCD].

12C5– 5(13) John L. Martin letter, Lincoln County, Ky., Sept. 8, 1852
Handwriting is blurred, and ink has bled through from the reverse side.

I am a native of Kentucky, being born in (I believe) Fincastle county, Virginia on the 28th of April 1786 (before the separation and location of the state of Kentucky) upon the Hanging Fork of Dick's River five miles west of Stanford and continued to reside in Kentucky until the death of my father on April 28, 1821.

(1) My ancestor Capt. John Martin was born and raised in Orange County, N.Y. near the Citty Goshen, was a soldier, a provisional grenadier for the king of Great Britain.

That my ancestor came to the western Country of Kentucky from Pennsylvania in the fall and winter of 1774 with Col. John Hinkston, and forty or fifty pioneer immigrants (viz) Michael Stoner, Samuel McMillian, Silas Train, Ozwell Townsend, John Woods, Michael Hogg, David Wilson, John, Samuel and Humphrey Lyons, John Haggin, Isaac Ruddle, and others. Stopped one month or more.

(2) The motives of those pioneer fathers in encountering dangers, captivity and more than probably death by conflagration at the stake, was to get a part of those luxurious fruitful lands described by Boone, Finley, ____, Scaggs, the two latter the long hunters from seventy two, up to seventy five [1772 – 1775]/ *Information on Hinkston's Station here is mostly illegible, as are several of the following pages.*

5(7) Siege of Boonesborough

5(9) Horse killed outside the fort by Indians

5(13) After the creation of this treasury warrant land law, a gentleman, whose name I have forgotten, came out from Virginia with a party of imigrants, bringing with him a trunk containing considerable amount of continentall money and original Treasury land Warrants. In a short time after his arival the virginian's trunk was missing and the suspicion fell upon a man by the name of Lytle and wife. And they were summarilly punished by whipping Lytle by linching and other wise exercizing terror and oppression upon his wife. Without getting from them any knowledge of the trunk or its contents and upon the establishment of the district County of Virginia, their holders in Danville, Ky., Litle and wife answered suits against Martin as commandant of his assistant spy ____ hunters for the station and Capt. Nathaniel Hart and recovered possibly nigh 300 pounds for the act.

At the time, without a solitary exception so far as my father ever knew or herd of in a short time, the Virginian stranger recovered his trunk, continental money and Treasury land warrants by hearing it was found in Col. John Holder's Negro quarters. If there ever was any ____ ____ between Lytle and wife and the Negroes, it was imposable to make it appere in a Court of Justice.

I will send in a few days the information of the prominent actors with there [sic] descendants where there is any left.

Accept my friendship,
John L. Martin

12C6-6(3) Major John L. Martin letter. *Ink has bled through from the other side. There are some errors in his account of the capture of the Boone and Callaway girls.*

Stanford [Ky.] Sept 27, 1851

My Dear Sir,

Yours of the 19th Inst is in my hands, and was received with great pleasure, having entertained douts of your health and existence from the appearance of the Historyical connection of the Pioneers of Western Country of Kentucky, Ohio and Tennessee &c, a work in which I feal a two fold interest (viz) the love of truth, and the reliving of the memory of a venerated father.

A man by the name of Harris mortally wounded during the siege of Logan's Station and whom died for a trust of land entered in the name of said Harris within six miles of said Station was ultimately sold for the taxation due thereon and William Logan, the son of the Colonel, became the purchaser.

Col. Benjamin Logan required no commendation and falsehoods or misstatements to the then inhabitants of the Country, or those that came at a subsequent time. He was befitted by nature for a way ____ in a wilderness, subjected to most frequently the covert attacks of the Northern and Southern Savages. He was a sober, discreet man of firmness and decision, and where he acted, he was most frequently successful. And as before indicated it was not his way to ellivate by contrast especially at the expense of truth. Col. Logan was ever, and ought to be, the pioneer of his own poision [position?] in relation to Kentucky and its early History.

When H. Marshall 's History of Kentucky and its settlement, defense and difficulties was maid out and published, William Logan, the son of Col. Benjamin **(1)** was the presiding Judge of the Court of Appeal of the Commonwealth of Kentucky. Previously and at the time the historian, H. Marshall, had pending a land suit or suits as assignee of Patty Harris for twenty four thousand acres of land lying in Bourbon County of the first quallaty in the State, every one of which he removed by the decision of the appellate Court agreeable to the original survey of a prior tract.

I wrote to Marshall [in] spring of 1832. Since the reception of your letter I have ___ of Bob Whitley who states that Vardaman and William Whitley are both dead and that Sollomon Whitley may still live, and William McKinley is living near Fulton, Missouri and Estess. McCormack still lives,

(2) That my father was at Boonesborough when the Callaway and Boon girls were taken prisoner in '76. They had gawn [gone] over the river to the north side in a canoe to collect wild roses growing on the bank or clifts of the stream and were captured by the indians who ware laying in ambush Untill the girls by there near approach had Neither the power to ___ away from danger or calling out for assistance. And they ware [Draper has over-written: forced] imediately into forests and cainbrakes. As soon as known in the station, I believe some eight strong active men volunteered in pursuit of the Indians. Daniel Boon was one of the party and evinced more excitement and agitation than ever manifested on any previous occasion of danger and difficulty knot [not] even knowing when in the act of starting that he was without his hat or cap untill called to by his friend.

The pursuit was prompt and vigerously continued untill they retook the girls on the same evening [it was three days later] in the campain on undelating lands between Kentucky river and Stoners or Hinkston fork of Licking, wether six or eight miles of the point where my ancestor raised his corne in 1775 and where his station was founded at a subsequent time.

My father was in Boonsborough during the long Siege by the savages. I could account many minor individual actions and incidents transpiring during the Siege. In the general Historys previously published so far as I have looked into them they are substantially true.
It is painfull to recount disappointment and want of success in any miscarriages that may of befallen us whether well founded or otherwise.

I have failled for the want of the means of progression by the faithlessness of an agent that received and kept from my knowlidge of the same **(3)** the means of preperation and success in the landed Suits and contests ... out of which all the ills of my life have flown.

Be pleased to accept my good wishes for your happiness and prosperity in every relation of life.

I bid you god speede

Respectfully yours, friend and Humble Servant

John L Martin

excuse the imperfect Scrall, and let me hear from you; my helth is not good and it would give me pleasure to shake your hand once more.

12C8-8(1) John Martin's Company Payroll for 20 April–May 27, 1781, 37 days. John Martin, Captain. Patt Harrigan, Lieutenant. David Adams, Ensign. Spies: Thos. Gilman, Stephen Huston.

New ____s: David Smith, Sgt. Major

Number of Privaturs

Wm. Stephens, Benj. Drake, Jno. Stapleton, Saml. Wilson, Jno. Jamison, Thos. Moon, Jno. Hardin, Geo. Hartt, Richd. Scaggs, Jos. Cartman, Jno. McEwen, Jno. Curd, Isaac Devine, Henry Boute[?], Ammaziah Vardiman, Jno. Vo__, Jno. Lee, Thos. McNeal, Lewis Rose, Jas. Harbison, Hugh Montgomery, Geo. Smith, Jno. Pringle, Jas. Alley, Thos. Stephenson, Jno. Ward, Jno. Simpson, Danl. Brown, Jacob Bushon, Danl. Hudg__, Wm. Hey__, Richd. Pennate, Rody Stafford, Leonard Graves, Thos. Davis, Jno. Bushon, Patt Carmichael, Edwd. Cather, Thos. Kerr, Anthony Lackey, Matt Robertson, Andrew Steele

This day came before me Jno. Martin, Capt. and was duly Sworn according to Law that the above List is a true Payroll.
Stephen Trigg
May 26th 1781

This tour of duty was accomplished within ___ ___ and 37 days & the most of them within 37 days

This transcript is perfect as a ___ ___ of the original Payroll will permit ___a day ___ ___ John L. Martin   Oct. 14th 1852.

Payroll of John Martin, Captain, and David Smith, Sgt. Major,

Lincoln County from 21 April to 27 May 1781.

"I do certify the above company, John Martin, Captain, were ordered upon duty that they carried out this tour.

       Stephen Trigg (signature)

Payroll of John Martin, April-May 1781. 12C8(1)

12C9 -10(11) Notes taken in the Fall of 1844 of Col. James Davidson, then State Treasurer of Kentucky, at Frankfort, Kentucky.

 Col. Logan's Expedition, Campaign of 1780

10(11) News came that an Indian party had been committing depredations, horse-sealing, or maybe killing some of the people. Logan and his men were desired to meet at a given place several miles off at daylight next morning. The dance would break up, men return home, put their rifles in order, run bullets, prepare provisions, and long before day be far on the way. Such, says Col. Davidson, frequently happened.

 Col. Davidson is quite sure that Gen. Logan did not, as Dr. Ben

Logan thinks, pursue the Indians who killed Robert McClure & chased Nathaniel Logan; that Nat. Logan then had no family captured, & probably had no family then. Nat. Logan was at Kings Mountain battle.

12C13-13(3) *The following pages are from Draper's small notebooks with two, three, or four pages on one microfilm page. Sequence is difficult to determine. More than one interview may appear on a page.*

LCD note: For brief Sketch of Col. Casey, see <u>Collins' Kentucky</u>, p. 331. For attack on Montgomery's Station, <u>Collins' Ky.</u> 405-7.

Col. Wm. Casey, of Kentucky
From his daughter Mrs. Ann Montgomery, Columbia, Ky., 1844.

Col. Wm. Casey died in Adair County, Ky., Dec. 1, 1816 in his 61st year. He settled Casey's station, near Russell's Creek, in 1789. He first engaged in public service at 14 years of age.

William Montgomery, Sr.'s Station was on Hanging Fork, Lincoln County [Ky.] 12 miles from Logan's Station. There were four families living there, viz. William. Montgomery Sr., his sons William Montgomery, Jr., John Montgomery, & his son-in-law Joseph Russell.

The elder Mrs. Montgomery went to Logan's Station the day before the attack to visit her daughter, Mrs. Ben. Logan. It was early in the morning. A Negro was carrying in a log of wood on his shoulder into William Montgomery, Sr.'s [cabin], when he was shot down as he entered the door. William Montgomery, Sr. then jumped out of bed & ran out of the door, and was shot down in the yard. Then his daughter Jane (then 18, & afterwards Mrs. Col. William Casey) barred the door. The Indians knocked with their war clubs and tomahawks, & Elizabeth Montgomery, then 16, called to her sister Jane to bring her brother's gun. There really was none, & it was from alarm & confusion that she did so. But the effect was fortunate, **(1)** for the Indians hearing the call for a gun, decamped. Elizabeth, in her alarm wanted to go out of the door, but Jane would not permit her to do so, & the frightened girl climbed out of the wooden chimney, half built up, & ran.

Elizabeth Montgomery, after being chased to the cabin & the Indians went back, left her hiding place & ran to a settlement or station 3 miles off, & gave the alarm. The Indians, seeing her, pursued. She ran into an unoccupied cabin without a door or even chinking between the logs. From some unaccountable course, the Indians did not prosecute the chase, but left the fair fugitive in quiet & undisputed possession of her pail [sic] place of refuge – whence she escaped.

In the house of William Montgomery, Sr., were several small children, & they implored their sister Jane not to go & leave them. Her heroism saved them.

John Montgomery (son of William, Sr.) was killed in his cabin & his wife **(2)** taken prisoner. Joseph Russell (son-in-law of William Montgomery, Sr.) himself escaped, while his wife & four children were captured.

William Montgomery, Jr., [whose cabin was near his father's – LCD] shot out of the port-hole of his cabin & killed one Indian dead & wounded another. A second shot killed another. The Indians now began to talk angrily among themselves, & gathered up their wounded Indians & prisoners & decamped.

During the fray, a Negro woman was pursued & knocked down, & her head scalped all over. Towards evening of that day, she was found by Jane Montgomery, brought in, & finally recovered.

The news was thence [brought] **(3)** to Logan's [Station] for aid to pursue. Benjamin Logan & party went in pursuit some 20 miles. When the prisoners saw the whites coming they (the prisoners) jumped behind trees to prevent being shot by their friends. The Indians seized Flora Russell, aged 12 years, daughter of Joseph Russell, tomahawked and scalped her. She had a long, flowing head of hair, which was doubtless a temptation to those who killed her. The Indians then ran off & the captives were all rescued. They represented that the Indians had taken their wounded companion, shot by William Montgomery, Jr., a little distance off the trail into a thicket, & there left him dead, the prisoners thought.

All returned to Montgomery's Station that night. It had been a day of mournful, toilsome, yet successful events.

Gen. Ben Logan's wife was Ann Montgomery, daughter of William Montgomery, Sr.; Alexander Montgomery, who was killed when Kenton was taken in 1778, was a son of William Montgomery, Sr.

12C14-14(7) Interview with Thomas Stotts of Adair County, Ky., in 1844, aged 65. Related to Col. Casey.

When Casey was in Casey's Station, a party of Indians [had] been doing mischief. Col. James Harrod happening there at the time, joined Casey & others & went in pursuit. Henry Renix, afterwards Colonel from Barren [County, Ky.] in the war of 1812, was along. Discovered the Indian camp on waters of Cumberland & delayed attacking till just before day – divided the men, Col. Casey commanded one party, & Col. Harrod the other party. One [Henry - LCD] Cook approached the camp. There was but a single Indian at the camp, & he cooking. Fired & wounded him. The Indian ran towards Col. Casey & Renix, near him, seeing the Indian coming, shot & killed him. Then returned. Were bothered by the Indians that day, but did not attack them.

Interview with Robert Fletcher, 78 yrs. Old [in] Feb. 1844, now of Adair County, Ky.

Came to Adair County in Nov., 1792. Col. Casey had settled his new station the Spring before.

Col. Casey was at the Point [Pleasant]. He & some others were ordered out some days after the fight. [They] were fired on & Casey wounded in his right side. (2) The bullet first past [sic] through a small pone of bread in his shot pouch, else he would have been killed.

Col. John Dickinson died soon after the close of the Revolution. His old Fort was on Cow Pasture River about 12 miles south of the Warm Springs.

Col. William Casey & family removed to Kentucky in December 1779, & camped that winter near where McKinney's station was subsequently located.

(3) Interview with William Dudley, now [age] 84, 9 October 1844.

Was in Cleveland's regiment at King's Mountain. The nine tories were hung in the night, towards day by firelight, a day or two after the battle. Don't know who got Ferguson's sword, nor to whom DePeyster surrendered. Believes Campbell did well & fought bravely. Cleveland's regiment was never attacked with the British bayonet. Always understood Campbell was brave.

John Tucker had a station 3 miles southeast of Casey's Old Station, abandoned it & went to Casey's & was about settling in the new place. Himself and wife started on foot, were fired upon & Mrs. Tucker killed on the spot. Tucker received 3 wounds in the body & yet ran for the Station, a quarter of a mile off, & was overtaken just before he reached it – killed him & took his scalp. The Indians were a small party who had been out on a hunt, & doubtless intended stealing horses. Failing there, killed Tucker & wife. Tucker was a Methodist preacher. This was in the spring of 1793.

Butler's Station was within a quarter of a mile of old Station, a skirt of woods between. William Butler, the father, part Indian, & his son John was particularly active & brave. William was with [William] Whitley at Nickojack.

Casey's old Station was located at "the old trading Spring," about 4 miles north of the present Columbia. Lived in this about 3 years, then located his ___ Station, near Butler's Fork of Russell's Creek, about 4 miles southwest of Columbia.

(4) 1776 – Wolf Hills. There were 48 men divided into 2 parties sent out – one half to go to mill with a grist; the other half under John Casey (the father of William) to gather flax about 2 miles from the fort, probably Black's.

Mrs. Casey & her party went out from Black's. William Casey was one. [They?] surrounded the Indian camp. At day-break, an Indian arose & gave a squawk like a goose. With that, the whites fired & all the Indians were killed, save one. Some in the river. Thinks there were 21 Indians. Harold was along.

Don't recollect about the Big Island battle.

Col. Casey was with his brother-in-law Logan on the Blue Lick campaign. Logan on one occasion was out scouting…not far from his Station when shot by an Indian & wounded in the arm.

When he went to Washington County, Virginia for aid, he went it in 4 days & nights – got 75 men, perhaps Daniel Trabue…

Was always with a loaded gun. The Indians would make the bullets rattle all around. One got out of bullets & had to run to the others to get a handful.

During the flight, Nancy's clothes caught in the bushes (this was before she had overtaken her brother & Harold.) She was thrown & an Indian came near enough grinning to have tomahawked her, when Wm. Casey, whose gun was empty, cursed the Indian, threatening to blow his brains out, when the Indian jumped to a tree & escaped. And Casey, as he ran, soon loaded his gun. This fight continued 2 miles & when Casey was all blackened with powder.

Nancy Casey, afterwards Mrs. Robert Fletcher, died in Adair County [Ky.] 6th October 1836, age 74.

Harold has passed away.

(5) At the Treaty of '77, an Indian saw & spoke of Nancy, & said he was the one who had the chance of killing her in the chase, but saved her, wishing, from her beautiful flowing hair, to make her a waiting maid for the Cherokee queen.

The Indians saw the two parties when they went from the fort & the Indians also divided & pursued each party. The mill party were fired on, and one Piper had one of his little fingers shot off. Henry Carswell was killed; the others escaped with the loss of the horses & grist.

The spies came and found where the Indians had camped on Holston...

(6) *omitted*

(7) Indians fired on & killed Christopher Mungle dead. All in the field jumped the fence & endeavored to escape. John Casey & his wife hid in the bushes. Another Blackburn, a lame man, was shot in the hip, overtaken, kicked down & scalped, & as the Indians returned from the pursuit, they scalped him again. Afterwards [he was] brought in & it was 9 days before he spoke. Finally recovered.

12C15 General James Ray – Original Notes by Mann Butler taken from his conversations in 1833. Three letters from Gen. Ray's son, Dr. John Ray, Madisonville, Ky., in 1843 & 1845 to L. Draper.

12C16-16(1-16) Dr. John Ray letter, Madisonville, Ky., 20th Feby., 1843

Dr Sir

In compliance with your request, I subjoin the principal Historical facts of my father, most of which are quite familiar with me up to the present time. My father was a man of Stern integrity and all matters emanating from him was considered unexceptionable.

The late Gen. James Ray of Mercer County, Kentucky emigrated from the State of North Carrolina (county not known) to Kentucky in the fall of 1775, was at that time about 14 years of age. He had a mother, a step Father, and two Brothers (all minors). His Mother was then married to Col. Hugh McGary.

They set out from North Carolina in company with Col. Daniel Boon and came to Kentucky together, [with] Col. Boon & Col. McGary as their guide & head. Gen. Ray's Mother came in company with the first white women that ever crossed the Mountains to the West. I think there ware some twenty or thirty families in the company. After coming through the Wilderness and arriving in the Kentucky Valleys, the Company divided. Col. Boon headed his particular party and went on and settled by a place in Kentucky called Boonsborough and built a Station or fortification. And Col. McGary pressed on with his particular party to a place now the City of Harrodsburg. Here they erected a temporary fortification in case of invasion.

(1) Everyone seemed to enjoy himself with a great deal of pleasure & happiness. Ample reward seemed to be promised for them in the vast richness of soil. They raised some crop the next season after their arrival in the Country, and occasionally an immigrant would arrive &

station with them, & in this way a little strength accumulated.

From the time of their arrival in the Country up to 6th March 1777, they had remained unmolested; they had not seen a foe in the yellow man. They ware entirely ungarded in all their intercourses & transactions, for they did not ever dream of Indians being in the Country. Every Man was at his diffarant station making his improvements Till the above Memorable 6th March '77. Gen. Ray and his Brother William, both boys then perhaps 16 and 18 years old, a young man 22 or 23 years of age and rather an elderly man name not recollected Ware all four at work clearing ground and boiling sugar water at their camp in the vicinity of their work.

About 12 O'clock, Gen. Ray & his brother, feeling a little tired, went to their camp to get some water & to rest themselves. They were lying down and after lying thare a little while, some noise was heard like moving animals they could not account for, yet it did not seem to excite them. But as it became more plain they cast a look in the direction from which it seemed to emanate – when to their great surprise they discovered a party of 47 picked or selected Shawnee Warriors running in file **(2)** within a few yards of them.

There was at that time Gen. Ray, his brother William, & the young man at the camp. They all sprang to their feet. William Ray had his Gun at the camp with him. Gen. Ray had left his Gun whare he had been at work. The young man I think was not a gunner & had not a gun at the place. When springing to their feet the General pointed out a course for his Brother & the young man to run, & he struck for the clearing to try and get his Gun left thare. But the Indians wishing to take him prisoner, a part of them ran heading him and succeeded in gitting between him and his gun. Seeing ___ he gave up a further effort to get his Gun and turned his course the way which he had directed William & the young man to run. He soon overtook William Ray but the young man was not with him. He and William then ran together for some distance. But William, being a fleshy young man & having a heavy Rifle to carry, could not make the speed that was necessary. He was not active & was not an expert runner. The General said that he felt every presence of mind about him, and being sensible that his Brother would soon be taken or shot, he told him as they ran together to throw down his arms and give himself up, that by doing so he would fare better. This it appears he was determined he would not do, but as the Indians approached pretty near him, he turned around and aimed to shoot them. An Indian seeming to anticipate him, fired at William, and at the crack of the gun, William fell. Gen. Ray then having **(3)** remained with his Brother until he could be of no further service to him made his own desperate effort to effect his own escape. He could himself have run much farther whilst with his Brother, but he could not brook the idea of leaving him disabled.

As soon as his Brother fell, He then set out at his full speed and in running something near a mile, he found that his leather leggings (which was common for all to wear in them days) was cramping his knees to such a degree that he found that if he could not get relieved, that the Indians must soon take him. He thought of this expedient as he ran, he drew his Butcher Knife and in descending a steep hill, he sprang behind a large tree and with 2 or 3 swipes with his knife, he cut close his leggings which was laced up with a strop and tore them both off.

While he was thus consealed, the Indians, some ten or fifteen, passed on ahead of him and fired off their guns in a tree top that lay near him, supposing that he must certainly be thare. About the time those guns ware fired he became extricated from his leggins. He sprang forward from his ambuscade. They then commenced firing at him as he ran, and throwing their war clubs, making a desperate effort to slay him. He soon out ran them **(4)** so far that they finally gave up the chase and turned back. After he found they had given up pursuit, he turned back himself, and followed on till he got back inside of the camp again & wished to ascertain if he could, what disposition they ware making of his Brother. He staid lurking about for some time, but could not see what they ware doing with him.

After finding that he could derive no satisfaction in relation to his Brother's fate, he now set out with all speed to the Fort at Harrodsburg, distant about four miles, which place he reached a little before night. The alarm was then sent out to all the men belonging to the fort who ware improving [building cabins, etc.] in various places. They ware all got in that night and the fort strengthened as well as they could for one night.

The next morning at dawn of day an Out House [a cabin outside the fort] situated a quarter of a mile from the Fort which contained some flax which they had raised the year before, was set on fire. This was done in order to draw the men out of the fort. This was Indian cunning, which the whites at that day had but little conception of. It had the desired effect – a portion of men spring out, but not without thur guns. They ran on toward the fire. The Indians ware lying in ambush on each side of the path leading from the Fort to the burning cabbin. Upon the approach of the whites, the Indians fired. The whites rather fell back a little to the cover of large Timber, made a stand and commenced the warfare. This firing soon drew from the fort. All its Male Strength made a stand, fought the Savages with desperation. The efforts of the whites ultimately prevailed, kept the ground and compelled the Indians to retreat with a loss of 5 or 6 of their number killed on the ground. Number of wounded not known. One of the Indians killed in this Battle had on the Buckskin hunting shirt which their victim William Ray had on when they [killed him].

(5) They did not intend to kill but to take them prisoner. By taking them, the necessary information could have been acquired to have enabled to take the fort almost without an occasion to fire a gun [had] Gen. Ray had not had the good luck to have made his escape.

Wretched inhabitants of the country would have been cut to pieces almost without opposition. And this occurrence would have deterred immigrants to the West for a Series of Years. I look upon this his successful effort to save the inhabitants in the forts an interposition of Divine Providence.

The men belonging to the Fort marched out next day after the fight at Harrodsburg, to the camp whare they ware routed from two days before. They found William Ray at the camp, striped [stripped], tomahawked, & scalped. They buried him near the spot whare he was killed.

The Indians seemed to lurk about for a day, making no other assaults, and left for their Country. As it was not long before they ware visited again by a more numerous train, attacking their fort, killing whenever they could kitch [catch] a man exposed, and killing up what little stock they had on hand. All the grain that was made in the Country the first year after Indian depridations commenced, was made while the labourers ware strongly guarded whilst at work, Indians making frequent assaults on the Forts. They at length came to the conclusion, that they could not storm the Fort and resolved on conquering the inmates by starvation. This strategy I think was commenced in the early part of the Summer (6) 1780.

There arrived a strong force from their country North of the Ohio River. Built an extension encampment within a quarter of a mile of the Fort. At this encampment they remained for the term of six or eight months with daily firing on the Fort so that no person could in safety venture out. This in truth seemed like subduing by starvation. It was soon settled that they could not long subsist in this way.

Gen. Ray, who was the most expert and celebrated hunter belonging to the Fort, proposed an expedient for relief. He kept within the Fort a noble horse, active and powerful. That he should leave the fort at a dead hour in the night, between midnight and day. When let out at the fort gate, he would put the spurrs to the steed and ride with rapidity till he thought he was out of the reach of the Indians. He would then ride moderately until he would get some ten or twelve miles from the fort. He would then kill as much meat as his horse could with convenience carry, having his Bridle always hung to his arm whilst butchering his game. He would then sally up some three or four miles of the Fort and stop, keeping a sharp lookout until a little before daybreak. He would then sally up and when coming on the dangerous ground, which was just around the Fort, he would again spur his horse and come into the fort in a brisk lope. This was his practice to do twice a week, which amply furnished the Fort with meat. This service was continued to be performed by him as long as their perilous situation required it.

After he had been performing these kinds of services for some months alone, two other men, names unknown, proposed that they would perform that service a while, if he had no objection, stating that it seemed a hardship to burden him with all this service. He was willing if they ware [were], they accordingly set out.

(7) The General was then of necessity impelled to resume his former occupation in furnishing the inmates of the Fort with Meat, as had been his custom for the length of time until it was known that the savages had raised the siege. After this siege was raised there seemed to be at all times squads of Savages lurking in the country ready to shoot down the whites at all times when exposed. This made it necessary that they should be at all times upon their guard.

Not long after the above incidents, and not being so frequently annoyed, the men of the fort had ventured out and raised some small crops of corn. A Major Bowman had raised a small crop of corn some 4 miles from the Harrodsburg Fort, and cribbed it on the premises. Sometime after it had been cribbed, the corn was kneeded [needed] in the Fort. A party consisting of Gen. Ray, Major Bowman & others went thare to shell a portion of the corn. They, all the party, ware in the crib shelling. Ray & Bowman had just started in a race of shelling 100 years [ears] upon a kind of bet. They had their butcher knives fixed in a log or block in a way in which enabled them to shell very **(8)** fast. Whilst under the pressure of a hard race, the Indians had crept up, poked their gun through cracks of the crib and fired upon them, I think without effect. Each individual sprang to his feet and bolted out of the crib, taking positions, fired upon the enemy, kept the ground and whipped them.

After raising the siege at Harrodsburg Fort, many other stations and Forts ware beginning to be erected in various sections of the Country. The flow of emigration seemed to be perpetual, notwithstanding the peril & risk. McAfee's Station near Harrodsburg, Bryant's Station near Lexington and many others ware alternately attacked and annoyed by the Savages.

In the progress of events Bryant's Station was besieged by a very formidable body. A heavy fire was kept up for several days. It become very doubtful with the whites whether they would be able to sustain the fort, & despatched an express to the Harrodsburg Fort for assistance. Immediately a ____ was equipped for the relief of Bryant's Station. This force was pretty formidable, headed by some gallant spirits. Upon their arrival at Bryant's Station, the enemy had raised the Siege some 12 hours previous to their arrival.

It was now resolved that the Indians should be pursued. The Number of Indians Ware Computed at 400, Whilst the Whites only numbered about 200.

The Whites ware commanded by Colonels Todd & Trigg. They ware pursued, and fought the celebrated Blue Lick Battle in which the Savages Ware Victorious, cutting the white ranks to pieces.

In this tragedy Gen. Ray was an actor. **(9)** The Licking River was occupied by the Savages. The river at that time was very deep fording, the whites crossing the same place whare the Indians had crossed it. By the time the whites ware fully across the River, the Indians commenced fire upon the front. The Indians being placed in an eligible situation and doubling the whites in number, produced an appaling shock to the whites.

Gen. Ray commanded a Battalion in front. At the first fire of the Savages, Gen. Ray dismounted, having Rifle, took a position at a Tree and fired twice. The second fire was deliberately aimed at a certain large Indian in the act of running down his Bullit. He knew it was with the desired effect as the shot seemed to double him. After firing this second round the Indians ware perceivably advancing upon him, which caused him to take a glance at his own party. And to his astonishment, found them retreating with precipitation, & all in disorder, of course. His only alternative was then to retreat also. After commensing his retreat, he found a great number of Savages before him & between him and the ford of the River. Here was his perilous situation: It did not look like there was any possibility for him to escape through a crowd of the enemy. He had jumped off his horse at the first onset and let him go. He was persuing on his course toward the ford of River with many Indeans ahead of him. This induced him to think thare was no chance to him to escape under Heaven. He was persued behind by Savages and his rout before him full. In this hazardous condition there came running by him nearly at full speed a fine large Bay Mare having lost the saddle, and the Bridle lying over her **(10)** neck, seemed to be truly frightened. As she ran by him he made a desparate effort, caught his hand in her mane. Thus mounted he used his gun and bridle both in his left hand. With his right he drew from his belt a long knife and as he would pass the Indians who ware before him, he would brandish his knife to deter them. He literally rode over many of them before reaching the River. He was fired at by an Indian before reaching the river at so close a distance that powder burnt his face.

When arriving at the ford for the River, the scene appeared awful. The Indians tomahawking & butchering the whites at an awful rate. He plunged into the water in the midst of the slaughter, and passed through in safety.

After crossing the River he discovered that many of the Savages had passed before him and ware still persuing the whites. He had not reached far after recrossing the river till he over took Capt. William McBride who called to him and asked if he could help him. McBride said that he was run down and the Indians in close persuit. Ray replied that he would help him, told him to step to a log which laid near and get up behind him. He took McBride by the hand, who was nearly exhausted, and pulled him up behind him, carried him out of the reach of the enemy, put him down and directed him the course to travel.

In this battle many of the choisest [choicest] spirits of Kentucky perished. Colonels Todd & Trigg both fell together with many other brave officers and soldiers.

The next morning after the battle, whilst the whites and Indians ware still scattered in a confused situation, Gen. Ray, reconnoitering the forest for the purpose of trying to collect his men, spied an Indian on horse back coming meeting him. As soon as the **(11)** Indian discovered that he was a white man, wheeled his horse to the right, and dashed off with full speed. The General pursued him, soon came up with his sword drawn. On coming in reach, the General commenced striking at him, aiming to cut him in the neck. The Indian seemed to keep his eye cocked on the General's motion and as he would strike at the Indian, he would throw up the Muzzel of his gun, glansing the stroke of the sword over his head. He struck at him very often in the chase. The Indian still continued to parry off the stroke. At length the Indian ran himself in the middle of a company of the whites. When the General discovered the whites, said Boys this is my pet, take care of him.

Upon this the Indian discovered that he was surrounded by the whites, sprang off his horse and raised his gun in a shooting position. Said Gen. Ray, take care, boys, there is danger in him. He seemed to point his gun first at one and then at another, without firing. They began to think his gun was not loaded. At length he pointed his gun at a Major Gray who was sitting on his horse. Upon discovering this, Major Gray wheeled his horse round, turning his back to the Indian. The Indian fired & with effect. Gray fell a dead man. The indian was then despatched forthwith. Upon examining the Indian's gun, it was found that the General had cut it full of gashes with his sword.

Incidents in Relation to the Fort at Harrodsburg

In the progress of events, some of the men of the Fort ware clearing a Turnip patch a short distance from the Fort. They at length discovered that there ware Indians watching their movements. **(12)** [Sent a] messenger to the Fort, giving the intelligence of the locality of the Indians. A small force [came] out, Gen. Ray being one of the party. Came round on the rear of the Indians, covered their position, fired upon them, killed some 4 or 5 of the Indians. One of the Indians crossing a fence was fired upon by Gen. Ray whilst on the fence. He ran but a short distance till he was come up with in a dying condition. For this dexterity in a youth, the Commander of the party gave Gen. Ray the Indian's Gun whom he had killed.

Whilst everybody was strictly confined to the Fort, danger being apparently at hand at all times, some gentleman of the fort was induced to believe his Gun did not shoot correctly. So about noon day, he fixed himself a target about a hundred yards distant from the Fort gate against a large tree, and shot out of the Fort gate at his target. He had shot some 3 or 4 times. He had just fired again and was walking on to his target when Gen. Ray stepped up to the gate whare he shot from as soon as the gentleman arrived at the tree. The General hallooed to him to know whare his Ball had struck. The Gentleman then exposed his Body a little around the Tree and putting his finger to the bullet hole. At this instant, he was fired upon by an Indian in ambush, and shot mortally. Gen. Ray then having his gun in his hand immediately sallied out. Meeting the wounded man on the way, merely passing him and keeping his eye strictly on the place where he saw the smoke of the Indians gun rise. He discovered the position of the Indian, but was not yet far enough to make a sure fire. Having his gun in a shooting position and walking on, but before he could see enough of him to shoot at, he was fired upon by a platoon of guns, he thinks not less than two hundred, none of which hit him. He wheeled and ran toward the Fort.

(13) When he reached it they had closed the gate & shut him out. The Indians pursued him & commenced a heavy firing upon the Fort. The General was now in the most hopeless condition. He ran around to the opposite side of the Fort and hid behind a stump till the inmates of the Fort dug a hole under a house and took him in.

During their confinement in this Fort, the General one day

sauntering about, viewing passing events, espied an Indian crawling on his side with his gun, adjacent to the Fort. He discovered in an instant his object. The Indian had discovered a Lady washing at the Fort spring which was enclosed by a kind of temporary walk adjacent to the Fort. The General saying not a word to any person, stept back into the Fort, picked up his gun, and slyly advanced to an eligible position to intercept the design of the Savage and awaited till he approached within gun shot. He fired at him, and at the crack of the gun, the Indian turned over on his back and continued to throw up his arms and feet for some time, as if in the agonies of Death. The Indian's aim was to shoot the Lady at the spring. The Indian remained where he was killed till night, and was then removed by his Savage friends.

A little Dutchman was attached to this Fort whose name was Barney Stagney [Stagner]. Often used the expression that the Indians could not kill him, that they had often shot at him unsuccessfully. One day when the Indians ware poaring [pouring] a tremendous fire upon the Fort, Gen. Ray said to Barney, Now Barney, you say the Indians can't kill you. Suppose We hoist you on the top of the Fort now and see what will be the consequence. **(14)** Sometime after this, he sauntered out of the Fort for purpose. The Indians killed him and cut off his Head.

As time progressed the Country gradually strengthened so that they became able to carry the War into the enemy's country. Many Campaigns ware carried on to the Indian Country, [a] diversified effort, I think. The first campaign was commanded by Gen. Harmer, who fell and his army cut to pieces. [Harmer's Defeat was many years later.] Gen. Clark then conducted campaigns into that country. Gen. Ray [was] in every battle that was faught with the Miami Indians.

Took a hand in nearly all the fighting which took place in Kentucky. He was very often imployed in persuing the Indians that had murdered or stolen horses. He one day whilst in the field plowing received intelligence that the Indians had stolen some horses out of a neighborhood 4 or 5 miles distant. He started fourth [sic] in pursuit of them, leaving his horse hitched to the plow and did not return again for nine or ten days.

He was at all times active in the prosecution of the Indian war till its termination which lasted seven years. What was the most surprising, he never received the slightest wound during the whole of his adventures.

He again embarked in the late war in 1812, joined that portion commanded by Gen. Hopkins. Gen. Ray was then 60 years of age. Upon Gen. Hopkins finding him attached to the army, immediately gave a promotion to his first Major General. This Campaign was the last Military service of his life.

15 [He held] every grade of Military officer from Captain to Major to General. He enjoyed a seat in the Legislature Counsils of State for about 20 years.

The General was at all times in easy circumstances, but never was very wealthy. He did not seem to thirst for wealth. He always appeared to be well satisfied. He was truly a philanthropist, never appearing to be as well satisfied & happy as when performing acts of kindness to his fellow men. The string of his Door latch was never found pulled in. My own opinion is that he died without leaving any human being his enemy. The poor and oppressed always found his House [an] Asylum.

Whither he left behind him any written sketches of Pioneerings, I am not able to say, as I reside some __ hundred miles from his late residence, but am inclined to think he left none.

Gen. Ray's first wife was Amelia Yocum. By her he had two sons. She died in early life. His second wife was My Mother, Elizabeth Talbott, sister of the late __ Isham Talbott, late Senator in the Congress of the U.S. from Kentucky. My Mother died in 1810[?].

My father then Continued to live a Widower till his death. He died [in] his old family Mansion in the County of Mercer [in] May 1834, aged about 81 years. [LCD: 73 – if 14 when he came to Kentucky vide deposition.]

(16) Col. McGary was an intrepid officer, performed many essential services to the Country. In battle he was thought more daring than cautionary.

I pray you to accept of my thanks for notices you may take of my venerable Father – as a Pioneer. And to consider me a subscriber [of] your work.

    I am With Much Respect

                          Your Obedient Servant
                          John Ray

N. B. Send Our Post Master A Prospectus, I think I can obtain subscribers here.
Memo: For some reference to Gen. Ray, Maj. Harlan & Capt. Gordon, see Edmund Jennings' pension papers. LCD

12C22-22(2) Mrs. Ann Harrod, Declaration of Dec. 1842
Boyle County, Ky. *LCD handwriting.*

                        Mrs. Ann Harrod
On this 3d day of December 1842 personally appeared before me

a justice of the peace for said county, Mrs. Ann Harrod, a resident of said county & state, aged eighty six years, & at this time infirm & confined to her bed, and unable to attend in open court, who first being duly sworn according to law, doth on her oath make the following Declaration in order to obtain the benefit of the provisions made by the act of Congress passed July 4th 1836. That she is the widow of Colonel James Harrod, who was a captain in the Virginia militia in the year 1776.

In that capacity with a company of men [he] explored a part of the State of Kentucky on the waters of Salt River & Kentucky River in the year 1774, & at that time laid off a town & built four or five cabins on the ground where the now town of Harrodsburg is built. That in the month of July in that year his company had one man killed by the Indians at a large spring called Fountain Blue northwest of their town [LCD: nearly 3 miles] by the name of James Cowan [LCD: not Jared - Gen R. B. McAfee] which compelled them to retract back to Holston in Virginia, where many of them reside. Soon after he raised a volunteer militia company which was called into service by the Governor of Virginia for three months & marched with Col. Lewis to the Battle of the Point [Pleasant] at the mouth of the East Kanawha & performed this duty, as her husband often told her.

That he was honorably discharged. That in the spring of 1775, Harrod returned to Kentucky & erected, with the aid of the then Capt. McGary, a fort at that place, of which Capt. Harrod had the principal command. That this deponent moved to Kentucky with her husband, she being then married (1) to a Mr. James McDonald in the fall of the year 1775. That next year, 1776, her said husband was killed by the Indians, & she removed to Col. Logan's Fort.

James Harrod continued in the command of the Fort at Harrodsburg, & in the fall of the year 1779, her then husband, James Harrod, moved to her present residence, Harrod's Station, 6 miles above & south of Harrodsburg, at which place her said husband still commanded as captain.

In the summer of 1780 he commanded as Colonel...on Col. Benjamin Logan's Expedition against the Indians at Pickaway at the Big Miami.

That from the fall of 1775 until the close of the Revolutionary war in 1783, her said husband was in continual service & in nearly all the skirmishes & attacks made by the Indians around Harrodsburg, during all of which time he was in command as a Captain at the Fort in Harrodsburg. The fact of his being a captain will appear from the records in Richmond in Virginia, his old company book, & his commission which was given to a Mr. William H. Todd to procure the back pay of her husband & either filed in Richmond or in the Pension Office, Washington City. She further states that her husband was a captain & commissioned officer in constant service in the Virginia State Line from the date of his Commission until the close of the Revolutionary War, about which time he was promoted to a colonel's commission. She further declares that she was married to the said Capt. James Harrod on __ [blank] in the year 1778. Her said husband was killed or died in a hunting expedition up the Kentucky River in the fall of the yeare 1792, & he has not been heard of since, a part of his clothes being found afterwards in the river. That she had remained a widow ever since that period as will more fully appear by reference to the proof herewith annexed, except for about 4 months I was united to a man, but we were (2) regularly divorced & I was restored to my former name <u>Ann Harrod,</u> & have been known as the widow of James Harrod for the 38 years last past.

Ann Harrod

  Benjamin Briggs of Lincoln [County, Ky.] deposes [that he] personally knew Capt. James Harrod in the year 1778. He was then a captain in the Virginia State Line troops in the regiment commanded by Col. Abraham Bowman. He further declares he was present at Logan's Station, called St. Asaph's.

  In the year 1778, as he verily believes, Capt. James Harrod & Ann (then Mrs. McDonald) [were] married by Col. Robert Todd, Esquire, then a justice of the peace for the county of Kentucky &c. That Capt. James Harrod was the founder & first settler of Harrodsburg & commanded as a captain at Harrodsburg & its vicinity & was engaged in nearly all the battles with the Indians at Harrodsburg & until the close of the Revolution.

  Mrs. Elizabeth Thomas deposes that she was 78 years old on the 4th Sept. 1842. That she came to Kentucky in 1775 & removed to Harrodsburg in '76 & then became acquainted with Capt. James Harrod who commanded as captain in the Virginia State troops. She also knew Mrs. Ann McDonald whose husband was killed the same year ['76: LCD] at Drennon's Lick. The said Ann in the year '78 was married to James Harrod, who continued to command as a captain & was out in nearly all the Expeditions until the close of the Revolutionary War in 1783. Part of the time [he] commanded as Colonel. Harrod was attached to Bowman's regiment. [He] was considered as a brave & faithful officer during the time I first knew him until his death about the year 1792. He was in constant service during the Revolutionary War, as our forts were in continual danger.

Note - Mrs. Harrod failed to get a pension. [She] often told Gen. McAfee her conviction that Col. Harrod was killed by Bridges, who had a suit pending in which Harrod was an important witness again him. LCD

12C22(3) Notes taken from Mrs. Harrod, Nov 23, 1842, by Gen. R. B. McAfee

Mrs. Ann Harrod's Declaration of Dec. 1842

In Kentucky in 1774, built cabins at Harrodsburg. The names of the party with him in '74 as copied by Gen. McAfee from Harrod's contemporary book, in possession of Major Fauntleroy, viz - Capt. James Harrod; James Davis; Mr. Venable; Mr. Arthur Campbell; Wm. Campbell; John Cowan; John Crow; Abraham Chapline; David Williams; James Kerr[?]; Silas Harlan; Azariah Davis; Joseph Blackford; Patrick Doran; James Sanders; David Glenn; James Cowan; Elijah Harlan; Wm. Crow; Wm. Myers; Wm. Fields; Wm. Mortimer; John Brown; Henry Dugan; John Smith; James Brown; Azariah Reese; Martin Stull; Wm. Garrett; John Clarke; James Wiley; John Shelp.

Col. Harrod left Kentucky in July '74; was at "the Point," returned to Kentucky in March '75, & still commanded a company & fought the Indians. In '76 he was commissioned a captain by Gov. Patrick Henry of Virginia. He was in Col. Bowman's regiment, fought at Pickaway in 1780, & was in active service during the whole time. Mrs. Harrod was married to him.

Col. Harrod was the second representative of Kentucky County to the Virginia Legislature. John Jones was the first representative. While Harrod was in the Legislature he got his marriage confirmed in that body (which is evidence that he was not representative till <u>after</u> his marriage in '78. LCD). Col. Harrod died or was killed trapping on Kentucky River in the fall 1792. Made his will 28th Nov. 1791. Wm. H. Todd got Col. Harrod's commission dated in 1776 from Patrick Henry, also other papers, pay rolls &c, which were got March 17th, 1834, & he filed them in the executive offices at Richmond, Va. - contract made with Todd on Novr. 20th,1833.

Col. Harrod was six feet one inch high, dark eyes & black hair, & trim made; 10 years older than his wife, she now 86 years old [which made him born in 1746 as the Family states. LCD]

12C23 *This letter was copied by Draper.* Col. Daniel Boone's Captivity by Tarleton, June 1781. Virginia Acts of June Session, 1781.
Col. Wm. Christian to Col. Wm. Preston

Mahanaim, Saturday June 30, 1781

The Assembly adjourned on this day ___ a week. Mr. ___ Madison came from Staunton but one day before I did, and, I suppose, has given you nearly all the news I have, but, as John Young is going over, I'll write what occurs to me.

Several laws were made respecting the War. The Militia law* is amended – martial law declared in force for twenty miles, around our army and also around the enemy's. All the powers of Government necessary for calling out militia and resources of every kind are vested in the Executive. Persons suspected of disaffection may be sent to the enemy after twenty days to dispose of their property. A law is passed allowing the ten thousand dollars for voluntary recruits for two years or the war. I think there are twenty two acts in all, but the above are the most material, except one I just remember for punishing those who may oppose the **(1)** laws by an armed force, declaring them to be civilly dead, and their estates to descend to their next of kin.

The lowland people are as fine and firm in the interest of America as any people in it. All I saw seemed to disregard property and only talk of independence. None despair in the least. They are more engaged for the state of South Carolina at present than Virginia. * * * Col. Knox took down a report about ten days ago that it (Ninety Six) was actually taken, &c. * * *

Some stores are saved, some lost. We had no certain accounts how much, either way. At Charlottesville, the damage was not great, perhaps about three hundred ___ destroyed, and some stores, but the greatest part had got out of town and Tarleton followed but one mile up the road. Col. Boone, who was with Lord Cornwallis, and since paroled, thinks the enemy about 6,000. * * * Deserters from Lord Cornwallis call his force 4500 and 5,000, reports call his horse 700.

Gibbs' Doc. Hist. 1776-82, p. 146, 147.

*See Newspaper Extracts, 1781, ii, p. 50. LCD

12C24-24(11) John Tayloe Griffin Fauntleroy, Sugar Creek, Buchanan County, Mo., 1845

John Fauntleroy lived with the James Harrod family for two years and married their daughter Margarett in 1802.

There had been some previous correspondence to this letter as Fauntleroy answered questioned which had been sen by Draper. The handwriting in this letter is legible, but ink has faded in places.

211

Punctuation has been added. Fauntleroy's own page numbering has been retained, "Pa 1, Pa 2". Draper's list of topics (some with page numbers) is given after Fauntleroy's introductory remark.

The within document contains information about the early settling of Kentucky and the postmaster whose office it pases [sic] through is requested to hurry it on to Baltimore City with speed.

Col. J. T. G. Fauntleroy, Jan. 13th, 1845.
Maj. John Fauntleroy
Mrs. Harrod & Mrs. Fauntleroy
Col. James Harrod - 2-3-7-10-11
Col. Wm. Harrod - 6 &c
The Coburn family - 2 &c - 9
McGary & the Blue Lick Defeat - 4
Capt. A. Chapline - 5
Mr. Oldham, E. Bulger, John Paul
 & Abm. Wickerhsham in '79 - 6
Silas Harlan - 7, 10
Jos. Blackford - 7
D. Boone - 7, S. Boone - 11
Jacob Stucker - 7
Wm. Pogue - 7, W. Daniel - 8
Crab Orchard Incident - 8
Col. Fauntleroy sugar making, about 1790,
 & man killed near him - 9
Knob Lick described - 9-10
John Gordon - 10
Capt. Harrod's papers burned - 11

(1) Pa 1   Dear Sir

Your letter of December 13, 1844 came safe to hand last week and I hasten to answer it to the best of my knowledge and recollection. But the Vast length of time and many difficulteys I have pased through has caused my mind to forget many things that I once knew to be now forgot.

Well, to begin, I must say something about myself By way of introduction. I was born in Queen Ann's County, Maryland, Sept. 1775. My father, Maj. John, whos name I bear, was Born in Virginia, moved to Maryland, thence to Kentucky in 1784 with my Godfather W. Keene[?] [Kune?], mother, Brother & one sister, 17 slaves &c &c. We landed at Limestone now Maysville... the only log cabbin was ther in the bushes, thence to the Blue lick fort and dined there Christmas day 1784 on Buffelow meat & Pumpkin py [pie], thence through the woods by a one horse path to Lexington.

My father was a very stout and active man and served the Maryland troops all the Continental War. I have his commission now as Major with the thanks of the Maryland assembly for his good services to the A.M. [American?] cause. Having much goods to move, undertook and did cut out the first waggon Road from Lime stone to Lexington, and some where at a place cald Daubins Station on Hingston or Stoner fork there fell a deep snow. He took the Pleurisy and died in Janry, 1785, leaving us all without any acquaintance in Kentucky in Lexington. He died and was Buried there.

My mother and all the family moved to the neighborhood of Danville, and in Danville from ther I went to live with Col. James Harrod in 1786[?], and went to the first Lattin School that was kept in Kentucky to a man named Malcolm W____y at Harrods Station, the Plaice I sold to move to Missouri.

I married Col. James Harrod's only child, Miss Margarett, May 2, 1802. By her I had seven sons and seven Daughters. All lived to be grown but the youngest. Samuel, 17 yrs. old, now going to the acadamy [sic] in Cadiz Kentucky. Mrs. Fauntleroy died August 25, 1841, aged 56 years.

Mrs. Harrod died April 14, 1843. Then pased away the last of the female pioneers of Kentucky, beloved and regreted by all her friends.

(2) Pa 2 The school then broke up in 1787. Myself and some more of the Boys went onto Elija Craigs at the Big Spring at George Town now, then in the ___ Bushes, only one little cabbin at the Place. Will McQuiddy lived in it. Indians about as thick as Butter but none of us got kild. Mr. Jones was our lattin teacher. Lexington twelve miles off. An odd notion to send little Boys a way yonder among the Indians to learn lattin. They had better sent us to learn Indian.

I returned then from home to Danville in 1791. I returned to Lexington in 1802 to get maried at Harrods Station. In 1843, then to the Platt purchase [Missouri] again among the Kickapoo Indians at Weston &c.

Your first inquirie is about James Cowan. He was killed at the Fountain Blue Spring in 1774 - August - but him alone was kild. The company then packed up and moved on through the Wilderness as it was then cald on to Holston. They Joined Col. Lewis's Ridgment [Regiment] and went on the Battle of the Point [Pleasant]. Col. Harrod was Captain and fought bravely and the whites were successful. The company then went home up to the Monongahala and disbanded.

Col. Harrod then returned to Kentucky in 1775 and settled at Harrodsburg. In 1778 [he] maried Mrs. Ann McDaniel, widow of James McDaniel who was killed by the Indians while making salt at a place cald Drennens lick in Henry county, Kentucky near to the Kentucky River in the above county - a fine man from Roan County, North Carolina, and his Brother Patrick McDaniel also. My wife heired two settlements and Preemptions by them.

Mrs. Harrod had her father killd by the Indians on the hanging fork of Dicks River a little above the road from Danville to Stanford. About twenty head of horses [were] stolen by the Indians, about 40 head of Cattle killed, her household goods burned at Harrodsburg by the Indians in sight of the fort &c &c. Her only brother was Capt. James Coburn, who was wounded at the Battle of the Blue Licks [in] August 1782. [He was] shot by the Indians in now Shelby County [Ky.] and died of the wound at her house.

(3) Pa 3 Mrs. Harrod in continuation, her only son by McDaniel burnt to death in time of lattin school being at her house, a fine boy about 10 or 11 years old, my schoolmate, James McDaniel. Oh I love him now - my wife's half brother. By him we heired the land on Gilbert's Creek, Lincoln and Garrard Countys. God bless him.

Col. James Harrod maried at Fort Asap [Asaph] then cald – afterward [called] Logan's Fort, so you may now know where that place was. He was a fine man ___ ___ ___ kind to a fault. His house and fire protected the travelor, all that cald on him, free of any charge. I lived with them (and my brother William who now lives) parts of two years so I know as much about him as any person could. Mrs. Harrod died at my house [18]43 at Harrods Station.

Col. Harrod was a Soldier every inch, every way, but good natured. Only when made angry which could not be done on trivial ocations. He served his country faithfully and it has neglected his memory and his heirs to this day. He killed many Indians in defending Kentucky, one at Pickaway, a big fellow, and took his finery from him and the Indian never forbid him. I suppose he forgot it - I proved that fact by old Mr. Lewis Vanlandingham of Owen County in taking depositions to get a pension for Mrs. Harrod. He commanded a ridgement out from Kentucky and furnished a large sum of money for the use of the men for which we never have received a dollar nor never will.

The Cherokee Indians were very bad on the traveler from the old settlement through the Wilderness on the Cumberland Trace as it was then cald. To put some check to their murders, Col. Harrod raised a company of men, went out, fell in with a party, defeated them, and he himself killed a chief ___ ___ full moon f___ and brought it home. He never did nor would scalp an Indian if he could do without. He killed one at Harrodsburg, Mrs. Harrod in the fort looking on, and scalped, kild him, with the Indians' own knife, so I have heard Mrs. Harrod say many times. While the tragedy was going, Mrs. Harrod thought it was the Indian killing the white man.

(4) Pa 4 The fact is Col. James Harrod was at all times ready and willing to serve his country and it is soon known who is willing to serve and them kind of men are the oftenest cald on, so he was often out. He did not go to the Battle of the Blue Lick, a great misfortune for Kentucky. He had the back ache so bad he could not get out of his house, but sent John Isaacs, who lived with him then, and Isaacs got back but forgot to bring a fine English mare or horse, rifle, buffalow robe, and all the other things he took out with him back, so the Colonel lost all them.

That was small loss to the loss of Silas Harlan, Col. J. Todd, Trigg and 60 of Kentucky's best Blood. What a loss at such a time, all by Maj. Hugh McGary's bad conduct. He went from Harrodsburg fort and joined the troops on north side and then on to the Blue Licks. A counsel was held what was best to be done; the better portion of the officers were for waiting for Col. Benjamin Logan's ridgement to come on. McGary, a great brag, or fool, or devil, or something worse, said in a loud voice, any man that was not a coward to follow him and spuring his horse, plunged into the Licking river, and of course the men had to follow.

The Indians were nicely fixed for to view them and oh god the fatal consequence. Sixty as good men as ever lived fell that day by McGary's bad doings. He was despised by everybody for it, not liked by the people and died at or near Harrodsburg. He was at my house since I was maried. I had ocation to take his deposition once in a land suit, but I despised him. He maried General James Ray's mother in North Carolina, moved to Harrodsburg [in] 1775, died in 180_, and buried at the residece [sic] of Gen. Ray at the Shawnee run big spring, Mercer County Kentucky. Mr. C. W. Davis, who maried my daughter, [I] am now living with says he has often visited his and other graves there.

(5) Pa 5 I must not forget to mention an Anecdote. Captain Abraham Chaplin, the father of the young gentleman you speak of, as told me by himself. McGary was very Insolent in his disposition, quarrelsom when he dared and took ocation to insult A. Chaplin who was as Brave as Brave could be. He cautiond Mc [McGary] to behave himself better, but that only made the matter worse, so the Captain challenged him to single combat and they striped of [stripped off] to the skin and went at it in good earnest. The good wishes of the women, men, Boys & Girls all for the

215

Captain and the fortunes of War died in favour of the Captain and he gave him a real good Beating to the real satisfaction of all in the fort.

I was acquainted with Capt. Abraham Chaplin. He often Visited my mother's when she lived in Danville in 1788 and he lived much at Col. J. Harrods before he maried to Miss ____. She died and he cald on me & Mrs. F. [Fauntleroy] to look him out another which I did in the shape and size of his last wife, a widow Moon adjoining us in Mercer. I attended the weding and his funeral, which was grandly conducted by the Infantry Company from Harrodsburg with The Honours of War & he left a widow, two sons and one Daughter named Ann for Mrs. Harrod. I forget the year he died. He was buried at his homeplace (peace to him).

He came to Kentucky with Capt. James Harrod in 1774, a soldier, was out [as] Ensign under Gen. George Rogers Clark at the taking of the Opost [Vincennes] and Gen. McAfee recovered $17,000 for his heirs since his death from Government. Thus you see the Soldier has gained over Captain Harrod, who his heirs or widow has as yet got not one Dollar.

You speak of being at Genl. R. B. McAfee's. I hope he and family were well then. Mrs. Harrod and myself gave the Gent. [Gentleman] a power of attorney some short time before I left Kentucky. Did he say anything to you about it, if he thought he could get something for us from government? I wish if you have ocation to write to him you would mention my case to him & I should think he could give you a great deal about Kentucky as he wrote a Book for Kentucky.

(6) Pa 6 You wish some information about Capt. William Harrod. He was older than James, a real Soldier, but I do not know he ever claimed Kentucky as his home, but was in Kentucky ocationally and at his Brother's often. He was maried and had some children, but Mrs. Harrod told me often they all died without issue. A Butiful girl maried a man by the name of M____y or some thing like it and [she] died. When speaking of her he would grit his hands together that you could hear them a distance. He was much of a man as to manhood. Few could stand him and he had ocation to try himself sometimes in that way. He commanded a company under Gen. George Rogers Clark at the taking of the Kaskaska (or some of the out posts) from the French and behaved with the greatest Vallor. He was upwards of six feet high, big boned, very stout.

The French had heard by some means that Clark could not get there and they had concluded to have a big dance and Ball. So all the Big ones [officers?] had gathered in a room for the Ocation and by some extraordinary luck the Americans reached the Town unobserved and the first object that met their astonished Eyes was this great giant William Harrod in the door with his big sword up lifted and in a Voice like Thunder proclaimed aloud "a thousand Bostonians are now upon you." It is easier to conceive the astonishment that fell upon them than describe it. He got some land in Indianna stiled [styled] Clark's grant but it passed from him without doing him or his heirs any good. He was at his Brother James's in Kentucky a short time before his death, staid a short time and returned to Monongahela and died there, pased a way a Brave man.

You wish a list of the mens names of his [William Harrod's?] company he commanded at Old Chillicotha in the year June 1779. They are mens Names: Joseph Phelps, Will Oldham, Edward Bulger, James Patten, Daniel Stull, Beverly Trent, James Guthry, Cap Sullivan, Solloman Carpenter, Samuel French, Peter Sturges, Michael Humble, Samuel Pottenger, James Stewart, Jonas Potts, Thomas Simpson, Angus Cameron, William Smily, John Hunt, Thomas Trible, H___ Hill , (7) Pa 7 John Crable, Henry Hall, John Paul, Dan Doak [crossed out], Daniel Driskin, John Kinney, Samuel Frazier, Jos. Frakes, Jacob Speck, Thomas Suttler, Reuben Pribble, Edward Murdock, Patrick McGee, John Stapleton, James Welch, Moses Kirkindall, Abraham Vanmeter, John Linus, Samuel Foster, Isaac Dye, Adam Wickersham*, Michael Vittils, Jacob Specke [twice named], Peter Bellos, and Jacob Wickerhsham.

Those are all the mens names I have a list of. It appears they enrold to go to the old Chillicothe and the Sale of the Plunder they took from the Indians amounted to [Pounds]: 10699. 8. 8, the company credit for Plunder.

The same made ___ for what they Purchased [in Pounds]: 7349.6,5 the above sum is scaled in November 1779 &c &c.

I have no list of names as to the Kaskaka affair. Whether these men was with him or not I cannot say.

You wish a list of the mens names who came with Capt. James Harrod in the year August 1774. They are as follows.

Mens Names: James Davis, Mr. Venable, Major Camble, James Harrod, John Cowan, John Crow, Abraham Chaplin, David Williams, James Kerr, Silas Harlan, Azariah Davis, Joseph Blackford, Patrick Dolan, James Sanders, David Glenn, Elijah Harlan, William Crow, William Mires, William Fields, William Mortimore, John Brown, Henry Dugan, John Smith, James Brown, Azor Rees, Martin Stull, William Garrot, John Clark, James Wiley, John Shelp, and William Camble. The above names is all I have of the men who came with Captain James Harrod to Kentucky in August 1774. Many I knew personally, the most of them that was not kild at the Blue Lick defeat.

I knew Daniel Boon well. He often cald at my store in Lexington and would take a drink of the Creatur with me in 1797. He moved to Missouri and died there in 18__ &c.

 I can say no more about Capt. Jacob Stucker than in my former letter. He was a brave man and has children living in Scott County, Kentucky, as I was informed a few days ago &c. William Pogue was killd by the Indians between Danville and Harrodsburg. That was the other Captain [that] A. Chaplin aluded to, I expect. But that was since 1777 from a book of accounts

[Note in the margin: "See John McCannan ____ __ __ in American Pioneer. LCD" No explanation is given for the asterisk after Adam Wickersham's name.]

 (8) Pa 8 [book of accounts] now in my possession of Capt. James Harrod but I have forgot the particulars. Walker Daniel was kild by the Indians some where on the waters toward Bairdstown. He was the man for whom Danvile in now Boyl County, Kentucky took its name. He, Daniel, bought fifty acres of Land of John Crow and caused a Town to grow up there. He was a fine Inteligent Gentleman, a Lawyer from Virginia, very much beliked and highly esteemd by all who knew him. But, poor man, he did not live to see his Town of Danvile flurrish as it does now and one of my heirs have at this present time a Lawsuit for Six hundred acres of land, including all Danville in right of their Mother, heir to Col. James Harrod. The issue is yet to be determined. If it is our right, I hope we may gain it, if not, I don't wish it &c &c.

 I must not omit to say that when a little Boy my Mother and stepfather, Capt. John L. Hunter of Danvil, saw cause to let me go to the now Town of Stanford in Lincoln County about 1787. While there the Indians saw cause to call and see a family a few miles from Town toward the Crab Orchard, say six or seven miles off. And before the family knew of danger, five fine Buck Indians stood before the door and one smarter than the rest rushed in the house after a Negro man. The door was shut to by some means. The Indian and Negro grappled and fell and a young woman by the name of Woods, I think, lifted the axe and stove it into the Indian's head and killd him. I have seen her since the affair happened myself.

 My stepfather, Capt. John L. Hunter, was the first keeper of the Kentucky Penitentiary in 1800, and returned to his farm at the Big Bridge at Eagle Creek, the road to Cincinnaty, and died there. He came to Kentucky in about 1785 and had for Dr. Hugh Shields the first waggon that crossed the Kentucky River by taking it apart on the north side, carrying it across and joining it again on the south side at the place known as the mouth of Hickman. Now there is a spanded bridge **(9)** Pa 9 across from Danville to Lexington 36 miles. When I went it was first a very moderate road, answered us Well.

  Capt. Hunter moved from Jacob Minns Station six miles from Danville to the neighbour hood of the mouth of Hickman about 1790 - 1791 and sent me and some of the Negroes to a place near George Town now about 3 or 4 miles on the road to Versails now. And there happened to be a good spel of weather to make sugar out of the sugar trees and I went at it like a heroe. And one Butiful night, Moon bright as could be, Bang went off a gun. I thought it was some body hunting Coons or something and kept on boiling my sugar water not thinking of harm. And in the morning the alarm came that such a neighbour was killd and scalped, his sugar fixings all broke up, sugar gone &c &c. It was about a mile from my camp but they were satisfied with killing him, poor fellow, and let this Child alone. And many more scrapes have gone through but now forgot &c &c.

  Mrs. Harrod was the only Daughter of Capt. Samuel Coburn who was as brave a man as ever lived. Moved from the Yadkin River, Roan County, N. Carolina in 1775, settled at the mouth of the Gilberts Creek in Lincoln County just above where the Road from Stanford crosses to Lancaster. He brought out a large stock of cattle and horses, some five or six Negroes. I knew them all at Col. Harrods. He and Mr. McDaniel moved to Harrods fort on account of the Indians breaking out and it was his cattle and horses that was killd and taken but all one family. Capt. Samuel Coburn got killd by the Indians. He went up to get some corn at Logan's and on his return to Harrods fort the Indians way laid them who was with him and killd them. He fought them bravely and no doubt the red Rascals paid for their enterprize.

  There is a remarkable curious knob cald the Knob lick about four miles south of Danvile. I often was at it when a boy and since [I] maried. You go up a small rise from the North side and good land close **(10)** Pa 10 a slate looking surface, steep and go round and look up, you wonder what Nature could have thought of in making. It is awfully sublime to look at. A drian [drain?] comes from the middle and on the sides you may pick thousands of round marbles of all sizes out of the sides.

  Ther is allum made in the neighboring[?] state in any quantity. Mr. Samuel Moore, the present owner, is the son of the man killd at Pickaway under Col. Harrod. They were own cousins. A fine brave man. Mr. Crawford showed me the oak tree he was killd behind on the bank of Mad River, Ohio above Dayton. The fight was on the side of the hill and river, I think. They had a Town named Boston at it....

The Mammoth Cave in Warren County is now thought one of the greatest wonders in the world and I wish if you write a Book you would give a MAP, and all the particulars of it - certainly it is a extraordinary place in nature's works.

January the 18, 1845. My writing is like Paddy's frog, skips about mitily. But I hope you can so understand it as to get the worth of your postage out of it &c &c.

Well, in conclusion I must wind up with Col. James Harrod. He was a man about six feet high, strait made - Roman nose, very black hair & beard. The Indians cald him black beard and wished very much to catch him. Simon Kenton told the Colonel never to be taken alive by them. They caut Kenton ones [once] and thout they had Harrod and was fixing to roast him when fortunately for Kenton they found out ther mistake and they were finally disapointed &c &c.

I now begin to give you a list of the mens names who belong to Capt. James Harrods Company in June 1777. They were Ambros Coffy, John Gordon, James Waters, James McCalley, Evan Hinton, Edward Worthington, George Clear, Patrick Shore, Benjamin Linn, John Masefield, William Coombs, Silas Harlan, Julius Sanders, William Morition, [small letters intended for insertions are illegible], William Pogue, John Brown, James Offin, Daniel Whealan, William Mims [Miers?], J. W. Paulson, William Stul, Barney Stagnard [Stagner], John Zebiah Applegate, **(11)** Pa 11 Abraham Chapline, Squire Boone, John Clerk, Marsham Brashear, John Masefield, William Fields, Patrick Doran, Agnus Cameron, William Stewart, Samuel Moon, James Harrod, Daniel Brown, James Waters, John Bailey. These appears to be all of the company in 1777.

Mrs. Harrod had her house burned by a man in 1833, September as we all thought, and I expect he did and burned Col. Harrod's sword. Two arrows that the Indians killd her husband, James McDaniel, with after they had scalped him &c - they laid the arrows across his breast and left him. One of the arrows was the handesomest I ever beheld. She lost her papers and all her household things, or nearly so. So you see what one has sufferd in Kentucky. I have seen two histories of Kentucky and a ____ in each Boon & G. R. Clark.

How would Col. Harrod do? He was as brave a man as ever trod Kentucky ground. So if you think proper He was elected to Virginia to the assembly and served in that honourable body for Kentucky.
I have not wrote but a small part of their losses but must conclude by wishing you health and prosperity in this world and a Blessed residence in

the world to come. Accept my best wishes and remain your sinceard [sic] friend &c

John Tayloe Griffin Faultleroy

Eleven miles North of Weston, fifteen [miles] North of Ft. Leavenworth on Sugar Creek that runs into Sugar Creek Lake in Buchanan County State of Missouri 1845

NB From what paper that did come into my hand the impression on my mind was that Col. James Harrod left home Feb. 1792 on a beaver traping excursion up the Kentucky River above the three forks on Trail ___ and never returned. He was killed by one of the party of three, James Bridges, or the Indians, it was never found out. If you make out a book and have any one to spare, I will accept of one copy cheerfully sent to Weston, my proper name printed in it - have a good many plates in it &c &c

JTG Fauntleroy

12C25 LCD: Mrs. Ann Harrod from the *Western Christian Advocate,* May 12, 1843.

Col. James Harrod lived at Harrodstown and in 1779 – 1780 [lived] seven miles southeast of town. Methodist Episcopal church. Buried at Harrod's Fort.

"O, we ought never to have left Carolina, for we were in good circumstances there, and since we have come here we have had a great many hardships to undergo. But I never could do much with a gun: I have tried it often, but never could succeed. I did manage to kill a cow (buffalo cow) and a bear, or the girls would never have got done laughing at me."

Some two years ago, at a celebration of the anniversary of the settlement of Kentucky, Mrs. Harrod attended, and received every possible mark of respect. She was placed in a splendid barouche, drawn by white horses elegantly caparisoned, and escorted by a company of cavalry mounted on white chargers.

12C26-30 Notes taken from Mrs. Elizabeth Pogue Thomas, born in Rockbridge, Virginia, Sept. 4, 1764. Residing near Harrodsburg, Ky., Oct., 1844

Mrs. Thomas's interview with John Dabney Shane was published in Filson History Quarterly, *vol 3, no. 5, pp. 226- 235 (1929). That interview is used here to supplement illegible copy. Shane's interview with Mrs. Thomas is found in DM 4CC85.*

Mrs. Thomas says her father, William Poage, in company with Col. Richard Callaway & family, passed from Holston to Boonesboro in September 1775. Col. Boone's family were then in Boonesboro, & his son-in-law, William Hays, and several other young men. Some had gone [back to Virginia] for their families. While there, a man was killed opposite to the Fort over Kentucky River, and a man with him escaped [Colonel Arthur Campbell]. They would not believe the story of the escaped man until they saw the dead body of his comrade. Thus one man, Young McQuinney, killed in '75.

In February 1776, William Poague & family started for Harrodsburg. On Gilberts Creek of Dicks River, [they] overtook Samuel Coburn, James McDaniel, & Julian Saunders & families [who were] camped. James Ray went to Boonesborogh to pilot Poague's family. Shortly after starting, a snow storm overtook them, & had to camp a day or two, & Ray killed a buffalo & supplied them with meat. Colonel Hugh McGary, Thomas Denton, Richard Hogan, Hugh Wilson, and their families were at Harrodsburg. Mrs. Wilson had the first child & it was called Harrod Wilson. Wilson had passed Poague and Calloway on the wilderness [road]. On the way, 10 Cherokees and a squaw came up to Callaway and Poague and were friendly and talked, near Cumberland River. After they left they killed a small buffalo, and divided with the whites.

Mrs. Thomas thinks it was in the spring of 1775 that [Benjamin] Logan, [William] Whitley, ___Clark, [William] Manifee and [Benjamin] Pettit, came to Harrodsburg. Logan got married on Holston not long before he came out.

James McDaniel and others took the kettles at the station and went to Dennin's [Drennan's] Lick about 1777 to make salt, and there McDaniel got killed. Left his wife with a young child. When some 7 or 8 years old, Harrod took him into the woods, and Harrod out [hunrinf?], the lad had evidently lain down by the fire, the leaves caught on fire and fired his clothing. He attempted to run to a branch [creek], and was found dead with his clothing burned off.

William Poague

In the summer of 1778 (14th Sept., was killed), Poague and others started for Logan's [Station, where Court was being held]. When near Harrod's Station, were fired on and Poague dropped his gun, fell from his horse and hid in the cane. His horse ran on after the others to Logan's Station. Poague was wounded by two balls, both from the same gun. One ball entered his side, the other in the shoulder. Hugh McGary and another

[man] a little behind, were shot at and wheeled and returned to Harrodsburg. It was thought the first party were all killed – some 8 or ten. John Hays one.

A party went from Logan's - Logan at their head – and came to their relief, and were fired on. Hugh Leeper was wounded; they made fight and the indians fled leaving Poague's gun.

Poague was wounded in the morning and lay in the cane till near night when a party relieved him. [They] took him to Cowan's or Harrod's cabin, where there then no families There [they] guarded all night, heard Indians around the house. Next day brought him to Harrodsburg, John Hays[?] sitting and holding him on the horse. Poague died the third day, leaving six children – one the late Gen. Robert Poague, who died in August of 1836, aged 70, of apoplexy, in Mason County, Kentucky.

William Combs, William Ray (younger than James), James Ray and one other man went out to Shawnee Run some five miles from Harrordsburg, clearing a place at the Shawnee Spring for McGary. A party of Indians fell upon them (some 30 or 40). Indians shot at them. Combs ran and hid under a log with his axe and gun and though Indians all around him, he escaped. William Ray was killed, and James Ray was reluctant to leave his brother to his fate. His moccasin was laced so tight as to hurt him, and he cut the string. His knee buckles too tight and loosened them or something, and ran to Harrodsburg. Black Fish said afterwards that there was a boy at Harrodsburg that outran all his warriors. The other man was never heard of afterwards. That night [James] Ray and a party went back, found Combs safe, and got William Ray's body.

Next morning, seeing smoke at some cabins a quarter of a mile up the creek where the people had evacuated the night before, a party consisting of McGary, Joseph Lindsay, John Gass, James Ray, Richard. Hogan, Ben Linn and others went there, found the cabins on fire. The Indians were secreted in the brush between the fort and the cabins and opened fire, broke McGary's arm, slightly wounded John Gass in the neck. McGary ran back to the fort. Gass and the others stayed, treed, killed one Indian by Linn, and drove [off] the Indians. Mrs. Thomas thinks that there were a second party (probably the McGary one) that ran out at the firing – and thus, on a very small scale is [Zachariah] Holliday's narrative corroborated. Gen. Clark could not have been there.

McConnell killed

Sometime after the above, perhaps a year, Francis McConnell and several went out to shoot at a mark to try their guns, in the morning. [They] were fired on, and McConnell [was] shot down a hundred yards from the fort, south of the fort at the foot of the hill. The others escaped to the fort. McConnell lay behind a log so that the Indians could not shoot him and during the day repeatedly waved his hand for the men to come to his relief. Near night a party concluded to go and bring him in, knowing the Indians who had watched him all day (no firing that day interchanged) would get him after dark. Several men got upon the cabins and fired towards where the Indians were hollering while Silas Harlan, James Ray and several others raised the yell and ran out for McConnell. The Indians ran alarmed from their covert and never fired again. Ray, when the others went into the fort and the gate was shut, he [was] left outside. Close to the gate was a large stump and between this and the cabin was scarcely room for him to squeeze (don't recollect whether the Indians fired and knocked up the dust around him) and the folks within dug a hole under the cabin, and he crept in.

Poor McConnell died shortly after being brought in, and was buried in an unoccupied bastion at the southwest corner. Saw no more of the Indians that time.

The Corn Crib

Corn had been raised at the Cove Spring near Harrod's run and some 5 miles [northeast] of Harrodsburg. A party went there to shell corn in the cribs, and the Indians came upon them. James Berry very severely wounded, and 2 killed and another wounded who subsequently died. The men fought. Nathaniel Randolph ran all the way to Harrodsburg, got help and returned. The men were still in possession and the Indians were moving off, saw bloody signs. Never heard about Ray's personal re-encounter.

(In the affair when McGary had his arm broke, Hogan ran off and returned to the fort in the night, and frankly acknowledged that he was a coward, and he did not care if they knew it. All thought he had been killed.)

Barney Stagner, Thomas Denton

Barney Stagner, an aged Dutchman, the father-in-law of Hugh Wilson, was by general consent appointed to watch the spring at the fort and keep it clean and keep the children from it. He would sometimes carelessly ramble off, saying the Indians would not kill so old a man as he. One day he went up the branch to its head, half a mile off, was killed, his head cut off and carried away. The little children were for a long time after fearful to go to the spring of evenings lest they should encounter the headless ghost of poor Barney Stagner. His son-in-law Hugh Wilson was shot from his horse near the fort, and the animal ran in with blood upon its back.

Thomas Denton, a brother-in-law of McGary's, went on horse back to Shawnee run, was shot at and had his arm broke. The Indians tried to catch him, but he evaded them, his horse jumping large logs, and escaped to Harrodsburg.

The Turnip Patch

One morning the cattle – cows – seemed much alarmed. One man was sent part way to the turnip patch which was on the far north of the fort, over the branch…while the men stole out of the south gate and circled around, stole upon their rear, and killed four [Indians] – the others escaped. The whites got their plunder – 15 bundles, indicative of the number. The whites were so secret as to fall upon the Indians undiscovered. McGary and Ray were of the number.

McAfee's

Samuel Adams, Nathan Linn and David Glenn were some distance below McAfee's. Linn was mortally wounded, and taken to McAfee's and died that night. Glenn pursued an Indian whose gun was empty, ran him down – nearly a mile – and tomahawked him.

Boone and Callaway Girls

One Sunday went out in a canoe pleasureing, Jemima Boone steering, went nearly a mile below [Boonesborough fort]. The Callaway girls wanted to go to the north shore, against Miss Boone's wishes – flowers or something else enticed them. As they touched the shore an Indian jumped into the canoe and one of the girls (Mrs. Thomas thinks it was Miss Boone) knocked the Indian over the head with the paddle. They were taken. [Samuel] Henderson who afterwards married Betsey [Callaway] was among the pursuers. [John] Holder married Fanny, the other [Callaway daughter].

Pendergrass, John Haggin, Bartlett Searcy

Pendergrass was killed within a hundred yards of the fort, his wife and family at the time looking out of the window and seeing it. Thinks Pendergrass was lame.

[John] Haggin was chased off by Indians – went to Boonesboro and was gone 2 weeks, and all had given him up for killed. One evening he returned and saluted his wife as though nothing had happened: "How are you by this time, Nancy?"

Bartlett Searcy was taken at the Blue Licks salt making, and subsequently escaped and got to Harrodsburg.

Blue Licks

Col. [Stephen] Trigg lived on Shawnee run. Capt. John Gordon lived near him, and a few others. Lewis Rose formed a settlement, McGary [and] Ray also lived on Shawnee run. Rose was taken and gone a year, given up for killed, and when he returned home his wife did not recognize him.

James Ledgerwood lived down Salt River, was taken prisoner, gone a year. His wife was about to be married when he returned.

There were 8 Harrodsburg people killed [at Blue Licks battle]: Joseph Lindsay, James Brown, John Kennedy, Capt. Clough Overton, Stevens, and 3 others. The Defeat occurred on 19th August '82. Thinks 8 or 12 were taken prisoner.

Hugh McGary

The people of Harrodsburg used to consider McGary as a blustering and rather cowardly man. Mrs. Thomas recollects seeing little John Gordon make McGary run.

Col. Harrod

Mrs. Harrod always thought one of the men killed him who was out hunting with him, for that man had an important land suit pending in which Harrod was a witness against him. He and [James] Ray, Robert Poague, perhaps, and others [were] the night hunters.

Maj. Silas Harlan, Capt. Henry Pawling

Major [Silas] Harlan was mostly with Clark in Illinois – had no family and resided in neighborhood of Harrodsburg.

Capt. Henry Pawling brought men to Boonesborough with [Col. John] Bowman.

Martin's and Ruddell's Stations

In 1780 when Martin's and Ruddell's Station were taken, the spies of Harrodsburg were on the lookout. If the enemy were found to be coming, the Harrodsburg people determined to waylay the Indians on the rocky banks of Kentucky River and prevent their passage. Ruddell and others [had] lived at Logan's Station, then [went] to Harrodsburg and then to Licking.

From Mrs. Elizabeth Thomas – 2nd interview

About 1778, Job Chapman and John Stapleton went out from Harrodsburg in the summer, some 150 yards from the Station, south in the field to get a piggin of beans. Indians [were] concealed in the corn field. Chapman was shot dead, a ball passing through the piggin and into his body. Stapleton had his arm broke and escaped to the fort, seized his gun and was about running out to pursue the Indians with his broken arm. [He] was with considerable persuasion prevented. A party went out, the Indians had gone, and Chapman was found scalped, and a spear sticking in his breast.

Cove Spring

Jarrett [was] killed and McDonald [McDaniel?] and [an?] Irishman, was the one doubtless who died that night.

It was Francis McConnell who was mortally wounded and died.

Col. Wm. Poague lived until the summer of '76 on a cabin place near Shawnee Run, cleared a piece of ground and planted corn.

A man, perhaps named Lee, was killed at Leestown, in summer of '76 and two lads named McConnell taken and escaped.

Then Poague and others went to Harrodsburg, built a cabin on the hill where [lived] McGary, Denton and Hogan, and George Clare, an Englishman, a hatter. He was the same who passed Poague on the wilderness near Clinch and he went direct to Harrodstown or burg Hugh Wilson and father-in-law [Barney] Stagner also passed Poague and went direct to Harrodsburg, now built cabins on the hill. [They were] forting the place, but not finished till next spring after Ray was killed. That night worked and fixed up some open places around the fort. Next morning the fight, when Ben Linn killed the Indian and McGary was wounded. This dead Indian was brought to the Fort for the women and children to look at, then dragged off and buried him.

Ben. Linn married Hannah Sovereigns, perhaps the first wedding. [She was] sister to John Sovereigns, who with his mother and sister had been captured by the Shawnees. His mother's tongue had been cut by them so she would not talk. Probably taken before they came to Kentucky. McGary married [officiated] several as [he was] magistrate.

1774

When James Cowan was killed 16th July, George Poague, (who came with Harrod and was a nephew of Col. William Poague's), was of the party at Fountain Blue. Was fired on. Cowan was killed, the others broke. Two Indians chased Poague who had his gun in his hand, but so closely pursued that he had not time to turn and shoot. They were so near that they tried to seize his gun, which he threw to one side. The Indians were now after it by which he gained on them. The Indians fired at him with his own gun, but missed. He escaped to Harrodsburg.

The Battle of Blue Licks

One of the 8 killed was William Harris. John McMurtry, Lewis Rose, Michael Humble and James Legerwood [were captured]. All these got back. John Kennedy was taken but was shot with some others on a branch near the battle ground.

Thinks McMurtry did get killed afterwards, and wife again married.

Harrod Wilson

Mrs. Thomas is certain that Harrod Wilson, child of Hugh Wilson was the first born at Harrodsburg – was a child [when we came].

Boonesboro

Mrs. [Daniel] Boone and Mrs (Susan Boone) Hays were the only women when Pogue and Calloway's families arrived in September 1775. Not more than half a dozen cabins had been built on the river bank perhaps a quarter [of a mile] below the Lick. Other cabins were building – a pretty good sized one was being erected for Col. Calloway. His son Caleb and nephew Flanders were there at Boonesboro and met Calloway and Poague a day's journey before reaching Boonesboro.

[There was] nothing like forting [picketing?] when Poague left there in February 1776. Found Col. [Richard] Henderson there, and left him there. The cabins were not in a row but scattering.

Harrodsburg

Harrod Wilson was some few weeks old when she went there [to Harrodsburg], born in one of the cabins where the battle was, about half way from the fort to the head of the branch. When the fight was, [they] had gone up to let pigs out of a pen.

Is certain Ben. Logan with his wife did not reach Harrodsburg till after Poague arrived, soon after, perhaps spring of 1776. Whitley, Pettit, Clark, Manifee &c came about the same time.

Squire Boone [living at Harrodsburg at the time], having seen an Indian show himself and several others following down the branch, Boone went ahead of the others. They cautioned him and told him the Indians would shoot him. A gun cracked and Boone was slightly wounded in the side, a flesh wound. The Indian was hid in the bushes, was not seen after. [Squire] Boone remained there at Harrodsburg some time, till he moved off to Shelby County.

It was in 1777 that little or no corn was made, and James Ray hunted so much, and hence were careful about saving what little there was, and hence the Cove Spring affair.

McGary reached home the night after the battle of Blue Licks and was the first to bring the news of the Defeat.

On a rough sketch of Harrodsburg Fort, Draper designated cabins belonging to McGary, the Linns as being on the west side; others were Harrod, Edward Worthington, William Pogue, Levi Todd, Ben Logan, Whitley, Clark, Manifee.

[Harrodsburg Fort]

A lad named John Miles went out near dark to get wood and was shot after the Blue Lick Defeat.

Levi and Robert Todd and John Todd – all lived there a while. Levi and John before they married, and Levi after.

But one big gate and that on the south side [of the fort]. Some two or more smaller gates. There was a stone wall around the spring. The ground on which the fort was, was a rising eminence, descending in every way except the south.

12C30 This closes the notes I took of Mrs. Thomas in Oct., 1844. See McAfee Papers for her replies to subsequent inquiries I sent to her through Gen. R. B. McAfee. LCD

Memo – Thos. Shores was 26 years old when captured at Shawnee Spring, [It was] March 6, 1777, when Wm. Ray was killed, & was from Baltimore, Md.

Certifies to good treatment from the British: Trip 1860, vol. vi, p. 127.

12C38-38(7) Herman Bowmar letter, Versailles, Ky., Jan 9, 1843

It gives me great pleasure to respond to your kind letter, written at Buffalo N. Y, November 26, 1842, enquiring of me facts in relation to the lives and character of the late Colonel John Bowman and Major Jonas Bowman, early adventurers to Kentucky. I was intimately acquainted with the former, but never saw the latter and I believe the name of the latter has been mistaken by your informants. I know his Character. Major Joseph Bowman, brother to John, was an officer in a Regular Regiment under the command of Gen. George Rogers Clarke, who marched to a large Garrison at the falls of Ohio, which I was at several times in the spring and Summer of 1780. This Fort had been erected some two years or a little more before I saw it and was occupied to the end of the War. Major Joseph Bowman was an officer in that Regiment, and had descended the River with Gen. Clarke on his Illinois Campaign before 1780. Troops were stationed [as] part of that Regiment at Kaskaskia and others at Vincennes, which was overtaken by our excellent General above named.

In 1780 or 1781 – I believe the former – Joseph Bowman was mortally wounded by a shot from an Indian in a bottom of the Mississippi River, being alone and was found some one or two days after still alive, but soon after expired. The melancholy intelligence was communicated to his brother above named. He then resided at a place he had settled, a large station about seven miles from Harrodsburgh called Bowman's Station in fall 1779 and Winter 1779 -80. The Writer's Father was one of the Tenants. In the 11th year of my age in the summer of 1780, I saw the Clothes of Joseph Bowman, more excellent cloth clothes than I had ever seen any one man have, as I believe. I remember that he was spoken of by many, then and after, as the pride of his **(1)** family.

I knew General Clark, have seen him at different places and several times at Col. John Bowman's after 1780. I was well acquainted in later years with Major John Crittenden who died about thirty or more years ago. He was aide de camp to General Clarke all the time the service continued. He was a Gentleman of high intelligence and character. I have heard him speak of Captain Joseph Bowman who had been killed on the Mississippi. The remarks amounted to this: "That he was an elegant man, amiable, intelligent & brave. "

Those Bowmans had a brother who continued to reside near Winchester, Virginia. I have seen him once in Kentucky many years ago. I presume his family or descendants are there yet. The Bowmans and Hites and Brinkers - their connections forty years ago resided near Winchester, Virginia. Col. John Bowman had but one son who departed this life over twenty years past. The Colonel has some family connections, but all who are living have been born since his death.

With respect to Col. John Bowman, I knew him well, perhaps more intimately than any man now living. My Father settled in his station of about twenty families, arrived there from Virginia in Feby. 1780.

There was a large Emigration to Kentucky in fall 1779. Some of the movers had been caught on the way by the severity of the Winter which commenced in November and they had to lie by on the way. Such was our Situation. The snow fell deep in November, and additions remained till near the first of March. It has been called the Hard Winter ever since. That emigration, I believe, doubled or more the inhabitants of 1779...

The state of Kentucky was then the County of Kentucky. And John Bowman, as I understand it, was then the Colonel Commandant of said County. For I believe that Virginia then had a Colonel Commandant of the Militia in every County then called County Lieutenants.

The County of Kentucky was, by an act of the Virginia Legislature, divided into Four Counties to take effect in November 1780. Col. Bowman by this Division resided in Lincoln County.

(2) Col. John Bowman made a crop of corn in 1778, a small field, I presume, at the Great Cove Spring five miles above Harrodsburgh towards the present city of Danville. His corn was cribbed there. He went there after it was gathered with about 9 or 10 men from Harrodsburgh, where he resided. While He and his party were shelling the corn, they were attacked suddenly by Indians, and two or three of his men killed. It was always Held That he made a bold stand of defense but his party taken by surprise. A thick and high cane brake coming up near the cribs, he and his party fell back into the cane, which saved them the loss of more men. What loss the Indians sustained was not ascertained. This was often spoken of as the battle of the corn cribs.

About thirty years ago, I had a conversation with a neighbor who was one of the party in the above skirmish, who described the affair to me.

In the spring or summer of 1779, the first Campaign that was ever made from the County of Kentucky and that by its Militia alone, was projected and commanded by Col. John Bowman. No doubt that some itinerant strangers, who had visited the County to explore it, joined them. I have no data from which to state their numbers of strength. This expedition was directed against Chillicothe on the Sciota and the expedition was successful in being undiscovered till they had arrived near the town, which they assaulted and carried the greater part of the Town. But the Indians who had given away at first rallied and in turn charged upon the whites and expelled them. Much plunder was brought away by Col. Bowman's troops.

(3) Pack horses afforded convenience for transporting copper kettles and many necessaries wrested from the Indians. A fine warmpun belt, several other bright & fanciful articles, some four dozen silver broches large and small. [I] made a present of several broches to my younger brothers.

Some gentleman, having moved to Alabama, visited Kentucky in

1825 and staid with me several weeks, [had] conversation on that campaign. I think he said our army was about three hundred strong. The late General John Logan was a Captain on that expedition. And after invading the Town several hours without success and convinced that the enemy were stronger than they had anticipated, a retreat was determined upon. They were pursued by the enemy and before their arrival at the Ohio River, were attack[ed] at Noon. The party made a Bold stand, gave Battle and repulsed the enemy which was the last they saw of the Indians.

This failure was regarded as unfortunate and principally ascribed to the circumstance of a number of the Soldiers being thrown off their guard by plundering and giving way to a sudden assault of the enemy. Col. John Bowman was then near fifty years of age, was personally as large a man as I had ever seen. He was tall and large wide frame and corpulent. He died in 1784 after two years of serious disease.

He was never again able to have served on a Campaign after 1780. He was a very Gentleman in his deportment and disposition as hospitable as any man.

(4) I presume that Col. John Bowman went out of office in 1780 as he did not go on the Campaign of this year. I remember in the summer of 1780 and afterwards that he wore a truss, which indicated a rupture, besides he was too large and heavy to have performed active service on Horseback.

The Division of the County as before named in 1780 would require probably new appointments. I think it probable that he resigned his office from the circumstances I have stated, which I know to be true. In conversation with this subject & it may not be amiss to mention that about July 1780, Gen. Clarke, then resident at his fort at the falls of Ohio (now Louisville), ordered out the Militia at the mouth of Licking, with his regulars and a field piece, went on and took and destroyed the Chillicothe. My father was one of the Militia. This army was ___ with the Indian corn as there was no bread in Kentucky except at the falls. Some corn had been Boated down the Ohio to that place by emigrants.

I have above mentioned that I had been there in spring & Summer, 1780, at the Fort at the falls. Some companies, say 15 to 20 men, armed, would be formed to go there to pack home corn to get a little bread and, more particular, to have meal to put into broth made of wild meat.

Gen. Clark's next Indian campaign was in fall 1782 after Blue Lick defeat. My father was also in both those. They have indelibly impressed my memory. The last campaign, I believe, took the Pickaway towns. I may be mistaken as to the Towns.

(5) I begin with Captain Simon Kenton. He was their chief and

___ Warrior of that in the vicinity of Maysville. He was amongst the first Settlers there. His services, adventures, and exploits were numerous, and of long duration, say from 1780 til 1794. The wars with the Sciota, Miami and Wabash Indians continued from 1776 until they were defeated by Gen. Wayne near Lake Erie on 20th August 1794, eleven years after the close of the revolution.

I trust you are furnished with incidents of his enterprize. I shall describe the person of the man. Stature full six feet, his form excellent and athletick, his deportment moral, and particularly genteel, no rude[ness] of manner, countenance grave and manly, his conversation interesting, unassuming and apparently unconscious of inferiority, void of austentation.

I have heard his fame as a soldier, had never seen him before 1793. He was then a Captain of Volunteer Militia from his neighborhood on Gen. Wayne's advance that year in which occupied Fort Greenville.

My position in the same corps happily inabled me to form an acquaintance with Capt. Kenton. I heard no boasting from him. In person neither beautiful nor ugly, but manly and an excellent man. He commanded a fine company without bestowing or blaming. Capt. Kenton was soon after appointed a Colonel of Militia and soon a General of Militia, in my opinion highly competent. I have not heard for several years whether he is still living. Before the late war he had emigrated to & settled in Ohio. He has never served in an army in higher rank than Captain.

The name of Jacob Stucker as a hero of Elkhorn from ___ deserves to be classed with Capt. Kenton. He was a youth of Dutch parentage residing at Bryant's Station at the time of the Siege of that place in August 1782. **(6)** Before & several years after that, went as a regular or spy with others and was very useful in pursuits when Indians broke into the settlements, and killed and plundered (generally) horses. His cautious movements and skill in pursuing and attacking, and then his bravery crown him with more success than any other man. It has been supposed that he had killed more Indians himself than any other man in Kentucky, unless Capt. Bland W. Ballard exceeded him.

An anecdod [sic] of Ballard, then about 20 years old. His father had settled in a small neighborhood near the present seat of Shelbyville, a most troubled Frontier about 1785 or '86. Bland W. Ballard had rose before day and went into the woods with his gun to bring up his plough Horses. As he returned and had got within two or three hundred yards of and in front of the House, he discovered a great smoke rising. He soon saw the flames appear through the cabin ___. He let go his Horse, he was riding side ways without a Bridle, and then saw a number of people in the yard, soon discovered they were Indians hurrying off loaded with plunder. As [he] ran through the yard, he saw his father [and] mother lying there murdered. This was in April. The Indians were passing through a cornstalk field and as they were crossing the fence he killed one. The Indians hurried on loaded with plunder. He reloaded and pursued and in this way he killed several.

    General Askin was at the treaty of Greenville made with the Indians by General Wayne in 1795, about nine years after this event. Askin got acquainted there with an old chief that could converse in English. Gen. Askin asked the chief where he had made war in Kentucky. He replied upon Beargrass, Floyd's fork and Brashears's creek. The Indian said, I killed old Ballard. The General told him that Bland Ballard says he killed five of your men. The Indian replied Bland Ballard's a liar, he killed four, the other one got [away?]. This tale may be exaggerated. I expect, after writing it, rather I should have omitted it. I did not get it from Gen. Askin myself, it was related by a clever man. I know not whether he obtained it from the General or some other. But nothing is more true than the killing [of] Ballard and wife & plundering and burning and that his son arrived in time to take some revenge and got his bold spirit & great efficiency, in Defending the settlements. I am acquainted with him. His character is justly very high.

    Dr. Sir. I regret that I cannot _____ . I am now Seventy four. I had received no Education except learning to read up to 1781. And as I have informed you, I was well acquainted with Col. Bowman. I will show how. My father was an excellent McCannick [mechanic], a first-rate millwright, and handy and capable with tools at about anything. Col. Bowman & he become very friendly.

    (7) In 1786 The Colonel employed my father to build a Mill on a small but good stream. I believe it was the best for its size I have ever known. Beginning of 1782, my father remained several miles from the Station and settled out with two other families. Soon after, a good teacher opened a School at Bowman's Station. I was entered to it, and boarded with Col. Bowman. His son was about my own age & was my companion. My father had been for many months engaged in Building a large Mill for the Colonel on Dicks River, about a mile from the Station. The Colonel died when it was about half done, and his widow gave up the mill to my father for a term of years to run and him for building it, which turned out well and parties satisfied.

    In 1785 an opinion prevailed there very favorably to the success I had in getting education and I was encouraged to open a school in that Station which I did. [I] was so fortunate as to please my employer and in course more approbation probably than I merited. My residence in that vicinity - ten years until I was grown - afforded the opportunities for my acquaintance and friendly intercourse. The Colonel's nephew married my sister. Their names are Bowman, mine is Bowmar.

The Honorable Mr. Campbell, so obliging as to inscribe the letter I am answering, will, I doubt not, transmit these two sheets, to his friend Mr. Draper. And oblige his Humble Servt
Herman Bowmar

PS as an apology for the clumsiness of this presentation. I plead age and infirmities.
H.B.

PPS Mr. Draper has my anxious desire for the ____ of his work. I desire to live to see it.
H.B.

The Bowmans – Kenton – B___ Stucker.
          From Col. C. H. Bowmar 9th Jan. 1843. LCD

12C39(11) *LCD notes on letter of Herman Bowman in 12C39-38(1-10) are dated March 22, 1845.* Major Herman Bowmar died at Carroll Point, Louisiana, Oct. 8th, 1855, formerly of Woodford County, Ky., aged 86 years. <u>Commonwealth,</u> Frankfort Ky., Nov. 6, 1855. LCD

[Memo – Dr. S. Threlkeld, who was in the battle of the Thames, Oct. 5, 1813, said to me, that "Capt. Jacob Stucker was a tall (6 feet) spare, quiet, taciturn, unassuming man; that Stucker was on the left of Capt. Johnson's attack on the Indians at the Thames." LCD.]

[LCD page numbers for Bowmar's statement:]
Major Herman Bowmar, 22 March 1845
Blue Lick defeat - 1, 2, 3, 5
Major Hugh McGary - 2 &C
Col. James Trotter - 2
Gen. James Ray - 3, 5
Maj. Fontaine - 3
Wm. McBride - 3
Humble & Hinch [wounded] at Blue Licks - 3
Maj. B. W. Ballard - T Arnold &c - 3, 4

Jac. Stucker - 4, 12
Col. W. Whitley – 4
Zach. Allen and other prisoners at Blue Licks - 5.
Capt. John Gordon - 5
Ezekiel Field - 5
Wayne's Campaigns, Scott - Todd, Busbee - 5 &c
Wm. Russell, John Adair, Wm. Shannon, Sam. Wells, John McDowell, Horatio Hall, & Maj. Bowmar - 6
Wm. Wells & party, 7-8
___ Price's spies - 7
Col. Boone's Narrative - 11

12C41 Col. Jos. McDowell, interviewed near Danville, Ky., Fall, 1844. LCD.

Capt. John McDowell...children, Sally[?] married Col. George Moffett. Joseph Lapsley, Richard Woods, Charles Hays, Jacob Anderson, a number of others at the battle where my father was killed.
I was with my step-father, Benjamin Borden, the younger, as a chain carrier [for the surveyors], when I was not more than eleven or twelve years old. I resided in the bounds of Borden's grant from the time my father settled where I formerly lived, which I was told in 1737, till the year 1783.

I was born (as appeared by the record kept by my father of the birth of his children) on the 27th October 1735, old style.
Benjamin Borden (the younger: LCD) died of small pox, I believe.
Botetourt & Greenbrier tracts... In 1781, he visited Kentucky, reached Lincoln County with his family in December 1783, was a commissioner before coming. He came with Caleb Wallace, a judge of the first District Court of Kentucky. Did not take part with Brown & Sebastian in the Spanish ___. He was over six feet [tall] & strongly made - over 200 lbs weight - fair skin, light complexion. He was an Elder in the Presbyterian Church, was liberal in business. His fourth child was Col. James McDowell.

12C44-44(2) Mary Logan Smith letter, Bardstown, Ky., Dec. 16, 1844
In the following two letters, Mary Logan Smith, daughter of Benjamin Logan, appears to be answering questions sent to her by Draper. The questions were not found with her letters.

Dear Sir

I am pleased to give you any information in my power in reference to the life of my father Benjamin Logan and should have taken an earlier opportunity to answer your letter concerning him.

You first desired to know the date & place of my father's birth. I cannot inform you where it was in Pennsylvania he was born, nor can I state certainly the date. He died in December 1802 and was then in his sixtieth year.

I can't say whether or not he was in Col. Christian's regiment.

As to the date of his emigration to Kentucky, I have repeatedly heard my mother say that my brother David, who was the oldest of the 9 children, was just commencing to walk when they came out. David was twenty years older lacking one day than my sister Ann Wickliffe, who was the youngest, and Ann was fifty years of age the 9th day of April last. From this I feel satisfied that my father came to Kentucky in the fall of 1774 or Spring of 1775. My brother William, I think, was born in Harrodsburg in 1776. There is a Bible I suppose in the hands of some [of] his children, most probably in the hands of Mrs. Jane Clark (Louisville) which gives the birth of all my father's children. I believe my father brought his family with him when he first came to Kentucky. It consisted of seven in number - himself & wife, one child (David) and a Negro woman with three children, the youngest of which was some older than my brother David.

Benjamin Petitt with his family came out with him and held land about 10 miles from my father's place at St. Asaph. I have heard my mother say that they were so anxious to get ground cleared & a crop in, that Petitt with his two sons, who were small, would come and help my father a week, and then he in time would assist Pettitt.

I have heard my mother say that she had no door to her cabin - a blanket in its stead. I have also heard her state that they were in Kentucky some months before the Indians found them out. It was certain from signs that the Indians had discovered them. Petitt came to my father with his family when they all proceeded to Harrodsburg in the night. This is the only abandonment **(1)** of St. Asaph, and this was before the fort was built. I do not know how long they remained at Harrodsburg, over a year perhaps, when he with others built the fort, they returned. My father, however, was to & fro during the time.

The incident you speak in reference to King occurred when the fort was besieged. My brother Benjamin is mistaken about King being shot. King made a bet with someone whose name I forget that he could climb a tree higher, feet foremost, than the other [man]. They had to go outside of the gate to get to the tree. King's companion started up first, &

as he was going up, an Indian who was concealed shot him in the heel. He dropd instantly, when King snatched him up & ran into the fort. This I have heard my mother repeatedly relate.

As to the name of the Individual who was wounded at the Fort and carried in by my father, I have heard my mother so frequently speak of the occurrence that there is no doubt but his name was Burr Harrison. It occurred thus - While the women were milking, there were several men guarding them. The guard was fired upon. One man was killed. I am under the impression his name was John Kennedy. Burr Harrison was wounded.

The rest with the women got safe into the fort though for a minute or so there was an alarm about my mother. The Negro woman not seeing her when she ran [in] at the gate, cried out to her master that her mistress was out. This was soon straightened, and then there was great anxiety about Harrison. It is a mistake about his having a wife & family for he was a single man, but was one of the bravest & most useful men in protecting the fort. Those in the fort when they saw he was alive called to him & told him to crawl nearer the gate. He told them he could not, and gave them to understand that the Indians would scalp him at night. My father determined to bring him in. I never heard that a proposition was made to or by [John] Martin to accompany him. I expect this is a mistake which might have grown out of Martin being a large stout man.

My father got a bed from my Mother and rolled it up & then tied it with chords [cords], rolled it before him till he reached Harrison, took him in his arms (leaving the bed) and ran into the fort with him, amid a heavy fire from the Indians. Harrison was exceedingly gratified stating that he knew he must die, but that he would **(2)** escape the loss of his scalp. He died that night or the next day & was buried under my father's cabin. I have heard my mother inquire whether Dr. Burr Harrison who now lives in Bardstown was related to the Burr Harrison who was buried under her floor at the cabin.

I have repeatedly heard my mother speak of my father's going to Holsten for ammunition. I think he took some one with him; who I do not recollect. Who & whether he came back I do not know.

After the siege was raised my father went out to have Kennedy burried, & being the first that got to him, found upon his body some papers which contained an offer of a commission in the British Army, and a certain amount of gold, I don't remember the amount, to anyone who would open the gate of the fort. He took the papers and gave them to my mother, telling her to hide them and let no one whatever see them. He did not permit them to be seen till they all left the fort for their respective homes. I have frequently heard my mother relate this as well as another incident.

  My father received word from Harrodsburg to examine & ascertain whether there were Indians still about. When he was about to start, someone in the fort insisted that he should ride his horse, which was a large white horse. When about three miles from the fort the Indians fired upon him and shattered his arm very badly. He lost his gun and the Indians were so near catching him, my father thought at the time. An Indian had the tail of his horse, but after a hard race, he escaped & got into the fort. The Indians thought they had killed him, and I think it was [to] Kenton that they boasted of killing Logan, but he undeceived them.

  His arm on account of bad management grew to his side or down by his side so as to be useless, until one day at the mill he had built near there, he fell through some hole about the mill, I forget how exactly, but it was too small for his body. His arms caught and were straightened out, & after that his arm was as well as ever.

  Ben is mistaken about McClure being killed at the time ___ Logan's family was captured; the capture and recapture you speak of was long before McClure's death

  I fear Sir I have written more than is necessary and especially as it will be of but small importance to you in the prosecution of your purpose which I suppose is write an historical account of my father's life - though I will [with] pleasure give you all the information I can.

      Your obedient Servant
        Mary L. Smith

12C45-45(4) Mary Logan Smith letter, Bardstown, Ky., April 25, 1845

       Bardstown April 25 1845

Sir
  Your letter of the 18th returned to my brother Dr. Logan was handed to me while on a visit to Shelby [County, Ky.] a short time since. I will answer your interrogatories and then give you, as far as I am enabled to do so, sketches of some incidents connected with my Father. As I did not retain a copy of my answer letter to you, I may unintentionally repeat what I have already communicated to you.

  My father died on the __ day of December 1802 while absent from home attending a sale near Shelbyville. Just before setting down to dine on the day of his death, he requested two of his friends (Whitaker & Simpson) to stand by him; they not comprehending correctly his meaning, took each a seat at his side. He sat down & spoke no more.

  As to the capture of my uncle Nathaniel Logan's family [which]

you allude to in your letter, you have been lead [sic] into some error as I never heard that his family was at any time captured by the Indians. On an occasion of his going to Russell's creek in Casey County, with Robert McClure, and a Negro woman - her three children with him - he was attacked by a party of Indians. McClure, who had in his hand the only gun they had with them, was shot and the four Negroes were captured. Owing to the eagerness of the Indians to plunder their packs & to seize upon the horses, my uncle made his escape. One Indian horseman pursued him and soon overtook him, but my uncle seized a chunk with which he knocked the Indian down, and made his escape. You may perhaps have confounded this occurrence with the capture of my aunt, Mrs. Russell & her family.

    My Grandfather, William Montgomery, moved his family from Virginia in the winter of 1779 and settled on the Hanging Fork about 10 miles from St. Asaph's. In the fall of 1780 (the month I do not recollect) the Indians made an attack on his cabins just at daybreak. A Negro man who was entering my grandfather's cabin with firewood was shot just as he opened the door of the cabin. He (my grandfather) immediately ran to the door to pull the Negro in & was shot just as he opened the door. His son William then drew him in and barred the door. He thrust his gun through the opening between the logs & shot [at] the Indians and drove them from his cabin. They however broke into the cabins of my Uncles, Mr. Russell & John Montgomery, killed John Montgomery and captured his wife, [and] Mrs. Russell & her four children (2 sons & 2 daughters). A report of the attack was immediately sent by Benjamin Petit, who resided about 2 miles from my Grandfather and heard the firing, to my Father. He with a sufficient number of men hastened to the spot and were soon in hot pursuit of the Indian left when overtaken **(1)** and the prisoners rescued & returned that day to the station.

    The eldest daughter of Mrs. Russell was killed by an Indian during the rescue. When one of the white men seized her to pull her from the grasp of the Indian who had her, he tomahawked her & fled. The Indians were retarded in their retreat by having to pack a wounded one. He was left when overtaken.

    I have two sisters living: the elder, Elizabeth, first married the late Col. Martin D. Hardin, son of Gen. John Hardin who was killed by the Indians in 1791. She is now the wife of Mr. Porter Clay and resides in Jacksonville, Illinois. The other and the youngest of my Father's children, Ann, married Mr. Nathaniel Wickliffe of this place.

    I have myself no recollection of the age of Col. Knox. My sister, Mrs. Wickliffe, recollects hearing my mother state his age at 82 years a short time before his death.

William Logan, my second brother, was born in Harrodsburg on the 8 day of December 1776 and died in Shelby [County, Ky.] on the 8th day of August 1822. He was the first male child born in Kentucky.

I regret exceedingly that I cannot state the county in Pennsylvania in which my Father was born, or the month. It was in the year 1742. His Father, David Logan, emigrated from Ireland and married Jane McKinly in Pennsylvania, who was also an emigrant from Ireland. In 1772, he married Ann Montgomery (of Irish descent) in Rockingham County, Virginia. Soon after his marriage he moved to Holsten on New River where he remained until the spring of 1775, when he came to Kentucky and settled at St. Asaphs. He was in Lord Dunmore's Campaign and from the fact of his being the largest and stoutest man in his regiment, the famous Shawnee Indian Logan assumed his name.

In the fall of the year 1775, [Benjamin Logan] returned to Virginia for his family and on the 8th day of March 1776, arrived at his station. Very soon after he had settled his family at St. Asaphs, the Indians discovered the settlement, the "sign" of their near approach to the settlement having been seen by my Father. As he and Benjamin Petit were the only persons with families in the station, they packed up and moved their families to Harrodsburg in the night about 20 miles distant. He remained at Harrodsburg until February 1777, and then returned to St. Asaphs, having previously picketed the cabins there and engaged men to Garrison the Station.

I have no papers that would enable me to give the names of the persons who returned with him to St. Asaphs.

(2) Of the two sieges by the Indians of St. Asaphs in the spring and summer of 1777 I need not write as they are both mentioned in Marshall's and Butler's so-called Histories of Kentucky and also in Bradford's Notes on Kentucky.

One occurrence which is not satisfactorily given in either of the above recited works I will mention. It was in the commencement of the second siege. One man of the Fort was shot down near the gate and after Nightfall my Father went out to carry in his body. He found the dead man lying on his back and upon his breast was placed a package addressed to Gen. Clark and Gen. Logan. He carried in the dead man and on examining the papers they were found to contain offers from the British Commander in Canada of a large amount of Gold and a commission in the British Army to every American who would join the British standard. My Father concealed the papers & their contents from the knowledge of everyone in the Fort from Apprehensions that some of the men might be induced to leave his Station, as their condition was at that time alarming - in fact, almost desperate. Before, however, the end of the 2nd siege, the men under the cautious management of my Father, regained confidence in their position & strength and assumed an air of defiance to the Indians.

I recollect an anecdote of that siege told by my Mother of John King who got one of the men in the humor of betting which could climb a tree <u>feet foremost</u> highest above the pickets. After several trials, each one going higher every trial, King's competitor (whose name I do not recollect) got shot by an Indian through the heel, which put a stop to their amusement.

As an offset to that game, one of the Indians one day of the siege managed to get into the Water Mellon patch, took a mellon in his hands and sprang behind a tree about one hundred yards from the pickets. To be imprudent he would step out from the tree some three feet, hold the mellon in the air, jump up & clap his feet together and spring back behind the Tree. After he had repeated that caper several times, one of the men in the Fort observed the exact position relative to the tree that he would take in going through his motions, placed his rifle in a loop hole and fastened it in a Fork to as to bear accurately on the place. He pulled while the Indian was in the act of cracking his heels together and shot him dead.

(3) My father built at St Asaphs the first frame house in Kentucky. He also built on the branch, a short distance below his Fort, the First Mill that was built in Kentucky. How he obtained the stones and the materials for it I know not

In 1794 he went to Shelby County & erected cabins & a water grist mill on Bull Skin [watercourse]. In 1797 after the birth of all his children, moved his family to Shelby.

I am not well acquainted with the political career of my Father. He was a Democrat of the Jefferson school. He was frequently during the Troubles with the Indians elected a Delegate to the Virginia legislature. In 1781 while attending the General Assembly of Virginia at Sharlottsville, during the invasion of Cornwallis into that state from South Carolina, Lord Cornwallis ordered a ___ under Col. Tarleton (I think, see Lee's Memoirs) to seize upon the Governor and the Assembly. The British Troops had almost reached the Assembly House before news of their approach was given; the Governor and members fled immediately, and my Father as being the stoutest man in the Assembly, picked up the bag containing the State Treasure in Gold & silver and carried it off "up the hill" in safety and beyond the reach of the British Plunderers.

He was a member of the first conventions that framed the two Constitutions of Kentucky. In 1796 he was a candidate for the office of

Governor against Garrard & Thomas Todd. There was a plurality of Electors on his ticket chosen by the people (by the old constitution the Governor was chosen by Electors elected by the people), but in the college of Electors they decided, notwithstanding the constitution was silent on the subject, that it required a majority of the Electors to choose a Governor, and in the College Todd withdrew & by intrigue Garrard received the votes of his Electors.

    David Logan, my Father's Father, had five sons, viz. Benjamin, John, Hugh, William, & Nathaniel, and three daughters, Mary, Elizabeth, and Margaret. His wife Jane McKinley came from Ireland at the age of 10 years. He, David Logan, died in 1762 in Virginia, and left the care and support of his family to his eldest son. My Father, who spurned the unjust operation of the Law of primogeniture, divided his Father's estate equally among all his Father's children. Ann Montgomery, my mother, was born in Virginia on the [blank] day of December 1751. **(4)** She was the second daughter of William and Jane Montgomery and married my father at the age of 20 years.

    The following is a transcript from the Bible in the possession of my Brother, Dr. Logan, the delay in receiving which has delayed this letter:

David Logan, son of Ann and Ben Logan, was born April 10th 1774
William Logan was born December 8th 1776
Jane Logan was born September 26 1779
May Logan was born April 8th 1782
Elizabeth Logan born May 22nd 1784
John Logan born December 15th 1780
Benjamin Logan born January 3rd 1789
Robert Logan born August 30 1791
Ann Logan April 9 1794

David Logan died Sept. 26 1816
Robert Logan was killed at the River Raisin on the 22 January 1813

Jane Allen died 27 February 1821 (Col. John Allen killed at the River Raisin Jan. 22, 1813)
William Logan died 9 August 1822
Ann Knox died October 18 1825
Col. Knox died in 1823

I have thrown these facts together without regard to method, and hoping they may serve you I subscribe myself

Very respectfully
Mary Smith

My sister Mrs. Wickliffe has reminded me of an anecdote connected with my Father which I well recollect. It was about the year 1788. He had a lot of beaves [beef] slaughtered at the Falls, Louisville, and boated it to New Orleans, where he sold it out but at a rate so low that he was apt to suffer considerable loss by his trip.

C____ , who had obtained their portion of his Boat load without paying half its worth for it, accosted him and very tauntingly asked him "Well, General when will you bring us another load of Beef?" He replied "when I bring men enough with me to eat it." There was that, in his manner, that struck consternation with those who heard his reply that they went off immediately & raised money to pay him his price and demands, which they paid him without further effort on his part.

12C46-46(5) John L. Ballinger letter, Frankfort, Ky., Jan. 11, 1845

Mr. Lyman C. Draper
    Dear Sir

Before leaving home for this place, my mother, Mrs. Jane Ballenger, put in my hands your Letter of the 6th of Oct. last with a request that I would answer it according to the best of her recollections on the subjects proposed by you to her. She is now an old woman in the seventy first year of her age, and the sole surviving child of the late Col. John Logan, my Grandfather.

Her Grandfather, she thinks was by the name of David Logan, died before she was born in the State of Pennsylvania. Her information is that he was a native of the North of Ireland and Emigrated when young to America. He died when the most of his children were young, who were afterwards raised by their mother.

Gen. Benjamin Logan was the oldest son and by the laws of primogeniture in force at that time was entitled to the real estate, but he made an equal distribution of the same amongst others. My Grandfather John Logan about or immediately after his marriage with Miss McClure moved on Holston River at or near where the Town of Abingdon now stands, at that time called Black's fort.

Whether his **(1)** elder brother Ben had preceded him, and where my mother was born, she recollects of his mother often telling her of the occurrences at that time [in Virginia]. She recollects indistinctly of the family having been seated at Dinner when news came of the Indians being in the Neigbourhood. Her mother with the children immediately sought refuge in Black's Fort and her father with a company pursued the Indians, overtook and defeated and killed the most of the Indians. She does not know any of the particulars of the Fight except that she always understood that it was in that battle her father lost one of his fingers. It was a Frontier Post, and her father was very often engaged in expeditions against the Indians. Gen. Benjamin Logan, she says, moved with his family to the now state of Kentucky in the year 1775, as she has always understood, and settled Logan's or St. Asaphs Fort.

John Logan visited Kentucky in 1778 and determined to remove with his family, and in the fall of 1779 carried his intention into effect. She knows that her father was on various military expeditions but she was too young to recollect distinctly the particulars. She has known him frequently to start at an hour's warning when news would come of the settlements being broken up and families murdered and it was seldom the Indians escaped.

Her father was **(2)** in some of Gen. Clark's Expeditions in the West and he and Hugh Leeper were the first men who ever brought cups & saucers to Kentucky, the people having previously eat out of Noggins.
The man Gen. Ben Logan brought into fort was named Harrison and he did it by rolling a Bed up & pushing it before him, he crawling after it. Then throwing it on his back he carried the man in, for Gen. Logan was a man of great personal strength.

Ben Logan was the Senior Officer & John the Second in command. Gen. Ben Logan was a man of great coolness, deliberation & prudence. His brother John had more impetuosity about him.

Col. John Logan died at Harrodsburg, Mercer County, Kentucky about the year 1808, aged as we suppose about 54. He had gone there for the benefit of the medical waters, his residence being in the Town of Frankfort. Although he was a very active, daring and even reckless soldier, he was remarkably taciturn and a man of but few words. He was the Treasurer of the State when he died.

My father, Joseph Ballinger, apprehended the Harps and had them guarded in his house for about three weeks. They had killed a Mr. Langford in the Wilderness and they were apprehended for this murder. After they were tried they were sent to the District prison at Danville where they continued to make their escape as was supposed by the aid of money, but this was only rumor.

Big Harp was upwards **(3)** of six feet high and remarkably strong and active. He was a man of very savage appearance with a remarkably black bushy head of hair, which fell over his ears & shoulders. His companion Little Harp was a small man with sandy colored hair and a pleasant agreeable appearance. They were first apprehended in their Camp upon Green River some twenty miles south west of Stanford where they had some two or three women with them. They were lively whilst in confinement and did not seem in the least depressed. Big Harp sang finely and amused himself in that way. After they broke jail in Danville, they went down into the southern part of the state of Kentucky, and whilst on their rout they killed young Trabue, a boy who was riding on a bag of meal, which they wanted. They afterwards attacked the family of a Mr. Stigall in his absence from home, murdered his wife & children, how many I do not know, and burnt them up in the house.

  The Citizens of the Country raised up in arms and pursued them with Stigall and amongst them was a tried soldier named John Leeper, a very large, strong and active man, who was placed upon the best & fleetest horse of the party. They got upon the Trail of the Harpes and found them **(4)** encamped, but the Harps saw them in time to mount their Horses and fly. Leeper being the best mounted soon outstripped his companions and gaining upon the Harps, they separated. Little Harp made his escape because Leeper paid no attention to him & he slipt away unperceived by the others. Leeper continued the chase with unabated ardour. His object was in view but was nearly as well mounted as himself and he being afraid he might escape, determined to risque a shot. He did so, and missed. Big Harp returned it and missed also & continued his flight. Leeper now abated his speed and loaded his Gun on Horseback still keeping the chase in view. They had now reached a long space of ascending ground and Harp urging his horse beyond his strength, the Horse failed & gave out. Leeper rode up to him, demanded of him to surrender which he refused to do, and supposing Leeper had not reloaded his gun, cursed him. Leeper then shot him in the thigh, breaking it & killing his horse at the same shot. [The horse] fell dead and caught Harpe's leg under him. He continued **(5)** in that position untill the Company came up, when some of them required Stigall to kill him. He did so very reluctantly at last by cutting off his head. Harp appealed to Leeper to protect him, but he refused to interfere and left him to his fate.

  Little Harp made his escape and was finally hung in Natchez, Mississippi after having committed a great many depredations with the robber Mason, whom Little Harp finally killed, cut off his head in order to get the reward of $1000 offered for it. In claiming the reward, was recognized & afterwards tried & hung.

  My Grandfather was on an expedition against the Miami Indians under Gen. Logan in 1782.

I have thus hastily thrown a few of the reminiscences of my mother concerning my Grandfather together and if they are of any use to you, you will know how to apply them, what to use and what to omit. I am sir

Respectfully yours,
John L. Ballinger

12C47 Interview with the Hon. John McKinley of the Supreme Court, Louisville, Ky., Fall, 1846. *The lower parts of pages 47(1) and 47(2) are in reverse order.*

Gen. Ben. Logan - He was bold, daring & taciturn, & when he spoke, it was always to the purpose. When he returned from the campaign of 1786, a young fop at Danville - a class for whom he ever entertained very little regard - after congratulating him on the success of the campaign, added he was sorry that he should have tarnished his well-earned fame by killing Moluntha. "I did not kill him" said Logan, "nor order him to be killed & as deeply regret the circumstance of his death as any man; but since you seem to sympathize so deeply in this case, you had better marry Moluntha's queen, whom I have among the prisoners."

In the Legislature of 1793, Logan was a member; in organizing the judiciary; he voted for the liberal salaries for the judges, voted that they should have one thousand dollars per annum. This was by peace-meal [sic] reduced **(1)** to three hundred dollars per annum. Gen. Logan arose, & simply remarked, "that a judge should be a gentleman; that very few men, in the then state of society, would be found to agree to behave themselves like gentlemen for $300 a year." This speech had great effect.

12C47(2) Interview with Mrs. Col. George Rogers Clark Floyd of Louisville, Ky., Nov. 17, 1846.

Col. John Floyd was 3 years teaching in Colonel William Preston's family [in Virginia]. Became engaged to Miss Jane Buchanan, then went to sea. On return as the vessel was entering Hampton road, he was captured. Floyd [was] taken to London & confined near 12 months in the Tower. A lady of nobility visited the prison to render kind offices. [She] asked Floyd who he was. He said he was an American &c & secured her sympathy. [She] said she would render him any service in her power. Floyd said that if she could send a letter, he would write to Dr. [Benjamin] Franklin. He thought the Doctor would use his efforts to get him released or exchanged. At length this lady managed in some way to effect his escape. Floyd went to Paris. Dr. Franklin befriended him, got clothes, a scarlet coat among other things, in which Floyd was subsequently married, & afterwards killed. The Doctor secured Floyd a passage home.

After marriage, he moved to Kentucky. [They were] 9 months without bread, & when a traveller presented Mrs. Floyd two ears of corn, she kept it in case of sickness. [This must have been in '80 after the hard winter. LCD] Built a cabin, had it lined with dressed skins &c.

When Col. Floyd was killed in April 1783, he had started for Harrodsburg to get some land titles consummated. He was accompanied by his brother, Charles Floyd, & Alexander Breckenridge. When near what is now the P____t Springs, in Bullit County, they were fired on, & Floyd shot through the body. He wore his scarlet coat, which he had been advised not to wear, as it rendered him so conspicuous. His brother Charles rode behind him after he was wounded (Indians having fled away) & helped him on. His entrails &c came out of wound. Took him to the river [several words illegible] to Stevens's Station where he died some 10 hours after receiving his wound. [He was wounded Tuesday, 8th April & died on Thursday the 10th, 1783. Col. Fleming's Diary. LCD]

When Mrs. Floyd (who afterward married Alex. Breckenridge) died, by her request the scarlet coat of her first husband was enclosed in the coffin.

12C48 Obituaries and Resolution for Benjamin Logan

Died on the 11th inst., General Benjamin Logan, while siting at supper. Between the hours of six and seven he was taken with an apoplectic fit, which terminated his existence in a few minutes.

By his death, the country is bereaved of a friend - his acquaintances of a beloved companion - his family of a fond husband and indulgent parent. To pronounce ___ upon the services he rendered his country, both as a soldier and Statesman, language must fail.

"Come then, expressive silence, muse his praise."

On Monday last the General Assembly passed the following resolution unanimously:

Resolved, That the Members of the General Assembly mourning in token of that high regard and respect which the people of Kentucky entertain for the memory of the deceased General Benjamin Logan, the firm defender of his country.

Palladium, Frankfort, Ky., Dec. 16, 1802

Gen. Benjamin Logan, living in Shelby County, died on Saturday evening, 11 December 1802, "of an appoplexy."
Kentucky Gazette II: 22, vol. XVI, No. 848, Tuesday, 14 Dec. 1802

The General Assembly of Kentucky passed a resolution regarding the death of Gen. Benjamin Logan.
Kentucky Gazette, vol. XVI, no. 849, Tues, 21 December 1802

12C49-49(15) From Elijah Farris, born 1762, notes taken in Paoli, Washington County, Ky., Nov., 1844 *This is the first of two somewhat disjointed interviews from Elijah Farris. They are written in one of Draper's small notebooks. Sequence and page numbers are difficult to determine. The main topic is Donelson's Expedition to Tennessee in 1780.*

Col. Donelson was some engaged against the enemy. He lived on George's Creek in Pittsylvania [County, Va.]. 640 acres to every man who would go & raise a corn crop on Cumberland.

There were altogether 300, including men, women & children. Elijah Farris enlisted, got to the Long Island late in the fall of 1779. Built cabins & camped along the bank of the river, & built 40 flat bottomed boats. Killed game, deer, turkies, geese & ducks, but not always enough. Sometimes could buy corn & bacon. About 200 souls embarked. A large number went by land, some 100 by land [doubtful - LCD]. Edmund Jennings went by land.

At the upper fort at [?] Chiccamauga, saw two Indians who ran off, & Donelson raised a flag, then they returned & were friendly. Donelson gave them presents and a canoe, & they said the whites could pass in safety.

The Indians soon commenced firing on the boats & fired on a man, perhaps Blackamore[?], who was shot through the body, lived 10 days. Stopped & buried him on the river bank. There were two boats with small pox, about 30 [persons ill with smallpox] in all. When first taken [captured?] a woman threw herself overboard & drowned, seeing which the Indians threw her small child in after her. Then went on down to the Suck [whirlpool]. The Indians run across the bend (perhaps 4 or 5 miles across & much further by land) to the suck, & there fired on the boats again. Jennings' boat was suffered to float along, the men laying down, until the boat ran on a rock. Several Indians attempted to swim to the boat, but old Jennings fired briskly on them & beat them back. Young John

Jennings & another man concluded to swim ashore & give themselves up, confident that they all would be taken. The young man was immediately tomahawked; & Jennings taken captive. The man killed was about [age] 30.

Old Jennings was now left alone, no man to help, & he commenced throwing out goods, & among other things a feather bed with a young suckling child – accidentally - the mother too late discovered the mistake. The Indians did not pursue below the <u>Suck</u>, & some half a mile below camped. The fight at Chiccamauga in the morning, & at the Suck the same day.

When the boats would get between him and the Indians… young Donelson [wanted] to go ashore & fight, but Col. Donelson thought it rash.

After dark heard a noise striking on the side of a boat. It turned out to be Jennings's boat, great rejoicing. His boat was riddled with bullets & almost sinking. His property was transferred & his boat soon after sunk.

It was thought there were 500 Indians lined the shore at Chiccamauga; the whites had the fairest kind of shots.

At the mouth of the Tennessee River was a large tree uprooted & the top at the Ohio [River], the current pretty strong, the river swollen. Two of the boats made several attempts to head around the top of the tree, but every time were forced back several hundred yards by the current. Finally floated off downstream calling out "Farewell, farewell."

Col. Donelson had a swivel [cannon] on his boat, & once or twice at Chiccamauga got his boat in a proper position to fire but made no impression. After that day, [Indians] would keep up fire of nights, when the whites would fire back at the blast. The Indians were about 3 days around & then waylaid the paths & killed several hunters for several days. Thomas Spencer was there.

One day soon after the attack, my informant, Farris, & two others went out hunting, & three miles off were fired on by a large party in ambush, & one of the men was shot through the thigh. All escaped into the fort; when near they saw a Negro cutting down a sapling, & warned him to retire to the fort. He said he would after he finished cutting his tree down. The others had scarcely reached the fort, when they heard ___ fire. The Negro ran some distance towards the fort & fell. A party run out, beat back the Indians, & brought in the Negro, who was found to have had the skin of his belly barely cut through, his entrails let out in the sand. He was carried in on a blanket, his entrails cleanly washed with warm water, greased & pushed in, & the cut sewed up. He soon recovered.

The man who had been shot in the thigh recovered in due time, & said he would not risk his life again for meat, for he would as soon starve as be killed. Poor fellow, in the fall of 1780, when one morning opening the fort gate, a concealed Indian shot him dead.

Freelyn's Station

In day time nearly sun down, some Indians stole up & seeing a little girl at play just within the fort gate, an Indian reached through & seized her & scalped her alive. The mother seized a hoe handle (the hoe had been taken off for baking pones on), & seeing which, & mistaking it for a gun, shot her through one of her breasts, & the Indians ran off. One night a party of Indians got into the station. A Negro opened the door of the house & went into the fort yard thinking the Indians were without, & was shot down. Major Lucas was killed. Three men in a house played so warmly in firing on the Indians that they clambered up over the houses & cleared off.

In the summer of 1780, while two men were out three fourths of mile back of the fort, grubbing [hoeing], they were some distance from each other. A party of six Creeks stole up & took one by surprise. While yet standing, one out with his knife cut & wrung off the man's head while others were holding him, & ran off with it. The other man, while the Indians were busy with their captive, squatted in the tall weeds & escaped (Haywood p. 113).

In the fall of 1780, a young lady who came in Blackamore's boat, was shot & killed when going to the spring for water.

In fall of 1780, old Mr. Jennings went up Cumberland in a canoe, about 2 miles above Nashville, was shot at, ran ashore, & while ascending the bank was mortally wounded. [He] returned to the boat & went to the fort & died next morning.

One day in 1786, Lucas & others, 5 or 6 in all, went out hunting on Harpeth [River]. Lucas got the main spring of his lock [rifle] broke, & while returning home was shot with an arrow which struck in his breast. He attempted to draw it from the wound, but the wooden portion came & left the bearded brass arrow. He escaped to the fort & with pincers had it extracted, fast in the breast bone.

One day in 1780, Farris & another man going out into the large field to work were shot at by Indians in ambush, the man shot dead. Two scalps taken & [enemy] decamped with the yell of victory. Farris escaped.

In the fall of 1781, James Farris & family, one Scaggs & family, & the Jennings family (Farris was old & could not use a gun - his son Elijah, Edmund Jennings & Scaggs had each a gun) - started for Kentucky, got horses & had plunder carried as far as Green river at the old crossing place. There were some empty cabins, & took possession. Then the horses (which had been hired) were returned.

It was the calculation for young Farris to go to the settlements in Kentucky & get horses to move there to Harrodsburg. But Scaggs, out a-hunting, discovered a party of fifty Indians, & he hastened to the cabins & all fled, leaving everything behind. The Indians in a few moments came up, plundered what they wished, fired [burned] the cabins & went off.

The people now concluded to make the best of their way to the settlements, & rambled ten days before reaching Wilson's Station, living all that time on ___. Jennings went up on Kentucky River. This trip was severe, waded streams, taking the children [over], & of nights lying on the cold ground, weather cold.

Wabash Campaign 1786

Col. Barnett of Lincoln, Major James Downey, Major Anthony Crockett. My informant Elijah Farris was a captain of horse. The Americans had sent word in to [George Rogers] Clark & others to come to their relief. One young Captain wrote a brief address to come to their relief. This produced the effect to induce many to go on the campaign. The Indians mixed friendly with the French & the few Americans were cooped up in the fort at Vincennes, & killed a good many, straggling. The Americans were greatly relieved when Clark came. Went up about 80 miles above Vincennes, got out of provisions & returned.

Scott's Campaign – 1791

Rendezvoused at Harrodsburg. Went to north of Kentucky River. Elijah Farris a pilot & spy. Struck the Indian town. The first house - two Indians in it, Capt. Price's Company in advance, the Indians ran out, dodged under the horses, & Farris shot one of them. The town was completely surprised, & the Indians ran for the river & many of them hid under the overhanging bank & finally would make a dash to cross & dive, but not one was known to have got over. Seven or 8 canoes with Indians in them were all emptied; occupants shot out. Took some 60 prisoners - 3 warriors among them. Doesn't acknowledge that they were lost returning, or that Hardin had the return piloting to himself, but my informant's memory not altogether the best on many points.

[William] Whitley

In 1782 about December, two Indians came & stole 3 horses. Whitley & 18 others went in pursuit some fifteen miles, overtook the Indians in camp in the night, & fired on them at their [camp] fire, &[were] both slightly wounded each in an arm at the fire as they were lying down.

Ran off; recovered the horses, & camped at their fire. Next morning, snow on the ground, tracked the Indians till about 10 o'clock when Nathan & Elijah Farris & William Hall were in advance, overtook.

Due to microfilm pages perhaps being out of order, the following two accounts about female captives are incomplete.

The two first nights they tied her, but did not the third night. She did not sleep, & when they were asleep, she stole off. After a while they missed her & ran in pursuit in every direction. She, hearing them, hid under some drift wood in a branch. Some of the Indians came very near, finally gave up & returned to camp. She resumed her flight. At day wearied & sleepy she sat down beside a tree & soon fell asleep. She dreamed her brother came to her & told her to take off to her right & she would get safe in. She followed this direction & in due time reached Blackamore's Fort, her clothes nearly all torn off, having eaten nothing from the time she left the Indians. She was 3 or 4 days getting in. (vide Haywood p. 259).

12C49(?) *fragment*

...went to the defeated camp on the waters of Rockcastle, trailed the Indians. In examining their tracks on the damp ground, was discovered that the Indians numbered ten or twelve, & that there was a shoe track of evidently a female.

Among the hills of Rockcastle & Laurel, overtook the Indians about mid-day, singing & dancing around the pile of plunder. The white woman prisoner sitting some ten steps off on a log and an Indian sitting by her side a part of the time. The whites crept up & fired. The Indians broke, making bloody trails, & ran down a small clifty branch.

12C50-53 Interview with Elijah Farris *Page numbers are unclear.*

December 1781, a party of nineteen – Elijah Farris & William Overall were of the party, & Julius Sanders was the leader. [They] left Nashville and went up Cumberland to Price's Settlement. Killed several buffalo & 130 bears. The buffalo were killed for meat for the present use of the party, & the bear meat to take home. All went up on horses. When about ready to start back, one of their out-camps (not their Station camp) was attacked one night by Indians & killed three out of six hunters. The Indians decamped.

Three large canoes of poplar were dug out, and loaded with meat, and three men to man each canoe…

The river was in full flood, & on the 28th of December they started for home. That night one of the canoes, in which was Elijah Farris, taking the lead, in the darkness they accidentally ran near shore which was flooded over. Amon the bushes and saplings the canoe upset & sunk. The three men seized hold of what they could. Farris got hold of a small sapling and clambered up it & it would bend down & let him in the water again, & so he kept doing… One third of the bear meat was lost…

52 LCD: Elijah Farris [4th Scrapbook. LCD]

About 1785, Elijah Farris & John Davis went from Wilson's [Station] down Kentucky River to hunt buffalo. Took up camp & Farris went out a little distance to make discoveries, and found where a bear had taken up its abode in a cave in the rocks. They had two dogs, a large & small one. The large dog was sent in, and returned no more, & then Farris took his gun & went in, saw the enraged animal's fiery eyes rolling, fired, & retreated out - the bear snuffing. Farris re-loaded, & re-entered the cave, & again fired at the glaring eyes, & again retreated. He now sent in the remaining dog, & as it did not bark, concluded the bear was dead. The two hunters then went in together, with the understanding if the bear was not dead, they could rouse it out. As the cave was small, they would lay down among the leaves, & let the bear run over them. They went in, Farris ahead, who felt the bear, & exclaimed "Davis, here he is," & with that, Davis, not overly bold, ran out on his hands and knees in such haste that the overhanging crag severely cut and lacerated his back. Farris tried to get him back, but could not. Farris finally got a long grape vine, went in, found the bear dead, **53** fastened the vine around it, & hitched Davis's horse to the end at the mouth of the cave, & drew out the bear, one of enormous size. He had killed the first dog out-right.

Another Hunting Adventure

At another time, Farris was out alone hunting with his dogs, & discovered a bear in a standing hollow poplar. The bear had crept in some fifty feet from the ground, & then went down the hollow tree. Farris clambered up a tree by its side, with a torch, and built a fire at the aperture, the fire dropping down soon roused out the bear, who came up & stuck out its nose, & then retreated back. Presently the fire growing warmer, the animal bulged up & out. Farris within reaching distance from the other tree, hurried the bear down by the application of the torch in its rear. The dogs kept it at bay until Farris got down & killed it.

Note by LCD – This affair was doubtless in Dec. 1780 – not 1781, for it will be seen by Mr. Farris's prior narrative that in the fall of 1781 he moved to Kentucky with his father & their families, & returned no more to reside in Tennessee. I did not note the contradiction – this conflicting of dates when I made the memorandum, but the correct date is sufficiently palpable. See <u>Haywood's Tennessee</u>, p. 116

fragment

One of Farris's children in the haste was left asleep on the bed & it was killed. A Negro woman of Nathan Farris had her arm broke with a ball, but the Indians did not further molest her. A Negro man who was out cutting timber, hearing the shooting, met Nathan Farris's wife & 2 children, & conducted them in safely. Though shot through the body, tomahawked & scalped, Nathan Farris recovered his senses & could talk after the Indian had gone off. The Negro woman bound up his head as well as she could with her arm broken. A relief party soon came from the Station (2 miles off, Elijah Farris thinks - & probably Casey's) & Farris soon after expired.

Jesse Yoakum, who lived on Shawnee Run, was taken at the Blue Licks & subsequently escaped & returned.

12C54-54(9) Interview with Armistead Miller, Lincoln County, Ky., born July 25th, 1768.

Capt. John Miller joined Col. John Donelson at the boat-yard at the Long Island of Holston. Spent the hard winter in camps strung for ten miles along the river, building boats. Killed plenty of deer. The cattle drives started in the fall - Josiah Ramsey – Winters - Lindsay - Solomon Turpin & others. The hard winter caused them to tarry in the cane, many died (many buffalo died of that hard winter) & when spring opened, the freshes drowned many other buffaloes. There were 40 boats, batteaux & canoes - started in spring, when the river opened. At Chiccamauga town Indians came to John Donelson, Sr.'s boat, & behind it was an army to attack, & he landed them. [The Indians] made profession of peace, but they parleyed only to gain time, & then commenced firing on all the boats. They wounded James Jones through the thigh & others took the two rear boats, [in which the passengers] had the small pox, & were kept behind. The Indians slipped in on them in their canoes & captured one woman. Seeing they were about to be taken, [she] jumped overboard & was drowned. The Indians took the small pox [boat?]. The Indians followed the same day along to the Suck, at which Indians reached first & were ready to receive the whites, & fired on the boats as they passed. Here as at Chiccamauga they had to row **(1)** at a hard rate. At the suck it was perilous, & had to keep close to one bank or the other to avoid the whirlpool. The Indians did no mischief after passing the Suck. No material accident over the Shoals, rapid work.

At the mouth of Tennessee River, held a council whether to go up or down. Some went to Natchez, allowing if they went up Cumberland they would all be destroyed. Going up Cumberland, killed game & cooked herbs for greens. Each was saving a little bunch of corn & pumpkin seed for planting. A little above the mouth of Red River, Solomon Turpin shot a bear in the river.

[Tthose in the company were] James Renfroe, Jesse Renfroe & their families; Isaac Renfroe; John Ban___ & family; Cartwright & wife & Mill___ Crutchfield; wife, several children; Johns & family; Jones & family; John White & wife; Capt. John Miller & family; Solomon Turpin & family; James & Thomas Jones & families - making sixteen families, about eighty souls & four Negroes. Went up Red River nine miles & settled on the bluff of the northern bank sometime in April. Made a camp-fort of half-faced camps - two rows from the river **(2)** [with the fort] ends open. Cut off some of the bushes, planted some corn & pumpkin without fence.

Moses Renfroe was the leading man of the settlement. He was a fine gunsmith, & made many a rifle. A "Renfroe rifle" was a passport all over the west. Moses, Jesse & Isaac Renfroe were all Baptists preachers; Isaac Renfroe preached Sunday at the station.

Turpin & Dewees went out one day hunting & when not exactly together, a panther sprang from a tree upon Turpin & stuck his claws into both shoulders, bit him on the head & tore his clothing with his hind claws. Would have killed him but for Dewees running up & knocking off the unwelcome visitor with the breech of his gun & killed him - fearing to shoot lest he should kill Turpin.

Young James Renfroe, a son of Moses, out a-hunting, got lost & was 2 nights gone before he got in. It was feared the Indians had killed him. Caught sturgeon (one six feet) & other fish; buffalo, deer, elk, bear, &c & ducks & geese. John Lumsden came there from one of the other stations.

One day in June while in a mulberry tree gathering fruit one Sunday evening, and others at their trees, three shadows were seen slipping thro the spice[?] bushes & all fired & killed Lumsden, scalped him & dodged off. The **(3)** whites carried in his body & buried it.

Next day Solomon Turpin went out hunting, & on his return was killed &

scalped within three hundred yards of the Station. His body was brought in & buried.

All was now consternation. Men were sent to Nashville, Eaton's & Manscoe's for aid to move to those stations. Several came with horses. Manscoe came with the others, carried a portion of the families & returned for a second load. Josiah Ramsey was along & Joseph Renfroe & Negroe came also. They took all [the] People & nearly all the property. Started about daylight, travelled all day without anything to eat, crossed Sulphur Fork & then up Miller's Creek, & camped at a spring running into Sycamore Creek, tied up the horses. That night Indians, howling like wolves, owls &c, but it could not be told whether it really was an enemy or not.

Between daylight & sun rise, Joseph Renfroe & a Negroe went to the spring to get water & were both shot down, & [Indians] then dashed & fired upon the company. One Indian ran up & tomahawked James Jones, then on a litter from his wound received coming down Tennessee. His brother Thomas shot the Indian.

(4) Isaiah Ramsey took with him (my informant), Armistead Miller & young John Johns & ran off. Johns was overtaken & tomahawked; & [Indians] took Moses Jones prisoner.

Old Mr. Jones fought till he shivered his gun to pieces, but was finally killed, taken with his wife & wounded son as stated. Mr. Crutchfield, wife, & Harry Crutchfield, old Mr. Johns' wife & daughter (& grandson John Johns, as already stated), Cartwright & wife & perhaps John White & wife, tho not certain - had got the idea that 16 were killed, but perhaps that may have included Sol. Turpin & Lumsden. Mrs. Jones, the wife of James Jones with her two children, one a boy named Shadrack some 3 years old, and a sucking child. She escaped & at a little distance hid under a shelving rock, & there remained until a party went next day to the defeated camp, & brought her & her children in.

Beside young Miller, two of Mr. Crutchfield's sons, Thomas & John, escaped, & Manscoe & others who came to aid. The heads of families remained with the families & fought & died in their defence. Young Miller & Ramsey hid under a fallen tree within half a mile of the camp, & there remained till sun rise, hearing the firing & cries. Then when all was still, they slipped off.

When the relief party came to the defeated camp, found the dead bodies **(5)** scattered around, scalped & mangled, one horse killed accidentally, the camp plundered. The Indian shot by Thomas Jones was found laid beside a log, with some jerked venison, pipe & tomahawk by his side.

The Indians were about 50 - Chickasaws. Moses Jones was kept by the Chickasaws nine years, & died but a few years ago on Kentucky River. About that same time they killed Ambrose Porter near Eaton's Station [while] cutting down a cedar tree. This was in June 1780. The families were scattered among the three stations - French Lick, Manscoe's & Eaton's.

When the massacre took place at the Clover Bottom, a party of Moses Mauldin, Jo Looney, John Hamilton & others pursued. Hamilton & Mauldin killed one & brought in his scalp to Manscoe's station. This Looney was a lazy fellow & at the Station would sneak the others' wood, & sing of nights (after he had been charged with it): "I'll sing you a song & sing it good, Let every one take care of his wood."

James Cain bored a hole in a stick of wood & put in some powder & plugged it up & placed it within Looney's reach. **(6)** [Looney] got it one evening, placed it under his kettle & blew it & broke it to pieces, a sad loss in those times.

In March of 1781, Miller, Col. Donelson, the Henrys, Renfroes, Turpins moved to Kentucky. Col. Donelson lived at Logan's a short time, at Whitley's & then built a station in the neighborhood of Col. John Bowman's, & in 1784 returned to Tennessee to Manscoe's Station.

Col. Harrod was like Moses, went out to view the promised land. He died, was buried in the valley of Moabe, & no one knew where his sepulchre was. See Deureronomy 34th Chap. v. 6.

Harrodsburg

In the spring of probably 1782, one morning the cows going out of the Station came running back alarmed. The men went out on their rear, killed two of the Indians secreted behind the brush near a new clearing & drove off the others. Gen. Ray was one of the whites. He was out on the Wabash Campaign.

Blue Licks

Paul Humble, of Mercer County, had his thigh broke, & **(7)** escaped on a horse with his knee shattered & got off on three legs. Walker Daniel with two others were killed on waters of Beargrass in 1783.

Cove Spring

A party went out from Harrod's to the Cove Spring, on Harrod's run, a mile from the station, & shelling corn. Indians fell on them, shot at the whites in the crib. One Indian was killed & another wounded. One white killed & James McCullock severely wounded. The Indians were driven off. Av reinforcement ran from Harrod's to their relief. (vide p. 34 – McCulloch, Ensign in '81 - vide Henry Wilkin's Notes p. 73. LCD)

John Miller, living on Rolling Fork, in the Spring of 1783, [Indians] fell upon him & family - self, wife & three children all tomahawked & scalped. Capt. Jeremiah **(8)** Briscoe & nineteen others (Armistead Miller one) pursued & would have taken them on surprise but Joseph Ayre's gun went off accidentally, alarmed the Indians. They lay down resting at a fire, the smoke of which was seen by the pursuers on a distant knob. They divided to surround them; the Indians broke - seven of them were Cherokees. The whites got but distant fires [shots], wounded one Indian, overtook & killed him. Got back the stolen plunder.

George Bright & 2 others were killed by a party under Watts on the Wilderness road, in the winter 1780-81. [Indians] took their horses & other property. Learned these facts from prisoners returned to whites.

Vannoy & family, Henry Howeshall, Maxwell, & Rounsevale, James Ferris & family - all came down Tennessee with Donelson in '80.

(9) Joseph Skidmore, of Lincoln [County, Ky.], says he was a soldier of Crockett's regiment composed of Capt. James Smith & James Barnett, about 100 men in all. Marched from Bottetourt & passed through Abingdon on New Years day, 1781, & joined Gen. Campbell at Eaton's Station, near the Big Island, & there they were dismissed.

Jos. Skidmore's uncle, Capt. John Skidmore, was wounded at "the Point" - shot through the leg, & another shot in his body.

12C55 *Isaac Shelby obituary*

"In the archives of his country and the page of <u>Faithful History</u>, His name will be presented to Posterity, For the ad----------- example of the Patriot, Warrior, Statesman and Private Citizen He was born December 11th, 1750; and on Feby 18th, 1826, Expired without a pang, Full in the Hope of Immortality."

The inscription is copied verbatim & covers two sides of the monument - the other sides are blank - nor does the monument stand to the cardinal points. Oct 15th?, 1844. LCD

12C55(1) LCD handwriting.

Here Rest the remains of Isaac Shelby [underlined 4 times] State Governor of Kentucky; To whose memory The Legislature of the State Have erected this MONUMENT. Maryland Gave him birth; He gave a life of Usefulness and Glory To the Nation."

Buried beside Gov. Shelby is Mrs. Susan Shelby, born Feb 18th, 1761; died June 19th, 1833. LCD

12C56-56(2) Interview with Sol. Clark, Pontotoc, Miss., June 1842

William Whitley's children, Nickojack, &c.

Robert Clark, a prisoner in 1786 or 1787 on Logan's Campaign to Piqua, son of George Clark [not George Rogers Clark], he married Whitley's sister Margaret. Whitley had 3 brothers.

Col. Wm. Whitley [the younger] - not known whether living near Crab Orchard. Children: Elizabeth married Robert Stinson - he is dead. She, if living, is at Huntsville. Solomon lives at St. Charles, Mo. - about 62 yrs [old?}. Levisa, as were the others, born in Kentucky about 1776.

William and Andrew both live near Crab Orchard. William lives on a splendid plantation called the "Double Springs." Easter [daughter of elder William Whitley] married a Colonel (perhaps Wm.) Lewis, lives near Frankfort, Kentucky. Polly married a Harper, near Versailles, Woodford County, Kentucky.

[William] Whitley married Easter Gill. Her father was in the Revolutionary army.

Nickojack. Some little time after the successful campaign, Whitley gave a public barbecue, & invited all who served under him on that occasion & his neighbors. The entertainment was a splendid one at his plantation - a fine one - some three miles from Crab Orchard, Lincoln County, Kentucky on the road to Stanford. The barbecue was in his yard in front of his brick house, a shaded & a beautiful grass-plat. The table was well supplied with viands, vegetables, & fruits. What called out roars of convulsive laughter was two shoats well roasted, with a Irish potato in the one end of each, a sweet potato the other. Some were so full of laugh,that they rolled off their seats upon the grass & over & over. Mrs. Solomon Clark was an eye witness.

12C62-62(46), 63 *Interviews here were taken in Lincoln County, Ky. during Draper's visit to Kentucky in the Fall of 1844. They were recorded in one of Draper's little notebooks and microfilmed four pages to each page. The first interview is with the son of William and Esther Whitley; he* *was also named William. His wife, Polly Shanks Whitley, was consulted during the interview. Interviews with George Nokes and Morgan Vardeman follow, but Draper did not clearly indicate when interviews began and ended. Sequence is difficult to determine.*

William Whitley of Lincoln County, Ky.

Col. William Whitley, born August 14, 1749. Esther Fuller [Fullen?], born May 10th, 1755 and died 20th Nov. 1833 at her daughter's, Mrs. William Harper's, in Woodford County, Ky. She died sitting in her chair. She married in 1770, had two daughters when they moved to Kentucky in 1775.

Mrs. Whitley had the two children packed on with her [on her horse] – one in her lap & the other behind – Elizabeth & Isabella. When little Elizabeth, the eldest and riding behind, would fall asleep, Mrs. Whitley would take the little one's head under her arm to prevent her from falling off. On one occasion in descending a steep bank of a creek, the horse's foot caught under a root & stumbled & pitched them all into the stream. Whitley was on this trip afoot and driving the stock. Very likely George Clark & family [were] along.

[William Whitley's] father was Solomon; his mother was Elizabeth Barnett. In after-times, both came out to Kentucky & died at Whitley's Station on the Hickory Flat. Both very aged & hence Solomon may have been of the Borden Emigration, & may have been brother to Paul Whitley. Paul was a family name.

(1) Mrs. Whitley was a better shot off- hand than Col. Whitley. In 1775 when Bowman's men first arrived, that evening they got in a match at shooting for the lead – i.e., the bullets themselves – for lead was then of moment. Whitley just coming from a hunt & learning what was going on. At that moment seeing Mrs. Whitley going to milk the cows, called out to her to come & take his gun & win the lead. She set down her milk pail, fired & beat them all. Not content with this, they kept up the firing until dark without equaling Esther Whitley's shot.

In 1795, soon after peace, a party of 21 Cherokees came & had a hunt on the Upper Cumberland River & brought in skins & furs to the Crab Orchard settlement to trade & barter. Doublehead [a Cherokee chief] & the other ___ & John Holly, a half-breed, were of the number.

An Indian was desirous of carrying off the palm at rifle target with the great white warrior, & challenged Whitley to shoot at a mark with him. Whitley said he was busy, but his squaw **(2)** could beat him. Mrs. Whitley accordingly went out & very early beat him, which very much mortified the Indian & the others laughed immoderately at his expense & advised him to give up his rifle to the Whitley squaw. Mrs. Whitley, to soothe his wounded pride, assured him, which was true, as regards shooting at any length that she could beat Col. Whitley the best day he ever saw. Many other anecdotes of her skill at rifle shooting are related.

In 1795, Whitley, at the head of ten men, started for the Cherokee Nation & took 3 canoes down Tennessee River to convey Logan's men over the river to attack the towns. Gen. Logan was to raise the men & take the nearest rout, while Whitley proceeded down with the canoes. Whitley had a dangerous time. When he reached the suck where the Tennessee River breaks so furiously through the Mountains, of which he had no previous knowledge, he lashed the canoes together & fortunately passed down in safety. At the appointed place, found no Logan, waited a few days & returned **(3)** leaving a written notification to that effect. But Logan was prevented – perhaps by Blount – Mrs. Whitley is not certain as to date, but think it was 1795.

Nickojack: Col. Whitley had 105 ____ as Mrs. Whitley thinks, & this agrees with one with Sampson Williams statement. Col. Whitley had several young lads along, whom he always encouraged ... He took pains to shew the young soldiers how to stitch on their patches to their rifle balls to facilitate loading in time of action. On his return from Nickojack he gave his men a barbecue, & roasted a beef whole. Several invited friends were present.

1812 & 1813 – went out on Hopkins' Campaign. Again in 1812 mounted his noble horse, "Emperor," & started on the campaign; shot an Indian on the morning of the 4th just at the water's edge on the opposite shore of the river, swam over on his fine animal, the bank was so abrupt he could not get up & worked it to get the ____ as he sat upon his horse **(4)** in the water.

He had often said he would prefer to die on the battlefield than in any other way & requested if killed that his companions should not suffer him to be scalped by the enemy. He wore a cocked hat; his fine-wrought powder horn & beaded belt on his noble steed made him, a six foot man, a conspicuous appearance, the moreso being as differently attired from the mounted riflemen. He was killed near the famous Tecumseh with 2 or 3 bullet holes through the body. His old horse "Emperor" lost an eye & several of his teeth, just survived several years.
Colonel Whitley was buried with military honors & logs burned over his grave to prevent discovery.

On his powder-horn, which he wore at the Thames, & which he himself very curiously[?] wrought out many years before, & which is sufficiently capacious to contain 3lbs. powder, is this poetic inscription of Whitley's own composition:

> "William Whitley, I am your horn,
> The truth I love – a lie I scorn;
> Fill me with the best of powder,
> We make your rifle crack the louder.
> See here the dread terrific ball,
> Makes Indians bleed & tories fall;
> You with powder I'll supply,
> For to defend your Liberty."

(5) Just after peace, Whitley took with him William Hartgrove & went to the Cherokee Nation after Gen. Ben Logan's Negroes. The anecdote occurred as Marshall relates it.

Levisa, [William Whitley's] third daughter, was named after the country as it was then called. Betsey Manifee & William Logan were all born about the same time & were the first births at Logan's Station.

Col. Whitley raised 3 sons & 8 daughters. One of the latter married Philip Sublett, the father of the present Col. William L. Sublett of St. Louis, Mo., who many years ago took over[?] the Rocky Mountains mine wagons loaded with goods. He let them down a Rocky precipice of 60 feet perpendicular with the aid of ropes. Returning loaded with skins & furs, ascended that difficult spot the same way. Had had many narrow escapes from the western Indians. (See Collier about Wm. Sublett. LCD)

Col. Whitley first settled at the Hazelnut Flat & there _____ (in 1779) & ever after known as Whitley's Station, about midway between the Crab Orchard & Logan's Station. In 1786, in the fall, (6) removed & settled within two miles of Crab Orchard & there lived ever after.

After the wars, the people were much troubled with thieves. Whitley headed the Regulators, sometimes whipping culprits & in flagrant instances, compel them to abandon the country.

Col. Whitley was several times chosen to the Legislature.

He was about six feet [tall], reddish, sandy hair, large aqualine nose, of great strength. He was never wounded except on one occasion – a ball or more likely a splinter of cane cut his nose slightly in an Indian fight.

Mrs. Daviess Taken

From George Nokes

Mrs. Daviess taken, as George Nokes thinks, it was 1784. Samuel

Daviess was then living at Gilmore's Lick 4 miles west of the Crab Orchard. He went out early one morning in his shirt tail with his rifle to see if there were any deer in the Lick. A party of Indians got in between him & the **(7)** house. Seeing his retreat was cut off, he ran off a mile to William Stone's & gave the alarm.

When Mrs. Daviess & her five children were taken, Mrs. Daviess exerted herself to detain the Indians by showing them different articles & advising them to catch the horses. Finally they started, Mrs. Daviess breaking twigs along the way. Finally when about two miles from the Lick among the knobs, she advised them to kill the dog, lest he might bark. An Indian gave him a blow and the dog yelped. The pursuing party, of which Nokes was one, some 40 in all & probably Whitley among them, hearing the dog (which Mrs. Daviess had hoped) give the yell, the Indians then scattered. One scalped James, some 6 years old. The youngest, a mere infant, little Polly, **(8)** [hit?] against a tree, and all fled. James in due time recovered. Polly's head was so injured as to require trepanning. She recovered & lived to a good old age. James was subsequently killed by the Indians.

The Otter Lifter [a Cherokee] was the leader – 12 Indians – he was invariably kind & humane to his prisoners. A one-eyed Northern Indian aided her up the rocky knobs while some of the others were for killing her.

Nickojack: William Whitley brought home 2 of the prisoners – a boy & girl & kept them 2 or 3 years. The boy was an ugly, ill-grained fellow, but the girl was kind, affectionate & very teachable, & learned rapidly to read & do housework. When sent to her people, she shed tears, so loath was she about leaving.

From George Nokes, of Lincoln [County, Ky.], born March 1766, came to Kentucky in 1782.

Whitley was with the reinforcement that joined Logan to bury the dead at the Blue Licks. He was a captain on the fall campaign of 1782. Nokes was not along. For his good service he was soon after **(9)** promoted to Major.

Logan had about 300 men to go to the Blue Licks, afterwards reinforced by about 200. Whitley was of one or the other parties. John Logan was not. He remained to guard the frontier, went to the foot of the Dry Ridge about 15 miles north of the Blue Licks & there met the fugitives.

Logan battled <u>there</u> until reinforcement came, & left there the 5th day & went & buried the dead. 66 bodies found, 12 taken prisoners, some burnt at May's Lick where they had 3 stakes at which they burned some or all.

Capt. Lafale, McBride was among the killed. Boone told Nokes he knocked down two Indians & ___ a third & then escaped. Netherland & a few others kept the Indians at bay.

Logan's Campaign, 1786.

Rendezvoused at Col. Henry Pawling's in the fork of Dick's & Kentucky Rivers, **(10)** September 10th [to?] October, fought at Mechacheck & got home 25th November.

Benjamin Logan [was] commander, John Logan a Colonel, Thomas Kennedy a Colonel, McGary a Colonel, Col. James Trotter of Fayette. Col. Boone was along but probably with no regiment. Col. Patterson. Simon Kenton was a volunteer & pilot. Capt. John Martin commanded a company.

Crossed the Ohio River at Limestone, up Eagle Creek on the north of Ohio to its forks to where the war trace crossed it leading from the Sandusky to the Shawnee towns. Followed that. On the 9th October a white man deserted who had got miffed. He was pursued by Kenton, Hugh Ross,& George Nokes to within ten miles of Meckacheck. Then they waited till Logan came up on the morning of the 10th, then pushed on (all mounted except 85) & reached the **(11)** town. Near the first town, perhaps a mile off, when McGary had been dispatched with his regiment of Mercer [County] men, perhaps some 200, he was met by the Indians in the prairies & rather worsted, when Ben & John Logan & the other troops, hearing the firing & hollowing, rushed up. In a few minutes the Indians fled, had fought altogether some 20 minutes.

Prior to this, at the town, Logan had taken 42 or 46 prisoners, 2 white women & 2 white children & a Frenchman trader.

In the fight several Indians were killed – 12 scalps were taken from the Indians and they were seen to carry off several of their dead and wounded. Of the whites, 6 were killed & 7 wounded. One of the latter was shot in the neck refused to have anything done for it, & mortified & died at the forks of Eagle Creek **(12)** on their return.

In the battle, an Indian shot one of McGary's men in the shoulder. Nokes seeing the smoke rise from the grass, ran up & shot him dead.

An Indian had his hip broke, crept to a briar thicket & backed himself up against a log. This was after the main body had broke. They shot Capt. William Rout & broke his thigh & Rout's men were gathered around him when Capt. Christopher Irvine came up & asked why they did not kill the Indian. He & several others rushed up & the Indian had by this time re-loaded & shot Irvine dead off his horse. The Indian was now well riddled with balls.

After the fight, Moluntha [was] among the prisoners, McGary came up & asked if he did not command at the Blue Licks? I did, said the Indian. Then McGary said "G___ d___n you, it was your day then, **(13)** it's mine now" - & with that, seized a squaw axe & at a single blow cleft his head in two, & he fell. The other Indians now raised a terrific yell, expecting they would all be killed.

Some blamed, others approved McGary's conduct & but for the interference of the men, McGary would have attacked Col. Trotter.

Among the Indian prisoners was a smart boy some 6 or 8 years old, whose skill at shooting with bow & arrow was frequently brought into the test. He took upon himself the name of Capt. Logan.

Mechacheck, McKee's Town, Moluntha's Town, Wapokonetta & near it a large blockhouse also burned. Destroyed a large quantity of corn &c, got a good many horses, a French store, & all the horses **(14)** the ownership of which were not proved by men along. They were sold at the town, the first they came to – he thinks it was Moluntha's – where the prisoners were taken & kept. The plunder – brass kettles, dry goods, horses, &c amounted to two dollars and a half a man, 885 men in all.

The first night on return, it was discovered that they were pursued. Indians were heard around. Next morning, before marching, Gen. Logan wrote a written notice, sticking on a stick saying if they killed a solder [sic] & stole a pack-horse, we would kill all the prisoners. We were pursued no farther.

The 2 women & 2 little girls had been taken prisoners in the Greenbriar country, near Donnelly's fort. The Indian prisoners were taken to Danville & kept until exchanged.

McGary was tried for killing the Indian chief, [tried] at Harrodsburg & broke of his commission – took out beeves, flour, ammunition &c on pack horses.

Page 15 contains crossed-out notes not pertinent here.
12C62(16) From George Nokes of Lincoln County, Ky., who came to Kentucky in fall of 1781. Continued – 2nd sheet. *There is no indication of a "1st sheet."* Notes of George Nokes Taken Oct. 1844. LCD

Donnelly's Fort

Capt. Michael Woods gave Mr. Nokes this information about the affair William Bryan & Philip Hammond were sent out as spies, discovered the Indians crossing at the mouth of Big Kanawha River, followed the Indians (the two spies had painted themselves in Indian style) near to within a day's march of Donnelly's up Greenbrier. There [they] passed through the Indians, when they were hailed[?], ran & escaped to the fort. Next day Indians came – killed a white man at the wood pile cutting in the morning. Then ran for Donnelly's house, through which it was necessary to pass to gain access to the fort. At the door they were met by old negro Will, of Donnelly's, & Phil. Hammond, Donnelly & Pryor. The Indians were endeavoring to force the door & partly succeeded. Hammond over night expecting the Indians, loaded old Will's large musket with 17 balls. Will asked "what shall I do, Massa?" **(17)** "Shoot," said Hammond, & Will poked out his gun between the door & jamb & fired away. Tumbled over three Indians. The other scampered off.

Two Indians, a large and a small one, got under the house. The dog made a fuss, & both were killed. That evening Hammond seeing something near a hay stack, grunting along. Pryor said it was a hog. Hammond doubted & shot. A fire brand now presented itself to view. An Indian in a bear skin was killed. This Indian remained 3 days around the fort. The hay stack would have set the fort on fire. Capt. Woods & others broke through a rye field filled with Indians & rushed into the fort.

Goose Creek Scout

In 1784, in the fall, it was reported by hunters that Indians were camped on Red Bird fork of Kentucky River. Logan, Capt. Thomas **(18)** Kennedy, about 40 men went out. At the mouth of Goose Creek, the men found a large number of wild geese just shed their wing feathers, & several of the men were engage in catching them, & others bathing in the river, when they heard 12 Indians raise the yell. The men put after them. Capt. Kennedy hotly pursued one up a hill, & finding he was about to be headed by others, he suddenly whirled & aimed a tomahawk blow at Kennedy. Being below him & running towards him, the blow struck his head with the handle & threw the instrument from the Indian's grasp. Kennedy fell to his knees, arose, seized & threw the Indian & gouged him when a man came up & shot the Indian

Gen. Logan & some others chased another Indian into the river & there shot him several times before they killed him. The others escaped. They found where the whole 12 had been in the cane.

(19) Bryan's Station

Recollect about the Indian being shot from the elm near the spring. In a cooper's shop adjoining the fort, Reynolds hearing a noise went there to see what it was. An Indian in the chimney shot at him, the ball passing through the brim of his hat. Then he shot the Indian. Thinks there was an old Colonel Bryan there.

Boonesboro

A negro, Pompey, ran off from Col. Grubb's Station, in Clark County now, & joined the Indians. Was killed in the subterranean ditch at the long siege, shot through the head, where he had posted himself to get good shots. [This could hardly have been so, as there is no evidence that Col. Higgason Grubbs, or any one else settled a station in Clark County till several years subsequent to the attack on Boonesboro in 1778. LCD]

About 1792, a party of Indians stole horses. A party pursued & at the mouth of Line Creek where it joins Rockcastle, met the Indians, fired over Rockcastle at their pursuers, killed Clark, & mortally wounded James Daviess. Johnson Ferris killed one of the Indians – the whites retreated. [Who was killed in 1782 with Daviess family? LCD]

12C62(20) The Crab Orchard Incident

On Sunday, in the fall of about the year 1783, a party of about 12 Indians secreted in the top of a black oak tree which had recently been fallen, approached the house of Capt. Michael Woods, a mile east of the Crab Orchard. Woods & his son William were absent on a scout. At the house were Mrs. Woods, her daughter Hannah, a young lady grown, & her sister Susan, younger, a Negro man Davy, & a small crippled boy of Mrs. Woods about six or eight years old. When the Indians came, Mrs. Woods seized her crippled boy on a deer skin in the yard & brought him into the house, barring the door. An Indian now made a ____ at the door & the ____ sent Mrs. Woods several feet. Again, she placed herself against the door & again the Indian would attempt to force the door. One Indian followed Mrs. Woods in.

Susan ran under the bed in terror. Davy got the gun to **(21)** shoot the Indian when the Indian seized Hannah by the arms & held her between himself & the Negro to prevent his shooting. Finally the Indian made a jump & seized the Negro, who dropped the gun, & the Indian was getting the better of the Negro pelting him with his fist, when Hannah seized a small hard broad axe & aimed a blow & entered between the shoulders. He fell back dead against the heroic girl.

By this time, the Indian who had been endeavoring to force the door desisted & with his tomahawk endeavored to get out a chunk[?] to shoot in, when James Hamilton now ran from Anthony Rogers' house, some 300 yards off, & shot the big Indian at the house. He fell & four of his companions carried him off.

(22) Some of the Indians had posted themselves between Woods & Col. John Snoddy's & Michael Ferris whose cabins were a quarter of a mile off. Snoddy & Ferris ran to the relief of Woods' family, when seeing they were intercepted, treed. The Indians now all scrampered off with their wounded man. My informant, George Nokes, now came up, having heard Hamilton's gun, found Hannah crying for joy.

Col. Snoddy & several others pursued them till night, & not overtaking them, returned. Hannah Woods was not hurt.

John Harper killed Tom Langford, a brother of Stephen's. (The peddler or trader, one Todd, was not killed by the Harpes[?], but by two Frenchmen who were hung.) They were taken by Capt. Joseph Ballinger & a party took them on the head waters of Green River. Took them to Stanford, tried them before a **(23)** Magistrate's Court. Evidence that overcoat, rifle, hat &c were Langford's. They were sent to Danville jail. There just before court, got a fro [froe?] as was supposed from a cooper by bribing him. With it, picked out [of jail]. The Two Harpes & 2 of the three women got off. One remained. She was tried and condemned to death. Got a rehearing on the ground that she had no one in her defence. At her second trial, Col. Joseph H. Daviess was assigned as her counsel, & cleared her.

At the magistrates trial, Big Harpe said he could whip any two men in town. No one paying attention to it, thinking it a <u>ruse</u> to create an excitement, throw the people off their guard & make their escape. [Moses Steele: Haywood p. 306, John Leeper, Haywood, p. 401. LCD]

McNitt's Big Defeat

A large party coming to Kentucky camped on Big Laurel River & were fell upon just before day. Seventeen were killed, chiefly young women. Some of the fugitives escaped to Col. Whitley's. He raised a party & **(24)** went to the scene of the disaster, buried the dead. Whitley got there the third day after the defeat. He found a Mrs. Bunch who had [hidden] in a hollow tree some distance from the defeated camp. And there amidst a bed of leaves, she gave birth to a child. Her older daughter was with her. Child & mother survived. It was just before Christmas & snow on the ground.

Notes of George Nokes of Lincoln County, Ky. Taken Oct., 1844. LCD. Continued.

Draper's Defeat 1793. Found a little girl. *Narrative does not continue.*

12C62(25) McFarland's Defeat

Some 30 or 40 men on Little Laurel River were attacked in broad day, by an attempt to get in between the men & women & children. The men divided – one portion to push ahead with the women & children while the others with McFarland were to remain & keep the Indians at bay. At the first onset before this division, they had rushed in, tomahawked a Mrs. Mitchell. She was carried in to English's Station a little over 2 miles from the Crab Orchard & there died.

In the fight, one Caruth[?] had his thumb shot off. A little girl who had been ___ a short time previous by a party of Indians now was retaken by the intrepid McFarland. He secreted her under a root for safety while the fight lasted. Finally a white man of the Indian party called out to McFarland **(26)** to leave his tree & come out & fight like a man. McFarland stepped out & both fired at the same time. The renegade white man fell dead.

McFarland had the tip of his powder horn shot off. The Indian beat back, & McFarland & men moved on, with the little rescued prisoner.

Whitley, with a party, went out, Nokes was one, to find the Indians. On the battle ground found considerable bloody sign. The white renegade killed was found covered up with brush & chunks in the fork of a fallen tree, a real white man: fair hair & blue eyes.

LCD commented that Vardeman verified the date of the next event, but this seems to be a continuation of statements by George Nokes, as there is no indication of a change of narrator.

Baughman's Defeat

In fall of 1783 (Vardeman thinks date correct), Henry Baughman with a large party camped on ___ Creek of Dick's River, were attacked just before day. Baughman & his mother & a boy about 10 years old were killed, & Philip Doley wounded **(27)** and the others escaped. Whitley with a party, Nokes one of them, were soon on the ground. Found Doley badly wounded in the body. He was sent in to English's [Station] & followed on the Indian trail without overtaking them. The Indians got the plunder of the defeated party.

The Minister's Defeat

Martin Haggart [Haggard], one Rice, & four others, all Baptist preachers going in to attend a religious convention to Philadelphia, were attacked while travelling near Richland in broad day and all killed. A party of four white men out hunting had killed a buffalo & were skinning it not far from Middleton's Station near Richland, were fired on by three persons whom they took to be Indians. The whites fled, leaving their horses. After going a little distance, one of the men said he did **(28)** not like to lose his horse in that way, that their enemy numbered only three & they [were] four. And it was agreed to return. Did so, crept up & fired on their foes. All fled, leaving signs of blood. The white party followed the trail to Middleton's Station. One John Rowe died that night at Middleton's of his wound.

Matt[?] Middleton was taken to Bean's Station & died in a few days, & the third, Green Middleton, was shot in the knee & recovered. Before his wound got well, he was a portion of the time bereft of his reason. He would call out "There they come! There they come! Here bloody they are – give the preachers their money!" And he would then swoon away.

McClure's Defeat

Camped at Scaggs' Creek & [were] fell on just before day – six or eight young people killed, the rest escaped. **(29)** Col. Whitley & Col. John Snoddy, Nokes along, with a party went to the scene of the defeat. A portion of the men were left to bury the dead, while Whitley, Snoddy, & Logan followed on the trail. Overtook the Indians in 6 or 8 miles & found them at the Horse Lick of Rockcastle.

Not apprehensive of pursuit, most of the Indians were dressed in the clothing they had taken at the defeat & were dancing & frolicking about in the Lick. They had taken a white girl & a Negro girl prisoners at the defeat.

John & Stephen English & George Nokes got in a deer gut within a short gun shot of the Indians, while Whitley, Snoddy & others were to their rear. It was after sun down. **(30)** Each of the Englishes selected their Indian to shoot at. Nokes was to shoot the Indian sitting beside the white girl on a log with a tomahawk in his hand. Stephen English wounded his Indian. At this moment, Whitley's party fired upon & wounded several.

John English & Nokes chased the Indian who was sitting beside the white girl up a ridge & both fired & brought him down dead. The other wounded fellows got off. The Negro girl & white girl were rejoiced at their deliverance. Retook a large amount of plunder taken at Mc____'s defeat. The goods were taken in to Whitley's Station where they were reclaimed by their owners. They gave Whitley & his party a fine steer **(31)** that they might have a barbecue. Mr. Nokes thinks Baughman's defeat was first, & then the others followed in order.

George Nokes, Senior - Station

The station was a mile and a half from the Crab Orchard.

In 1782, just before Christmas, Abram Nokes, a son of old George, was then living at Richardson's Station, some 3 miles from the Crab Orchard. He had gone to hunt a horse in the woods and was taken prisoner & killed.

On the night of the 25th July 1789, the Otter Lifter with a party came to the Station, killed Benjamin Nokes, wounded his sister Betsey, & killed a little boy of Jacob Trumbow's. They decamped. A party pursued two of the party. They came to a fallen tree in top of which the Otter Lifter lay concealed, as he afterwards himself said.

.**12C62(32)** From George Nokes, 3rd Statement. Oct. 16, 1844.

At the time that Abram Nokes was killed, Whitley, with a party, pursued. They discovered an unusually large Indian on a cliff on a snowy morning in January 1783. He was no doubt a spy. Ben. Nokes, Nathan Ferris, & James Finney gave chase, run him nearly three miles. All their guns were wet & finally the Indian jumped down a cliff of 10 or 12 feet. All three jumped after him. Each, Indian and all, tried & snapped their guns, & then seized the Indian, bound him, & brought him in. He was fully 6 feet 6 inches & powerfully made. He was taken to English's Station & there was shot by Ben. Nokes & Michael Ferris. This was Big Jim Butler. He had done much mischief on the frontier. His foot track was 14 inches long. He had often been seen in the country. **(33)** Subsequently Jesse Nokes & another brother was killed.

Whitley's Fight on Fishing Creek

On Fishing Creek of Cumberland River, Whitley was pursuing the Otter Lifter & a party that stole horses from Lt. Nathan McClure, John Hartgrove, Benjamin Langford & others. Whitley's party was small, perhaps not over seven or eight men. They overtook the Indians near midday in a fine bottom along the creek. Their horses were feeding. The Indians were about double the number of the whites. The Indians at first broke & ran & the whites went to gathering up the horses. While thus engaged, the Indians returned & shot Benjamin Langford through the wrist while he was unhoppling a horse. Then the fight commenced. Alexander Walker was wounded in **(34)** the cheek badly. Lt. Nathan McClure, as he was picking his flint to make a second fire, he was himself shot through the thigh & fell.

McClure, at his first shot, killed an Indian. John P___ killed another. McClure was very careless & had held up his foot while picking his flint. Two Indians charged upon P___ but seeing Col. Whitley nearby, they wheeled. Whitley fired at one close by & brought down the one he shot at & the other was not in range. The same bullet passed on & wounded the other, so that he afterward died. [This is misplaced by Nokes. It was on Goose Creek, 1784. LCD]

But for the ball first hitting the end of the first Indian's powder horn, the ball losing some of its force, the last Indian must have been killed on the spot.

The Indians now hauled off, & the whites, crippled as they were, were as ready. Col. Whitley took charge of Walker & some two were assigned[?] **(35)** & some 30 men pursued.

It was Christmas Eve [when they] overtook the Indians at their camp, having first heard the horse bell rattle, their horses being turned out. The Indians had a good fire. Then snowing, the [pursuers] had tracked them by snow. This camp was on Ba___y's branch of Breck[?] Creek. They crept up & shot at the Indians. One of the men even bawled out "a Merry Christmas to you." The Indians decamped, without guns or moccasins.

The whites camped there that night. Next day about noon they overtook the two barefooted Indians. One hid in a tree top, & as he ran off, Micajah Ferris shot him dead. Capt. Nathan Ferris took after the other on foot, determined to take him prisoner. After a long chase, Ferris overtook him. They clinched, & the Indian **(36)** threw him & had well nigh got Ferris's knife from its scabbard, to prevent which Ferris got one of his hands considerably cut. Finally after a few moments William Hall came up with an old sword. He gave the Indian a heavy cut across the back of his neck, nearly severed his head from his body. Ferris allowed if he had not been relieved as soon as he was, the Indian would have killed him, for he was well nigh giving out. He thought he would hardly attempt taking another Indian alive.

From Morgan Vardeman, near Crab Orchard, Lincoln County, Ky. Born 16 Dec. 1766. Came to Kentucky in fall of 1779.

Nickojack

He was out with William Whitley. He did not swim the river as Gen. ___ thinks, but couldn't swim. **(37)** Went over the river in the hide boat. Some of the men did not get over the river till the sun was an hour high. They attacked the town about 9 o'clock. Some of the Indians were hunting. They were on that day to have a green corn dance at Running Water.

Col. Whitley & men were not pleased with one being placed over him. Whitley's men were in the night in the attack. The men ___ the heaviest of the firing was over, Whitley with seven of his men, & a few Cumberland men, ran off for Running Water [Town]. They met the Indians. Thomas was shot. Rutherford, one of Whitley's men, then shot the Indian as he stuck his head from the tree behind which he was posted. Shot him through the head – ran up & scalped him. The Indians then ran.

Next morning, Whitley, Brown (Joseph, probably), & Alexander McFarland, who had fought the Indians on the Wilderness Road & now of ____. Five men started over after horses & were shot at & retreated[?]. Took 18 prisoners – killed about 60.

12C62(38) Col. Whitley

Mr. Vardeman does not doubt but that he was on a campaign in 1780. He led the party that rescued Mrs. Daviess & children. James Daviess, who was on this occasion scalped near the whole of his head, was subsequently mortally wounded. Whitley was not along. Place correct as stated by Nokes. Found the river swollen & then raining. It was not thought prudent to cross. As the whites wheeled to return, Joshua Clark & Daviess standing on some driftwood were fired at by an Indian on the opposite shore. Clark died on the way home & Daviess survived a few days after he was brought home to the Crab Orchard where his people then lived. No recollection about Joshua Ferris killing an Indian.

Whitley was rather too venturesome. He would make any risk to rescue prisoners, or chastise the Indians. Sometimes he would mount his horse in an alarm without hat or saddle, & dash to the place of danger with his rifle **(39)** in his hand & horse at full speed at the head of a little troop as valiant & as hastily equipped as himself. Never was defeated when he had the chief command & engagement.

The campaign of Bowman's, & the Wabash affair of 1790, & the failure of Clark's campaign of 1780 were the only exceptions. Together with the failure of 1795 to the Cherokee towns - & these were rather failures than repulses. This attempt against the Cherokees was certainly in 1795.

Ferris Killed

When Nathan & Isaac Ferris, & John Pointer & another were killed, Isaac Ferris & Pointer were first shot. Ferris ran to the camp & died in a few moments. Pointer dropped after a step or two. Nathan Ferris fought the Indians & by his conduct & self-sacrifice saved the women & children - & himself killed. Whitley raised a party – Vardeman one - & pursued. They crossed Cumberland River, found the Indians' hunting camp & they gone. Whitley returned from great difficulty in crossing the Cumberland with the horses from the abruptness of the banks. This was prior to 1793. Ferris had not been there over two weeks when killed.

12C62(40) William Whitley

His men were known as <u>Whitley's Minutemen</u>. They were the protectors & saviors of the frontier of Lincoln for a period of fifteen years. Ever ready, ever on the alert, rescued many defeated and scattered emigrants on the Wilderness Road. Sometimes would overtake & chastise the Indians & was the barrier between them & the more thickly settled parts of Lincoln [County]. Whitley's men were the Ferrises, McClures, Vardemans, Daviesses, Nokeses, & others.

Big Defeat on Big Laurel

This was known as McNitt's defeat. Ford, Bunch, some 60 or 70 in all. That evening they were greatly elated, & joyous, expecting to reach the Crab Orchard & be beyond the apprehension of an attack. They set up pretty late. Finally, with sentinels placed out, fell asleep. When the Indians ran in with their tomahawks & war clubs, the sentinels fired on them. The Indians killed 22, many women & children. Of one whole family, of some eight persons, not one escaped.

(41) All were found tomahawked in this camp, as though each was tomahawked while asleep, & had put his hand to his head and in the agonies of death, nearly all had some of their fingers cut off. Mrs. McNitt was among the slain & received shocking treatment. Mrs. ___ [Bunch is crossed out] had a child under a chestnut tree that night, which lived.

Whitley went out with a party, rescued the scattered survivors. Found a little girl. Pursued the Indians. Got one horse back, but the enemy had scattered & thus escaped. Old Mr. McNitt was also killed. A son of his escaped at the defeat, collected the cattle & selected for Whitley & his men a steer & shot it for they were needy. This defeat was in October, perhaps 1786.

Moore's Defeat

Sam. Moore & a large party were defeated. Moore & several others were killed. Forty head of cattle of More's were saved & his brother Robert gave a steer to Whitley & his men for a barbecue – for good service performed on that occasion. About the same time of McNitt's...

(42) ... from Nicojack the first [day] was rainy. La___ talked some & died the night following. He was said to have been a good soldier & killed several Indians.

That day (the second from Nicojack), was the sale – amounted to $1000. Col. Whitley packed out the cannon or swivel on his horse & went out on foot. He was left on the bank of Tennessee [River] at the crossing, not being able to carry it over.

At Nickojack one ___ of seven Indians got off. They had crept along under the south bank down some distance before pushing into the stream, & thus escaped.

Nathan McClure's Fight

This was in the spring of 1792. McClure's fine horse had been stolen. He, John O____, Benjamin Langford, Alexander Walker, & James Hurstgrove went in pursuit. Whitley was collecting a larger party. McClure found his horse hoppled, & Langford ran to unloose him & was fired on & shot through the wrist by the Indians in an ambush. At the crack of the gun, the men treed. McClure got behind a double oak with a small space **(43)** between. McClure tried to shelter behind both & was shot between the two, & had his thigh broke. He called to Walker & Hurstgrove to place him on his horse, & while the two men were picking him up, Walker received a very severe wound in his face, the ball having entered near his nose & out near his ear on the same side of his head. Mr. Vardeman thinks the whites did not fire. Pr___ had several snaps with an Indian in good view. When McClure was placed on his horse, the Indians did not pursue, hence the Indians could not have numbered over 3 or 4 as Mr. Vardeman thinks.

After a little distance in ascending a steep declivity, McClure was pitched from his horse & rolled down the hill, his broken leg doubling in every way. McClure was carried but a short distance further & there, beside a log on his blanket, his horse standing by him, saddled. Some said McClure advised that he should be left, that was a **(44)** cold rainy night. Whitley's party reached the battle field that evening, having followed on the trail out, but missed Walker & the others [crossed out: found McClure's & Walker's guns near the double oak]. That night Whitley's party camped in a rock-house not over 150 yards from where McClure lay.

Next morning a third party arrived – Vardeman one of them. Hurstgrove was along to show where McClure was left. Then they found the guns of the McClure & Walker near the double oak. They searched for McClure, found his horse, & his bones a hundred and 30 yards up a steep hill with the flesh all eaten off by wolves. It was supposed he had clambered up the hill to hide himself from Indians & there found a bed of leaves near where his remains were found.

These were buried. This occurred perhaps on waters of Fishing Creek, not on the creek itself.

Mr. Vardeman does not think Whitley was in this fight, nor does he recollect anything about the shot of Whitley killing one & wounding another Indian.

The Indians when they fired on McClure & his party were posted in a laurel thicket **(45)**. James Farris & ____ McKinney were the captains & Butler with a small command, perhaps. Cravens[?] would put himself forward, but really lead no command. ___ Thomas would shoot. Cravens[?] ran off. Had a few over one hundred men.

It was Capt. Murrell who thought he heard the platoon fire, in the mountain in the dark of the evening. [There] were 12 picket guards, of whom Su___ was one. Now 60 others were sent out, & then rest of the army under arms. Had fallen asleep & when the 12 saw the additional company coming with a fire-brand to find the path, & at first suspecting it was the enemy, roused up ____ who ran off. They scarcely thought anything about it, & in a short time they heard something fall some distance off, like a water-soaked ___ ____. Next morning S____ was found by some of the men looking for their horses, his hips all ____ to pieces...

End of 12C62-62(45)

12C63 Nickojack Barbecue

Whitley gave a barbecue, roasted a beef whole, erected a tall pole with a flag on an Indian mound.

Beside the Minister's Defeat, at which Haggart & others were killed, there was another defeat of Dunkard preachers on Rockcastle, four or five killed.

The Board of Officers had the two Stations – Middleton's & Woods's - placed on the Wilderness Road for the protection of emigrants. Middleton's was located a day's march from Cumberland Gap. John Woods's was located on Little Rockcastle [River] about midway between Middleton's & the Crab Orchard, calculated for the two stations to answer for the two nights in the rout, about 100 miles. Capt. Watt Middleton at one with a few men. The Middletons proved as treacherous as Indians. The narrative of their being shot, as Nokes states, is correct.

Edmund Jennings's family moved from New River to Blackamore's fort. His brother, Robert, was killed or scalped. John Vardeman, Edmund Jennings, & Nall with Boone cutting road. Nall [was] bit by a mad wolf...

End of Vardeman Notes except a separate sketch of his brother, Rev. Jeremiah Vardeman here appended and an incident at Estill's Station, also appended. LCD

12C64-64(1) Taken from Morgan Vardeman in Lincoln County, Ky. [May not possibly be accurate – date of birth. LCD]

Jeremiah Vardiman was born in what is now Wythe County, then old Fincastle, on New River about 12 miles above Fort Chiswell in the commencement of year 1776. His father was John Vardeman, who came to Kentucky to mark the road in company with Sam Drake's brother & Squire Boone, & others in the Spring of 1775. He died at his son's in Missouri about the year 1827, aged about one hundred & nine years old, a native of Sweden. At seven years old his father & family emigrated to America & settled in South Carolina, & there the old man (John Vardeman, Sr.) died at the advanced age of 125 years - a man of piety, of the Established Church.

John Vardeman, Jr. married Elizabeth Betsy Morgan, a native of Wales, in South Carolina, & soon after removed & settled in Bedford County, Va., & there both united with the Baptists, & ever after continued as religious professors.

About the year 1767, removed to New River; in 1777 removed to Clinch, & there forted at Shadrach White's in the neighborhood of the Maiden Spring fork of Clinch. The Skeggs [Skaggs], James & Henry, & Richard, all noted hunters, & their families, all forted at the same time at White's.

In the fall of 1779, removed to Kentucky & settled within three miles of the Crab Orchard & the family took part in the early Indian wars. John Vardeman, the father of Jeremiah, was too old to take an active part in the wars, but stood guard. His three sons, John, Amaziah & Morgan (my informant) all were frequently engaged in the Indian wars. His eldest son, William, was at the Point Pleasant battle, & settled first in Kentucky, & finally in the Natchez country. Both John & Amaziah were soldiers on Clark's campaign of 1782 & Amaziah & Morgan [were] with Whitley at Nickojack.

Jeremiah was old enough at the close of the Indian wars to act as scout frequently for the last year or two. His chance for schooling was very limited - all in Kentucky. Could read, write & cypher but ordinarily. One day when about seventeen, with his brother Morgan in Cedar Creek on which his father resided, Jeremiah heard in the air the sound of a choir of voices, & asked his brother if he heard it? When replied to negatively, he seemed somewhat alarmed, & it troubled him considerably. Shortly after (early in 1792), a revival broke out in the Cedar Creek Church under the preaching of John Bailey. **(1)** Had at first when he got a hope, a strong conviction impressed on him that he must preach the gospel. He kept in the church very comfortably for about two years until two or three companions of his own age who were not in the church, & so influenced him by representing that there was a time to be merry & a time to be sad, and while young ... to enjoy himself. He partly yielded to their influence. Was persuaded to attend a dancing school at the Crab Orchard & when he joined by setting his name to the paper, and very much against his wishes, he afterwards said he felt like a man condemned to death, but braved it out & went through the course of the school. Up to this time he had never attended a dancing school, never had been profane nor otherwise an outbreaking sinner, having been brought up by religious parents, his mother having joined the Baptists about the same time of his father. (His brother Morgan, now 78, wept as he related this part) & endeavored his brother Morgan to look at his dance. But he replied that he would sooner see him buried. This chide did not seem to affect him.

About this time, he married Elizabeth James, not then religious. but subsequently she became convicted under her husband's preaching. When at school he became enamored of the viollin, purchased one & in the course of two or three years became skilful in its performance. Now paid his attentions to Miss James. Her father, Squire John James & wife, members of the Cedar Creek Church, were opposed to the match. [They] said young Vardeman spent & wasted too much of his time playing the violin. His wife's parents, the best of people, became reconciled to it, when opposition was no longer of use, & with them moved to Pulaski [County], Kentucky. There he was the leader among the young people in mirth & amusement. (Soon after he went first to dancing school he left the church.) At Pulaski was Thomas Hansford, a Baptist preacher of great zeal, piety & success in his labors, was preaching from the text about the backsliding sinner, was powerfully wrought on & awakened.

After this sermon, he retired a day or two by himself, & during this time in the woods, & like a drunken man he viewed himself in a similar situation to Jonah who had neglected his command to preach. Vardeman was powerfully impressed or convicted of his duty to go forth the rest of his days. He made an appointment to preach at Pulaski. This was but a few days after the awakening sermon of Mr. Hanford… His family & relations particularly trembled for him lest he should fail. But it was a solemn discourse & he spoke with great freedom, neither wasting words nor substance.

When in the woods he looked upon himself situated as was Jonah – and the promise of the Lord was to him (Malachi, 4th Chapter). "We shall go forth and grow up as calves of the stall." And during that & several succeeding sermons, some twenty or more young persons… became convicted or converted.

Taken from Morgan Vardeman, brother of Jeremiah (who died 28th May 1842, Ralls County, Mo.).

17th Oct. 1844 – Addenda – Jeremiah Vardeman was the youngest of twelve children.

12C65-66 Morgan Vardeman interview, Oct. 17, 1844.

Estill's Station Incident - About the time of Estill's Defeat, my informant's [brother] John Vardeman was out guarding at Estill's Station. James Cain was at work in the field, & Vardeman sitting on the fence, when a party of Indians sent forward. One of their number stole upon Vardeman, came within close gun-shot, & crept behind a log. Vardeman hearing something, looked, and saw the Indian's back protrude over the log. Vardeman levelled his gun, and sent a ball through the Indian's back, so that he died & Vardeman ran for the fort, closely pursued by the other Indians. In the race, Vardeman put his ankle out of joint, & but for Cain's good conduct in keeping the Indians at bay, he would have been overtaken & killed. An incident about one Whitesides on Clinch was told me by Mr. Vardeman, & not putting down at the time, was forgotten. LCD.

12C67-67(6) From Gen. Christopher Rife, Casey County, Ky., Nov. __, 1844

The following pages are from another of Draper's small notebooks which have been microfilmed four to one page. Sequence cannot be determined. Pages numbered 7 and 8 are crossed out but are included here.

Whitley's Men – 1794

Capt. John McKinney & George Murrell, Major Jesse Cravens & Capt. William Butler, the two latter not regularly in command, but yet taking some command. Butler was something of a backwoods surgeon & extracted the ball from Don____'s heel. The night before crossing, Whitley swam the river & was absent some time to reconnoiter & see if the Indians had any spies out. Went half a mile from the landing spot on the opposite shore, all silent, & he returned, then set to work & crossed. Whitley sent some 20 men opposite to the town [Indian town not named] under Capt. McKinney, & killed several Indians. After the fight, one of the squaws in the canoes under Capt. McKinney jumped out into the river, dove & came up several feet & then down again & notwithstanding 12 or 15 shots, she escaped. And when she reached shore, clapped herself in derision.

Reached the town when the Indians were eating breakfast. They were intending to have a green corn dance that day at Running water. (1) A simpleton got a forked stick and stuck it up in the bank of the river. Seeing an Indian in a canoe far beyond shooting distance, he pulled the trigger. The ball struck the water within the bank, glanced off, & finally to the astonishment of every one, passed through the Indian & killed him.

The supplies at Nashville were voluntarily furnished by the people. Manscoe was liberal, as was Robertson, who was very kind.

The place of rendezvous was at a block house. There they chose officers & had an Indian dance in which fully 400 participated. Gen. Robertson & Manscoe were there. James Ferris was grand master or adjutant. Ferris now lives near Liberty, Ky.

(2) Whitley was probably not out in the fall of 1781 – was not along in 1786, was out in 1790 up the Wabash & joined Hamtramck. James Ferris was out...

The Crab Orchard Incident

This Indian came to Daviess's Station at the Crab Orchard, in the night. Seeing a house detached some 120 yards off, an Indian ran down to see. Peeped into the house through a crack & saw only an old Negro, an old white woman & daughter, then set down his gun & bursted into the home. He seized the Negro & had a scuffle... the Indian endeavored to get his knife from the scabbard, but the Negro prevented his doing it. The white girl seized a broad axe & struck the Indian between the shoulders & sunk it to the handle, & killed him at that single blow. The Negro now jumped up & barred the door, for other Indians hearing the fray now came (3) dashing there. One put his hand through the crack of the door & the girl cut if off outright. Then the Indian shot in beside the door & wounded the brave girl in the thigh. The old lady now seized an old gun without a lock, & thrusted it through a port-hole. Seeing this, the Indians decamped.

Gen. Logan sent for the wounded girl & had her placed under the care of a surgeon at Danville, and she recovered.

McNitt's Defeat

McNitt's or the big defeat on the Wilderness Road – a woman escaped & had a child in the woods, which survived.

The Minister's Defeat

Going from Kentucky, one Shephard Sweeney was along & escaped. A letter that had been committed to his care to convey to Virginia was found at Nickojack. Gen. Rife commanded a regiment on Shelby's Campaign, 1813, & remained in command & care of camps where fence was made across the peninsula & horses kept near mouth of ____ ____. Oct. 1844.

In the following paragraphs sequence cannot be determined.

(5?) Not long after, James Burton was out ploughing & his son Ben[?] riding horse. They were waylaid in the field. Burton was shot dead & his son beat on the head with a war-club so that his brains oozed out. He survived but a few days.

The wife of James Doolan, a son-in-law of McKinney's, who lived in a cabin a small distance from the station, was killed. Her infant child was unharmed. Two larger children ran off & hid in an adjoining rye-field & were thus saved.

In the spring of 1793, Dan[?] McKinney was preparing a new place on the waters of Green River on the frontier of Lincoln County. While cutting down a tree, Indians (a party of 5) crept upon him & shot him. James McCormick, Sr. heard the gun, raised two or three men, went out & found McKinney yet alive. He said it was a white man who scalped him; he survived about two hours.

(6) His father, Daniel McCormick, with his family came to Kentucky late in 1779. Reached the Hanging Fork in Lincoln County in December. Camped all winter with his own family only. That winter very many families wintered on the road, & none were molested that winter by Indians.

In 1780, south of Kentucky River, they were not annoyed by Indians, but in 1781 some persons were killed. McCormick started his station on Hanging Fork. Benjamin Pettit settled his station that year (see p. 20. LCD), five miles south of McCormick's. In the summer of 1781, an Indian party waylaid the trail between these two stations & killed a man named Smith who had gone out after his horse. They took his son, about 12 years old, prisoner & kept him several years. Michael Stoner then lived at Pettit's Station.

Starns's Defeat

Adam & Frederick Starns & others were going from Boonsboro to Holston, where their families were. Several others with them were defeated. Both these brothers killed, & Adam had a son-in-law killed. Jacob Starns, afterwards Captain, & son of Frederick, escaped & probably two others were killed.

John Walker went out from McCormick's Station to look for horses. About 2 miles from the Station was killed by the Indians. His horse that he was riding came dashing up to the Station with his ear slightly wounded. This was in 1781.

John Sloane & his two sons, Robert & Alexander, in Feb. 1790, went from the neighborhood of McCormicks' Station to Martin's Creek of Rolling Fork of Salt River to salt their cattle. Wintering there, encamped & had a fire. Indians crept up in the night & fired, (7?) killed the oldest man & Robert. They got hold of Alexander, but he knicked them with his fists & escaped. This date is correct for Mrs. McCormick had a child born shortly after (March 4?) and cannot be mistaken.

Logan's Scout

Indians stole horses & were pursued. When Logan's party found their trail & found they had horses with them, they determined to follow till they should overtake them. Discovered the Indian camp, & waited till day break. Indian dogs made a great fuss. One Indian crept out just at break of day, & Hugh Ross shot him. Then commenced the fight. Daniel McCormick, Jr. & Joseph Dobson pursued after two Indians. Both fired at one of the Indians & he fell dead. The other Indian instantly fired at McCormick & wounded him, the ball entered his side & circled around to his back-bone. Brought him in on a horse-litter. One John King extracted the ball – skillful in such operations. One white man was killed.

(8?) Gen. Ben Logan

Intelligence of Indian sign, so Logan said he would ride out & see if there was any reality to it. Went to the Flat Lick, about a mile and a half from his fort, was waylaid & fired at, & broke his arm. He escaped to the fort.

Benjamin Pettit…who had been several years with the Indians &

learned their mode of treating broken limbs, cured Logan, for which Logan gave him a tract of land. Logan went out of the Fort during the siege to bring in Burr Harris [Harrison] & did so with a feather bed to shelter himself. Always understood it was John Martin who went to Holston after the powder, either during the siege or about that time, during a period of extreme danger.

McKinney's Station

Daniel McKinney & connexion settled a station in the neighborhood of Pettit's Station & between the head waters of Hanging Fork of Dick's River & Green River – about the Spring of 1781.

(9?) Indians came of an evening & shot & killed a negro woman sitting by the fire in John Carpenter's kitchen. Next morning a party went in pursuit, were waylaid, & Isaac Neely was killed. A ball passed through Conrad Carpenter's clothes. The Indians escaped. Where Neely was killed was among the knobs toward the Rolling Fork, & the place since called Neely's Gap.

Boone & Callaway's Daughters Taken

They were taken on a Sunday. John Martin was one of the pursuers. The girls broke twigs (Martin never spoke of shreds) & the Indians to prevent pursuit took the shoes from the girls & gave them moccasons. [Rescuers] overtook them as the Indians were about to encamp. The girls were sitting on a log. The whites fired on the Indians and rushed up. The girls were frantic with joy, ran and embraced their deliverers. October 1844

12C68 Col. James Knox, James Dysart, William Miller & probably others – Long hunters - went to Kentucky. On waters of Green River had their Station Camp. Killed 1500 deer & got their skins, covered them up & returned to Virginia. When they returned for them, the bears had torn off the shelter & all spoiled. This was the Miller who acted so badly in Estill's Defeat. He died on Paint Lick Creek in Garrard [County, Ky.] within a few years at a very advanced age.

Gen. Logan when speaking of the Blue Lick defeat used to be affected even to tears, saying if he had been there, those gallant men would not have been so wantonly sacrificed.

Carpenter's Station

John Carpenter located his station at the head waters of Hanging Fork of Dick's River.

12C73 Samuel Davis letter, Harrodsburg, Ky., Nov. 11th,, 1854

Dear Sir

Yours of the 28th Oct is now before me. In order to answer your inquiries I must State Some circumstances which I consider connected with the inquiries you have made.

Samuel Davis, the father of James Davis, emigrated to Kentucky in the year 1779, settled in Lincoln County at a place called Gilmour Lick which was at that time an ___ frontier. In August 1782, a party of Indians, five in number, came to her cabbin one morning early and watched Until the Door was opened by my uncle and he had steped a few paces when to her surprise the five Indians took possession of the Door so that he could not enter his house. With great Dificulty he made his escape to the nearest station which was about five miles distant. He raised a party of men and returned in pursuit of the Indians, who had left his House and carried off his wife and seven children. After a pursuit of about three miles from his home they overtook the Indians with his family. The Indians, after a few shots, fled, but before they took to flight they knocked down James, the oldest son, sculpd or skelped him so that he was much disfigured afterwards. He was at the time only 11 or 12 years old. He recovered from the injury except being disfigured and grew to be a stout man.

In the year 1791 or 1792, a party of Indians stole some Horses from the Neighbourhood of his father's and he raised a party of men and pursued them as far as the Cumberland River. The Indians who had concealed themselves in the cane on the opposite side shot across and wounded young Davis, who died in about __ days, at the age of about 21 years.

Her father was my uncle and lived but a short time after the Death of his Son. I hope you have nearly finished your work. Any other information I can give you I will do so with pleasure.

I am Yours Respectfully
Saml. Davis

12C74 Mrs. M. T. Daviess letter to J. B. Bowman, written from Hayfields, Harrodsburg, Ky., 1865. Care of Maj. W. Daviess.

To Mr. J. B. Bowman
Dear Sir

Duties that cannot be postponed prevented me from answering your communication of Monday. I feel much gratified & interested in the undertaking of Mr. Draper and wish him all success.

I presume a great mass of matter that would have been interesting to him was burned in town last spring when our old home perished. I will take occasion at my earliest leisure to look over what we have left and will send to Mr. Draper **(1)** any pioneer incidents or traditions that I find.

As to Col. Daviess's papers, I have commenced examining and clipping them with a view to perhaps weaving ___ ___ ___ and changeable threads of his life. Such of his correspondence as I thought would [be] interesting to the public or if I should find the matter too complicated for my own Handling to turn it over to some one who could do Col. Daviess and his contemporaries justice.

I know not yet what these papers contain. Although alphabetically arranged, every paper has to be examined, as its initial does not indicate whether it is a family, political, or business document. I fear the other papers, the most interesting of all, are not extant.

Capt. [sic] Daviess had a kind heart & was strongly appealed to by descendants of men undoubtedly implicated in that conspiracy, to destroy them.

Col. Daviess's correspondence with the statesmen of his day is interesting and the only ___ I have of his own production – very much so as it was chiefly on the Federal relations, so strongly disputed and tested now. But these papers would be ___ to Mr. Draper's purpose.

I will furnish Mr. Draper a sketch of Col. Daviess...

James McAfee of Danville (Col. R. B. McAfee's son) has probably a good deal of matter of the kind that would interest Mr. Draper. His Father was fond of such research and in preparing a history in his youth, probably gathered up a good deal that would be interesting.

You may assure Mr. Draper of my sending him what he wishes – but it must be some time hence as I cannot command my time for immediate investigation.

Most respectfully,

M. T. Daviess

12C76 Interview with Samuel Frazee, Bracken County, Ky., November 1845. Born in New Jersey, Nov. 1754. Died March 17, 1855. LCD

Was out in Capt. William Harrod's Company on Bowman's Campaign in 1779. Edward Bulger was along. John Moredock was killed.

Saw two whites wounded beside a cabin, & the other whites retreating. Frazee saw two Indians approach the two wounded men, & he shot one of them. This attack was in May 1779. Harrod's men were posted about the center of the town. Got a good many horses.

12C77 Jeff Patterson[?] interview[?], son of Col. Patterson, who served in May 1779, served as an Ensign in Levi Todd's Company on Bowman's Campaign against Chillicothe on Little Miami.

Jeff. Patterson (1843) said his father related that an officer (Captain or Lieutenant) was wounded in one of the fights on the retreat, & was carried home on a horse litter.

Col. Patterson never attached any blame to Bowman. The moveable battery or breastwork was only designed for the use of a few, to use in firing cabins near the stockade.

Capt. Levi Todd's Company were joined to Logan's party in attacking the town.

Col. [Robert] Patterson's deposition, May 15, 1815 in a land case.

That Levi Todd, [John] Holder, Harrod, & Logan commanded companies under Col. Bowman. Marched from Lexington about the 15th of May 1779, camped the first night on the Little North Fork of Elkhorn, near the mouth of the same. Second night encamped on a small branch of Mill Creek about 2 miles northwardly from Lee's Lick. The men turned out as volunteers, so no draft was made, which would otherwise have been resorted. A day was appointed to meet the volunteers at mouth of Licking [River], & met accordingly.

There were about 70 men in Capt. W. Harrod's Company from the Falls of Ohio, & about 30 men from Lexington under Capt. Haggin, who met at the mouth of Licking, & about 200 men in our party. Bowman went by Licking Station [?] to get men & met at mouth of Licking.

12C78 [fragment in LCD handwriting]
May 30th – fighting, & commenced the retreat, fight near night, & Black Fish killed. Followed down Cesar's Creek that night.
May 30th – Kept on. Didn't hunt that night, worn down, took some repose.
June 1 – Early this day reached the Ohio just above the mouth of the Little Miami. Crossed the river – went some 3 or 4 miles to hills skirting the river. Found a large spring. Hunted, fished, & got supplies.

12C81 Bowman's Campaign.
Richard Rue's statement

"The second night after we left the Licking [River] we came in sight of the enemy undiscovered. A hard battle ensued, & we set fire to some of the Indian huts but were not able to storm the town as we had no field pieces. About ten o'clock, Col. Bowman commenced marching homewards, having had nine men killed and some wounded. We had not marched more than 18 miles before the Indians overtook us, & another battle ensued in which we stood our ground."

Samuel Davis' Statement
"In Capt. Ben. Logan's Company I marched from Harrodsburg to Elkhorn Station, near where Lexington now stands – there met with several companies, & marched to Ruddell's Station, at which place after being detained some time for provisions, we marched to a new town of the Shawnee, on the little Missouri – crossing the Ohio a short distance above the mouth of Licking."

Volume 13C contains 219 numbered pages.

13C9(3) V. B. Young letter, Owingsville, Ky., July 28, 1883

James Wade was born in North Carolina (the date I am not informed). He came to Kentucky in 1775 and was intimate with Daniel Boone. He settled on Puled Oak in Bath County [Kentucky] at a very early day and was appointed a Justice of the Peace in this county in 1813. He held the office until he was appointed Sheriff of this County in 1825, which office he held two years. James Wade was a man of fine natural ability and was a leader among men. He had several children. His daughter Peggy married Jefferson Butts in April 1815.

James Wade died in 1834 at the age of 82, so he must have been born in 1756.

I will see some of his grand children and find out where his son lives and let you know.

Daniel Boon's name, very old, date not given, appears on a beech tree at a large spring on Licking river 7 miles N. E. of this town.

You have a copy of an address delivered by me in 1876. If you can look on page 17 of that speech you will find when Boon was in this country in 1776.

13C13 LCD notes: About the whisky bottle incident, & the real facts – see Shane's Historical Collections. Vol. 1, pp. 8 & 9. No date – in winter –

probably winter 1779-1780, when a deep snow fell in December 1779.

With the whisky bottle affair, there is no certainty that Boone was present when it was deposited, yet it may have been so. His "camp" was there at "Three Forks of Kentucky" – no doubt when he surveyed lands for Col. Thomas Hart & others. As it was in June 1780, when Boone lost the money of Hart & others in Virginia for entry of these lands, no doubt, Boone had selected for them – it would appear to have been prior to that date. [In margin: Hart County.]

13C14-14(1) H. C. Anderson letter, Haywood County, Tenn., June 1, 1884

I am a great lover of just such incidents in the early history of our states as you seem to seek. They bring out in bold relief the home life detail of our early Fathers. How interesting for us, their children & grand children, to know the actions, thoughts, & interests of their lives, just as our children in the future so earnestly will desire to know the daily incidents of our lives.

The incident to which you refer in your letter about Col. Daniel Boone and the whiskey bottle I saw in print but in what paper I cannot now remember. I take the Louisville Post, the New York Sun, the N Y Times, the Nashville American, religious papers & a great many agricultural papers.

Col. Boone was with a party of surveyors. They had come to a certain place near some stream or noted hill. The man who made the chops on the trees had just finished this operation on a certain tree when Boone became aware of a party of Indians. The two chops had been made on this tree, when Boone said we have a bottle of whiskey with us. If the Indians capture us & get drunk on this whiskey they will become uncontrollable. Give me the whiskey & I will hide it. In this tree there was a small hollow near a limb & in this hollow Boone **(1)** put into it the whiskey bottle, corked & more than half full of whiskey. They left, making a hasty retreat.

More than 40 years afterwards, some parties being interested in this very line that was being run the 40 years previous by Boone & his party, had a dispute about something with regard to corners or lines, I think. Boone remembered the incident of the whiskey bottle & the Indians, & said he believed he could designate the spot. He went with them, followed the chops made with the hatchet, & came to the spot. The last tree chopped was found, but no hollow was visible. Boone was certain that the tree was the one into which he placed the whiskey bottle 40 years previous, & said cut it down & split it open or cut into it, you will find it. It was done. Sure enough, there was the bottle with cork in, but no whiskey - all having evaporated.

13C15-19, 22 LCD notes on Daniel Boone in 1781 and his list of sources concerning Tarleton's attempt to capture members of the Virginia Legislature in June 1781.

17 In conversation with Col. Thomas J. Randolph, grandson of Pres. Jefferson, in August 1871, then, I think, 79 years old, he said:
That in June 1781, there were 1,000 riflemen at Rockfish Gap, Va., to guard the Legislature at Staunton just after Tarleton had driven them from Charlottesville. They captured one of the members at least, Col. Daniel Boone, & kept him a few days, when he again took his seat as a member at Staunton. Lieut. Brooke, at the head of eighty men, suddenly made ___ which alarmed the Legislature, and produced a stampede. Lossing, ii, note 3431, Brooke's Nar., 19, 20.

18 Tarleton's Irruption – June 1781, Madison's Writing: I, 46. Its effect on Jefferson's popularity: "Letters & Times of the Tylers" I, 87.
Col. Daniel Boone attended the Virginia Assembly Session of Nov. 1781 to Jan. 1782 representing Fayette County [on] several important committees.
See Journal of that Session, p. 61, & several preceding pages, where his name is underscored with blue pencil – viz: pages 7, 20, 28, 40, 46
Tarleton's Irruption – see Jefferson's writings – vol. ii, 425 &c, vii, 449, ix, 219, 273 &c.

19 Capt. John Jouett – Trip, vol. ii, 132. Virginia Historical Collections vi, 73, 135. Destruction of property – Howe's Virginia, 167.

After the summer session of the Virginia Legislature adjourned June 28th, I infer Boone made a visit to Bucks County. Pa., & was there Oct 20th, 1781. He must have returned from there to Richmond in time for the November Session.
On the whole, I conclude after the adjournment on June 23rd, Boone returned to Kentucky – staid there till well along in September – & then went up the Ohio – then to Bucks County, Pennsylvania where he was Oct. 20th. Though the Virginia Legislature re-assembled, after several attempts for a governor, Nov. 8th – Boone's name does not appear til Nov. 19 in the printed Journal, though he may have been there earlier as no roll-call is given.
Nor does Boone's name occur in the printed Journal after its

dispersion by Tarleton June 4th – adjourning June 23rd. LCD.

13C20-20(1) Tarleton, Charlottesville, 1781.
Thomas Walker letter to Mr. Lewis[?], August 1, 1781

   I hope to be at your house at the 17th at farthest. The bad weather prevented my seeing you sooner.
   My friend Mr. Rutherford waits on you with sundry warrants & ___ down the Ohio with the claimants. Unless you can spare an able assistant or two to attend them, he would gladly accept a deputation under you. Mr. Rutherford is so well known to you that saying anything of his probity or ability appears to me needless. Were it necessary I could with justice say as much for him as any man of my acquaintance.
   I should be obliged to you if convenient & agreeable to ___ ___ that Mr. Doak or Mr. Smith may do any business I may have to do. Please to give my compliments to your Lady, I am
         Thomas Walker (copy of original)

Mr. Lewis, August March ye 1st, 1774.

LCD note: Dr. Walker's Letter about Mr. Rutherford to Col. William Preston. Memo: The preceding newspaper scrap was copied, together with Dr. Thomas Walker's letter, by Mrs. Jos. B. Boyd, of Maysville, Ky., in 1858, for Charles H. Morse, Washington D.C. & Mr. Morse sent them to Col. A. G. Boone, B____ 's Springs, Kansas, May 16, 1878 - & that letter sent then to me. Feb. 13, 1883.

       A Revolutionary Incident.
   The <u>Charlottesville (Va.) Chronicle</u> says: It is a fact well known that during the Revolutionary war the British Colonel Tarleton came very near capturing the Virginia Legislature, then in session in Charlottesville. Tradition has it that the members were indebted for their escape to the thieving propensities of Tarleton's own soldiers.
   It is related that the dashing cavalry Leader called on Dr. Walker at "Castle Hill" and ordered breakfast. After waiting some time he complained that the cook was not as brisk as he might be, and the doctor went to the kitchen to hurry up the cook. He was informed that breakfast had been cooked twice and consumed by the soldiers, who, as hungry as wolves, had made a rush for the smoking viands. Tarleton at once placed a guard at the entrance to the kitchen, and in due time sat down to a comfortable meal.

In the meantime, Jack Jouett saw the soldiers at the place, mounted a fine horse and reached Charlottesville two hours before Tarleton. The members of the Legislature, availing themselves of this timely information, adjourned unanimously and made tracks for Staunton.

Col. John Archer had a few mounted men in town, and was the last who attempted to escape. He was cut down near the Stone Tavern, the residence of Dr. John Gilmer, whose wife went to Tarleton at the head of his troop and asked that the gallant Col. Archer, the friend of her husband, might be brought into her house. The request was cheerfully complied with and a guard placed at her door. Col. Archer was carefully nursed and recovered. On his deathbed he called Hon. William S. Archer and Dr. Branch Archer to his side and charged them over to regard Dr. Gilmer and his family with the same affection bestowed on those of his own blood. The gentlemen who restate this incident travelled with Dr. Archer in 1832 and had the statement from him.

Col. Boone captured by Tarleton, June 1781

13C21 Col. Daniel Boone, June 1781 [June 23d, say British & American Chronicles, was when Tarleton was at Charlottesville. LCD]

Ms. Letter of Col. William Preston to Col. John Floyd, Fort Chiswell, June 17, 1781, he says: "I shall, however, write you more at large by Col. Boone or Logan on their return from Charlottesville, which is now the Seat of Government."

Since writing the above, a gentleman came here from Staunton, to which the Assembly is adjourned, being routed at Charlottesville by Tarleton and a body of Light Horse who marched there from Hanover Court House in a short time to surprise the whole. They however took three or four, amongst whom are Col. Syme, Col. Boone, and a member of Congress from South Carolina called Kinlow. Syme was parolled, but Boone was still with them. Tarleton returned immediately after destroying a magazine.

The above was sent me as a copy from the original by Ben. Rush Floyd, from Wythe Court House in 1846. LCD

W. D. Hixson, Maysville, Ky., Feb. 1, 1886, sent me this item giving his authority for it – hence some tradition that he had picked up: "Boone's Capture, 1781 – On taking his Seat in the Legislature, Boone was objected to as a legislator because when captain he had taken the oaths to the English Government." I have no complete set of the House Journals, & cannot therefore give the year.

Nothing in printed Journal on the subject of Christian's letter following & Campbell's Virginia, show Boone was paroled. LCD

13C22 LCD: Daniel Boone in 1781

Capture of Charlottesville – "So important was it in the opinion of the British to get possession of the Governor and Council and the members of the Legislature, that we find them, after the unsuccessful effort made at Richmond, making a forced march to Charlottesville, from which place the officers of the Government were actually going out at one end of the town while the enemy were marching into the other." Frankfort, Ky., Palladium, July 10, 1800.

Note on Col. Christian's letter following 2 pages – which says he left Staunton a few days before – probably at time of adjournment. Must have met Boone there & learned his views of Cornwallis' strength, & that Boone had been paroled. This shows Boone when paroled repaired to Staunton & took his seat there as member. [LCD gave sources here.]

Col. Richard Butler's Journal, 11th June 1781 says: "The enemy surprised Charlottesville, & took several of the Assembly in and about that place, also a member of Congress, Mr. Kinla, & destroyed some of our arms & military stores that lay there. These gentlemen they sent out on parole ___, I believe not practiced nor admissible in the rules of war in other nations. But it is a conduct that answers both parties a good purpose, as it ties up any of those that are men of influence in the country from acting and those who wish to ___ ___ can easily put themselves in the enemy's power for the very purpose of being paroled [remainder illegible].

Coroner of Fayette County, Ky. Trip 1860, iii.19.
Meade's Old Churches of Virginia, I, 322.

13C23-23(1) Col. Daniel Boone's Captivity by Tarleton, June 1781. Virginia Acts of June Session 1781

Col. Wm. Christian to Col. Wm. Preston:

Mahanaim, Saturday June 30, 1781

The Assembly adjourned on this day. Mr. W. Madison came from Staunton but one day before I did, and, I suppose, has given you nearly all the news I have, but as John Young is going over, I'll write what occurs to me.

Several laws were made respecting the War. The militia law* is amended – martial law declared in force for twenty miles around our army and also around the enemy's. All the power of Government necessary for calling out militia, and resources of every kind, are vested in the Executive. Persons suspected of disaffection may be sent to the Enemy after twenty days to dispose of their property. A law is passed allowing ten thousand dollars for voluntary military recruits for two years. There are twenty two acts in all, but the above are the most material except one, I just remember, for punishing those who may oppose laws by an armed force, declaring them to be **(1)** civilly dead, and their estates to descend to the next of kin.

*see Newspaper extracts 1781, p. 50

The lowland people are as true and firm in the interest of America as any people in it. All I saw seemed to disregard property and only talk of independence. None despair in the least. They are more engaged for the fate of South Carolina at present than Virginia. Col. Knox took down a report about ten days ago that it (Ninety Six) has actually taken &c.

Some stores are saved, some lost. We had no certain accounts how much, either way. At Charlottesville, the danger was not great, perhaps about three hundred guns destroyed, and some stores, but the greatest part had got out of town and Tarleton followed but one mile up the road. Col. Boone, who was with Lord Cornwallis, and since paroled, thinks the enemy about 6,000. Deserters from Lord Cornwallis call his force 4,500 and 5,000. Reports call his horse 700.

Gibbs' Doc. Hist. 1776 – 82, p. 146. 147.
Margin note on Tarleton is illegible.

13C24-24(1-4) Tarleton ___ Virginia Legislature, June 1781
From Hon. J. Marshall McCue's Ms. loaned me, to return. LCD

Mount Pleasant (Augusta County, Virginia)
There is upon the old Col. George Moffett farm of Revolutionary memory, lately owned by Bailey Dunlap, & yet belonging to his heirs - a conical shaped hill, that bears the above name. We remember when comparatively young to have heard our mother detail the incidents connected with the removal of the Legislature from Charlottesville to Staunton; & then under the impression that Tarleton would follow them there, that some of them found a shelter, and as they supposed, a safe retreat in this hill. Before they had arranged their c____, they made application to Mrs. Moffett, in the absence of her husband, who

was in the army, for a meal. She cheerfully assented, and when at the table, and she began to understand the situation, and that they were members of the Legislature, she remarked that there was one member of the body she felt very sure wouldn't flee before Tarleton, meaning Patrick Henry, and was much mortified to find that he was one of the party.

(1) Adjournment of the body from Charlottesville, in conversation with young Mr. Tyler, and mentioning the incident above, he said that his grandfather had presented the facts of an incident of a similar character, and gave me the [printed] narrative. There had evidently been much romance connected with it, and the circumstances as detailed here have no doubt been made the foundation for the diverse versions given of it.

Mr. Tyler's Narrative

Sometime in 1781 – '82, the Legislature, of which Mr. Tyler was a member, were assembled at Charlottesville. Lord Cornwallis had invaded Virginia, and Colonel Tarleton, at the head of his regiment, determined to make a sudden descent on that town, with a view of surprising the Legislature and capturing its leading members, among whom was reckoned Mr. Henry, Mr. Tyler, Benjamin Harrison (the father of the late President, and then Speaker of the House of Delegates) and Colonel Christian, afterward a famous Indian fighter in Kentucky, and several others.

A countryman named Jewett [Jouett] got intelligence of Tarleton's intended movement and, by dint of hard riding [to] Charlottesville **(2)** in time to give warning of the approaching danger. Finding his admonition unheeded by the Speaker, and the greater part of the members, as being the effect of a causeless fight, he addressed himself with great earnestness to Mr. Henry and Mr. Tyler, begging, at least, that they would fly, and save themselves since the Assembly refused to believe him. They, at last convinced of the truth of his assertions, proposed an adjournment to Staunton, a town some forty miles distant, which was finally agreed to.

On their way thither, many of the country people were met, two or three upon a horse, riding in the defence of the town, the news of Tarleton's march having already spread over the neighboring country.

Late in the day, Mssrs. Henry, Tyler, Harrison, and Christian, who had ridden together, fatigued and hungry, stopped their horses at the door of a small hut, in a gorge of the hills, and asked for refreshment. A woman, the sole occupant of the house, inquired of them who they were, and where from?

"We are members of the Legislature," said Mr. Henry, "And have just been compelled to leave Charlottesville on account **(3)** of the approach of the enemy." "Ride on then, cowardly knaves," replied the old woman, in a tone of excessive indignation; "here have my husband and sons just gone to Charlottesville to fight for ye, and you running away with all your might. Clear out – ye shall have nothing here."

"But," Mr. Henry rejoined, in an expostulating tone, "we were obliged to fly; it would not do for the Legislature to be broken up by the enemy. Here is Mr. Speaker Harrison. You don't think he would have fled had it not been necessary." "I always thought a great deal of Mr. Harrison till now," the old woman answered; "but he'd no business to run from the enemy," and she was about to shut the door in their faces.

"Wait a moment, my good woman," again interposed Mr. Henry, "You would hardly believe that Mr. Tyler or Colonel Christian would take to flight if there were not good cause for so doing." "No, indeed, that I wouldn't," she replied. "But Mr. Tyler and Colonel Christian are here," said he. "They are! Well, I never would have thought it," and she stood a moment as if in doubt, but finally, **(4)** added Mrs. Moffett, "We love those gentlemen, and I don't suppose they would ever run away from the British; but since they have, they shall have nothing to eat in my house. You may ride along."

As a last resort, Mr. Tyler then stepped forward and said, "What would you say, my good woman, if I were to tell you that Patrick Henry fled with the rest of us?" "Patrick Henry! I would tell ye there wasn't a word of truth in it," she answered angrily. "Patrick Henry would never do such a cowardly thing." "But this *is* Mr. Henry," rejoined Mr. Tyler, pointing him out. The old woman looked astonished. After a moment's consideration, and a convulsive twitch or two at her apron string, by way of recovering her scattered thoughts, she said, "Well, then, if that is Patrick Henry it must be right. Come in, and ye shall have the best I have in my house."

Perhaps no higher compliment was ever paid to the patriotism of Patrick Henry, than this simple tribute of praise from the mouth of that poor but noble woman." Life & Times of the Tylers, I, 81-88.

13C25 Among the several delegates caught was Col. Lyons of Hanover, and Francis Kinlow, a member of Congress from South Carolina, who was also caught at Mr. John Walker's, whose daughter he had raised some time before. Gov. Jefferson had a narrow escape. Tarleton's party retreated with as much celerity as it had advanced.

Tarleton had been sent with all the celerity possible to surprise and take the General Assembly and Executive, who had retreated from Richardson to Charlottesville. The vigilance of a young gentleman who discovered the design, and rode express to Charlottesville prevented a complete surprise. As it was, several delegates were caught, and the rest were within an hour of sharing the same fate. Works of Madison i, 46

Capt. Jos. Sanders (in vol. 1, Clark's Campaigns) says: About May 1781, he was sent on to Virginia (from Falls of Ohio) for money and supplies for the troops. He was captured at Charlottesville by Tarleton, together with Daniel Boone & Thomas Swearingan, then delegates from Kentucky to the Virginia Legislature.

Thomas Swearingan was a Justice in Boonesboro, went to Kentucky in 1779 with G. M. Bedinger, was in the Virginia Legislature from Kentucky. [LCD sources omitted here are only partly illegible.]

13C33 *LCD list and chart of those killed and wounded and those who escaped at the Battle of Blue Licks on August 19, 1782. Shane's collection is cited along with other sources. The dead were buried on August 24, 1782 (citing "Clark Papers.")*

13C34 LCD notes on Col. Daniel Boone – 1782
Aug. 2nd 1782 – John Callaway & Jones Hoy captured in melon patch
    [captured probably August 14]
    Shane's Collections, xvi, 104
    Kercheval's Hist. of the Valley 2nd, edn., 325
    Pension Statements, no. 2, p. 4
    Shane's Collections, ii, Montgomery County, 68__
    Capt. Saml. Boone's Notes & letters
    Shane ii, Montgomery County [Ky.], 68-69, & 83
Aug. 14th – Holder's Defeat – Capt. Buchanan's death – Shane, xv
    Shane's Collections, ii, Fleming County, [Ky.] 14-15
    Shane's Collections, xvi, 44
    Capt. Wm. Buchanan killed - Note Book "2", 120
    Illinois Papers No. 2, p. 30
    Va. Calendar of State Papers, iii. 280
April – Boone orders out relief parties: Pension Statements no. 2, p.4

13C38 W. D. Hixson, Maysville, Ky., Feb 1, 1886
Diagram of Estill's Battleground

References:

1. the place where Estill was killed
2. the place where McNeely was killed
3. the place where John South was killed
4. the place where John Colefoot was killed
5. the place where Jonathan McMillan was killed
6. the place where David Cook was wounded
7. the place where a gun was found

LCD note: The above map references are carefully and faithfully copied by one of the company and drawn by Robert Morrow, 1817, by order of Montgomery [County, Ky.] Circuit Court, where the case had its origins. The record does not mention (except in the above references) about Cook being wounded.

13C38(1) John F. Estill letter, Lewisburg, W.Va., August 24, 1891

My friend, Mr. Virgil A. Lewis, has given me your address, and advised me to write you for some information concerning the Estill family. Mr. Lewis and I are getting together the materials for a sketch of the family. My great-grandfather, Wallace Estill, married Mary Ann Campbell in Augusta County [Va.] in 1747, but I do not know her father's name. She must have been the daughter of the John Campbell, to whom you refer in your "Heroes of Kings Mountain."

In an old record of the family, I find the following - Mary Anne Campbell's father was a Scotchman who married in Ireland. He moved from Ireland when she was ten years old, bringing ten children with them - settled first in Pennsylvania, and then moved to Virginia. She is said to have been but fourteen when she was married, and if this be true, was born about the time the family moved to Augusta County, say 1730. You may have some notes or data on the Estills and Campbells.

MAP OF ESTILLS DEFEAT.
FROM CONNELLYS HEIRS VS. SMITH.
5. J. MARSHALL. 304.

1. Where Estill fell.
2. " McNeely "
3. " Jno. South "
4. " " Coldfoot "
5. " Jonathan McMillen fell.
6. " B. Cook was wounded.
7. " gun was found.
A.A. Buffalo trace.

MEM. Carpenter was buried with Estill.
Forbes was buried with McMillen.

> 7.
> 1. Where Estill fell.
> 2. " McNeely   "
> 3. " Jno. South "
> 4. " " Coldfoot "
> 5. " Jonathan McMillen fell.
> 6. " D. Cook was wounded.
> 7. " gun was found.
> A.A. Buffalo trace.
> Carpenter was buried with Estill.
> Forbes was buried with McMillen.

Enlarged key to map of Estill's Battleground. 13C46

13C39-48(1) Taken from the record of Conley's Heirs vs. Chile in the Kentucky Court of Appeals, Spring Term, 1831. Chief Justice Robertson. Copied from the original record, Frankfort, Ky., 28th Nov. 1845.

Depositions of Joseph Proctor, Enoch Smith, John Lane, Frederick Couchman, Stephen Hendricks, Samuel South & James Berry, John Harper, Higgason Grubbs, David Lynch

Nathaniel Hart gives, in letter appended to Butler's Kentucky, an account of Estill's Defeat.

13C40 Joseph Proctor's Deposition, Dec. 20, 1816

Sometime the last of February or first of March 1782, he, in company with James Estill & others, pursued the Indians to this place, and engaged with them in battle, in which James Estill was killed, also Adam Caperton, John South, Jonathan McMillan, John Colefoot, McNeely and a young man by the name of Forbes. The number of whites engaged in the battle was twenty-five, a part [were] from Boonesborough, Paint Lick, and Estill's Station. Estill was a Captain, and commanded the company that fought the battle. During the battle he saw an Indian kill Capt. Estill. He saw him sink.

In about three [days] after the battle, he in company of between 50 & 60 men, some from Boonesborough and others from Boone's Station, McGee's Station, Strode's Station, and White Oak Station, returned to bury the dead. [We] found Capt. Estill lying nigh the spot on the sign we left, where we fought by shooting bullets in trees & scalping them might have been seen for several years. This whole bounds that we fought on was about 8 or 10 acres, on the southern bank of Kentucky River. The battle ground was about a mile & half below the Little Mountain, between the mouth of two branches putting into Hinksons [Creek], the east side, about 300 yards apart. The lower branch ran into the Creek like it ___ of the creek. The fighting was principally between the two branches &c.

13C42 James Berry's Deposition taken in 1818, Madison County, Ky.

Came to Boonesborough in March 1777 – was in Estill's defeat, & got wounded in the action. The cane was low where the conflict took place, but further up the ridge as they [whites, doubtless - LCD] drew off from where the fight commenced, the cane became higher, as high or higher than a man's head, not thick nor strong. Cane gets nearly its growth, generally, as to height & thickness, in one year, but afterwards gets more bushy & heavy about the top, & in my opinion, gets high or low according to the soil on which it grew.

On the left hand side of the creek as you go down was a bottom, & in that bottom the Indians made their first stand that I saw on the right hand side of the creek as you go down. A while after the battle began, we drew farther off from the creek to the top of the ridge, where the ground was more level, & being driven from the top of the ridge, retreated down a small drain, & crossed the creek below where they commenced.

John Lane's Deposition

That in the year 1776, himself & Enoch Smith raised corn & potatoes & lived at the place where said Smith afterwards obtained his Settlement & preemption, near the Little Mountain. Lived ___ during that year and frequently visited by the inhabitants of Boonesborough, which was then the nearest Station.

Stephen Hendricks' Deposition taken in 1818

That he came to Boonesborough in January 1776, & in the fall of 1777 moved his family to Estill's Station. Was not at Estill's defeat nor burial ... that he & his brother set out to go with Estill, but before they got out of sight [perhaps Estill had gone on ahead & the two Hancocks (Hendricks) intended to follow on & join him. LCD] of Estill's Station. The Indians attacked some Negroes, & a daughter of Capt. Gass at the sugar camp. He and his brother returned to defend the women and children until Estill's return.

Enoch Smith's Deposition taken April 1818
Settled in 1776 near the Little Mountain, had ground in cultivation &c.

David Lynch's Deposition taken in 1817
Was in the battle with the Indians under Capt. James Estill, 22d March 1782, when Capt. Estill was killed, together with Adam Caperton, John South, Jonathan McMillen, John Coltfoot, McNeely, & Forbes.

13C43 Frederick Couchman's Deposition
At the time of Estill's Defeat, [we] went out of Strode's Station with the party to bury the dead. Some of those that had escaped from the defeat piloted the balance of the way. Had neither axe nor other tools. Laid the dead beside logs and covered them with logs and &c.

13C44-44(1), 45 Samuel South's Deposition taken June 16, 1818
Resided at Boonesborough, was in Estill's Defeat. It was stated and believed that the battle was a hard fought one, said to be the hardest ever fought in Kentucky. David Cook, William Crim, Whitson George, James Berry, Joseph Proctor, David Linch, Henry Boyers, and Beal Kelly were in the engagement; Cook was very near me, also Col. Irvine.

The battle was fought from one and one half to 2 ½ miles below the Little Mountain, and on the creek which passes by the little Mountain. The engagement commenced on the east side of the main creek leading from small mountain, between two branches that put in on the same side ___, which deponent believes not more than 100 **(1)** or 150 yards apart. The ground between the two branches very level, but becomes ___ as you ascend the point, and particularly on the north side of the rise and the head of the branches came nearer together as you go from the creek. The battle was fought principally between the two branches and on the east side of the main creek.

I believe Forbes was killed on the west side of the main creek. The Lieutenant was with Forbes, and so soon as fired at, came over to the east side to Estill's party, and immediately ran off, carrying with him six men.

The battle ground was bare of cane, and [there was] but little under-wood. But the cane was knee high after we retreated about 80 yards. My impression is that the battle ground was not more than 125 yards wide and 200 long, and that Estill was killed between 80 and 100 yards from the creek and on the south side of the cane brake.

45 I speak of the ground occupied by the white people, and the

Indians followed us up very close. Strode's Station was the closest station to the battleground - and that 16 to 18 miles. The intermediate country was an entire wilderness thickly covered with the rich growth common to the country, cane, vines, &c.

John Harper's Deposition

Thinks the distance between the two branches where the battle was fought was two hundred or more yards. The main stream was generally called Little Mountain, but known to be Hinkson's Fork of Licking [River].

13C46 *Draper's handwriting.*
1. The place where Estill was killed
2. The place where McNeally [sic] was killed
3. The place where John South was killed
4. The place where John Colefoot was killed
5. The place where Jonathan McMillen was killed
6. The place where David Cook was wounded
7. The place where a gun was found

Carpenter was buried with Estill.
Forbes was buried with McMillen.

13C48(1) From J. J. Marshall's Court of Appeals – Vol. 5 – Conley's Heirs vs. Chiles. Chief Justice Robertson delivered the opinion.

The battle was fought on the 22d of March 1782, in the now county of Montgomery, and in the vicinity of Mount Sterling. It is a memorable incident, and perhaps one of the most remarkable in the interesting history of the settlement of Kentucky. The usefulness and popularity of Captain Estill; the deep and universal sensibility excited by the premature death of a citizen so gallant and so beloved; the emphatic character of his associates in battle; the masterly skill and daring displayed throughout the action ("every man to his man, and each to his tree"); the grief and despondence produced by the catastrophe, all contributed to give to "Estill's Defeat" a most signal notoriety and importance, especially among "the early settlers."

All the story with all its circumstances of locality, and of "the fight" was told and told again and again, until even the children knew it "by heart." No legendary tale was ever listened to with as intense anxiety, or was inscribed in as vivid and indelible an impress on the hearts of the few of both sexes who then contributed the hope and strength of Kentucky.

Such is the traditional, well-recorded history of this legendary battle between the white men and the Indians, & such, too, is the testimony embodied in this cause.

It could scarcely be credited, that the site of such a ____ could not have been formed by any rational man, exercising the usual and ordinary diligence.

But the testimony in this case proves satisfactorily that not only the scite [sic] of the battle, but even the spot where the intrepid leader of the little Spartan band fell, might, in 1783, have been found without any difficulty. The dead were buried, or rather covered, with logs, by persons from the several "stations" and in fact from all the stations as were the same at Boonesborough.

A trace led from Boonesborough to Caulk's [William Calk's?] Cabin near the creek, and about three miles and the scars made on the trees and other vestiges remained visible to identify and define the theatre.

It has been proved by the testimony of several of the surviving combatants & others. It was also proved that the bones of some of the dead, and the scars made on the trees by the bullets and other vestiges remained visible for several years to identity and define the theatre of this remarkable battle, a circle with a diameter of two hundred yards would have enclosed it. The two branches were not more than two hundred yards apart."

Margin note: Estill's Defeat – Chief Justice Robertson's Opinion – Conley's Heirs vs. Chiles – Kentucky Court of Appeals.

13C50(2) Envelope addressed to Draper and postmarked ____tsville, April 30. LCD note: From D. W. Hazlerigg, 29 April 1842. Draper's notes on envelope: Capt. James Estill from D. W. Hazlerigg [sic], 29th April 1842.

13C50(3) …To make your personal acquaintance possible you may visit Kentucky before I do Mississippi. I should be happy to greet you by the hand at my residence. Accept my heartfelt wishes for your happiness and success.

          Very respectfully Yours &c.
          Dillard W. Hazelrigg

13C51-51(4) Dillard W. Hazlerigg essay on James and Samuel Estill

James Estill was born on the 9th of November 1750, in Augusta

County, Virginia. He removed from Greenbriar County to Kentucky in 1777, previous to which he had explored the Country.

In 1776 he made the settlement required by law and obtained preemption to 1000 acres of land on the head waters of Muddy Creek and Otter Creek in Madison County [Kentucky]. In 1778 he moved his family to Boonsborough and raised a crop in the following year. In 1780 he left Boonsboro and built a fort 16 miles distant on the head waters of Otter Creek.

In the Spring of 1780, James Estill and John Callaway reconnoitered their new fort to discover if any hostile movements of an enemy were being made. Some 7 or 8 miles from the fort, in Big Muddy Creek, they crossed an Indian trail [of] about 16 in number making directly to the Fort. They followed the trail until they arrived within 6 or 8 miles of the fort when they perceived a smoke proceeding from the center of a Cane brake surrounded on every side by forest oak.

Ascertaining that the Indians had encamped, they held a consultation and agreed to tie their horses and each one conceal himself and kill an Indian. Estill's gun fired and killed one on the spot. They then returned, sprang to their horses, one going on each side of the encampment at full speed and making the woods ring again with "Come on boys! Come on boys!" The warriors, panic struck, fled, leaving everything but their guns. The two daring young warriors loaded their horses with Knapsacks, Cooking utensils, one gun etc., and returned in Safety to the fort.

In the spring 1781, a company of Dutch settlers left Estill's fort to establish a new fort on Muddy Creek about 5 miles distant. The advance guard had proceeded one mile on this way when Samuel Estill (brother of James Estill) discovered Indians concealed. He gave the alarm to his brother James, who was in place in front and was fired upon while in the act of stoping his horse.

When he heard Sam, he checked his horse and instantly received a shot through his right arm just above the elbow. His arm fell at his side with so much violence that it came near throwing the reins of his bridle over the horse's head. His horse instantly wheeled and ran off at full speed. His horse had run some distance when he managed to get hold of the bridle with the left hand, by holding his gun under his chin, his right arm which was dangling by his side and liable every moment to be torn off by limbs and canebrakes. He got hold the thumb [of his right hand] in his mouth and in this condition his horse went full speed to the fort.

Samuel Estill sprang from his horse on the same side with the Indians to a tree and while they intently engaged observing the result of their fire, Sam killed two at one shot. At the 1st fire of the Indians, a little

Dutchman who was in the Company had his horse shot under him. The horse fell and Caught the Dutchman. Estill's gun was empty. He saw a tall painted Savage making directly to him with tomahawk in hand. Sam, who was the largest man in Kentucky if not on the Continent, drew his heavy battle ax and presented himself to the Indian in full battle array. The astonished Indian, seeing a man of such dimensions with battle ax uplifted and daring him **(2)** to the contest, wheeled and fled. He bent his course towards the little Dutchman who had just succeeded in extricating himself from his horse and seeing the Indian running towards him, cried out to Estill to "Shoot the Indian! Shoot the Indian." Estill replied in no ceremonious manner to "Shoot him yourself! My gun is empty." The Dutchman shot the Indian when he was so near as to powder burn his clothes. The Indian on being shot raised a yell and the other Indians stopt as they came up, thus giving time for the moving party to return in safety to the fort.

Sam Estill was more fortunate than James for at the 1st fire, allthough his clothes were <u>riddled with balls,</u> yet strange to tell, he did not receive a wound.

Campaign of '82

Early in the spring of 1782, a number of men from different forts assembled at Estill's, formed a company of 20 men, and with one accord, appointed James Estill Captain. They set out on a scouting expedition and to discover Indian traces. They left the fort on Saturday 19th day of March, and on Sunday 20th, Savages to the number of 25 appeared before the fort, murdered the daughter of Capt. Gist [Jenny, daughter of Capt. David Gass] in sight of the fort, and captured Monk, a shrewd and faithful old servant belonging to Estill. The case of Miss Gist [Gass] was painful. When she saw Indians she ran towards the fort, her friends seeing and hearing, called to her to run, but she was tomahawked before she could reach [the fort]. The Indians dragged her behind a tree and while scalping her, was fired on by her brother* from the fort, which in connection with information they derived from old Monk, caused the Indians to leave immediately and thus saved the fort.

Jenny had four brothers: William, John, James, and David. John Gass would have been in his teens in 1782. He never mentioned having fired at the Indians in any of his interviews or letters to Draper when asked about his sister Jenny being killed.

This Old Monk told them that there were 20 white men in the

fort and that it could not be taken. There was not a half dozen guns in the fort. An express was sent to Estill, distant 25 miles at what is now called the Estill White Sulphur Springs. Estill, to intercept the enemies' retreat, set off by forced marches and on Monday night, March 21st, lay within ½ mile of the enemy. When they left next morning, they travelled about that distance when they arrived at the encampment which the Indians had just left. They set off full speed and came in sight of the Indians after sun rise. They were crossing a small creek about one mile north of Mt. Sterling in Montgomery County.

After the first fire, the Indian chief was shot down in the creek, but he concealed himself and continued giving orders during the battle. He divided his men and sent a party round to flank Estill and capture the horses. Estill perceiving their design, formed his men into 3 divisions of 8 men each. The command of one division was given to the ensign, one to the Lieutenant, and the other he commanded in person. He ordered the Lieutenant with his division to the rear to defend the horses. In a few minutes that point was attacked. The Lieutenant and his division <u>fled</u> without firing a gun. This base desertion of one division left the rear uncovered and the first notice he had of the desertion was the Indian firing on the rear.

He remarked **(3)** during the battle that it was not planned, little dreaming that a whole division had deserted its post. In the commencement of the action a man named McMillion rode full speed amongst the indians, swearing he would have a shot at an Indian and was instantly killed from his horse, having received 3 balls. Early in the action, Adam Caperton, an intelligent and respectable man of family, was shot in the mouth and through the head. The shot produced instant derangement and he followed Capt. Estill during the battle, making signs and trying to talk. Estill could not avoid him and thus he was a mark continually for the Indians, who perceiving Caperton's situation would not shoot him.

After the battle had been raging some hours and the shots had become less frequent, Joseph Proctor, a private in the ensigns division (and the only man in the battle that is now living), was in full view of Capt. Estill. He addressed Estill thus: "Capt. Estill! I am going to leave the ground. Every man in my division is killed excepting myself, and there are but three or four of your men not killed." Estill requested him to wait and he would go with him directly.

At this instant a brother of Joseph Proctor called loudly for him to shoot an Indian who was pursuing him. He shot the Indian and reloaded his gun as quick as possible. Estill now left his position to go to Proctor and was instantly pursued by an Indian. Faint from the loss of blood, he dropt his gun and retreated slowly. The Indian rapidly advanced upon him, keeping Estill between him and Proctor. Perceiving that he was overtaken, he wheeled and grappled with his foe, who drew a knife and stabbed him through. Estill fell and Proctor shot instantly, shot the Indian dead and he fell by the side of the Captain.

Proctor had finished reloading his gun while the Indian was pursuing Estill and immediately levelled at the Indian. The Indian being aware of it, kept Estill between him and danger. Proctor would not entertain the idea of shooting his Captain, and at no instant could he have shot the Indian without being in danger of shooting his Captain until he fell.

Proctor saw from Estill's white hunting shirt that he was bleeding at many places. The number of shots he received before he fell can never be known as the Indians mangled his body most strikingly to break their vengeance upon him. This shot from Proctor, killing the Indian who fell by the side of Estill, was the last gun fired on the battle ground. When Proctor left his position and found the few remaining men left, and proposed to them to leave the ground, they refused to go and leave their Captain until Proctor told them that he saw Estill fall.

There were but five men on the ground when Estill fell. They were not pursued by the Indians; when they left the ground not an Indian was to be seen. The Indians returned to the ground, or probably did not leave it, buried their dead, carried off what guns they could and buried the rest. Thus fell Capt. James Estill in the prime and vigor of life.

At the commencement of this battle the parties were equal, 25 on each side. Each Commander divided his men into 3 divisions. But the Indian Chief had decided advantages. His men had been trained by him, had often fought **(4)** by his side, and one of them would Sooner die than leave him. They were brave, cunning and farless [fearless] picked warriors and close marksmen and declared to Old Monk that they could whip any 40 white men in Kentucky.

Mrs. Margaret Polly,* a prisoner among the Indians, states that 25 of their finest warriors left for Kentucky. They said they had wounded the great man in Kentucky last faul [fall], and they were then going to kill the great Man and also the Big Man [James and Samuel Estill]. They told Mrs. Polly that the great man crept up on them and killed one of their warriors and then stole their provisions &c. and they were then going to kill him first. They also told her that the big man killed two of their warriors at one shot when they wounded the great Man and for that, they intended to kill him. She states that but five returned and their Chief was among the missing. They said they had killed the great Man whom they knew by his broken arm. She says when they returned there was the greatest yelling and screaming she ever heard for the loss of their warriors, indeed so many of their distinguished men fell in that battle that not an Indian was seen in Kentucky for some 5 or 7 years.

Capt. Estill had but Seventeen of such warriors with him, not one of which left the ground until he fell. The other eight from this fort were not men of Estill's training, and left their post at the commencement of the action. The whites lost 13, leaving 4 of their fighting men. The Indians lost 20, leaving five of their fighting men. This is thought to be the most closely contested and hardest fought battle fought in America.

James Estill was about 5 feet 10 inches in height, slender and rather delicate in appearance, though very active and athletic. He was of regular features, handsome countenance, and amiable disposition and a great favorite with his friends and acquaintances. He was well educated, pleasant in conversation and a good speaker. He had been in Kentucky but a short time when he was sent on a Special Mission to the Virginia Legislature. It had passed some law which the settlers deemed destructive to their interests. Estill appeared before the Legislature in the garb of the hardy western pioneer: Buckskin Moccasons and pants, and hunting shirt, and by his masterly address, obtained a repeal of the odious law. He was a man of industry and business habits and being a stranger to fear, he had entered land for many of the settlers. He had entered 40,000 acres of land for himself and friends when he fell, which nearly all lost, as the witnesses who were fearless and went with him to enter the land, were brave enough to fall with him in battle.

*Mrs. Margaret Pauley, captured in Virginia in 1779, was still living in Piqua in 1782.

13C52-52(1-2) William Estill, Winchester, Tenn., Sept 13, 1845

Dear Sir
      Yours of the 2nd inst. was received by last nights mail.
You are mistaken in supposing me to be a son of Col. Samuel Estill. My father (Isaac Estill) was the youngest brother of James & Samuel Estill and emigrated to this country from Virginia in 1817.

There are none of the descendants of my uncle Samuel Estill in this section of Tennessee of whom I have any knowledge. The old man died some few years since, as I am informed, at the house of a son-in-law who at that time resided, I believe, in Fentress County in this state. Whether [his son-in-law] still lives there or not, at this time, I am certainly unable to say.

Col. Samuel Estill lived for many years in Madison County, Kentucky near Richmond, and [was] a near neighbour to Wallace & James Estill, sons of Capt. James Estill, both of whom were living a short time since. I have no doubt [they] can give more satisfactory information in relation to their uncle than any of his family. There is also a sister (Mrs. Ruth Cavanaugh), daughter of Col. Estill, living in that neighbourhood that can give you much **(1)** useful and interesting information as to the life and adventures of her brothers, as well as many other of the Pioneers.

I think you would do well to visit Richmond while in Kentucky. The distance is not great. There are a great many of the descendants of the early settlers of Kentucky in Madison County. If you have not seen the obituary notice of the Rev. Joseph Proctor, who died some months since in that section of Kentucky, try and procure it as it might be of use to you. It contains some interesting historical facts. Should it fall into my hands again, I will send you, least [lest] you might fail to get it. I do not now remember the paper it was published in.

I have seen Mr. John Handley, and he informs me that he had failed to get your letter, but that he would, as soon as practicable, furnish you with all the information he can as to his father's history &c. I will see Col. Richard Calaway in a few days, and also a daughter of Col. John Holder's, and present your requests to them, together with your memorandum of interogatories &c.

I regret very much indeed that this work had not have commenced some twelve years ago, as my father, and another older brother, Capt. William Estill, were then living. They could **(2)** have furnished a mass of valuable & interesting matters although neither of them were engaged in the Indians wars of Kentucky.

Capt. William Estill served in the Virginia lines during the Revolution, and was in command of a company at the siege of York. He had the most astonishing memory of any man I ever met. Having emigrated to Kentucky at an early day, had made himself entirely familiar with all the important historical incidents attending the first settling of that country. Neither he nor my father left any papers that could be of any use to you.

Col. Calaway, I imagine, will be able to give you a great many facts, both in relation to his father, and his near relative, Col. Holder, as his memory is remarkably good. They will be forwarded to you, so soon as they can be pursued.

Mr. Hutchins is much pleased to hear once more from his old, and highly esteemed friend Mr. Re----n, and desires to be affectionately remembered to him.

                    Respectfully, your obedient Servant
                    Wm Estill
                    L. C. Draper Esqr

PS Excuse this hurried scrawl. W. E.

13C un-numbered page: LCD handwriting: Dr. Wm. Estill, Sept. 13, 1845. Postmark: Sept. 11, Winchester, Tennessee.

13C53-53(1), 54-54(1-3) Wallace Estill, Pleasant Hill, Madison County, Kentucky, April 20, 1846.

Wallace Estill was a son of Captain James Estill. He inherited Monk, the servant of James Estill who took part in the battle and whose account Wallace Estill gave to Draper. Monk Estill, known for his skill in making gunpowder, was appraised at 80 pounds in James Estill's estate; he was freed by Wallace Estill. The accounts of the battle were also gleaned from his uncle, Samuel Estill. Throughout this letter, ""the" is used when ""they" is meant. Other spelling is unaltered.

Captain James Estill was born November 9th, 1750 at Bullpasture, Augusta County, Virginia. Visited Kentucky in 1776, returned home to Greenbrier County the same year and in the year of 1778 removed his family to Boonesborough, the first immigrants after its noted siege by the Indians.

About the year of 1775 as should have been first stated, in Greenbrier County, Virginia, James Estill went with a considerable number of men up to relieve Donley's Fort. They secreted themselves in a Rye field. The fort was invaded by about 300 Indians. At the approach of daylight they made a charge to the fort, Estill going foremost. All got in the fort safe after a travel on foot 40 miles the previous day.

After this he moved to Kentucky. Raised a crop of corn in 1779 and early in the year of 1780 he settled a station on the headwaters of Otter Creek which he resided at until his death.

He was one of the number of General Clark's campain against the Shawney Indian towns which happened sometime from 1779 to 1781.

Early in the spring of the year 1780, Captain James Estill and a man by the name of Calloway made a cursory tower [tour] some 10 or 12 miles in the woods in a circuitous manner, came across the trail of about 12 or 15 Indians who were making a straight course to Estill's Station.

After trailing their sign they saw the sine [sign] of fire by smoke in a small pach [patch] of cane about 3 miles distant from Estill's Station. They rode cautously [cautiously] towards the fire, hich't [hitched] their Horses in about 40 or 50 yards of the Indians. All their blankets were hanging to the sun to dry as the sun had just shone out from a considerable wet spel, each then picked out his Indian to shoot at the same time. Calloway's gun snap't and Estill's gun fired, killing his Indian. They boath then Retreated to their horses, parted to come up in opposite directions boath crying out as they rode up to the Indians fire come on boys, here they are. Estill requested Calloway to stand about 20 paces from the fire the way the Indians had fled while he would scalp and gather up all the booty they had left which was shortly sold at Estill's Station at about $50 in a very hard time to get money.

Some time after, the same year, about one mile from the fort, Estill saw the Cane shaking near the path before him. Keeping his eye on the spot when coming up, saw plenty of mokison tracks in the path, they placed intentionally in different directions, and sent back to the fort for more men. When reinforced they made a regular search in different parts, but the Indians had made their escape on their back track and fled. They ware followed until they came ___ the mountains where they separated in different directions.

In the spring of the year of 1781, Captain James Estill was solicited by some German settlers to go with them to assist in settling a Station some 7 or 8 miles [away]. When about one Mile and a quarter from Estill's Station, they ware attact with about 15 Indians who ware lying in ambush. Samuel Estill, brother of James Estill, being the next man behind James Estill, some 10 or 12 ___ saw the Indians behind a sapling tree **(1)** to the right hand about 28 steps, Samuel Estill cal'd out to his brother, Captain James Estill, there was Indians. Samuel Estill sprang from his horse and as his feet struck the ground the Indians guns fired braking Capt. Estill's arm between the shoulder and elbow, taking away about 3 inches of the bone, giving his arm such a jerk it threw the bridle rains out of his hand. Lighting alone to the horses was Capt. Estill, finding his arm broke and his horse being well trained for the woods, stood quite stile while Estill gathered up his bridle with his left hand and still holding to his gun, put off his horse by the hook of the bridle at nearly half speed going straight forward while geting out of sight then wheeling to the right made a circuitous rout back to the fort.

Again about the middle of March in 1782, Capt. James Estill sent a request to some of the neighbouring stations for men to [scout] the country for the enemy. Accordingly, Saturday, the 19th of March 1782, they started out from Estill's Station, went out to a lick known then as the Sweet Lick on the Kentucky River.

The Indians came to Estill's Station the same day at night near morning. They attact some hands [workers] sent out to get firewood, and ___ some sugar trees, killed a daughter of Capt. Gass about 14 years old and took a Negroe man and two horses of Capt. James Estill. [They] made much of the Negroe on the strength of the fort, and suspecting they would not be able to take it, they hurried off with the booty for the Indian town.

As soon as the Indians were gone, two runners were sent out after Capt. James Estill from the fort who came up with the company of men at the before-mentioned Sweet Lick, informing Capt. Estill what was done. He instantly started down the Kentucky River on the north side to find the Indian trail as this was Quite easy as ther was snow on the ground. They found their trail much where they expected, following on that day untill night, finding the men not far behind the Indians. There was a consultation held wheather to attact that night or in the morning.

They finally concluded on the latter, so early in the morning by daylight, they started briskly on the trail, leaving some few men at camp who were not well prepared to travel Briskly. When they proceeded some 2 or 2 ½ miles, they came up with the Indians who were skinning a Buffalo they had killed. The Indians hearing the sound of the Horses feet, sprung to their guns, urged Monk the Negroe to run. Monk making great speed but shortly found himself entirely behind the Indians, then stop't and met his master Capt. Estill, who was in front of his men. Ordered Monk to take charge of all the mens horses which he did. The whites got the first fire, wounding the Indian Commander as they were crossing a small creek. The Indian commander concealed himself under the leaning cane that grew on the opposite Bank while the ballance of the Indians formed their line and Returned the fire from the opposite bank under the Command of their leader - who gave his loud hollow [yell] at the time of the battle. Capt. Estill, knowing the Indian mode of fighting by Flanking, ordered **54** Lieut. Miller to defend the Left wing where the Horses were stationed with the Negroe man, Monk.

In a short time the Indians began to flank to the Right and left. Capt. Miller seeing the Indians Running Round on his side on something of Elevated ground and taking a great alarm cried out to his men Boys let us run or we shall be killd. Monk at the same time criing [crying] out to Mr. Miller, Pray do not leave us. Miller made a small halt, but hearing another gun fire at his men, they all Broke and Ran off the ground. Not one of Miller's men or himself were Firing a gun, which left the Ballance of the men nearly Surrounded by the Indians.

Thus our men fought untill they weare nearly all cut down on the Right wing but Capt. Estill, and him mortally wounded and Quite Bloody. He then attempted to Retreat to the ballance of his men who had been more in the center and a man by the name of Joseph Proctor, seeing his Captain coming, he made himself ready. Estill being very faint with the loss of blood, the Indian came up to Estill. Estill turning round to the Indian, placing his hands on the Indians sholders as if to make Resistance but was too weak with the loss of Blood. The Indian drew his knife making a stab at Estill, who fell, when Proctor instantly presented his gun, shot the Indian in the brest who fell forward, quite over Capt. Estill. The ballance of Estill's men, about 4 or 5 in number, retreated after Runing about 50 yards slowly off the battleground.

According to a statement of a prisoner at that time in the Shawnee village by the Name of Peggy Polly, there was only 8 Indians Returned to their towns out of 25 picked warriors of the Wyandott tribe. Thus ended the life of Capt. James Estill in the prime of life, Beloved and Respected by all who knew him, on the 22 of March 1782, in the County now known as the County of Montgomery.

Col. Samuel Estill, brother of Capt. James Estill, was born in the Bullpasture in Augusta County, Virginia, September 10th, 1755. On the 10th of October 1774, Samuel Estill was out with a Boddy of Militia under the command of Gen. Lewis encamp't at the point where Pittsburg now stands and where the River takes the name of Ohio. The spies that were out that morning came running into camp, criing out as they ran from the line of battle, the Indians are upon you. The army Just about taking breakfast, many however charged at the line of battle without taking a bite. Samuel Estill, then a soldier just 19 years & a month old, and a Mr. Robert Carlisle, being mess mates, Rushed on to the line that was forming about a ½ mile from one River to the Other. They boath got behind a large oak tree shortly after which they were boath Nocked down by the bark of the tree being knocked off by enemy balls. Estill lay sometime, supposing his mess mate dead, feeling of his own face to find wheather he was wounded. Thus lying he discovered the mode of Indian warfare, which was to ly flat on the ground and shoot. Roll over to a fresh place, **54(1)** lye on his back and load his gun, Rolling each time under the smoke of his gun. This was the battle fought that Estill says Learned him to fight Indians. Thus the battle continued from the rising to the setting of the sun under a perfect cloud of smoke. Estill said the whole day did not appear to him to be over 2 hours long, the Indians Retiring at the setting of the sun. A relief guard was then ordered out to Relieve those men who had fought all day.

In their Returning to camp the most wonderful scene accurred.

Joy and grief intermingled in the most expressive manner. Brothers embracing each Other with tears of Joy having expected never to see each other again. Here Estill and his mess mate at camp who was Nocked down at the tree in the battle, and while many others ware in the most agonising pain being shot through the bowels Imploreing some one to shoot them in the hed to put end to their misery, such was the awful shock that one Soldier the same night after the Battle and report said there could not be a wound found on him.

Some time in the year of 1775, Samuel Estill under the Command of his Brother Capt. James Estill [was sent] to Relieve an attact on Donley's Fort in Greenbriar County, Virginia. Marched all day and part of the night about 40 miles, got into a Rye field after night out at the approach of Daylight. All the company made a rush to the Fort and got in safe (while about 300 Indians was Round the fort at the same time) to the great Joy of its inhabitants. After this Samuel Estill was more or less Imploying himself in the woods Hunting or in Manufacturing Gunpowder untile Capt James Estill started to Kentucky in the fall of the year 1778, arriving **54(2)** at Boonesborough shortly after the noted siege of the Indians at that place.

Samuel Estill being a single young man at that time, made his brother's house his home, and undertook to supply them with wild meat. Went on a hunting tower [tour] with one Jack Webber. They had both their horses loaded coming towards the fort of Boonesborough and in sight of the Boonesboro Fields. Estill became alarmed at the affrighted cattle that ran from him on the pathway. Knowing there was 2 gaps made in the fence not very distant apart he took to the most unfrequented one and when in a short distance of the gap, he saw the muzzle of the Indians guns pointing through the cracks of the fence at him. Having no time to get off deliberately, he threw himself off in a sidling position rather backwards and Webber with him. Boath ran about 40 or 50 paces and squatted in some tall weeds. The Indians came running up to their horses, pushed their hands into Estill's saddlebags, took out a twist of tobacco, dividing it up amongst them. Estill said he could have shot any of them at the time but his comrade Webber begged him not to shoot, that if he did, he would certainly fall into their hands. One Indian came on their trail within 30 feet of them, but Estill determined not to shoot until the Indian saw them. The Indian turned round without raising his head, walked back to his company holding as it seemed a parley. Some went to the left and some to the right. Estill concluding it would not do to stay longer, lest they would surround him, they then ran and the Indians after them untill they came to a small opening in the cane and some twenty yards across.

54(3) When they stopped at the farther side of the opening, the Indians came to the edge of the opening and stoped some time when Estill, fearing they might flank round Estill & and Webber, both started again and the Indians pursued untill they came to a similar opening in the cane. Estill calls his halt on the farther side again, the Indians approaching up as before, stoping at the edge of the open ground. Estill concocts another plan, tells Webber for him to go ahead while he might get a shot at their pursuers. But the Indians being cautious would not approach the opening, stood parleying some time and as night was approaching, they retreated back to their booty, got his horses and load of wild meat.

At the retreat of the Indians, Estill followed his comrade Webber where they Boath concealed themselves at the approach of night under the top limbs of a large Black oak tree that had fallen the previous summer, Clothed with its leaves, the Indians passing near them. In the night about 12 o'clock occationally ___ in their chargers, here the men lay until the rising of the Morning Star when they started for the fort at Boonesborough, came to the mouth of Otter Creek, went down the River to the fort. Gave information of the Indians taking of horses and on examination found all their horses were taken belonging to Boonesborough. Thus the Indians escaped pursuit that time, [the men] having no horses to follow them.

Estill was with the Company the Time Capt. James Estill got his arm Broke, the Indians lying in ambush behind a Large Blackoak tree. He cried out to James Estill, chekd his horse and sprang off by the side of a small tree at hand and shot a ball through 2 Indians, killing the hind most Indian ded on the spot and the other died in short time after. One Indian run at him as he was leaving the ground with a drawn tomahawk. Estill then stopt and drew his tomahawk from his belt which so deterred the Indian that he left Estill and ran at a small man that his horse shot down under him. He cried out to Estill, Shoot the Indian. Estill [said] Shoot your self, I have shot which caused him to recollect his gun, wheeled round and shot the Indian which was also killd making 3 ded Indians to 1 wounded man. Samuel Estill on returning to fort found on examination that there was 7 bullet holes shot through his under shirt though he supposed one ball might have made several of the holes.

He has been in nearly all the Campains against the Indians in his day when he was in Kentucky but never having blood drawn by anyone at any time. Being always in danger, extremely cautious and as brave as the brave, having the most acute sight and great knowledge of Indian life. He knew when to look and guard for them and seeing almost everything that would move in a half circle before him. In traveling when he suspected danger, he left all paths and roads and arrive at forts on licks in some obscure way that was not generally traveled. This great caution seemed to be the guardian angel of his life, passing many perilous dangers without much harm. He died in a good old age in the state of Tennessee on 9th Feb. 1837.

13C55 Wallace Estill letter, Pleasant Hill, Madison County, Ky., May 25, 1846

Mr. Lyman C. Draper, Baltimore, Md.
Dear Sir in Complyance with your Request I forward to you by Mail some of the sketches of the acts of My Father James Estill & also of his Brother Samuel Estill in their lifetimes. Much more I presume would have been given hand [had] this application been made years back by those better Acquainted with him in Early life who are now like himself - no more.

    I was, at his death, only between 7 & 8 years of age and at his Removal to Kentucky left with my grandparents. All which I have stated about him I learnt from others. I owned the servant that took care of their Horses while the battle went on the [that] terminated the life of my Father, [and] who has related to me often the action of the Battle. Many or nearly all the statements relative to Col. Samuel Estill I have had from his own statements.

    The Request you have made Respecting Elverton [Yelverton] Payton & Joseph Kenedy - boath are ded. I have had no communication with the Mrs. Fieldses, not having been in Richmond since Receiving your letter but will shew them your letter on the earliest opportunity. I know of no old papers of James and Samuel Estill that [would] be of any use to you. I expect my Father James Estill might have been on some Campaigns against the Indians but have no knowledge myself.

    According to Family information, the Estills came to the United States from Europe about the year 1620, settling in Jersey and have been progressing westward Ever since. I shall Expect you Sir to make just such use of what I send you as you may think proper. Change it and form Just as it suits you. Cripled as I am with Siattic [sciatic] pains in the hips, I am very seldom in Company. I woul[d] be Quite happy in being the means of forwarding to you any thing that would advance the Caus you have under taken. With Sentiments of Respect I subscribe myself your Friend and Obedient Servant,

                                                   Wallace Estill

Died on the 7th Ult., three days before completing his 86th Year, a son of the noted Capt. James Estill, who emigrated to Kentucky in 1779. <u>World</u>,

Oct 12, 1860.

13C56-56(1) *Interview by "FF" with David Cook of Lincoln County, Ky. in 1820 for* Hunt's Western Review. *The interview was published in June 1820. Other newspaper clippings here concern the Bryan's Station siege.*

"Mr. Hunt,

I haven't not long since to fall into company with Mr. David Cook, of Lincoln County, a gentleman of respectability and unimpeached veracity... expert, intrepid, successful warrior during the early defenders of our soil. Taking a deposition to promote as far as I am able your design of perpetuating these incidents in our history which are threatened with oblivion, I have procured from him the following narrative ...

In March 1782, fifteen [were] ordered by Col. Logan to join Capt. James Estill at Estill's Station near the present site of Richmond, Kentucky and thence to march under his command as a kind of reconnoitering party to different parts of that section of the country, at the discretion of the Captain. They accordingly marched in company with as many as could be spared from the stations, amounting altogether to the number of 40, to the Kentucky River, a few miles below the mouth of Station Camp Creek. Here they commenced digging a canal [canoe? LCD] for the purpose of enabling the company to pass and repass the river with facility and even expedition should any exigency require it.

A day or two after they had left the station, a body of Indians arrived there, killed a daughter of Capt. Innes [Gass, LCD] in sight of the fortification, and committed some other depredations. As soon as this news reached Estill's company, five of those who had families within the fort, being unwilling to trust them to the care to the few who remained, returned themselves to the fort. The company next marching crossed the river and took the direction in which they expected the Indians had retreated. After having gone about 10 or 12 miles, **(1)** they fell into the track, or as they termed it, the trail of the Indians, pursued them expeditiously as possible the remainder of the day, and encamped the ensuing night near Little Mountain, the present site of Mount Sterling.

Early next morning they again took up the line of march, leaving behind ten of their men whose horses were so fatigued that they were unable to proceed. The company, now reduced to the number of 25, had not gone far before they discovered by the appearance of the track of the Indians that they were not very distant. They then marched in four lines until about an hour before sunset when they discovered six of the enemy helping themselves to rations from the body of a buffalo. The company were ordered immediately to dismount. Capt. Estill fired his piece with effect and the Indians fled. Mr. Cook, our narrator, naturally ardent and exceedingly active, had proceeded some distance before the company and taking an Indian halt, raised his gun and fired. At the same moment, a second Indian passed on the opposite side and he leveled them both at one shot.

This fact is well attested, and being in view of nearly the whole company, inspired them with a high degree of ardor and confidence. In the meantime the main body of the enemy had heard the alarm and returned, and a general engagement commenced at this moment.

Lieut. William Miller, who commanded the left line, took a panic and fled from the contest and his division, consisting of six men, through courtesy followed him without firing a gun. This flank immediatley became unprotected and the enemy made an effort to join their rear.

As soon as Capt. Estill discovered this, he ordered Cook, who was an Ensign, with three other men, to occupy Miller's ground and repel the enemy in that quarter. He accordingly took the lead and others followed, one of whom discovered an Indian and shot him. When the three retreated to a little ___, since they thought they could do greater execution with less danger, continued to advance, not discovering the absence of his comrades until he had discharged his gun with effect. Then he immediately retreated. Some distance toward a large tree, near which he intended to shelter himself, he unfortunately got entangled in the tops of some fallen trees, which circumstance occasioned him to halt for a moment, and a ball struck him just below the shoulder blade and came out near his collar bone.

In the meantime, the captain and the rest of the company kept up a tremendous fire. The gallant Capt. Estill expired with his fourth wound. Second Lieutenant Samuel South experienced the same fate after perhaps one of the most sanguinary and bloody conflicts ever fought in Kentucky for the number of men engaged, which continued for the space for 1 hour and 3/4. Both parties then seemed to withdraw and the contest subsided by mutual consent.

Of Estill's company there were 8 killed and 3 wounded. Mrs. Gatliffe,* a woman who was then a prisoner with the Indians, and also a Negro who that day was captured by the whites, stated that the Indians were 25 in number, 17 of whom were killed and 2 wounded. This battle was fought on the same day as the Battle of Blue Licks. [Signed] FF

The closing sentence is all wrong, Estill's was fought in March, Blue Licks in August, etc. LCD.

* *Mrs. Faulconer, in her interview with John D. Shane, named Mrs. Gatliff and her children among those captured at the attack on Martin's and Ruddle's Stations in June 1780 (DM11CC 135-138). Mrs. Gatliff told of seeing the Indians who returned from Estill's Defeat while she was still a prisoner. DM 3Q116*

13C63-66 *In the following, two newspaper accounts are combined to tell of the Siege at Bryan's Station of August 1782. The statements were "phonographically" recorded and published in* The Christian Union, *New York, on April 12, 1876 and May 16, 1876.*

Grandmother Tomlinson's Story - by Irvine Beman

The following story is strictly authentic, as recited by one of its heroines, Grandmother Tomlinson, and phonographically reported as it fell from her lips.

There were forty or fifty families occupying log cabins built near together and surrounded by a fence of logs, called a stockade. A stockade was made by digging a deep, narrow ditch, and then planting in it large long logs, upright and tight together, and filling in the soil around them. Such a fence was fifteen or twenty feet high, and an excellent fortification when the enemy had no cannon with which to destroy it. It was built with crooks or angles, called bastions, and was pierced with many port-holes, through which those inside could discharge their rifles at a foe outside.

At one point was a huge gate of logs, swinging on great wooden hinges, which, when closed, was as strong as any part of the walls.

A few words about our heroine, and we are ready for the story. Grandmother Tomlinson's life began in Western Pennsylvania, ten years before the Declaration of Independence, or, as she used to say, "before the first Fourth of July," and closed in Kentucky when she was above ninety years of age. At the recital of this incident she was a sweet old lady, the soul of piety and truth.

In the spring of 1782, when she was nearly sixteen, her parents, with several younger children, removed from Pennsylvania to Bryan's [Station], in a rough boat down the Ohio River to Maysville [Ky.], thence on horseback some sixty miles to their new home.

These were perilous times on the frontier: the Indians, incited by British agents, waging a fiercer war against the settlers than anything in the Atlantic States. Kentucky was aptly styled "the dark and bloody ground." Now for Grandmother Tomlinson's story.

It was the morning of the 15th of August, just a week after my birthday. Most of the night mother and I had been helping father mould bullets and prepare for an early march with the garrison to Hoy's stockade, near which Captain Holder had recently been defeated by the Indians. Little did we imagine that nearly a thousand warriors were gathering then in the fields and woods about us, eager for our scalps.

At early dawn all the men in the stockade paraded with their guns and accoutrements and food enough for four days. The women and children were all out to say good-bye, and the gate was about to be opened for their departure, when suddenly on the back side of the stockade there was heard the most unearthly noise of guns and shouting and screaming, so that many of the children began to cry for fear.

We all ran to the picketing and saw, through the portholes, a party of thirty or forty Indians standing among the corn, brandishing their tomahawks, firing guns, and yelling.

Some of the young men were for rushing out [but others] who understood Indians better, said "No!" for it was only a decoy party to draw us out where some larger concealed force would destroy us.

But nothing was in sight yet. However, a keen watch was kept up as the sun rose, and pretty soon those best qualified to judge decided that a large force of warriors was concealed in the low bushes beyond the spring. As soon as this was certain it was resolved to send somebody to Lexington to warn the people there, and to obtain assistance. There were horses in this stockade, and young Tomlinson, afterward your grandfather, and another man, volunteered to undertake this service.

Mounting two of the swiftest animals, the gate was thrown open, and they rode out as hard as they could run down the Lexington road. We expected the Indians by the spring would fire at them, but they did not, showing that they thought themselves undiscovered, and were so numerous as to not fear any reinforcements that might come from Lexington. The Indians among the corn were not in sight of the gate and the road, but they still kept up the most horrible noise.

Some of the old Indian fighters now held a council to consider what to do, for although in every way well-armed for the struggle, our garrison was but a handful beside the enemy.

It was decided to act for a while as if we did not suspect the ambuscade by the spring, and thus see if they would not expose themselves to our advantage.

But one difficulty of an alarming nature was discovered – we had no water in the stockade. The spring inside the picketing had been dry for many days, as it was a very hot summer, and we had been bringing water from the outside spring near which so many Indians were concealed.

Not a bucket of water was there inside the fort, as we used it all during the night in preparing for the early march so suddenly interrupted. If the siege should continue even twenty-four hours we should suffer fearfully in the parching August weather, and it might hold out for several days, in which case we should actually perish from thirst, as cruel a foe as the bloodthirsty savages.

"What shall be done?" went from lip to lip, and even our bravest men seemed alarmed at our peril from this lack of water.

At length a plan was proposed. The old Indian fighters said that the principal force of the Indians was near the spring, concealed, and would not show themselves until their leaders saw a chance to capture the stockade at a rush. The party in the corn was intended to draw our attention away from their main body, and make us careless on our gate front. But as long as we seemed on our guard, no general attack would be made. Therefore a few persons might safely go after water, if the garrison would make a show of watchfulness in their defense.

At this suggestion, one of the mothers proposed that the women should go after the water in their usual way, while the men made show of being on the alert. "Probably," she said, "the women could go to the spring and return unharmed if they would do so without acting as if they suspected an enemy nearer than the corn. The Indians would not forfeit their hope of taking the stockade by surprise, just for the sake of killing a few women."

This bold project met at first much opposition. Some of the men would not listen to the proposal that their wives and daughters should run such risk; a few children, catching the idea, set up a frightened wailing. Certain of the women, as was natural, had no relish for the dangerous undertaking.

I remember one in particular, a boastful creature, who had always seemed to consider herself as brave as the bravest man, but now showed herself a great coward exclaiming, "Let the men bring the water. We are not bullet proof! The savages will take a woman's scalp as soon as a man's!"

65 But so many of the older women were in favor of it that in a few minutes all agreed to the plan. It was decided that every women in the stockade able to bring a pail of water should go, so as to show no partiality. We were not to go all in a crowd, but stringing along two or three together, as naturally as possible, so as to excite no suspicion among the Indians.

Then we got out buckets, some of us carrying two. Oh, how plainly I remember those few minutes. Many of us wore shoes, or moccasins, but we all took them off so as to run the faster if we need.

We stood all together by the picketing, and a paler-faced crowd of women was never seen. But there was no fainting, as in these days is so common among ladies.

The men, each with two or three loaded guns, gathered along the stockade at the portholes, ready to fire on the Indians if they attacked us. Two of the strongest were to manage the gate.

Finally, when all were ready my mother suggested that a prayer should be offered before we went out, for, said she, "If God does not shield us we shall never come back." This pleased all, both men and women.

Mr. Reynolds, whose son was captain of the garrison, knelt down on the ground, while everybody knelt around him, and such a prayer as that old man prayed! The people in those days, ministers and all, do not know how to pray as folks prayed in those bloody times. You do not feel your need of God as you would if a thousand wild Indians were at your very doors panting to kill you and all your loved ones. You do not nowadays, hourly, hold your lives in your hands, and feel that you have no hope but in the Lord.

This white-haired old man in a quavering voice told God our very hearts, and it did seem as if God was right there to hear him. How wives were going forth from husbands into the jaws of death; how young daughters were running the risk of a captivity worse than death; how mothers were leaving their babes whom they loved more dearly than life – thus he prayed. We all felt such a prayerful earnestness as people do not feel in the splendid modern churches, where prayers are almost a mere form. And he besought God, weeping, that every soul in Bryan's stockade might that day and that minute, be born again, and thus fitted to die or live. I was not until then a Christian, but while I was kneeling there on the hard-trodden earth I felt I must give myself to God, and I did. And from that awful hour I date my hope of heaven. And I was not the only one; every poor sinner in the fort did the same. It was a great revival within fifteen minutes, and nearly two score persons were then and there converted. When we rose from our knees, men and all were in tears, and we knew God would take care of us, die or live.

There was a moment of sad and fond farewells, and we began to slip through the gate and start for the spring. How vivid it is yet to me, though it was about seventy years ago! I can see and feel it all, as if it were now before me. The sun was some two hours high, and the very air seemed as still as death. There were moccasins we had removed standing in a row by the picketing. The little children were crying by the cabin doors. The men were going to their guns by the portholes.

I went out with my mother, and as we were passing through the gate she said in a low tone: "Walk behind me, Hetty, so if they shoot they will not hit you till they kill me."

But I replied: "for Father's sake and the children, I will keep between you and the Indians."

66 And I did. Going to the spring I walked before her, and returning I kept behind her. When we were dipping up the water, I chanced to see under the bushes the feet of one Indian and the hand of another grasping a tomahawk.

Within a few minutes everyone was safe back in the stockade and the Indians had not fired a shot. But some of the buckets were not very full, for it is not an easy task when you shake like the leaves to carry water without spilling.

Authors may write about the courage of soldiers in battle, but I think if they had it all so deathly still, without a drum beat or bugle, they might not be braver than we women were.

The Indians attacked the stockade that afternoon, but the men fired accurately and we women kept their guns loaded.

After the Indians had lost nearly fifty of their number, their chiefs began to talk of retreating. But the renegade white man, Simon Girty, opposed such a step. He proposed to try upon us the effect of parleying and threats. Creeping to a stump about half-way from the woods to the stockade, he hid behind it, and hailed the garrison. As soon as the guard heard his voice, Capt. Reynolds was sent for, and nearly every person in the fort hastened to hear what was said. When Girty was asked what he wanted, he began to praise the courage of the garrison, but lamented that our courage was worse than vain, as it only the more enraged the thousand warriors with him. When they should capture us they would take every scalp in the fort, and it would be impossible for him to stop them. To this Capt. Reynolds answered, "Do not count your chickens till they are hatched. It will require a braver thousand red-skins than yours to take our scalps."

Girty replied, "If it needs more to capture your little fort, they are coming; every hour new parties of warriors are arriving. You should surrender now."

In less than forty-eight hours, they became discouraged, and they all stole away through the great forests. We afterwards found out that when we went to the spring, we were within short rifle shot of more than six hundred warriors.

Two days after, this same army of Indians fought and defeated the Kentuckians in the bloody battle of the Blue Licks in which more than sixty of the best men were killed. So you see, if we had fallen into their hands, the Indians would have made short work of us.

13C74-74(4) Joseph Ficklin letter, Lexington, Ky., June 26, 1845
Joseph Ficklin answered numbered questions concerning the siege at Bryan's Station. The list of questions was not found. In the list of names given, some are marked with "x" to designate names of men who were killed during the siege. The list was taken from the Appendix to Bryan's Station Heroes and Heroines (Virginia Webb Howard), Lexington, Ky., 1932

Dr Sir
I give the following facts in answer to your letter of yesterday on condition that you forbid the publication in form I give it, which is not fit for print until it be prepared by a competent person.

1. Robert Johnson, the father of Col. R.M. Johnson, was a Captain of the militia but at the time he was in Virginia & no one took on themselves any command but John Craig...the head of the population in the absence of Capt. Johnson.
2. There were 44 men in the fort in the morning, two of whom - Nicholas Tomlinson & Thomas Bell - were sent off to Lexington for help; now remaining 42 who had guns & rated as fighting men. The names of all cannot now be given. I name them as their Houses stood beginning with the corner near the big spring:

1. John Williams; 2. Wm. Beasley Senior.; 3. Charles [Beasley]; 4. John [Beasley]; 5. James [Beasley - Wm Beasley's] 3 sons; 6. Wm. Lay, sick; 7. John Craig, Senior; 8. John Craig Junr, his son; 9. Jeremiah Craig; 10. Philip Drake;11. David Williams; 12. D. Suggett, very old; 13.John Suggett; 14.Wm Childress; 15.Wm. Arnold; 16. Matthew Gayle; 17 Josiah Gayle, his son; 16 Jacob Stucker; 19. David Stucker; 20. Michael Stucker; 21. x Daniel Mitchell; 22 David Mitchell his son; **(1)** 23. x John Adkins; 24 Wm. Tomlinson; 25 Nicholas [Tomlinson], his son; 26. Wm. T[omlinson], another son; 27. Thomas Ficklin; 28. John Ficklin; 29. David Hernden; 30. Henry Herndon; 31. Wm Gatewood; 32. Mr? Campbell at Col. Johnson's; 33.Wm Campbell; 34. John Guill?; 35. Lewis Vanlandingham; 36. Wm. Bradley; 37. Aaron Reynolds; 38. Wm. Rogers;

38. [sic] Thos. Bell.

3. The alarm was given before sun rise by the fire of many guns at Mr. Tomlinson, Senior, when he opened his door
4. The great body of the Indians moved off in 24 hours.
5. There were a few houses about 60 feet outside of the Picketts which were abandoned at the first alarm & occupied by the Indians for a time and set on fire. A favorable change of the wind to northeast blew the flames the opposite direction & saved the whole population from the flames & death or capture.
6. In the dusk of the evening, Simon Girty approached the Picketts in a thick ___ & secured himself behind a large stump of a tree within 5 yards of the house of John Williams & [told] the place to surrender. John Craig's son answered, replied it would not be done. Girty lamented the dredful consequences which must follow on the arrival of the cannon, it would not then be in his power to save the women & children from the fury of the Indians. He gave his name as the commander of 600 Indians. This was heard by all within the fort & produced great alarm, but Aron Reynolds, a young man known & beloved for his pleasant manner replied that his ___ was well known & boldly ___ that he had named his two dogs one Simon & the other Girty. On this Girty assured Reynolds it was an awful subject & not to be **(2)** treated lightly. Reynolds replyed he and his naked followers were just cowards, that the brave men in the fort would use nothing but switches on their yellow birds if they attempted to brake into the fort. This produced a fine feeling & restored confidence. Girty made a few more attempts to alarm & departed.
7. Behind a stump as stated in no. 6.
8. First day as stated in no. 6
9. No recollection of the Commander of 16 horse men [who] got in 1st day… None of the horse men were killed or wound[ed] but almost 30 men on foot were driven off & two of them killed, both horse & foot had left Lexington on their way to Boons Station in what is now Clark County. When overtaken by the express from Bryants returned on B__ ___ and met on the Lexington road ___ ___. The foot [men] passed through the corn field & the horse men went round to the lane from Lexington & when fired on the foot [men] instead of making their way to the fort, made for the firing & when they arrived the horse men were safe in the Fort & 200 or 300 Indians ready to meet the foot [men] & between them & the fort, so they made a break to Lexington that evening.
10. I can not say whether Col. Todd was of ___; he did not get into the fort – a cane brake near the head of the land saved the foot men from death.

11. Can give no more information than in No. 10. There was many fortunate escapes among them.

12. When the alarm of the morning came and siege was expected & all the females, boys, Girls &c went to the little spring as it was called. Filled their vessels, & were not disturbed altho the Indians were in the high weeds near the spring. But the Indians waited for the signal on the other side, expecting all the men to run out that way. But after aplenty of water was secured & and vacant places of pickets filled up, say in two or 3 hours, about 15 men went out on the lane to Lexington & many fired on. Then the great body of Indians started to **(3)** the fort believing the men were all out. When the Indians approached in about 50 yards, the men fired on them & all fell back except the party behind the out houses. Many Indians were killed; some of them got up to the Houses – 2 men were killed at this ___. Mr. Mitchell was shot dead above the eye, & J. Adkins in the side & died that day. Nicholas Tomlinson was wounded slightly in the arm in the evening after he returned with the 15 horsemen, or a short time before then.

13. Jacob Stucker shot an Indian about 120 yards from the fort near the little spring. [The Indian] was behind a stump peeping over, the ball struck in the top of the head & passed through part of his back between the shoulders.

14. This has been answered. The Indians had nearly 40 killed – all were taken off except the one shot by Jacob Stucker, but Charles Beasly at the distance of nearly 200 yards fired aiming at the head ____ . The Indian was found hid.

In giving over the names I may have omitted some half a Dozen. It would be unjust to say any thing unfavorable. All done their duty but there were many more certain than the rest: Jeremiah Craig, Jacob Stucker, Nicholas Tomlinson, Thomas Bell, Aron Reynolds, __. Mr. Beasly I recollect at this late date. The horses were mostly in the fort, the ___ hogs were nearly all killed. John Beasly & Reynolds were both taken [captured] a few days after at the Blue Licks, but got back safely. James Beasly was killed & Charley [Beasley] taken but returned. The ___ ___ **(4)** in the deepest distress never to return – but both John & Charles l[Beasley] lived to good old ages in the state of Ohio. I do not know a soul living to consult except John Craig, Junr. is still living. Mrs. Gen. Payne, the eldest sister of R. M. Johnson, is still living and might be able to give you names left out by me. There was Wilcox in the Fort but whether he was killed before or after the siege I am not able to tell.

Yours &c

Joseph Ficklin

13C76-76(1-7), 77 The History of Black Hoof, a Chief of the Shawnee Nation. *Sent to Draper by Joseph Ficklin.*

During the late war, the volunteers from Kentucky became acquainted with Black Hoof, who remained friendly to the American cause as did Logan [who had been captured by Benjamin Logan when young] and many other northwest Indians. In frequent conversations with Black Hoof, Gentlemen from Kentucky learned that he had observed French traders who were fine smiths, working silver into ornaments for the Indians at the old town of Lulbegrud on the waters of Kentucky River 8 or 10 miles north of Mt. Sterling, Kentucky. The idea expressed by Black hoof was that the silver was the produce of ore near said town of Lulbegrud which took with the Gentleman at once. They had long believed in a mine of silver in that quarter of the state & prevailed upon Black Hoof to visit Kentucky in 1815. While here he gave the following historical facts to the Rev. J. H. Ficklin of Scott County, Kentucky, which were esteemed correct in all but dates which could only be conjectured.

Black Hoof said that he had it from his father that when the great body of the Shawney nations removed from East of the Alleghany Mountains, a split took place between the chiefs. A large portion of more **(1)** than 1000 men, women, & children separated from the Nation and crossed the Ohio & found a small prairie well supplied with a fine stream on which they settled as if supposed about the year 1690. Prosperity attended this settlement for about 20 years when the northern Indians frequently killed them and messengers from old Chillicothe & the Shawney towns near it called & urged return of this Kentucky party. But they still refused, suspecting that the injury done to them had been set on by their nation on the Scioto River to force their return. The wars with the northern Indians becoming more alarming, the Lulbegrud town agreed to break up. To punish their own people, [they] refused to return but accepted the invitation of the Cherokees & went among them on the Tennessee river from below where Knoxville stands.

At this time Black Hoof was a boy of about 10 years of age. How long the Lulbegrud party remained in Tennessee could not be stated but supposed to be 10 or 15 years, which brings it to about 1730 when messengers again appeared from their friends in Ohio & intreated **(2)** them to return.

National feeling & a difference arising with the Cherokee

people, on sundry occasions, the Lulbegrud tribe agreed to return & set out mustering nearly 200 warriors, & about 1000 women & children with all their horses & property. Not possessing a sufficient supply of horses to convey all the young & old & infirm comfortably, the plan of reaching the Cumberland river and use canoes was adopted. At some point not well described by Black Hoof, the tribe halted and were preparing canoes when nearly all their horses were stolen by Indians and the impression was pretty general that it was by the Cherokees who had become unfriendly. Everything being ready, the baggage and helpless part of the tribe were placed in canoes and the able-bodied went by land as a guard.

When the party entered the Ohio river, the spring floods was comeing down. By great exertion the canoes ascended to within a few miles of the Wabash River & stopped at the point now called Shawney town in the state of Illinois and formed their camp near the river to protect their canoes. The river continued to swell until Banks or Mounds of earth were raised, which still may be seen.

The French had a short time before settled at Kaskaskia from Europe & formed a considerable town. The tribe were **(3)** invited there by some of the French traders. To avoid the danger of hostile tribes & to procure provisions, agreed to remove a distance of only 90 miles by land. At Kaskaskia the tribe remained two years & after a strong party of their nation arrived from Ohio, conducted them back to Old Chillicothe where they arrived as supposed about pla.

When Black Hoof arrived in Kentucky in 1815, he supposed his age to be 109. Those who conversed with him had the utmost confidence in his statements. He could tell his age to be 50 when Gen. Braddock was defeated and many points of History to confirm his story.

Although he had not been at Lulbegrud for about 100 years, he could describe the face of the Country & the Creek. When approaching the spot within a few miles, his recollection improved & he pointed out the spot & country around before he was in sight. His activity was equal to that of most men at 80. He road [sic] well & could walk without a staff.

Note: The word Chillicothe was explained to me – Fire not going out or fire that could not be put out. It burned all ways at the legal or proper time. This is the only explanation ever given of this word. LCD

(4) 6 Cases of Indian Depredations

It was the practice of the early settlers near the great crossings to find small boys of 12 or 14 years of age [to go] 5 or 6 miles to [work?] the mill of Col. Robert Johnson at the Great Crossings. The people had fought through the dangers of _____ & could not believe in the danger around them. The following cases are samples of the times.

The first occurred before the removal from Bryan Station. Early one morning a lad by the name of Lay was first out to cut a bundle of green cane to feed horses. The lad about 16 years of age imprudently crossed the creek near the big spring near where a Baptist meeting house now stands when he was shot in the leg & his horse badly wounded & fell. The lad was overtaken & killed & scalped. Had he in his escape taken the nearest route after his horse fell, he would have met a party from the fort & been saved.

In the Spring of 1787, a boy about 14 by the name of Jones was first out near Major Thomas Herndon's 4 miles from the Great Crossings, to drive up the cattle & was shot down & scalped.

About the same time a boy about 12 by the name of Rees was just to the mill of the Great Crossings when in about a mile of the mill his horse was shot off & the boy killed & scalped.

About this time William Ficklin, a young man nearly grown & the son of Thomas Ficklin, went out early in the morning to drive home **(5)** the horses when it appeared that two Indians on foot had just passed. He hastened to the house of Mr. Rogers near the place obtained [sentences illegible] & they followed the trail though the Indians fled leaving behind their packs of Halters & some fine bloody clothing which was supposed to be from the party killed on the Ohio River where John May fell...after whom Maysville and Mays Lick were named.

Many pioneers were killed descending the Ohio River in what are still called Kentucky boats & small parties of Indians crossed into Kentucky to steal horses [and] to take the plunder of the boats.

In one case, a single Indian came into the settlement on Dry Run near George Town & stole two horses. One he had to leave from being lame & not content with one horse, passed into Mercer County & had taken 4 others. He was discovered & killed by Simon Kenton & a party of men near Maysville.

The case of Capt. Hubble, the son-in-law of the Rev. __ Ganoe, should be stated in full. By his _____ bravery, he caused a few men to resist a large party of Indians on the Ohio, and after killing some, drove the rest from the boat. Hubble died at an old age near Georgetown, Ky.

About this time, Mr. Applegate was killed near Georgetown. His son now keeps Tavern in that place.

(6) Three Cases of Indian Depredations

In October 1786, two young men, Henry Herndon & William

Ficklin, at sunset, left the house of Thomas Ficklin about 4 mles below the Great Crossings to kill deer by a bright moon light at D___'s Lick on North Elkhorn a mile below. At about midnight a party of 6 Indians who had been __ __ Mr. Denny near that place to steal horses, had been driven off by the fierce dogs after securing horses. This party of Indians arrived on the Bank of the creek behind a standing hollow tree occupied by Herndon & Ficklin. One Indian on foot and one on the stolen horses passed the root of the tree into the edge of the water within a few feet of the two white men who sprung out & had to pass through the party of Indians on the bank. Both parties fired & fled. The young men collected a party in the morning & visited the Battle ground. The Indians had thrown off all their Baggage, halters, Blankets, meats, & every thing & escaped with only the horse of Mr. Denny – neither of the two were injured. The rout of the Indians was complete. They fled from the settlements with all haste.

In the spring of 1785, the Indians attacked the Negro of a Mr. John Scott on the north bank of the Creek 4 miles below the Great Crossing. The Negroes were preparing a new field for corn & were alarmed of their danger **(7)** by Lewis Flanagan who was in the woods near the spot. The Negroes all reached the house, two only slightly wounded, but Mr. Flanagan was pursued by some of the Indians near the house of Thomas Ficklin on the other side of the Creek. One of the Indians out stripping the rest, was at one time within a few feet of Flanagan. Neither of their guns loaded, all depended on speed…

The opinion prevailed in most parts of Kentucky up to a late date that such depredations existed in many spots of Kentucky. This was rather an unfortunate thing & led at various times to the loss of time & waste of blood.

Some time in the summer of 1786, a party of working hands & hunters built a small stockade fort on the Kentucky river at Drennons Lick & commenced working in Lead. A quantity of very rich ore was secured in the fort. The cold winter approached & the most of the men left for the settlement on North Elkhorn about the Great Crossings to spend their Christmas, apprehending no danger at that inclement season. But when the party returned in January, the fort was burned down & a Mr. Ray – highly esteemed – had been killed & also the two or three left with him.

13C77-77(1) Joseph Ficklin letter, Lexington, Ky., May 13, 1846 with LCD notes on Ficklin's statements pertaining to Col. Robert Johnson, Maj. Thomas Herndon, Col. Thomas A. Russell, and Robert Wickliffe.

13C78-78(1) Joseph Ficklin letter, Lexington, Ky., Oct. 9, 1846

This letter addresses the possibility of the papers of the Rev. Campbell[?] being housed in Mason County, Ky. at the house of A___ Pickett. A manuscript prepared by Mr. Wickliff is mentioned as having been destroyed because Draper had not called on Mr. Wickliff. Joseph Ficklin wrote: "I can tell you it was no great loss."

13C79-79(1-25) Interview with Joseph Ficklin, Esqr., of Lexington, Fall 1846. Diagram of Bryan's Station at the Siege – Fort about 250 x 600 feet, about 12 houses on a side and 4 at each end.

Shown are the original fort, an addition made in 1781, a provisions building afterwards used for a school house, three cabins and a stable about 100 feet from the fort. These buildings were unoccupied during the siege except for the stable. The cabins were referred to as "out houses." Resdients of those cabins probably moved into the fort in times of danger. Indians occupied them during the siege.

There were 44 men – Childers was one – don't recollect about Adams. Before sun-rise a Negro, Jim, out in the lane, was shot at & ball passed **(1)** through his clothes. He escaped to the fort. At the same time [they] shot at William Tomlinson, Sr. as he stood in the door of his cabin, missed him & lodged by the door side. It was customary when such an alarm sounded for the men to snatch up their guns and run out towards the report & no doubt the Indians expected & desired this, but the word passed quickly around "don't go out! don't go out!"

Nicholas Tomlinson and Thomas Bell were despatched on horseback as express to Lexington, went up a little branch but were unmolested, though the Indians were in that quarter. The women now milked the cows in the calf pasture bordering along the branch by the little spring, & on the spring side of the branch, while the others & the blacks went to bringing water, and though the Indians were posted mostly in the tall weeds & close [to] the women, yet they did not choose to molest them.

The men were busy preparing their guns &c. There were several spaces between the cabins where stockading had never been placed in the new part of the fort. These were at once placed, as the ditches were already dry & stockading split and placed. It was now **(2)** about eight o'clock, & the Indians still quiet. Tubs &c filled with water.   It was now thought best that a party should go out up the lane & see what produced the firing early in the morning. Thirteen went & Jerry Craig among them, & he the leader. They had proceeded about 100 yards from the fort when they discovered Indians in the corners of the lane fence. Shots were exchanged, but without effect, & Craig's party made good their retreat to the fort.

The Indians now – by this firing – particularly in the calf pasture near the spring, evidently thinking the men had been enticed from the fort, & rushed up expecting, doubtless, an easy conquest. Took possession of cabins [the deserted cabins outside the fort], & some below the cabins. As they ascended the gentle acclivity, they received a fire & were driven back with considerable loss. Those at the cabins fired into the upper end of the fort, killed Michael Mitchell (not David Mitchell as mentioned in Ms. Statement) dead in his cooper shop, & mortally wounded John Adkins in the side. He, a few hours after, desired a piece of watermelon; it was given him & he immediately expired. Mrs. Mitchell afterwards said she "would rather have lost her best cow, Patty, than her **(3)** dear husband, but was thankful his eye was not shot out." He was shot through the forehead.

The Indians in the [deserted] cabins were, in some fifteen minutes, glad to retreat from them, so hotly were they received & several supposed to have been killed. Before leaving them, they set them on fire, & some two or three horses were burned up in the stable. Does not recollect about Jerry Craig firing from a cabin roof in the fort, & killing an Indian.

In the fort was an old parson, David Suggett, who now set to praying (then near 80 years old), & the wind, light, now suddenly & providentially veered & blew so as to drive the flames from the fort & thus, as all admitted, was the fort saved from destruction. The fort nearest the burning cabins was scorched, as it was.

This was soon after 8 o'clock. No marching to a fife, as Gatewood says. After this there was no attempted attack on the fort, except by creeping up as near as they safely could, & firing from under the bank.

Mentioned here is Holder's Defeat, in which John Holder and his men went in pursuit of Indians who had captured two little boys from a watermelon patch at Hoy's Station.

(The night before, news came of Holder's defeat, & a request for all the **(4)** men that could be spared to meet next day at Hoys Station to go & bury the dead. They set up part of the night preparing for [a morning departure], men grinding corn at the hand mills, & was baking bread, & had the Indians delayed their firing half an hour later in the morning, all the efficient part of the garrison would have been absent.)

After retreating from the cabins, set them on fire, the Indians kept up an occasional yelling & firing, but in the main kept pretty quiet. About 12 o'clock, Tomlinson & Bell returned direct from Boone's Station,

& came through the big cornfield, & were astonished to find all peace & no sign of Indians, but soon were told of the attack. They reported that all that could be spared at Lexington had gone to Hoy's Station. They pursued on & overtook them about half way on the road from Lexington to Boone's Station; & the messengers said the party would shortly come to their relief. Some one of the Lexington party went express to Boone's Station & the Boone Station men had formed then to go to Hoy's....

About one o'clock, the Lexington party arrived in the rear of the big corn field. It was arranged that **(5)** some 18 of them were to pass direct through the corn. The horsemen rode at their usual gait until in the lane they found the Indians on either side of them. They put their horses to full gallop, & though fired on, enveloped in their own dust, they escaped & got into the fort. As the gate on the side was fastened, had not time to open it, they were admitted through the cabin doors at the upper end of the fort adjoining the lane. Man nor horse injured of this party.   This firing was heard by the Boone Station men, 4 or 5 horsemen & some 12 footmen, who were then a quarter of a mile off. They now hastened their speed, directing their course to the head of the lane. The footmen at the cornfield, on hearing the firing at the head of the lane on the horsemen, instead of pushing for the fort, changed their course for the firing at the head of the lane, to aid if need be, the horsemen whom they supposed engaged in a fight. They & Boone Station men met in the woods at the head of the lane at the same time. Found some 300 Indians in the lane, some 10 minutes after the horsemen had been fired on in the lane between them **(6)** and the fort. Fortunately the most of the Indians guns were empty having discharged them at the horsemen.

It only remained to retreat. The tall cane was close at hand, & all broke for it, being fired on by some of the enemy having loaded guns. Here Capt. Hays & the others were wounded & one killed – (certainly one killed on the spot, & one mortally wounded – Charles Hunter – who died afterwards). The Indians when they got his scalp raised the scalp halloo. There was chasing to the cane (none whatever in the cornfield). The cane commenced about a quarter of a mile from the head of the lane. The Indians in squads of four or five, pressed the fugitives. James Girty was with one of the partys, pursued a fugitive, who would turn with his gun & check the pursuers, until finally Girty concluded his gun was empty, & pushed in with his tomahawking & the man shot. Girty was only singed by several pieces of leather he had got at the big spring & tied to his shot pouch...

John Sharp, an aged & rather infirm man, though closely pursued in this way, by reserving **(7)** his fire, kept the Indians off, &

escaped. While passing through the cane, as he jumped a log, he roused up a bear – both were equally scared. The Indians did not enter into the cane, but kept the trace, & about half way to Lexington, overtook & killed one McConnell.

The Indians could & did repass from the big spring to the head of the lane through the big cornfield without being observed. The Indians now returned to the big spring, & commenced preparations for dinner – or rather those who had not already eaten, for from their smoke they were cooking down there before & at the time of the arrival of the Todd party of Lexington. The Indians had killed several beeves, & were now cooking & feasting on them. After dinner, from the hemp field, the Indians fired into the fort without injury

In the morning, soon after they had fired from the cabins, Jacob Stucker, seeing an Indian near the little spring behind a stump & had fallen back out of gunshot as they supposed, only his **(8)** head to view, fired away. At a distance of 120 yards, shot him dead through the head. Stucker's rifle was not an unusually large one.

Not long after, John Beasley (a brother of Gen. Nathaniel Beasley of Ohio, not then there, or too young) espying several Indians over the branch opposite the lower end of the fort, at a watermelon patch & some broom corn (mellons growing in the corn) – sitting down eating them. One of the Indians, fully six feet four inches tall jumped up & cut up a good many pranks, striking his breast, as if defying those in the fort. Beasley took good aim at his forehead, calculating for so long a shot – 150 yards – the ball would fall; & took him through the body near the pit of the stomach. His body was afterwards found, sunk in the creek.

The only Indian found where shot, was the one Stucker killed. The others must have been afraid to come there by day light, & perhaps could not find the body by night.

During that afternoon the Indians occasionally fired **(9)** on the fort from the hemp patch, but spent much of their time killing cattle, hogs & sheep – about 80 cattle altogether, about 150 hogs, & all the sheep, some 80. Towards night, Nicholas Tomlinson received a chance shot, passing the thin part of a house log, & slightly in his arm.

Soon after sun down & while yet sufficiently light to distinguish, Girty got behind a tall stump some 10 feet high, where a tree had broken off, within about forty steps of the fort – in the hemp patch. He called for the commander of the fort. Capt. John Craig, Sr. appeared (who acted as such in the absence of Capt. Robert Johnson) & Girty announced his object – his name & assumed to be commander of the Indians. Said that he had a force of about 600, with a company of artillerymen, & that his cannon would be up that night & would be able to destroy the fort He claimed to have great humanity, but if compelled to take the fort by assault, the natural excitement of the Indians would take them beyond his control & he could not be accountable for the consequence. He was particularly distressed at the thought of the inevitable destruction of the women & children that could follow. Surrender was the only remedy, if this would be done **(10)** before the cannon appeared; in this case, all should be protected & saved.

To this Capt. Craig replied that he would not surrender, that the fort was sufficiently strong to resist any force Girty & the Indians could bring to bear against it, & added that the fort had received a reinforcement. Girty now spoke again & said it was a solemn occasion, & could not bear the idea of such a bloody massacre as must ensue if they persisted in their resolution & begged them to reconsider the matter.

The women & children & nearly all the men of the fort were collected at the end of the garrison & a deep gloom seemed to rest particularly on the females & the children. Observing this, Aaron Reynolds, wishing to dissipate the gloom & produce cheerfulness & self-reliance, mounted the stump & called out to Girty, assuring him that he was well known, that he had worthless dogs - one he named Simon, the other Girty, to express his contempt for the man. There was no fear or concern felt in the fort of being taken if his **(11)** Indians were to break in at any point, that they could lash & drive their yellow hides out with switches alone, of which they had a great number purposely prepared, without resorting to their guns.

Girty interrupted him – said he was no blackguard, that he had come there upon a solemn occasion & upon a mission of peace & good will, to save the effusion of blood. Reynolds said "it is you yellow rascals who ought to be concerned for the effusion of blood" that you have lost ten to our one, & that if you don't make haste out of this country, there would not be one of you left to cross the Ohio. Girty observed, seeing he could not coax a surrender, "since you have got such a reinforcement, leave the women & children in the fort & come out and fight like men." Then Reynolds observed "Yes, & if we were to leave the fort to fight you, you would send in your cowardly rascals to murder our women & children – we'll never trust such a treacherous set." This produced the greatest…good feeling among all, & confidence took the place of fear & alarm. Reynolds proposed to take the men & go out & try & take Girty, but it was objected **(12)** to, as it was thought he had a large party all around him to prevent any such attempt. No recollection about a gun being fired at him.

It was subsequently ascertained from prisoners taken at the Blue Licks [on August 19], that abandoning all idea of taking the fort either by bravery or stratagem, Girty & his Indians left early in the night, leaving a party of 30 or 40 to keep up appearances, who kept up a yelling & distant firing all night – nothing more.

The men in the fort were up & vigilant, reserving their fire, in case of any renewal to storm the place. Soon after sun rise, all being quiet, a party went out to the spring, tied a cord around the neck of the Indian that Stucker had killed, & dragged him around the fort in a sort of triumph. It was now found that the Indians had all left, leaving behind them sad evidence of destruction, particularly the stock. Not much of the corn was destroyed. Miss Nancy Tomlinson (a sister of Nicholas Tomlinson) a young lady of about 18 was particularly useful, & greatly exerted herself **(13)** to keep up the spirits of the garrison & constantly engaged in running bullets. Mrs. Robert Johnson was there, & she was a daughter of Parson Suggett. After the 16 horsemen got safely in to the fort, the Indians fenced up the upper part of the lane.

Blue Lick Campaign

The evening of the same day, the men began to collect at Bryan's. If the attack on the fort was the 15th of August – then the men began to gather there on the evening of the 16th, marched sometime in the forenoon of the 17th & the 18th to within two miles of the Blue Lick. But if the march from the Station to within two miles of the Lick was effected in a single day, then the attack on Bryan's was on the morning of the 16th. The distance was fully forty miles, the way the buffalo trace went, from Bryan's to the Blue Licks – too great a march, one would suppose, for one day, especially as they must have been guarded to avoid a surprise.

Of the council at Bryan's, it may be well presumed that Henry Wilson's statement is correct – that McGary did urge pursuit &c.

Major Harlan came to Bryan's with a cocked hat, & apprehensive **(14)** of the danger of going into an Indian fight with such a Conspicuous Mark, proposed exchanging it; but did not, & very likely lost his life the sooner for it.

Ben. Netherland, afterwards Major, did make an effort to rally a few men at the ford, & in a small way succeeded. Among the Bryan's Station men who went to the Blue Licks, were Aaron Reynolds, John Beasley, Jacob Stucker.

Major Bulger was shot on horseback, the ball entering low down his back & out at his shoulder. Thomas Gist (son of Gen. Nathaniel Gist) accompanied Bulger. When a mile or two over the river, Bulger unable to ride any further, left the few in whose company he was, & turned off & went to a sink-hole. Thomas Gist, then a lad not quite grown (afterwards Major Thomas Gist of Smithland, where he died) not being able to persuade any one to join him, went alone with his horse to aid Bulger. He made a litter using Bulger's horse as his own, & stretching a blanket across a couple of **(15)** poles, fastened on either side of the horses, one ahead of the other. Placed Bulger on the litter, & keeping off the trace to avoid the Indians, reached Bryan's the next evening, having travelled thirty six hours without stopping. Bulger was taken to Capt. John Craig's, & lived two or three weeks before he died. For the kind act, Gist was greatly thought of. He died about 1810. Bulger was a tall man, heavy man, red hair, [wore] a leather hunting shirt at the Blue Licks.

Reynolds fought on foot. On retreat, saw the horse of Ezekiel Field, the dead body of Field with his foot fastened to the stirrup, Reynolds caught the horse & instantly cut the girth, & stripped off the saddle & entanglement, mounted & soon overtook Capt. Robert Patterson, exhausted. Patterson asked to ride behind Reynolds & the latter dismounted & gave up his horse to Patterson [who] escaped. [Patterson] afterwards gave Reynolds one hundred acres of good land. Reynolds swam the river below the ford, his gun & shot pouch he threw away[?] and swimming the river, thereby escaped. Reynolds swam the river before the ford, & finding wet clothing retarding his progress, sat down & disencumbered **(16)** himself of some portion of them. Three Indians stole upon him with their guns pointed, took him before he had notice of their approach. At that instant one of the fugitives appearing in view, two of the Indians ran after him, leaving Reynolds with the third, whose gun Reynolds thought to be empty from the fact of the flint being in the pan. After walking a little distance, the Indian loosened his hold on Reynolds & stopped to tie his moccasin – when, not fearing a shot, Reynolds broke & ran & made his escape. The Indian ran after some little distance, when finding himself far outstripped, & the distance widening every moment, stopped short & hollowed. Avoiding the road, Reynolds reached Bryan's the evening of the next day, with only a shirt on. When first seen, he had an ear of green corn in his hand eating, with which, half starved, he had been careful to provide himself as he came to the cornfield adjoining the fort.

John Beasley, of the Bryan's Station men, after swimming the **(17)** river & losing his rifle in the river, was captured. He was sent to Detroit, thence to Montreal, & finally exchanged & sent to Albany, thence to Kentucky, where, after a year's absence, he arrived. Afterwards settled in Ohio, near Manchester, where as a Colonel or General, he died.

(His brother Charles Bealsey, some time after, went out from Bryan's on a hunt on Licking, was captured, but escaped, stealing a gun & horse. Just at night, made a raft – swimming his horse ahead, he took his gun & swam with it, & finally had to drop it, & with difficulty reached the southern shore. It now being dark, lost view of his horse. He finally got back to Bryan's before his brother reached there, living part of the time on turtle's eggs. Charles also lived near Manchester.)

James Beasley, about 1785, while with a party to Blue Licks to make salt, 850 gallons of water to make a bushel of salt, one day when out by himself hunting he was killed. [It was in fall of 1786 he was killed – Howe's Ohio p. 301; see also John Craig's notes. LCD]

Jacob Stucker in the [Blue Licks] battle was the first to reach Bryan's Station. He arrived near night on the day of the battle, & brought the mournful intelligence of the **(18)** dismal defeat, producing the most gloomy aspect & talked of breaking up the Station & retiring south of Kentucky [River]. That night fugitives kept coming in, & so till next evening. The timely arrival of Logan dissipated these fears, & tended to restore confidence with his 400 men. Mr. Ficklin thinks he arrived on the evening of August 19th or morning of the 20th.

The story of the Indians losing 4 more at the Blue Licks than the whites must be fabulous; such a story <u>was</u> told at that day, with this correction, that the Indians included among their killed those killed at Bryan's Station. Mr. Ficklin does not credit the story, has no recollection of hearing Beasley say that any were killed or tortured to death. It was a matter of policy to keep & sell their prisoners.

Chillicothe means, according to Black Hoof, <u>fire that won't go out.</u> This much resembles a Jewish (& other nations) meaning in sacred fire. LCD

Jacob Stucker was in Logan's Campaign, 1786 – Howe's ___ ___. LCD

(19) Col. Danl. Boone

When Col. Tarleton made his descent on Charlottesville, John Jouett (since Major. Jouett) at Richmond, got wind of the plan to take Gov. [Thomas] Jefferson & the Legislature. He dashed ahead, though a very heavy man, gave notices [of the danger], & the members dispersed. Boon & the others took the Lynchburg road, & were soon overtaken by an officer & some dragoons, and not taking these to be those they were seeking after, conversed with them as they rode along. Finally Boone's companion seeing a road turn off, & thinking it best to leave the present company says,

"Colonel, this is our road!" "Ah, a Colonel," said the British officer – perhaps Tarleton himself – "You are just such prisoner as we want," & thereupon took them both prisoners, but not confining them. Boone soon found an opportunity to escape. *Other versions of this account say that Boone was confined in a coal bin overnight and taken before an officer the next morning, appearing dirty and undistinguished, and talked his way out of the situation. He was released.*

The family of a widow Shanks were killed on Cooper's [sentence illegible] **79(20)** ...found three girls in one house weaving; killed two & took the other prisoner. One of the girls killed [had] previously killed one of the Indians with a butcher knife she had in her hand to cut threads. Mrs. Shanks and a widowed daughter with one small child & two sons, grown, were in an adjoining house. This the Indians fired [burned]. They remained in the house until the fire lighted up the yard around & rendered their escape the less probable. They were compelled to abandon the burning building, the Indians, the while keeping around in the dark & on the watch.

One of the young men took charge of his mother, and the other of his sister & her child, and all dashed out at the same time. The son & mother were killed. The others escaped. Next day, Col. Edwards pursued & took some dogs along & near night as they neared the Indians, then stopping a short time to rest, one of the horses accidentally tread on a dog's foot & his yelping **(21)** alarmed the Indians. They tomahawked their prisoner, & dashed off except two who remained behind. By their yells & running to & fro from tree to tree, induced the whole party to dismount, & exchanged shots, the Indians reserving theirs as long as they could, (evidently, as it afterwards appeared) to gain time for their comrades. One was killed, & the other wounded mortally as was supposed, but made his escape. This Indian party had travelled hard all the preceding night, and the snow began to fall while they were at Mrs. Shanks' house, & they were apprehensive of an easy pursuit. They were overtaken on water of the Raven Creek, in what is now Harrison County. They packed off considerable plunder, making Miss Hanks carry a heavy load. This was on Easter Sunday, about 10th or 11th of April.

Col. Robert Johnson's negroes were fired on one Sunday evening returning from [church] meeting, on Cane Run, less than **(22)** a mile from Col. Thomas's house. Raised 52 men & pursued. At the Ohio, met a flat boat loaded with iron going to Louisville, prevailed on this boat to convey them over, & await their return. Col. Johnson & 26 men pursued on about 15 miles (the others remaining to guard the boat – 25 of them), following the trail, discovered a large camp of about 40 warriors & 100 women & children on ___ Creek. This was discovered after dark.

After the Indians had retired to rest, the whites set about & caught all the Indians' horses, about 50, & got them secured about a quarter of a mile from camp. A guard of five men was placed over them. The others – 22 – approached the camp on opposite sides & awaited the approach of day; one half on one side ___ ___ fired on the camp. When the Indians ran out on the other side, (where Col. Johnson & Stucker were) & treed, when Johnson's party fired on them, & Stucker fired & not knowing at the time that it was a squaw **(23)** he fired at, killed two of her children in her arms, for which he ever after felt regret.

The Indians now fled, leaving at least ten of their number dead on the ground. In a moment, they heard the yell of Indians & barking of dogs up the creek a short distance, which convinced them that there was another camp close by. Then Johnson's party retreated for the horses, got them, & the Indians now began to pursue, & the horses not bridled, only b__ halters & no saddles, & rode ___. The Indians at the place where the horses had been kept killed Moses Grant (probably Moses [was] first killed) & Samuel Grant, inquiring for his brother, was also killed. Another man was also killed. Then Indians pursued them to the river once or twice coming in sight of them. Swam the horses over, the boat had barely left the northern shore when the Indians came up & fired on the boat, but without injury. Fully a hundred **(24)** warriors made their appearance. The horses when part way over, turned & swam out the same side they were driven in, & thus lost to the captors. Mr. Ficklin, having heard this matter fully discussed in the Grant & Johnson families, gives Johnson full credit for his conduct on this Expedition. Both of the Ruddells were with the Indians & afterwards confirmed the story of the two encampments & the large number of the enemy. [See Extract, from Kentucky Gazette for 1789. Also notes of John Gatewood, Mrs. Lemon's letter, Howe's Ohio, p. 99, Hannan? Papers. LCD]

The Buried Canoe

This story, told in <u>Notes on Kentucky</u>, was furnished by Mr. Ficklin: An old Indian, his son grown, & a young adopted white man came to steal horses in Bourbon [County, Ky.]. Had killed a considerable game on Little Miami, the old man left his squaw & children to go with the young men to get horses to pack home their game. The old man was opposed to it from the start, & predicted that evil would come of it, but yielded to the importunities of the young men. Crossed the Ohio, hid their canoe in the willows just below the mouth of Licking. Went about 15 miles

& camped, & there hid a kettle & some provisions until their return to camp another night, near the settlement. The old man heard some peculiar tone of an owl hooting & declared **(25)** that it was a sure foreboding of his misfortune, & insisted on returning. But the young men urged a prosecution of the enterprise. The old man was so disturbed in his mind, that he would not agree to sleep in that camp, & all moved some distance, it being warm weather & no fire necessary. The next night they came into a settlement on Townsend creek, in Bourbon. In approaching a house to steal some horse tied up for safety in the yard, the dogs flew out at them, & in the night they separated & took to a cornfield. And after a long meditated plan, the young white man now resolved on rejoining the whites. The next day he washed the paint off himself & went to the house, & by signs & some few English words he could make himself understood, that he had been captured when a boy either in West Pennsylvania or West Virginia. Doubts arising as to the truth of his story, he was called on to pilot a party in pursuit of the Indians. Although very reluctant, he faithfully did so, led them to the camp where the kettle & provisions were hid, where the old Indian & his son were. There killed the old man, the son escaping. The **(13C80)** young white man shed a profusion of tears for the death of his adopted father, chiding himself bitterly for the act and desired the party to return to the settlement, but the whites insisted on his conducting them to the canoe, which he did, and with so much speed, that they arrived there before the young warrior, and secreted themselves. The young Indian soon appeared and ran down the bank to within a few steps of the canoe, when he was shot down. Here again the young white man gave renewed vent to his sorrow, shedding tears, &c. The party returned, & the young man, dejected, started to go to his friends when he was captured, never was heard of after. He was about twenty years of age – his name not recollected.

End of Jos. Ficklin's Notes, taken in fall of 1846. LCD
Mr. Ficklin died Jan. 8^{th,} 1859.

Memo. – The youth mentioned in the preceding narrative was named John Griste. He was captured on Wheeling Creek in August of 1777. He was living in Belmont, Monroe County, Ohio, as late as 1820. See notes of Mrs. Lydia Cruger & Vachel Dickerson – the latter taken in 1860. LCD

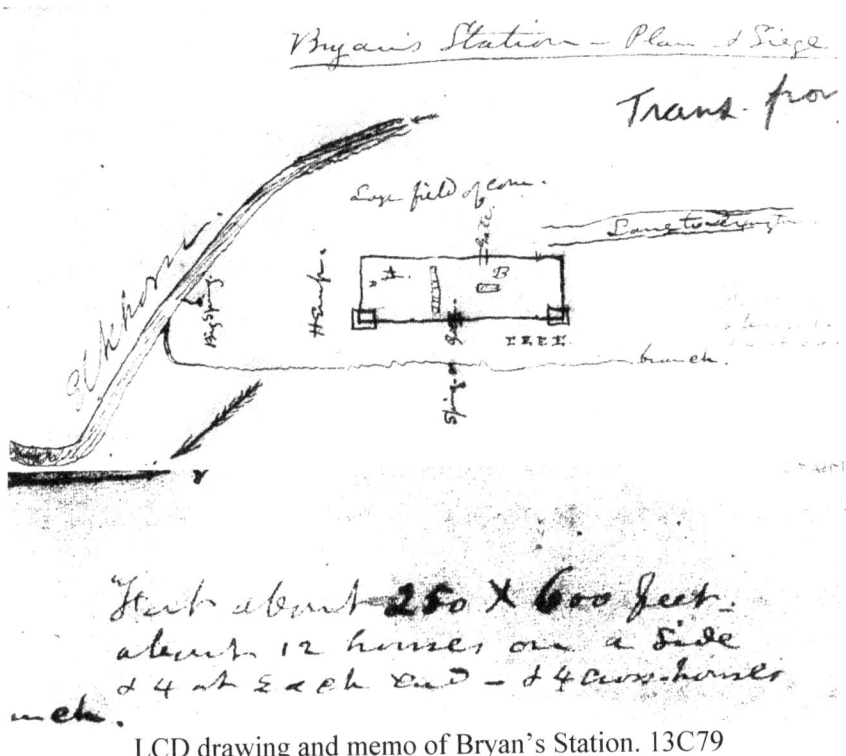

LCD drawing and memo of Bryan's Station. 13C79

13C85-85(1) LCD from Baltimore, Md., to Joseph Ficklin, April 1, 1847.

My Dr. Sir

    I ought long ago to have acknowledged your great kindness in sending to me the box of old papers & their safe arrival, after some little delay. I found much to my purpose among them, & esteem them highly. Of course there was also much of no sort of value.

    In the latter part of February, I commenced a good ____ on <u>The Life & Times of Gen. G. R. Clark</u>, which will probably make a couple of good volumes (& I think will require a cheap abridged edition in one volume). I wrote quite a number of pages in regular order on Clark's life up to 1773 – when, waiting for some additional facts before progressing upon the eventful year in 1774, I dropped for a while the thread of the narrative & went to work on a preliminary chapter on <u>the history of the Shawnanoes –</u> being the only Indians, so far as I know, who ever occupied Kentucky. To aid me in the labor, I have several rare works – Collins' History of the Five Nations. I have your Lulbegrud narrative before me & confess I am not a little puzzled. You record from Black Hoof – who, when he gave it, in 1815, professed to be 109 – which would have given 1706 as **(1)** the year of his birth & according to his narrative it made Lulbegrud the place of his birth – for he **was** but about 10 years old when his people abandoned the settlement & went south, after they occupied the Lulbegrud settlement some 20 or 30 years. Then went south about 1716 – stayed there some 10 or 15 years &c.

  I repeat these dates, as a sort of text for ___ comments, & as the foundation for my troubles. You do not say in the statement that Black Hoof claimed to have been at Braddock's defeat in 1755, but mention his professing to be some 50 years old at the time of that event. It has been said on authority of the venerable Col. John Johnston of Ohio – who went out with Wayne in 1793, & was for a great many years after the Treaty of 1795 Indian agent for the Shawanoes, &c - well knew Black Hoof – that, this old chief <u>was</u> at Braddock's defeat. I doubt it, & will soon explain.

  In an article furnished the American Antiquarian Society by Col. J. Johnston in 1819, & published in the 1st vol. of their Transactions, now before me, he speaks of Black Hoof then being eight-five years old - & born in Florida. Here you see two very material differences. This would make the date of Black Hoof's birth in 1734 – which I believe to be correct.

Memo – I find no reply to the preceding. LCD

13C96-96(1-3) Joseph Ficklin letter, Lexington, Ky., 21 Sept. 1854

Dear Sir

  In hope of a ___ place I left home for a White Sulphur watering place and found your letter of the 15 ult unanswered. My health remained good & today welcome a change & a bright prospect of rain & I reply to your 5 enquiries as follows.

(1) 1st I was born in Spotsylvania County, Virginia 21 Sept. 1775. My father's name was Thomas. He removed with his wife & 6 children to Kentucky in 1781 and settled in Bryan's Station early in 1782.

2. I have never seen a good likeness of Col. John B. Campbell. The only one I had I sent a few years ago to Mrs. ___.

3. Gov. Charles Scott has a grandson near here & he may be able to inform me, but if any likeness exists it must be at Frankfort.

4. There is a daughter of Col. ___ near this place. She was born at Boonsboro in 1779 & may recollect the places near her father's station. Her recollection is said to be very good.

                Joseph Ficklin

(1) I write on my birthday & will write again…

13C100 Joseph Ficklin comments on Robert Todd

Major Robert Todd, a Gentleman of great enterprize, married a miss Lytle near Lexington [Kentucky] & settled on the Georgetown & Frankfort road 10 miles from the latter place. He was engaged in surveying & often called into the woods. Returning home sometime in 1792 [was] killed by the Indians about ½ a mile west of Frankfort, leaving a young wife & two small sons, one of whom resides near Lexington

The connection of this Gentleman with the Lytle family may be said to have laid the foundation of the fortune of Gen. William Lytle, the brother of Mrs. Todd, by engaging in the surveying & Land business under the instruction of Major Todd. General Lytle died in Cincinnati; leaving a respectable family behind him.

13C101 T.[?] Russell letter, Lexington, Ky., Nov. 25, 1859

I regret to inform you that Joseph Ficklin, Esq. died on 8th of Jany. last. I have opened your letter to him, having been entrusted with his business, but know nothing of the history of the Gentlemen of whom you make inquiry.

Yours Respectfully
T[?] Russell

13C103 Joseph Ficklin's notes on the geography & streams of the Green River in 1823. Found in the fall of 1846 in the papers of John Bradford at Lexington, Ky. in papers of his son, Dan'l Bradford. LCD

13C110-110(2) Mrs. Elizabeth Arnold as told to Benjamin C. Bradley, Clerk of Baptist Church, Versailles, Ky., 25th day of June 1845.

Mrs. Elizabeth Arnold was born in Fauquier County, Virginia on the 12th day of March 1759. She was the daughter of Peter & Sarah Heitt. She was married to John Arnold on August 29, 1775 in the same county. He was the son of Nicholas and Margaret Arnold. He was born Jany 10th, 1754 and died May 4th, 1818.

Mr. and Mrs. Arnold emigrated to Kentucky in August 1781 in company with about 180 persons including men, women, children, and Negroes. They first stopped at Bryants Station. The number of men in the Station was about 40, with a number of women, children &c.

The siege took place in August 1781 [1782]. Capt. Jno. Craig was the commander; Lyman Stucker and his Brother Jacob were Soldiers, and not many other names recollected.

The Indians [were] first discovered on Friday morning by an old Negro man. The Indians fired Two shots at him but he escaped unhurt and got in to the fort.

About a dozen Young men took their guns and started towards Lexington and were fired at by Indians in the cornfield but none were hurt. They fired at the Indians and returned to the fort. The Indians then attempted to fence the lane to keep others from passing to & fro, but before they succeeded, horse-men from Lexington charged on them. They were fired at by the Indians, but the horsemen raised such **(1)** a dust among them that they could shoot with no certainty and none were hurt. All got in to the fort safe, and flustrated [sic] the arrangement of the Indians.

[Battle of Blue Licks]

The Indians were discovered Friday morning and left Saturday about 9 o'clock a.m. They crossed the Licking River at the Blue Licks and divided on each side of a Point coming down to the River. About 30 men followed across, the Indian men about surrounding them. Col. John Todd commanded his men to retreat. Others by that time had come up and they had some fireing across the river and many of our men were killed, but the names not recollected. The dead were buried about a week after they were killed.

[Siege of Bryan's Staiton]

[Aaron] Reynolds asked who was commander; Symon Girty replied he was, and there were many in the fort who knew him. Reynolds told him to shew himself, that he had enough Powder and Lead to whip such a son of a Bitch as he was (or) if he would show himself he would come and Snitch him, but Girty's men surrounded him so he could not be seen.

The Indians stayed around all night in a trench. Some of them were killed. This took place in the first day in the morning.

The commander of the Troops from Lexington not recollected, only 14 of them, and all got in the fort in Safety.

(2) The reinforcement of footmen not recollected, who was commander – how many – or where from.

The whites made the attact in the cornfield when the fight ensued and one of our men was killed.

The Indians were on the right of the fort and the Spring on the left. Several women packed water in to the fort to put out fire in case it was needed. Mrs. Arnold, Mrs. Ficklin, & her daughter were 3 [of the women] and the others are not recollected.

Lyman Stucker and another man were in basteens at the corner of the fort. They saw an Indian in the top of a tree. Both shot at the same time, was only herd as one gun. The Indian was killed but it was unknown which killed him. The shot was a very long one. Nick Tomlin was shot at one of the port holes and wounded in the arm. John Mitchell (a cooper) was standing in the door of his Shop peeping over and was shot dead – the Bullit entering the brain. There was one other young man from Fredericksburg, Virginia killed, his name not recollected.

Capt. John Craig told the women to take the Hoes and Axes and go in the house and if the Indians attempted to scale the walls to fight till they died, as he intended to fight as long as one man would stand by him.

The above facts were communicated by Mrs. Elizabeth Arnold of Woodford County, Ky. in March 1845 and carefully written out by the undersigned in compliance with a request of Lyman C. Draper of Baltimore, Md.. Given under my hand, Benj. C. Bradley, Clerk of Baptist Church, Versailles, Ky. this 25th day of June 1845.

13C114-114(1) "Blue Licks Campaign – British Account"
From <u>Albach's Annals of the West,</u> Edition 1857, 395-6

In regard to this expedition, the following statement is made by an individual who was in the party of the enemy, and who afterward emigrated from Canada and settled in the Miami Valley:

In the summer of 1782, the British commandant at Detroit ordered Major Caldwell to take Simon Girty, a few traders, a company of Provincial Militia, together with whatever Indians could be collected at Detroit, and with these forces, to attack and destroy the settlements the rebels were making south of the Ohio.

Caldwell collected his men, was joined by a party of Indians at Detroit, and by other parties on the Maumee, on the Great Miami, and from other points along the line of march. When he reached the Ohio, his forces, thus increased, amounted to about four hundred men. It was Caldwell's intention to attack the station at Beargrass (Louisville) first. Receiving information that [George Rogers] Clark was there, and that the place was supplied with cannon, he changed his plan, and led his forces up the Kentucky River, and thence to Bryan's Station. Before they arrived there, they were discovered, and the inhabitants were so well fortified, that a siege of two days and a half made no impression upon them, and gave no hope that they could be compelled to surrender.

Under these circumstances, Caldwell withdrew his forces from the Station, and fell back as far as the Blue Licks, where game was supposed to be sufficiently abundant **(1)** to support them until he could find some other and weaker point of attack.

At first the Indians were unwilling to alarm the buffaloes by encamping too near the Licks; but Caldwell, a vigilant and efficient commander, suspecting the Kentuckians were in pursuit, over-ruled their objection, and selected a position near the Licks most favorable for defence. They had not been twenty-four hours in their new location, before the Long Knives came. They were supposed to number about two hundred men, many of whom fought on horseback, and appeared to have several commanders. All of them who were fairly brought into action fought desperately; but it seemed that they were more blind than brave, for in a battle of one hour only, their loss was sixty-five killed, and many wounded. Of these, several were carried off by their companions, and the remainder were massacred by the Indians. Many more of the Kentuckians must have fallen, had the Indians continued to fight instead of scrambling after spoils, and even fighting among themselves for choice rifles, which were found near the dead, and in some instances, wounded men. Immediately after the battle, as provisions were very scarce, and the savages unwilling to remain embodied, and even hard to control under any circumstances, Major Caldwell retired with his troops to Canada, and the Indians, after crossing the Ohio, separated, and returned to their homes.

13C115-115(2) Elizabeth (Betsy) Payne letter, Scott County, Ky., January 14, 1846 *Elizabeth "Betsy" Johnson was living at Bryan's Station when it was attacked in 1782. She married Gen. John Payne.*

Mr. Draper.

Your favour of Dececember propounding 12 questions to me in relation to occurences during the Siege at Bryans Station in and about the year 1782 came to hand. I was but about 10 years of age at this time and can only answer to best of my recollection. I cannot give dates as I was too young to have known. I shall now proceed to answer your querys in the order they occur.

1st My Father Robt. Johnson, was Captain of the men in Bryan Station but was absent at the time [of the attack] and the command devolved on Lieut. Bennet Rogers.
2nd The footmen and horsemen agreed on leaving Lexington to take different directions in reaching the station and in the event of either being attact, the other was to come to their relief. The horsemen in reaching the

mouth of the lane that leads down to the fort was attact by a party of Indians and fired upon. They however rushed by and reached the fort without the loss of a man. The footmen from Lexington hearing this firing hastened to the spot to release the horsemen. At this moment the Indians made a attact on them.

(1) Simon Girty called to know who commanded them – Capt. Craig answered - Capt. Craig – and asked Girty who commanded them. He answered Simon Girty. [He told] Capt. Craig to put all his women and children in a house and come out and fight like men. Capt. Craig answered they would not, he recollected the fate of Martins and Riddles Stations. Girty answered and said cannons would be here in the morning and he would then make them give up. Capt. Craig answered and told him they would not give up and to come on, every man determined to fight until he died. Girty then commenced humming a song that they had plenty of potatoes, corn, pork, beef &c.

Col. R. Johnson was born 17th day ___, 1761 and died 15th Oct. 1815 – as taken from his tomb stone at Great Crossings, Scott County Kentucky.

(2) There was 43 fighting men and five too old to do service, about 32 women and 64 children contributed to the population of Bryans station.

I have no recollection of a man by the name of Martin Whetzle coming to the station having escaped from the Indians, but I recollect a man that was found and brought in who had escaped from the Indians by the name of Mr. ____ Beasley.

I have thus given you a correct statement [as] it is possible for me to do and I hope you will be able to collect a sufficiency of matter to do ample justice to the Early Pioneers who had many Hardships to undergo – and that your Book may be both respected and [your] undertaking adequately Rewarded.

Yours
Elizabeth Payne
By George Offutt.

I should say Mr. Suggett was at least 70. I recollect only 2 men too old to fight. I will suggest Tomlinson.

13C117-117(6) Betsy Payne letter, July 25, 1846

Dear Sir

I received yours a short time since in which you seem to be

well pleased with my former communication to you but as you did not keep your letter to me in which I replyed, you were not able to understand some of my answers as they [were] by numbers. I have no copy of your former letter nor my reply to same. I have carefully read your letter to me several times and will endeavor to give you the information you request without stating your Questions.

My father, Col. Robert Johnson, was born July __, 1745 in Culpepper County, Virginia on the Rapidan River and marryed to Jemima Suggett in Orange County, Va. in June 1771 and [he] died 15th October 1815 in Kentucky & his remains now lie intered on the Family burying place at the Great Crossing, the place he lived at for upwards of 30 years.

I was born (his first child) April 16th, 1772 in Culpepper County, Virginia. His family about the time or after my birth moved to Orange County, Virginia, and lived in that County till my Father had 4 Children: myself, James, William & Sally, afterwards Sally Ward. In the year 1779 in the fall [left] for Kentucky with all His family. when we arrived at Red Stone on the Monongahela River. **(1)** Richard M. Johnson, his 5th child, was born in September 1780. In fall my father and all his family moved to Bryant's Station now Fayette County, Kentucky. While we were living at the place, say in August 1782, in morning about sun rise, my Father's negro man by the name of Lancaster went out of the fort. He got wood on the lane towards Lexington on the west side of the fort. He was fired on by the Indians. We heard the report of 6 Guns but he ran in safety to the fort. This was the first and only alarm we had of any Indians near us.

An Express was then sent to Lexington who went out of the fort in a back way through a cornfield. The men of the fort drew powder, and had of my mother who had kept it (in the absence of my Father who had gone to Virginia to the Legislature). They barred up the gates of the Fort, put up stockading that was down &c &c.

My Father was Captain of the Company that Commanded the fort but in his absence, Barnett Rogers was Lieutenant Commander.

About 10 o'clock Barnett Rogers proposed that 6 men would go out **(2)** and retreated back to the Fort [in] a heavy fire from the Indians. They all got in safe and the door was closed. While this was going on the Indians made a desperate charge on the East side of the Fort where their main body laid. they formed & rushed up towards the fort with their tomahawks in their hands, all painted, some red, some black & others red & black. Our men were at their posts and as they came up, gave them a very distinctive fire out of the Port holes killing a great many and wounding others. They gave him the fire so warm that they were forced to return but not until a great many had been killed. The firing lasted for about one hour. When all was silent except now & then, when an Indian showed himself, he was pretty sure to be shot.

About this time, say about 11 o'clock, our Express from Lexington returned. About 1 o'clock p.m. the horsemen from Lexington came to the mouth of the cane toward Lexington on the west side of the Fort. They saw about 60 Indians who were all in the act of eating their dinner. The horseman pushed on to the fort running a heavy fire from the Indians. They halted with their horses, got in to the Fort safe. The Indians had built a fence across the land to prevent the horsemen from getting to the Fort, but they had made so poor a fence (not being in the habit of making fences), had stacked the rails so that the horsemen easily pushed it when they came to it. It was not much in their way. There was about as many footmen as horsemen who were to enter the Fort through the corn field. The footmen & horsemen had made an agreement that if either was attacked, **(3)** the other was to go to their relief.

All pretty quiet again till in the evening. A while before sun set two Indians had ___ up a very large tall Syckamore down on Elkhorn Creek & was shooting. The women were all told to go into their houses. Before I went I looked & saw the two Indians up in the long tall Syckamore near its top. Jacob Stucker fired at them & one of them fell to the ground, supposed to be shot dead but he was so high if the bullet did not kill him the fall would, & the other got down very Quickly keeping the tree between him & the fort.

After sun down in the evening, Simon Girty hollowed to the fort & asked who commanded the fort. Capt. John Craig answered and said he, Capt. Craig, commanded & asked in return who commanded the Indians. The answer was Simon Girty. He then told Craig to put all his women & children in a house and come out and fight like men or to surrender. Craig told him he would not for he had not forgotten Martins Station & Ruddle's Station - that all in the fort intended to fight till they were killed. Girty answered & said our Cannon will be here in the morning & we will make you. Craig told him the Cannon would make no difference; they would never surrender. Girty then said they never lived better in their Lives. They had plenty of good fat Beef, Mutton hogs, Corn & watermellons &c. The Indians killed a good many cows, cattle, sheep, hogs &c & destroyed some of the corn being **(4)** too lazy to cut up much cane. In the night about 2 or 3 hours before day, the Indians commenced a yell which went all around the Fort which we afterward ___ as a signal for a retreat as they soon all pretty well gone by day light in the morning.

My Father commanded a Company and went out on a Campaign when he lived at Floid's[?] Station, and commanded a company and was out on a campaign when he lived at Bryant's Station, I think against the Shawnee Indians. He moved to the Great Crossing, now Scott County, Kentucky in the fall, 1783, and had a station at that place well stockaded in with two good gates.

The Indians were very troublesome till after Scott's Campaign in May 1791 in which my husband John Payne commanded a Company. My Brother James Johnson was in said Campaign being about 17 years old. In Scott's Campaign the troops crossed the Ohio River in which I think now is Indiana. Some Indian towns over there had been troublesome to our settlements. They got in a very large Prairie when they could see so far as the Eye would let them without any obstructions in way of timber or hill whatsoever. They discovered something at a great distance in said Prairie, very small, something like a small spot. At length they discovered the object they saw moved and seemed to move towards them as it came. It was at length discovered to be a man on horseback, no doubt an Indian, as he still advanced towards the Army. General Scott ___ out a number of his men with ___ to pursue said Indian ___ should attempt to make a retreat. At length saw the army, and went on his horse as fast as he could go, pursued by the Army and the select horsemen General Scott had detached to pursue him. They gained very much on the Indian but he, the Indian, arrived a little **(5)** a head of the Army to their towns on the River. When our army & men arrived at the town there was a good many canoes[?], all full, many women and children trying to make their escape across the river but in attempting to cross most was drowned and killed by our men. They took a good many prisoners of women & children who were left in the town & could not have time to Cross. Their prisoners brought through Kentucky by the Great Crossings & I saw them. [They were] conveyed to Maysville, Kentucky, then [called] Limestone, where they were kept till an exchange of prisoners at a treaty made. After this never was much troubled with the Indians – perhaps occasionally a few horses stolen.

Jacob Stucker, the man who killed the Indian out of the tree at Bryant's Station, died June 10th, 1820 in his 56 year of his age, would have been 56 years old the 11th August, 1820. He was of dutch descent and was born in Germany, was at the Battle of the Blue Licks and in 1813 Commanded a Company in Col. R. M. Johnson's Mounted Regiment & faught bravely on 5th October 1813 at the Battle of the Thames. He married the niece of my Father, my cousin Elizabeth Rogers. His youngest child Polly Stucker lives with me in my house.

John Craig is still alive and lives near Burlington, Kentucky. Cave Johnson, my Uncle, married John Craig, Sr.'s [?] daughter. [He] is now alive about 84 or 85 years old, a very nimble, intelligent man & has not as yet lost his memory, which I think is good. First write a letter to him. You may get a great deal of usefull information. I have no doubt he **(6)** would answer your inquerys with great ____ which may be relyed upon.

Respectfully yours
Betsy Payne

Mrs. Elizabeth Payne Aug 25, 1846
Envelope addressed to LCD at Baltimore Maryland.
Return address: Great Xings [Great Crossings] Aug 18. LCD notes on envelope:
Mrs. Elizabeth Payne – Aug 25 – 1846.
Col. Robt Johnson
Siege of Bryan's Station
Jacob Stucker
R M. & Jos. Johnson
Scott's Expedition.

13C119 Elias Kincheloe letter, Chaplain, Ky., June 16, 1847

My Dear Sir,

    Mr. C. Slaughter shewed me a letter dated 24th May Directed to Judge James Slaughter who is no more. he departed life some five or six months past.

    Descendants of Capt. William Kincheloe whose station was taken and burned by the Indians in 1782 - I am one of his sons & there is only one other liveing. My Father removed from Virginia in 1781 perhaps five or six miles above Middleburg in Louden [County] but my father was a citizen of Fauquier County. Colonel Cox was killed about twelve miles below where I now live in Nelson County – perhaps in the year of 1786. As to that I do not recollect the exact time, though I well recollect the day. I was a small boy and out on business at the time the Colonel was killed & brot the news in to our neighbourhood. The Land that I now live on my Father settled on in 1785. I know of no further information that you desire of me.

Respectfully Yours
Elias Kincheloe

13C120 *Obituary (printed) for William Polk who died in 1843 in Ft. Wayne, Indiana.*

William Polk, a native of Virginia, whence with his father's family, he emigrated to Kentucky in 1782. Soon afterwards he was captured by a party of Indians, and carried to Detroit, where he remained in captivity for a period of about twelve months. At the age of nineteen, he enlisted in Gen. Wayne's division. In 1808 he removed from Kentucky, and settled in Knox County, Indiana Territory, and in 1811 he was slightly wounded at the battle of Tippecanoe. He was a member of the Convention which formed the Constitution of Indiana, and at different periods, he discharged the duties of various offices of trust and honor, under the State government. At the time of his death, he held the office of register of the U.S. Land Office at Fort Wayne, and he was justly beloved and esteemed by a large circle of relatives and acquaintances. A_____ Almanac, 1844, p. 338.

Mr. Polk, then a child, with his mother & other children, were taken at Kincheloe's Station in 1782 – alluded in the following letters of Elias Kincheloe. LCD.

13C121-121(1) Elias Kincheloe letter, Chaplain, Ky., August 11, 1847

I think he served a Second tour in the Carolinas. Perhaps my father was born in Prince William or Fairfax but volunteered from Fauquier County and removed to Kentucky in the spring, 1781, departed life in Feb. 1797. he was killed by a limb falling off of a tree. He had left the station before it was taken and settled in the woods alone because the Setlers in the fort would not fortify in a more substantial manner against the enemy. Father departed life about [age] fifty eight years. At this time I do not remember more.
Colonel Cox settled his station in about five miles of my Fathers Station and was killed in a few miles of his home when Surveying. He was a man of good Character here.
(1) Mr. David Cox, Brother to Col. Isaac Cox, died near Bardstown in Nelson County, Kentucky perhaps twenty five years ago. He has one daughter yet living near Bardstown, a widow, Mary Cox, the widow of Gen. James Cox. I am not sure where Capt. Linn died. When I new him I was a boy. Capt. Linn lived two or three miles below Bardstown.
John Sovereign lived within one mile of where I now live & Emigrated to Indiana about forty eight years past; I do not recolect Colonel Brown but it was on St. Clair's defeated ground,
You want my age. Born 1776, Nov. 29, & my Brother lives in

Muhlenburg County [Ky.].

13C122-122(1) Elias Kincheloe letter, Chaplain, Ky., November 10, 1847. *The letter is mostly illegible.*

My Father was living on the same ___ that I am now on when he was killd; my brother that is living is eight younger than myself, his name is William. I was born 29th November 1776 about fifteen miles n.e. of Bards Town and one mile from Chaplain. Severns [Sovereign?] [was] about five feet 10 or 11 inches in hite, very singular in appearance & Severns took the name from S____s. Settling there alone and as soon as others began to locate around him, he left and settled within four or five miles of Bardstown, staid but a short time before he left, no person knowing when he left or where he went. Gen. Lewis Kincheloe found him in **(1)** a fallen down hollow tree with his wife & two little children perhaps in 1787 & shortly after brot him into our neighbourhood and there he remained till about 1799, left for Indianna. I think he settled in the neighbor hood of vinsens [Vincennes] but I have no knowledge of his death nor do I know whether his Daughter or son is living. His son was named John after him Self and I do not know who the Daughter Married. Severns had quite a wild appear[ance] and as much so in his deportment.

13C123–123(1) LCD to Elias Kincheloe, from Philadelphia, Nov. 1, 1848. *Oct 25th is marked out. This must be a rough draft of questions Draper intended sending to Elias Kincheloe. Many lines are crossed out and questions re-worded. Topics include Cox's Station and names of persons killed and captured when Kincheloe's Station was attacked. Draper asked about George Walls and Maj. Andrew Hynes, who served under Gen. Clark. He asked about writing to a a son-in-law of George Walls named Samuel Patton who lived near Elizabethtown. Other questions involved Capt. Harmon Consola, Richard McCary, and Angus Cameron, who were officers under George Rogers Clark.*

My Dear Sir,
You will, I am sure, excuse me for imposing so much labor upon you – but recollect I am toiling to place before the present & future generations a full & faithful account of the early settlement of the west, that they may see something of the sufferings undergone, & blood expended, in reclaiming the wilds of Kentucky from the grasp of the Red Man, & thereby inspire them with patriotic ardor to perpetuate the freedom thus purchased at a cost incalculably great.

With renewed wishes for your health,
I remain very Truly Yours,
Lyman Draper

13C124 -124(3) Elias Kincheloe letter, Chaplain, Ky., December 14, 1848

My dear Sir

I received yours dated Nov 1st and I must correct my mistake as to the Settling of Kincheloes Station. My father did not remove his Family until Eighty one [1781] but in the fall of 1779 he came out and Brot Two of his Sons & two Blacks, a woman & a Boy, and in 1780 raised a small crop and in the fall went on to Virginia after his family. From cause was detained until the spring following and in his absence Stephen Kincheloe, the son of my Father, was with Gen. Clark on his Campaign in Illinois.

You wish to know the killed at the taking of Kincheloes Station: Cornelius Davis & his second child, a daughter; Mrs. Randolph and her small child & Mrs. Ash was all that was killed, I beleave.

Cornelius Davis's oldest child, a son about six years old, was taken & a black woman and three of her Children was taken and a Mrs. Polk, the wife of Capt. Charles Polk. Her maiden name was Field. She was taken on to Detroit and after elapse of time, Capt. Polk went out and Mrs. Polk and Isaac Davis, the son of Cornelius, was exchanged.

(1) My Father had removed about eight miles from the Station previous to the taking of the Station and raised a small crop of corn. He moved to Bardstown & in ___ removed to where I now live, all in the same County of Nelson.

My Father's Family was not disturbed at the time the Station was taken but they [the Indians] had been at his field a short time before & killed a cow & gathered Corn out of his field, roasted the corn & barbecued the Cow and when the feast was over they then stole three of my Father's Horses & started, but there was men gathered and pursued them, killed one Indian and retook the Horses. The number of Indians was five

I would not wish to be understood that I was Born in Kentucky. I was born in Virginia Nov. 1776, the 29th.

I have not a distinct memory of Maj Walls. I have known some thing of his Character. Maj. Andrew Hynes was Colonel at his death. He died near Bardstown, Nelson County, and I am now married to a Daughter in law of Colonel Hyneses. There is a son of the Colonel's, Doctor Alfred Hynes, now living in Bards Town. The Colonel's descendants are all dead but two.

(2) You wish to know which of Clarks Campaigns my Brothers Servd on. Stephen Kincheloe served on the first. Stephen & Lewis served on the Second.

You now speak of the ___ of Thompson Randolph. William Harrison Randolph killed two Indians in his cabbin and made his escape through his loft and the roof of his cabbin & so cleared himself with his little son, six years old, & got to my Father's.

Mrs. Davis, the wife of Cornelius Davis that was killed, & Mr. Harrison made their escape through where a black man pulled up a stockade and made their way to Coxes station.

Mrs. Bland[?] roved through the woods for five days, was at length met by a Boy the name of Ash come a-hunting and carried her to Coxes Station, a mere Skeliton with her Clotheing all in rags. Her maiden name I do not know. Mrs. Davis did not change her name in her first marage. Mrs. Harrison's maiden name was Davis but a distant relation of the others. Mr. Randolph was ___ before Randolph made his escape. He fought valiantly but did not leave until after the death of his wife.

(3) The Indians that tooke Kincheloes Station was not of the party that fought at the Blue licks but was a part of the party that Sieged Harrods Station.

[The] Commander of Kincheloes Station I supposed was Capt. Charles Polk who was not there when the Station was taken & burned, but was in pursuit of the party that had invaded Harrods Station.

Sir, I now recollect Capt. Wm. May well. He died near Bards Town 16 or 18 years ago.

Mrs. Davis lived with in one mile of me for more than fifty years and is buried on my Farm within fifty yards of my House.

Respectpully yours
Elias Kincheloe

13C125 *Newspaper article on attack at Kincheloe's Station in September 1782 just after the Battle of Blue Licks. Mrs. Bland escaped through the woods after 18 days and was taken to Linn's Station. Mrs. Polk and 4 children were among captives who were advertised in the newspaper. They had been bought by the British. Mrs. Chapline's husband brought them home from Detroit.*

13C126 LCD Notes: Kincheloe's Station taken – 1782.

Col. Ben. Logan, Aug 31, 1782 writes: "Since writing the foregoing, I have received certain information that Kincheloe's Station, in Jefferson [County, Ky.] was burned and 37 souls made prisoners." Trip

1860, vol. 3d [3rd] p. 15. LCD

13C129 "Pioneer Incidents of Kentucky"
LCD: Clipped from <u>Columbian & Great West.,</u> Feb.13, 1851. *The topic is Philemon Waters' Indian captivity.*

Early in the winter of 1781 and '82, the northwest Indians becoming suspicious that the British armies had been overthrown by the American army, sent a party into the "dark and bloody ground" to take a prisoner from whom they could obtain information on the matter as the British agents in Canada concealed from them the news of Cornwallis' surrender to Washington.

Col. Philemon Waters had settled on a spot near the present town of Springfield, and had erected a cabin near the fort at Cartright's creek, about where the road from Springfield to Lebanon crosses that stream.

On an occasion of being out chopping logs, a short distance from the fort, and after finishing his day's work, he had started on his return to his cabin, but before reaching it discovered that he had left his knife, and returned for it. Finding it, he again started back home. He had made but few steps when a party of four Indians, who had been guided to the spot by his chopping, sprung from behind trees on each side of his path, and presented their rifles, motioning him to surrender. Waters instantly fled and outran their fleetest man – a half blood, who had been sent for the special purpose of capturing a prisoner. But being seized with violent pains in his side, Waters dropped and was captured. He was bound and taken to the Blue Licks, where the main body of Indians were under the command of Tecumseh-ka, then only fifteen years old and afterwards the renowned Tecumseh in the northwest war.

Waters was questioned with great scrutiny as to the affairs of the British army, and threatened with death by burning if he told a "lie." He informed them that Cornwallis had surrendered to Gen. Washington, which they were reluctant to believe. He was interrogated for a whole week concerning it, accompanying the renewal of their questions with threats of burning.

Still dubious about the matter, they took him to their towns, and called on one of the British agents to know if Waters' report was true. He answered that it was.

Before leaving Kentucky, they captured three other white men, all to be burnt to atone for the death of a relative of one of the Indians in their party. After, however, getting from Waters information of the defeat of the British army, the one who was to be appeased painted himself: one half of his face and body black, and the other half red. This was his aspect when he entered the towns, and which indicated that he submitted the fate of the prisoners to the war chiefs in council. Their decision was to run the gauntlet.

At the appointed time, and as the chiefs were assembled for the performance, Waters marched out, singing a song that had been taught him. As he reached the starting point, a furious warrior dealt him a blow with his tomahawk on the forehead that drew the blood most copiously. Waters sang on till he had finished his song, and in consideration of the blow, was reprieved. The ceremony was finished with a dance around Waters, tied to a stake, after which the Indian who had struck him apologized, telling him he meant it for a "how-d'ye do!"

Waters soon ingratiated himself into the confidence of the chiefs, and was allowed gradually increased freedom, until he got enough to make his escape. Young Tecumseh was extremely kind to him, associated with him a great deal to learn the English language, and evinced an extraordinary ambition to learn the arts of the white man. And in return for the information Waters would impart to him, Tecumseh divided with him his jerked venison and salt. Waters regarded Tecumseh as a noble Indian of great talent and as one above the cruel arts of the savage.

13C130 Frank Waters letter, February, 1862. *There is mention at the end of this barely-legible letter of "papers left in his effects relative to Clark." This letter perhaps introduced the following essay on The Early Pioneers of Kentucky beginning on 13C131(1). The essay is in different handwriting than that of Frank Waters.*

Dr Sir   In answer to your letter to my Father, Maj. Thomas H. Waters, he desired me to say he recollects of my Grandfather's early life. Col. Philemon Waters was born in Winchester, Va., his father having built the first cabin in that place. He afterwards removed to Kentucky and died in ___ county in July 1829. He was born in March 1750…

Yrs &c
Frank Waters

13C131(1)–131(9), 132   The Early Pioneers of Kentucky

Col. Philemon Waters

The early history of Kentucky is full of examples of daring and adventure and tradition brings down to us the exploits of the early pioneers who in "the dark and bloody ground" found a field for their love of wild adventures and the display of the times, hardihood and courage. Among the earliest of the hard adventurers who sought Kentucky was the subject of this sketch. He was a Virginian by birth, a man of iron nerve, indomitable character and great personal strength which he seems to have inherited. His Father had in the town of Winchester, Va., shouldered, carried forty yards, and thrown down before the tavern door a large rock which no one for many years after had been able to lift higher than the knee.

During the year 1780, Col. Philemon Waters was one of the garrison of Gen. Clark in the log fort where the city of Louisville now stands. "Indian signs" having been reported by the hunters, Gen. Clark started three of the most experienced of the garrison, Waters, Morehead and Brown, as a scouting party to ascertain the truth of these reports.

The scouts had proceeded some distance from the fort without finding any "signs" and at length, to avoid the labor of struggling through the cane, descended to the bed of a creek which wound along in the direction they were pursuing. They had however been discovered by a party of Indians, about forty in number. On account of the numerous bends of the stream, the Indians were enabled to approach to within a short distance of them unperceived, just as the scouts, as yet unaware of the presence of Indians, had turned a sharp angle of the creek. Waters proposed to mount a steep bank leading up from the Stream. The party had proceeded about half way up the ascent, **(2)** Waters leading, when Brown who was in the rear looking back discovered the Indians within fifteen steps. He called to his companions that "The Indians were upon them" which was answered by a volley from the Indians. At the first alarm, Waters had thrown himself upon all fours and commenced scrambling to the top of the bank. One of the enemy's balls struck his knapsack and knocked it around upon his breast. Quietly disengaging it, he sprang to the ridge and thinking, as he said afterwards, that he could run as well with an empty gun as a loaded one, he wheeled to get a shot. Although some of the Indians were within ten steps, the first object which came in range as he wheeled was Brown, wounded and down upon one elbow with his other arm raised to ward off the blow of a tomahawk which a warrior standing over him had drawn to split his skull. Quick as thought Waters fired and sprang into the cane with which the top of the bank was covered, but before he had proceeded two steps, he became entangled in a grape [vine] and finding all efforts to advance fruitless. He stood perfectly still. He could hear Morehead breaking through the cane and the whole body of the Indians with a dog running upon the trail in pursuit.

The chase was soon out of hearing and Waters, backing out the way he had entered, cautiously struck back upon the former trail. As he descended the hill, he turned his head and saw the dead body of Brown with that of a warrior lying beside it. Following the track back for some distance, he then made a wide circuit to avoid the Indians on his return to the fort. At last, however, he heard the dog belonging to the Indians running in his direction. Supposing Morehead either killed or taken and the Savages now upon his trail, he **(3)** doubled his speed until coming to a large pond. He swam across in order to lose the dog or kill him. While in the water with this intention and with the hope that he might get another shot at the Indians as they came up to the opposite bank, he sprang behind a tree. But the dog, after swimming to within a short distance, turned off in another direction. It was still upon Morehead's trail and the latter, with the same intention of killing the dog in the water, had made for the pond, but catching a glimpse of Waters as he sprang behind the tree, mistook him for an Indian and turned off on another course.

Waters proceeded safely to the Fort and late in the evening entered at one gate reporting "Brown dead and Morehead dead or taken," while Morehead, who had succeeded in eluding pursuit, entered at another gate and reported "Brown dead and Waters dead or taken."

Waters, in his report to Gen. Clark, stated that he had shot the Indian who was about to tomahawk Brown with an ounce ball, in the hollow of the armpit. Clark replying somewhat incredulously that "a man could hardly tell the result of a shot made with forty Indians in ten paces of him." Waters, fixing his eye upon a small blaze in a tree about a hundred yards distant, threw his rifle to his face and struck the center of the mark – thus turning haughtily to Gen. Clark, he exclaimed, "as sure as I hit that mark my bullet burst that Indian's heart."

The next day Waters piloted a party to the spot and there found the body of Brown tomahawked and scalped and by it the Indian that Waters had killed, shot in armpit as he had stated. Both bodies laid side by side and wrapped in Morehead's blanket which was the best of three the Indians had taken. This consideration to a "pale face," placing him side by side in burial with an **(4)** Indian warrior was the only such instance ever known in Kentucky. This was considered as a token of respect to the bravery of his comrade. Waters, who in the presence of such odds, stopped and emptied his gun to save his companion. For the scalp of the Indian thus killed, Waters received from the Government 40 lbs. with which he pre-empted the farm in Washington County upon which he afterwards resided.

Early in the Winter of 1781-82, the Northwest Indians, becoming suspicious that the British force had been overthrown by the American armies, sent a party into Kentucky to take a prisoner from whom they could obtain the information concealed from them by the British agents in Canada. Col. Waters had then settled on a spot near the present town of Springfield, Washington County, Ky. He erected a cabin by a small stream, not far from the Fort on Cartwright's Creek about where the present road from Springfield to Lebanon crosses that stream.

Indian signs having been reported, he removed with his wife to the Fort and finding all the houses in it occupied by the settlers, went into the woods to cut logs with which to build one. In the evening, after having cut logs sufficient for his cabin, he returned to the Fort, but discovering he had lost his knife, expressed his determination of returning for it. His youthful wife teased him to be allowed to accompany him, but Waters not desiring to be delayed and being a powerful man, playfully put his hand on her head and spun her around until becoming dizzy, she fell – he then ran off and left her.

As he proceeded with his head down looking for his knife, he was discovered by a party of Indians who had been attracted by his chopping, but had arrived after he had left. Concealing themselves they allowed him to pass within four or five steps, but when they were between him and **(5)** the fort sprang into the path and levelling their rifles, called upon him to surrender. He, however, sprang off like a deer and three of the fastest Indians throwing their guns to their companions, started in pursuit. Waters made a wide circle, confident in his speed to outrun the Indians and reach the fort upon the other side.

After running about three quarters of a mile, two of the Indians were out of sight and the third, a half-breed who had been sent for the special purpose of capturing a prisoner, was some distance behind. Waters, being seized with a violent stitch in the side, clapped his hand upon it and proceeded until it became so painful as to prevent his running. He then stopped and held out his hand to the half breed, exclaiming, "Howdy-d'ye do." But the wary Indian, drawing a small pocket pistol, kept him at bay until the others came up. He was then bound and taken to the Blue Licks where the main body of the Indians was and with them Tecumseh-Ka, then only 15 years of age, afterwards the renowned Tecumseh of the North West war.

The trail which the Indians took after the capture of Waters led within a short distance though not in sight of his cabin, and one of them seeing hog tracks leading down a path asked in broken English "house? how far?" Waters, unwilling [to lose] the few stores he had been compelled to leave behind should he be plundered by the Indians, answered "don't know." "Lie lie – killee you!" returned the Indian, but passed on leaving the cabin undisturbed.

From the Blue Licks, Waters was then taken to the Indian town at Pickaway near the present site of Chillicothe, Ohio. The day before they reached the town, an Indian who was to be appeased for the death of a relative at the hands of the Whites by the burning of the next prisoner taken, seemed sullen and silent **(6)** and at length appeared with his face painted one half black and the other half red, indicating that being himself a warrior, he would leave the prisoner's fate to the decision of the Warriors. They decided that the prisoner should run the gauntlet before being questioned.

The next day as they approached the town, they were met by a great crowd of boys and women shouting, yelling, and brandishing their clubs in high glee with the expectation of the prisoner's being compelled to run the gauntlet.

At their head was a white boy who had been taken some time before, who seemed as much delighted at the prospect of the prisoner's torture as any of the savages. Waters recognizing the boy as one to whom during periods of distress at the Fort at Louisville, he had given buffalo bones and venison procured by his superior courage and wariness, spoke to him, calling him by name. The boy instantly shrank back into the crowd.

A consultation of the Indians was held and at length the boys and women sent back to the town. A body of "Braves," all decked in their war paint and fully armed, then came out to meet the prisoner. Waters still tied, singing an Indian song which had been taught him, advanced steadily until the foremost Indian, a gigantic warrior whirling his tomahawk, aimed a blow at the prisoner's head. Waters received it without moving a muscle, but the Indian just as the weapon descended, turned it and struck the captive with the flat side, upon the forehead, cutting a gash to the bone. The blood spurted in a stream and then ran down the face. Waters never ceased chanting his song and the Indian who struck him exclaimed "God damn you – that's a how dye do for you!" The remainder of the Indians offered no further violence, but each one pulled at some portion of the prisoner's **(7)** clothes, uttering exclamations he did not then understand, but which he afterwards learned were meant as salutations. He was told that the blow was in lieu of the gauntlet and it was considered a great honor for a prisoner to be struck by a warrior instead of being handed over to the boys and women.

This was owing to his recognition by the white boy and was a mark of their admiration for a brave and gallant enemy.

Waters was then questioned with great scrutiny as to the affairs of the British Army and repeatedly cautioned that if caught in a "lie" he would suffer death by burning. He told them of the Surrender of Cornwallis to Gen. Washington which they were reluctant to believe. For nearly three weeks they continued their inquisition in the hope of catching the prisoner in a lie.

Once he noticed an unusual ____ amongst the council and upon enquiry was told by the interpreter that he had crossed his track – he immediately explained any supposed discrepancy when one of the Indians remarked "it was no use to question him for if they caught him in a lie he was to get out of it."

Twice they tied the prisoner to the stake but the British agent at a neighboring town substantiating his statement, he was adopted by the Indians into their tribe under the name of Tucubia.

The watch kept upon him for some time was very strict and every move that he made was known to the Indians. Although after sometime when the vigilance of the enemy relaxed, Waters made preparations to escape. One night the Indians had gone to a war dance at a neighboring town and he determined upon the effort. An old Negro woman who was also a prisoner shared with him an eggshell full of salt and gave him several pounds of jerked venison.

When Waters went out to find the horse he had hobbled, **(8)** upon which to escape, he could not find it, but came across one belonging to an old Indian who had been very kind to him while a prisoner. It was the old Indian's only horse. Waters however mounted him and took a course due north. After proceeding a short distance, he came upon the horse he had hobbled and though the one he rode was the best of the two, he was unwilling to take the only horse of the old Savage, and dismounting, changed horses.

He then made a wide circle to the west and pushed on for the Ohio river. The night before he reached the river, he suddenly heard the horse bells of a hunting party encamped nearby. Cautiously, he proceeded, and as he rose in crossing a small stream up a steep bank, he suddenly came upon the Indians lying on their blankets around a fire, not 15 steps before him. A silently as possible, he reined his horse back the descent and struck off undiscovered.

Reaching the Ohio River, he tied his horse and tying a few chunks together with grapevine, floated down the stream. The weather was very cold and he was compelled to keep his feet in the water to keep them from freezing. The circle which he had made was so large that the Indians never struck his trail and he reached the fort at the Falls in safety.

Years after, Col. Waters met a Shawnee, one of the tribe who had captured him, and upon discovering his Indian name of Tucubia, the Indian instantly recognized him and seemed almost frantic with delight at having again met "his Brother."

Col. Waters was a thousand times exposed to the most imminent danger. During seasons of scarcity at the forts, he would steal out at the dead hour of night and dodging the **(9)** Indians, proceed far enough to be outside the range as they watched the Fort. He would then hunt during the day and at night steal into the Fort with the game he had killed.

Once while thus employed in hunting, he heard the gobble of a wild Turkey within a short distance and hid behind a tree in order to get a shot. In the bush a few yards to one side he heard the call of the female Turkey, but the Gobbler being in open ground, he waited till it should approach in range. At last just as he had brought his rifle to his face and his rifle cracked, he heard the call and an Indian warrior sprang forward to the gobbler he had killed. Waters, although undiscovered, was afraid to shoot the Indian, not knowing how close his companions might be, and crept silently back until some distance from the spot.

Upon another occasion the watch of the Indians had been so rigid that Waters was prevented from making his night excursions. The food in the fort had been exhausted and the garrison was upon the point of starvation. When they were in their last extremity a hawk lit upon the limb of a tree just outside the fort but in such a position that if killed instantly it would fall inside the wall. Waters raised his rifle and fired, and the hawk dropped headless within the walls. Waters had scarcely loaded before another hawk lit upon the same limb. This one was served in the same manner. They were made into soup and sustained the garrison until the Indians, becoming disheartened, raised the siege.

Col. Waters lived to the advanced age of 80 years and for many years after the settlement of Kentucky held legislative office
(132) as in the General Assembly of the Commonwealth. His undaunted courage and strong intellect gave him a state reputation and were preserved until a short time previous to his death. Two of his sons are still living in Kentucky.

See Cist's <u>Cincinnati Advertiser</u>, July 4, 1851, for a notice of Col. P. Waters, & the Brown & Morehead adventure. LCD.

13C133-136 LCD questions to Frank Waters dated March 8, 1862.

Col. Frank Waters:
    My Dear Sir:

I have most sincerely to thank you for your obliging favor, together with the statement of your father's recollections of his father's early pioneer services. Your father's statement I am exceedingly glad to obtain.

I deeply regret that your father's papers relative to Clark's Kentucky Expedition have been lost or mislaid. Is there the least possible hope of their recovery?

Permit me to make some additional inquiries.

1st. What was the name of Col. Philemon Waters' father – where was he a native of, & from what region moved from when he settled at Winchester, Va?

2nd What was Philemon Waters' occupation prior to going to Kentucky - & did he first go there as an adventurer, or as a soldier in some company? In a newspaper account of the adventures of Waters, Brown & Morehead, which I have – appeared in a Cincinnati paper in 1861 - it is stated that Waters came to Kentucky with Gen. Clark in 1780. I think Col. Slaughter took a reinforcement from Virginia to Clark in 1780 & Waters may have been among them, but Clark took no man personally in 1780 from Virginia.

3rd What were Brown's & Morehead's first names?

4th *pages or questions are out of order* Has your father any knowledge of the date or the year upon the adventure in which Brown lost his life occurred?

5th When P. Waters was captured in 1781 & '82, the name of Tecumseh is mentioned. From published accounts, it would appear that he was too young...

Unnumbered questions
Who was the white boy with the Indians, whom your grandfather formerly knew at Louisville, who was disposed to aid in torturing him? What became of him? What was the meaning of the Indian name Tucubia given to your grandfather? How long was he in captivity and at what period did he effect his escape? When he left his horse, & crossed the Ohio, when effecting his escape, did he return & get the horse?

6th Was P. Waters in either of Clark's Indian campaigns – in the summer of 1780, & fall of 1782, against the Shawanoes, & in 1786 up the Wabash?

7th You say Philemon Waters was born in March 1750 & died in July 1829, which would have made him in his 89th year & in another place you say he was in his 84th year. Is the latter an error?

8th. Describe P. Waters size, personal appearance, & leading traits of character. I presume there is no portrait of him – let me know if there is.

Send his autograph signature, if you can, that I may use for an engraved illustration.

9th. "Two of his sons are living in Kentucky" – who is the one beside your father, where reside, & their respective ages? **135** What finally became of Morehead, where settled & died, his character and has he any descendants to whom your father can refer me? On what creek, how far and which was from Louisville, was Brown killed, & to the pond where P. Waters waylaid the Indians' dog?

13C137 Frank Waters, grandson of Philemon Waters, letter, 1872. *Much is illegible due to faded ink. Answers are numbered, apparently for questions from 13C133, despite the discrepancy in the dates recoded by Draper..* Reply to my inquiries of March 8th, 1872. LCD

        In answer to your inquiries, My Father requests me to make the following:

Answer 1: Thos. Waters – a native of Virginia, born near Winchester – died in 1751.

Answer 2: A farmer and an adventurer.

Answer 3: Don't know Brown's or Morehead's first names. Both were killed by the Indians. The ford[?] where the dog was killed is not known. The creek was known as Harrods Creek.

Answer 4: None! Except it was in the fall.

Answer 5: We are certain about Tecumseh. He was only 15 years old. My Grandfather taught him English. He spoke very highly of Tecumseh. He was a captive about 40 days. The name Tucubia meant "Brother" because the Indians considered him a great warrior and worthy to be a brother to them. He escaped in the fall. He left the horse tied on the bank of the Ohio so the Indians could find it and [he] floated down the river on a raft

Answer 6: He guided Clark's forces back to the Indian towns in the Kentucky Expedition against the Shawnees.

Answer 7: He was born March 10, 1751, and died 30 May 1829.

Answer 8: He was about 5 feet 11 inches in height and weighed 184 pounds, and said by those who remember him to have been the most fearfully formed man for heavy activity & strength they ever knew. His [sic] wore No. 6 boots and No. 7 1/2 hats. [He had] yellowish hair, a clear blue eye, square-cut massive features, thin straight lips, and square long jaw. He was considered as an _____ handsome man. He was a proud man, rather haughty and commanding. Clark said he was as brave a man as ever threw a gun to his shoulder. An iron intellect which in spite of want of education gave him a command over his fellow man until his

Death. We have no portrait. I send you his autograph and first commission.

Answer 9: My uncle, Phil B. Waters, now ___ in Barren County near Glasgow. My Father Thomas H. is in his 71st year, my uncle in his 78th year.

My Grand Mother was a lineal descendant & one of the most remarkable women of her days who married a Waters in the early part of last century. From her descended the Wickliffes of Kentucky and the Bullins of South Carolina.

My Grand Father was a "rebel" in 1776 and I am a "Rebel" in 1862.

Very Truly,
Frank Waters

13C138, 138(1), 139 [LCD handwriting] From <u>Cist's (Cincinnati) Advertiser</u>, July 4, 1851

Incident of Early Settlement in Kentucky.

Col. Philemon Waters, late of Washington County, came to Kentucky with Col. George Rogers Clark in 1780, and formed one of Col. Clark's garrison in his Fort near the Falls of the Ohio. On one occasion, Waters and two of his comrades, by the names of Brown and Morehead, were out on some excursion into the country, Their trail was struck by forty Indians, who followed them unperceived, until they commenced ascending a very steep bank of a creek, not very distant from the Fort. Waters, by an angular turn in the pathway, placed himself in front, and Brown in the rear. While the three in Indian file were clambering up the bank, [Brown] discovering the Indians but a short distance from him, called out to the two in front, that the Indians were on them, which was instantly followed by a fire from the Indians. Waters reached the top of the bank, and looking back saw Brown prostrate, with his right hand raised to ward off the blow of an Indian standing over him with an uplifted tomahawk, and in the act of sending it into his brain. He instantly raised his rifle, and sent his ball immediately under the arm that held the **(1)** tomahawk in the air. He then fled into the cane, but after running a few yards, he became entangled in a grape-vine. Not being able to extricate himself before the Indians would be upon him, he laid perfectly still until they had passed him in pursuit of Morehead, with a dog running on his trail, and who passed within ten feet of Waters. He then retreated across the creek, and in a very short time heard the Indian dog following, as he thought, his trail. Coming to a pond he crossed it, and determined to kill the dog in the act of swimming the pond, and thus elude further pursuit. Just as he threw himself behind a tree to wait on the dog, Morehead reached the pond, following the same course, and resolved upon that stratagem to get rid of the dog. But he saw Waters as he jumped behind the tree, and mistaking him for an Indian, changed his course. Both reached the Fort about the same time, entering at opposite sides; each reported that he supposed the other was either killed or captured, and that Brown was killed. A party was immediately sent out in search of Brown. His body was found near the spot where he was shot, tomahawked and scalped, and rolled up in Morehead's blanket with the Indian Waters had shot. Both Morehead and Waters had dropped **139** their knapsacks when they commenced the fight. The laying of Brown in the same blanket with, and by the side of the dead Indian, is the only instance of such a burial that I have ever known. It must have indicated some extraordinary occurrence in the encounter.

13C140 Appointment of Philemon Water to Captain of Militia by Gov. Benjamin Harrison, 1784.

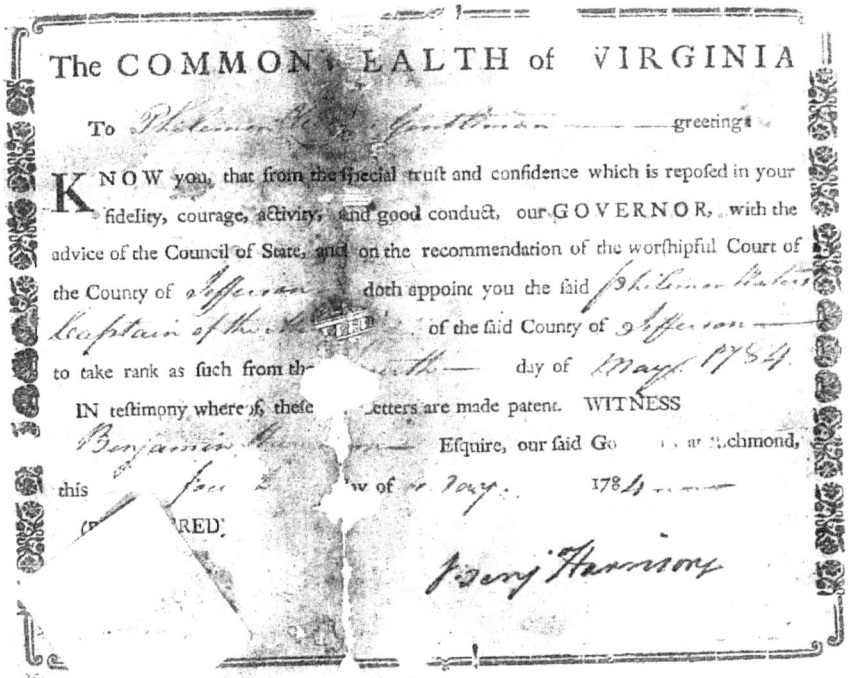

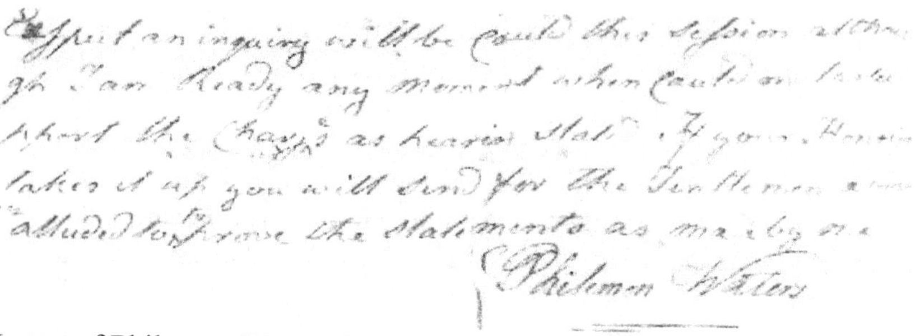

[handwritten text, partially legible:]

...expect an inquiry will be made this session although I am ready any moment when called on... about the charge as having stated... If you have taken it up you will send for the gentlemen... alluded to, prove the statements as ... by me

Philemon Waters

Letter of Philemon Waters. including the original document appointing him Captain of Militia in 1784. 13C140

13C141 *LCD questions to Maj. Thomas H. Waters in 1862 about Philemon Waters The return letters from Thomas Waters are illegible because of faded ink.*

13C145-145(1) Thomas C. Waters letter, Lexington, Ky. Oct 23, 1862
Dear Sir:
  Owing to the cessation of mails to this place, yours of August 30th did not reach me until two days since. Regarding the discrepancies in my brother's and my account of my father's early pioneer life, I can only say that though he is some years older than myself, yet we were more particularly interested in my father's adventures, at about the same age, and parental rules being stricter in those days than now, we rarely presumed to ask questions when my father was relating them to older listeners, so that it is a matter of memory between us.
  I am perfectly satisfied that my brother is mistaken in locating the incident I communicated to you on Beargrass. The fort was at the mouth of Beargrass in the present site of Louisville and this went some distance from the fort to a much larger stream, which I have always thought was Harrods Creek, though might possibly be mistaken, but it was most certainly <u>not</u> Beargrass Creek, which is so insignificant a stream that it scarcely deserves a name.
  (1) While my father was going up the bank, which was just there a ridge, they fired, as I before described. I asked my father when I was a man about their position at the time and am confident I am right.
  A story which my father used to tell, of his having once on the Ohio River, when he was leading a small body of men, stopped on a sand bar, or small island, expecting an attack from a party of Indians on shore,

who however did not come over in their canoes. My father, taking aim at the head of a large Indian, fired & heard him yell & saw him leap into the air as if mortally wounded. The Indian fired once upon the party but the guns being short range the balls knocked up the sand around them & injured no one.

I still think my father said that the Indian party numbered about forty. My father was taken prisoner to an Indian town in Ohio in the Shawnee nation called Pickaway. It was an impression that it was a black woman that he got salt & venison from, though I will not be perfectly certain. I remember she said to him "Don't let them yaller devils ketch you they'll skelp you."

About "Tecumseh Kah" as he was called, my father spoke frequently, telling no particular incident except his always sharing his venison & other food with him, for his teaching him English, which he took the utmost pains to learn. Indeed he said he never saw a man who was so determined a student as Tecumseh was of the English language, **(2)** the character of a noble-minded man. [Waters] regretted much that a Kentuckian, Richard Johnson, should have been the means of the death of this splendid looking savage, whose intellect & natural good qualities would have made him an ornament to civilized society.

I know very little of Clark, as my father was not a soldier under him, but a civilian who was employed by him occasionally to lead Scouts. Brown & Morehead were also civilians employed for the same service & the late expedition which I before related, Clark promised them forty pounds English money for every scalp taken. My father received his money & with it he bought a pre-emption claim near Springfield, Kentucky, where he built a house & lived until his death.

My father built himself a flat boat to go down to New Orleans, & was, in fact, the first white trader from Kentucky that ever accomplished that trip. After loading it with salt, bacon &c., he hired me to go with him as hunter to provide the boat with fresh venison &c. When they got down to Yellow Banks, my father & two of the men went out in search **(3)** of game, leaving the boat tied to the bank in charge of the other two. When they returned they found the boat on the opposite side of the river, but there being a canoe moored on the side nearest them, they got in & easily rowed across and owing to the lowness of the river they were not floated down stream. When they reached the boat they found one of the men lying before the fire with his head cut off & his body ripped open, his heart taken out & laid upon the head of a salt barrel, with the intention of being eaten no doubt. Tthe Indians were frightened away by the idea they supposed of superior numbers coming. The other man they could find no trace of, whether he was shot in swimming the river and sunk or whether he was taken prisoner they could never tell. I don't know the name of the men that were hired hunters.

I am more than ever assured of the fact of my father's companion name's being Morehead and have always been under the impression that he was an ancestor of Gov. Charles Morehead of Kentucky, or some relation. I think my brother had confounded his name with that of another Indian hunter John Morelock of whom you will find a particular account in Harper's Magazine for October. I did not communicate the story to the newspaper in 1851 & am ignorant who did. I read the account at the time & struck me as being correct.

(4) My father was a member of the Baptist Church from the time he was a grown man. My impression is that he ___ the Church in Virginia.

My Grandfather Harrison had no active part in the Indian warfare that I know of but there is an incident I have often heard related of his daughter, my aunt, which may interest you.

She was just grown at the time & was staying with a Mr. and Mrs. Harris at Burnt Station, when it was attacked by the Indians. The man escaped out of the window and the two women lifting up the puncheons of the floor, got down into a hole beneath it, leaving a little black child in the corner. The Indians came into the cabin & seized upon the little negro when he shrieked out "Please Massa Indian don't kill me; plenty white folks under the puncheons." The Indian however did not understand him. They then took the **(5)** fire from the fire place, & put up on the mantle shelf to set the house on fire. The affrighted women could see the fire blazing through the cracks in the puncheons. The Indians then left the house but the fire did not burn. They then set fire to it on the outside & the two women taking advantage of the smoke & confusion & the Indians by this time had become very drunk, they made their escape to the woods. The next day the Indians saw them & tracked them but they crouched down in some underbrush & covered their heads with a horse shawl they had with them. It being the color of the leaves, though the Indians passed within touch of them several times, they were not discovered. After the Indians had left the pursuit these women made the best of their way to the nearest settlement half starved & wearied.

My aunt's name was Sally Harrison, afterwards Mrs. Isaac Frommer.*

Hoping my answers to your inquiries will be satisfactory, I am
Yours respt.
Thomas E. Waters

*See <u>Marshall's Ky.</u>, p. 144

13C153-153(1) Thomas C. Waters letter, Lexington, Ky., February 16, 1863

Lyman C. Draper
    Dear Sir
    Your last favor was duly received. In answer to your inquiries my replies are:
    The man whom I called Harris was called both Harris and Harrison and was related to the Harrisons in an indirect way so the Scandal whispered. He is the same man spoken of in Marshall's History though the ___ adventures of the two females. They escaped from the burning house as I described. I have only a faint remembrance of ever having heard the names of the persons who were at the Burnt Station with the name of Col. Brown but no particulars concerning them.
    My Grandfather's name was Thomas Harrison and he came to Kentucky in 1780 & settled at Falls of Ohio. He afterwards moved to Washington Co [Ky.] near Springfield where he died Dec. 1827 at the age of 96. My father & Mother were married at Falls of Ohio in 1782 & she died near Springfield on Oct 9, 1824 in 68th year of her age. She was younger than my Aunt Sally. I can give no particulars in regard to the White you speak of. I was not in service in 1812 & can tell you nothing of Capt. Tommy.
    I cannot tell where my Aunt ___ died or at what age. They moved to the place near Flint Island on the Ohio & my Uncle started from that place to Post Vincent on a fine horse & with all his money to enter the land he had taken possession of. He was never heard of afterwards but there was found upon what was called "the trace" a scull with a bullet hole through it supposed to be his.
    (1) Mrs. Fanny Young may not have received your letter as the address could not be certainly given, but her Mother's name is at present Mrs. ___ Craft, who resides near Mrs. Young. Mrs. Craft had another daughter living in Carrollton (town), Carroll County, Missouri. Whole name is Sally Campbell. Mr. James Campbell, her husband, is quite an intelligent gentleman & to him you could address a letter, enclosing your enquiries to Mrs. Craft whom you will find an interesting lady with a mind well stored with memories of the past and incidents of the early times as told her by her relatives. From the fact of losing her father as supposed Mr. Foreman, it may readily be supposed her reminescences would be of

a vivid character.

Respectfully
Thos C. Waters

13C154 Fanny Young letter, Millville, ____ County, Mo., Feb 25, 1863
This is an account of the Indian attack at Kincheloe's Station, also called Burnt Station.

Dear Sir

    I have concluded to write you after so long a time. The reason that I did not write sooner was that I have an Aunt that lived in Carroll County that was older than my Mother and would give me more satisfaction, but she did not – therefore I thought I would write to my regret without giving but little or no satisfaction – but by the aid of my Mother I will do the best I can.

    As to the name and place of the station, Mother thinks you are correct. My Grand Mother was a young lady about 18 years old and she lived in Coxe's Station and was there at the Burnt Station on a visit when it was attacked but by what tribe Mother doesn't know. But I will tell you the circumstances as near as I can: Grandfather said that there was a young lad that was in the fort. He went out one day from the fort and he saw a tribe of Indians coming and he hid behind a log till they passed and he said that they ware so long in passing by that he got tired laying on one side and turned over. So if that be the case, there must have been a good many: this boy was brought up and he swore to it.

    The Colonel had all the men paraded & sent out after them. The night after the men left, the Indians came in on them unprepared for them. They came and destroyed every thing and burnt all of the houses. **(1)** There with her cousin, William Harison, his house was the last that was attacked. While this was burning, and the Indians were murdering the rest, he put Grand mother and his wife in the celler and then he made his escape. He had a keg of whisky and when they came in they murdered a little black boy that was under the bed. Then took the whisky and set the house afire then left to divide the whisky and then these two women left and ran out into some hemp that was close by there. They wandered about for nine days before they was found. They was naked and starved and had sat down for the laste time when some man was out hunting stock and came across them and took them in Coxe's Station. They was all murdered or taken prisoners except those I speake of as fare [far] as I can find out. Grand Mother Froman died in the year 1832. She died in Perry County Indiana State. I thought I would tell you the circumstances as my Mother gave it to me so you might gather all you could. That is all that Mother knows about it. She don't know the tribe nor the number nor the time. I think that I will gather more about it, and if so I will write to you. Please excuse my bad dictating and writing.

Fanny Young

13C155-160 LCD questions to relatives of Philemon Waters

13C160 April 16, 1862 *Letter to "Mr. Lamon E. Drapor" from a son of Philemon Waters is barely legible due to ink blots.*

Dr Sir Agreeable to your request and inquiries I will give you my best recollection of all your inquires concerning my father, Philemon Waters, who emigrated to the Falls of the Ohio in 1779 or '80 where he found a few families. Indians were vary troublesome. They went to work picketing [the fort]. My father would take his horse out some 3 or 4 miles from the fort.

13C161-161(14) Frank Waters, April 16, 1862.
Memo: This letter was post-marked Cave City Ky., April 25, 1862.
Much of this letter is illegible; some pages are omitted.

Sir Agreeable to your request and inquiries I will give you my best recollection concerning my father, Philemon Waters, who Imigrated to the Falls of the Ohio in the year 1779 or 1780 when he found a few families forted. The Indians were very trubelsome, and the whites about to desert the fort. He encouraged them to stay & they ___ picket in the fort. They would divide up the work and allot to every man his portion. He would do his portion of the picketing, and he went to hunt & kill meat for all to live if they would stay. They agreed to do so, laid off every man his part to do, so they agreed to stay. They went to work picketing. My father would take his horse of nights and go out some 3 or 4 miles from the fort, turn out his horse & strike camp, and wait till day, then take his gain. Go out hunting & kill all the game he could that day & **(2)** when night would come, he would pack up his horse and take it in the fort and then go to work at his picketing. And that is the way they did till they got the picketing done.

In 1781 my father, Moredock & Brown ... *ink blots obscure the story, which is told in another account.*

(5) Philemon Waters' captivity in Ohio
Before they got to their [Indian] town, they learned him a song and told him he must sing it when he got in town. The words of the song were "she-gawana he-hew." When they got in sight of their town, he commenced singing "she-go-wa-ne-heho." The Indians formed themselves into being a few feet apart. He was ordered to march between the lines which he did, repeating his song without being molested until he got nearly through when an Indian, painted, a tomahawk in his hand, wavering & grinning, and as if he was going to split his head open, turning the edge and letting the side strike my father, which cut and like to have knocked him down. My father repeated his song marching along till he got through, sat down, bloody. The Indian went into council, and one went to him and told him "no kill you" and dressed his wound, and adopted him into an Indian family, and named him "Tuck-a-p___. His Indian Daddy's name was k k kin-a-thick-her. They had him a prisoner forty days. He could shoot at a mark several times.

13C183 *Hand-drawn map of Blue Licks Battleground; writing below map is illegible but begins:* "Thinking perhaps you never had a complete diagram of the battle ground at Blue Licks, I Pencil out one."

13C188(3) last page of letter of W. T. Sterling, 1886
The is an account of the siege at Bryan's Station of August 1782 as told to him by his mother, Elizabeth Harper Sterling, who was born in 1779 and died in 1860. He also stated: "My grandfather Jacob Harper came to Kentucky in 1779 from Harper's Ferry."

I do not know the number of men in the fort. But when the water supply gave out it was the only alternative to ___ and surrender Which] would be followed by a great massacre. A call was made for volunteers to get water. Three girls volunteered – Elizabeth Harper, Sarah Patterson, and another whose name I do not recollect. They went in a playful manner with their sun bonnets in one hand and wooden pails, which they called piggins, in the other. My mother used to tell that 500 arrows were pointed at them but not one fired. They returned safely with the water to the fort. About the 6th or 7th day of the siege Mother told me she took her breakfast from the pewter dish she used and before noon the dish was run into bullets and she then had to eat out of the pot.

My Mother, Elizabeth Harper Sterling, died in Cass County, Missouri, Dec. 4, 1860 aged 90 years. She was consequently 12 years old at the time of the attack at Bryant's.

W. T. Sterling

13C192 John Vawter letter, 1854, Morgantown, Indiana.

The story is told of a family arriving at Bryan Station on the night of Nov. 15, 1779. Daniel Boone was then at Cross Plains. Jesse Vawter, father of the writer, and wife Elizabeth went to North Carolina about 1780[?]. Holston River, and Tennessee are mentioned and information is given on Blue Licks, William McMurtry, etc.

13C193(1,2,3) *John Vawter writing for Phoebe Vancleve Harris, a daughter of William Vancleve. John Vawte s statements on his life as a Baptist minister and his service in War of 1812 in Indiana are omitted.*

Morgantown, Indiana, 20 June 1854

My Dear Sir

Religious, and social or Family obligations have delayed my answer to yours of the 15 of May until now. Today I called on our good old Baptist Sister Phoebe Harris, Read her your Interogatories. And recorded her answers as follows.

1st She does not distinctly remember noted Stations or places of Boon & his party (being very young). She Remembers Crossing the Big Yadkin, James, & New Rivers. The number of Families she does not recollect, but there were 100 or upwards.

2nd The company had what was called a Swivel, but what became of it she does not remember.

3rd Col. Daniel Boon and the party he had collected set out on their Journey for Kentucky, Levisa, on 20th day of September 1779. The party with which she was a member landed at Bryants Station, at nyte on the 15th day of November 1779. The whole of Boons Party arrived at Boonesborough on the previous Sunday.

4th [She] cannot say how many or who they were who stoped with Col. Boon at the Cross Plains, her association and recollection being confined principally or altogether to the party and names to [those who] made Bryants Station their point of destination.

5th Cannot say what detained Col. Boone in North Carolina one year after his return home, and after his captivity. But as he frequently visited her Father in the time, supposed and believed it was to recruit and raise a Strong migrating party.

(2) 6th Says she does not know anything about John Finley, Joseph Holden,

or William Cooley.

7th She does not know anything of Andrew Johnson.

8th Col. Boone, with others of her acquaintance, were at the Blue Lick defeat. She has a distinct recollection of the account of the Slaughter, and massacre at the Blue Lick. Col. Boone's son, Israel Boone, was killed there.

9th She recollects Col. Whitley with others, her husband being one of the party (before married), went into the Indiana country and destroyed or Burnt the Shawanee Towns, but she does not recollect where those towns were Located.

10th She says Squire Boone's wife was an own Sister to her father, William Vancleve.

11th Says she knows nothing about Sevier or the early pioneers of Tennessee.

12th Says no part of the larger Company were disturbed or interrupted by the Indians on their way from North Carolina to the New Country [in 1779]. Says it was one of the most delightfull falls [autumns] she had ever seen.

13th She recollects that, Between Boons Station, & Linns Station, the Indians attacked on emigrating party, killing 4 of the party. Of the number killed, Her Sister Sally Vancleve was one of the number.

(3) Also her Aunt Molly Vancleve & 2 of her children were Slain (and some few were taken prisoners, names not now recollected). They being the wife and children of her Uncle John Vancleve.

She has a perfect recollection of the attack at Bryants Station, although She did not live there at the time. The Indians continued the siege for 5 days and nights. Prior to the Siege, and while she lived there, the Indians killed old Mr. William Bryant.

She recollects that before the Siege at Bryants Station, the Indians had destroyed Ruddles & Stroud's [Martin's] Stations. There are many other incidents of early times. If you were present to make the inquiries, I have not a doubt would be interesting to you and valuable in your History of Kentucky. She is very Intelligent for a woman of her age. Cannot see [well?]. Craves death, deserves to be absent from the Body & present with the Lord. Has been for a very great many years a pious, devoted Christian of the Baptist order. She cannot remain with us Long.

You invite me to say something about my Humble Self. I am not averse to any man, or Set of men... (4) I was born of Humble, but Honest Parents, 18th January 1782 in Orange County, Virginia. My father when I was but a few months old moved into North Carolina, now one of the upper counties in east Tennessee. Although very young, I recollect

____ of Sevier & Tipton. My Father was an ensign ... that went out against the Hostile Indians... In 1788 he visited Kentucky, and in 1789 or 1790, moved with his family to Kentucky. Although very young, I became a close observer of passing evens until the present day, hold an Ensign's Commission in Kentucky, under its first Constitution. Married in Kentucky in 1805. Visited Indiana Territory in search of a Home, visited it again in 1806, moved my family, Wife and one child into the wilderness of Indiana in March 1807. Settled near Madison, before it was laid out..

John Vawter

13C194-194(1) Philip S. Bush letter, Covington, Ky. April 27, 1867. Letterhead: United Fire and Marine Insurance Company of Kentucky.

    Capt. John Craig was the oldest son of Toliver Craig and Mary Hawkins, his wife, of Culpepper County, Virginia. They are supposed to be descendants of "John Craig who was a colleague of John Knox and as appears from the records of the Church of Scotland to have been minister at Halierudehouse (Holyrood) in the year 1562 and in that year was conjoined with Knox in the ministry of Edinburgh." The proclamation of the bands [banns] of marriage was reluctantly performed by John Craig, the colleague of Knox, between Mary Stewart the Queen and Lord Bothwell on the 11th May 1567.

    John Craig was the oldest child of Toliver Craig who had seven sons and four daughters. Three of his sons were Baptist preachers of notoriety in Virginia, all of whom emigrated to Kentucky at a very **(1)** early date. John, who had served in the war of the revolution of 1776, upon removing to Kentucky settled at and Commanded Bryant Station when it was attacked by the British and Indians under Colonel ____ and the celebrated Simon Girty and ably and successfully defended the fort with a small force. Jacob Stucker and Jeremiah Craig were always spoken of as the two warriors of the Fort. Jere killed two Indians in view of many witnesses, one who had secreted himself behind a stump and ventured to peep over the top of it was shot in the forehead. The other had ascended a tree in the night and was firing into the fort. The flashes of his gun gave Craig the opportunity to mark him and he brought him to the ground the first shot.

    The author of these lines is the son of Sally Craig, the daughter of John, who had detailed the accounts and events of that attack on Bryans Station frequently in his hearing.

Philip S. Bush

13C195 LCD notes: Capt. John & Jeremiah Craig – Bryant's Station, 1782.

Capt. John Craig
1785[?] in Danville Convention – Collins' Kentucky., i. 354
1787 in Fayette County – Collins' Kentucky, ii, 193
1790 represents Woodford County [taken from Fayette County] in Va. Legislature, Collins' i, 366
1794 Justice of Campbell County. Collins' ii. 111
1796 in Legislature. Collins' ii, 773.

Jeremiah Craig
1792 in Legislature – Collins' Kentucky, ii, 182
    Indian fighter – Collins' Kentucky, ii, 767.

13C196-196(1-5) William McMurtry letter, Oakland, Ca., April 24, 1890

    I possess no knowledge whatever of the locality in North Carolina where Samuel McMurtry, the father of Capt. John, resided and where Capt. Johnson was born.
    Of the services of Gen. George Rogers Clark, I know nothing except what you may find recorded by Collins in his History of Kentucky. **(2?)** The incidents following the Blue Licks battle & defeat, of which you sent me an extract, as related to their families and others after their return home from their imprisonment, Capt. John McMurtry related (as my memory serves me, told to me by my Mother).
    That the night after the battle, he found himself and several other of whose names he knew not, prisoners of war. That the Indians painted them all black as the signal of torture and death. These five prisoners were **(3)** stripped and placed in a line on a log, Capt. McMurtry being at one extremety of the row. The Cruel Captors, beginning at the other end, commenced the slaughter, by one of the braves advancing in front and raising the captor to his feet and his arms to right angles with his body, while another with a long knife, advanced in the rear and finished the execution by plunging the knife to its hilt in the heart, one by one. But when they came to the only survivor, though they raised him up also, and drew the bloody knife to strike under the uplifted arm, they paused, and after a long pow-wow, spared his life. Why, he never knew. The next day he was placed under the same guard with Capt. Rose and Jesse Yocum.
    Yocum was the individual person who ran the gauntlet with McMurtry & Rose. **(4)** [This was] told by Capt. Rose to his family and

others and recorded in Collins' History of Kentucky. I could relate to you the interesting narrative of their captivity, their miraculous escape from being burned at the stake, after having been bound to the stake and the fagots collected for the purpose. The gauntlets that they were forced to run in the villages through which they passed, for the amusement of their women and children until they arrived at Detroit, when they were delivered into the hands of the British – if you wished me to do so. I could also inform you of the campaign Service they performed, after the Blue Licks affair, should you wish.

The reason for my not doing so in my former letter, was that the **(5)** entire narrative in my possession was communicated to Collins previously.

Yours Most truly
Wm. McMurtry

13C198 LCD notes: Lewis Rose, son of George Rose, of Germany who had 3 sons – Lewis, Martin, & Matthias. Lewis was at the Blue Licks, captured, exchanged & returned home in August 1783. His brother Matthias settled in St. Louis County, Mo., and left many descendants.

Pioneer Families of Missouri, p. 409.

13C199-199(2) William McMurtry letter, Oakland, Ca., May 13, 1890

In relation to the narrative of the captivity of McMurtry, Rose & Yocum, of which you spoke, allow me to make the following remarks.

The published narrative of said Captivity found in Collins' <u>History of Kentucky</u>, vol. 2, pages 662 &3, embraces in substance all in relation thereto, except what I have heretofore communicated that I am able to furnish. In verification, however, of the truth of Collins' narrative, I can say that I knew of my grandfather, Capt. Rose, spending a few days with Gen. R. B. McAfee at his country residence three miles northwest of Harrodsburg, Kentucky, at which time he dictated the Biographical Sketch of his **(1)** life, which was furnished with an obituary by McAfee. It was published in the Harrodsburg <u>Central Watchtower</u> on Feb. 28th, 1829, from which Collins extracted and together from tradition, furnished by Rev. Aaron A. Hogue (a grandson of Capt. McMurtry) in 1871, particulars in the life of Capt. McMurtry which together make up the narrative of Collins, the truth of which may be relied upon.

Jesse Yocum was a farmer and resided all his life near Ma—ville, Washington County, where he was living with a numerous family in the early part of the present century. His age I know not, but believe it to have been ten years younger than either Rose or McMurtry. I feel quite sure that John Yocum, of whom you mentioned, is a descendant. His Post Office is Ma---ville, Washington County, Ky.

I have no knowledge of Brashear of whom you made inquiry. **(2)** Abraham Chapline I knew well in my boyhood. His residence was three miles n. e. of Harrodsburg, on the great road leading to Lexington, by way of Pleasant Hill. His landed possessions were extensive and valuable. His character above reproach. His life was quiet and happy.

I knew his sons, Abraham and Isaac. In my manhood they were working and highly respected Citizens, and occupied a portion of the old homestead.

Permit me to call to notice to one of Mercer County's earliest and most respected persons, Major Thomas Allen. He was one of the early Surveyors. He was Clerk of Mercer County at my earliest recollection and has been succeeded in the same office by his sons, one after another, down to the present time, when his youngest Son, Benjamin Allen, 80 years of age **(3)** continues in said office.

Should you hereafter wish information concerning any person, place, or thing ancient or modernn, within the bounds of Mercer County, he above any other man now living is most competent to furnish it.

13C202-202(1) Capt. Lewis Rose, John McMurtry, James Ledgerwood, from notes of Gen. R. B. McAfee, Jan. 10, 1849 (copied by LCD)

As to Lewis Rose and John McMurtry, I have now before me a sketch of Mr. Rose's life, written by myself from his own mouth, a few weeks before his death. He was born on the 11th day of October 1749, in a small village near the City of Bingen, on the river Rhine, in one of the Paletinates of Germany. His father Cudliff[?], or Godlove, and Barbery Rose were members of the Lutheran Church, and were respectable and industrious citizens. His father and grandfather were iron-founders, and in consequence of the peace of 1763, their business having declined, they removed to this country in 1764, landing at Alexandria, Va., near Washington City now. In 1765, his father moved to Grant's Iron Works in Frederick County, Maryland, and in 1770, removed into Bedford County, Pennsylvania, where he bought a tract of land and commenced farming. Here, on the 31st of March 1772, Lewis Rose married Miss Barbara ____, a German lady. In 1777 & 1778, he served several terms with the Pennsylvania militia in the Revolutionary War.

In the Spring of 1779, he came to Kentucky and aided in raising a crop of corn in the town of Harrodsburg, partly where the court-house

(1) now stands and north of it. In May 1781 he assisted in relieving McAfee's Station, then attacked by the Indians, and in August 1782, he was taken prisoner at the battle of the Blue Licks with John McMurtry and James Ledgerwood. Rose was taken by the Ottawas and carried to Detroit, and sold to the British commandant, and returned home by the way of Montreal, and got back the 28th of August 1783.

He was so altered that his wife did not know him for some time.

McMurtry was taken to the Miami Village, near Fort Wayne, where he ran the gauntlet, & was taken to Detroit, and got home some weeks after Rose. [See Illinois Papers, ii, p. 20 LCD.] *Remainder of notes illegible.*

James Ledgerwood was taken to Mackinaw, and did not get back till the fall of 1784. He was my uncle, having married my mother's sister (Elizabeth McCoun.) His return was despaired of, and his wife had several offers of marriage, but rejected or postponed them until her husband got back to his great joy.

Lewis Rose lost his first wife in 1792, and in 1793, he married Mrs. McMurtry, the widow of John McMutry who was killed in Harmar's defeat. But it was not positive for a long time that he was killed, and Mrs. Rose was at first rejected, but he finally married her, and even then, it was reported that McMurtry was alive to their great annoyance. But Gen. Robert Caldwell having last seen him surrounded by the Indians, put that matter to rest.

Rose became an elder in the Presbyterian Church at Cane Run and Harrodsburg in the place of McMurtry and continued until his death about ___ 29th, 1829.

It was on McMurtry's return after the Battle of Blue Licks that Mrs. McMurtry exclaimed, as Judge Robertson relates, "That's John's gun."

13C202-202(8) Capt. McMurtry & Rose & Jesse Yocum.

Your kind reply of the 19th inst. to my Communication of late date.

Rev. A. A. Hogue is not living and the copy of the Central Watch Tower which he possessed was furnished to Collins.

(2) McMurtry family connections, etc.

(3) *continuing an account of the Battle of Blue Licks*

They cautiously but quickly ascended the gradual but exposed Slope of the second main bank of the creek to the west of the trail taken by the main body of the routed, with the hope of avoiding the foe. When arriving on the top of the bank, an open forest with trees of large size only here and there, toward one of which they directed their course with quickened pace, running near to each other, when the crack of a rifle rang through the forest and McBride fell to rise no more.*

*See Wm. McBride's statements in Shane, Woodford County p. 20-21 show that Capt. Joseph McBride settled a station near Harrodsburg.

Rose increased his speed, keeping the large tree steadfast in view, arriving at which and throwing himself behind the same, cast a backward glance, beheld an Indian half bent over his victim in the act of taking his scalp. Quick as thought his trusty rifle was brought to a rest by side of the tree with knee resting on the ground and the trigger was sprung. The stalwart savage warrior fell dead **(4)** and not waiting to reload, Rose renewed his retreat to the distance of a mile or more, when suddenly he was brought to a halt by four swarthy warriors who obstructed his path and demanded his gun or his life. When he handed up his gun, they blew in the muzzle, and finding it empty, they returned it to him, and marched him back the way he came, observing McBride and the dead Indian at some distance to the side of the course they were traveling. They turned aside to examine the bodies, which created in Rose no little alarm, fearing that they would reasonably conclude from finding his gun empty that he was the slayer of the Indian, and dispatch him upon the spot. Not so, for although they turned them over and examined the wounds, they seemed not to suspect him in the leased [sic] and went on. That night they placed him under **(5)** guard with McMurtry and Yocum.

Of the prisoners taken, 4 were killed by the Indians, in a most barborous manner as I have related to you heretofore, and the other 3, Lewis Rose, John McMurtry, and Jesse Yocum* [*See Shane ii, Bath County, p. 33. LCD] were packed to the extent of their strength with the spoils of the day. With their captors, they were hurried next day across the Ohio River at the mouth of Eagle Creek, 7 miles below Limestone Creek. Thence passed Upper and Lower Sandusky, and foot of the Miami rapids (afterwards Fort Meigs), to Detroit, where they arrived on Sept. 4th and were delivered into the hands of the British.

The above is a quotation from Collins History of Kentucky with which you are doubtless familiar.

I am not in possession of any Indian villages through which the **(6)** captors with their captives passed, nor the name of any Chief connected therewith.

I am not a little Surprised at learning that the children of Capt.

McMurtry should ever have entertained notions or feeling for Capt. Rose (their step-father) other than that of kindness and affection of a parental nature, all of which he exhibited towards them and their father in an unmistakable and eminent degree from their first acquaintance to the day of his death. No Sir, Capt. Rose was a representative Specimen of the honest German - honest, truthful, faithful to his promises, Steadfast in friendship, a devout Christian.

In contradiction to such false charges, I will relate in as few words as possible the true condition of the two men and their families during the 8 years from 1782 to 1790, the time of Harmar's defeat. It is not denied that McMurtry & Rose reached home at the same time from their captivities of one year and 9 days, on the **(7)** 28th day of August 1783. Rose's wife was now living, mark you, and My Mother was born during the year 1782, and her Mother lived to bear a daughter and a Son after her birth. I am not in possession of the account of my Grand Mother Rose's death, but I can not put it earlier than 1787. Therefore my Grandfather Rose was not a widower earlier than that date. It is nowhere asserted that McMurtry was again in captivity after the Blue Licks affair. You See at once the fallacy of the charge that Rose was not quite pleased with McMurtry's return from captivity. Rose was in the expedition with Benjamin Logan against the Shawnees on the Miami in 1786, and again after the death of Capt. McMurtry and previous to his marriage with his widow, he was on the campaign in 1791, with Gen. Charles Scott against the towns of the Wea Indians on the Wabash, in which 32 warriors were Slain and 58 prisoners taken.

(8) Capt. Rose's marriage with McMurtry's widow was in 1792. His age was then 43 and ____ ____. He had 6 children and She 7, and they had one son born to them in 1793. Now I do not doubt from what Dr. William T. McMurtry told you, that the McMurtry Children, after their father's death, was not altogether pleased with Rose, for encouraging their father to go on Harmer's Campaign, and much more displeased when they learned of his proposal of marriage to their Mother. Children scarcely ever are willing for their widowed parents to remarry.

Rose and McMurtry were eminently patriotic, and it was natural for them to believe that it was the duty of one, or both of them, to go on Harmer's Campaign, and consulted with each other upon the subject. Thus, Rose would say, My wife is dead, I have 3 Motherless children under 8 years old and you, McMurtry, have a Mother [to take care of the children.]

13C203-204 William McMurtry letter, July 14, 1890, Oakland, Ca., with LCD notes

1st. Of John Morgan, captured at the Blue Licks, &c. I know nothing, not having ever learned of any such capture.

2nd. I never knew or heard of any such name as "McMurtry" in Kentucky and suppose the person referred to was my Grand father Joseph McMurtry of Lexington, a pioneer of 1776 or 1777.

Of Harrodsburg, Kentucky - for information in relation to Samuel Moore, perhaps his grandfather.

LCD notes:
Capt. Joseph McMurtry wounded on Clark's Shawnee Campaign of 1780
See Henry's Wilson's Notes, before p. 21, 22, 98
1782 in Arthur Crockett's Company on Clark's Campaign 1780
Illinois Papers, ii. 24.
1791 commanded rangers on frontier, Kentucky Gazette Extracts, 6, p. 85

13C203(1) From Kentucky Gazette, Saturday, April 16, 1791

Extract of a letter from Capt. Joseph McMurtry, dated Fort Scott, 12th April 1791.

"The Indians daily make sign about our garrison; five of my rangers yesterday fell in with seven Indians, six miles below this post on the Ohio. A skirmish ensued in which our people kept the ground, capturing 4 horses & some colts stolen from Loudon's Station on Drennon's Lick waters, & took seven blankets, with kettles and deer skins, wounding two of the savages badly."

Kentucky Gazette Extracts, "6" p. 85.

Fort Scott was Gen. Scott's first location at mouth of Kentucky River.

Several references given by LCD omitted.

13C204 *End of letter from William McMurtry.*

May Heaven bless you my Dear friend, with health, happiness and length of days even beyond that, which your humble friend, with all the delightful enjoyments of which he is free to boast, is the fervent hope and prayer of your ever true and

Obedient friend

Wm. McMurtry

576 Thirty Fifth St.

13C205 *No address, date, or salutation. Not LCD handwriting*

    There was a son of James McMurtry and Nancy Todd (aunt of Col. John and Generals Robert and Levi Todd, of early pioneer memory). First cousin of Capt. John McMurtry and was born in RockBridge County, Va., about the year 1737. Married a Miss Campbell of Virginia, and immigrated from thence to Lexington, Kentucky with his wife & several children A. D. 1777. Purchased a farm within the immediate suburbs where he continued to reside during his life, following the vocation of a farmer. This life was prolonged to near his three score and ten years, but more definitely this deponent sayeth not.

    3rd. I must refer you to Dr. Moore, President of one of the two National Banks.

13C211-213 William McMurtry letter, Los Gatos, Ca., Jan. 31, 1890. *The writer was the grandson of John McMurtry.*

The McMurtrys are Scotch-Welch, started early in Pennsylvania & thence emigrated down the Shenandoah Valley, & finally to Kentucky about the close of the Revolution.

    The McMurtry family reached Kentucky late in 1779, reaching what is now Garrard County the night before the commencement of the big snow storm, which lasted perhaps some six weeks, & the winter became known as the hard winter. Had to camp where the storm caught them - & the men could easily kill game – deer & turkeys, &c – the deep snow preventing their escape. Afterward crossed Dick's river & settled in Mercer County.

    At the battle of the Blue Licks, McMurtry, Lewis Rose & another, at the defeat, kept together. Rose was a tall, athletic, raw-boned man, well adapted to backwoods life & Indian fighting. They were followed at the Blue Licks retreat by a party of seven Indians. Rose only of the three had his gun loaded, & felt like aiding his two companions, though he felt that he could escape. He told them to go ahead & he would protect them, & try to kill one of the pursuing party. It so happened, that when he sheltered himself & waited the approach of the Indians all in Indian file, & as he fired at the front one, another at that instant got in the rear or side of the front one, so that the **(212)** same shot killed both. He directed McMurtry & his companion to load their guns the first opportunity. They had got into a bend of the river, & see if they could not each kill one of the surviving Indians, & then manage to dispatch the other two. But McMurtry & Rose were so beset by the Indians that they had to present the buts of their guns in token of surrendering, while the other said he would not take the chance of surrendering, so attempted to escape, but was shot down as he ascended the opposite river bank. Rose managed, in a night or two after reaching the Ohio, to escape.

McMurtry was captured & made the prisoner of a young warrior who appeared to take a liking to him – adopted him as a brother. First gave him a gun to hunt, & finally when full confidence was had in him, permitted him to go out hunting alone. One night he ran off with his gun & thought he knew he was ___, would be scalped.

He had agreed with his wife when would reach within hearing distance of his home, he would fire off his rifle as a signal of his near approach. When all had given him up as lost, she agreed to marry Lewis Rose, a neighbor & widower, & the wedding day appointed, & when accordingly a rifle was heard in the distance, when Mrs. McMurtry said "That's John's Gun." So it proved, & the wedding was abandoned.

Mrs. McMurtry was Mary Hutton. Col. McMurtry had become an elder in one of Dr. Rice's churches, & when men were called for to leave on Harmar's Campaign in 1790, a number of the young men of the settlement said if they could go out under Capt. McMurtry, they would enlist or volunteer **(213)** & as a sense of duty, thought he ought to be exempt from the service, he finally yielded, & went & was killed in Harmar's defeat, having been shot through the body about the time the retreat commenced. When a neighbor, one Wood, on horseback, took him up behind him, hoping to escape. But finding within a short distance of being pursued, & could not hope both to escape, McMurtry said to Wood, as he was mortally wounded, to lay him down, & save himself, which was done.

Then Rose married the widow. He died about 1822, aged 82 years & Mrs. Rose about 1840, fully 80 years of age. She when young was beautiful, black expressive eye, handsome features. In her old age became quite corpulent.

Capt. McMurtry had established a station – McMurtry's Station adjoining Shaker Village in Mercer County.

A tradition in the McMurtry family says that Rose was not quite pleased with McMurtry's return, perhaps about a year, and did all he could to encourage him to go out on Harmar's Campaign, thinking perhaps he might not live to return. Mrs. McMurtry had one child, who died young.

John McMurtry's mother was a Todd & was Mary Hutton's

mother's ___ . Hence McMurtry married his cousin. Their mothers were sisters of the pioneer Todds of Kentucky.

In pioneer times in Kentucky, as turkey meat was dry, it was served instead of bread, while venison & bear meats, being more juicy, served as animal food. [See Roosevelt's <u>Winning of the West</u>, ii. 99. LCD]

Appendix Volumes 4-13 Findings Without Transcriptions or Notes

Volume 4
Hon. James Veech letter, 1858 ....4C7
Account of Fort Blackmore or Blackamore and Daniel Boone,
 1769... 4C28, 8(1-8)
LCD: map, location of Boone & Bryan Settlements ....4C32, 32(1)
Daniel Pennington, c.1854... 4C99
Daniel Boone's Kentucky Explorations, 1772-1773 .... 4C128-128(1)

Volume 5
Bryan's Station battle, map 5C52-53
E. M. Leavell letter to LCD 5C67

Volume 6
Powell's Valley Defeat 6C7, 14, 16, 18
LCD notes on Daniel Boone in 1773... 6C17
Brief note on Blue Jacket..6C17(4)
Map Clinch River, Powell's Valley area 6C40
Map Holston/ Tennessee/Virginia, 1884 .... 6C65
J. H. Huff, 1883: three--page map of Western Virginia-Kentucky.............
 .... page after 6C88 (1)
J. H. Huff. 1888: map Powell's and Clinch Valleys................... 6C88-90

Volume 7
Map of lands ceded by the Cherokee Indians 7C6
Memo of Henderson's Treaty at Watauga, 1775 .... 7C7
LCD notes on Col. Daniel Boone in 1775 .... 7C8,9
Benjamin Sharp letter (grandson of Benjamin Sharp) 7C26
D. B. Wenler[?], 1884[?] map: Head of Long Island and Fort Patrick
 Henry..7C28(2)
Map of Fort Patrick Henry and surroundings 7C29
R. J. Fickle, 1884, Battle of Long Island Flats 7C32
Battle of Island Flats, July 20, 1776..7C33
E .L. Wood letter, 1883... 7C36-36(1)
LCD notes on Teas Valley captivity story 7C50

Map: Teas Valley area, West Virginia... 7C54
Thomas Teas discussed... 7C56 (1-5)
LCD to William Callaway, 1884 .... 7C61-62
Thomas Callaway discussed 7C65-67
William S. Callaway letter, 1885...................................... 7C68
Henderson's Treaty, 1775 and William Crawford 7C75
LCD notes on Edward Boone killed in 1780 .... 7C82
V. B. Young, 1885 map, Bath County, Ky. 7C90
LCD notes for location of re-capture of girls................... 7C92
LCD list of persons telling of girls' capture, locations 7C93
LCD: "Where [Boone and Callaway] Girls Recaptured" 7C95
George Hamilton[?], Mt. Sterling, Ky., rough map of Flat Creek
  area 7C104
Boone and Callaway girls' captured 7C106 (1)
B. F. Maxey: map showing where girls rescued 7C107-108

Volume 8

LCD notes on Indian warfare in Rowan County, N.C. in 1760........... 8C1
LCD notes on attack at Fort Dobbs in 1760 .... 8C1 (1)
LCD notes on Indian forays in North Carolina in 1760... 8C1 (3)
LCD notes on Indian forays on the Yadkin in April 1759.... 8C39
Plats of Boone land grants in North Carolina in 1753 ..... 8C92
Capture of Boone and Callaway girls. 8C181
J. Rumpley, 1883 Map of Rowan County, NC. 8C188

Volume 9

W. E. White, 1887, map of Wilkes Co., N.C. 9C2
D. B. Dougherty, 1885, re: Jesse Boone land in Wilkes Co., N. C. ....
....9C50-50(2)
T. C. Land, 1885 map Watauga area 9C84
Lewis Green, 1886, map Yadkin River area..................... 9C90
Daniel Boone in Watauga and Wilkes Co., N.C. 9C99
Jonathan Horton, 1884, map Yadkin area......................... 9C102
Holander's map, Lewis Green, Benjamin Cutbirth......... 9C134
Map: Baker's House 9C147
Map: Stone Mountain area 9C162

LCD questions to Jesse Yates at Stony Hill, N.C., 1883 ....9C191-192
LCD questions to Jesse Yates, 1883 .... 9C199
Map: Yadkin area 9C223
Map: "Town of Boone" .... 9C after 223
Map: Boone's Camp 9C225

Volume 10
Elijah Dougherty, 1884, map Baker's Gap, Johnson Co., Tn. 10C35
Elijah Dougherty, 1884, map Cove Creek area 10C40
J. D. Imboden, map, southwest Virginia 10C50
D. B. Dougherty, 1884, map Boone Co., N.C. 10C56
W. H. Weaver, 1884, map Three Forks of South Fork of New
   River.. 10C58
W. H. Weaver, 1884 re: "Daniel Boone killed a bar" tree .... 10C69-69(4)
LCD notes: Boone's route over the mountains .... 10C73-73(1)
J. D. Imboden, 1884: Three-page map: Boone's possible route to
   Kentucky in 1769.. 10C77
Boone at Roan's Creek 10C79

Volume 11
LCD references for Ansel Goodman .... 11C23(1)
Rebecca Boone returned to North Carolina 11C29
LCD notes re: Josiah Phelps 11C51
Col. William Russell's Services 11C52
LCD notes: "A List of William Russell's letters to Col. Preston
   1775-1780" 11C54-55
LCD notes for Daniel Boone in 1778 .... 11C56-58
LCD sources for Paint Creek Expedition in 1778........................... 11C57
LCD notes re: Bartlett Searcy 11C71
LCD notes on Daniel Boone in 1778 .... 11C77-86
David Thompson re: saltmakers 11C81
Rebecca Boone returned to North Carolina in 1778 .... 11C83
Notes on Pompey, Negro interpreter 11C84,87
William Pogue's plat 11C88
Map: Limestone, Kenton's cabin, etc. 11C93
Douglas Brynner[?] letter, 1884 .... 11C95

H. D. Hixson Memos, 1886 .... 11C97

Volume 12
Long Hunters of Kentucky 12C68
LCD Notes on Bowman's Campaign 12C79-80

Volume 13
LCD notes on Daniel Boone in 1780 .... 13C1-7
LCD notes on Daniel Boone in 1782 .... 13C28-34
Joseph Ficklin letter, Jan 1, 1847. .... 13C80[?]
LCD notes: Patterson Papers, McClelland & Marshall's Note on
    KY .... 13C81-81(3)
Joseph Ficklin letter, Feb. 7 1847. LCD notes: John Steel, Dr.
    Dudley 13C82
Joseph Ficklin letter, Feb. 10, 1847. LCD notes: Box of Patterson
    Papers sent .... 13C83-83(1)
Joseph Ficklin letter, 1847 .... 13C84
Joseph Ficklin letter, 1847 .... 13C86-86(1)
LCD questions to Maj. Thomas H. Waters, 1862 .... 13C141
LCD questions to relatives of Philemon Waters 13C155-160
Map: Upper Blue Licks, Licking River, and streams 13C178
Map: Blue Licks Battleground 13C183
Diagram of Bryan Station as in 1782 .... 13C191

ACKNOWLEDGEMENTS AND GLOSSARY

After transcribing, with its adventures in frustration and discovery, I needed much help to make this work presentable. I would like to thank Linda Ward and Harry Enoch. Librarians, as always, are to be thanked as well: Andy Gary, Senior Archivist, and Daniel Aken, both at Clark County, Kentucky Public Library; Jackie Couture, Archivist at Eastern Kentucky University; Lee Grady, Reference Archivist at Wisconsin Historical Society.

GLOSSARY

& - and

&c – et cetera

Caintuck - Kentucky

Express – a messenger sent on horseback to a neighboring fort or to Virginia for help

fly – flee, escape

haws – edible fruit of the hawthorn tree

hollow - yell

Licking – Licking River in north central Kentucky

Shawnee / Shawnese / Shawanoes – spellings for Shawnee tribe

suck – an eddy or whirlpool

stroud - a coarse woolen cloth, blanket, or garment formerly used by the British in bartering with the North American Indians. [from Wikipedia]

swivel - cannon

treed - hid behind a tree

trepanning – drilling a burr hole through the skull after a head injury

INDEX

Draper's system of numbering pages is retained throughout the body of this work, including the index. The first number is the volume number, the letter following it is the series (C in this work), and the next number is the page number. For instance, an interview appearing in volume 7 on page 5 would be numbered 7C5.

To account for interviews with more than one page, Draper additionally assigned numbers 1,2,3, etc.. So if the interview contained 3 pages it would appear as 7C5-5(1,2,3). Cardinal numbers are omitted within letters/interviews. After the first page, numbering appears within a letter or interview as **(1), (2),** etc. Therefore the last page of 7C5-5(1,2,3) would be designated **(3)**.

ADAMS 13C79
    Capt. 12C2(16)
    David, Ensign 12C8(1)
    Samuel 12C26
ADAIR, James 13C85
ADKINS, John 13C74, 13C74(2), 13C79(1,2)
ALCORN, George 12C2(11)
ALEXANDER, Mark 7C14
ALLEY, James 12C8
    Samuel 6C70(1,2)
ALLEN, Col. John 12C44(2), 12C45(4)
    Thomas, Maj. 13C199(2)
    Zach 13C38(5)
ANDERSON, Col. 7C24(1,2)
    H. C. 13C14
    Jacob 12C41
APPLEGATE, John Zebiah 12C24(10)
ARBUCKLE, Matthew, Capt.7C17, 7C77(2)
ARCHER, Dr. Branch 13C20
    John, Col. 13C20
    Hon. William S. 13c20
ARMSTRONG 11C62(19)
ARNOLD, Elizabeth 13C110-110(2)
    John 13C110
    Margaret 13C110
    Mrs. 13C110(2)
    Nicholas 13C110
    William, 13C74
ARTER, John 4C24, 4C24(4, 12, 16)

ASH 13C124(2)
    George 11C62(36)
    Mrs. 13C124
ASHBY, John, Capt. 6C94
ASKIN, Gen. 12C38(6)
ATTAKULAKULLA, 7C6
ASBURY, Daniel 11C62, 11C62(10)
AYRE, Joseph 12C54(8)

BAILEY, John 12C24(11), 12C64
BALLARD 11C62(35), 12C38(6)
    Bland 12C2(11)
    Bland W., Capt. 12C38(6)
    Bland W., Maj. 12C2(11)
BALLENGER/BALLINGER
    Jane 12C46
    John L. 12C46
    Joseph 12C46(2)
    Joseph, Capt. 12C62(23)
BAPTISTS 12C62(27-28), 12C64
BARBOUR, James 12C2(9,11)
BARNETT, Col. 12C49(1)
    Elizabeth 12C62
    James 12C54(9)
BARTON, Benjamin 4C86
BAUBIN, Charles,11C96
BAUGHMAN'S DEFEAT 1783 12C62(26-27)
    Henry 12C62(26)
    his mother 12C62(26)
BEAN'S STATION 12C62(28)
BEARGRASS 11C62(28), 12C38(6),

Page numbering order: Volume number, series number, page number (with page numbers within interviews cited parenthetically after the primary citation) Ex: 7C5-5(1,2,3).

12C54(6) 13C114, 13C145
BEARS 9C204(3)
BEASLEY 13C79(18)
    Charles 13C74, 13C74(3), 13C79(16,17)
    James, 7C21, 13C74(3), 13C79(16)
    John 13C74, 13C74(3), 13C79(8, 14, 16, 17)
    Major 7C1, 7C3
    Mr. 13C74(3), 13C115(1)
    Nathaniel, Gen. 13C79(8)
    William, 7C1, 7C3
    William, Sr. 13C74
BEDINGER, G. M. 13C25
    Maj., 11C62(19)
BELL 13C79(4)
    Thomas 13C74, 13C74(3), 13C79(1)
BELLOS, Peter 12C24(7)
BENTON, 4C31
BERMAN, Irvine 13C63
BERRY, Benjamin 7C3
    Francis 7C21
    James 12C26, 13C39, 13C42, 13C44
BEVAN, James 4C61
BIBB'S *KENTUCKY REPORTS*, 11C113(2)
BICKLEY, William 11C97
BIG BONE LICK 12C1(1)
BIG LUMP 9C60, 9C74, 9C79, 9C130(2)
BIG SANDY RIVER 4C26(8), 4C30
BIRD, Col. 12C2(12)
    Henry 11C108
BLACK, James 4C75
    Joseph 7C23
BLACK FISH / Cotta-wa-na-go 4C26(14), 4C46, 11C98, 12C1(2)
BLACK HOOF 11C62(22, 37), 13C76-76(1), 13C77, 13C85
BLACK STUMP 11C62(17)
BLACKAMORE 12C49
BLACKAMORE/BLACKMORE FORT 4C28(1-8), 6C70(1,2), 6C93,
6C96, 7C11, 12C49(1), 12C62(63)
BLACKBURN 12C14(7)
    Arthur 7C21
BLACKFORD,
    Joseph 12C22(3), 12C23,12C24(7)
BLACKMAN, James 6C103
BLACK'S FORT 7C11, 12C46(1)
BLEDSOE, A., Col. 7C23
    Sally 7C25
BLOCK HOUSE (Martin's Old Station) 6C93
BLOUNT, 12C62(3)
    John Gray, 7C20
BLUE JACKET 6C17(4)
BLUE LICKS 4C26(12), 4C30(map), 4C31(map), 4C32(2), 4C33, 4C44, 4C50, 4C130, 6C104, 7C 1st page, 7C80(1), 7C107(map), 9C88(1), 11C12, 11C28, 11C33, 11C44, 11C46, 11C62(2), 11C62(14),13C139, 13C178, 13C192,13C193
    Lower Blue Licks 4C30, 7C80(1),7C81, 7C82, 7C85,7C86, 7C93(map)
    Upper Blue Licks 7C80, 7C81, 7C82,7C84, 7C85,7C86,7C87, 7C91, 7C92, 7C95, 11C11(1),11C12, 13C178 (map),
BLUE LICKS BATTLE 4C31, 4C50, 7C115(3), 11C22, 11C62(30), 11C62(32), 11C98, 12C1, 12C1(12), 12C2(8,9), 12C24, 12C24(2,4,7), 12C26-29, 12C38(1,2,3,5), 12C54(6),13C56(1), 13C66, 13C79(12,13,14,17,18), 13C178 (map), 13C13C183, 13C193(2), 13C198, 13C200, 13C200(3)
BLUE LICKS BATTLE – British Account
13C114-114(1)
BOGGS, Henry 4C43(1)
BOONE MANUSCRIPT, destroyed 7C26
BOONE, A. G. 13C20
    BOONE, Daniel 4C83-87,

Page numbering order: Volume number, series number, page number (with page numbers within interviews cited parenthetically after the primary citation) Ex: 7C5-5(1,2,3).

404

5C54(5), 12C2(10), 12C23
alcohol or whiskey
4C33(5)
account book 4C75
adopted 4C46,
11C62(10), 11C81
and Henry Hamilton
11C108, 11C110
and Simon Girty
11C62(35)
and cannon 11C108-109
appearance 4C55,
in old age 7C25
appointed Justice of
Peace for Transylvania
Company 7C20
at Blue Licks 4C5,
13C193(2)
at Boonesborough,
11C6, 11C10, 11C11,
11C24, 11C25(1),
11C28, 12C26
at Cross Plains 13C192
at Three Forks of
Johnson 11C89
at Three Forks of
Kentucky 13C13
books 4C55
Boone's camp 9C225
Boone's cave 4C31,
4C133
Boone's Company
12C2(6)
Boone's first fort 4C31
Boone's intials on tree
13C9(3)
Boone's Knob 4C157
Boone's Lick 4C61
Boone's new fort, east
side of Lick Branch,
4C31
Boone's Station 4C31,
4C44, 12C2(6), 13C40,
13C79(4)

bringing family to
Kentucky 11C105,
13C193, 12C26
burial in Kentucky
4C33(2)
burial of Edward Boone
7C82, 7C83, 7C85,
7C87
captivity and escape
4C33(3), 4C44, 4C46,
9C58(1, 2, 3), 9C68,
9C79(1-4), 11C28,
11C33, 11C38, 11C44,
11C62(2,34,5,6,7,8,
11,12), 11C96,
11C96(3),11C97
captured by Tarleton
12C23
LCD references:
13C 15-19, 21,22
character 11C108
coffin 4C57
Colonel 12C62(10)
court martial 11C61
death 7C25
depositions 6C103,
6C105,
7C80-81), 7C91, 11C64
father 8C11
gun Tick-licker 4C33(4)
homeplace in North
Carolina 10C79 (map)
hunting in Missouri,
4C36, 11C100. 4C61,
4C43, 4C44, 4C53,
4C55, 7C43(1)
in Charleston. SC
4C75(1), 11C107-108
in Missouri 11C98,
11C100, 11C105,106
in North Carolina,
4C48, 9C58, 9C60,
9C84, 9C99, 13C193(1)
map
Yadkin area 9C2

Page numbering order: Volume number, series number, page number (with page numbers within interviews cited parenthetically after the primary citation) Ex: 7C5-5(1,2,3).

in Ohio during captivity 11C62(11-12)
in Pennsylvania in 1781 13C19
in Virginia Legislature, 1781 13C15, 13C18, 19
Indian attacks
Powell's Valley 6C7, 6C14, 6C16, 6C18, 7C23(3), 7C25
Twitty's 4C81, 7C76
"killed a bar" 10C69(1)
killed Indian 4C45, 7C27, 9C79(2)
last illness 4C57
LCD notes/chronology
1772-1773 4C128-128(1)
1773 6C17
1775 7C10-13
1776-1776 7C15
1778 11C 56-68, 77-86
1780 13C1-7
1781 13C1-7, 15, 16, 19, 22
1782 13C28-34
Letters to Col. Arthur Campbell from William Fleming – Boone delivers gunpowder 7C15
to William Preston 4C77
Evan Shelby 4C80
mentioned in: Arthur Campbell, 6C96
long absence 6C70(2), 9C137, 11C100-101
Militia 11C75
Militia Company in Rowan Co. NC.11C107
Narrative 12C39(11)
officiated at marriage 7C15
opinion of *Mountain Muse* 7C43(1)
on Indian campaign to Piqua 7C22
Paint Creek Expedition 11C62(14,15), 11C65, 11C66
pamphlet 9C139
promise to surrender 11C62(12,13)11C76, 11C98
rescue of captive girls 4C49, 7C77(1,2), 7C97, 11C64, 12C6(2)
return to Kentucky from Missouri 4C51, 4C59, 4C61
return to North Carolina from Kentucky 11C61
route over the mountains, 10C73
rumor of death 7C15(1)
saltmakers 11C17, 11C61, 62, 11C62(14), 11C71
settlement and pre-emption right 11C112-113, 113(1-3)
siege of Boonesborough 4C33(4), 4C46, 9C60-60(1), 9C68, 11C62(16), 11C76, 11C98
siege of Boonesborough Treaty 11C76, 11C98
tobacco story 4C52
understanding of Indian warfare 6C70(1)
visitor in Missouri 7C43-43(5)
whiskey bottle incident 13C13, 13C14
with George Rogers Clark 11C14
with John T. Fauntleroy 12C24(6)
with John Yates 9C60,

Page numbering order: Volume number, series number, page number (with page numbers within interviews cited parenthetically after the primary citation) Ex: 7C5-5(1,2,3).

9C202
with Hugh McGary
12C16
with Michael Stoner
4C132
to recall surveyors
6C94, 6C104
with James Wade
13C9(3)
with tame beavers
6C75(1)

BOONE, Daniel M. (son of Daniel)
character 4C55
hunting in Missouri 4C51
not a hunter 4C55

BOONE, Edward (brother of Daniel)
hunting with Daniel 9C68(5)
killed, in 1780 7C80, 7C81, 7C82, 7C83, 7C84, 7C91
where killed 4C31
"Neddie", 9C68(5)

BOONE, George (brother of Daniel)
mentioned 9C130
land in North Carolina, 8C92

BOONE, Hannah (sister of Daniel)
children 4C99
married Pennington 4C99
widow of John Stuart 4C99

BOONE, Harriet (daughter of Jesse, granddaughter of Daniel)
joke 11C111(5)

BOONE, Israel (son of Daniel)
7C81, 7C85, 13C193(2)

BOONE, James (son of Daniel)
killed 4C26(6), 9C130

BOONE, Jemima (daughter of Daniel)
appearance 4C51,4C1
captured - see capture [3] of
Boone and Callaway girls
mentioned 12C26
wedding 4C49

BOONE, Jesse
appearance 9C91
character 9C91
funeral mentioned 4C55
hunting with Daniel 4C33, 4C33(1), 4C60, 9C87, 9C88(1), 9C90
in North Carolina 9C50
in Tennessee, 9C88(1) 9C90

BOONE, John 8C11
land in North Carolina 8C82

BOONE, Mrs. 12C26

BOONE, Nathan (son of Daniel) 4C43(1)
and Daniel's illness 4C55,4C59, 7C11
hunting in Missouri 4C51, C52, 4C55
mentioned 11C107, 11C111(3)

BOONE, Rebecca, wife of Daniel 4C48
birth of child 7C11,12C100-101
mentioned 12C26-29
not at Siege 4C46
profane letter 11C61
returned to North Carolina in 1778 4C33,11C29, 11C83,11C107

BOONE, S. 12C23

BOONE, Sallie (daughter of Jesse) 9C91

Page numbering order: Volume number, series number, page number (with page numbers within interviews cited parenthetically after the primary citation) Ex: 7C5-5(1,2,3).

BOONE, Samuel (brother of Daniel) 4C66,12C107
BOONE, Samuel (nephew of Daniel) 12C107
BOONE, Samuel, Capt.13C34
BOONE, Squire (brother of Daniel) 12C26, 12C64, 13C193
    a Tory, 11C107
    at Harrodsburg 12C24(10), 12C26
    at Siege 11C104
    at Snoddy's Fort 4C 26(9)
    cannon 4C33,4C46,4C47, 4C48, 13C191
    disagreement 4C26,4C27
    family wilentucky in 1779 4C26(9)
    land in North Carolina 8C92
    in Shelby Co. Ky. 12C26
    officiated wedding 1776 7C97
    wife 13C193(2)
    wounded in heel 4C33,4C46
BOONE, Squire (father of Daniel) 8C11
BOONE, North Carolina, 10C41
BOONE'S STATION 12C2(6), 13C40
BOONESBOROUGH 4C24, 4C24(15), 4C30,4C31, 4C33(4,6), 4C66, 4C77(1), 4C79, 4C80, 4C133, 4C133(1), 7C3, 7C11,7C14, 7C22, 7C72, 7C95, 7C97, 7C115, 8C181, 9C77, 11C6, 11C10, 11C16, 11C21, 11C24, 11C25, 11C25(1),11C28, 11C33, 1C38,11C46, 11C51, 11C61, 11C62, 11C62(1, 3,4,5,6, 11, 13, 14, 15), 11C65, 11C83, 11C96(3), 11C108, 11C110, 11C111, 11C111(1), 11C111(5). 12C2(7,10,11,25), 12C6(2), 12C16(2), 12C26-29
BOONESBOROUGH, SIEGE 4C24, 4C24(11), 4C33(2), 4C44, 4C46, 4C47, 4C78, 4C79, 7C22, 9C58, 11C62(16), 11C76, 11C88, 11C98, 11C101, 12C2(15,16,18,20,21,23), 12C5(7), 12C16(2)
BOONESBOROUGH SCHOOL 11C111, 11C111(2)
BOONESBOROUGH TWO FORTS 9C68(6)
BORDEN, Benjamin 12C41
BORDEN'S Grant 12C41
BORDEN IMMIGRATION 12C62
BOSTON, 4C81
BOTHWELL, Lord 13C194
BOUCHELLE, Thomas 9C68, 9C129(2)
BOUTE?, Henry 12C8
BOWMAN 11C62(11,17, 19, 22, 24), 12C1(4,5,8,9), 12C62(1)
    Col, 4C26(12), 12C38(7)
    Abraham Col. 12C22(2)
    J.B., 12C74
    John, Col. 12C2(4,9), 12C26, 12C38, 12C38(1,2,4)
    John 12C38(1)
    Joseph, Capt. 12C38(1)
    Maj. 12C16(7)
    Jonas, Maj.12C38
    Joseph, Maj. 12C38
BOWMAN'S CAMPAIGN 4C26(13,14,15), 11C51, 11C62(17,22,24), 11C108, 12C1-1(12), 12C38, 12C62(39) 12C81
BOWMAN'S REGIMENT 12C22(2)
BOWMAN'S STATION 12C38,

Page numbering order: Volume number, series number, page number (with page numbers within interviews cited parenthetically after the primary citation) Ex: 7C5-5(1,2,3).

12C38(7)
BOWMAR, Herman 12C38-38(7)
 obituary 12C39(11)
BOYD, Mrs. Joseph B. 11C110, 13C20
BOYERS, Henry 13C44
BRADDOCK'S DEFEAT 11C62(11,17,19, 22, 24), 13C85
BRADDOCK, Gen. 13C76(3)
BRADFORD, Daniel 13C103
 John 13C103
BRADLEY, Benjamin C. 13C110, 13C110(3)
 William 13C74
BRASHEAR, Marsham 12C24(11)
BRECKENRIDGE, Alexander 12C47
BRIANT, David 7C25
BRIDGES 12C22(2)
 James 12C24(11)
BRIGGS, Benjamin 12C2(17,19), 12C22(2)
BRIGHT, George 12C54(8)
BRINKER, 12C38(1)
BRISCOE, Jeremiah 12C54(8)
BROADHURST, ___ 4C82
BROOKE, Lt 13C17
BROOKS, Samuel 11C62, 11C62(10)
 William 11C62, 11C62(10)
BROWN 12C62(37), 13C131(1), 13C139, 13C145(2), 13C161
 Col. 13C121(1)
 Daniel 12C8, 12C24(11)
 Ham A. 9C68(10)
 Hamilton 9C68(10)
 James 12C22(3), 12C26-29
 Jemima, Mrs. 9C68(1-11)
 John 9C137, 11C75, 12C22(3), 12C24(7), 12C24(10)
 Joseph C. 11C103
 Sarah 9C68(10, 11C75
BRYAN/BRYANT,
 Abner 4C43(10, 4C45, 4C50, 4C53, 4C55, 11C105
 David 4C48
 Daniel 7C43
 Elijah 4C33(6), 4C34-34(1,2), 4C55, 11C105
 Emily 4C40
 Etta 9C139
 George 7C93
 Henry, 4C60
 James, 4C33(6), 4C41(1), 4C42, 4C48, 4C55,4C62, 11C105
 J. Wiseman, son of Abner 11C105
 Jonathan 4C33(6), 4C48, 4C50, 4C55, 11C105
 Mary 4C41(1), 4C42
 Mr. 4C54, 4C59, 4C59, 4C60
 Mrs. 4C58
 Polly 9C139
 Susan 4C60
 William 12C62(16), 13C193(3)
BRYAN'S/BRYANT'S STATION 4C31, 4C32(1), 4C48, 4C49, 5C53, 7C21, 7C86, 11C105, 11C107, 12C2(6,8), 12C38(6), 12C62(19), 13C56, 13C63-66, 13C74, 13C79(1,2,13,14,16,17), 13C110, 13C114, 13C115, 13C117(6), 13C117(1), 13C188(3), 13C195
BRYAN'S STATION SIEGE 13C63-66, 13C191 diagram
BUCHANAN, Capt. 7C21
 Jane 12C47(2)
 William, Capt. 13C34

Page numbering order: Volume number, series number, page number (with page numbers within interviews cited parenthetically after the primary citation) Ex: 7C5-5(1,2,3).

BUFORD, A. 6C105
BULGER, E. 12C23
    Edward 12C1(1, 7), 12C24(6), 13C79(14)
    Maj. 13C79(14, 15)
BULL PASTURE 13C53, 13C54
BULLOCK, Nathaniel 11C62, 62(10)
BUNCH family at McNitt's Defeat 12C62(23)
    Mrs. 12C62(33, 41)
BURNT STATION – see 6Kincheloe's Station
BUSH, Elkanah 12C2(22)
    Philip S. 1C194
    Pleasant 4C66
    William 7C11
BUSH SETTLEMENT 4C66
BUSH, William, Capt. 4C66
    Willis 4C66
BUSHON, Jacob 12C8
    John 12C8
BUTLER, ___ 12C62(44)
    Big Jim 12C62(32)
    John 12C14(3)
    Mann 12C15
    "Old Butler", servant 11C103
    Richard, Col. 13C22
    Simon – see Kenton
    William 12C14(3)
BUTLER'S HISTORY 13C39
BUTLER'S STATION 12C14(3)
BUTTS, Jefferson 13C9(3)
    Peggy Wade 13C9(3)
BYNUM, Hon. W. P. 7C20

CADE, Baylus 7C41
CAIN, James 12C54(5), 12C65
CALDWELL, Gen. Robert 13C200(1)
    Major 13C114, 13C114(1)
CALIFORNIA 4C43(1)
CALK, William 7C3

CALLAWAY 13C53
    family 7C11, 7C77(2)
    Betsy 7C15, 7C97, 7C15-16
    Caleb 12C26
    Col. 13C52(2)
    Elijah 7C67
    Fanny 4C67, 9C68(7), 12C26
    Flanders 4C33(2), 4C34(1), 4C54, 6C105, 7C20, 7C43(1), 7C81, 7C87, 7C97, 9C68(7), 11C6(1), 11C62(5),12C26
    James, Capt. 4C34(1), 4C54
    Col. 12C26
    James, Dr. 7C67
    James 11C62, 11C62(8,9,10)
    Jan Denes 9C137-138
    Jemima Boone 4C51, 4C55
    John (Jack) 13C34
    John 7C61, 7C65, 7C68(7), 11C65, 13C34, 13C51
    John B. 7C80-81
    Joseph 7C67
    Micajah 11C62,62(10)
    Prudence 9C134, 9C135, 9C138, 9C140
    Richard, Col. 4C79, 4C80, 7C22, 7C87, 7C87(8), 7C130(1), 11C62(28), 12C2(24),12C26-29
    Richard (son of Col.) 13C52(1)
    Samuel 7C67, 9C137-138
    T. S., 9C130(1,2), 9C133
    Thomas 7C65, 7C67

Page numbering order: Volume number, series number, page number (with page numbers within interviews cited parenthetically after the primary citation) Ex: 7C5-5(1,2,3).

William 7C65
CALMES, Marquis, Sr., Col. 7C3
    Marquis, Jr. 7C3
CAMBLE, Major 12C24(7)
    William 12C24(7)
CAMERON, Angus 12C24(6,11), 13C123
CAMPBELL 7C23, 7C24, 7C76, 12C14(3)
    Arthur 4C78, 4C80, 4C81, 7C bef 15
    Arthur, Mr. 12C22(3)
    Arthur, Col. 12C26
    Col., 6C96
    Maj. 4C77 4C77(1), 6C96
    John 13C38(1)
    John, Capt. 7C21, 7C23, 11C62(23,26)
    John B., Col. 13C96(1)
    Gen. 12C54(9)
    Miss 13C205
    Mr. 12C38(7), 13C74
    James 13C153(1)
    Mary Anne 13C38(1)
    Mrs. 13C153(1)
    Sally 13C153(1)
    William 7C21, 11C62(23), 12C22(3)
CAMPBELL and CLEVELAND, Tories 7C22(1)
CANADA 12C45(2)
CANNON 11C108-9, 12C49, 12C62(42), 12C107
CAPERTON, Adam 13C40, 13C42, 13C51
CAPTAIN TOMMY 13C153
CAPTURE OF BOONE AND CALLAWAY GIRLS IN 1776 4C31, 4C49, 4C66, 4C67(1), 7C15, 7C17, 7C20(1), 7C43(4), 7C44, 7C67, 7C72-72(1), 7C72-72(1), 7C80-81, 7C84, 7C92, 7C93, 7C95, 7C97, 7C99, 7C100(2), 7C106(1), 7C107, 7C115, 8C181, 9C68, 9C68(6), 12C6(2), 12C26-29
CAPTURED AT BLUE LICKS, 1782
    Allen, Zach 12C38(5), 12C39(11)
    Beasley, Charles 13C74(3), 13C79(17)
    Beasley, John 13C 74, 74(3), 13C79(17)
    Humble, Michael 12C26-29
    Ledgerwood, James 12C26-29, 13C200(1)
    McMurtry, John 12C26-29, 13C96(2,3,4) 13C200(1, 4, 13C211-213
    Morgan, John 13C203
    Reynolds, ___ 13C74
    Rose, Lewis 12C26-29, 13C96(2,3,4), 13C200(1), 13C211-212
    Yocum, Jesse 13C50, 13C96(2,3,4) 13C200(4, 7)
    Captured and shot: Kennedy, John 12C26-29
CAPTURED by BRITISH
    Boone, Daniel in 1781, 13C17, 13C21, 13C22
    Floyd, John 12C47(2)
    Lyons, Col. 13C25
    Kinlow, Francis 13C25
    Sanders, Joseph, Capt. 13C25
    Swearingen, Thomas 13C25
CAPTURED by INDIANS – see saltmakers
    Ash, George at Loughey's Defeat,

Page numbering order: Volume number, series number, page number (with page numbers within interviews cited parenthetically after the primary citation) Ex: 7C5-5(1,2,3).

411

11C62(36)
Callaway, John (Jack) in 1782, 13C34
Campbell, [William] 11C62(23)
Clark, George 12C62
John 12C56[10]
Cowan, Mrs. John 4C26(5)
Crawford, Wm., Col. 7C56(4)
Daviess, Mrs. and 5 children, 12C62(6)
James 12C62(38)
Polly 12C62(7)
Davis, Isaac, son of Cornelius, 13C124
Estill, Monk 7C22, 13C51
Gatliffe, Mrs. 13C45, 1356(1)
Grieste, John 13C45(15)
Hamblin family 7C21(1)
Hoy, Jones in 1782, 13C34
Jennings 12C49, 49(1)
Jones, Moses 12C54(4,5)
Jones, Mrs., and son 12C54(4,5)
Kennedy, John 13C79(24)
Kenton, Simon 4C54, 11C62(6, 7, 10),12C13(13), 12C26-29, 12C62(10)
Long, ___ 5C54(6)
Mrs. 11C62(30)
Maginty and companion. 1753, 7C first unnumbered pages
McConnell boys escaped 12C26-29
Jones, Mrs., and son 12C54(4,5)

McIlvaine, Moses 11C110
Montgomery, Mrs. John, two sons and two daughters 12C13(1,2-3), 12C2(24), 12C13(2-3), 12C45
Negro woman 4C26(13) and 3 children 12C45-45(4), 13C124
Pey, Margaret /Peggy Polly 13C54, 3C51
Polk, Mrs. and four children 11C62(36), 13C120, 13C125
Polk, William 13C120
Pompey 11C84, 87, 12C62(19)
Rogers, Joseph 11C62(29)
Ruddell, Abram and Stephen 11C63
Russell, Mrs. and four children 12C13(2)
Russell, Mrs., and family 12C45-45(4)
Sanders, Samuel 7C14
Searcy, Barlett 12C26-29
Shanks girls 13C79
Shores, Thomas in 1777 12C30
Sovereigns, Mrs. and daughter 12C26-29
Stewart/Stuart, John 4C59
Tackett, Hannah in 1774 7C45(1)
Teas, Thomas in 1774, 7C35-35(1-5), 7C36(1-3), 7C56(1-5)
Walker, Ann 4C26(2)
Waters, Philemon 13C16(1-14), 13C96(2,3,4), 13CC129,

Page numbering order: Volume number, series number, page number (with page numbers within interviews cited parenthetically after the primary citation) Ex: 7C5-5(1,2,3).

13C131131(9),13C132. 13C133-136, 13C137, 13C138-139
    White, Ambrose 11C110
CAPTURED BY KENTUCKIANS on Logan's Campaign, 12C1(11),12C47, 47(2), 12C62(11)
    "Capt. Logan" 12C62(13)
    Moluntha's queen 11C62(30), 12C47
CARA___, Andrew, 7C21
CARLETON, Guy 11C91(1,2,3)
CARMICHAEL, Patt 12C8
CARTER 4C27(2)
    Col. 11C107, 11C109
    Catherine 4C26
    Thomas W. 4C26, 6C94
CARPENTER, Sollomon 12C24(6)
CARSWELL, Henry 7C14(7), 12C14(5), 12C26-29
CARTMAN, Jos. 12C8
CARTWRIGHT & wife 12C49(4)
CASEY 7C23, 7C24(2)
    Col. 12C13, 13C14
    John 12C14(4,5)
    Mrs. Col. William 12C13
    Nancy 12C14(4)
    William, 7C21
    William, Col. 12C13, 12C14(2,4,7)
CASEY'S STATION 12C14(3)
CASSITY, Jacob 7C100(2)
CASTLEWOOD(S) 4C24, 4C26, 4C26(4), 4C47(2), 6C96, 7C21(1)
CATHER, Edward
CATHEY, John 11C107
CATON, Jesse 4C53
CAVANAUGH, Ruth Estill 13C52
CHAPLINE. Abraham 12C22(3), 12C24(7), 12C24(11), 13C199(2)
    Abraham, Capt. 12C23,

12C24(5,7)
    Isaac 13C199(2)
CHAPMAN, Job 12C26
CHARETTE 4C33(6), 6C75(1)
    Creek, 4C41(1)
    Village, 4C34(1)
CHARLESTON, SC 4C75(1)
CHEROKEE 4C8, 4C21, 4C22, 22(1), 4C81, 6C96, 7C6 map of lands ceded by, 7C17, 7C24(1), 7C77(1, 2), 9C129(1,2), 9C204(1), 11C61(31), 12C14(5), 12C24(3), 12C26-29, 12C54(8), 12C62(1), 13C76(1,2,3)
CHEROKEE WAR 7C6, 7C17, 7C21
CHILDERS 13C79
CHILDRESS, William 13C74
CHILLICOTHE 4C79, 11C48, 11C62 (26,29), 13C76(3), 13C79(18),13C131, 13C131(5)
    Little Chillicothe 11C62(10, 12, 24, 25, 29, 32),12C1(1), 12C24(2), 12C38(4), 13C76(1)
    New Chillicothe 11C14, 11C62(10,12, 17, 23
    Old Chillicothe 12C1(1), 12C24(2), 13C76(10, 12C38(4), 13C76(1,3)
CHRISTMAS 5C54(3), 12C62 (31,34,35)
CHRISTIAN 13C21, 13C22
    Expedition 7C21(1), 11C52
    Regiment 12C44
    Col. 12C44, 13C21, 13C22, 13C24(1)
    William, Col. 13C23
    Mr. 13C24(2, 3)
CHRISTIAN UNION 13C63
CINCINNATI 4C30
CIST'S *Cincinnati Advertiser* 13C138-139

Page numbering order: Volume number, series number, page number (with page numbers within interviews cited parenthetically after the primary citation) Ex: 7C5-5(1,2,3).

CLARK 11C62(24, 25), 12C26, 13C114
   George 12C56
   John 12C56
   Robert 12C45
CLARK, GEORGE ROGERS 12C2(5,13), 12C16(14), 12C24(5,6)
   Campaign - 1780
     4C31, 11C16, 11C48, 11C62(28, 29), 11C80, 12C2(12),12C38 12C62(39), 13C53, 13C79, 13C203
   Campaign – 1782
     11C16, 11C48, 11C62(30), 11C80, 12C1-12, 12C1(19, 12C6412C2(18), 12C38(4), 12C64
   at Kaskaskia
     1C48, 12C2(18), 12C24(6), 13C76(2,3)
   at Piqua
     11C62(18)
   at Vincennes
     7C24(1), 12C49(1)
   North Western Regiment 12C2(14)
   Col. 7C24, 12C2(14, 15, 16)
   General 4C31, 11C10, 11C11, 11C14, 11C26, 11C33, 11C51, 11C62(14, 24, 32), 12C2(5,6, 3), 12C16, 12C26-29, 12C38, 12C38(1), 12C44, 12C45(2), 12C49, 12C52, 13C53, 13C196
   Robert 12C52
     Sol 12C52, 12C56-56(2)
CLARK, Henry C., Col. 7C24(2),
   Jane, Mrs. 12C44
   John 7C25, 12C22(3) 12C24(7
   Joshua 12C62(38)
   Robert 12C56
   Solomon, Mrs. 12C52(2), 12C56(1)
CLARKE, John 12C22(3)
CLAY, Porter 12C45(1)
   Elizabeth 12C45(1)
   Mrs. Porter 12C45(1)
CLAYTON, Ralph 7C3
CLEAR, George 12C24(10)
CLERK, John 12C24(11)
CLEVELAND 7C23, 7C24
   Ben 7C24(2)
   Ben, Col. 9C58
CLEVELAND'S REGIMENT 12C14(3)
CLINCH MOUNTAIN 4C26(6)
CLINCH RIVER 6C40, 13C123, 13C124
   Old Neil Ford at, 4C26(6)
CLINCH VALLEY 6C89
CLINGMAN, T.C. 10C69(1)
COALTER, John 4C54
COBURN Family 12C 24
   James, Capt. 12C24(2)
   John, Judge 11C110
   Samuel, Capt. 12C24(2), 12C26
COCK, Capt. 7C21
   William, Capt. 7C75
COFER/COPHER, Jesse 4C66, 11C62, 11C62(10)
COFFY, Ambros(e) 12C24(10)
COLDEN, Cadwallader, 13C85
COLEFOOT/COLTFOOT, John 13C38, 13C40, 13C42, 13C88
COLLINS, Elisha 4C86
COLVILLE, Andrew 7C21
COMBS, Benjamin 7C3
   Cuthbert 7C3
   Enos 7C3

Page numbering order: Volume number, series number, page number (with page numbers within interviews cited parenthetically after the primary citation) Ex: 7C5-5(1,2,3).

John 7C3
Joseph 7C3
CONJURERS 11C62(19, 27, 31, 32)
CONLEY'S HEIRS vs. CHILES 13C39-48(1)
CONSOLA, Harmon, Capt. 13C123
COOK, David 13C38, 13C44, 13C56-56(1)
    Henry 12C14
COOLEY 8C11(1)
    William, 9C138, 9C149, 13C193(2)
COOMBS, William 12C24(10)
COOPER, Ben, Col. 11C98
    Betty 11C103
    Frank 11C98-104
    James 7C17
    Joseph 11C102
    Sarshall 11C98- 103-104
    Stephen 11C98-104
COOPER'S FORT 11C102
COOPER SHOP
    at Bryan's Station 12C62(19)
    at Danville 12C62(23)
CORN CRIB EVENT 12C26-29, 12C38(2)
CORN PONE 12C49
CORNSTALK, Shawnee Chief 4C8, 4C81, 7C17, 7C77(2)
CORNWALLIS 13C22, 13C131(7)
    Lord 12C45(3),13C23(1)
COSHOW, Jonathan 4C57
    Mrs, 4C57
COUNCIL HOUSE 11C62(18, 19)
COUCHMAN, Frederick 13C39, 13C43
COURT-MARTIAL 11C33
COWAN 4C27(2), 12C26
    killed, 6C94

Ann 4C26(4-16)
James 12C22, 22(3), 12C24(2), 12C26-29
John 4C24, 4C26(4), 12C22(3), 12C24(7)
John, Mrs. 4C26(5)
William 4C24, 4C26, 4C26(2)
COX, Col. 13C119, 13C121
    David 13C121(1)
    Isaac, Col. 13C121(1)
    James, Gen. 13C121(1)
    Mary 13C121(1)
COX'S STATION 13C123, 13C124(2), 13C154
CRAB ORCHARD, KY 4C26(2), 12C24(8), 12C56, 12C62-62(1-45), 12C64, 12C64(1)
CRAB ORCHARD INCIDENT, 1783 12C62(20-23)
CRAFT, Mrs. 13C153(1)
CRABLE, John 12C24(7)
CRABTREE, Isaac 7C24
    William 6C95
CRADLEBAUGH, William 12C2(6)
CRAIG, Capt. 13C79(10), 13C115
    Elijah 12C24(2)
    James, Rev. 4C57
    Jeremiah 13C74, 13C74(3), 13C194(1), 13C195
    Jerry 13C79(2)
    John 13C74, 13C117(5), 13C194(1)
    John, Capt. 13C110, 110(2), 13C117(3), 13C194-195
    John, Jr. 13C74, 13C74(1, 4)
    John, Sr. 13C74, 13C79(9)
    Mary Hawkins 13C194

Page numbering order: Volume number, series number, page number (with page numbers within interviews cited parenthetically after the primary citation) Ex: 7C5-5(1,2,3).

Sally 13C194(1)
Toliver 13C194
CRAVENS[?] ___ 12C62(45)
CRAWFORD 12C24(10)
    Wm., Col. 7C56(3,4), 11C62(33, 34)
CREEK WAR, General Jackson's 7C25
CREWS, James 12C2(14)
CRIM, William 13C44
CRITTENDEN, John, Maj. 12C38(1)
CROCKETT, Maj. Anthony 12C49(1)
    Arthur 13C203
CROGHAN. George (Journal) 11C112(1)
CROSS PLAINS 13C193(1)
CROW, John 12C22(3), 12C24(7)
    William 12C22(3), 12C24(7)
CRUTCHFIELD 12C54(1)
    Mr. 12C49(4)
    Mrs. 12C49(4)
    John 12C49(4)
    Thomas 12C49(4)
CUMBERLAND GAP 6C52, 6C17, 6C80 (map), 6C88(1) (map)
CUMMINGS. Charles, Rev. 7C21
CUNNINGHAM. Mrs, 7C93
CUPS AND SAUCERS 12C46(2)
CURD, John 12C8
    Joseph 6C94
CUTBIRTH, Benjamin, 9C130, 9C133

DANIEL, Walker 12C54(7)
DANCING SCHOOL 12C64(1)
DANIEL, W. 12C23
    Walker 12C54(7)
DANVILLE, KY 4C67
DAVIDSON, James, Col. 12C9(1), 12C10
DAVIESS 12C62(40)
    Col. 12C74-74(4)
    James 12C62(38)
    Col. Joseph H. 12C62(23)
    Mrs. 12C62(6)
    Mrs. and 5 children 12C62(38)
    Mrs. M. T. 12C74(4)
DAVIS 12C73
    Azariah 12C22(3), 12C24(7)
    C. W. 12C24(4)
    Clark 4C60, 4C62
    Cornelius 13C124, 13C124(2)
    Cornelius, Mrs. 13C124(2,3)
    Isaac 13C124
    James 7C76, 12C22(3), 12C24(7), 12C73
    John 12C51
    Samuel 12C73
    Thomas 12C8
DAVY, at Crab Orchard Event 12C62(20)
DELAWARES 7C17
DENNY, Mr. 13C76(6)
DENTON, Thomas 12C26
DePEYSTER 12C14(3)
DERRY (servant) 4C53
DETROIT 4C77(1), 4C79, 4C81, 7C14, 7C21(2,3), 11C33, 11C52 11C62(10, 14, 22,25, 30, 35,36), 11C71, 11C110, 12C1(5), 12C2(24), 13C79(17), 13C96(4), 13C114, 13C120, 13C124, 13C125, 13C196(4), 13C200(1,5)
DEVINE, Isaac 12C8
DEVIL'S RACE PATH 4C26(6)
DEWEES 12C54(2)
DICK, Cherokee 5C54(2)
DICKENSON 4C27(2)

Page numbering order: Volume number, series number, page number (with page numbers within interviews cited parenthetically after the primary citation) Ex: 7C5-5(1,2,3).

DICKINSON, John, Col. 12C14(2)
DICK'S RIVER 4C30, 4C31, 5C54(3)
DOAK, Dan 12C24(7)
    Mr. 13C20
DODGE 11C103
DOLAN, Patrick 12C24(7)
DOLEY, Philip 12C62(26-27)
DONELSON 12C54(9)
    Col. 12C49, 12C54(6)
    John, Col. 12C54
    John, Sr. 12C54
DONIPHAN, Gen. A. W. 11C111, 11C111(4)
    George 11C111(5)
    John, Capt. 13C79(15)
    Joseph 11C111(1), taught school at Boonesborough 11C111
    Margarett 11C111(5)
    Tom 11C111(5)
DONNELLY'S/DONLEY'S FORT 12C62(14, 16-17), 13C53, 13C54(1)
DORAN, Patrick 12C22(3), 12C24(11)
DORSEY, L. P. 7C84
DOUBLEHEAD, Cherokee chief 12C62(1)
DOUGLAS, ___ 5C54(2),
    John 7C21(1)
DOUGHERTY. Elijah 10C24, 10C25 (map), 10C40, 10C41
    Nelly 11C62(37)
DOWNEY, Maj. James 12C49(1)
DRAKE, Benjamin 12C8
    Joseph 12C2(7)
    Philip 13C74
    Sam 12C64
DRENNONS LICK 12C26, 13C76(7)
DRISKIN, Daniel 12C24(7)
DROUILLARD/DREWYER, 11C76

DUBUQUE? Julien 11C103
DUCHANE ISLAND 4C54
DUDLEY, Dr. 13C82
    William 12C14(3)
DUFF, J. H. 6C after p. 88-89
DUGAN, Henry 12C22(3)
DULA, John 9C137
    Susan 9C137, 9C139
    nee Ellison 9C137
DUNCAN, Capt. 7C24
    John 7C21
    Samuel McAfee 4C133, 4C157
DUNMORE, Gov. 6C103, 6C105
    Lord 7C76 12C45(1)
DUNN, John? 11C62
DUNN, Jack 11C62, 11C62(10,13)
DUQUESNE 4C46, 5C54(5)
DURRETT, R. T. 11C113(1-3)
DUTCH COLLEGE   4C34(1)
DUTCH SETTLERS ATTACKED 13C51(1)
DYE, Isaac 12C24(7)

EATON'S STATION 7C21,12C49(5), 12C54(3),12C65
EDMONDSON, Mr. 9C91
EDWARDS, Col. 13C79(20)
ELLIOTT, 11C62(36)
ELLISON, Susan 9C137
EMPEROR, Whitley's horse 12C62(3)
ENGLISH, ___ 12C62(30)
    John 12C62(29-30)
    Stephen 12C62(29)
ENGLISH'S STATION 12C62(25, 27, 32)
ERSKINE, Mrs. 7C56(3)
ESKIPPIKTHIKI 7C (beginning)
ESTESS 12C26(1)
    Abraham 12C2(19)
ESTILL, Isaac 13C52
    James 13C38, 13C42, 13C44(1)

Page numbering order: Volume number, series number, page number (with page numbers within interviews cited parenthetically after the primary citation) Ex: 7C5-5(1,2,

appearance 13C51(4)
arm broken in 1781
7C22, 13C51(1),
13C54(3)
in battle, killed 13C40,
13C51, 13C52,
13C53-13C53(1-4),13C54-54(4),
13C54(1), 13C55,
13C58
in Virginia Legislature
13C51(4)
Ruth 13C52
Samuel, appearance
13C51(1)
in battle 13C51, 13C52,
13C53(1),13C54,
13C54(2,3), 13C55
John F. 13C38(1)
Wallace 13C38(1),
1353-53(1),
13C54-54(1-3), 13C55
W. E., Capt. 13C52(2)
William 13C52
William, Dr. after 13C52
ESTILL'S DEFEAT 7C22(1),
13C38 (diagram of
battleground), 4C159, 12C65,
13C38,13C39-48(1), 13C51-51(4), 13C53-54(1,2,3), 13C56-56(1)
ESTILL'S STATION 11C113(2),
13C42
    Attacked 12C65
EVANS 11C112
EUROPE 13C55

FAIN, Lilas 12C2(33)
FALLS OF OHIO 7C35(1),
7C36(1),11C28,11C113,12C1,12C2(6,12),12C38, 12C38(4),
12C45(4), 13C25, 13C131(8),
13C138, 13C153,
13C160,13C161
FARRIS/FERRIS 12C62(40)

Elijah 12C49-49(15),
12C50-53
Isaac 12C62(39)
James 12C49(9),
12C62(19, 45)
Johnson 2C62(19)
Joshua 12C62(38)
Micajah 12C62(35)
Michael 12C62(22)
Nathan 12C49(1),
12C62(32,39)
FASSETTS, J. W. 7C99
FAUNTLEROY, Col. 12C23
John T. 12C24-24(10)
Samuel 12C24
William 12C24(3)
FEAR, Edmund 11C65
FERGUSON 12C14(3)
FICKLIN, J. H., Rev. 13C76
John 13C74
Joseph 13C74-74(4),
13C77-77(1), 13C78-78(1-25), 13C79,
13C81, 13C82, 13C84,
13C85, 13C86-86(1),
13C96(1-3), 13C100,
13C103
Mrs. 13C110(2)
Thomas 13C74,
13C76(4,7), 13C96(1)
William 13C76(4),
13C76(6)
FIELD, Ezekiel 13C79(15)
John, Col. 4C75(1)
Mrs. 13C124
FIELDS, William 12C22(3),
12C24(7), 12C24(11)
FINDLAY 4C31
FINLAY/FINLEY 5C54(5), 7C
beginning, 12C5(2)
John 13C193(1)
FISH 4C59
FISHING CREEK FIGHT
12C62(33)
FLANAGAN, Lewis 13C76(7)

Page numbering order: Volume number, series number, page number (with page numbers within interviews cited parenthetically after the primary citation) Ex: 7C5-5(1,2,3).

FLAT BOAT 13C79(22),
13C145(2), 13C154(1)
FLEMING, William, 4C78, 7C15,
7C17, 12C47
    William, Col. 7C77(2)
FLETCHER, Mrs. Robert
12C14(4)
FLORIDA EXPEDITION 4C75(1)
FLOYD 6C96, 7C17, 7C92
    Charles 12C47
    John 12C44(2)
    John, Col. 4C66,
4C77, 7C97,
        12C47(2), 13C21
    John, Gov. 12C2(4)
    Mrs. Col. G. R. C.
12C47(2)
FLOYD'S STATION 13C117(4)
FONTAINE, Maj., 11C62(36)
FORBES 13C40, 13C42, 13C44,
13C44(1), 13C88
FORD FAMILY at McNitt's
Defeat 12C62(40)
FOREMAN, Mr. 13C153(1)
FORT – see Boonesborough
FORT ASAPH see Logan's Fort
FORT BIRD 6C93
FORT CHISWELL 13C21
FORT DOBBS 8C1(1)
FORT DONLEY 13C53,
13C54(1)
FORT ERIE 11C62(28)
FORT HEMPSTEAD 11C101
FORT JEFFERSON 11C108
FORT PATRICK HENRY 7C29
FORT PITT 7C35, 7C36,
11C62(26), 11C96(3)
FORT PRESTON 6C93
FORT RANDOLPH 7C17,
7C77(2)
FORT SCOTT 13C203(1)
FOSTER, Samuel 12C24(7)
FRAKES, Joseph 12C24(7)
FRANKLIN, Benjamin 12C47(2)
FRAZEE. W. D. 11C111

FRAZIER. Samuel 12C24(7)
    William 7C4
FREELYN'S STATION 12C49
FRENCH, Samuel 12C24(6)
FRENCH TRADERS 13C76
FROMAN, Grandmother
13C154(1)

GARRARD 12C45(3)
    James, Col. 12C1(10)
GARRETT, Wm. 12C22(3)
GARROTT, William 12C24(7)
GASS, Capt. 13C42, 13C53(1)
13C54(2)
    David 6C93
    John 12C26
    Jenny (Miss) 7C32,
13C54(2)
GATLFF, Charles 7C81, 7C82,
7C83, 7C85, 7C86
    Mrs. 13C45, 13C56(1)
GAUNTLET 4C46, 11C62(10,
23, 25, 26), 13C129,
13C131(6,7), 13C196(3,4),
13C200(1)
GATEWOOD, John 13C79(24)
    William 13C74
GAYLE, Josiah,13C74
    Matthew 13C74
GEORGE, Whitson 13C44
GERMANY 13C117(5), 13C198
    Bingen 13C200
    Palitinates 13C200
GILMAN, Thomas (spy) 12C8(1)
GILMER, Dr. John 13C20
GIRTY, George 11C62(31,35),
13C115
    James 11C62(35),
13C79(6)
    Simon 4C26(5),
11C62(13, 27), 13C66,
13C74(1,2), 13C79(9,
10, 11, 12), 13C110(1),
13C114, 13C117(3),
13C194(1)

Page numbering order: Volume number, series number, page number (with page numbers within interviews cited parenthetically after the primary citation) Ex: 7C5-5(1,2,3).

GIRTYS 11C62(6, 30, 33, 34, 35)
GIST 11C112(1)
    Nathaniel 13C79(14)
    Thomas 13C79(14)
GLENN, David 12C22(3), 12C24(7), 12C26
GOE 4C67
    Phillip 4C66, 4C67
GOODMAN, Ansel, 11C62, 11C62(9, 14,16)
GOOSE CREEK EVENT 12C62(17-18, 32,34)
GORDON, Ann 9C58
    Capt. 12C16(16)
    John 12C24, 12C24(10),12C26
GRAND OSAGE 4C61
GRAND RIVER 4C53, 4C62
GRANT family 13C79(24)
    Moses 13C79(22)
    Mrs. 4C57
    Samuel 13C79(22)
    Squire, Gen, 12C2(6)
GRANT'S IRON WORKS 13C200
GRANTS, SPANISH 11C62(17)
GRANT'S STATION 12C2(6)
GRAVES, Leonard 12C8
GRAY, Major 12C16(11)
GREAT CROSSINGS 13C76(4, 6) 13C115(1,3, 5)
GREEN, Lewis 9C120
    Lewis, Expedition 9C87(1)
GREEN RIVER EXPEDITION 4C59
GILL, Easter 12C56(1)
GRIFFITH, William 7C76
GRISTE, John 13C45(15), 13C80
GRUBBS STATION 12C62(19)
    Higgason 12C61(19)13C39
GUILFORD 5C54(1)

GUNPOWDER 5C54(1), 7C15, 13C53,54(1)
GUTHRY, James 12C24(6)

HACKETT, Peter 7C22
HAGGARD/HAGGART, Martin 12C62(27-28)
HAGGIN, John 7C82, 12C1(1), 12C2(23), 12C5(1), 12C26
    Nancy 12C26
HALBERT, N. S. 7C37
HALL, Henry 121(1,9,10), 12C24(7)
    Leonard 4C86, 87
    William 12C49(1), 12C62(36)
HAMBLIN family 7C21(1)
    Henry 7C21
    Mrs. 7C21
HAMILTON, George 7C72
    Henry, Gov. 11C91(1,23), 11C108, 11C110
    James 12C62(21)
    John 12C49(5), 12C54(5)
HAMILTON'S PLACE 7C95
HAMMOND, ___ 4C84
    Philip 12C62(16-17)
HAMTRAMACK 11C62(37)
HANCOCK 11C111(1), 13C42
    Ruth 11C98
    Stephen 11C98, 4C54, 11C66
    William 4C79, 11C62, 11C62(10, 13)
HANDLEY, John 13C52
HANGING MAW (Scolacutta), 4C21, 4C22, 4C22(1,2,)
HANSFORD, Thomas 12C64(1)
HANSON, Thomas   6C96
HARBISON, Jas. 12C8
HARDIN 12C49(1)
    Col. 5C54(2)
    Elizabeth 12C45(1)
    Martin D. 12C45(1)

Page numbering order: Volume number, series number, page number (with page numbers within interviews cited parenthetically after the primary citation) Ex: 7C5-5(1,2,3).

John, Gen. 12C45(1)
HARLAN, Elijah 12C22(3), 24C24(7)
    Maj. 12C16(16), 13C79(13)
    Silas 12C23, 12C24(4), 12C26, 12C22(3), 12C24(7), 12C24(10)
HARMAR 11C62(11, 17, 29, 22, 24, 35)
    General 12C16(14)
HARMAR'S CAMPAIGN 4C62, 6C66(1), 13C213
HARP/HARPE, 12C62(23)
    Big Harp 12C46(3,4), 12C62(23)
    Little Harp 12C46(3,4 5)
    Brothers 12C46(2)
    appearance 12C46(3)
    Mrs. William 12C62
HARPER, Elizabeth 13C188(3)
    Jacob 13C188(3)
    John 13C39, 13C44(1), 12C62(22)
HARPER'S FERRY 13C188(3)
HARPER'S MAGAZINE 13C145(3)
HARRIGAN, Lt. Patt 12C8(1)
HARRIS 12C26, 13C153
    Mr. and Mrs. 13C145(4)
    Patty 12C6(1)
    Phoebe Vancleve 13C193-193(1)
    William 12C26
HARRISON 13C145(4), 13C153
    Benjamin 12C1(10), 13C24(1.3), 13C140
    Burr 12C44(1), 12C46(2)
    Burr, Dr. 12C44(2)
    Mr. 13C124(2)
    Sally 13C145(5), 13C153
    Thomas 13C153
    William 13C154

HARROD, Ann 12C22, 12C25
    Capt. 12C23
    James 12C22(1), 12C22(3), 12C24(1), 12C26-29
    James, Capt. 12C14, 12c22(1,2)
    James, Col. 12C26-29
    Jarrett 12C26-29
    Margaret 12C24
    Mrs. 12C24(2,3), 12C26
HARROD'S COMPANY 11C28
    in 1774 12C22(3)
    in 1777 12C24(10)
    William – Company 12C1(1,10), 12C24(6)
HARROD'S CREEK, 13C145
HARROD, Ann 12C22, 12C22(2,3), 12C24(2, 3, 5, 6, 9, 11)
    James 12C24, 12C22, 22(1,2,3), 12C24,12C24(3, 4, 5, 6,8,9,10,11), 12C25, 12C26-29, 12C54(5)
    Robert 7C21
    William 7C28, 11C33, 12C1, 12C1(3,11), 12C2, 12C24(2,6)
    Wiliam Harrod's Company in 1779 12C24(6)
HARRODSBURG/HARROD'S STATION
4C30, 4C31,7C10, 7C11, 7C17, 11C2(6,17), 11C16(5, 8, 11), 11C33,12C2(6,17), 12C16, 12C16(5,8,11), 12C22, 12C22(1,2,3,4,5,7), 12C24(2,3,5,6,9), 12C25, 12C26-29, 12C38, 12C38(1,2), 12C47(2), 12C49(1,6),12C54(5), 12C73, 12C81, 13C124(2, 3),13C199, 13C199(1,2),

---

Page numbering order: Volume number, series number, page number (with page numbers within interviews cited parenthetically after the primary citation) Ex: 7C5-5(1,2,3).

13C200(1), 13C203
HARRODSBURG MEN KILLED AT BATTLE OF BLUE LICKS 12C26-29
HART, Nathaniel 7C76, 13C39
    Nathaniel, Capt. 12C5(13)
    Thomas 13C13
HARTT, Geo. 12C8
HARTGROVE, John 12C62(33)
    William 12C62(5)
HATTEN 12C1(2)
HAWKINS, Mary 13C194
HAYS, Capt. 13C79(6)
    Charles 12C41
    Daniel 4C58
    John 12C26-29
    Mrs .4242
    Susan 4C50
    Susan Boone 12C26
    Susannah Boone 4C58, 4C60
    William, Capt. 4C58
HAZEL, Edward 11C96(3)
HAZELRIGG/HAZLERIGG, Dillard W. 13C50(2, 3), 13C51-54(4)
HEITT, Peter 13C110
    Sarah 13C110
HEMP 13C79(7,9), 13C154(1)
HEMPSTEAD, Capt. 11C101, 102
HENDERSON, Col. 7C76
    Richard 4C84, 7C5, 7C7, 7C11, 7C76, 7C76(2), 11C21, 11C112, 11C113(2)
    Richard, Col. 12C26
    Samuel 7C97, 7C15-16, 7C20(1), 12C26-29
HENDERSON'S GRANT TO BOONE 11C112-112(1)
HENDERSON'S TREATY AT WATAUGA 7C7, 7C75
HENDRICKS, George 11C62, 11C62(14,16)
    Stephen 13C39, 13C42
HENRY, family 12C54(6)
    Patrick 13C24-24(1,2,3,4)
HERNDEN, David 13C74
    Henry 13C74
HERNDON, Henry 13C76(6)
    Thomas 13C76(4)
    Maj. Thomas 13C77(1)
HEY, William 12C8
HICKMAN 6C103
    William 12C1(3)
HICKS, Allen 9C138
HILL, H. 12C24(6)
HINKSTON, John, Capt. 12C2(23, 12C5(1)
HINKSTON'S STATION 7C17, 12C2(23), 12C5(2)
HINTON, Evan 12C24(10)
HITE, 12C38(1)
HIXSON, W. D. 6C103-105, 7C21, 7C23, 7C77(3), 7C81, 11C89, 13C21,13C38
HOCKADAY/HOCKIDAY 11C111(5, 5)
HODGES, Jesse 11C62, 11C62(1, 22), 11C65, 11C66, 12C2(9,20)
HOGAN, Richard 12C26
HOGG, Michael 12C5(1)
HOGUE, Aaron A. 13C199(1)
    Rev. A. A. 13C200(1?)
HOLDEN 8C11(1)
    John 9C138
    Joseph 9C140,13C193(2)
HOLDER, Col. 4C66, 4C67
    John, Col. 12C5(13)
    John 7115(4), 12C5(13), 13C52(1)
HOLDER'S DEFEAT 13C34, 13C63, 3C79(3)
HOLLEY, John 11C62, 11C62(10, 14, 31)

Page numbering order: Volume number, series number, page number (with page numbers within interviews cited parenthetically after the primary citation) Ex: 7C5-5(1,2,3).

HOLLY, John 12C62(1)
HOLLIDAY, Zachariah 12C26
HOLMAN, Thomas 9C87
HOLSTON 6C65 map, 6C89-90 map, 7C6 (map), 7C21, 7C22, 7C23(3), 7C24(1), 7C32 map, 7C76, 9C130, 11C48, 11C52, 12C2(15, 16), 12C22, 12C24(2), 12C26-29, 12C54, 13C192
HONEYCUTT, Peter 4C24
HOPKINS' CAMPAIGN 12C62(3)
HOPKINS, General 12C16(14)
HORTON, Jonathan 9C102 (map)
    Widow 9C137
HOSSEY RAID 9C129(1,2)
HOWARD, Benjamin 5C54(1), 9C142
    Gen. Benjamin 5C54(2)
    Cornelius 9C139, 9C142
    John 5C54(1)
    Joshua 9C138, 139, 9C142
    Sallie 5C54(1)
    Virginia Webb 13C74
HOWELL, Susan 4C33(1)
HOWESHALL 12C54(8)
HOY, Jones 13C34
HOY'S STATION 13C63, 13C79(4)
HUDG___, Daniel 12C8
HUMBLE, Michael 12C24(6), 12C26- 29,12C54(6)
HUNT, John 12C24(6)
    Mr. 13C56
HUNTER, Charles 13C79(6)
    John L., Capt. 12C24(8)
HUNT'S *WESTERN REVIEW* 13C56
HURSBURNE'S FIGHT 11C62(37)
HURSTGROVE, James 12C62(42-44
HUSTON, Stephen (spy) 128(1)

HUTCHINS, Mr. 13C52(2)
HUTTON, 12C1(2)
    Mary 13C212, 213
HYNES, Dr Alfred 13C124
    Maj. Andrew 13C123, 13C124

IJAMES, Beal 8C11(1-3)
ILLINOIS, 5C54(1)
ILLINOIS CAMPAIGN 12C2(5), 12C38, 13C124
IMBODEN, 10C79 (map)
    J. D. 6C80 (map)
INDIAN CAMP, plat 4C31
INDIAN MODE OF FIGHTING 13C54-54(1)
INDIAN MODE OF SLEEPING 9C79, 79(1)
INDIAN OLD FIELDS 7C1, 7C4
INDIAN OLD TOWN 4C31
INDIAN PHILLIPS see Phil Nail 4C33(6), 4C34(1), 4C54, 8C11(2)
INDIANA 9C204(3)
IRELAND 4C24, 4C26, 4C26(4), 12C45(3),13C38(1)
IRON 4C48, 13C79(22), 13C200
IRVINE 4C67
    Capt. 12C1(10, 11)
    Capt. Christopher 12C62(12)
    Col. 7C22, 13C44
ISAACS, John 12C24(4)
ISLAND FLATTS 7C21-22

JACKSON, James 4C59
    Joseph 11C62-62(32), 12C1(1)
    Mr. 12C1(2)
JAMES, Elizabeth 12C64(1)
    John N. 11C76
    John and wife 12C64(1)
    Squire 12C64(1)
JAMISON, John 12C8

Page numbering order: Volume number, series number, page number (with page numbers within interviews cited parenthetically after the primary citation) Ex: 7C5-5(1,2,3).

JARRETT 12C26
JEFFERSON, Gov. 13C25
    Thomas 13C17, 13C79(19)
JENNINGS 12C49, 12C49(1)
    family 12C49(1)
    Edmund 12C49, 12C62(63)
    John 12C49
JOHNS, John 12C49(4)
    family 12C54(1)
JOHNSON, family 13C79(24)
    Andrew 13C193(2)
    Capt. 13C196
    Judge Fryman 5C54(7)
    James 13C117, 117(4)
    R. M., Col. 13C74
    Richard Johnson 13C145(2)
    Richard M. 13C117(1)
    Robert, Capt. 13C79(9,21,22,23), 13C115-115(1)
    Robert, Col. 13C74(4),13C77(1)
    Robert, Mrs. 13C79(13)
    Robert, 13C74 13C117
    Sally 13C117
    William 13C117
JOHNSTON, Col. 13C85
    J., Col. 13C85
    William 11C113
JONES, Dr.4C55
    James 12C49(4), 12C54, 12C54(3)
    and family 12C54(1)
    Mr. 12C24(2), 12C49(4), 12C54(4)
    Lewis 4C60
    Moses 12C49(4), 12C54(4)
    Shacrack 12C49(4)
    Thomas 12C49(5)
    and family 12C54(1)
JORDAN, Annie 9C68(1)
    William 5C54(5)
JOUETT, Jack 13C20
    John, Capt. 13C19
    John 13C79(19)
KASKASKIA 5C54(5), 11C48, 11C51, 11C62(24), 12C2(18), 12C24(7), 12C38, 12C76(2)
KEA 11C111(1,2)
KEDAN, John 11C62(24)
KEENE?, W. 12C24
KELLEY, Benjamin 11C62, 11C62(10, 13)
KELLY, Beal 13C44
KENNEDY, John 11C65, 12C26-29
    Joseph 13C55
    Joseph, Major 12C2(10)
    Thomas 12C1(10)
    Thomas, Capt. 12C62(18)
    Thomas, Col. 12C62(10)
    Tom 4C50-54
KENTON, Simon 5C54,11C62(6, 7,10, 14), 11C65, 11C76, 2C13(13), 12C24(10), 12C26-29, 12C44(2)
    Simon, Capt. 12C38(5)
    Simon, Gen. 12C2(13)
KERR? James 12C22(3), 12C24(7)
KERR, Thomas 12C8
KILLED
    Adkins, John 13C79(1,2)
    Allen, Col. John at River Raisin, 12C45(4)
    Armstrong ___, 11C62(19)
    Ash, Mrs. at Kincheloe's, 13C124
    Ballard, ___ 12C38(6)
    Baptist ministers 12C62(63)
    Baughman, Henry

Page numbering order: Volume number, series number, page number (with page numbers within interviews cited parenthetically after the primary citation) Ex: 7C5-5(1,2,3).

12C62(26-27)
Baughman, Mrs. ___ 12C62(27)
Baughman, ___ 12C62(27)
Beasley, James at Blue Licks, 13C74(3), 13C79(17)
Boone, Edward 7C80, 7C82, 7C83, 7C84, 7C92
Boone, Israel at Blue Licks, 13C193(2)
Boone, James at Powell's Valley, 4C26(6)
Bowman, Capt. Joseph 12C38(1)
Bright, George 12C54(8)
Brown, ___ at Falls of Ohio 13C131(1), 13C139
Brown, James at Blue Licks 12C26-29
Bryant, William 13C193(3)
Buchanan, Wm., Capt. 13C34
Bulger, Edward at Blue Licks 12C1, 13C79(14)
Callaway, Richard 12C2(24)
Campbell and Cleveland, Tories, at Point Pleasant, 7C22(1)
Caperton, Adam at Estill's 13C40, 13C51
Cara___, Andrew 7C21
Carswell, Henry 7C14(7)
Chapman, Job 12C26-29
Children at Thomas

Teas's 7C56(3)
Clark, ___ in 1792, 12C62(19)
Coburn, James, Capt. 12C24(2)
Colefoot/Coltfoot, John at Estill's 13C40, 13C42, 3C88
Cooper, James 7C17
Cowan, ___ 6C93
Cowan, James 12C22, 12C24, 12C26-29
Cowan, John 4C26(4)
Cox, Col. 13C119, 13C121
Crawford, Col. William 7C56(3)
Daniel, Walker 12C54(7)
David, Cornelius and daughter at Kincheloe's 13C124
Daviess, Polly 12C62(8)
Daviess, James 12C62(8, 19))
Davis, ___ 12C73
Douglas, John 7C21(1)
Dunn, John? 11C62
Estill, James 13C38, 13C40, 13C42, 13C44(1)
Farris/Ferris Isaac 12C62(39)
Farris/Ferris Nathan 12C62(39)
Field, Ezekiel 13C79(15)
Field, John, Col. at Point Pleasant 4C75(1)
Floyd, John 12C44(2)
Forbes, ___ at Estill's, 13C42, 13C44, 13C44(1), 13C88
Gass, Jenny at Estill's, 13C42, 13C53
Grant, Moses 13C79(22)

Page numbering order: Volume number, series number, page number (with page numbers within interviews cited parenthetically after the primary citation) Ex: 7C5-5(1,2,3).

Grant, Samuel 13C79(22)
Gray, Major 12C16(11)
Hamblin, Mrs. 7C21(1)
Hamlton, John 12C54(5)
Hanging Maw (Scolacutta), 4C22
Hardin, Gen. John 12C45(1),
Harrison, Burr 12C44(1)
Harrod, James 12C22(1), 12C22(3), 12C24(1), 12C26-29
Jarrett 12C26-29
Hays, John 12C26-29
Hays, William, in a fight, 4C58
Hunter, Charles 13C79(6)
Indian Chief on the Great Miami at Piqua Battle, 7C22(1)
Jennings, Mr. 12C49(1)
Jennings, Robert 12C62(63)
Johns family 12C49(4)
Jones, Mr. 12C54(4)
Jones, James 12C54(3)
Kennedy, John at Blue Licks, 12C26-29
Langford, Mr., killed by the Harpes, 12C46(2)
Benjamin 12C62(33)
Lay, ___ 13C76(4)
Lee, ___ 12C26
Lindsay, Joseph at Blue Licks 12C26-29
Linn, Nathan, 12C26-29
Logan, Robert at River Rasin, 12C45(4)
Lumsden , ___ 12C54(2)
Lucas, Major 12C49, 12C49(1)

McClure, Robert 12C10(11)
McConnell, ___ 5C54(1), 12C26-29,13C78(7)
McDaniel, James 12C24(2), 12C26-29
McDonald, James 12C22(1,2), 12C24(2, 12C26-29)
McDowell, ___ 12C41
McMillion, ___ 13C51(3)
McMillan/McMillen, Jonathan at Estill's 13C40, 13C42, 13C88
McMurtry, John 12C26-29, 13C200(1), 13C200(1-8),13C213
McNeely, ___ at Estill's 13C40, 13C42, 13C88
McNitt, Mr. and Mrs. 12C62(23,41)
McQuinney/McWhinney, William in 1775, 7C14, 12C26-29
Maulden, Moses 12C54(5)
Mauldin, ___ 12C54(3)
Middleton, Matt 12C62(28)
Mitchell, John 13C110(2)
Mr. 13C74(3)
Mrs. 12C62(25)
Michael 13C79(1,2)
Moluntha 11C62(33), 12C47
killed 12C62(12-13)
Montgomery, Alexander 11C65
on Paint Creek Expedition, 11C62(24, 25), 12C13(3)
Montgomery, John 12C13(1), 12C45

Page numbering order: Volume number, series number, page number (with page numbers within interviews cited parenthetically after the primary citation) Ex: 7C5-5(1,2,3).

Mooney, James at Point Pleasant, 6C93
Mungle, Christopher 12C14(7)
    Daniel 7C210
Napper, Fannie and five children 6C70(1)
Nokes, Abram 12C62(32)
    Benjamin 12C62(31)
    Betsy 12C62(31)
    Jesse 12C62(32)
    ___ 12C62(32)
Overton, Capt. Clough at Blue Licks 12C26-29
Pendergrass, ___,12C26-29
Pogue, Wm. 12C24(7)
Pompey 11C62(15)
Porter, Ambrose 12C54(4)
Ramsey, Mrs. 4C53
Randolph, Mrs. and child at Kincheloe's, 13C124
    Thomas J., Col. 13C17
Rawlings, Pemberton 12C1(24)
Ray, William 12C16(4), 12C26-29, 12C30
Rees, ___ 13C76(4)
Rogers, ___ 11C63
Russell, ___ eldest daughter 12C45(1)
Shanks family 13C79(19.20)
South, Jerry 12C1(5)
South, John at Estill's 13C40, 13C42, 13C56(1), 13C88
Stagner, Barney 12C16(14), 12C26-29

Stevens, ___ at Blue Licks 12C26-29
Stigall, Mrs., and children 12C46(3)
Stuart, John 4C99
Todd, John 11C25(1)
Todd, Maj. Robert 13C100
Trabue, ___ killed by the Harpes, 12C46(3)
Trumbow, ___ son of Jacob 12C62(33)
Tucker, Mrs. 12C14(3)
Turpin, Solomon 12C54(3)
Twitty, William in 1775, 4C81
    and servant, 4C81
VanCleve, Molly and 2 children, 13C193(3)
Wilcox, Isaiah at Blue Licks 9C63(1)
Young, James 7C21(1)
    and servant,7C21(1)
KINCANNONS FORT 7C24
KINCHELOE'S STATION 11C12, 11C62(35), 13C119, 13C123-123(1), 13C124, 13C124(1,2), 13C125, 13C126, 13C145(4), 13C153-154
    captured at: Mrs. Polk 11C62(36)
    prisoners at, 13C126
KINCHELOE, Elias 13C119, 13C120, 13C121-121(1), 13C122, 13C123-121(1), 13C124
    Lewis, Gen. 13C122
    Stephen 13C124, 13C124(2)
    William 13C119, 13C122
KING 12C44(1)
    John 12C45(2)

Page numbering order: Volume number, series number, page number (with page numbers within interviews cited parenthetically after the primary citation) Ex: 7C5-5(1,2,3).

KING'S MOUNTAIN 7C23, 7C24(1,2), 12C10, 12C14(3)
KING'S MOUNTAIN BATTLE 4C33(2, 6), 4C75(1), 4C78, 4C81, 7C24(2), 9C58,12C14(3), 13C38(1)
KINKEAD'S FORT 11C101
KINLA, Mr. 13C22
KINLOW, Francis 13C25
KINNEY, John 12C24(7)
KIRKENDALL, Moses 12C24(7)
KNOB LICK 12C23
KNOX, Col. 5C54(3-4-5-6), 13C23(1)
    Col. James 5C54(2)
    Ann 12C44(2)
    John 13C194
KUNE? , W. 12C24

LACKEY, Anthony 12C8
LANCASTER, servant 13C117(1)
LAND COMMISSIONERS 12C2(9)
LANE, Capt. 7C115(3)
    James 7C115, 7C115(4)
    John 13C39, 13C42
LANGFORD, Mr. 12C46(2)
    Benjamin 12C62(42)
    Tom, 12C62(22)
    Stephen 12C62(22)
LAUGHLIN 7C23
    Col. 7C24, 7C25
    Samuel H. 7C21
LAY 13C76(4)
LEAD 13C76(7)
LEAVELL, E. M. 5C87
LEDGERWOOD, James 12C26-29, 13C200(1)
LEE, 12C26
    Gen. 12C1(11)
LEEPER, Hugh 12C26
LEWIS, Bear fight, 9C60
    Col. 12C22, 12C24(2)
    Andrew, Col. 6C106
    General 6C105, 13C54

Mr. 13C20
    Virgil A. 13C38(1)
LAMME, William T. 4C34(1)
LAMMES, T. 4C33(2)
LAND, T. C. (map) 9C84, 9C91
LAPSLEY, Joseph 12C41
LARAMIE (French trader),11C62(17,28)
LARAMIE'S STORE 11C62(32)
LAWRENCE & BRACKEN, 4C23
LAY 13C76(4)
    William 13C74
LEDGERWOOD, James 12C26-29.13C200(1)
LEE, John 12C8
LEEPER, Hugh 12C46(2, 4)
LEWIS, Col.,   4C26(15)
LEWIS AND CLARK, 4C60
LIMESTONE, 5C54(1)
LINDSAY, Joseph 12C26-29
LINN, Benjamin 12C24(10), 12C26
    Capt. 13C121(1)
    Nathan 12C26-29
LINN'S STATION 13C193(2)
LINUS, John 12C24(7)
LITLE/LITTLE and wife 12C5(13)
    Samuel, 8C11(3)
LITTLE MOUNTAIN 13C40, 13C42, 13C44, 13C56(1)
LOGAN 13C21, 13C79(18), 12C62(2,3)
    Ann 12C44, 12C44(2), 12C45(1,4), 12C62(29)
    Ben 7C23, 7C24
    Benjamin 4C54, 12C1(1), 12C2(15,24), 12C6, 12C10, 12C13(3), 12C24(4),12C26, 12C44, 12C44(3),12C45(3), 12C62(9,10,11)
    Obituary 12C48

Page numbering order: Volume number, series number, page number (with page numbers within interviews cited parenthetically after the primary citation) Ex: 7C5-5(1,2,3).

Col. 7C21, 13C56
Dr. 12C45
Dr. Ben 12C10
David 12C44, 12C44(2), 12C45(1, 3, 4), 12C46
General 5C54(6), 12C10, 12C62(14, 18)
Benjamin, Gen. 7C24(2), 12C44-44(2), 12C45-45(4), 12C4712C46, 12C46(1, 2, 5), 12C47
Elizabeth 12C45(3)
H. Ben. 12C26
John, Col. 12C62(9, 10, 11)
John, Gen. 12C38(2)
H. 4C53
Henry 4C62
Hugh 12C45(3)
Jane 12C45(4)
Jim (Native American) 12C45(1), 13C76
Job 12C45(3)
John 721, 7C23, 11C65, 12C44(2), 12C46, 12C46(1)
Margaret 12C45(3)
Mary 12C45(3,4)
Ben, Mrs. 12C13, 12C26
Nathaniel 12C10, 12C45, 12C45(3)
Robert 12C44(2)
William 12C6, 12C44, 12C44(2), 12C45(1,3,4), 12C62(5)
LOGAN'S CAMPAIGN 4C50,11C62(32), 12C1(10), 12C2(24), 12C9, 12C13, 12C22(1), 12C56, 12C62(10-14), 12C81, 13C79(18)
LOGAN'S EXPEDITION 12C2(24, 12C9, 12C22(1)
LOGAN FAMILY BIBLE 12C45(4)
LOGAN'S FORT/STATION 4C30, 4C31, 12C1(10,15,17), 12C2(6, 15, 16), 12C13, 12C13(3), 12C22, 12C22(2), 12C24(3), 12C45(2), 12C24(9), 12C26-29, 12C46(6)
LOGAN'S FORT SIEGE 12C45(2)
LONG, Mrs. 11C62(30)
LONG HUNTERS 5C54(3-4)
LONG ISLAND OF HOLSTON 7C29, 7C21(1), 7C22, 7C28(2) (map), 7C29 (map) 7C32 (map), 7C49. 12C54
LOONEY 12C54(5)
LORIMER 11C96
LOUGHEY'S DEFEAT 11C62(36)
LOUTRE ISLAND and CREEK 4C33(6), 43C34, 34(1,2), 4C54
LUCAS, Major 12C49, 12C49(1)
LULBEGRUD 13C76(1), 13C85, 13C96
LUMSDEN 12C54(2)
LYNCH, David 13C39, 13C42
LYNE, Edmund 12C2(9)
LYON, Mr, 7C21
LYONS, Col. 13C25
    Humphrey 12C5(1)
    John 12C5(1)
    Samuel 12C5(1)
LYTLE, and wife 12C5(13)
    Miss 13C100
    William, Gen. 13C100

McAFEE, Gen. 12C24(5)
    James 5C54(4,5)
    R. B., Gen. 12C22, 12C30, 12C74, 13C199, 13C200
    Robert 5C54(4,5)
McAFEE'S LIST of HARROD'S COMPANY in 1774 12C22(3)
McAFEE'S STATION 12C2(6), 12C16(8), 12C22, 12C26,

Page numbering order: Volume number, series number, page number (with page numbers within interviews cited parenthetically after the primary citation) Ex: 7C5-5(1,2,3).

13C200
McBRIDE, William, Capt. 12C16(10)
    William 13C200(3,4)
McCALL, ___ 5C54(6)
McCALLY, James 12C24(10)
McCANNON, John 12C24
McCARY, Richard 13C123
McCLELLAN'S STATION 12C22(23)
McCLUNG, Mr. 11C76
McCLURE 12C44(2), 12C45, 12C62(40)
    Miss 12C46
    Nathan 12C62(33,42-45)
    Nathan, Capt. 12C62(35)
    Nathan, Lt. 12C62(35)
McCLURE'S DEFEAT 12C62(28-31)
    Robert 12C10(11)
McCONNELL 5C54(1),12C26-29, 13C78(7)
    Boys, escaped 12C26-29
    Francis 12C26
    William 7C83
McCORMACK 12C26(1)
McCOUN, Elizabeth 13C200(1)
McCUE 13C24
McCULLOCK, James 12C54(7)
McDANIEL 12C24(3, 9)
    Ann 12C24(2)
    James 12C22(1,2),12C24(2, 3,), 12C26-29
    Patrick 12C24(2)
McDONALD, James 12C22(1), 12C26
    Mrs. 12C22(2)
McDOWELL 12C41
    James, Col. 12C41
    Joseph, Col. 12C41
McEWEN, John 12C8

McFarland, ___ 12C62(25-26)
    Alexander 12C62(37)
McFARLAND'S DEFEAT 12C62(25)
McGEE'S STATION 13C40
McGEE, Patrick 12C24(7)
McGARY 7C11, 11C62(32, 33), 12C23, 12C24(5), 12C26, 12C62(12-13), 13C79(13)
    Capt. 12C22
    Col. 12C16(16)
    Hugh 12C1(10, 11, 12), 12C15, 12C24(4), 12C26. 12C62(10, 14)
McILVAINE, Moses 11C110
McINTOSH, Gen. 4C78
McINTYRE, John 7C87
McKEE 11C62(36), 11C96(3)
McKEE'S TOWN 12C1(12), 12C62(13)
McKINLEY, William 12C6(1)
McKINLY, Jane 12C45(1, 3)
McKINNEY, ___ 12C62(45)
    Alexander 4C41(1)
    Henry G. 11C105
    John 11C105
    Hon. John 12C47
    Marion, 4C41(1)
McKINNEY'S STATION 12C14(2)
McMILLAN/McMILLEN, Jonathan 13C38, 13C42, 13C51
McMILLEN, Samuel 12C2(23), 12C5(1)
McMILLION 13C51(3)
McMURTRY, Capt. 13C199(1)
    John 12C26-29, 13C96(2,3,4), 13C196-196(5), 13C200, 13C203, 13C205, 13C211-213
    Joseph, Capt. 13C293(1)
    Mrs. John 13C200(1)
    Mary Hutton 13C212
    Samuel 13C196

Page numbering order: Volume number, series number, page number (with page numbers within interviews cited parenthetically after the primary citation) Ex: 7C5-5(1,2,3).

William 13C196, 13C199, 13C203, 13C211
McNEAL, Thos. 12C8
McNEELY 13C40, 13C42, 13C88
McNITT, Mr. and Mrs. 12C62(23,41)
McNITT'S DEFEAT 12C62(23,41)
McQUIDDY, Will 12C24(2)
McMcQuinney/McWhinney
    William, 7C bef 15, 12C26-29
MADISON, Mr. W. 13C23
MAGINTY 7C beginning
MAMMOTH CAVE 12C24(10)
MANIFEE 12C26
    Betsy 12C62(5)
    William 12C26
MANLEY, John 4C34(1)
MANSCOE 12C49(4)
MANSCOE'S 12C54(3, 6)
MARBLE CREEK CAVE 4C133
MARSHALL, H. *History of Kentucky*
    12C6(1)
    Hon. J. 13C24
    J. J. 13C48
MARTIN, John 11C62(15), 12C44(2), 12C62(10)
    John, Capt. 12C8(1)
    John L., Maj. 12C2(2-24), 12C5(13)
    Joseph, Col. 7C23
MARTIN'S AND RUDDLE'S STATIONS 13C115, 13C193(3)
MARTIN'S OLD STATION 6C93
MARTIN'S PAYROLL 12C2(5), 12C8(1)
MARTIN'S STATION 7C21, 12C26-29, 13C193(2)
MARYLAND 12C55
    Queen Anne's County 12C24

MASEFIELD, John 12C24(10, 11)
MASON, "robber" 12C46(5)
MAULDEN/MAULDIN 12C54(3,5)
    Moses 12C49(5)
MAXEY, B. F. 7C100, 107, 108
MAXWELL 12C54(8)
MAY, George 11C113(3)
    John 13C76(5)
    William 13C124(3)
MECHACHECK 12C62(10, 13)
MERIWETHER
    George 11C112, 11C113(2)
MIDDLETON'S STATION 12C62(28,45)
MIDDLETON, Green 12C62(28)
    Matt, 12C62(28,63)
MIERS, Henry 12C24(7)
MILES, John 12C26
MILLER 12C54(6)
    Armistead 12C49, 12C54-12C 54(1-9)
    Capt. 13C54
    John, Capt. 12C54
    family 12C54(1)
    John 12C54(7)
    Lieut. 13C54
    Lieut. William 13C56(1)
    Mr. 12C62(41),13C54
    Mrs. 12C62(41)
    William 4C130
MILLS, Edward 7C bef 15
    John 7C14
MIMS?, William 12C24(10)
MINGOE, 7C17
MINISTERS' DEFEAT 12C62(27-28,45)
MINNS, Jacob 12C24(9)
MISSOURI
    Cape Girardeau, 11C62(17)
    Femme Osage 4C48, 11C106

Page numbering order: Volume number, series number, page number (with page numbers within interviews cited parenthetically after the primary citation) Ex: 7C5-5(1,2,3).

Green's Bottom 4C36
Marthasville 4C34(1), 4C53
Nevada 4C41(1), 4C61, 11C105
Osage 4C34(1)
St. Charles 4C33(1), 4C50, 4C61, 7C25
MITCHELL, Daniel 13C74
David 13C74
John 13C110(2)
Michael 13C79(1,2)
Mr. 13C74(3)
Mrs. 12C 62(25), 13C79
MODE of carrying on operations 12C1(8)
MOFFETT/MOFFITT, Col. George 12C41, 13C24
Mrs. 13C24, 24(4)
MOLUNTHA 4C50, 12C47
MOLUNTHA'S TOWN 12C1(11,12, 14)
MONK (Estill) 7C22, 12C62(13), 13C51(2,4), 13C53, 13C53(1),) 13C54
MONTGOMERY, Alexander 11C62(24, 25), 11C65, 12C13(3)
Ann 12C13(3), 12C45(1,3)
Elizabeth 12C13(2)
Family 12C2(24)
Hugh 12C8
James, Capt. 7C23
Jane 12C13, 12C45(3)
John, Col. 7C23, 7C24(1,2)
John 12C13, 12C45
John, Mrs. 12C13(1,2,3)
Mrs. 12C13
William 12C45, 12C45(4)
William Jr. 12C13(3)
William Sr. 12C13(3)
MONTGOMERY'S STATION 12C13

MONTREAL 11C33, 11C38, 13C79(17), 13C200(1)
MOON, Samuel 12C24(10)
Thomas 12C8
Widow 12C24(5)
William 12C24(11)
MOONER 4C24, 9C77(2)
MOONEY, James 6C93
MOORE'S FORT 6C93
MOORE, Capt. M. 9C129(2)
Dr. 13C205
Robert 12C62(41)
Robin 7C93
Samuel 12C62(41,13C203
William 4C75
MORAVIAN TOWNS 11C62(34)
MOREHEAD 13C138-139, 13C145(2), 161
Charles, Gov. 13C145(3)
MOREDOCK, John 12C1(6)
MORELOCK, John 13C145(3)
MORGAN'S STATION 7C115(4)
MORGAN, Elizabeth/Betsy 12C64
John 13C203
Mr. at Fort Pitt 11C96(3)
MORITION, William 12C24(10)
MORROW, Robert 13C38
MORSE, Charles H. 13C20
MORTIMER, Wm. 12C22(3)
MORTIMORE, William 12C24(7)
MORTON, John 11C75
MOUNTAIN MUSE, 7C43
MUNGLE, Christopher 12C14(7)
Daniel 7C21
MUNSSKA 11C62C32, 33)
MURDOCK, Edward 12C24(7)
MURRELL, Capt. 12C62(45)
MYERS, William 12C22(3)

NAIL, Phil 8C11(1-3)
see Indian Phillips

Page numbering order: Volume number, series number, page number (with page numbers within interviews cited parenthetically after the primary citation) Ex: 7C5-5(1,2,3).

NALL, ___ 12C62(63)
NAPPER, Fannie 6C70(1,2)
NEAL, ___ 5C54(2)
NEW JERSEY 13C55
NEW ORLEANS 12C45(4), 13C145(2)
NETHERLAND, Ben 13C79(14)
NEWELL, Col. Sam, 7C23
    Samuel 7C76
NEW YORK
    Orange County 12C5(1)
NICKOJACK 12C62(3,8,42), 12C64
NOGGINS 12C46(2)
NOKES, Abram 12C62(32)
    Benjamin 12C62(31)
    Betsy 12C62(31)
    George 12C62(10-40)
    Jesse 12C62(33)
NORTH CAROLINA
    Roan County, 7C22, 8C1
    Wilkes County, 9C68(1-11), Map, 9C84

OFFIN, James 12C24(10)
OFFUTT, George 13C115(1)
OLDHAM 12C23
    Will 12C24C(6)
ORE, James 4C22-22(1)
OTTAWAS 7C17
OTTER LIFTER (Cherokee) 12C62(8, 31,33)
OVERALL, William 12C50
OVERTON, Clough 12C26-29

PAINT CREEK EXPEDITION 4C44-61, 11C62(14,15, 24,25), 11C65, 11C66
PARKERSON, John R. 12C2(14)
PATTEN, James 12C24(6)
    William 12C2(15)
PATTERSON, Col. 12C62(10)
    Jef. Col. 11C62(30)
    Robert, Capt. 13C79(15)

    Sarah 13C188(3)
PATTERSON PAPERS 13C83
PATTON, Samuel 13C123
PAUL, John 12C24(7)
PAULEY, Margaret /"Peggy Polly" 13C51, 13C54
PAULSON, J. W. 12C24(10)
PAWLING, Capt. Henry 12C26, 12C62(9)
PAYNE, Elizabeth "Betsy" 13C115-115(2), 13C117-117(6)
    Mrs. General 13C74(4)
    John, Gen. 13C115
    John 13C117(4)
PEAK, Mr. 11C101
PEMBERTON, Col. 7C24(1,2)
PEN___, Richard 12C8
PENDERGRASS 12C26-29
PENDLETON, Edmund 7C15
PENNINGTON, Abigail 4C99
    Daniel 4C99
    Joshua 4C99
    Richard 4C99
PENNSYLVANIA 4C7, 7C21, 7C43(1), 9C62, 11C33, 12C2(22), 12C44, 12C45(1), 12C46, 12C126(1), 13C38(1), 13C63, 13C79(25), 13C200, 13C211, 13C63, 13C211
    Bucks County 13C19
PETTIT 12C26
    Benjamin 12C26, 13C44
PEYTON, Yelverton 13C55
PHELPS, Joseph 12C24(6)
PHILADELPHIA 4C26(2), 12C1(1), 12C27)
PHILLIPS, William, 9C68
PICKAWAY – see Piqua
PIPER 12C14(5)
    James 7C21,
PIQUA 4C31, 7C22, 7C22(1), 11C62(14,24,27,28,29,30,31), 12(18), 12C22(3), 12C24(10), 12C38(4), 12C56, 13C131(5),

---

Page numbering order: Volume number, series number, page number (with page numbers within interviews cited parenthetically after the primary citation) Ex: 7C5-5(1,2,3).

13C145(1)
PITTSBURG 5C54(5)
PLUNDER, sale of 12C1(10)
POAGUE, George 12C26
    Robert, Gen. 12C26
    Robert 12C2(6)
    William 12C23,
    12C24(7), 12C26
POGUE. Roger 11C88
    William 11C88,
    12C24(7,10)
POINT PLEASANT 4C27(2), 4C75(1), 6C93, 7C22(1), 12C14, 12C22, 12C54(9), 12C64
POLK. Charles, Capt. 13C124, 124(3)
    Mrs. 11C62(36), 13C120, 13C124
    William 13C120
POINTER, John 12C62(39)
POMPEY 11C62(6, 15), 11C84, 87, 11C98
PORTER, Ambrose 12C54(4)
    Patrick 4C24, 4C26, 4C26(2, 4,13,16)
    Samuel 4C24, 4C26(6), 6C94
PORTER'S FORT 4C24, 4C26(10)
POTTENGER, Samuel 12C24(6)
POTTS, Jonas 12C24(6)
POWELL'S VALLEY 4C33(6), 4C44-61, 5C54(2), 6C7, 6C14, 6C16, 6C18, 6C after p. 88-89, 7C11, 7C23
PRESTON 6C103
    Col. 7C15, 13C20, 13C21, 13C23
    William 4C44
    Wm., Col. 5C5491), 12C47(2)
PRIBBLE, Reuben 12C24(7)
PRICE, Capt. 12C49(1)
PRICE'S SETTLEMENT 12C50
PRINGLE, John 12C8[28]

PROCTOR, Rev. Joseph 7C22, 13C52
    Joseph, 13C39, 13C40, 13C44, 13C51(3), 13C54
PROFITT. Mr. 9C87, 9C87(1), 9C88, 9C90
    Wm. 9C91
PRYOR, ___ at Donnelly's Fort 12C62(16-17)
PUNCHEONS 13C145(4)

RAMSEY, Isaiah 12C49(4)
    Josiah 12C54, 54(3)
    Mrs.4C53
    Robert 4C53
    Thomas, Col. 13C17
RANDOLPH, Mrs. 13C124(2)
    Nathaniel 12C26
    Thompson 13C124(2)
    Wm. Harrison 13C124(2)
RATLIFF, Caleb 7C72
RAWLINGS, Pemberton 12C1(24)
RAY, General 12C65(7)
    James, Gen.12C2(6), 12C15, 1216(15), 12C26
    James 7C82
    Dr. John 12C15, 12C16(16)
    Mr. 13C76(7)
    William 12C16(1-5), 12C26-29, 12C30
REES 13C76(4)
    Azor 12C24(7)
REESE, Azariah 12C22(3)
REID, Nathan 7C24
RENFRO/RENFROE family 12C54(6)
    Isaac 12C54(1,2)
    James 12C54(1,2)
    Jess 12C54(1)
    Joseph 12C54(3)

Page numbering order: Volume number, series number, page number (with page numbers within interviews cited parenthetically after the primary citation) Ex: 7C5-5(1,2,3).

Moses 12C54(2)
RENIX, Henry 12C14
REYNOLDS, ___ 12C62(19)
 Aaron 13C74, 74(1,2,3), 13C79(10, 11, 14, 15), 13C110(1)
 Capt. 13C66
 Mr. 13C65
RICE [David], 12C62(27-28)
RICHARDSON'S STATION 12C62(31)
RIDDLE's/RUDDELL'S STATION 12C2(12), 12C26
RIGGS, Lt. Jonathan 4C54
ROBERTSON, Chief Justice 13C39
 Opinion 13C48-48(1)
 Matt 12C8
ROBINSON, Richard 7C22
RODGERS, Edmund 5C54(6)
RODMAN, Will B. 7C20
ROGERS' DEFEAT 11C62(23)
ROGERS 4C49, 11C63
 Anthony 12C62(21)
 Bennet, Lieut. 13C115
 Barnett 13C117(1)
 Elizabeth 13C117(5)
 Joseph 11C62(29)
 Mr. 13C76(5)
 William 13C74
ROSE 13C199
 Barbery 13C200
 Capt. 196(4)
 Cudliff? / Godlove 13C200
 George 13C198
 Lewis 12C8, 13C196(3,4), 13C200, 13C200(3-8), 13C211-213
 Martin 13C198
 Matthias 13C198
 Mrs. 13C200(1)
ROSS, Hugh 12C62(10)
ROUNSEVALE 12C54(8)

ROUT, Capt. William 12C62(12)
ROWE, John 12C62(28)
ROWLAND, Widow 7C80
ROYAL SPRING 7C17
RUDDELL 13C79(24)
 Abraham 11C63
 Stephen 11C63
RUDDELL'S/RIDDLE'S STATION 7C21, 11C63, 12C2(12), 12C26, 12C81, 13C117(3), 13C193(2)
RUSH, Ben 13C21
RUSSELL, 7C24
 Capt. 6C96
 Thomas A, Col. 13C77(1)
 Daughter 12C45(1)
 Flora 12C13(3)
 Joseph 12C13(2)
 Mr. 12C45, 45(1)
 Mrs. 12C13(2), 12C45-45(4)
 T.? 13C101
RUTHERFORD, ___ 12C62(37)
 General 11C107
 Mr. 13C20
SALT 4C26(8), 4C31, 4C33, 41C44, 7C11, 7C35(2,4), 7C45(2,5), 9C88(1), 11C28, 11C33, 11C44, 11C62, 11C62(4, 5, 8, 12, 24), 11C107, 12C24(2), 12C26-29, 13C79(17), 13C79(16), 13C131(7), 13C145(2)
SALTMAKERS 11C28-32, 11C33, 11C38-39, 11C44, 11C62, 11C75, 11C81
 adopted 11C62(10)
 captured 4C44, 11C12, 11C33, 11C38, 11C44, 11C46, 11C62-62(37), 11C92(1,2,3), 12C26-29
 escape 11C62(10)
 sold at Detroit 11C62(10)

Page numbering order: Volume number, series number, page number (with page numbers within interviews cited parenthetically after the primary citation) Ex: 7C5-5(1,2,3).

SANDERS, James 12C22(3), 12C24(7)
    Joseph, Capt. 13C25
    Julius 12C24(10), 12C50
    Samuel 7C14
    William 12C24(7)
SAUNDERS, Julian 12C26
SCAGGS//Skaggs,Skeggs 12C5(2)
    family 12C49(1)
    Henry 5C54(4, 6), 12C64
    James 12C64
    Richard 12C8, 12C64
SCARY CREEK 7C56, 7C84
SCHOLL, Joseph 4C87
    Peter 4C62
    Septimus 7C93
SCOTT, Col. 7C24(1)
    Gen. 12C39(11), 13C117(4), 13C200, 13C117(4), 13C201(1)
    Mrs. 4C26
    Charles, Gen. 13C96(1), 13C200(7)
    Charles, Gov. 13C96(1)
    John 13C76(6)
    Patrick 11C62
SCOTT'S CAMPAIGN 1791 12C49(1), 13C117(4,5,6), 13C200(7)
SEARCY, Bartlett 7C87, 12C26
    captured 11C65, 12C26-29
SHAKER VILLAGE 13C213
SHANE, John Dabney 12C2(23, 12C16
SHANKS family 13C79(19,20)
    Miss 13C79(21)
    Mrs. 13C79(20, 21)
    Widow 13C79(19,20)
SHARP,____ 5C54(1)
    Benjamin 7C21-25
    John 13C(6)
    Thomas 7C21, 7C24
SHAWNEE 4C8, 4C33(3), 4C45, 4C59, 4C81, 7C17, 11C96, 12C2(12), 12C45(1),13C76-76(1), 13C77, 13C145(1)
SHELBY 6C96, 7C24
    D. 7C25
    Evan 4C80
    Isaac, obituary, 12C55
    Ivan, Col. 7C21
    Sarah 7C21
SHELP, John 12C22(3), 12C24(7)
SHIELDS, Dr. Hugh 12C24(8)
SHOEMAKER, Peter 7C76
SHORE, Patrick 12C24(10)
SHORES, Thomas 12C30
SILVER MINE 13C76, 13C86
SIMPSON 12C45
    John 12C8
    Thomas 12C24(6)
SINK HOLE BATTLE 4C52
SKIDMORE, Capt. John 12C54(9)
    Joseph 12C54(9)
SLAUGHTER, C. 13C119
    Lawrence 7C77(2)
SMILY, William 12C24(6)
SMITH, Bob, Capt.11C111
    Col. 4C26(12)
    Daniel, Capt. 6C96
    Daniel 7C21, 12C8(1) (Journal)
    David, Sgt. Major 12C8(1)
    Edmond 4C75
    Elizabeth 12C45(1)
    Enoch 7C3, 13C39, 13C42
    George 12C8
    James, Capt. 12C54(9)
    John 12C22(3)
    Mary Logan 12C44-44(2), 12C45-45(4)
    Mr. 13C20

Page numbering order: Volume number, series number, page number (with page numbers within interviews cited parenthetically after the primary citation) Ex: 7C5-5(1,2,3).

William B. 4C80
William Bailey, Maj. 4C78
SNODDY, Capt. 7C24
    John 4C2, 4C6(1), 4C26(4,16), 4C27(2)
    John, Col. 12C62(22, 29)
    R. M. 4C2, 4C6(1)
    William 4C26(2)
SNODDY'S FORT 4C26(2, 4, 5, 6, 10, 15, 16), 4C27(1, 2)
SOUTH, Jerry 12C1(5)
    John 11C111(2), 13C38, 39, 40, 13C56(1), 13C88
    Samuel, Gen. 7C22
    Samuel 13C44-44(1)-45, 13C56(1)
SOVEREIGN(S) 13C122
    Hannah 12C26-29
    John 12C26, 13C121(1)
SPANIARD 11C111(1)
SPANISH GRANTS 11C62(17)
SPECK/SPECKE, Jacob 12C24(7)
SPENCER, Thomas 12C49
SPRATT, J. B. 4C149
SPY Thomas Gilmer 12C8(1)
    Stephen Huston, 12C8(1))
ST. CLAIR 11C62(11, 22, 24), 13C121(1)
STAFFORD, Rhody 12C1(11)
    Rody 12C8
STAGNER, Barney 12C16(14) 12C24(10), 12C26-29
STAPLETON, John 11C65, 12C8, 12C24(7), 12C26
STEELE, Andrew 12C8
STEPHENS, Wm. 12C8
STEPHENSON, Thos. 12C8
STERLING, Elizabeth Harper 13C188(3)
    W. T. 13C188(3)
STEVENS 12C26-29

STEVENSON 7C43(2)
STEWART/STUART 4C33(1), 4C43(1), 4C50, 4C61
    James 12C24(6)
    John 4C59, 4C99
    Mary the Queen 13C194
    William 12C24(11)
STIGALL, Mr. 12C46(3, 5)
    Mrs. 12C46(3)
STOCKFIELD 11C112-112(1), 11C113(1-3)
STONE, ___ 5C54(5)
    William 12C62(6)
STONER. George, 7C22
    Michael 4C130, 6C94, 6C104, 12C2(23, 12C5(1)
STONESTREET. James S. 4C66, 4C67
STOTTS, Thomas 12C14
STRODE'S STATION 13C40, 13C43, 13C44(1)
STUART, John 4C99, 6C94
STUCKER 13C79(7)
    David 13C74
    Jacob 7C81, 12C23, 12C38(5,6), 12C39(11), 13C74, 13C74(3), 13C79(14,16, 19), 13C110, 13C117(3,5), 13C194(1)
    Jacob, Capt. 12C24(7)
    Lyman 13C110, 110(1)
    Michael 13C74
    Polly 13C117(5)
STULL, Daniel 12C24(6)
    Martin 12C22(3), 12C24(7)
    William 12C24(10)
STURGES, Peter 12C24(6)
SUBLETT, Philip 12C62(5)
    Col. William L. 12C62(5)
SUDDITH, William 7C115(4)
SUGGETT, David 13C74, 13C79(3)

Page numbering order: Volume number, series number, page number (with page numbers within interviews cited parenthetically after the primary citation) Ex: 7C5-5(1,2,3).

John 13C74
Mr.13C115(1)
Parson 13C79(13)
SULLIVAN, Capt. 12C24(6)
SUTTLER, Thomas 12C24(7)
SUTTON, Ed 4C23
SWEARINGEN, Thomas 13C25
SWEDEN 12C64
SYME, Kindlow 13C21
TACKETT, Hannah 7C45(`), 7C56(3)
TALBOTT, Hale Col. 4C33(6), 4C34(1,2)
    Isham 12C16(15)
TANNER, John 11C107
TARLETON, Banastre 12C45(3), 13C20-20(1),13C23(1), 13C24-24(4), 13C25, 13C79(19, 21)
    LCD sources for: 13C 15-16-17-18-1913C22
TEAS/TEASS, John T. 735
    Stephen 7C56
    Thomas 7C35-35(1-5) 7C36(1-3), 7C56(1-5), 7C58
TEASS' VALLEY 7C35(4)
TECUMSEH 12C62(4), 13C131(5), 13C145(1)
TENNESSEE 4C22-22(1)
THAMES Battle 12C62(4)
THOMAS, Col. 13C79(22)
    Elizabeth 13C22(2, 13C26
    Elizabeth Pogue 12C26-29
THOMPSON, Capt. 11C62(27)
    David, 11C81
    David H. 11C76
    James 7C23
    John H. 9C139, 9C140, 9C142
THRELKELD, Dr. S. 12C39(11)
TICONDEROGA 12C2(24)
TODD 4C50, 12C62(22)

Col. 5C54(6), 13C74(2)
John 5C54(1), 11C25(1), 11C71
John, Col. 13C110(1)
Levi, 5C54(1), 12C1(1), 12C26-29
Levi, Col. 6C103
Levi, Gen. 12C26-29
Robert, Col. 12C22(2)
Robert, Maj. 13C100
___, McMurtry's mother 13C213
Thomas 12C45(3)
William H. 12C22
TOMLIN, Nick 13C110(2)
TOMLINSON 13C63, 13C79(4), 13C115(1)
    Grandmother (Hetty) 13C63-66
    Nancy 13C79(12)
    Nicholas 13C74, 13C74(3), 13C79(1, 9, 12)
    William 13C74
    William, Sr. 13C79(1)
    William, son 13C74
TOWNSEND, Oswald 12C2(23, 12C5(1)
TRABUE 12C46(3)
    Daniel, Col. 12C2(14)
TRACEY, William 11C62, 11C62(10)
TRAIN, Silas 12C5(1)
TRANSYLVANIA COMPANY 7C20(1), 11C107, 11C112(2), 11C113(2)
TRENT, Beverly 12C24(6)
TRIBLE, Thomas 12C24(6)
TRIGG 4C50, 12C24(4)
    Col. 12C16(8,10)
    Maj. 5C56(7)
    Stephen 12C2(9), 12C8(1), 12C26
TRIMBLE, E. D. 6C105
TRISTAN, Thomas L., Col.

Page numbering order: Volume number, series number, page number (with page numbers within interviews cited parenthetically after the primary citation) Ex: 7C5-5(1,2,3).

10C69(1)
TROTTER, Col. 12C62(13)
    Col. James 12C62(10)
TRUMBO, John 7C115(4)
TRUMBOW, Jacob 12C62(31)
    ___, son of Jacob
12C62(33)
TUCKER, John 12C14(3)
    Mrs. 12C14(3)
TURF and TWIG 7C75
TURNIP PATCH 12C26-29
TURPIN 12C54(2)
    family 12C54(6)
    Solomon 4C81, 12C54,
54(1,2)
    and family 12C54(1)
TUSCARORAS 9C129(2)
TWITTY, William 4C81
TYLER, Mr. 13C24(1,2,3,4)

VANCLEVE, John 13C193(2)
    Molly 13C193(3)
    Sally 13C193(2)
    William 13C193,
13C193(2)
VANLANDINGHAM, Lewis
12C24(3), 13C74
VANMETER, Abraham
12C24(7)
VANNOY & family 12C54(8)
VARDEMAN/VARDIMAN
12C6(1)
    Amaziah 12C8
    Betsy Morgan 12C64
    Jeremiah 12C64
    John 12C64, 12C65
    John, Sr. 12C64
    Morgan 12C62(36-
37,)12C64, 12C65-66
VAUGHN, Mrs. 4C66, 4C67
VAWTER, John 13C192,
13C193-193(1)
VEECH, Hon. James 4C7
VENABLE, Mr. 12C22(3),
12C24(7

VINCENNES 11C71, 12C2(18),
12C24(5), 12C38-38(1),
12C49(1), 13C122(1), 13C153
VIRGINIA COUNTIES
    Amelia 7C76(1)
    Augusta 7C43,
13C38(1), 13C51,
13C53, 13C54
    Bedford 11C16, 11C38,
11C41,
11C41(1),11C62, 12C64
    Botetourt
5C54(1),11C41,
12C41
    Buckingham 11C48
    Culpepper 13C117,
13C194
    Fauquier 13C110,
13C119
    Fayette 13C18
    Fincastle
7C21(1), 7C15,12C5,
12C64
    Goochland 11C16
    Greenbriar 12C41,
13C51, 13C53,
13C54(1)
    Lee 7C21
    Lincoln 11C11
    Louden 13C119
    Mecklenburg 11C22,
11C33
    Montgomery 4C78
    Orange 4C62, 4C66,
13C117
    Pittsylvania 12C49
    Prince William
11C11(1), 13C121
    Rockbridge 13C205
    Rockingham 12C45(1)
    Russell 4C26
    Scott 4C24
    Spottsylvania 13C96(1)
    Washington 4C78
    Wythe 12C6, 12C64

Page numbering order: Volume number, series number, page number (with page numbers within interviews cited parenthetically after the primary citation) Ex: 7C5-5(1,2,3).

VIRGINIA LEGISLATURE 12C45(3), 12C38(1), 13C17, 13C79(19)
VITTILS, Michael 12C24(7)
VO___, John 12C8

W____Y, Malcolm (at Harrod's Station) 12C24
WABASH CAMPAIGN 12C49(1, 6), 12C54(6), 12C62(39)
WABASH RIVER 12C38(5), 13C76(1), 13C134, 13C76(2), 13C200(7)
WADE, Dawson 7C115
    J. A. 7C115(4)
    James 13C9(3)
    Peggy 13C9(3)
    Richard 11C75
WALES 12C64
WALES, Maj., 5C54(2)
WALKER 7C17
    Alexander 12C62(33,42)
    Ann 4C26(2)
    John 13C25
    Thomas 13C20
WALLACE, Caleb 12C41
WALLEN/WALLIN
    Creek 4C24, 4C26(6)
    Ridge 4C26(6), 7C23
WALLS, Alfred 13C124
    George 13C123
    Major 13C124
WAPAKONETTA 12C62(13)
WAR ROAD(S), 4C84 7C95
WARD, Frances 4C130
    John 12C8
    Sally 13C117
    Thomas 6C104
WARNER, John 7C115(4)
WASHINGTON, General 11C111, 13C131(7)
WATERMELON 12C45(2), 13C79(2), 13C117(3)
WATERS, Frank 13C133, 13C137
    James 12C24(10, 11)
    Philemon 13C16(1-14), 13C96(2,3,4), 13C129, 13C131-131(9), 13C133-136, 13C137, 13C138-139-140, 13C145-145(1), 13C155, 13C160, 13C161(1-14)
    Indian name 13C13
    Thomas 13C145
    Thomas C. 13C153
WATKINS. Charles G., Capt. 11C62(11)
WATSON, William, 4C 83, 7C91
WATTS 12C54(8)
WAYNE 13C85, 13C120
    Gen. 4C26(5), 11C62(35), 12C38(5,6)
WEBBER 13C54(3)
WEIGHT, John E. 12C2(19)
WELCH, James 12C24(7)
WELLS, Widow 8C11(3)
WESTERN CHRISTIAN ADVOCATE 7C22
WETZEL/WHETZEL, Martin 13C115(1)
WHEALAN, James 12C24(10)
WHEELING 11C62(13)
WHITAKER 12C45
WHITE, Ambrose 11C110
    John & family 12C49(4), 12C54(1)
    Shadrach 12C64
    W.E. 9C2
WHITE OAK STATION 13C40
WHITESIDES, ___ 12C64(1)+
WHITE SULPHUR SPRINGS 13C51(3)
WHITLEDGE, Robert 7C3
    Thomas 11C113(3)
    Willia 7C20
WHITLEY 11C62(37), 12C26, 12C49(1)
    Bob 12C6(1)

Page numbering order: Volume number, series number, page number (with page numbers within interviews cited parenthetically after the primary citation) Ex: 7C5-5(1,2,3).

Col. 13C193(2)
Ester Fuller/Fullen Gill
12C56, 12C62
Family to Kentucky
12C62
Paul 12C62
Solomon 12C62(1)
William, Col. 12C6(1),
12C10, 12C14(3),
12C26, 12C56,
12C56(1), 12C62(1-46)
appearance 12C62(4,5)
horse Emperor
12C62(3)
killed 12C62(4)
powder horn 12C62(4)
Mrs. Esther 12C62(1-3)
Shooting match
12C62(2)
Levisa 12C62(5)
Mrs. [Polly] 12C62(1-3)
Children : 12C56:
Andrew, Easter,
Elizabeth, Lewis, Polly,
Solomon, William
Elizabeth 12C62
Isabella 12C62
WHITLEY'S MINUTEMEN
12C62(40)
WHITLEY'S STATION 12C54(6).
12C62-62(1-45)
WHITLEY'S BARBECUE /
PICNIC 12C56(1), 12C62(63)
WICKERSHAM, Abraham 12C23
Adam 12C24(7)
Jacob 12C24(7)
John Paul 12C23
WICKLIFFE, Ann Logan
12C44,12C45(1, 4)
Charles 5C54(2)
Nathaniel 12C45(1)
Robert 5C54(1-7),
13C77(1)
WILCOX 9C63(1), 13C74(4)
Isaiah 9C63(1)

Samuel 9C58
Sarah 9C58
WILCOXEN 9C68(3)
Samuel, 9C68
WILDERNESS ROAD
7C87, 12C26-29, 12C54(8)
12C62, 12C62(37)
WILEY 7C20
James 12C22(3),
12C24(7)
WILKINS, Henry 12C54(7)
WILL, at Donnelly's Fort
12C62(16-17)
WILLIAMS, David 12C22(3),
12C24(7), 13C74
Jenkin 4C54
John 13C74, 13C74(1)
Sampson 12C62(3)
WILLIAMSON 11C62(34)
WILSON, David 12C5(1)
Harrod 12C26
Henry 5C54, 54(7),
13C79(13)
Hugh 12C26
Mrs. 12C26
Samuel 12C8
WILSON'S STATION 12C49(1)
WOLF HILLS 12C14(4)
WOOD 13C213
family attacked, 11C101
married Betty Cooper,
11C101
D. M. 4C27(1)
Ed, Mrs. 7C35
E. L. 7C36
Elizabeth L. 7C58
M. B., Judge 4C26,
4C27(5)
Richard 12C41
WOODS 12C24(8)
Capt. At Donnelly's Fort
12C62(17)
Family, under siege
12C62(22)
Hannah 12C62(20-21)

Page numbering order: Volume number, series number, page number (with page numbers within interviews cited parenthetically after the primary citation) Ex: 7C5-5(1,2,3).

441

John 12C5(1)
Michael, Capt. 12C62(16, 20)
Susan 12C62(20)
Mrs. William 12C62(20)
William, 12C62(20
WOODS'S FORT/STATION 12C62(63)
WORTHINGTON, C. Edward 12C26
    Edward 12C24(10)
WYANDOTT 7C22, 11C62(14, 34, 36), 13C54

YADKIN 4C33(6), 4C75(1), 12C24(9), 9C102 (map), 9C134 (map)
YAGER (gun) 4C24, 4C26(11)
YATES, A. S. 9C79
    Aley 9C75, 9C204(3)
    Hugh 9C68
    Jesse 9C191-192, 9C199
    John 9C58, 9C60, 9C202
    S. A. 9C58, 9C61, 9C62
    Sally 9C68
    Sarah 9C60
    William 12C56
YELLOW HAWK 11C62(17)
YELLOWSTONE RIVER 4C62
YOCUM 13C199
    Amelia 12C16(15)
    Jesse 13C50, 13C96(2,3,4) 3C200(4, 7), 13C196(3), 13C199(1), 13C200(1-8)
YORK, siege of 13C52(2)
YOUNG'S SALT WORKS, 4C31
YOUNG, Fanny 13C154
    J. 6C105
    James 7C21(1)
    Mrs. 13C153(1)
    V. B. 7C99 13C9(3)

Page numbering order: Volume number, series number, page number (with page numbers within interviews cited parenthetically after the primary citation) Ex: 7C5-5(1,2,3).

www.ingramcontent.com/pod-product-compliance
Lightning Source LLC
Chambersburg PA
CBHW060910300426
44112CB00011B/1414